Praise for SLAVERY REPARATIONS TIME

"The book presents an arguable case that at the
.... a *prima facie* case for the illegality of slavery,
the practice followed in the colonies. ... My thanks to Ms. Wittmann, particularly
for the wealth of material she has unearthed."
- **Patrick Robinson**, (Former President) Judge of the UN International Criminal
Tribunal for the Former Yugoslavia

"This book should be welcomed as an addition to the growing number of works
on the subject of reparation. It advances the cause and constructs a sound basis
for legal redress."
- **Verene Shepherd**, UWI Professor and Chairwoman of the UN Working Group
of Experts on People of African Descent

"Dr. Nora Wittmann, a passionate advocate for the cause of reparations, has
written a brilliant work of deeply researched scholarship. Her theme is that the
international trade in African people for the purposes of slavery, practiced by
many European countries over four centuries, was a crime against humanity.
When slavery was abolished, the slave-owners in the English colonies received
huge sums by way of compensation for the loss of their 'property'. The former
slaves were left to fend for themselves, and their descendants continue to suffer the economic and psychological consequences of the crime. Therefore, under
well-established principles of international law, reparation is due from the former
slave-trading powers, who themselves were massively enriched.
Dr. Wittmann's scholarly analysis is interspersed with eloquent contemporary
quotations describing the enormity of what was done, from the seizure of whole
communities in Africa, to the horrors of the 'Middle Passage', to the barbarities
of the slavery system in the Americas. The perpetrators were contemptuous of
human life, treating Black people as chattels who could be worked to death and
replaced by new arrivals. Hence Dr. Wittmann argues that they, and the governments which supported them, were guilty also of genocide.
The book is particularly valuable in refuting the arguments commonly advanced
against the payment of reparations. I encountered these arguments when I raised
the issue of reparations in the House of Lords in 1996. 'The government was not
involved, only private traders' – Dr. Wittmann traces how slave trading was instigated at the highest levels of power, from King John of Portugal onwards. 'Africans held people in slavery' – she explains the total contrast between the relatively dignified treatment of African prisoners of war, and the racist system of
dehumanization practiced by the Europeans. 'It all happened too long ago' – she
sets out the legal doctrines by which there is no limitation on claims for crimes

against humanity.

Most significantly, she rebuts the argument that 'slavery was legal at the time'. Ranging over legal precedents and scholastic writings from many countries, she demonstrates how in most nations involved in the transatlantic deportation, slavery was rejected as contrary to natural and positive law. To the extent that colonial laws upheld slavery, she proves that laws passed in order to justify a crime against humanity cannot be used as a defence to the crime. In all that I have read on the subject, this argument has never been presented with such wide-ranging and convincing research.

The movement for reparations is gaining momentum, especially in the Caribbean. Dr. Wittmann rightly says that the demand will not be willingly conceded, nor are there courts which will grant it. There will have to be, she concludes, an expression of people's power, through the raising of consciousness, before the right to reparations can be vindicated. Dr. Wittmann is to be highly praised for the huge contribution to the raising of consciousness which she herself has made, through her work on this eloquent, readable and scholarly book."

– **Lord Anthony Gifford**, QC, lawyer in Jamaica and the UK, legal pioneer for slavery reparations

"For The Journey out of Bondage : EXODUS 12:35-36 : "Now the children of Israel had done according to the word of Moses, and they asked from the Egyptians articles of silver, articles of gold, and clothing / And the Lord gave the people favour   in the sight of the Egyptians, so that they granted them what they requested.'

Exposing lies claiming justice - REPARATIONS for Slavery NOW ! Dr. Nora Wittmann's book is of elegant erudite judicial passion. Elegantly, she sizes up standard arguments against reparations like - 'slavery' wasn't illegal and thus 'non-retroactivity' would bar the route to justice claims . . she exposes European imposed transatlantic 'chattel-slavery' as egregiously distinct from any treatment of human beings called 'slaves' or 'serfs' internationally under laws or prevailing practices international including Europe preceding its global dominance. Since as Cicero of Rome reasoned 'Where human beings exist laws exist' - whether of 'Tribe' or 'State' - the writer's erudition obliges the reader to acknowledge a range of appropriate precedent, other references, and patterns of history . . of methodical jabbing forth precedents from different angles wearing down 'the body of lies' drooping for the knockout which this lawyer clinically delivers to other arguments against reparations like 'Why should a State be responsible for reparations for benefit gained by private entrepreneurs building international empires facilitated by 'State' for wielding power worldwide ?!' The power of the gun & iron for tools marketed by European enslavers would in time nigh compel African tribes involvement for survival against each other and the white man playing off mere 'blacks' against each other for 'white' profit. The author urges understanding for reconciliation between continental & diasporic Africans . .

let shared music & culture help build the fire of consciousness unapologetically demanding the right of reparations for a people acknowledging shared self of eternity . . of Mother Africa's sense of self for The World needing reconciliation with 'Mother-Father' for shared Prosperity with Peace. So, what of the created continuing consequences of definition 'black' nurtured of chattel-slavery , and of continuing imposed compromise of 'self' in neo-colonialism inimical to exodus of 'self' African ? This daughter of Austria describes herself as 'universal', not 'white', thus it seems to follow - 'judicial passion' for 're-balancing' the Globe for Justice for the idea, or apparently often unseen reality, that all humanity & creation come of One Creator. REPARATIONS for Slavery NOW - an international legal assessment cornering stinging consciences exposing lies claiming long overdue justice from those who so pride themselves on the idea of The Rule of Law . . or the lie of all equal under law which is in fact influenced by power blocs of Big Business, like 'Slavery'. Comprehensive penetrating legal argument, easily in the reach of the average reader. I Rastafari would further underline Dr. Nora Wittmann's acutely convincing submission for reparations for slavery NOW - by asking a question basic to shared hallowed principles of law European , and Beyond Before worldwide : What of Principle in Precedent ?

– **Ras Tekla Mekfet**, scholar and writer

Slavery Reparations Time Is Now

Exposing Lies, Claiming Justice for Global Survival
An International Legal Assessment

Nora Wittmann, Ph.D.

Power of the TrInIty Publishers
Vienna
Afreeka
Universe

Power of the TrInIty Publishers

Visit our website at www.powerofthetrinity.net or www.pot-publishers.com

Book design by Alexander Franz and Nora Wittmann

FIRST EDITION PUBLISHED BY POWER OF THE TRINITY PUBLISHERS / Nora Wittmann 2013.

Books are available at quantity discounts for educational, business or promotional use. Please contact info@powerofthetrinity.net

ISBN: 978-3-200-03155-5

To my still unborn children and to all children in this world.

... that this book be a, however small, contribution that you will have a future here ...

CONTENTS

ACKNOWLEDGMENTS

First and foremost I give thanks for the inspiration and strength to conceive and realize this book to the Universe, the Most I, the Power of the TrInIty, Haile Selassie I, Empress Menen I for shining the light and guiding my steps.

Then, of course, my greatest gratitude goes out to my mother Elisabeth Goldschmid and to my father Erich Wittmann for the continuing support and love. I acknowledge this is not always easy for them, because although they sent me on the way, they cannot always understand where I am going. Yet from how they raised me, it is really only logical that I got to where I am now. Mutti, thank you for the warmth always, for being there with a solution countless times, and for the material support without which this research would have been totally impossible to carry out. Papa, thank you for raising me from the very start on that great love for books and knowledge and justice, and for growing me to love to live healthy, for being so kind and patient with me at all times and also for the continuing financial support that made it possible to get this work out in the way it is supposed to. Thank you both for letting me choose you.

I am also most grateful to my grandmother Rosa Wittmann, one of the strongest women I will ever know, for always supporting me more than anyone else could have on the small means she had and who strove to understand why I am doing what I am doing, although she came from a time so different in many ways. Omi, I am so proud that you are my granny, you have built from nothing. It still hurts much that you had to go.

I am also very thankful to my other grandparents, Josef and Maria Goldschmid, who have given me such long-lasting material support as well. I am proud to come from farmers, the base on whom we all depend. Opa and Oma, you could not witness my development in the physical, but I know you are always here with me.

My brother Raffael and sister Lisa Goldschmid, your smiles mean the world to me and since the days you have been born my heart has expanded. I hope that you forgive me for sometimes being so unavailable to you because of my works.

Johanna Grillitsch, my sister from another mother and father, without you this book simply wouldn't exist. The Universe knows why we linked up, you and I know too. I give thanks for you.

My friends Karin and Petra, thank you for giving me strength by listening to my little madnesses and always being there for reasoning.

Stéphane Labrador ... Stickee ... Stenli, I give thanks for your existence. Without you I may never have gone to Paris to study international law with the aim of working for reparations. I already knew the mission, but bwoi, you were so nice and handsome and that made that move a lot easier. Give thanks for the reasonings, intellectual procreation, for telling me that lawyer can be a very creative occupation. Give thanks for your helping me research in "French" Guiana. Give thanks also for inspiring me to conceive the Power of the TrInIty.

Rosette, it is mainly because of you that I sometimes miss living in Paris. You are a beautiful soul, such as it is rare to meet one, and although we had not known each other for long you have been there for me so many times. Although you are conscious and come from an African country that has been imposed so much violence and suffering by Europeans for centuries, you have always extended much love to me. Go hard in your studies, knowledge is power, and I hope we will be able to do some serious works together.

I am deeply grateful to Anthony Gifford for encouraging me to come to Jamaica at an early phase of this research, giving me the possibility to accompany the National Commission for Reparations to some meetings, for the continuing guidance and encouragement at so many moments, for the review of this book, and for the friendship and help when I was far away from my family.

I am also thankful to the late Prof. Barry Chevannes who, as Chairman of that Commission, made it possible for me to use the library of the University of the West Indies, Mona Campus, where I unearthed a great deal of information that found its way into this book.

I am also indebted to Judge Patrick Robinson of the International Tribunal for the former Yugoslavia for taking the effort to read my manuscript, setting, in his own words, a "personal record reading 484 pages in about 3 days", and for his extensive and critical comments that have helped me sharpen my argumentation and bring some aspects more on point.

Thanks also go to Prof. Faye Harrison for her continuous encouragements for my research works and for sending me a package of her writings a few years ago, although we have never met face to face. Her works have been a great inspiration and guide for my own journey.

I want to thank Prof. Verene Shepherd and Prof. Hilary Beckles for the positive comments on this book and my work.

I also want to express my gratitude to Ayi Kwei Armah, one of my very favourite writers, for taking the time to reason with me on reparations via email. This communication certainly made me realize some important aspects and is reflected in this book.

Many thanks also to Prof. Irmgard Marboe who has supervised my dissertation in international law that forms the basis for this book. The same goes for Prof. René Kuppe, whom I also thank for his strong and heartfelt words of encouragement.

I-Nation, respect for catering the knowledge to the people. Your mission is crucial in this revolution for global survival.

Dutty Bookman, thanks for the productive feed-forwards and advice, even if finally we did not work together on this project.

Acheampong, give thanks for that palm kernel ring you gave me about ten years ago in Ghana, telling me that when I wear it the ancestors will be with me. I have been wearing it every day since.

Slash, nuff respect for keeping up the guard at Clignancourt and for always uplifting my mood when I passed while dodging through the last intense stages of this research.

Kahleb, I give thanks for the many words of encouragement for my being and mission and for the strength while completing the manuscript.

I am very grateful to Jaqueline Lubin for welcoming me into her house while I was working on this book in "French" Guiana.

I also need to express my thanks from the bottom of my heart to Susanne Kamann, my elementary school teacher, the best instructor I could get at that time. She made school an adventure, a chance for growing at my own rhythm, not a duty. With another teacher I would have taken another route. I also thank Ingrid Englitsch for giving me opportunity to train my composition and writing skills in high school. I always looked forward to our German creative writing exams.

Many thanks of course to all the comrades from the reparations movement in France and in the French colonies, Rosita Destival, Martin Okeke, Théo Lubin, Peter Lema, Rosa Amélia Plumelle-Uribe, Apa Mumia Makeba, Claudette Duhamel and Alain Manville for the reasonsing, the strength and the love.

I am most thankful and indebted to my friend and comrade Dr. Fanta Kaba for the continuing stream of information, knowledge, advice, love and encouragement. You are one of the most humble and competent persons I have ever known, a rare combination. I give thanks for your existence and that the ancestors made us connect. You have triggered a great deal of reflections in me that are now expressed in this book and have opened many doors for me. Thank you also for helping me find my copy-editor.

I am grateful to Viola Zimunya, my copy-editor, for assuring that despite her other workload and moving across a continent we kept our deadline. I very much appreciate all the advice that was not even part of the copy-editing job. Thanks also to Bankie Forster Bankie for establishing that link.

I thank Alexander Franz for always so well assuring any graphic designs I need, including the cover and set-up of this book.

Many thanks to all the vocal artists such as dead prez (Stic.Man and M-1), Peter Tosh, Bob Marley, I-Wayne, Queen Omega, Tanya Stephens, Lutan Fyah, Sizzla, Tarrus Riley, Sa-Roc and thousand more as well as their beatmakers and producers who provided me with the vibrational soundtrack that was responsible for many inspirational moments and necessary to get this book done. Most definitely, without them this work wouldn't have been possible.

I am more than indebted to the great ancestor Dr. Walter Rodney, forever one of my greatest inspirations and guides.

Last but not least, my heartfelt gratitude goes out to the people in Port Antonio, Kingston, Cayenne, Apatou and Saint Laurent that have reasoned with me on reparations and thus contributed to the research that is the base of this book. Millicent, Joanne, Max, Sunny, Miss Claudia, Shane, Kenjah, Joy, Fuzzy, Son, Pauline, Mr William, Kenneth, Ms Rachel, Johnny Clarke, Jaycee, Ms Firth, L'Artisto, Kéké, Pinouche, Jean-Pierre Sida, and all others, thank you.

"When African righteous people come together, the world will come together. This is our divine destiny." – Haile Selassie I

I. The Foundational Crime of Transatlantic Slavery and the Need to Re-Balance the World. Introductory Remarks

According to a UNESCO conference summary report, "African losses during the four centuries of the Atlantic Slave Trade must be put at some 210 million human beings".[1] This estimate takes account of those who arrived in the Americas as well as those who perished during the razzias, in the dungeons and on the ships. Scholars speak of a 1:4 ratio, that is, for every African who reached American shores, four more had died in the process of enslavement on the African continent or in the ships.[2] As horrid as they are, these numbers do not yet take account of those who were born into slavery in the Americas, nor their descendants who after the abolition of slavery were subjected to segregation, lynching, racism and continued colonial and neo-colonial occupation. Up to today, African people globally suffer from the legacy of transatlantic slavery and the continuing crime of the Maafa[3]. Also, when considering the numbers of victims of transatlantic deportation, it is important to keep in mind that traders often declared the numbers of people forced and pressed into their ships below real figures in order to circumvent tax laws.[4]

---

1   United Nations Educational, Scientific and Cultural Organization (ed.) (1978). Meeting of Experts on the African Slave-Trade, Final Report, Port-au-Prince, Haiti, January 31-February 4, 1978, downloaded from http://unesdoc.unesco.org/images/0003/000333/033360eb.pdf (accessed 21.6.2012); see also: Patric, Adibe/ Boateng, Osei (2000). Portugal, the mother of all slavers, in: New African, No. 385, London: IC Publications, 20.

2   Ki-Zerbo, Joseph (1978). Histoire de l'Afrique Noire, Paris: Hatier, 218.

3   Some reparation activists employ the concept of Maafa in designating the crime (comprising its different stages of slavery, colonialism and neo-colonialism) for which reparation is sought. Maafa is a Kiswahili word meaning "disaster", and is used to describe over 500 years of warfare and genocide experienced by African people under enslavement and colonialism and their continued impact on African people throughout the world. The term was introduced by anthropologist Marimba Ani (see: Ani, Marimba (1988). Let The Circle Be Unbroken: The Implications of African Spirituality in the Diaspora. New York: Nkonimfo Publications).

4   Inikori, Joseph E. (1992b). The Chaining of a Continent. Export Demand for Captives and the History of Africa South of the Sahara, 1450-1870, Kingston: Institute of Social and Economic Research, UWI, 3.

In view of this most terrible horror that the world has ever seen, the aim of this book is to explore to what extent international law provides an affirmative basis for reparation claims for transatlantic chattel slavery. One pillar of this undertaking is the deconstruction of the very foundations of the dominant and accepted legal opinion on the subject.[5] Although members of no other group of humans were ever subjected over a comparable period of time to attacks so serious to their physical and mental integrity as Africans in the transatlantic slavery[6] system and their descendants[7], no reparation whatsoever has been made. The prevalent scholarly opinion categorically shuts the door on such claims for justice by referring to the principle of *non-retroactivity* and to the allegation, presented as if it were a fact, that transatlantic slavery would have been "legal" at its time. This is indeed *the* basic argument that European and US ex-enslaver states always come up with first and last. In fact, this is really the principal argument that they persistently repeat each time they are confronted with the topic, indicating that this is where the crux of the legal matter lies.

Now, this principle of *non-retroactivity*, a tenet of international law, has the effect that a state can only be found legally responsible if that state committed an act that was "internationally wrongful" at the time it occurred. Recently, the principle that has long been central in customary international law has been taken up in the Articles on the Responsibility of States for Internationally Wrongful Acts (thereafter called "ILC Articles"). These Articles will be frequently referred to in the course of this work since they frame the applicable international law on state responsibility today, and one of the principal aims of this book is to assess the legal responsibility of ex-enslaver states with respect to reparations claims. According to international law, such as expressed in Art. 2 of the ILC Articles, an act (action or omission) of a state is internationally wrongful and engages its international responsibility only if the act is by international law attributable to that state, *and* if it constitutes a violation of an obligation that the state owes

---

5   Chattel slavery: people are treated as the personal property, chattels, of an owner and are bought and sold as commodities.

6   I use the term "transatlantic slavery" and strive to avoid the more common transatlantic "slave trade and slavery", because the latter implicitly suggests that the African victims would have been slaves awaiting sale in Africa, which is contradicted by the historical facts. Most of those shipped to the Americas had been free people on the African continent. The violent seizure of people did not entail any transaction, and many affected African communities were not involved in business deals. The "literature that focuses on the commercial part of the process does not capture the experience of the vast majority of the affected Africans. It is no exaggeration to assume that the tens of millions who suffered, directly and indirectly, from this immense disaster were primarily concerned with elaborating strategies to counter its consequences on themselves, their loved ones, and their communities" (Diouf, Sylvaine A. (2003). "Introduction", in: Sylvaine A. Diouf (ed.): Fighting the Slave Trade. West African Strategies, Athens: Ohio University Press, IX-XXVII, XI.).

7   Plumelle-Uribe, Rosa Amelia (2004). 'Les crimes contre l'humanité et le devoir de réparation', in: de Chazournes/Quéguiner/Villalpando (ed.): Crimes de l'histoire et réparations: les réponses du droit et de la justice, Brussels: Editions Bruylant, 187-202, 194.

under international law.[8] Legal responsibility for transatlantic slavery can thus only be attributed to states if it was illegal by international law at that time, and if that illegality was binding on states. So, *non-retroactivity* basically means that a fact must be assessed in the light of the law in force at the time when the act was realized, whereby the qualification as "internationally wrongful" is not affected by any differing legal qualifications in national or internal law (Art. 3).

Adopted in the form of a resolution by the UN General Assembly[9], the Articles initially only had declarative value. However, the International Court of Justice (ICJ) had already made reference to their draft provision, adopted on first reading in 1996, in the *Gabĉikovo-Nagymaros* decision.[10] Since then, the ICJ and international tribunals have referred to the ILC Articles in numerous instances.[11] In *Application of the Convention on the Prevention and Punishment of the Crime of Genocide* and in *Legal Consequences of the Construction of a Wall in the Occupied Palestinian Territory*[12], the Court declared that the standards stipulated reflect customary international law[13]. The Articles have also been frequently relied upon in investment treaty arbitrations, such as in *CMS Gas Transmission Company v. Argentine Republic*[14], *Eureko BV v. Republic of Poland*[15], *Noble Ventures v. Romania*[16] or *EnCana Corp. v. Ecuador*[17]. Art. 38 of the Statute of the International Court of Justice is commonly considered the inventory of legal sources of international law and mentions "judicial decisions" as "subsidiary means for the determination of rules of law". Thus, if we are arguing the case for reparations in international law today, the ILC Articles need to be taken into account.

But *non-retroactivity* has also long before featured as a general principle of international customary law. The ILC Articles really only concretized its content

---

8   International Law Commission (2001). Draft Articles on Responsibility of States for Internationally Wrongful Acts, November 2001, Supplement No. 10 (A/56/10), chp.IV.E.1, downloaded from http://www.unhcr.org/refworld/docid/3ddb8f804.html (accessed 23.6.2012).

9   UN General Assembly, Responsibility of States for internationally wrongful acts: Resolution adopted by the General Assembly, January 28, 2002, A/RES/56/83, available at http://www.unhcr.org/refworld/docid/3da44ad10.html (accessed 2.4.2012).

10   Gabĉikovo-Nagymaros Project (Hungary v. Slovakia), Judgement of September 25, 1997, ICJ Reports 1997, 7.

11   Ollesson, Simon (2007). The Impact of the ILC's Articles on Responsibility of States for Internationlly Wrongful Acts, London: British Institute of International and Comparative Law, 98.

12   Legal Consequences of the Construction of a Wall in the Occupied Palestinian Territory, Advisory Opinion of July 9, 2004, ICJ Reports 2004, 136.

13   Application of the Convention on the Prevention and Punishment of the Crime of Genocide (Bosnia and
Herzegovina v Serbia and Montenegro), Judgement of February 26, 2007, ICJ Reports 2007, 420.

14   CMS Gas Transmission Co. v. Argentina, Final Award of May 12, 2005, ICSID Case No. ARB/01/8; cited in: Ollesson (2007), 186.

15   Eureko B.V. v. Republic of Poland, Arbitral Award of August 19, 2005, Ad hoc Arbitration, Brussels; cited in: Ollesson (2007), 70.

16   Noble Ventures Inc. v. Romania, Award of October 12, 2005, ICSID Case No. ARB/01/11; cited in: Ollesson (2007), 70.

17   EnCana Corp. v. Ecuador, Award of February 3, 2006, London Court of International Arbitration, 45 ILM 655 (2006); cited in: Ollesson (2007), 72.

and scope. There was no cut between ancient international law developments and the present-day international law regime. The later developed out of the former. It is really not so much international law norms as such that are imperialist, as often contended, but rather international law practice. Many of the norms indeed trace their roots way back and are grounded in natural law.

Coming back to the main argument of the opponents of reparations and the dominant legal opinion, it is the combination of the allegation of international "legality" of slavery at that time with this principle of *non-retroactivity* that is invoked to categorically block transatlantic slavery reparation claims. This is not a scientifically pertinent and tenable position, however. When one contends that "slavery" was "legal", it needs to be asked by whose standards it is supposed to have been legal. The allegation of legality is based solely on the colonial laws that European enslaver states passed after they had been the driving force in transatlantic slavery for already more than a century. However, transatlantic slavery was not legal by the laws of affected Africans, nor was it compliant with international law standards of the time. It was not even "legal" by the laws of European enslaver states, most of which had come to pass, in developments up to the 16th century, legislation abolishing, or at least severely restricting, slavery and outlawing chattel slavery. In their majority, these laws were never abrogated and thus continued to be in force throughout the transatlantic slavery period. The present work investigates the law that was actually in force at that time, thereby enabling an honest and thorough legal appraisal of reparation claims, while at the same time remaining respectful of contemporary and current international law principles, such as *non-retroactivity*, and their legal ratio.

Pursuant to that endeavour, we will first engage in an investigation of the development and state of "international law" up to the time when transatlantic slavery was started. Legal regulation of "international", or "inter-polity", contact can be traced back to a far distant past. Before the time of transatlantic slavery, many regions of Africa were active participators in international relations, and many African societies had highly developed political and social institutions. Contrary to what we are often made to believe, African political entities of that time were as much creators, actors and subjects of international law as their European counterparts, if the accepted elements of definition are applied in a non-biased manner. In order to sustain the idea that transatlantic slavery would have been "legal", the dominant opinion alleges or implies that African political organization would have been primitive, incapable of maintaining stable international legal relations and thus excluded from participation in the moulding of international law. However, since it really is documented that many African societies were politically and socially organized as states that were highly respective of the law in both their internal and external dealings, the logical conclusion is that their legal perspectives and contributions to the international legal status of slavery must be included in any assessment of the same. In the 17th and 18th centuries, when European nations started to legislate on transatlantic slavery, international law was no *tabula rasa*. And Europeans, having always been only a global minority (and before transatlantic slavery not a particularly powerful one), could neither unilaterally impose what international law was, nor change it.

And contrary to hegemonic opinion, historical sources referring to African, European and international law show that transatlantic slavery was indeed illegal at its time. Now, the concept of legal responsibility and its ensuing obligation to make reparation for wrongful conduct too was, in one form or another, historically present in all legal systems concerned – African, European and international. Once the illegality of transatlantic slavery can be established and responsibility legally attributed, in appliance of the law of the time of facts, reparation is due for this most massive crime.

Transatlantic slavery was not only fundamentally illegal; it was arguably the biggest genocide ever, a genocide that is still continuing today in the form of neo-colonialism. Although African and solidary activists globally maintain that transatlantic slavery is and was genocide, this is not accepted by the dominant legal opinion. The required element of "intent" would not be given, since – it is contended – European enslavers would not have aimed at exterminating Africans "as such". Yet, from the available documentation it is pertinently assessed in this work that transatlantic slavery does in fact meet the legal requirements of genocide. It is also in this context of genocide that Nobel Peace Prize laureate Albert Schweitzer made the following statement: "How did the Whites of all nationalities deal with the Indigenous since the discoveries of new lands? What signifies the fact alone that wherever Europeans went, in the name of Jesus, such a great number of peoples have perished already? (...) A debt weighs on us. The good we owe them is no act of charity but of reparations. And when we will have done all that is in our power, we will only have repaired a small part of the wrongs committed"[18].

So, as a next step, this book elaborates on the fact that transatlantic slavery was one phase of the continuing crime and violation of international law that is the Maafa, and rendering that perspective legally relevant. The legal concept of the continuing violation of international law renders possible a direct application of present-day international law, of the jurisdiction of today's institutions of international jurisprudence such as the International Court of Justice or the International Criminal Court, and, since we are dealing with genocide, puts *all* states into a *legal obligation* to make efforts to bring that global illegal situation to an end.

---

18   A. Schweitzer quoted in: Baba Kaké, Ibrahima (1998). La vulgarisation de l'histoire de la traite negrière'', in: Doudou Diene (ed.): La chaine et le lien. Une vision de la traite negriere, Paris: UNES-CO, 25-29, 26.

This is followed by an assessment of the legacy of genocidal transatlantic slavery and of the consequences of the continuing crime of the Maafa through discussing a few examples of the general reality of global apartheid.

Reparations opponents also love to postulate that transatlantic slavery would be a matter of old, far-back history, and that it could not be possible to go back "indefinitely" with reparation claims, that at some point one just needs to look ahead. Legally and technically speaking, this kind of discourse refers to the doctrine of *laches*, which holds that a claim can no longer be brought forth after too much time has passed. We will see that with regards to transatlantic slavery, *laches* is without any relevance since, one, the crime is continuing and *laches* logically concerns only completed acts, and because, two, the claim has in fact been brought forth since the first deportations of Africans over the Atlantic. Perpetrator states have only never accepted them.

We will also look into additional recent and significant developments in international law that strengthen the legal claim for reparations further. These include the fact that slavery is today considered contrary to *ius cogens*, and that several former enslaver states have in the past few years expressed their "regrets" in one form or another. In other contexts, international jurisprudence found fair solutions when confronted with other sensitive matters, even when positive law at first sight seemed to deny any such possibilities.

But in those other cases where jurisprudence found innovative solutions to get to justice, lobbying and power was decisive to one extent or another. As in life in general, in international law too nothing moves by itself, and given the fact that no state today is in a realistic position to push forward the claim to full global African reparation, it is people's power that we have to build upon in this. Even more so since it would be delusionary to think or even hope that European ex-enslaver states and the USA would ever make the reparations that they are in a legal obligation to make, even when confronted with the most solid legal argument. They have consistently proven by their conduct in perpetrating the Maafa during the past 500 years that they will never by their own volition desist from this genocidal behaviour. Furthermore, full reparations for transatlantic slavery, if sticking to international law requirements, would translate to the end of the current capitalist world system, as will be elaborated towards the end of this book. So, even though reparations are about much more than money, we see what interests are at stake.

That being given, it is important to substantiate and shout it loud again and again that African people have a clear legal entitlement to reparations, whereas European states are in a legal obligation to make reparations and in a permanent grave violation of international law for genocide. The building of awareness and consciousness by African people about their legal right to reparation can, so I hope, form a strong engine to *take* reparations.

In a next section we will familiarize ourselves with different forms of reparations, such as provided by international law, and their relevance with regard to transatlantic slavery and the Maafa. This is done within a hopeful perspective that elaborating, showing and discussing for and with the people about what it is that is concretely due to them legally as reparations for transatlantic slavery can motivate them into action to get it when it is not willingly given by perpetrators.

The 1996 debate on reparations in the British House of Lords was the first time that a government of a former slaver nation was obliged to set out its reasons for being against reparations. Lord Chesham on behalf of that government contended that "first, slavery was practised by Arabs and Africans as well as Europeans [thus alluding to the allegation of its legality]. Second, African leaders were active participants in the slave trade. Third, it was not the British Government which traded in slaves but individual traders and companies. Fourth, there was no evidence that the effects of slavery were still being felt by Africans now living in Africa and the Diaspora. Fifth, racism was not just a Black and White problem, but occurs between different ethnic groups all over the world"[19]. All of these arguments, forming the ideological foundation of the position of the whole entity of former European slaver states, are deconstructed in the course of this work.

Already in the very early phases of this research that extended over almost four years, the few international lawyers that were exposed to its basic ideas and premises thereupon changed their legal opinion, such as my tutor at the Institut des Hautes Etudes Internationales (IHEI) in Paris where I started the research. After transmitting an early research paper to Anthony Gifford, a pioneer in the legal reparations struggle, he informed me that he thought my ideas worth pursuing, so I went to Jamaica to continue to research from there. I am very grateful to Tony for inviting me to accompany the Jamaican National Commission on Reparations to some of their public sittings, as well as to the late Professor Barry Chevannes, chairmen of that Commission, who made it possible for me to use the library of the University of the West Indies on Mona Campus, where I found a great amount of very useful evidence and literature for the legal argument now presented in this book.

While I was in Jamaica, the National Commission on Reparations asked Patrick Robinson, then President of the International Criminal Tribunal for the former Yugoslavia, for his opinion on the matter of transatlantic slavery reparations. He initially responded echoing the dominant position, maintaining that he saw no legal basis for this reparations claim since "slavery" would have been "legal" at its time and that he would advise the Jamaican government to pursue reparations on a purely diplomatic and moral level. Yet upon being exposed to my manuscript,

---

19   Gifford, Anthony (2007). The Passionate Advocate, Kingston: Arawak Publications, 259 et seq.

he conceded that I established *prima facie* that transatlantic slavery was illegal at the time of facts, with all the consequences that this would legally entail when it comes to reparations.[20]

Beyond the legal case for reparations, today the fact remains that Africa was and is the resource-richest continent of the globe. Before transatlantic slavery, these resources were not taken from the continent but remained for the benefit of its people. But after transatlantic slavery and up until now, structures were put firmly in place to drain the wealth of Africa and make hundreds of millions of Africans suffer from hunger. These are simple and readily observable facts and they should suffice to make every sensible human being understand the necessity of reparation.

Reparation, the healing of Africa, is also vital for the indispensable re-balancing of our planet. The western system which has emerged out of transatlantic slavery and is still dependent on mechanisms and structures laid down in transatlantic slavery, has not only killed off unimaginable numbers of people during the past centuries, but has also brought our planet to the verge of collapse. This system that is also responsible for the massive environmental catastrophe that we are currently faced with has its foundation in the enslavement of African people and of Africa. Reparation, if sticking to international law, also translates into the abolition of this system. Africa has a right grounded in international law to be free from the threat of nuclear holocaust. Reparation would also mean the abandonment of the traditional western political system which has come under much fire recently from the Occupy-movement and other social justice movements globally. The western democratic system basically relies on the principle that those who can lie best and furnish most short-term material benefits, even if coming with huge hidden long-term costs, to their constituencies, will win the election. Such a system is doomed to bring our planet to collapse. One of our great challenges in these times is to grasp the signs of the moment and get the global social justice and environmental movements to understand that their claims are in fact connected to the claim for transatlantic slavery reparations, and that it is a claim that is well grounded in international law. We have a legal entitlement to the end of capitalism, of genocide, of racism and of massive industrial and nuclear pollution.

Looking at our world, any sound thinking person should easily see that it is in serious and urgent need of re-balancing and healing, if we are to stay here. Transatlantic slavery reparation is fundamental to this healing. And since it seems as if we are at last dependent on people's power, and cannot rely on states or politicians to accomplish this goal of redeeming humanity and our planet, we will need to engage cultural movements such as hip-hop and reggae to reach out to the

20   National Commission on Reparations. Commentary by Lord Anthony Gifford QC on Judge Robinson's Paper, December 29, 2009; E-Mail from Judge Patrick Robsinson, October 16, 2012 (on file with author).

youth of this earth, African and other, and make them know the truth about what is rightfully theirs in these times of confusion and weapons of mass distraction.

Before really getting started though and for the case that some of you are wondering how as a young woman of immediate physical European ancestry from Austria I came to do this work, let me state that I consider myself universal. The truth remains the truth for all, just as the imminent threat to human existence from the system that was founded on transatlantic slavery and continues to shed so much blood and generate so much pollution that our planet can no longer take it, is also the same for all of us. Beyond that, it probably also had some kind of influence that Africa has always given me so much joy through people, music, food, literature, vibration and much more. If the planet has a future, Africa is that future.

II. Europeans Were Always Only a Global Minority – The Evolution and State of International Law Before Transatlantic Slavery

Tragically but hardly surprisingly, reparation claims for transatlantic slavery are generally ignored or ridiculed in Western academic, legal and political discourses, based on the contention that "slavery" would have been "legal" under international law at the time in question. This allegation of "legality", combined with the fundamental international law principle of *non-retroactivity*, is employed to maintain that no internationally wrongful act could be attributable to the European states involved in transatlantic slavery, and that therefore international law would provide no basis for reparation claims in this matter.

This is really the heart piece of the international political and legal reparations debate. I do not wish to contest in the least that it is indeed "the international regulation applicable at the time when the tragedy of the transatlantic slave trade took place"[21] which is decisive in order to assess legal responsibility for this most massive crime. It is a long accepted tenet of international law that facts can only be judged by the law that was valid when they were realized. This was consistently maintained by international legal jurisprudence, such as in the *Island of Palmas* case where judge Max Huber stated that "[a] juridical fact must be appreciated in the light of the law contemporary with it, and not the law in force at the time when a dispute in regard to it arises or falls to be settled"[22]. And the principle does not stem from recent imperialist international law developments, but is really anchored in natural law and the logical demands of justice, so there is no way around it when dealing with transatlantic slavery reparations from a legal perspective. However, and contrary to reparation negationists who are always so eager to stress this legal requirement, I do not think that the endeavour can

---

21   Boschiero, Nerina (2004). "La traite transatlantique et la responsabilité internationale des Etats", in: Laurence Boisson de Chazournes, Jean-François Quéguinerand Santiago Villalpando (ed.): Crimes de l'histoire et réparations: les réponses du droit et de la justice, Brussels: Editions Bruylant, 203-262, 217.
22   Island of Palmas (Netherlands v. USA), Award of April 4, 1928, R.I.A.A. (2), 829-871.

be accomplished satisfactorily by limiting the historical legal investigation to the concepts of European enslaver states who were able to impose a global predominance, including law norms declaring de-humanizing chattel slavery as "legal", onto Africa and the rest of the world. That they were able to do this was itself a consequence of the crime of transatlantic slavery.

Ancient African law knew non-retroactivity, too. "To fulfil their preventative function, punishments had to be determined before an act was committed. (...) Through continuous massacres, deportations and genocides, many written supports of legal traditions have been lost, but [this knowledge] still survived thanks to the memory of the elite of the griots."[23]

Indeed, prior to transatlantic slavery Africa participated as much as Europe in the formation of international law, as will be shown throughout this chapter. And it is by the standards of this "pre-transatlantic-slavery" international law that the legal status of transatlantic slavery has to be assessed; not by the norms that enslaver states passed in the middle of their crime, to enable them to carry out the crime. This point has been insisted upon in various communications and claims by descendants of enslaved Africans, such as in a draft paper titled "Charting an African Self-Determined Path of Legal Struggle for Reparations", presented in 1993 at the conference of the African Reparations Movement – United Kingdom Committee (ARM-UKC).[24] Its authors Julie Affiong Southey and Kofi Mawuli Klu maintained that the essential questions in the struggle for reparations concern "whose framework, whose Law and whose Justice"[25] are employed. They insisted on pressing the matter from an "African perspective of Law and Justice, within the principled framework of the popular democratic rule of just International Law"[26], and stressed that "the interests of imperialism were directly written into the rules of International Law"[27]. Though I would rather say that the interests of imperialism were written into the practice of international law, not the rules themselves, the question of the legal status of transatlantic slavery is indeed the angle point of the whole international debate about reparations. This is indicated by the fact that it is always the first, and often only, argument that Western governments come up with when confronted with reparation claims. For example, not long ago the British High Commissioner in Jamaica, in the name of the Queen of England, responded to a claim by the Rastafari movement that "(...) the historic slave trade was not a crime against humanity or contrary to international law at the time

---

23   Camara, Fatou Kiné (2004). Pouvoir et Justice dans la Tradition des Peuples Noires. Philosophie et Pratique, Paris: L'Harmattan, 38 (t.b.a.).
24   Affiong Southey, Julie/Klu, Kofi Mawuli (1993). Charting an African Self-Determined Path of Legal Struggle for Reparations, Birmingham: African Reparations Movement-United Kingdom Committee.
25   Ibid., 1.
26   Ibid.
27   Ibid.

when the UK Government condoned it. It is a fundamental principle of international law that events have to be judged against the law as it stood at the time when they occurred. We regret and condemn the inequities of the historic slave trade, but these shameful activities belong to the past. Governments today cannot take responsibility for what happened over 150 years ago".[28]

However, as Rastafari insisted, "there was no historical era when Englishmen or Europeans constituted the total family of humanity; nor was there a period of the history of mankind when the European concept of International Law and Justice was globally accepted or universally enforced"[29]. They recalled the "ancient legal maxim that ignorance of the law does not constitute an excuse or defence for its violation. It is important to mention here that there is no statute of limitations in law for the crimes of murder, genocide and enslavement"[30].

Even legal scholars have commenced to recognize that "the views of both the 'great powers' as well as those subject to their colonial domination ought to be considered. (...) The fact that a continent was colonised and its statesmen and leaders silenced, does not mean that we should accept the views of the oppressors as the only source of the content of international law at the time"[31]. Yet so far, there has been no serious undertaking to reconstruct the real international law pertaining to transatlantic slavery at its time and to assess reparations claims on that legal basis. This book takes up that task.

The necessity to thoroughly research and reconstruct the law applicable to transatlantic slavery requires us to look far back in the history of international law, and to deal with some fundamental questions. Since when does "international law" exist? Who participated in its genesis and development? If we accept the notion of *ubi societas ibi ius* – where there is a human society, there is law –, a provision of Roman law still highly esteemed by contemporary lawyers[32] and one of the first things that any law student hears in college, we must conclude that international law had existed for quite some time before the late 15th century when the first Africans were subjected to transatlantic slavery, because an "international" society that maintained peaceful contacts, mostly via commerce, did exist. It has been maintained by sociologists and international law scholars, such

---

28   Letter of January 2, 2003 by Gavin Tech, Deputy British High Commissioner, to "the RastafarI Brethren of Jamaica", c/o Mr. Howard Hamilton, Public Defender, 78 Harbour Street, Kingston (on file with author).

29   Letter of January 15, 2003 by the All Mansion's Secretariat of the Ethiopian Peace Foundation, Jamaica Branch, International RastafarI Community, RastafarI Brethren of Jamaica, to Her Royal Majesty Queen Elizabeth II, Buckingham Palace, Attention: Mrs. Kay Brock, Assistant Private Secretary, c/o Mr. Gavin Tech, Deputy British High Commissioner, Kingston, 3et seq (on file with author).

30   Ibid.

31   Peté, Stephen & Du Plessis, Max (2007). "Reparations for Gross Violations of Human Rights in Context", in: Max du Plessis and Stephen Peté (ed.): Repairing the Past? International Perspectives on Reparations for Gross Human Rights Abuses, Antwerpen/Oxford: Intersentia, 3-28, 25 (t.b.a.).

32   Scelle, Georges (1934b). Précis de Droit des Gens. Vol.2, Paris: Librairie du Recueil Sirey, 61.

as Georges Scelle, that every *de facto* society is at the same time a society *de jure* for there can be no enduring social practice without emission of rules regulating interactions.[33]

1. ROOTS

"If one perceives (...) international law as the set of rules, written and non-written, applicable to subjects and situations that do not exclusively pertain to internal law, it is permissible to affirm that it has always existed."[34]

It is generally accepted that international law has its origins in international commerce.[35] According to western international law scholars, provisions of international law can also be traced back to the Bible, the practice of Ancient Greece's city-states or the Roman Empire, all of which left a footprint that is still present in contemporary international law.[36] In this context, one should keep in mind that numerous passages in the Bible make reference to Africa, and that both Ancient Greece and the Roman Empire maintained, economic and other, relations with African societies.[37] As shown by Georges James in *Stolen Legacy*, Ancient Greece indeed took many of the concepts that are generally credited to it from Kemet, that is, Africa. Many Biblical and Rabbinic sources point to the political and military power of the people of Kush – Africans – their wealth and international influence, as well as their role in international trade.[38]

Historical records leave no doubt that Africans were involved in international trade at least as much as Europeans prior to the late 15th century. In antiquity, the Axum kingdom of Ethiopia was a leading power in world commerce, with its own gold, silver and copper money, dominating maritime traffic from the Red Sea to the Persian Gulf, India, Ceylon, South-East and Oriental Asia, and from the Gulf of Aden on the coast of Somalia downwards oriental Africa. Original records from this trade still exist, and they contain nothing that would indicate regular export of slaves, yet Axum's Adoulis was the most important port in the Red Sea.[39] The time between 500 and 1500 CE was the millennium during when the commerce

---

33 Scelle, Georges (1934a). Précis de Droit des Gens. Vol.1, Paris: Librairie du Recueil Sirey, 4.
34 Carreau, Dominique (2007). Droit international, Paris: Editions Pedone, 30.
35 Hummer, Waldemar/Neuhold, Hanspeter/Schreuer, Christoph (1997). Österreichisches Handbuch des Völkerrechts, Vol.1, Wien: Manz, 14-17.
36 Carreau (2007), 30 et seq.
37 James, George (1993). Stolen legacy, New York: Africa World Press.
38 Isaac, Ephraim (1985). "Genesis, Judaism, and the 'Sons of Ham'", in: John Ralph Willis (ed.): Slaves and Slavery in Muslim Africa, Volume I. Islam and the Ideology of Enslavement, London: Frank Cass and Company, 75-91, 80.
39 Popo, Klah (2010). Histoire des‚Traites Négrières'. Critique afrocentrée d'une négrophobie académique, Paris: Anibwe, 29.

between East Africa and countries bordering the Indian Ocean was at its height.[40] For several centuries the wealth and industry of Africa, often denominated as Sudan in historic documents, never ceased to attract Arabs and Berbers, Jews and Christians. We were also left with accounts of the interrelations between the East African littoral and the Chinese for purposes of trade, exploration, and adventure.[41]

Indeed, Africa had become a veritable myth in Europe, and was sometimes referred to as "land of gold".[42] Africa contributed significantly to the world economy. In fact, securing a better part of the very lucrative trade just described may well have been one major motive for the Portuguese and Spanish to come to West Africa in the beginning of the 15th century.[43] Other European rulers also had their eyes on it. Ramusio, secretary to the rulers in Venice, was urging the merchants of Italy in 1563, to "go and do business with the King of Timbuktu and Mali (...). There is no doubt they will be well received there with their ships and their goods and treated well, and granted the favours that they ask."[44] Thus we see that the trade of gold, ivory, silk and spices between Africa, Persia, India, China and Europe had taken place for centuries before Europeans began to enslave people in Africa.[45]

Legal-historical scholars have confirmed that intense international legal relations, especially economic, were maintained in the Mediterranean region, encompassing North Africa, from the 8th century onwards.[46] Since the 12th century, there existed a merchant maritime "international code so that traders from all parts were familiar with the rights and obligations it enforced"[47].

Ample evidence exists that, much earlier, dynastic Egypt had a system of tributary relations with its smaller neighbors, and that these arrangements were regulated by treaty, whereby the juridical construction of "making peace" was combined with the Egyptian obligation to "be generous" and to "do good" to the new vassals.[48] One of the best known "international" legal treaties of antiquity,

40   Davidson, Basil (1961). The African Slave Trade, Boston/New York: Back Bay Books.

41   Elias, T.O. (1975). "International Relations in Africa: A Historical Survey", in: A.K. Mensah-Brown (ed.): African International Legal History, New York: UNITAR, 87-106, 87 et seq.

42   M'Bokolo, Elikia (1995b). "La rencontre des deux mondes et ses repercussions: la part de l'Afrique (1492-1992)", in: Elikia M'Bokolo (ed.): L'Afrique entre l'Europe et l'Amerique. Le role de l'Afrique dans la rencontre de deux mondes 1492-1992, UNESCO, Paris, 13-30, 21.

43   Chinweizu (1987). The West and the Rest of Us, Lagos: Pero Press, 3.

44   Davidson (1961), 26.

45   Hess, Penny (2000). Overturning the Culture of Violence, St.Petersburg: Burning Spear Uhuru Publications, 5.

46   Fischer, Peter/Köck, Franz Heribert (2004). Völkerrecht. Das Recht der universellen Staatengemeinschaft, 6. Auflage, Wien: Linde Verlag, 50 et seq.

47   Miéville, China (2006). Between Equal Rights. A Marxist Theory of International Law, Brill: Leiden, 197.

48   Bederman, David L. (2001). International Law in Antiquity, Cambridge: Cambridge University

involving an African party, is the peace and alliance treaty concluded in 1279 BC between Ramses II of Egypt and Hattusili II of the Hittites.[49]

Once concluded, such agreements had to be strictly respected.[50] Thus, we find here one of the most basic premises of international law, the principle of *pacta sunt servanda* ("agreements must be kept"). *Pacta sunt servanda* has also been a fundamental precept in Islamic law, even in dealings with non-Muslim entities.[51] In African legal traditions, the principle of pacta sunt servanda was a legal precept as well.[52] Good faith was a related legal maxim that seems to have been well accepted in ancient times. "As an idea, it was adopted by nearly all ancient civilizations as a means of recognizing the integrity of promises made both within a social order and in the international realm. (...) States had no obligation to make promises; but once they did, they were compelled to keep them."[53]

Those ancient times also knew the legal requirements of diplomatic immunity. "Ambassadors had to be well treated and their person was inviolable, every breach of this principle constituting a wrongful act that could justify to resort to war. Isn't it here that we find the origin of 'diplomatic immunities' that never ceased to be one of the most fundamental and elementary institutions of international society (...)? The condition of strangers was the object of frequent developments in the Bible: basically it states their equality of treatment with 'nationals' and ordains their protection."[54]

The available historical evidence shows that these rules of international relations were known and respected by African states in their encounters with European officials and traders before and at the beginning of transatlantic slavery. Tragically, this conformity with international law was not reciprocated by their European counterparts who disrespected agreements, ignored the sovereignty of African states and violently deposed rulers who were unwilling to collaborate with them in enslavement.[55] We will come back to this in more detail later.

Moreover, the existence of a natural "international" law was explicitly recognized in antiquity, and indeed up to the 19th century. Roman jurist and statesman Cicero had provided the following definition:

Press, 146 et seq.

49   Nussbaum, Arthur (1954). A Concise History of the Law of Nations, New York: Macmillan Co., 4 et seq.

50   Carreau (2007), 31.

51   Lohlker, Rüdiger (2006). Islamisches Völkerrecht. Studien am Beispiel Granada, Bremen: Kleio Humanities, 91.

52   Alexandrowicz, Charles H. (1975). "The Role of Treaties in the European-African Confrontation in the Nineteenth Century", in: A.K. Mensah-Brown (ed.): African International Legal History, New York: UNITAR, 27-68, 48.

53   Bederman (2001), 52.

54   Carreau (2007), 31 (t.b.a.).

55   Clarke, John Henrik (1998). Christopher Columbus and the Afrikan Holocaust. Slavery and the Rise of European Capitalism, New York: A&B Publisher Group, 16.

"Law in the proper sense is right reason in harmony with nature. It is spread through the whole human community, unchanging and eternal, calling people to their duty by its commands and deterring them from wrong-doing by its prohibitions. This law cannot be countermanded, nor can it be in any way rescinded. We cannot be exempted from this law by any decree of the senate or the people. (...) There will not be one such law in Rome and one such law in Athens, one now and another in the future, but all peoples at all times will be embraced by a single and eternal and unchangeable law; and there will be, as it were, one lord and master of us all – the god who is the author, proposer and interpreter of that law."[56]

Roman *ius gentium* (law of nations), regulating relations concluded between Roman citizens and foreigners, established minimal obligations with regard to foreigners. It is maintained by scholars that this position of principle has ever since remained part of international law, and was thus valid at the time of transatlantic slavery. Roman law also recognized the inviolability of envoys as a standard in international (or, inter-polity) relations.[57]

The Roman Empire was obliged to maintain relations with its unconquerable adversaries on the basis of international law and agreements. During and between the Punic wars, their adversaries and agreement partners were Africans. In the treaties between the Roman Empire and Carthage in 509, 306, and 279 BCE, heavy maritime restrictions were laid upon the Romans, whose ships were excluded from important African coastal waters.[58] The Carthagian hinterland was far-flung into Africa. However, the exclusion of Greeks and Romans from African seaways seems to account for the lack of information about this in the writings of classical authors. What we know is that Carthage traded intensively with West Africa and closed the North/West African coast to all foreigners.[59] In the 5th century BCE, Carthage sent out an expedition under Hanno to found trading posts on the African coast, passing by the Senegal River, Gambia estuary, Sierra Leone, Cameroon, and Gabon River. Gold was one important object of the expedition. Centuries later, Prince Henry the Navigator, who desired to discover the source of the gold imported into Morocco overland, sent out Portuguese seamen to follow the route of Hanno.[60] Carthage concluded a treaty with Macedon in 215 BCE under the authority of Hannibal, a treaty that has been described as containing "extraordinary detail and complexity of its provisions"[61].

---

56   Cicero (ed.1998). The Republic and The Laws, trans. by N. Rudd, Oxford: Oxford University Press, 68f; cited in: Peté/Du Plessis (2007), 26.
57   Ibid.
58   Nussbaum (1954), 4et seq.
59   Elias, Taslim O. (1972). Africa and the Development of International Law, Leiden: A.W. Sijthoff, 3 et seq.
60   Elias, Taslim O. (1975). "International Relations in Africa: A Historical Survey", in: A.K. Mensah-Brown (ed.): African International Legal History, New York: UNITAR, 87-106, 87 et seq.
61   Bederman (2001), 188.

Yet, there are some scholars who maintain that there would have been no "international law" in antiquity because "nations", in the sense of independent political communities vested with sovereign power, would not yet have existed at that time. Without sovereign nation-states, there could be no law whose subjects are those nation-states, it is sustained.[62] Though there is some internal logic to this argument, it is mostly of semantic value. One may substitute terms such as "global" or "interpolity" law for "international law", but the fact remains that there were global and interpolity legal regulations. Nothing forces one to reduce the term and concept of international law to a law between "sovereign" and "equal" states.[63]

In substance, international legal intercourse and even individual institutions of international law trace their history to the most ancient periods of society. "To the extent that exchange was not initially made between individuals, but among tribes and communities, it may be affirmed that the institutions of international law are the most ancient of legal institutions in general."[64] It has indeed been maintained that "many, if not all, concepts of present-day international law can be followed down the evolutionary ladder to their primeval stage".[65]

Renowned scholars and legal experts such as Ago[66] and Paradisi[67] have further highlighted the fact of the existence of the ancient state and the reality of "international" relations in antiquity. Bederman in his research revealed that in each of the times and places considered, covering 2,500 years of human history and a region encompassing north-eastern Africa, there existed states conscious of their own status and sovereignty, actually conducting international relations along predictable patterns which emphasized the necessity of diplomatic relations, the sanctity of agreements, and controls on the initiation and conduct of war.[68]

So when it is asserted that since modern times Europe and North America had determined world politics and therefore fashioned "classic international law" to their liking, this does not imply that there was no system of international law before these "modern times". Conventional authors maintain that fundaments of international law existed not only in Europe, but equally in the Middle East, India and Ancient China. Furthermore, scholars have ascertained that in spite of cul-

---

62   Miéville (2006), 159.
63   Grewe, Wilhelm G. (1984). Epochen der Völkerrechtsgeschichte, Baden-Baden: Nomos Verlagsgesellschaft, 26 et seq.
64   Miéville (2006), 160.
65   Parkinson, F. (1975). "Pre-Colonial International Law", in: A.K. Mensah-Brown (ed.): African International Legal History, New York: UNITAR, 11-26, 11.
66   Ago, Robert (1983). TheFirst International Communities in the Mediterranean World, British Year Book of International Law, Oxford: Clarendon Press, 1983, 53, 213 et seq.; see also: Bederman (2001), 21.
67   Paradisi, Bruno (1951). L'amitié internationale: les phases critiques de son ancienne histoire, in: Recueil des cours, Académie de Droit International de La Haye, Vol.78, 325-378,355; see also: Bederman (2001), 21.
68   Bederman (2001), 21.

tural and social differences, identical legal solutions to problems were provided in these regions, such as immunity being guaranteed to emissaries.[69] We have already seen that the immunity of ambassadors was respected by African states prior to transatlantic slavery.

Some original accounts make explicit reference to "international law" or the "law of nations" well before the 17th century, the generally accepted birth period of "modern" international law. For example, a council of jurists came together in Almeirim in 1569 where they promulgated the "Resolutions des Lettrés" ("resolutions of the learned") which mentioned the "inviolability conceded to ambassadors in accordance with the law of nations"[70]. In 1588 Alberto Gentili wrote that "piracy is contrary to the law of nations and the league of human society. Therefore war should be made against pirates by all men (...)"[71]. As early as in the 1500's, piracy was considered a customary international crime, entailing legal responsibility.[72] Indeed, ancient peoples apparently spoke regularly of a law of nations.[73]

So let us not become confused by semantic debates that only serve to shift focus from what is really essential, and that remains that there was law, whether we term it international or intergroup, at the time up to transatlantic slavery.

What is equally important to realize is that there "is no question that Western legal scholars knew of, and were influenced by regulated behavior, even the legal form, between non-Western polities. Grotius (1583-1645) pointed out in his *Mare Librum* that '(t)hese islands of which we speak, now have and always have had their own kings, their own government, their own laws, and their own legal systems. The Portuguese do not go there as sovereigns but as foreigners. Indeed they only reside there by sufferance'"[74]. In his monumental *De Iure Belli ac Pacis*, Grotius outlined the history of arbitration, and was manifestly inspired in this by Eméric Crusé's *Nouveau Cyrée, ou discours d'Etat réprésentant les occasions et moyens d'establir [sic] une paix générale et la liberté du commerce par tout le monde,* containing a proposal for a scheme of international consultation and arbitration on a truly universal, and not only European, scale.[75]

69   Hummer/Neuhold/Schreuer (1997), 14.

70   Capela, José (2002). 'Ethique et representation de l'esclavage colonial au Mozambique', in: Isabel Castro Henriques and Louis Sala-Molins (ed.): Déraison, esclavage et droit. Les fondements ideologiques et juridiques de la traite negriere et de l'esclavage, Paris: EDITIONS Unesco, 329- 348, 340 et seq.

71   Rubin, Alfred P. (1968). "The Use of Piracy in Malayan Waters", in: Charles H. Alexandrowicz (ed.): Studies in the history of the laws of nations, The Hague: Grotian Press Society, 111-135, 111 et seq.

72   Bassiouni, M. Cherif (1992). Crimes Against Humanity in International Criminal Law, Dordrecht/Boston/London: Martinus Nijhoff Publishers, 194 et seq.

73   Bederman (2001), 276.

74   Miéville (2006), 168.

75   Purves, R. (1968). "Prolegomena to Utopian International Projects", in: Charles H. Alexandro-

Thus, we see clearly that, regardless of the semantic term, some sort of "international" law did exist. Many general principles of international law have their origin in rules and institutions of ancient and Roman law.[76] Legal scholars have well established that there is an unbroken continuity in international law from antiquity up to the present.[77] Indeed, it is somewhat interesting that international lawyers today will come a long way to defend their discipline against the charge that it would be anything less than "real" law. However, when it comes to state relations in the ancient world, many will readily concede that such were "unprincipled, devoid of any sense of legal obligation, and without effective sanctions. In short, they acknowledge for antiquity what they deny for the modern law of nations".[78] Why is all of this important for us? Because what international law was historically is essential to legally ground the reparations claim for transatlantic slavery.

Researchers and scholars have established that prior to the 19th century treaties were characterized by a relative absence of colonialism. That is nothing to say about the practice, but the law applied by all parties globally in their relations was the classic law of nations which was dominated by natural law doctrine. Thus we see that natural law was recognized and considered a part of the positive and applicable law at the times of transatlantic slavery. It was rooted in the universality of the family of nations irrespective of race, creed, civilization, or continent. This is also evidenced by the nature of early treaties and diplomatic relations between Portuguese and other European state officials and African sovereigns.[79]

Even much earlier, in antiquity, Greek deputies explicitly relied on natural law as applicable law when they sustained that the Thebans "came not only in time of peace, but at a holy season, and attempted to seize our city; we righteously and in accordance with universal law defended ourselves and punished the aggressor."[80] Again, Cicero had maintained, speaking of natural law, that "there will not be different laws at Rome and at Athens, or different laws now and in the future, but one eternal and unchangeable law will be valid for all nations and for all times".[81] Scholarship has therefore concluded that there was "a common idea held in antiquity that international relations were to be based on the rule of law. The embrace of that idea, and not any particular structure of process or doctrine, is what qualifies ancient international law as something more than 'primitive'"[82].

---

wicz (ed.): Studies in the history of the laws of nations, The Hague: Grotian Press Society, 100-110, 106.

76   Carreau (2007), 33.
77   Fischer/Köck (2004), 49.
78   Bederman (2001), 48.
79   Alexandrowicz (1975), 32 et seq.
80   Bederman (2001), 253.
81   Ibid., 280.
82   Ibid., 267.

Isidor of Seville (560-636) stated that *ius gentium* was called by that name because all people were making use of it. This conceptualization entered the *Decretum Gratiani* and was upheld by Thomas of Aquinas, who defined *ius gentium* as all norms that men recognize by reason to be necessary in human relations and which could therefore be observed with all people.[83] Examples of this, again, were said to be the inviolability of embassies and *pacta sunt servanda*, documentedly respected in Africa. A letter from the pope to the King of Sicily in 1272 makes explicit reference to the necessity of *ius gentium* that envoys dwell in absolute security when abroad. Numerous arbitral sentences were also grounded in *ius gentium*.[84]

Within these ancient lines of international or inter-polity law, the duty to make reparation for wrongs had long been recognized. "The principles of Mosaic, Islamic, and even English common law are all rooted in *compensation for injury* caused by another (...)"[85] The parties of the mentioned treaty concluded between King Ramses II of Egypt and Hittite King Hattusilis III regarded their consensual obligations as legally binding and accepted that any breach of it involved a duty to make reparation.[86]

In African legal traditions, reparation was a well-established legal concept. African legal systems placed more importance on limiting the damage for the victim than on retaliating against the aggressor. Thus naturally, reparation and reconciliation were accorded a high level of importance.[87]

In Europe, after the collapse of the Roman Empire there was hardly any law at all, and its reconstruction was greatly the work of the church. The *Corpus iuris canonici* contained rules of secular power that were, in the sphere of international relations, far more coercive than those presented by the international law of our day, because consequences of their breach included excommunication, disposal of kings, massive fines, disqualification from public office, threat of losing capacity to make a will or acquire property by succession.[88]

In this context one should keep in mind that in medieval Europe and later, professors, although sometimes appointed to university chairs by rulers, were not authorized to make law in the strict sense. However, they did hold a non-negli-

---

83   See Grewe (1984), 108 et seq.

84   Ibid.

85   Winbush, Omari L. (2003). "Reflections on Homer Plessy and Reparations", in: Raymond A. Winbush (ed.): Should America pay? Slavery and the raging debate on reparations, New York: Amistad, 150-162, 150.

86   Schwarzenberger, Georg (1976). "Towards a Comparative History of International Law", in: M.K. Nawaz (ed.): Essays on International Law. In Honour of Krishne Rao, Leiden: Sijthoff Publishing, 92-106, 102.

87   Kiné Camara, Fatou (2004). Pouvoir et justice dans la tradition des peuples noirs, Paris: L'Harmattan.

88   Nussbaum (1954), 20.

gible influence on law-making in the sense that it was their job to interpret the *Corpus Iuris Civilis*. The reception of Roman law in most European states and the law-making powers of the law professors went hand in hand. "The heroes of Continental law before codification are law professors."[89] Please consider that much of the European law pertaining to slavery was taken from Roman law. The official Spanish position, influenced by the crown jurist Sepulveda, was at first to negate that the peoples of the Americas were subjects of the law of nations. However, the leading legal scholars of the University of Salamanca at that time maintained that the relations of all people repose in natural law. De Vitoria wrote in *Reflectio de Indis* (1532) that a Christian state could not rightfully claim dominion over a non-Christian state. He saw the law of nations as valid for all humanity because it flows from natural law, whereas the formation of detailed rules demands practice and agreements. Grotius too, who was heavily influenced by the Spanish school, followed this in claiming that the fundamentals were rooted in natural law, whereas the details were to be explicitly or tacitly agreed upon. Soto upheld explicitly that in the law of nations there was no difference between Christian and "heathen" nations. Ayala, Gentili and Grotius also subscribed to this.[90] Suarez also conceptualized the community of the law of nations as englobing all mankind, although for him the material law of nations reposed on the will of states.[91] Vitoria maintained that a *titulus naturalis societatis et communicationis* gave the Spaniards the right to travel to indigenous people, to dwell in their lands and engage in trade. Only if the indigenous people showed themselves unapproachable or resorted to violence, did the law professors concede the Europeans a right to self-defence in the limits of necessity, meaning that even then they did not have the right to kill or rob them or take over their cities.[92]

It was only as late as in the 19th century that international law theory and practice lost this grounding in natural law, and that the European positivist point of view became prevalent and non-European peoples were denied an international legal personality in international law practice, which was by then controlled by Europeans as a consequence of their foundational crime of transatlantic slavery.[93] But since natural law was recognized as valid law at that time of transatlantic slavery, it has to be included in the assessment of the legal status of the same. "In practice and theory, the law of nations was conceived of as universal during the whole era of the European expansion from the age of 'discoveries'."[94] Until

---

89   Watson, Alan (1989). Slave Law in the Americas, Athens/London: The University of Georgia Press, 3 et seq.
90   Grewe (1984), 225.
91   Ibid., 226.
92   Grewe (1984), 243.
93   Fischer/Köck (2004), 20.
94   Schulte-Tenckhoff, Isabelle (1998). "The Function of Otherness in Treaty Making", in: E. van Rouveroy van Niewaal and Werner Zips (ed.): Sovereignty, Legitimacy and Power in West African

the mid-19th century a non-discriminatory and universal concept of the law of nations based on natural law had prevailed, which had considered all organised political entities, including those "overseas", as free and equal. It is important to keep in mind that treaty making is "one of the essential attributes of external sovereignty", and that Europeans concluded an abundance of treaties with African rulers over the centuries.

From all of this, we see that it is way too simplistic to contend that "the practices of slavery and slave trade by certain states were not prohibited by the law of international society as they were tolerated by the legal orders of the majority of the components of this society"[95]. Yet this is indeed just what reparations negationists rely upon principally and chiefly in their argumentation to bash reparations claims. But we know that from ancient times, "international society" was not limited to Europe. A contrary stance not only reproduces a vision of a colonial legal system that was itself an integral part of colonialism, but is also factually wrong.

Before we go on to excavate the actually relevant legal provisions of African and European states concerning transatlantic slavery, we should dwell a bit on the characteristics of affected African societies in order to pertinently demonstrate once and for all that they were subjects of international law whose legal perspectives are relevant when assessing and reconstructing the legal status of transatlantic slavery. Some might, rightfully, interject that the qualification of historical African societies as states should really be no point warranting debate, but I esteem such a clarification important still, precisely because representatives of responsible European states, the United States of America and Canada[96] as well as other reparation negationists, regularly try to make the point that African and indigenous nations would not have been states, with the ensuing implications that treaties with them would not have had binding character and that they would not have been relevant in the historical formation of international law.

2. LEGAL CRITERIA OF STATEHOOD, AND AFRICAN STATES AND SOCIETIES BEFORE AND DURING TRANSATLANTIC SLAVERY

The proposition that transatlantic slavery would have been legal indeed goes hand in hand with, and is to a large extent dependent on, the contention that no African states would have existed at that time. However, in the context of the

---

Societies, Hamburg: Lit-Verlag, 9-21, 11 et seq.
95   Boschiero (2004), 209 (t.b.a.).
96   Daes, Erica-Irene (2009). The Contribution of the Working Group on Indigenous Populations to the Genesis and Evolution of the UN Declaration on the Rights of Indigenous Peoples, in: Rodolfo Stavenhagen & Claire Charters (ed.): Making the Declaration Work. The United Nations Declaration on the Rights of Indigenous Peoples, Copenhagen: IWGIA, 48-78, 58f.

UN Programme of Assistance in the Teaching, Study, Dissemination and Wider Appreciation of International Law, set up by Resolution 2099 (XX) of the General Assembly, UN experts and researchers assessed that "[f]or too long, an image has been conveyed of Black Africa before European colonization as a collection of primitive tribes living in anarchy or under the arbitrary rule of a chief, perpetually at war with each other. With such a view, one could not admit to the existence of 'States' in Africa – in the sense of a defined territory and population under the control of one central authority – still less to any system of international law, which by definition is a body of rules regulating relations among sovereign States. (...) The existence of sophisticated forms of government in pre-colonial Africa is now beyond doubt."[97]

Research today has established clearly that there existed kingdoms, often of a surface comparable to that of the whole of Europe, in Africa as far back as in the 4th century. In West Africa Ghana, Songhai, Mali, Wagadu, Kanem and Walata were examples of such empires; in East-South Africa Zulu, Barotse, Bunyoro, Swazi, Lesotho and Basutos; in Central Africa Monomotapa; and in East Africa the ancient Bunyoro Empire and the Buganda kingdom. Some of them, like Kanem-Bornu or Songhay, existed for as long as one millennium.[98] By the 14th century, many African societies called their leaders *mansa, mai, oba* or *ntemi*, for example, and these terms translate to *king*. Some kings and emperors, like Mansa Musa and Askia the Great, acquired an intercontinental reputation. When Mansa Musa, emperor of Mali, came to the throne in 1307, he made a pilgrimage to Mecca, his caravan carrying tons of gold. But already prior to this, the fame of Mali had spread to Europe and the Middle East. This is why around 1600 the Portuguese sent embassies to the kings of Timbuktu and Mossi. They wished to conciliate their goodwill for trade.[99] The Malian city Timbuktu had become a great center of scholarship and culture, known to medieval Europe and attracting scholars and students from various parts of the world.[100] Other known universities with high quality scholarship were, for example, Longor, Mbakhol, Niomre, Coki, Ngalele, Thilogne, Gao or Djenne in Senegambia and Mali.[101]

Thus, thorough and honest analysis of African forms of political organization around the 16th century and earlier, along the line of criteria elaborated and used by contemporary doctrine and jurisprudence to define a state, leads unambigu-

---

97   Davidson, Nicol (1975). "Preface", in: A.K. Mensah-Brown (ed.): African International Legal History, New York: UNITAR, i-ii, i.
98   Nmehielle, Vincent O. (2001). The African Human Rights System. Its Laws, Practice, and Institutions, The Hague/NY: Martinus Nijhoff Publishers, 8; see also Elias (1975), 93.
99   Elias (1972), 3 et seq.
100   Elias (1975), 90.
101   Thiam, Iba D. (1995). "L'Afrique Noire a la veille de la découverte de l'Amerique", in: Elikia M'Bokolo (ed.): L'Afrique entre l'Europe et l'Amerique. Le role de l'Afrique dans la rencontre de deux mondes 1492-1992, Paris: UNESCO, 83-92, 87.

ously to the conclusion that African legal perspectives on slavery, servile labor and "human rights" must be included in any assessment of the legal status of transatlantic slavery. The allegation that slavery was "legal" depends fundamentally on the assumption that the political and social organization of African societies did not allow to qualify them as subjects of international law. Even Western scholars who otherwise might be considered progressive stick to this purely fictional point of view that "at this time, such 'political' entities certainly did not constitute subjects of international law in accordance to the State model (...), that is a political and legal expression of a collective identity sufficiently cohesive and stable to be able to enter into relations with other political entities in the framework of the principles of international law and to assure the full exercise of the sovereign competences and prerogatives recognized by this law"[102].

It could be interjected at this point that it would be another biased analytical pitfall to appraise the international legal personality of African societies by definitional standards enunciated post-factum by Western international jurisprudence and practice. However, it seems very likely that these elements of definition have essentially remained the same since the emergence of the roots of international law long before transatlantic slavery, because they basically refer to the factual capacity of territorial entities to maintain contacts at an international level. They stem from logic, such as recognized also from time immemorial in natural law, and have ever since remained with us, globally. Let us therefore now take a closer look into the various definitional elements of statehood: territory, population and sovereignty.

A. TERRITORY

The criterion of territory in international law refers to the geographical limits within which the authority of a state is exclusively exercised. The legal practice recognizes this criterion as fulfilled even if a state exercises effective power only on a core territory while the exact frontiers are not yet defined.[103] It has been clarified by jurisprudence and scholarship that it is irrelevant for legal purposes whether there is effective administration by a state right up to its boundary, defined as the line which marks the legal termination of the territory of one state and the commencement of the territory of another. This is relevant, for example, with regard to the Yoruba and Ewe kingdoms (Dahomey, ...) at the time before and during transatlantic slavery, where the exact frontiers of the kingdoms were represented by the limits of effective control or acknowledged overlordship.[104] Research has shown that most African societies had a territorial basis, even if it

---

102   Boschiero (2004), 250 (t.b.a.).
103   Hummer/Neuhold/Schreuer (1997), 142.
104   Allott, Antony (1975). "Boundaries in Africa: A Legal and Historical Survey", in: A.K. Mensah-Brown (ed.): African International Legal History, New York: UNITAR, 69- 86, 70 et seq.

was not precisely demarcated; and that "many modern States would fail the test if one required too high a standard of precision in the definition of the extent of their territories"[105].

B. POPULATION

Concerning the criterion of population or people, the administrative court of Cologne stated in the *Duchy of Sealand* case that "whilst size was irrelevant, in order to constitute a people the group of persons in question must form a cohesive vibrant community. (...) The State, as an amalgamation of many individuals, complements the family, which consists of only a few members, and has the duty to promote communal life. (...) It must be aimed at the maintenance of an essentially permanent form of communal life in the sense of sharing a common destiny"[106]. In international legal practice and doctrine, a people is generally defined as constituting a community with a common history and solidarity ties in the present and towards the future.[107] Such communal solidarity links, tied to a common history, have always been very important in African societies.

In Akan society, one was obliged by birth to contribute to the defense of the state in one way or another, complemented by the right to protection one's person, property, and dignity, not only in his own state but even outside it. In traditional African settings, securing the freedom of their citizens abroad, or avenging their mistreatment, were considered legally legitimate reasons to go to war.[108]

C. SOVEREIGNTY

Finally, sovereignty rests on the monopoly of public administration, the capacity to edict a rule and the ability to have it respected. It is reflected, for example, in the maintenance of a unified army. There were African regents, like Queen Nzinga, who fought the enslavers in their territory over a long time with strong, organised armies and disposed of very well administered kingdoms.[109] In the *Lotus* case, the Permanent Court of International Justice made it clear that in case of doubt, a limitation of sovereignty must be construed restrictively.[110] This same standard must also be upheld when it comes to African states.

In the *Greenland* affair, the PCIJ recalled that "legislation is one of the most

---

105   Ibid., 79.

106   Duchy of Sealand, Judgement of May 3, 1978, Administrative Court of Cologne, ILR 1989, 687.

107   Carreau (2007).

108   Mutua, Makau (2002). "The Banjul Charter: The Case for an African Cultural Fingerprint", in: Abdullahi A. An-Na'im (ed.): Cultural Transformation and Human Rights in Africa, London: Zed Books, 68- 107, 81 et seq.

109   Hess (2000), 43.

110   Carreau (2007), 352.

obvious forms of the exercise of sovereign power"[111]. Complex legislation by historical African states is evidenced in records of European traders who complained about taxation laws.[112] A sophisticated system of tax regulation on exports and imports is documented for the Empire of Songhay, for example.[113] Similar facts can be established for other African states at the time, such as for the kingdoms of Zambezi (Zimbabwe, Zambia and Malawi) who were engaged in the trade of gold, silver, iron and copper.[114]

Gluckman assessed in his renowned study that Loziland was a traditional African society with a fairly advanced legal system, consisting of rules of varying types and origin. "These in their own right are the various sources of law as commonly defined in Western jurisprudence. He found that in Lozi, as in Western jurisprudence, these sources consisted of customs, judicial precedents, legislation, laws of natural morality and of nations, good morals and equity."[115] Other anthropologists argued along the same lines and concluded that the norms governing conduct in African societies did not diverge very profoundly from those of European societies. "What were crimes or torts to Europeans were for the most part crimes or torts to the African societies."[116]

Regarding contentions and assumptions that pre-Maafa Africa would not have known sophisticated political and legal systems, it is worth noting that Congo's legal system, for example, was similar, and in some regards much more humane, than those of many European nations at that time. Due to the increasing importance of private property in Europe, theft was punished with an ever-increasing brutality there. For example, a child in England could be hanged for stealing even so little as a rag of cotton in 1740. In the Congo, comparatively little importance was attached to theft. "Small thefts were punished by fines or 'public shame' (...). Larger thefts were generally punished by enslavement or by a fine equal to the value of a slave. Such slaves were not chattel slaves, of course, but domestic slaves who could generally expect to win their freedom. On murder the sanctions were evidently much the same in Portugal and Congo: death except in the case of reasonable self-defence. High treason and rape were also punished in the same way in both countries."[117]

In a collection published in 1767, it was reported with regard to the kingdom of Jalof "(t)hat the King has under him several ministers of state, who assist him in the exercise of justice. The grand Jerafo is the chief justice thro' all the King's

---

111   Legal Status of Eastern Greenland (Denmark v. Norway), Judgment of April 5, 1933, PCIJ, Ser. A./B., No. 53, 28.
112   Chinweizu (1987), 36.
113   Ibid., 191.
114   Ibid., 199.
115   Nmehielle (2001), 10.
116   Ibid.
117   Davidson (1961), 163 et seq.

dominions, and goes in circuit from time to time to hear complaints, and determine controversies. The King's treasurer exercises the same employment, and has under him Alkairs, who are governors of towns or villages. That the Kondi, or Viceroy, goes the circuit with the chief justice, both to hear causes, and inspect into the behaviour of the Alkadi, or chief magistrate of every village in their several districts."[118]

Grotius, one of the founding fathers of European international law doctrine, classified Egypt and Ethiopia as monarchies governed by sovereigns with a highly centralized power in *De Iure Belli ac Pacis*.[119] Alexandrowicz went on to assess that internal clashes in Kush/Ethiopia had significant repercussions for the pattern of government in other parts of Africa. The royal family of Kush, after leaving its kingdom, exercised influence on the region between the Nile Valley and Lake Chad. Thus, the Ethiopian-Egyptian idea of kingship and state organization was spread throughout the Sudan and gradually penetrated to the West coast of Africa and to the South.[120]

Grotius also made it clear in the 17th century that extra-European territories "now have and always have had their own kings, their own government, their own laws, and their own legal systems. (...) The Portuguese (...) do not go there as sovereigns but as foreigners. Indeed they only reside there on sufferance"[121]. In that regard it is interesting that it is also documented that some African rulers ceased to extend protection to their Portuguese guests and the rest of the population adopted an unfriendly attitude, as it became apparent that the Portuguese attempted to wrest sovereignty from them during the latter part of the 16th century.[122]

As much as Europeans rely today on the argument that they would have been states and Africans not, fact is that even within European law doctrine the first explicit theoretical enunciation of sovereignty as one of the essential criteria of the state was given by Jean Bodin only in 1576.[123] Therefore, at the time of the arrival of the first European slave expeditions in Africa at the end of the 15th century, it was the European political entities that were not defined as "sovereign states" because they did not yet know the concept. This leads the argument that African states were not sovereign and therefore, contrary to Europeans, not participants of international law *ad absurdum*. Let us remember at this point also that, in contrast to "sovereignty" which was not yet conceptualized in Europe,

---

118   Benezet, Anthony (1767). Some Historical Account of Guinea, Cirencester: The Echo Library (2005 ed.), 11.
119   Grotius, Hugo (1625). The Rights of War and Peace, Indianapolis: Liberty Fund (ed. 2005).
120   Alexandrowicz (1975), 32 et seq.
121   Grotius, Hugo(1609). The Freedom of the Sea, Ontario, Batoche Books (ed.2000), 14.
122   Rodney, Walter (1970). A History of the Upper Guina Coast 1545-1800, New York: Monthly Review Press, 88.
123   Carreau (2007), 305.

"international" law and some of its fundamental rules did exist at the time of the beginning of transatlantic slavery.[124]

Coming back to Bodin, he defined the essence of a state as the unity of its government, the *summa potestas* or sovereignty. Sovereignty encompasses the capacity to make laws and to enforce them, restricted only by divine law, the law of nature and reason, common to all nations.[125] Building on Bodin, European scholars then came to identify the elements of the state (territory, population/people, sovereignty) which remain valid up to today.

In that context, we should remember what eminent historian Chinweizu reported, that:

"The hundred years between 1450 et 1550 were a period of social reforms and of innovations in statecraft in the kingdoms and empires of Africa. Like their contemporaries elsewhere in the world, such as Henry III in England and the founders of Mogul India, African princes of that era were busy expanding and consolidating their rule, curbing unruly nobles, elevating king's men to important offices, establishing or reforming imperial administrations, and creating professional, full-time armies to replace the draft armies of their past. On the lower Niger at Benin, Oba Ewuare, after he came to the throne in 1440, vigorously extended the kingdom, taking and incorporating over 200 new towns. He built good roads in Benin City, added new walls and ditches to the city's defences, and being a patron of the arts, he encouraged wood and ivory carving. By forming the State Council of Benin, he gave to the kingdom a strong central government (...)"[126].

Ki-Zerbo, also with regard to Benin, stated that the capital of Benin was a city that outrivaled in urbanism most big European cities at that time. The palace of the king seems to have been especially impressive and there were apartments with large and beautiful galleries as big as those of the Bourse of Amsterdam for the ministers. It also appears to have been a remarkably clean city. The people were said to have good laws, to live in accordance to them, to have an orderly police force and to be very hospitable to strangers. The Oba (king) could mobilize an army of 20,000 men in one day, and of 100,000 with little delay.[127] Lourenco Pinto, captain of a Portuguese missionary ship wrote in 1691 that "Great Benin, where the king resides, is larger than Lisbon; all the streets run straight and as far as the eye can see. The houses are large, especially that of the king which is richly decorated and has fine columns. The city is wealthy and industrious. It is so well governed that theft is unknown and the people live in such security that they have no doors to their houses. The artisans have their places carefully allocated in the squares which are divided up in such a manner that in one square he count-

---

124   Ibid.
125   Ibid., 34.
126   Chinweizu (1987), 188 et seq.
127   Ki-Zerbo, Joseph (1978), 163 et seq.

ed altogether 120 goldsmith's workshops, all working continuously".[128] European travellers to Benin often expressed surprise over the occasion of human sacrifice at the "great custom", that this was "nothing else than the execution of all the criminals of the year"[129].

From all accounts, Europeans from the time of intensifying contact at the end of the 15th century onwards were overwhelmed by the number, organization, solidity and opulence of African states.[130] While keeping in mind that "sovereignty" was conceptualized in Europe only in the late 16th century, it is additionally important to fully grasp that sovereignty can neither be denied on grounds that the sovereign rights of African rulers were conceptualized as derived from dynastic or divine origin. For similar claims were made by the absolute monarchs in Europe at that time. And in contrast to them, rulers and kings in Africa were not generally considered absolute, but their state organization usually relied on democratic tradition.[131]

It is essential to highlight that once the criteria are met, a state exists. "The form of internal political organization and the constitutional provisions are mere facts, although it is necessary to take them into consideration in order to determine the Government's way over the population and the territory. (...) The existence or disappearance of the State is a question of fact; (...) the effects of recognition by other States are purely declaratory."[132] Yet, recognition retains some legal significance in that it indicates statehood. Those recognizing are bound by it and subsequently are obliged to deal with the recognized party on a basis of legal equality. Recognition in international law is not subjected to formal constraint; it can be given tacitly, for example through the establishment of diplomatic relations.

i. Recognition of African statehood by European states

As such, sovereignty of African states was recognized by Europeans in numerous treaties and official communications. In 1512, the Portuguese crown addressed the King of Congo as "Most Powerful and excellent King of the Congo"[133]. In 1840, a treaty between Great Britain and the King of Combo (sic) read that "all Sovereignty of the before specified territory is now vested in the said King of Combo and has descended to him from his ancestors"[134]. Even the Congo Declaration of 1885 that was exchanged between the Belgian government and the International Association of the Congo and which laid the pseudo-legal foundation for the murder of millions of Congolese Africans, referred to treaties "concluded with the

---

128   Elias (1972), 3 et seq.
129   Camara (2004), 28.
130   M'Bokolo (1995b), 20.
131   Ibid.
132   Ibid.
133   Alexandrowicz (1975), 31.
134   Ibid, 45.

legitimate Sovereigns in the basin of the Congo"[135]. "Zulu Sovereignty" was also the term used in British government statements when referring to Zululand. Such treaties most often also contained references to African customary law.[136]

So when, in 1482, the Portuguese built their first fort on the Gold Coast, El Mina (meaning "the mine" from their belief that it would enable them to tap the sources of African gold), they built this fort by agreement with the chief of the region. This chief consented to the building of the fort only after a long process of pleading by the Portuguese, but on condition that "peace and truth must be kept". Diplomatic missions of friendship and alliance were exchanged subsequently.[137] King John of Portugal also ordered in these early days of contact that messengers dispatched by African rulers be accompanied back to their country.

More treaties were concluded which granted rights of transit to Europeans for commercial purposes. Others were ally treaties, whereby African states sought to reinforce themselves against invasion by neighboring states. "All these were prompted, no doubt, by the ideals of the universal law of nations: peace and prosperity among mankind! (...) [There is] ample documentary and oral evidence for the proposition that the continent contributed by State practices to the ideals of the universal law of nations which influenced the theoreticians of international law in Europe."[138]

The initial official communications between "royal brothers" of Portugal and Congo from 1487 onwards were couched in terms of complete equality of status. Emissaries went back and forth between them. Relations were also established between Congo and the Vatican, and a son of the Mani-Congo was appointed in Rome as bishop of his country.[139] Now, even in much more ancient states like Greek city-states, Rome and Egypt, the universality of rules of diplomatic conduct had been accompanied by the principle that only legitimate states had the right to send and receive embassies.[140]

Mensah-Brown, chief coordinator of the earlier mentioned UNITAR research project, stated that the

"Historical contribution of Africa lies in the state practices which were aimed at the promotion of peaceful interstate relations. (...) Akin to those state practices in ancient Greece and Rome (...) native state practices were governed to a certain extent by the same law of nations, customary or based on the explicit consent of the States concerned, to which appeal was made in Europe in internation-state

---

135 Ibid.
136 Ibid, 60.
137 Davidson (1961), 28 et seq.
138 Mensah-Brown, A.K. (1975b). "Notes on Internartional Law and Pre-Colonial Legal History of Modern Ghana", in: A.K. Mensah-Brown (ed.): African International Legal History, New York: UNI-TAR, 107-124, 123.
139 Davidson (1961), 136.
140 Bederman (2001), 95.

relations. This seems to be evidenced by the fact that the early European nation state representatives did encounter indigenous policies with which they dealt as states according to the European ideals of the law of nations in which they had been brought up. (...) Some indigenous state practices in the pre-colonial legal history of modern Ghana which were similar to, if not the same as, what international lawyers have come to identify as forming the roots of modern international law or law of nations."[141]

This UNITAR research project also confirmed that oral tradition and other documentation strongly indicates that pre-Maafa African states considered themselves bound by them in their dealings with one another. The researchers furthermore assessed that historically in Africa, as elsewhere, some universally acknowledged law justifying causes of war, dictating negotiations before war, and the conduct of the war itself, was recognized and applied.[142]

Europeans, through the conclusion of treaties and the establishment of diplomatic contacts, not only recognized African states on the continent but also on the other side of the Atlantic. For example in 1678, the governor of Pernambouc, as a representative of the King of Portugal, concluded a peace treaty with the Republic of Palmares, thereby recognizing this Republic of self-liberated Africans as equal and as a state. In 1685, the King of Portugal Pedro II himself sent a communication to the leader of the Palmares, Zumbi.[143] Even though the Republic of Palmares was finally destroyed by the Portuguese after having upheld its resistance for more than 100 years, other *quilombos* (Maroon communities) existed in Brazil from the first half of the 16th century and persevered to the end of slavery in 1888.[144]

Very interesting with regard to the question of statehood of pre-Maafa African societies is the advisory opinion rendered by the International Court of Justice in the *Western Sahara* affair. The Court stated that, "State practice of the relevant period indicates that territories inhabited by tribes or peoples having a social and political organization were not regarded as *terrae nullius*. It shows that in the case of such territories the acquisition of sovereignty was not generally considered as effected unilaterally through 'occupation' of *terra nullius* by original title, but through agreements concluded with local rulers (...)"[145]. If historic nomadic societies, as in Western Sahara, were recognized as sovereign by the ICJ, then the sedentary African kingdoms and empires affected by transatlantic slavery must be considered sovereign too.

So to sum up, historical documents clearly show that European officials initial-

---

141   Mensah-Brown (1975b), 110.
142   Ibid., 111.
143   Police, Gerard (2003). Quilombos dos Palmares.Lecture sur un marronnage bresilien, Guyane: Ibis Rouge Editions, 96.
144   Ibid., 13et seq.
145   Western Sahara, Advisory Opinion, ICJ Reports 1975, 80, par. 31.

ly recognized African states and sovereigns as equals. Why this attitude subsequently changed and Europeans started to regard treaties with African states as non-binding, despite the presence of all state elements in these "African political entities", cannot be satisfactorily answered here. Immense greed, wickedness and jealousy all probably played a role. At this point, it suffices to emphasize that in any way disregard of facts cannot turn criminal and genocidal behavior into legally acceptable conduct. Alleging that people who by all standards were sovereign and equal, would not have been subjects of and could therefore not contribute to the development and content of international law, does not turn such an allegation into reality. Concluding from such an allegation that genocide and enslaving would have been legal would render the concept of law meaningless, and constitute a negation of law itself.

ii. Decentralized African societies

Although many of the African societies affected were indeed states by the standards of international law enunciated by European scholars in the late 16th century, others were really decentralized societies, lacking a sovereign administrating force and may therefore not qualify as states by those legal requirements. Yet these societies knew and practiced law, including individual and human rights (see Chapter II.3.a. iii; vii; viii).[146] In comparative studies on historic human rights conceptions in decentralized and in state societies in Africa, it has been documented that both types of African societies knew and protected notions of human rights. The Akamba of East Africa made up an example of a less rigidly organized society, whereas the Akan of West Africa were a state society. Both recognized that, as an inherently valuable being, the individual was naturally endowed with certain basic rights. According to Wiredu, "it was an absolute principle of Akan justice that no human being could be punished without trial".[147] Approximately 30 per cent of Africa's area at the onset of transatlantic slavery was occupied by states with a surface area larger than 50,000 square kilometers; the rest was occupied by smaller communities.[148] However, as assessed in the Barotse Arbitration case where the King of Italy was the arbitrator, "a Paramount Ruler is he who exercises governmental authority according to customary law, that is, by appoint-

---

146   See, e.g., An-Na'im, Abdullahi A. (ed.) (2002a). Cultural Transformation and Human Rights in Africa, London: Zed Books; An-Na'im, Abdullahi/Deng, Francis M. (ed.) (1990a). Human Rights in Africa. Cross-Cultural Perspectives, Washington DC: The Brookings Institution; Mutua, Makau (2002). "The Banjul Charter: The Case for an African Cultural Fingerprint", in: Abdullahi A. An-Na'im (ed.): Cultural Transformation and Human Rights in Africa, London: Zed Books, 68- 107; Cohen, Ronald/ Hyden, Goran (ed.) (1993). Human Rights and Governance in Africa, Gainesville: University of Florida Press.
147   Wiredu, Kwasi (1990). "An Akan Perspective on Human Rights", in: An-Na'im/Deng (ed.): Human Rights in Africa: Cross-Cultural Perspectives, Washington DC, Brookings Institution, 243-60, 252.
148   Thornton, John (1992). Africa and Africans in the Making of the Atlantic World, 1400- 1680. Cambridge: Cambridge University Press, 104.

ing the subordinate Chiefs, or by granting them investiture, by deciding disputes between those chiefs, by deposing them where circumstances call for it and by obliging them to recognize him as their Paramount Ruler". This was classified as an "important definition for international lawyers immunising the legal notion of chief and paramount chief against the vagaries of non-legal classification in some of the literature about Africa"[149].

On the Upper Guinea Coast, where decentralized societies were the norm and which was later ravaged by transatlantic slavery, an ohai, an offence against law, always necessitated a "palaver", which means it went into the local courts. "The customary law of the Upper Guinea Coast was not so foreign to the experience of the Portuguese that they could not understand it. To fell timber in many areas of Europe would have been an offense, so that on the Upper Guinea Coast, to fell trees which had not only an economic but also tremendous religious significance, was obviously going to bring the Portuguese into conflict with the Africans."[150] Recent investigations in that region have shown that the Papels have a juridical system based on five categories of property and revealed the complexities of Diola law.[151]

In that context, it is illuminating that the International Court of Justice in an opinion sustained that "from the moment that organizations exercise legal competencies of the same type as those of States, it seemed logical that the same consequences should attach to the actions of both one and another".[152] Thus, to the extent that they were engaging in legal dealings with other states and communities, historical decentralized societies were subjects and participants of international law. As T.O. Elias stated, there are and were legal champions in quasi-totality of African societies, from the most to the least organized.[153]

Considering all these facts, synthesized with historic and present international law theory and practice, there can be no doubt that African societies' legal perspectives as well as natural law, both of which were bodies of law considered valid and in force at that time, must be included in any assessment of the legal status of transatlantic slavery.

---

149   Alexandrowicz (1975), 40.
150   Rodney (1970), 85.
151   Ibid., 28.
152   Pellet, Allan (2010). The Definition of Responsibility in International Law, in: James Crawford/ Alain Pellet/Simon Olleson (ed.) The Law of International Responsibility, Oxford: OxfordUniversity Press, 4-15,4f; (Reparation for Injuries Suffered in The Service of the United Nations, ICJ Reports 1949, p 174, 178.)
153   Camara (2004), 39.

3. AFRICAN AND EUROPEAN LEGAL CONCEPTIONS AND PRACTICES OF SERVILE LABOR AND SLAVERY

"During this long stretch of time, the captain and indeed every member of the crew assumed that the people brought on board were held against their will and that they would do anything possible to escape captivity. The captain's power depended first and foremost on brute force. (...) Newton saw 'unmerciful whippings, continued till the poor creatures have not had power to groan under their misery, and hardly a sign of life has remained. 'He saw the enslaved agonizing for hours and indeed days in thumbscrews. He knew one captain who 'studied, with no small attention, how to make death as excruciating as possible.' (...) After failed resurrection (...) Captain Jackson sentenced the rebellious slaves to die, and then selected their mode of punishment. The first group 'he jointed; that is, he cut off, with an axe, first their feet, then their legs below the knee, then their thighs; in like manner their hands, then their arms below the elbow, an then at their shoulders, till their bodies remained only like the trunk of a tree when all the branches are looped away; and, lastly, their heads. And, as he proceeded in his operation, he threw the reeking members and heads in the midst of the bulk of the trembling slaves, who were chained upon the main-deck.' (...) Captain Jackson then punished the second group: 'He tied round the upper parts of the heads of others a small soft platted rope, which the sailors call a point, so loosely as to admit a short lever: by continuing to turn the lever, he drew the point more and more tight, till as length he forced their eyes to stand out of their heads; and when he had satiated himself with their torments, he cut their heads off.'"[154]

Quite obviously, the assessment alone that African states were subjects of international law does not yet tell us anything about the legal status of transatlantic slavery at the time it was effectuated. In order to get there, a thorough historical investigation into the laws and legal concepts of both European and African states, and their confrontation with the ferocious reality of transatlantic slavery, is necessary. Such a review, also considering historical examples from world regions other than Africa and Europe concerning the legal status of servile labor and slavery, will allow us to come to the assess general principles of law, which are, next to treaty and customary law, one recognized source of international law and are generally defined as legal principles common to a large number of systems of national or municipal law.

Reparation detractors regularly contend that Africans would have "enslaved" one another from time immemorial; and that they would have actively and voluntarily participated in transatlantic enslavement. Both contentions are of high legal significance because they serve to basically bolster the allegation that transatlan-

---

154   Rediker, Marcus (2008). The Slave Ship. A Human History, London: John Murray, 216 et seq.

tic slavery would have been "legal". The above quote, however, already illustrates drastically that transatlantic slavery was not "slavery" such as practised in some African societies, but indeed a crime against humanity and genocide. Transatlantic slavery was essentially different from African systems of slavery and servile institutions, and this will clearly be exposed in this chapter. The section will be a bit lengthy since it is expedient to incorporate as many examples as evidence as possible, to make the accuracy of the legal argument maintained here unassailable.

One point that needs to be highlighted time and again is that "slavery" in African societies was not racialized, as it was in the Americas.[155] In transatlantic slavery, the mere fact of being of African or Black was presumptive of slave status, and slave status was forever. With the advancement of time, manumission became increasingly difficult and often impossible, such as in the United States. An early law of Maryland, dating from 1633, declared that "All Negroes or other slaves within the province, all Negroes to be hereafter imported, shall serve *durante vita*: but their children were to serve likewise. (...) A South Carolina law of 1740 provided that 'any free Negro should be sold at public auction if he had harboured a runaway slave, or was charged 'with any other criminal matter'"[156]. A Black person in Mississippi could be sold as a slave unless he was able to prove himself free. In Georgia, as late as 1818, a law imposed a fine of one thousand dollars on anyone who gave effect to a last will and testament freeing a slave or allowing him to work on his own account.[157]

Documents and notes by contemporary European officials testify that transatlantic slavery was totally different from African servile labor through the former's complete disregard of the humanity of its victims. Thus, for example, Pruneau de Pommegorge who worked for the *Compagnie des Indes* noted that sucklings of women who were sold to the Americas were taken from them and thrown to the wolves.[158] On the ships, sick people and toddlers, weak and prone to sickness, were often thrown overboard.[159] The average life expectance of a person enslaved in the transatlantic system, once he or she passed childhood and was put to work on the plantation, was five to seven years.[160] In contrast, in African societies "slaves" were gradually integrated into the lineage.

Common punishments in transatlantic slavery included the putting into facial or whole-body gibbets, with metal spikes on the inside; the utilization of thumb-

---

155   Palmer, Colin A. (1998a). "Introduction", in: Colin Palmer (ed.): The Worlds of Unfree Labour: From Servitude to Slavery, New York: Ashgate, 1-11, 8.
156   Davidson (1961), 38 et seq.
157   Ibid.
158   de Pommegorge, Pruneau (1789). Description de la Nigritie, Amsterdam/Paris: Maradan, 210 et seq.
159   Ki-Zerbo (1978), 216.
160   Ibid., 222.

screws; extreme lashing and smearing of wounds with salt and hot pepper; limb amputation; alive muring; covering the enslaved person entirely with honey and then putting him or her on a tree for days so that bees, ants and mosquitos would cover and bite every inch of the body.[161] No laws protected the African from any cruelty the European masters could conceive. Men, women, and children were at their complete mercy. "For looking a white man in the eye the enslaved person could have his or her eyes blinded with hot irons. For speaking up in defence of a wife or woman a man could have his right hand severed. (...) The enslaved person could be roasted over a slow-burning fire, left to die after having both legs and arms broken, oiled and greased and then set afire while hanging from a tree's limb, or being killed slowly as the slave owner cut the enslaved person's phallus or breasts. A person could be placed on the ground, stomach first, stretched so that each hand was tied to a pole and each foot was tied to a pole. Then the slave master would beat the person's naked body until the flesh was torn off the buttocks and the blood ran down to the ground."[162]

The Middle Passage from Africa to the plantation colonies took approximately three months during which the people remained enchained in darkness on minimum space, the living, sick and dead side by side, laying in their excrements and vomit, and without any possibility of movement.

No reparation detractor has ever been able to come up with documentation of any such institutionalized barbarities happening in pre-Maafa African "slavery" because they simply did not exist there.

A. AFRICAN SERVILE LABOR AND "SLAVERY"

It is interesting to note that it was at the very same period of time when the international movement for reparations for transatlantic slavery gained some amplitude in the 1970s and 80s that studies on "slavery" in Africa increasingly became a major subject among European and North American historians and anthropologists, after years of neglect.[163] The "information" that such studies produced was then appropriated and used by reparation negationists. Contending that "slavery" would have been an inherent African institution makes it easier to claim that transatlantic slavery would have been "legal" and to deny reparations on that ground. Not accepting this and looking beyond semantic labels and terms, this section will shed some light on what the reality behind "slavery" and servile labor in many pre-Maafa African societies was. One must keep in mind that

---

161   Peret, Benjamin (1999). La Commune des Palmares, Paris: Editions Syllepse, 36 et seq.

162   Asante, Molefi Kete (2003). "The African American Warrant for Reparations", in: Ray Winbush (ed.): Should Americapay? Slavery and the raging debate on reparations, New York: Amistad, 3-13, 7 et seq.

163   Inikori, Joesph E. (1999). "Slaves or Serfs? A Comparative Study of Slavery and Serfdom in Europe and in Africa", in: Isidore Okpewho/Carole Boyce Davies/Ali A. Mazrui (ed.): The African diaspora: African origins and New World Identities, Bloomington: Indiana University Press, 49-75, 49.

the use of the same semantic term to describe disparate social realities changes nothing to this disparate reality, and must neither influence their legal appraisals. The people who were eagerly qualified as inner-African "slaves" were not submitted to the dehumanization that was really constitutive to transatlantic slavery.[164] African slaves did not have their ears cut off, the name of their master was not iron-branded on their breasts, their babies were not killed when bothering the sleep of the mistress[165], they were not cruelly tortured for minor "infractions" or roasted alive over several days, and dogs were not trained to drink their blood and nourish off their flesh[166]. The European colonial slave codes defined the status of slaves as movable property and provided for all these atrocities. Such dehumanization was unknown to African societies. The concept and reality of African "slavery" coincided rather with the meaning of the European terms "servile labour" or "serfdom"[167], terms that many European scholars regrettably prefer to reserve for the description of situations where Europeans subjugated other Europeans. Ironically, despite this common denomination of European forced laborers as serfs and Africans as slaves, the term "slave" itself stems from the old European Christian practice of enslaving "pagans" of Eastern Europe, the Slavs. A lucrative commerce of these slaves was organized between Venice and Arabs until the 13th century. The term *slavus*, designating the "pagan" people of East-Central-Europe, was then transformed to "Sclavus".[168]

Honest review and research into the available evidence about pre-Maafa African "slaves" shows that "a more precise use of terms, in the manner of modern historians of pre-capitalist Europe, would compel scholars to describe the vast majority of them as serfs"[169]. It is important to discern that, "although some slaves in antiquity were by no means completely without property, the distinction between slaves and serfs is based on the fact that, on the whole, slaves were the chattels of their master, employed as instruments of production in agriculture or industry, receiving food, clothing and shelter from the master and possessing nothing (...)."[170]

Despite the fact that this co-existence of slave and non-slave servile categories has been carefully studied concerning Europe, this distinction is not maintained when it comes to Africa.[171] Inikori has shown that the distinction made between

---

164   Asare, William Kweku (2002). Slavery reparations in perspective, Victoria: Trafford Publishing, 20.

165   Hess (2000), 130.

166   Plumelle-Uribe, Rosa Amelia (2001). La férocité blanche. Des non-Blancs aux non-Aryens: génocides occultés de 1492 à nos jours, Paris: Editions Albin Michel, 74.

167   Scelle (1934a), 55 et seq.

168   Ajavon, Lawoetey-Pierre (2005). Traite et Esclavage des Noirs. Quelle responsabilité Africaine? Paris: Editions MENAIBUC, 17.

169   Inikori (1999), 63.

170   Hilton, R.H. (1969). The Decline of Serfdom in Medieval England, London: Macmillan, 9-11.

171   Inikori (1999), 50.

serfs and other dependent categories on the one side and slaves on the other in European societies incorporates certain unambiguous elements. The serfs, or non-slave dependent, people must possess means of production of their own (mainly land) large enough to provide a potential income that could support a household with unproductive children and old members. Furthermore, they must have enough free time to realize this potential income and they must be allowed to keep for themselves and do as they please with this income realized. Also, their residences must be physically separated from those of their lords.[172] As we shall see, this was the case in most instances of pre-Maafa African "slavery".

Language and its manipulation indeed have such an important place in the transatlantic slavery reparations debate. Scholars have pointed out that even though French and English-speaking Diola (southern Senegal, Gambia, Guinea-Bissau), for example, translate the terms *amiekele* and *agoutch* with "esclave" or "slave", there are significant differences between transatlantic slavery and what is described by these terms in Diola societies. Labor requisitions were the same tasks also performed by free-born Diola. Diola slaves married, had their own homes and their own land, though rice and livestock could be taken by their masters. Slaves enjoyed a considerable amount of protection against violence or physical abuse.[173]

In the Twi language of Ghana there are several terms that have been equalized with "slave". *Domum* is a captive, either directly taken as a prisoner of war or one who had been collected as a result of tribute arrangements. *Odonko* actually means foreigner, thus designating a recently acquired captive. *Akoa* means someone else's man and is used to signify a master-servant relationship. "Not to have a 'master' was to be an outsider with no network of familial connections. (...) Nearly everyone in Akan society was someone else's akoa. On the average the labor requirements imposed on the average household slave in the Akan and Adangme regions of the Gold Coast were (...) not oppressive in comparison with the classic plantation-type of the Americas during the 18th century."[174]

In the Zambezi region, different categories of "slaves" were recorded by early Portuguese chroniclers. The *achicunda* formed a veritable warrior caste and assumed the function of police. They themselves had slaves to their service. They are also said to have raised armed revolts at several occasions against the European colonists when these aimed at abolishing "slavery" there in the 19th century. Their African indigenous "slave" status assured them certain privileges such as

---

172   Ibid., 55 et seq.
173   Baum, Robert (2010). "Slaves without Rulers: Domestic Slavery among the Diola of Senegambia", in: Stephanie Beswick and Jay Spaulding (ed.): African Systems of Slavery, Trenton: Africa World Press, 45-66, 45 et seq.
174   Dumett, Raymond E. (2010). "The Work of Slaves in the Akan and Adangme Regions of Ghana in the Nineteenth Century", in: Stephanie Beswick and Jay Spaulding (ed.): African Systems of Slavery, Trenton/Asmara: Africa World Press, 67-104, 67 et seq.

being exempted from taxes and from certain servile labor tasks, while the European colonizers wanted to subject them to paying taxes and recruit them to forced labor. Bichos were slaves attached to a master's residence and accompanied the important ladies of the society. One Portuguese witness wrote that there was "no Negro who did not aspire to serve the King" in this area.[175]

Generally speaking, in many pre-Maafa African societies "slaves" or their descendants gradually became members of the lineage, like young people eventually became elders. The tasks of these "slaves" may have been more menial, but still they were often granted responsibilities in trade, craft production, and other occupations, and were treated very much as members of the household.[176] Such observations are recorded for every part of Africa where the outside world had contact. Martin Delany, for example, speaking of Nigeria, made it very clear that "it is simply preposterous to talk about slavery, as that term is understood, either being legalized or existing in this part of Africa. It is nonsense. The system is a patriarchal one, there being no actual difference socially, between the slave (called by their protector son or daughter) and the children of the person with whom they live. Such persons intermarry and frequently become the heads of state. And where this is not the case, it either arises from some innovation among them or those exceptional cases of despotism to be found in every country."[177]

The role of servile labor in assimilating outsiders into the host society in Africa has also been stressed by anthropologists Kopytoff and Miers. For other African societies, researchers have assessed that "a slave's principal function in the village is his or her procreation on behalf of the lineage group in whose care and power he or she is".[178]

In several African societies, "slaves" held positions in the ranks of high society. The King of Kayor employed slaves as war leaders, province governors, preceptors, and other such functions. Slaves gave commands to free men and possessed goods, chattel, land and even slaves. Slaves were not for sale. Sometimes, "they made and unmade kings".[179] Such was the case, for example, in Samory's 19th century Mali, in Benin, and at Maradi where most royal title-holders were systematically divorced from administration responsibility, judicial and economic power and economic resources, but depended on the largesse of senior officials who were royal slaves. "All princes were under the eunuch Galadima's jurisdiction,

---

175   Capela (2002), 336.

176   Lovejoy, Paul (2000). Transformations in Slavery. A History of Slavery in Africa, Second Edition, Cambridge: Cambridge University Press, 14-15.

177   Davidson, Basil (1961). The African Slave Trade, Back Bay Books, Boston/New York. 38f.

178   MacGaffey, Wyatt (2010). "Indigenous Slavery and the Atlantic Trade: Kongo Texts", in: Stephanie Beswick and Jay Spaulding (ed.): African Systems of Slavery, Trenton/Asmara: Africa World Press, 173-201, 192.

179   Meillassoux, Claude (1986). Anthropologie de l'esclavage, Paris: Quadrige Presse Universitaires de France, 185 et seq.

their behaviour being reviewed critically to select the most suitable successor."[180]

Historical evidence leaves no doubt that various forms of servile institutions existed in pre-Maafa Black Africa independent of external demand for captives. However, these institutions were part of a process through which aliens were incorporated into kin groups, and the general tendency was full integration as free people. A multitude of scholars has retraced that phenomena of servile institutions approximating chattel slavery were new in Black Africa, and that their development was linked strongly to the growth of export demand for captives, first across the Sahara and later, at a much greater amplitude, across the Atlantic.[181] A UNESCO report of experts assessed in 1978 that "the traditionally organized authorities, for example in Jolof, Cayor, Balol, Songhay, Congo and Zimbabwe, were in various ways and at various times, confronted with the pressure of European and Muslim demand for slaves. They were all upset by this pressure. Such upsets were accompanied by an increase of social tensions, a worsening of servitude, especially quantitatively and by a transformation of the former processes of social integration that the various forms of personal dependence provided in African society prior to the 15th century. (...) None of the experts present disputed the idea that the slave trade was responsible for the economic backwardness of Black Africa."[182]

Eminent historian Basil Davidson underscored an important difference: "This was not slavery as Europe understood the word – chattel slavery, the stripping of a man of all his rights and property – but serfdom, vassalship, 'domestic slavery'. Degrees of servility and obligation would immensely vary with time and place, as they would elsewhere; but this vassalship in Africa would have many institutional parallels with that of Europe."[183] He assessed that "the 'slave' peoples of the hierarchical or 'centralizing' States, whether near the coast or inland across the Sudanese grasslands, were in truth serfs and 'clients' (...) with valued individual rights. Their status was altogether different from the human cattle of the slave ships and the American plantations"[184]. Davidson also pointed out that at the beginning of transatlantic slavery semantic manipulation was employed by European traders to justify their dealings. It is important to see clearly and acknowledge that this very same manipulative argument is still used today to fend off reparations claims. The slave traders were arguing that slavery, slave-raiding and slave trade had always been part of African lifestyle. "This propaganda was delivered so efficiently that in the nineteenth century it had become fashionable among the general public and most European travellers to Africa. Lord Luggard asserted that

---

180   Ibid.
181   Inikori (1992b), 38.
182   Inikori, Joseph E. (1982). Forced Migration. The impact of he export slave trade on African societies, New York: Africana Publishing Company, 58 et seq.
183   Davidson (1961), 30.
184   Ibid, 38 et seq.

'slavery' has been an African institution for 1,000 years (...)."[185]

Yet in reality, what was translated with "slavery" in the general African context was something categorically different from what was designated by the same word in the transatlantic context. The great Cheikh Anta Diop has shown that "slaves" of the emperor of Mali and the Askia of Goa enjoyed total liberty of movement. There were also entire tribes who were "slaves" of the Askia, such as the Diam-Ouali, Diam-Téné and Sorobanna, yet they occupied an entire country of their own where they cultivated at their gain and only gave a pre-fixed part to the emperor. In such African societies, "slaves" could get very rich, reside at the imperial court and occupy high political functions.[186]

Therefore, it needs to be stressed time and again that terminological manipulation and confusion does not alter the disparate social realities of indigenous African systems of servile labor and of transatlantic chattel slavery, and must neither influence their legal appreciation. The monopoly of words and definitions is not neutral. It is part of the manipulation of history and of the control of its interpretation. It is here that the implications of a legal qualification appear in their whole striking amplitude.[187] We therefore now need to look into the available documentation on African servile institutions and "slavery" as the next step in the assessment of the true and veritable legal status of transatlantic slavery.

Now, records testify that people of the Gold Coast bought around 500 slaves from the European sailors who came mostly from the Nigerian and Congolese/Angolan coasts, to use them as domestic labor or commerce in the time span from the 15th to the mid-16th century.[188] However, the existent records also tell us that the use and treatment of these "slaves" was totally different from what captives who went through transatlantic slavery had to endure.

Although there is evidence for the existence of pre-European and pre-Arab African servile institutions, there is absolutely no evidence that these "slaves" were treated in the barbarous way that was an integral part of the transatlantic slavery experience, quite on the contrary. Many of them lived and worked just as their so-called masters did, and Europeans, and often even other Africans, could not tell them apart. Many such "slaves" were not considered saleable.[189] It is also important to consider that even the criterion of saleability is a relative one, as the establishment of relations with spouses, children, and kin-group members may

---

185   Inikori. (1982), 38.
186   Popo (2010), 73; see also Diop, Cheikh A. (1987). L'Afrique noire précoloniale, Paris: Présence Africaine, 146 et seq.
187   Plumelle-Uribe (2001), 30.
188   Diop-Maes, Louise Marie (1996). Afrique Noire. Démographie, Sol et Histoire, Paris: Presence Africaine/Khepera, 218.
189   Kopytoff, Igor/Miers, Suzanne (1977a). "African 'Slavery' as an Institution of Marginality", in: Suzanne Miers and Igor Kopytoff (ed.): Slavery in Africa: Historical and Anthropological Perspectives, Madison: University of Wisconsin Press, 3-81, 3 et seq.

involve material transactions in many African societies.[190]

One of the most pertinent disquisitions about African systems of servile labor and slavery has been made by Inikori. In his seminal article "Slaves or serfs?"[191], Inikori applied to African evidence the formula employed by modern historians to distinguish slaves from serfs in pre-capitalist Europe, and concluded that

"it is (...) clear that the chattel slavery experienced by Africans in the Americas was something new for them. (...) The claim that the pre-existence of chattel slavery in the coastal societies of western Africa facilitated the growth and development of the trans-Atlantic slave trade is not borne out of evidence. (...) For the few who were already in bondage before capture and forced transportation to the Americas, their socio-economic conditions in Africa were much closer (in many cases even superior) to those of serfs in medieval Europe than to those of chattel slaves. All of this may help explain the phenomenon observed by students of slave societies in the Americas that the greater the proportion of African-born people in the population, the greater the incidence of resistance or revolt"[192].

Despite the rigor and pertinence of Inikori's analysis, anthropological and historical studies that ignore its lesson and insist on using the term "slavery" while describing African institutions of serfdom, continue to be published.[193]

Equiano, an enslaved African, with his autobiography left us an account of his life that displays very instructively the fundamental difference between African servile labor and transatlantic slavery. Equiano was born in the Nri-Awka/Isuama region in central Nigeria, where he was kidnapped in 1756. He noted that his father had many "slaves", yet added that this was a "slavery" in which "slaves" lived with and were treated like family, in contrast to the cruel system of the same name to be found in the Americas.[194] Equiano related that, while on the European slave ship, "(a)fter experiencing the stench of the lower deck and a flogging for refusing food, he longed to trade places with 'the meanest slave in my own country'". Finally, he wished in utter despair 'for the last friend, Death, to relieve me'."[195] He also drew a clear picture of the efforts of African people, his father included, to protect people from illegal seizure and slavery into the transatlantic system. This account is of special significance because Equiano's father owned "slaves" himself and was involved in the process of the enslavement of criminals within his home society. Equiano himself was first sold to an African blacksmith and then to Europeans, and he clearly related the fundamental difference in treatment between the two. This makes his account very instructive for the purpose

---

190   Ibid., 12.
191   Inikori (2001).
192   Ibid., 68.
193   See e.g. Spauling/Beswick (ed.) (2010). African Systems of Slavery, Trenton, Africa World Press.
194   Rediker (2008), 110.
195   Ibid., 117.

of comparing indigenous African and transatlantic slavery. "The prisoners which were not sold or redeemed were kept as slaves: but how different was their condition from that of the slaves in the West Indies? With us they do no more work than other members of the community, even their master. Their food, clothing, and lodging, were nearly the same as theirs, except that they were not permitted to eat with those who were free born; and there were scarce any other difference between them than a superior degree of importance which the head of family possesses in our state, and that authority which, as such, he exercises over every part of his household. Some of the slaves have even slaves under them as their own property and for their own use."[196]

Equiano's father was involved in legal proceedings by which slave merchants passing through were customarily questioned in order to determine the legality of their merchandise. "Only prisoners of war and criminals convicted of kidnapping, adultery, and murder were considered legitimate slaves."[197] It is significant that Equiano was, after being kidnapped, first sold to an African master where he stayed with the master's family, who treated him well and where he worked as a smith. In contrast, he described transatlantic slavery, beginning with the stay in the dungeons before being embarked on the Middle Passage, as nothing but most hellish. "They always carry slaves through our land; but the strictest account is exacted of their manner of procuring them before they are suffered to pass. Sometimes indeed we sold slaves to them, but they were only prisoners of war, or such among us who had been convicted of kidnapping, or adultery, and some other crime, which we esteemed heinous."[198] There existed a legal obligation of determining the legitimacy of a slave's status, although not everyone complied with this obligation. Elsewhere in Africa, similar legal requirements existed. For example, King Afonso of Congo in the 16th century established courts of enquiry designated to investigate illegal enslavement.[199]

In order to pertinently deconstruct the assertion that "slavery" would have been widespread in pre-Maafa Africa, a concrete review of numerous examples of institutions of forced labor throughout Africa is what we will embark on over the next pages. The reparation negationists' allegations that Africans would historically have sold one another massively are factually wrong and thus unable to bolster or substantiate any pretention of "legality" of transatlantic slavery and the denial of reparation claims. It seems expedient to begin this review with examples of the African societies that were the very first massively impacted and transformed by transatlantic slavery.

---

196   Lovejoy (2000), 125.
197   Ibid.
198   Ibid., 89.
199   Ibid., 89.

i. Congo

In Congo, where the Portuguese started large-scale slaving operations in the early 16thcentury, "slaves" traditionally had a right of appeal against sale to another country. This legal provision became routinely dismissed once the Congolese elite and collaborators became increasingly entangled in transatlantic slavery, yet it was the legal standard. A French observer in Loango noted in 1776 that "every slave in the kingdom is under the protection of the Mfuka [one of the king's chief brokers] and may appeal against his master, should he be inclined to sell him to the Europeans, unless he has given him that right through his own misconduct"[200].

In general, African "slaves" were well integrated into the family of the masters. In Congo, the master called the "slave" *nvana* (son). A European doctor wrote that "in truth, the Congolese slave is a supplementary element of the family. He is a false member, an artificial child".[201]

Even though their society was brutalized for centuries at the hand of European and African slavers, Congolese "slavery" still retained some of its humane features even with the passage of time. Thus, when the Swedish missionary K.E. Laman conducted ethnographic research around 1915, he found that "when slaves were oppressed by their *mfumu* and wanted to run away, they could go to commit themselves by *bula banda*, to break a taboo, to whomever they chose. A slave would break a plate or mug, or tread on the prospect with his foot, *kundyatila tambi*, saying: I will not be paying you the money [in compensation] but my master, who is a tyrant. Then the new *mfumu* is paid by the previous owner. If the previous owner does not want to let the person out of his hands he will have to pay a very large amount to the protector"[202].

The dehumanization and brutality of transatlantic enslavement was not accepted by Congolese law at all, but it was to be violently imposed on the people in that region over several centuries. Comprehensive reparation endeavours must acknowledge this, and also aim at healing the deep wounds that African societies suffered as a result of the continuing and structural violation of their traditional legal standards.

The letters that King Affonso I (see Chapter IV) sent to the Portuguese Crown in protest of the wanton enslavement of his people at the beginning of the 16th century further evidence to the fact that chattel slavery was not a normal condition for Africans, such as portrayed by European slavers and reparation negationists.[203]

---

200 Davidson (1961), 163et seq.
201 Ki-Zerbo (1978), 210.
202 MacGaffey (2010), 189.
203 Bailey, Anne C. (2007). African Voices of the Atlantic Slave Trade, Kingston/Miami: Ian Randle Publishers, 93.

ii. Dahomey and Benin

Even in "pre-European" Dahomey, whose elite became deeply involved in transatlantic enslavement at a later time, individual masters did not have the right of life and death over their slaves. Only the sovereign king had this right over human beings, and anyone who contravened this legal prohibition was punished by decapitation. Benin nobility was not exempt from this.[204]

In a letter that Francisco de Gois, enslaver captain of Sao Jorge da Mina, sent to King Manuel of Portugal on August 19, 1513, he stated that his ship had already been waiting for five months because the Oba (king) of Benin refused to sell slaves. Thus, we see that even in this region that was to become one of the most important bases for transatlantic enslavement, slaves had initially not been abundantly available before European intervention.[205]

In Benin, captives who ended up in the ships headed for the Americas in the 18th century were not "prisoners of war", as advocates of the slave trade maintained at that time to justify their dealings, but rather kidnapped by groups of nomadic and independent warlords, armed and recruited by European slavers. A contemporary British witness testified for the region that he "made continuous inquiries but never heard of any wars".[206]

Concerning Dahomey, early European observers left us documentation testifying that "the country appears full of towns and villages; and being a rich soil, and well cultivated, looks like an entire garden"[207]. There was no property in ground, people went out in troops to cultivate the king's fields, "afterwards, they in like manner sow the ground, allotted for their neighbors, diligently as that of the King's, by whom they are also feasted; and so continue to work in a body for the public benefit, till every man's ground is tilled and sowed. None but the King, and a few great men, are exempted from this labour".[208] A certain Bosman related that "(t)hat when a Negro finds he cannot subsist, he binds himself for a certain sum of money, and the master to whom he is bound is obliged to find him necessaries; that the master sets him a sort of task, which is not in the least slavish, being chiefly to defend his master on occasions; or in sowing time to work as much as he himself pleases."[209] How could anyone have the audacity to compare this social arrangement to bloody, genocidal transatlantic slavery?

In Dahomey, though children of slaves remained slaves, those born within the family could not be sold. Only those captured in just wars or condemned crim-

---

204   Avajon (2005), 38 et seq.
205   Popo (2010), 166 et seq.
206   Rediker (2008), 146.
207   Benezet, Anthony (1767). Some Historical Account of Guinea, Cirencester: The Echo Library (2005 ed.), 19.
208   Ibid.
209   Benezet, Anthony (1767). Some Historical Account of Guinea, Cirencester: The Echo Library (2005 ed.), 20 et seq.

inals could be disposed of through trade or were employed as slaves for royalty in accordance with traditional legal precepts.[210] Yet, local slavery was on the rise as transatlantic enslavement became an inescapable reality in the region. However, historian and slavery expert Robin Law assessed that "those retained in local slavery were, in comparative terms, the fortunate ones, in escaping the brutality of the middle passage and the harsher exploitation that was generally the fate of those taken into slavery in the Americas. (...) Partly in recognition of this, the descendants of slaves in Ouidah tend to maintain identification as clients with those of their ancestors' owners, even when not actually absorbed into the family through intermarriage"[211]. Thus, we see once again that even in a society like Dahomey, which arguably grew out of the brutality and corruption of transatlantic slavery, local slavery remained qualitatively distinct from the transatlantic experience, a distinction that is legally significant. To quote again Law,

"Slaves in Dahomey enjoyed legal protection against ill-treatment: 'the government protects the slave who can, if he is mistreated, appeal to the authorities who can oblige a master to fulfil his duties better or take away the slave'. Many slaves in urban centres such as Ouidah also had a measure of economic independence. In the 1840s it was said to be 'general practice' for masters to allow slaves to prosecute their own affairs, and to receive in exchange for this concession of their time, a stipulated monthly sum derived from their labour (...)".[212]

Slaves could also rise in the state hierarchy to positions of power. Thus the Tegan (viceroy of Ouidah) of 1743-5 was a slave of the royal palace, originally a captive taken by the Dahomian army.[213] Slaves in Dahomey were traditionally foreigners, captives taken in just wars or purchased from outside the country (and enslaved through one of the legitimate means of enslavement; criminal conviction, war captivity, ...). Dahomians could be enslaved only as punishment for some specific and serious offence. When some kings of Dahomey, in default of sufficient supplies of foreign slaves to satisfy European demand, resorted to selling their own subjects (as did kings Tegbesu and Gezo in the late 18th and early 19th centuries), this was considered aberrant and illegitimate.[214] In Igboland, another nearby region from where many captives were deported to the Americas, the loss of freedom was a form of punishment and not at all comparable to chattel slavery.[215]

Hope Waddel, a missionary in Calabar and Bonny in the Benin region in the

---

210   Manning, Patrick (1982). Slavery, colonialism and economic growth in Dahomey, 1640-1960, New York: University of Cambridge Press, 39.
211   Law, Robin (2004). Ouidah. The Social History of a West African Slaving 'Port' 1727-1892, Oxford: James Currey, 15et seq.
212   Ibid., 78.
213   Ibid., 106.
214   Ibid., 149.
215   Oriji, John N. (2003). "Igboland, Slavery, and the Drums of War and Heroism", in: Sylvaine Diouf (ed.): Fighting the Slave Trade. West African Strategies, Athens: OhioUniversity Press, 62-78.

1850s, explicitly contrasted domestic and transatlantic slavery: "Most of the slaves are employed in farming and trading. The former cultivate a portion of land, allotted by their masters for their own use, and generally supply the town markets with produce. Their labour is much less continuous and severe than that of West Indian slaves. If called into towns to work, they receive a small allowance. (...).”[216] It is also significant that at Calabar slaves formed an association that struggled successfully to end the sacrifice of slaves at funerals through a series of demonstrations and riots, but they did not challenge the institutions of slavery as such, whereas slave rebellions in the Americas always sought to end slavery in its totality because there it was in its totality and in its essence an inhuman, illegal and genocidal institution.[217]

Contemporary testimonies and records show that in the 19th century, many European observers gained the impression that the population of Ouidah consisted mainly of "slaves". It is clear that these accounts sometimes suffer from conceptual imprecision, confusing categories of slaves, pawns (whose labor was pledged for the security of debts) and even free clients. However, reality also seems to be that a substantial proportion of the population had indeed been relegated to a servile status by the 18th century as a consequence of the entrenchment of the transatlantic enslavement system in the region. "In Ouidah, as throughout West Africa, the growth of internal slavery was closely linked to that of the export trade in slaves (...)." [218]

iii. Ashante / Akan

Another African society documented to have sold many fellow Africans to European slavers in the 18th and 19th centuries was the Ashante kingdom in the territory of modern Ghana. Traditionally however, before its elite had become corrupted by European slave demand and before the slave-gun cycle had been constructed into an inescapable reality in the region, masters did not have the right to kill a slave on Ashante territory. Anyone who killed a human being, free or slave, without royal permission, was persecuted for murder. Mutilating slaves without permission was also forbidden. The slave was considered a human being, not chattel, as in the transatlantic system.[219] Davidson reported of a contemporary British witness who documented that even in times of transatlantic enslavement, in Ashante "a slave might marry; own property; himself own a slave; swear an oath; be competent witness; and ultimately become heir to his master. Such briefly were the rights of an Ashanti slave. They seemed in many cases practically the ordinary privileges of an Ashanti free man. An Ashanti slave, in nine cases out of ten, possibly became an adopted member of the family, and in time his de-

---

216   Lovejoy (2000), 188.
217   Ibid., 188.
218   Law (2004), 77et seq.
219   Testart, Alain (2001). L'esclave, la dette et le pouvoir, Paris: Errance, 50 et seq.

scendants so merged and intermarried with the owner's kinsmen that only a few would know their origin."[220]

Documentation clearly suggests that before the arrival of the Portuguese and other Europeans at the end of the 15th century, some kind of "slavery" existed in the societies of the territory of both historical and present-day Ghana. Some of the earliest accounts of the encounter between the Portuguese and Africans on the coast mention slaves being offered to the Europeans in trade. Such is the case with the reports of Diego Gomes about the Wolof (1445) and the Serer (1458), of Pacheco Pereira about the Tukolor (1507) and the Temne, Yoruba and Bakongo[221], and of Cadamosto about the Gambia region (1456). Eustache de la Fosse wrote about the Grain Coast (1479) that "they brought us women and children for sale. (...) (W)e resold these without difficulty on the Gold Coast"[222]. Without categorically denying any truth to such reports, it is essential to maintain a critical perspective as well. More than a few contemporary European observers at the time of transatlantic slavery issued statements about numerous African societies, to the like of "all men are slaves to the king". It is rather evident that the term "slave" such as used by European observers in those times does not necessarily reflect what "slave" meant in the transatlantic slavery system. In fact, in these records "slave" is very often employed more or less interchangeably with "servant", "serf", "pawn", "client" or even "subject".[223] In this context it is also important to consider that even kings could not be defined as totally "free", since they were conceived to be dependants of the ancestors.

Additionally, most of the cited European observers were illegal enslavers themselves or at least had displayed racism and violent behavior towards Africans. Thus, it is crucial to reflect critically on European testimonies, and the ideological status of their authors, when speaking of African "slaves". Pacheco Perreira, for example, penned a report in 1505 about Benin, stating that "the trade one can conduct here, is the trade in slaves (and) and in elephant's tusks"[224]. Yet, Pacheco Perreira was a blatant racist who thought of all Africans as slaves and "dogs". The statement must also be qualified in the light of other documents which show that the traders found that objection was taken in Benin to the enslavement of the natives of the country. By custom and by moral law, slaves had to be men and women captured from neighboring peoples in battles, whose objective was not to procure slaves. This rule was often broken; yet it was very widely admitted.[225]

---

220   Davidson (1961), 38 et seq.
221   Fage, J.D. (1980). Slaves and Society in Western Africa, c. 1445-c. 1770, in: The Journal of African History 1980 (21), 289-310, 298.
222   Ibid., 298et seq.
223   Ibid., 296.
224   Davidson (1961), 40 et seq.
225   Ibid.

Ghanaian historian Akosua Perbi writes that when the Portuguese first set foot to the region in 1471, they immediately began to participate in the indigenous southern coastal slave trade between Senegal and Ghana.[226] This, however, tells us nothing yet about the numbers of such "slaves", their condition and treatment, or of the legitimate reasons for enslavement in this region. In that regard Perbi argues that "the characterization of a slave as a chattel was not (...) part of the Ghanaian slavery experience. In Ghana the slave was regarded as a human being and was entitled to certain rights and privileges. (...) (T)he slave in Ghana was 'a person in a state of servitude guarded by rights".[227] There were avenues for social, economic and political mobility for enslaved persons. That there existed five categories of voluntary and involuntary subordination possibly added to misrepresentation of Akan African "slavery" in European perception and records. The "slave" as such was a person who had been bought or acquired through various means and was taken from his home, family, state, country into another family, home or country.[228] A slave was never a chattel in Ghana however. He was recognized and regarded as a human being, entitled to certain rights and privileges. His position was that "of a person in a state of servitude guarded by rights".[229] Slave status was terminated if an enslaved person married a free person. Manumission could also be attained by seeking sanctuary at the shrine of a traditional priest or king. No slave owner had the right of life or death over a slave. Following Ghanaian tradition, an acquired slave was immediately integrated into the family structure.[230]

Some male slaves did in all probability work in gold mines. This required hard work and was a dangerous, risky job.[231] Yet, this too must be considered within the context of legally proscribed limited causes for enslavement. Those employed in such mines were convicted criminals or war captives. Gold was the most important trade commodity across the Sahara and the Atlantic before transatlantic slavery. And according to Meillassoux, one of the most accredited anthropologists on the subject of slavery and servile labor, "the production of gold was mostly the work, not of slaves belonging to a ruler, but of independent populations"[232]. This assessment is in concordance with the testimony of John Barnes who was resident in West Africa for 13 years in the 18th century and British governor of Senegambia from 1763 to 1766. "In 1789 Barnes told a committee of the British House of Commons that in areas of West Africa where gold was obtained from mines, the gold so collected was distributed to the different people working for it:

---

226   Akosua Perbi (2004). A History of Indigenous Slavery in Ghana: From the 15th to the 19th century, Accra: Ghana: Sub Saharan Publishers, 4
227   Ibid.
228   Ibid., 3.
229   Ibid., 4.
230   Hickling, Frederick W. (2009). The Cycles of Elmina: Healing Our Memories,Overcoming the Wounds of Our History, Kingston: CARIMENSA, 7et seq.
231   Perbi (2004), 85.
232   Cited in: Inikori (1982), 39 et seq.

the Prince has a share; the clergy has a share; and the labouring workman has the remainder."[233] Thus, the indication is that servile labor was not very important in gold production. The next important good in trade was pepper, and there is absolutely no evidence that pepper was produced by slave labor. Since the two most prominent export products from the region did not rely extensively on slave labor, it seems rather logical that there were not many slaves in this society.[234]

All of this notwithstanding, oral and documentary records confirm that the few existent "slaves" formed the lowest social group in pre-colonial Ghana. Treatment depended to a large extent on the owner, the family and the household, yet was set within a legal and customary framework that provided some protection and rights to the slave. One such rule was that a slave was integrated as part of the family and household of the owner, and treated as such. The enslaved had the right to food, clothing and shelter, and some privileges of children while staying with their owners. They had a right to marry and to pursue an independent income. A child born of a marriage between a free royal male and an enslaved woman could be enstooled as a chief.[235] Children born of a marriage between an enslaved person and his or her owner or also between the enslaved and a relative of his or her owner were recognized as free. All of this stands in striking contrast to transatlantic practice and legislation. [236]

Those who had been completely integrated into the family had the privilege of attending family meetings, discussing family affairs and even inheriting. Enslaved persons were eligible for summons as witnesses in traditional court cases. They could sue and be sued. They could swear the state oaths and they could act as witnesses in legal actions and "drink the gods" to prove their words.[237] There was a rule for every child to be polite and respectful to everyone, including slaves. Slave owners were obliged to make themselves accessible to their slaves. This is reflected in the Akan proverb *wo nkoa suro anim asem a, wonni nim mma wo* (if your slaves/servants fear to speak to you, they will not gain victories for you). There was indeed a system of checks and balances in place in pre-Maafa Ghana with respect to slave treatment.[238]

Oral tradition confirms the rule that slaves had to be kindly treated and paints a picture of peaceful co-existence between masters and their slaves in pre-Maafa times. Oral traditions of Kwamankese, Komenda, Odompo, Katakyiase and Dagomba communities state that slaves were humanely treated, as relatives, or "nicely". In fact, all ethnic groups studied by Perbi carry oral traditions that stress how slaves were generally well treated in pre-Maafa Ghana. Even in later times,

---

233   Inikori (1982), 39 et seq.
234   Ibid., 39 et seq.
235   Perbi (2004), 135.
236   Ibid., 114.
237   Ibid., 122 et seq.
238   Ibid., 117 et seq.

outside observers, such as Freeman, Klose, Madden, Beecham, Crowther and other British Commissioners, expressed pleasant surprise at the humane treatment of slaves. "Freeman remarked that slavery in Ghana was very different from that of Europe, North America and the West Indies. A certain District Commissioner Crowther who had worked in Ghana at the turn of the 20th century described slaves in Ghana as 'more like adopted children'."[239]

Such slaves still suffered from several discriminations. An enslaved person was supposed to be unassuming and not to mix too openly with free men and women. If these prescriptions were not respected, an enslaved person who became too presumptuous could be sacrificed.[240] Please consider in that context that slaves were usually convicted criminals or war captives, and that there were no prisons. Customary law permitted kings and chiefs to kill slaves for ritual and other purposes. This happened occasionally but was by no means a regular occurrence, and a slave could not be killed by his owner, whatever his offence. To kill a slave was recognized as murder and punished as such. This contrasts strikingly with what prevailed in transatlantic slavery Europe and the Americas where slave owners, irrespective of their rank, and even other "whites"[241], claimed the power of life and death over their slaves and indeed over any African.[242]

A slave who was being cruelly treated by his owner could have recourse to several remedies in pre-Maafa Ghana. He could run away and seek protection at a traditional grove or at the royal mausoleum. He could get another person to adopt him, in which case that person paid compensation to the owner.[243] The branding of slaves, one of the many genocidal features of transatlantic slavery was not a Ghanaian practice. European observers have at many times misinterpreted the various ethnic markings displayed by many of their African captives as brandings.[244]

---

239   Ibid.
240   Ibid., 131.
241   I put the term "white" as a designation for humans under quotation marks because it is necessary to highlight that the self-categorization of European people as "white", with a strong connotation of superiority and "purity", was a deliberate social construction that went hand in hand with transatlantic slavery and the diabolization of anything "Black" (black sheep, black heart, black Friday, etc...). "Whiteness" was and is constitutive for the functioning of colonialism and "white" global supremacism. However, no humans are really white, as European's skin color is really beige or pinkish. See Cleaver, Kathleen Neal (1995). The Antidemocratic Power of Whiteness, Chicago: Kent Law Review 70, 1375-1387. I accept that African/Black people refer to me as a "white" person. The fact that European descended people have over centuries constructed themselves as white has been constitutive in the violent exclusion and genocide of African/Black people. This social reality needs to be addressed, and African/Black people need to identify their oppressors, that is the global "white" collective. Personally, I "burn" whiteness and the violence and genocide that it encompasses, and rather conceive of myself as beige in terms of skin color, which is actually a much more accurate and realistic description.
242   Perbi (2004), 7.
243   Ibid., 117 et seq.
244   Ibid., 120.

A further indication of the benign nature of Ghanaian slavery compared to transatlantic slavery stems from the examination of available records showing only five instances of rebellions from the 15th to the 19th century. And some of these were very probably related to the violence that the transatlantic slavery system had engendered. In 1640, a slave in Assin killed his master, who was an important person in the state and as such surely involved in transatlantic slavery. Subsequently the caravan trade between Assin and the districts to the north were disrupted. Assin was an important market and entrepot town in the hinterland of the Ghanaian coast through which many captives were channelled in order to reach the slave dungeons of the port towns of Elmina and Cape Coast. At about the same time three enslaved women burnt down all the granaries of the king in Elmina. The King of Elmina was one of the chief collaborators in transatlantic slavery, so a relation between his criminal enterprise and the fire attack seems more than likely.

The available historical evidence seems to confirm that in pre-Maafa times, people who had been enslaved by one of the legitimate means (war captivity, criminal punishment, pawning) were traded between some African societies. On the Gold Coast, relatives of those legally condemned to death could be put under "slavery". Another reason for legitimate enslavement was not being able to pay one's debts.[245] However, this trade was never large-scale, and the treatment of these slaves, though not enviable, was by no means comparable with the transatlantic experience.

Portuguese records testify to the existence of a trade in goods and slaves between Ghana and its coastal neighbours. Eustache de la Fosse and Pacheco Pereira who visited the coast of Ghana in the 15th century wrote about a maritime trade in cloth, beads and slaves between the Nigerian coast and Elmina in Ghana. The slaves acquired through this trade were used in iron working, pottery making and fishing industries.[246] But even in later times, when Akan society and its institutions of servile labour had already deteriorated and been corrupted after centuries of transatlantic slavery, "expatriate observers, even those few who knew the Akan and Adangme cultures relatively well and who had observed village life at close hand, often could not differentiate between who was a slave and who was not"[247].

This type of slavery was in line with the Akan conception of the human being perceived as an expression of the life principle, *okra*, carrying a divine element. As such, every person has the same intrinsic value. The doctrine of okra recognizes the right of each person, as the recipient of a destiny, to pursue that unique desti-

---

245   Fage (1980), 298 et seq.
246   Perbi (2004), 20.
247   Dumett, Raymond E. (2010). "The Work of Slaves in the Akan and Adangme Regions of Ghana in the Nineteenth Century", in: Stephanie Beswick and Jay Spaulding (ed.): African Systems of Slavery, Trenton/Asmara: Africa World Press, 67-104, 67 et seq.

ny assigned to him by God.[248]

Akan people recognized rights "that people have simply because they are human beings. (...) If every Akan was thus obliged by birth to contribute to defense in one way or another, there was also the complementary fact that he had a right to the protection of his person, property, and dignity, not only in his own state but also outside it"[249]. It was an absolute principle in Akan society that no human being could be punished without trial. "Neither at the lineage level nor any other level of Akan society could a citizen be subjected to any sort of sanctions without proof of wrongdoing."[250] Since there were no such institutions as prisons, slavery was one of the logic means of punishment by which a convicted wrongdoer also indemnified society through the value of his work.

A British official stated that about Ashante society: "a slave might marry; own property; himself own a slave; swear an oath; be competent witness; and ultimately become heir to his master. (...) Such briefly were the rights of an Ashanti slave. They seemed in many cases practically the ordinary privileges of an Ashanti free man. (...) An Ashanti slave, in nine cases out of ten, possibly became an adopted member of the family, and in time his descendants so merged and intermarried with the owner's kinsmen that only a few would know their origin."[251] Captives became gradually free, and free men became gradually chiefs, vassals became free men; whereas in the transatlantic system, the mere fact of being African was presumptive of slave status, and this slave status was for ever, such exemplified by laws passed in several US states in the 17th, 18th and 19th centuries. In Mississippi, any Black person could be sold as a slave unless they were able to show him or herself free. Georgia lawmakers imposed a fine of one thousand dollars on anyone who gave effect to a last will and testament freeing a slave or allowing him to work on his own account.[252]

In contrast, European accounts reveal that in the region of the Akan and particularly the Ashanti, whose kingdom was one of those most heavily involved in transatlantic slaving, many slaves worked in the fields alongside their masters as late as 1904, thus at a time when the transatlantic system and all the turmoil it had engendered had been at work for centuries. "For the Abron and above all for the Kulango agriculturalist, a slave is an assistant who enables him to increase the area he cultivates or who lessens the burden of heavy field work. The master himself works alongside his captives. A sort of intimacy which lessens the distinctions between them and renders the captive a servant rather than a slave grows out of their daily contact."[253]

---

248   Wiredu (1990), 244 et seq.
249   Ibid., 249.
250   Ibid., 252.
251   Davidson (1961), 38 et seq.
252   Ibid.
253   Lovejoy (2000), 171.

In traditional Akan society, slaves were not readily distinguishable culturally from free men. Still, they suffered from forms of discrimination and did not enjoy rights that free men did, such as the participation in the control of land distribution.[254] Yet, the whole cultural and social pattern of slavery here was totally different from that of the transatlantic system. The emphasis on owning domestic slaves in Africa was on their incorporation into the family unit as they became successively acculturated and proved their loyalty. Once culturally assimilated, they could expect to be treated as full members of the family.[255]

Not far from Ashanti, Quobna Ottobah Cugoano was born into Fantee society. He was first enslaved to the Caribbean and then to England. As an adult, he related in his autobiography that in his home country,

"(...) a bond-servant was generally the steward in a man's house, this is a particular custom in the country of Fantee, a faithful servant, or slave, as so called, generally becomes steward of his master's household, and frequently his heir. There was no harm in buying a man who was in a state of captivity and bondage by others, and keeping him in servitude till such time as his purchase was redeemed by his labour and service. (...) And so in general, whether they had been bought or sold in order to pay their just debts when they became poor, or were bought from such as held them in an unlawful captivity, the state of bondage which they and their children fell under, among the Israelites, was into that of a vassalage state, which rather might be termed a deliverance from debt and captivity, than a state of slavery. In that vassalage state which they were reduced to, they had a tax of some service to pay, which might only be reckoned equivalent to a poor man in England paying rent for his cottage. In this fair land of liberty, there are many thousands of the inhabitants who have no right to so much land as an inch of ground to set their foot upon, so as to take up their residence upon it – and yet the whole community is free from slavery. And so, likewise, those who were reduced to a state of servitude, or vassalage, in the land of Israel, were not negotiable like chattels and goods; (...) or ever transferred or disposed of without their own consent. (...) The service which was required by the people of Israel in old time, was of a far milder nature than that which became the prevalent practice of other different and barbarous nations; and, if compared with modern slavery, it might be called liberty, equity, and felicity, in respect to that abominable, mean, beastly, cruel, bloody slavery carried on by the inhuman, barbarous Europeans, against the poor unfortunate Black Africans."[256]

Numerous reports by European observers also confirmed that "slavery" on the

---

254   Ibid., 175.
255   Ibid, 176 et seq.
256   Cugoano, Quobna Ottobah (1787). Thoughts and Sentiments on the Evil of Slavery, London: Penguin Classics (ed. 1999), 125 et seq.

Gold Coast was fundamentally different from transatlantic slavery, such as one by a British man in the mid-18th century:

"By an inquiry into the laws and customs formerly in use, and still in force amongst the Negroes, particularly on the Gold Coast, it will be found that provision was made for the general peace, and for the safety of individuals; even in W. Bosman's time, long after the Europeans had established the slave-trade, the natives were not publicly enslaved, any otherwise than in punishment for crimes, when prisoners of war, or by violent exertion of the power of their corrupted Kings. Where any of the natives were stolen, in order to be sold to the Europeans, it was done secretly, or at least, only connived at by those in power: this appears from Barbot and Bosman's account of the matter; both agreeing that man-stealing was not allowed on the Gold Coast. (...) Hence it may be concluded, that the sale of the greatest part of the negroes to the Europeans is supported by violence, in defiance of the laws, through the knavery of their principal men, who, (as is too often the case with those in European countries) under pretence of encouraging trade, and increasing the public revenue, disregard the dictates of justice."[257]

For the Anlo Ewe community in South-eastern Ghana which later became called "Slave Coast" by Europeans, domestic slaves had usually been criminals or debtors sold into slavery in pre-Maafa times. Domestic slavery took on the role that prisons serve in modern societies. There is ample evidence that slavery was a marginal economic and social force before transatlantic slavery. "In fact, domestic slavery became a significant phenomenon in Africa only by the 19th century when it was influenced by global forces and demand."[258]

By the time of abolition of the "slave" "trade" by colonial Europe, not only on the territory of modern-day Ghana, but in large parts of Africa, "instead of resorting to traditional legal means of redress", the powerful in many African societies had under the pressure of the transatlantic system and for personal greed "turned to the slave trade. The custom of Nyiko, which included a trial and whose verdict had to be approved by the chief and elders, was summarily bypassed. (...) One effect of the slave trade was to corrupt indigenous legal institutions."[259]

iv. (Upper) Guinea Coast

Walter Rodney assessed that the slavery that undoubtedly had existed on the Upper Guinea coast in the 19th century was not indigenous to the region, but rather developed directly out of transatlantic slavery.[260] In fact, European records of the 16th and 17th centuries confirm this in that they display a striking absence of references to local African slavery in the Upper Guinea coast region. The term "slave" was employed sometimes, but so loosely as to apply to all the common

---

257   Benezet (1767), 51.
258   Bailey (2007), 11.
259   Ibid., 50.
260   Inikori (1982), 39.

people. The Jesuit priest Alonso de Sandoval related that "all Negroes"[261] were slaves of absolute kings. Regarding such utilization of the term "slave" in European documents, Rodney therefore rightfully stated that "in this arbitrary and figurative sense, the word 'slave' is equally applicable not only to the common people of Europe at that time but also to the proletariat of the capitalist world."[262] The same is valid for other parts of Africa where transatlantic slavery stimulated the growth and development of the local institutions of slavery.[263]

But even then, as elsewhere in Africa, domestic slaves were members of their masters' households on the Upper Guinea Coast and could not be sold, except for serious offences which would have made them subject to enslavement and sale even if they had been free. They had their own plots of land and rights to property of the fruits of their labor. They could get married.[264]

In the Sierra Leone region at the beginning of the 17th century a person encountering problems in his home community could flee to the jurisdiction of another king and place him or herself at his mercy. Thus, he became that king's "slave", also liable for sale. It is in this context that the Portuguese chronicler Valentim Fernandes wrote in 1507: "The king has no servants other than his slaves. Sometimes a young stranger arrives and seeks the protection of the king, who looks upon the young man as his own."[265] By all that we see that the occasional references to "slaves" on the Upper Guinea Coast in the 16th and 17th centuries have to be carefully scrutinized. They only point to the presence of a small number of political clients in the households of the kings and chiefs of the area. It is difficult to conceive that any observers would possibly have overlooked the presence of chattel slaves, agricultural slaves, or even household servants if these had been numerous and markedly unprivileged, especially since several descriptions by Portuguese from the 16th and 17th centuries are replete with details of the structure of African society on this section of the West African coast. In these reports the only distinction that is consistently emphasized is that between rulers and subjects. In matters of trade they are scrupulous in recording details and show that the Portuguese even knew of trade routes between the Futa Djalon and the coast in the 16th century. Yet, in enumerating what was exchanged there, they never once mentioned slaves, but only cloths, pieces of dried indigo, iron bars, etc.[266] This indicates, even more so in combination with the rest of the evidence discussed in this book, that this part of Africa had not known indigenous chattel slavery.

According to Rodney, the Balanta of the Upper Guinea Coast were initially

---

261   Cited in: Rodney, Walter (1966), 393.
262   Rodney, Walter (1966), 393 et seq.
263   Inikori (1982), 39.
264   Rodney (1982), 393 et seq.
265   Ibid.
266   Ibid., 393 et seq.

"hostile to the slave trade"[267], and the region's transatlantic enslavement business was monopolized by a net of corrupted kings. More recent research shows that decentralized societies of this region, like the Balanta, were drawn into the transatlantic system as suppliers of slaves once it had become so firmly entrenched that they could not escape it.[268] Yet, researchers also made it clear that it was warfare, drought, disease, political instability, and economic decline, all consequences of transatlantic slavery, which initially and continually placed strains on societies. Participation in the slave trade most times offered the only means people had to acquire the resources necessary to defend themselves. Now of course there are also some wicked individuals practically everywhere, and why should the Balanta have been an exception? But that does not change the fact that their society knew no chattel slavery and that they had initially actively opposed illegal transatlantic slavery. "Out of greed or as a desperate attempt to aid kin or community, some kidnapped strangers and others organized small-scale raids, selling their captives to merchants for valuable imported goods. (....) In very few instances can we point to people who were passively tossed in the currents of change or who allowed themselves to be plucked from the sands of Africa's shores. Those living in decentralized societies and on the frontiers of predatory states adopted strategies through which to cope with the broad structural changes unfolding around them."[269] That research also showed that in the Guinea-Bissau region, because of the rise of insecurity and slave raiding through the transatlantic system, communities had to uproot themselves from their difficult-to-defend upland homelands and went to settle in isolated, marshy, and riverine coastal zones. They gave their houses new architectural designs and concentrated houses into fortified villages. Most significant for our purpose is the fact that because they were residing in terribly dangerous places and times, farmers needed weapons for protection when they went out to their fields. European guns played a part, but since at that time they were still somewhat inaccurate and difficult to repair, iron core that the Europeans traded exclusively for slaves also played an important role in some regions. Without any large-scale iron core exploitation in the region, coastal farmers needed iron, from which they themselves could forge spears, swords, knives, and arrows made of or tipped with iron. Before transatlantic slavery, they had traded for iron with traders to the east, but the transatlantic system had shifted trade patterns. Most traders now came from the west, and they did not want salt or coastal products, but only slaves.

"So to obtain iron from which to forge weapons to defend communities, many coastal people produced slaves. (...) Individuals themselves could not hope to alter the structural realities of the Atlantic system; they could only seek to make the

---

267 Hawthorne, Walter (2003a). Planting Rice and Harvesting Slaves. Transformations along the Guinea-BissauCoast, 1400-1900, Portsmouth: Heinemann, 2 et seq.

268 Ibid.

269 Ibid., 10 et seq.

best of the options presented to them at the most local levels. One of the cruel iro-nies of the Atlantic slave trade was that, in desperate times, individuals living on the frontiers of powerful regional States might one day have feared being swept up in an attack by a large army but the next day might have used the power they wielded locally to participate in the kidnapping of a stranger for sale abroad."[270]

Other people of the region, such as the Papel who lived on one of the islands off the coast, were also drawn into the slave "trade" due to the same pattern. By the beginning of the 17th century, members of this group convicted of various "crimes" were subjected to being sold. In 1686, Spanish Capuchins described how bands of Papel left their island to raid coastal communities.[271]

All of this needs to be considered in the context that the Portuguese and their Luso-African offspring had soon after their arrival established a tight and flexible commercial network in this decentralized region.[272] In this situation,

"(h)owever they restructured their societies, many residents of the coastal reaches of the Upper Guinea Coast found it necessary to produce slave exports in order to garner the imports needed for protection. What coastal people wanted most from Atlantic merchants was iron, which could be fashioned into defensive weapons. Hence, in order to obtain iron needed to defend themselves from sla-vers, decentralized societies produced and marketed captives. The 'iron-slave cy-cle' fuelled the conflicts that generated slaves in this politically fractured region. (...) Unable to generate sufficient numbers of captives through attacks on outsid-ers, they often enslaved 'insiders', people within their own communities. They did so by transforming judicial institutions so that those found guilty of various 'crimes' could be sentenced to sale"[273].

Since this went on during a time spanning several centuries, it is indeed logical to conclude that transatlantic slavery is at the root of long-lasting inner-and in-ter-group conflicts that are still relevant today and need to be sorted out through comprehensive reparations.

In this particular region, by the mid-16th century, the local Cassanga King had become wealthy by directing military institutions and corrupting judicial in-stitutions toward producing slaves who were sold to Atlantic merchants. Such an assessment is generally accurate for much of Africa. A mixed population of Cassanga, Mandinka, Felupe, Balanta, Brame, and Banyun became incorporat-ed in the Casa Manga (Casamance) kingdom, while other communities of these same communities remained independent. Casa Mansa's militia attacked Banyun, Brame, and Balanta communities between and around the Rio Casamance and Rio Cacheu to enslave and sell them. Transatlantic slavery provided the Casa Mansa

---

270   Ibid., 10 et seq.
271   Ibid., 65.
272   Ibid., 82.
273   Ibid., 93.

rulers and many other African rulers and collaborators with an easy way to eliminate rivals as well as unwanted or rebellious commoners by condemning them to captivity and sale for whatever "crimes" they may have committed.

Of course these developments had grave consequences for the relations between the different communities living in an area. The vicious cycle of fighting constantly fuelled by the need of each and every group to get access to European arms and/or iron, among the decentralized groups around the Rio Cacheu was a major contributor to the volume of slave exports from the region. By the mid-17th century, even Felupe communities, sometimes referred to as the ancestors of the Diola and also living in the Senegambia region, who had up to then actively fought the slavers and attacked slave vessels, were drawn into the trade in captives. Previously, Felupe communities had seen themselves increasingly becoming victims of organized raids staged by groups like the Cassanga and Mandinka, and were thus compelled to find ways to improve their defences against threats from slave-raiding. The Portuguese Almada documented that some Felupe had been captured while eating at the river. Other groups already involved in active slave raiding did so with the help of the iron obtained from Europeans. The Felupe therefore also had to acquire iron to be able to defend themselves, and to do so, they had to make and market increasing numbers of captives.[274]

Even though societies like the Felupe underwent massive internal changes because of transatlantic slavery, among them the emergence and rise of internal slavery, it is important to see that even then, such internal captives were not "slaves" in the western plantation sense of the word. They were regularly given menial or labor-intensive tasks, but lived within the community. "In the late 19th and early 20th centuries, 'slaves' (...) of (...) decentralized groups in the area were said to live 'with the families of their owners'. Some observers were struck by the nature of the 'master-slave'-relationship: 'We spoke with some female slaves of Nalu origin who reported how they were captured and treated: well like people of the family'."[275] A contemporary European witness had reported concerning the societies on the coast of Guinea that "(...) they have not many slaves on the coast; none but the King or nobles are permitted to buy or sell any; so that they are allowed only what are necessary for their families, or tilling the ground. (...) they generally use their slaves well, and seldom correct them."[276]

Even then, testimonies recorded in Equatorial Guinea for a UNESCO research project on oral traditions about transatlantic slavery relate that during the first years of Portuguese presence in the early 16th century, the character of family slavery and other servile institutions changed and "slavery" acquired a new, more oppressive sense.[277]

---

274   Ibid., 98 et seq.
275   Ibid., 139 et seq.
276   Benezet (1767), 35.
277   Kwenzi-Mikala, Jérome T. (ed.) (2003). Tradition orale liée à la traite négriere et à l'esclavage en

v. Senegambia

In Senegambia, also one of the areas impacted the earliest by transatlantic slavery; traditionally "slave-owners (...) did not have powers of life and death over their slaves. They could not deliberately kill them. Slaves could change masters by destroying the property of a kinder master and getting themselves given to them *in lieu* of damages".[278]

European observers stated in the mid-17th century that man-stealing was "discountenanced by the Negroe Governments on the river Gambia", and declared that the enslaving of peaceable inhabitants was "a violence which only happens under a corrupt administration of justice"[279]. They blamed the native

"King's insatiable thirst for brandy that his subjects' freedoms and families are in so precarious a situation. Whenever this King wants goods or brandy, he sends a messenger to the English Governor at James Fort, to desire he should send a sloop there with a cargo: this news, being not at all unwelcome, the Governor sends accordingly; against the arrival of the sloop, the King goes and ransacks some of his enemies towns, seizing the people, and selling them for such commodities as he is on want of, which commonly are brandy, guns, powder, balls, pistols, and cutlasses"[280].

One William Moor, another contemporary European observer, reported that,

"tho' some of the Negroes have many house slaves, which are their greatest glory; that those slaves live so well and easy, that it is sometimes a hard matter to know the slaves from their masters or mistresses. And that though in some parts of Africa they sell their slaves born in the family, yet on the river Gambia they think it a very wicked thing."

He stated that he never heard of any case but one when a slave born into a household had been sold, except as for such "crimes as they would have been sold for if they had been free"[281].

Amadou-Makhtar M'Bow, former director-general of UNESCO, substantiated concerning Saint Louis in present-day Senegal that although at the end of the 18th century approximately two thirds of its population were enslaved (the rest were mostly colonialists and traders), the situation of these slaves was altogether different from that of slaves on the plantations and the mines of the Americas.[282]

Afrique centrale, Paris: Unesco, 68.

278   Barry, Boubacar (1998). Senegambia and the Atlantic Slave Trade, Cambridge: Cambridge University Press, 115.

279   Benezet (1767), 51.

280   Ibid.

281   Ibid., 35.

282   M'Bow, Mahtar Amadou (2002). "Les théories esclavagistes à travers la presentation du cahier des doléances de Saint-Louis du Senegal aux Etats bénéraux de 1789", in: Isabel Castro Henriques and Louis Sala-Molins (ed.): Déraison, esclavage et droit. Les fondements ideologiques et juridiques de la traite negriere et de l'esclavage, Paris: EDITIONS Unesco, 284- 300, 285.

It is also documented that Bambara slaves still lived, worked, ate, and slept side by side with their masters and were in all outward appearance indistinguishable from them in the early 20th century.[283]

Language indeed holds a very central and critical place in the debate about transatlantic slavery reparations, yet one that is only rarely acknowledged in public discourse. The Diola who live in southern Senegal, Gambia and Guinea-Bissau translate *amiekele* and *agoutchas* "esclave" or "slave". It is essential to disseminate that, however, there are significant differences between transatlantic chattel slavery and what is described in Diola society by these terms. Diola forms of "slavery" really conform to the model of the servile laborer. In Diola society this is the lowest social group, yet legally and socially its members are acknowledged as fully human, in contrast to the transatlantic system. Additionally, labor requisitions were limited to tasks that were also performed by free-born Diola such as farming, livestock herding, and the maintenance of the household. "Slaves" married, had their own homes and their own land. They were defined as strangers in the community and subject to some degree of social disdain, and excluded from intermarriage and priestly offices. As such, they conform to the defining characteristics of Miers and Kopytoff's qualification of African slaves as kinless strangers within a kinship based society,[284] and not to that of chattel slaves illegally held in the genocidal concentration complex of the transatlantic colonial slavery system.

These characteristics of servile labor in African societies also explain why, given the relative freedom of movement to and from the agricultural work sites, the laborers did not take flight. They were incorporated into the society as junior kin, were allowed to marry and had access to land to work for themselves and their families. As already mentioned before, it also resorts from early documents that the Felupe, one of the communities that later became identified as the Diola, did not have a system of servile labor at all. It is documented that up to the late 16th century they refused to engage in any commerce with Europeans. The sporadic participation of other Diola groups in early transatlantic slave trading grew out of the practice of taking war prisoners and of capturing cattle-thieves who were then "enslaved". While awaiting a possible ransom by their families or friends, they were kept in the vicinity of the major family shrine of Hupila, had a wooden fetter attached to their legs to prevent escape, and could be made to perform agricultural labor under the close supervision of their captors. A shortage of cattle for ransom, the unwillingness of family to pay it, or absence of kin could create a situation where captives might find themselves being sold into slavery. Yet, at all times rules governing the proper treatment of the captives while awaiting ransom, and the requirement to allow sufficient time for families to ransom their

---

283   Brevié, J.C. (1904). Rapport sur l'esclavage, Bamako: ASAOF, 1819.
284   Baum (2010), 45 et seq.

relatives, were enforced.[285]

In 1594, Alvares de Almada had penned about Diola society that "(t)hey used to kill all of our people whom they captured when ships were wrecked, without trying to sell them [for money] or exchange them [for goods]."[286] It must be noted that this had happened at a time when transatlantic enslavement had already started, and the Diola knew what the purpose of their Portuguese "visitors" was. They killed the European crew of shipwrecked ships as part of their resistance to illegal transatlantic enslavement. However, the Buramos, another community in the region, eventually arranged for the Portuguese that the Diola no longer killed the so captured Europeans but exchanged them. The Diola in return got arms, for which they had an increasing need with the steady rise of slave raiding in the region. Their inclusion in the inescapable reality of the slave-arm-cycle led to a development in which the Diola too ended up selling captives raided from neighboring communities. All of these developments involved a series of changes in Diola lifestyle. People began to work rice fields in groups, rarely wandered far from home and built both homes and villages so as to better protect themselves. Often areas around villages were left uncleared and houses were built without windows and with a single entrance that could be bolted. The Diola did not develop any significant "slave" population within their communities until the 19thcentury, but when they finally did start keeping "slaves" this system was highly integrative. "Slaves lived within the family, could marry free women and were treated as junior kin."[287] It was when during official colonialism the French imposed peanut monoculture in Senegal and the Gambia that the demand for Diola rice increased, because large parts of the working force had to farm peanuts for the French. To meet the basic nutritional demand of the community, the use of servile labor for rice cultivation within Diola society increased. But even then the "slaves" were treated as members of the family, were eventually able to marry free women and could only be sold in cases of absolute necessity. "Slaves" enjoyed a considerable amount of protection against violence or physical abuse, but were subjected to humiliating treatment in some regards. For example, neither slave men or women could readily speak up in village assemblies or be buried in the main cemeteries. Still, adult slaves consumed most of what they produced.[288]

A similar fate befell the Balanta, who had also initially displayed little interest in trading with the Portuguese. As slave raids began taking their toll on them, the Balanta needed to change their way of life and moved into densely packed villages

---

285   Baum (2010), 45 et seq.
286   Cited in: Klein, Martin A. (2010). "Slavery in the Western Sudan", in: Stephanie Beswick and Jay Spaulding (ed.): African Systems of Slavery, Trenton/Asmara: Africa World Press, 11- 43, 19 et seq.
287   Ibid.
288   Baum (2010), 52 et seq.

in defensible locations. They started to grow rice instead of yam, probably because it provided a higher yield per acre and was thus safer to work due to the personal insecurity situation resulting from transatlantic slavery. To be able to purchase the iron needed for rice cultivation tools, they started raiding other communities for slaves. For both the Diola and Balanta, and many other African communities, transatlantic slavery created a paranoid, fear-driven environment in which people felt insecure outside their village walls, and often even within them.[289]

vi. Mali

Ibn Battuta, the Moroccan scholar who traversed Africa and travelled as far east as China, wrote in 1352 that "one of the good features [of the government and people of Mali] is their lack of oppression. They are the farthest removed from it. Another of their good features is the security which embraces the whole country. Neither the traveller nor the man who stays at home has anything to fear from thief or from usurper."[290]

When Sundiata Keita founded the Mali Empire in 1213, its Great Assembly explicitly prohibited slavery in rather unambiguous terms throughout its territory that was as vast as Europe and comprised most of the nations of West Africa.[291] This government organized anti-slavery brigades to fight Muslim, Arab and other slavers. Indeed, one reason for the establishment of the Empire itself was to put to an end to the aggression against Black Africans by invading Arab slavers. And don't be fooled, the Mali Empire was no small thing; it stretched from the Senegambian Atlantic coast to the Middle Niger bend. The Manden Charter furthermore contained an explicit recognition of human rights: "Every human life is a life. One life is not superior to another. Every wrong done to a life demands reparation."[292] This *Dunya Makilikan* is considered the first declaration of human rights[293], and it was African. It read in part:

"The children of Sanènè et Kontron declare:

Hunger is not a good thing,

Slavery is not a good thing;

There is no worse calamity than these things, in this low world.

As long as we dispose of quiver and ark,

Hunger will kill no one in Mandé,

If by chance famine arises;

War will never again destroy villages to raid slaves;

This means that no one will henceforth place spits in the mouths of his fellow

---

289   Klein (2010), 19.
290   Robinson, Randall (2000). The Debt. What America Owes to Blacks, New York: Penguin Group, 20.
291   Popo (2010), 151.
292   Plumelle-Uribe, Rosa Amelia (2008). Traite des Blancs, Traite des Noirs. Aspects méconnus et conséquences actuelles, Paris: L'Harmattan, 52.
293   Cissé, Youssouf Tata (1991). Soundjata, la Gloire du Mali, Paris: Karthala-Arsan.

man
To go sell him;
No one will be beaten henceforth,
Much less killed
Because he is the son of a slave"[294].

Even in places like Djenne and Timbuktu where the course of economic development coupled with pressures from both transatlantic and trans-sahara slavery led to an expansion of domestic slavery at later times, this slavery was altogether different from the transatlantic institution. Slaves lived with their families and were attached to a certain occupation, and would thus more appropriately rather be called serfs.[295]

The Banamba in Mali have been labelled a "slave society" by some researchers. Yet, their "slaves" had a right to free time and to a plot of land. An incident is documented where a master requested millet beyond his rightful share. After consultation, the "slaves" responded through their elder spokesman:

"Mahmady, I salute you; all who are here are your captives. They salute you. You have asked us for millet but you know that the millet which is in our granaries is ours, because we planted it. If we do not want to sell, it is because we want to conserve it. We will not sell it today. We have given you the part that belongs to you, because you are our master. But you shall not get more until the next harvest. Mahmady, do not count on our millet, because we will keep it for the winter"[296].

It is totally unimaginable that slaves on a plantation in the Americas would have said such a thing to a master. Yet, this took place in a society that was described as having a slave system that was "clearly among the harshest in West Africa"[297], and that also had previously experienced centuries of enslavement by Arabs. Young slaves, even if working for a different master, lived with parents. "The slave family was an important institution. The slave had the company of a mate and the slave household was a social and economic unit."[298] There existed physical punishment and the life of such a slave was certainly not a lot to be envied. Yet still, this institution was something fundamentally different from genocidal transatlantic slavery.

It is beyond doubt that the Bambara states of Segu and Kaarta engaged in slave-raiding. Yet again it must be acknowledged that these kingdoms consolidat-

---

294   Popo (2010), 259.
295   Ki-Zerbo (1978), 210.
296   Péroz, Etienne (1889). Au Soudan Francais: Souvenirs de Guerre et de Mission, Paris: C.Lévy, 189-90; cited in: Roberts, Richard/Klein, Martin (1980). The Banamba Slave Exodus of 1905, in: Journal of African History, Vol. 21, Nr. 3, 375-394, 381.
297   Ibid., 379.
298   Roberts, Richard/Klein, Martin (1980). The Banamba Slave Exodus of 1905, in: Journal of African History, Vol. 21, Nr.3, 375-394, 381.

ed themselves only in the 18th century, thus at a time when both trans-saharan and transatlantic slavery had ravaged the continent for centuries and influenced indigenous servile institutions. Additionally and fundamentally, Bambara slaves generally worked in the fields together with their master and his family. They shared the same way of life and became integrated into the Bambara society after two or three generations.[299] With the Bambara, a slave was purchased by a community. As soon as a slave woman bore a child, she acquired the status of woloso (born in the house). A man could also acquire this status once his master had sufficient confidence in him. After reaching the status of woloso, they could no longer be sold, and also had a right to property and to transmit it to their children. As such, their living conditions, if not their status, were preferable to those of poor free men.[300]

vii. Dinka

Francis Deng, presently UN Special Adviser on the Prevention of Genocide at the level of Under-Secretary-General, assessed that "there can hardly be any doubt that some notions of human rights are defined and observed by the Dinka as part of their total value system. Respect for human dignity as they see it is an integral part of the principles of conduct that guide and regulate human relationships and constitutes the sum total of the moral code and the social order. (...) Certain obligations toward fellow human beings are universally prescribed"[301]. Thus, an elder of the Dinka, who live mostly in today's South Sudan which at the time of Deng's research was still part of the state of Sudan, when questioned about slavery stated that "if you see a man walking on his two legs, do not despise him; he is a human being. Bring him close to you and treat him like a human being. That is how you will secure your own life. (...)"[302]. A chief claimed with regard to the disdain the Arab-Muslim North of Sudan has toward Black people of the South that "our brothers [the northerners] thought that we should be treated that way because we were in their eyes like fools. I have never heard of any man being such a fool. A human being who speaks with is mouth cannot be such a fool. Whatever way he lives, he remains a human being. And whatever he does must be thought of as the behavior of a human being"[303]. In Dinka society, the sanctity of life and

---

299   Levtzion, Nehemia (1985). "Slavery and Islamization in Africa: A Comparative Study", in: John Ralph Willis (ed.): Slaves and Slavery in Muslim Africa, Volume I. Islam and the Ideology of Enslavement, London: Frank Cass and Company, 182-198, 194 et seq.
300   Barry, Boubacar (1992). "Senegambia from the sixteenth to the eighteenth century: Evolution of the Wolof, Sereer and 'Tukuloor'", in: B.A. Ogot (ed.): General History of Africa V. Africa from the Sixteenth to the Eighteenth Century, Paris: UNESCO, 262-299, 362.
301   Deng, Francis M. (1990). "A Cultural Approach to Human Rights Among the Dinka", in: Abdullahi An-Na'im and Francis M. Deng. (ed.): Human Rights in Africa. Cross-Cultural Perspectives, Washington DC: The Brookings Institution. 261- 289, 272 et seq.
302   Ibid.
303   Ibid.

of the human body was well established, and appropriate measures were taken to remedy any violation. Even in fights with other communities, war ethics dictated that any enemy outside the battlefield must not be attacked. For example, injured warriors, physically sheltered by a woman for protection, were not to be killed or subjected to any torture.[304]

In this regard, Deng stressed that in "traditional African society, (...) there is no clear-cut line between religious values, moral precepts, and laws. On the contrary, they are interrelated. And if it is conceded that African societies have their own institutions and enforcement procedures that might differ from those of the west but are nonetheless effective within their own context, then it goes without saying that the rights and obligations derived from religious, moral, and cultural values associated with human dignity in traditional society are enforceable and, indeed, enforced against and for the benefit of both the community and the individual."[305]

viii. Examples from various other African societies

Incidences are documented for the Zaire Basin in which a slave holder lost his wealth gambling and subsequently became the slave of one of his own former slaves.[306] Such a situation was totally unimaginable for the genocidal American colonies where Black skin was generally considered synonymous with slave status in a society built on white supremacism.

Basil Davidson stated that the

"'slave' peoples of the hierarchical States, whether near the coast or inland across the Sudanese grasslands, were in truth serfs with valued individual rights. Their status was altogether different from the human cattle of the slave ships and the American plantations. Accounts by early European traders on the Coast, though freely misusing the word 'slave', repeatedly document this. Bosman, for example, reported of the Guinea Coast around the year 1700 that 'those who come from the inward part of the country to traffick [sic] with us, are chiefly slaves: one of which, on whom the master reposes the greatest trust, is appointed the chief of the caravan. But when he comes to us he is not treated as a slave, but as a very great merchant whom we take all possible care to oblige. Indeed, I have observed that some of these slaves have more authority than their masters; for having long exercised command over their masters' dependants, by their own trading they are become possessors of some slaves themselves, and in process of time are grown so powerful that their patrons are obliged to see with their eyes only (...)'"[307].

---

304   Deng (1990), 272 et seq.
305   An-Na'im, Abdullahi/Deng, Francis M. (1990). "Introduction", in: Abdullahi An-Na'im and Francis M. Deng (ed.): Human Rights in Africa. Cross-Cultural Perspectives, Washington DC: The Brookings Institution 1-14, 3.
306   Brooks, Roy L. (2004). Atonement and Forgiveness. A New Model for Black Reparations, Berkeley: University of California Press, 182.
307   Davidson (1961), 38 et seq.

Similar contemporary observations are recorded for every part of Africa.[308]

A research project for UNESCO about African oral traditions concerning trans-atlantic slavery revealed that in Cameroun, the *Nanda* were subjects who had worked exclusively for the chief. *Nanda* is designated as a form of "slavery", but this "slave" had his house and family where he went to sleep.[309] In the Bamoun kingdom of Cameroun masters also did not have the right of life and death or even of harsh physical punishment over their slaves. Every act of mistreatment of a servile laborer was severely dealt with and could lead to the imposition of a death sentence for a master if the servile laborer had died.[310]

The Dschang of Cameroun provide yet another example of the African practice of "slavery" where the "slave" was not denied his humanity. The traditional practice of "slavery" conformed to the ethics of the society. Criminals, supposed vampires and witches who were considered as incorrigible in their home society could make themselves a new life in a new community through this social institution of "slavery".[311]

Harms assessed that

"for those captives who remained in Equatorial Africa, their tasks differed little from those of free people. Slaves did domestic chores, worked in agriculture, fishing, and commerce, paddled canoes, and transported goods on their backs or heads. (...) The fields worked by slaves were indistinguishable from those worked by the master's wives and children or by free families that lacked slaves. (...) Slave women would harvest extra cassava and bring it as a 'gift' to the master. Although the 'gift' itself was obligatory, the size of the gift was negotiable."[312]

There were also people who did not practice any forced labor at all, like the Fang of equatorial Africa.[313] Generally speaking, earliest Portuguese sources testify of an abundance of indigenous occurrences of African "slavery" that were fundamentally distinct from transatlantic slavery. The slaves of the *Cheuas de Macanaga*, for example, were integrated into the families. Whether they were war captives or enslaved following a judicial conviction, they were encouraged to marry free persons. Sometimes the owner even married a slave with a free woman of his own lineage, because this had the advantage of having no obligations to the husband's family attached. It happened quite often that an owner married a slave woman himself, for several reasons. There was no bride dowry to pay; the

---

308   Ibid.
309   Kwenzi-Mikala, Jérome T. (ed.) (2003). Tradition orale liée à la traite négriere et à l'esclavage en Afrique centrale, Paris: Unesco, 17.
310   Ajavon (2005), 40 et seq.
311   Ibid., 48 et seq.
312   Harms, Robert (2010). "Slavery in the Politically Decentralized Societies of Equatorial Africa", in: Stephanie Beswick and Jay Spaulding (ed.): African Systems of Slavery, Trenton/Asmara: Africa World Press, 161- 172, 165 et seq.
313   Ki-Zerbo (1978), 210.

husband did not have to fear any intrusion by the family of the wife; and he could be sure to reign undisputed over his children from such a union.

According to the slave trade memories recorded by UNESCO, transfer of slaves for the transatlantic system in Nigeria in the late 18th and 19th centuries was usually done secretly, at night and through back streets, to the extent possible.[314] This is an indication that slavery, in its transatlantic implementation, was not considered normal by traditional African standards, but was esteemed highly problematic and illicit. According to that report, popular memory of the local people still recalls the practice of this kind of slavery with a lot of distaste. Oral tradition in Benin holds the greed of the kings of Dahomey as causal for this catastrophe, and maintains that legally it was not the king's subjects who could be sold into slavery, but only captives of war, though this legal precept was often violated.[315] Thus we see how crucial it is to differentiate between the legal standards and rules in a given society and the actions of individual African rulers and corrupted individuals. Up to now, I have seen no pertinent historical source testifying of any traditional setting of chattel slavery in Africa.

But it should not be denied either that there existed physical punishment in traditional African slavery and that the life of a slave could be a hard lot. However, young slaves, even if working for a different master, lived with parents. The "slave" family was a respected institution.[316] One European explorer, a certain Monseigneur Cuvelie, wrote that the institution of "slavery" in Congo (one of the regions where the Portuguese first started massive enslavement operations) appeared tolerable, and that an honest slave could even become deputy chief. Forced laborers had civil and property rights, and there were multiple procedures for manumission, several of which could be taken up on the sole initiative of the slave.[317]

Ethiopia was never successfully colonized or made part of the transatlantic slavery system. The Ethiopian Fetha Negast (Law of the Kings) came into force around 1440 and bore strong Roman/clerical influences. The Fetha Negast states that

"(...) if one who flogs, has flogged him [slave] a great deal, or if one has killed him with poison or burned him with fire, he must be punished as a murderer. (...) Should one's servant be guilty of fault deserving the punishment of death, his master must bring his servant to the judge so that he may be punished for his crime"[318].

---

314   Simpson, Alaba (ed.) (2004). Oral tradition relating to slavery and slave trade in Nigeria, Ghana and Benin, Paris: Unesco, 20.
315   Simpson (2004), 33.
316   Ibid., 381.
317   Ki-Zerbo (1978), 210.
318   Strauss, Peter L. (ed.) (2002). The Fetha Negast. The Law of the Kings, Kingston: Miguel Lorne

Though this type of slavery was undoubtedly accompanied with harsh living conditions, there remains a fundamental difference to transatlantic slavery where any African was considered a slave, a slave was considered a chattel, and murdering him was not punished. He could be killed because of nothing at all by any "white" person.

The Fetha Negast also recognizes, just like other laws at the time of its creation, whether African or European, that "the state of liberty is in accord with the law of reason, for all men share liberty on the basis of natural law. But war and strength of horses bring some to the service of others, because the law of war and of victory makes the vanquished slaves of the victors. (...) To manumit is one of the deeds of perfection which must be done, for it is an excellent form of alms"[319]. If a slave chose to become a monk, he became free. The Fetha Negast never overthrew the customary legal systems of Ethiopia that continued to be in force along with it. According to these customary laws, slavery was domestic and slaves were regarded as second-class minor members of the family they stayed with. They roamed around freely and conducted business in the same way as free people. They had complete freedom of religion and culture.[320]

Generally in East Africa, a master granted slaves or servants a series of privileges, such as guaranteed food, clothing and shelter. This gave them, in some regards, an enviable status when compared to the poor free population and explains how the residential areas along the Zambezi River could maintain such high concentrations of servile populations without revolts. When slave revolts did take place in the second half of the 19th century they were not directed against "slavery" as such, but rather for the maintenance of the status quo every time it was to be altered because "slaves" feared that they were to lose these guarantees.[321]

Zanzibar, on the east coast of the African continent and as such not readily associated with transatlantic slavery, is usually considered as a society historically characterized by a strong prevalence of slavery. Some degree of a slave mode of production seems indeed to have become widespread in this region from 1810 onwards. A slave trade developed here on a scale unparalleled in Eastern Africa. Yet again, European action was instrumental in bringing about this social change. From the 1770s, the French, via a base they had taken at the Mascarene Islands, developed an intense slave trade with the Swahili coast and accelerated the slave trade in East Africa that had previously been directed to Arab countries. Most of the historians of Swahili society admit the existence of slave trading, but maintain that before the end of the 18th century, it remained a minor part of the coastal

---

Publishers, 175.
319   Ibid., 175 et seq.
320   African slave trade, downloaded from: http://en.wikipedia.org/wiki/African_slave_trade#cite_ note-Ethiopian_Slave_Systems-7 (accessed 23.3.2011).
321   Capela (2002), 329 et seq.

trade compared to the trade in ivory or gold.[322] Generally speaking, medieval geographers rarely mentioned a slave trade on the Swahili coast. Moreover, slaves in Swahili society were considered more like personal clients and not chattels. With increasing European domination and oppression, slavery expanded. "Chattel slavery, as opposed to dependency based on client relationships, seems to have been introduced on the Swahili coast by foreigners: mainly Portuguese (...). This state of affairs is confirmed in the records of contemporary chroniclers".[323]

ix. Maroon communities

When reconstructing African legal perspectives on chattel slavery, African communities in the Americas must also be taken into consideration. In this regard, the Maroon communities are of special importance. The Republic of Palmares in Brazil lasted for over a century, its people maintaining resistance against the Portuguese enslavers. It is sometimes contended that the Palmares Maroons would themselves have held slaves. This is a serious allegation. A closer examination sheds a differentiated light, however. Historical evidence indicates that forced labour in the Palmares started only after the Portuguese had heightened their military attacks on the Maroons. Defence and agriculture were both essential to the survival of the community. With intensified assaults by the Portuguese, all forces were needed for immediate defence, making it necessary to oblige newly freed individuals to do the farming.

There is absolutely no indication that "slavery" would have existed in the Palmares before the Europeans started to undertake large-scale expeditions against the self-liberated Africans. It was from that moment when they found themselves confronted with the necessity to accomplish two major tasks, both of which demanded all their force – the defense of the Palmares and agriculture – that they were obliged to resort to servile labor. It is very likely that "slavery" in the Palmares Maroon society was preceded by a period of systematic labor division where one part of the population consecrated itself to agriculture and the other one to protection and defense. With little doubt were the fields entrusted to the women, such as is still the case with numerous African societies. However, the attacks by the Europeans resulted in the loss of both the women and the agricultural produce. Permanently faced with the necessity of defense, it was impossible for the Maroon warriors to also assure the cultivation of the fields. They therefore really had no other practical choice than to put those recently liberated from the plantations at the agricultural tasks.[324]

A new member also first had to liberate another enslaved African from the

---

322   Vernet, Thomas (2009). "Slave Trade and Slavery on the SwahiliCoast, 1500-1750", in: Behnaz A. Mazrui, Ismael Musah Montana and Paul E. Lovejoy (ed.): Slavery, Islam and Diaspora, Trenton: Africa World Press, 37-76, 39 et seq.
323   Ibid., 52 et seq.
324   Peret (1999), 92 et seq.

plantations, thereby proving his loyalty, before he was granted full liberty in the Palmares and could participate in the defence of the community. This made sense because treason was always a high risk factor for all Maroon settlements. Many Maroon communities perished because of traitors. It was such a newly liberated ex-slave who betrayed Zumbi, the last great leader of Palmares, and made it possible for the Europeans to capture and execute him. It was for the same reason that the death penalty was imposed for newcomers who then fled the community. The fugitive was perceived as a potential traitor.[325] Thus, even if a certain kind of forced labor existed in the Palmares, there was good reason to it. Furthermore, the sole assessment of its existence reveals nothing about how those "un-free" people were really treated. There is no historical evidence about any individual ownership over these laborers. Their un-free status was not fixed to eternity, but rather depended to a large degree on the actions of the individual person who could gain full freedom by proving loyalty to the community.[326]

It is indeed very improbable that the Palmares could have oppressed larger numbers of their members. Such actions would have proved counter-productive and would have resulted in a house divided against itself. But the historical records speak only rarely of any major problems and confrontations within this Maroon community. Where any such problems are mentioned, they result from leadership issues rather than being a revolt of the "enslaved". Furthermore, Maroons who were captured by the enslavers or returned for some reason to the plantation, sometimes alleged that other Maroons had abducted them, in order to escape punishment.[327]

It is important to stress whenever this internal slavery allegation against Maroon societies is brought up, that in order to survive Maroon societies had to guard themselves against the ever-present danger of betrayal. Nieuhof related in 1704 that those reaching the Palmares Confederation on their own volition would become free immediately, but those liberated in attacks on plantations would remain "enslaved" until they had redeemed themselves by liberating another. Runaways were received with extreme caution, because they might turn out to be spies for the European authorities. Instead of executing those suspected of being spies, they could be put to a regimen of hard work. But such Maroon "enslavement" was not permanent. [328]

A documented testimony of a woman from the Aluku or Boni Maroons, who today live mostly in Suriname and "French" Guiana, relates that Boni, the leader of that community, did not trust any of his followers with firearms until they had

---

325   Ibid.
326   Ibid., 92 et seq.
327   Thompson, Alvin O. (2006). Flight to Freedom. African Runaways and Maroon in the Americas, Kingston: University of the West Indies Press, 224.
328   Ibid., 225.

served in "slavery" for some years and proved their unquestioning loyalty to the community. Yet, the woman said, Boni was more loved than feared because he governed with a strict but just hand, and people also understood why this was so.[329] Research has brought forth evidence that suggests that Maroon communities were generally administered on humane principles. If justice was sometimes harsh, this was born out of an imperative of survival.[330]

It is also relevant to consider that scholars established that the Brazilian Maroon communities, *quilombos*, were founded mainly in laws and customs from the Western Bantu people.[331] Thus, to a certain extent conclusions can be drawn from what the Maroons considered legitimate servile labor to what might have been considered legitimate "slavery" and servile institutions in continental African home societies.

Zips stated concerning Maroons in Jamaica that newcomers were also reduced to slavery, but at the same time assessed that they remained in a subordinate position only until their initiation was completed.[332] Because I could not find more information to substantiate this further, I benefited from my research stay in Jamaica to journey to Charles Town, one of the remaining Maroon communities. I reasoned with Colonel Lumsden, current leader of the community, and with the custodian of the museum and a few others. What they told me illuminates several controversial aspects of the Maroon past, such as the problematic fact that the peace treaties that Jamaican Maroons signed with the British obliged them to return any new runaway and to help the British suppress slave revolts.[333] This remains a somewhat controversial topic in Jamaica even today, over which some resentment between Maroons and other Jamaicans still boils.

While it is true that the British were never able to conquer the Maroons, they still rendered life immensely hard and difficult for them. Maroons were not near defeat, but they continuously lost many of their members and were prevented from leading a peaceful and healthy life. When, because of treachery or other reasons, Maroon settlements were discovered, they had to abandon them at once, leaving everything and even small children behind. Colonel Lumdsen told me that life conditions were rendered so hard by the British that deadly food poisonings augmented because people were hungry and just had to eat anything they could find. Children caught by the British were often cut in the Achilles and left to bleed to death. This was the background for the Maroons signing those treaties and compromising to suppress rebellions and return runaways. Yet even when faced with those adverse conditions, Nanny, legendary woman leader of Jamaican Ma-

---

329   Thompson (2006), 214.
330   Ibid., 218.
331   Davidson (1969), 53.
332   Thompson (2006), 227 et seq.
333   Conversation with Colonel Frank Lumsden, Somerset Falls, Jamaica, 20.2.2011.

roons and Jamaican national hero, refused to sign such a treaty with the British to the end. Additionally, even though stipulated in the treaty, Maroons refused to come out on most occasions when called to crush rebellions.

Concerning another critical point, namely the allegation that Maroons would have held slaves themselves, I was given some highly significant information by my interlocutors, information that coincides with what has just been summarized concerning other Maroon communities, such as those in Suriname and Brazil. First of all, I was told that Maroon society in general retained many features of African social organization and culture. Jamaican Maroons trace their roots to the Ashante, where, according to Jamaican Maroon memory, "slaves were confortable and integrated in society"[334]. Significantly, the descendants of Maroon "slaves" still live in the Maroon communities today and have completely mingled with the rest, thus proving that this type of "slavery" was not at all comparable to transatlantic slavery. Colonel Lumsden substantiated that there were 47 "slaves" in the Maroon community of Charles Town in 1831. He gave me a copy of a persona census that documents this.[335] It is highly significant that "slaves" were listed by the Maroon in their persona register and not as property, as was the case in plantation slavery in Jamaica and elsewhere.[336] Now, one of jobs of these Maroon slaves was to collect wild honey. Most slaves were runaways who had reached the community by one way or another, and who had not yet taken the blood oath of loyalty. By the terms of the treaty, Maroons were in principle obliged to return these runaways to the British authorities and thus to barbarous cruelty. However, to circumvent this, Maroons kept fingers and cut-off ears of men who had died in battle and handed them over to the British, pretending to have taken them from slain runaways.[337]

Maroon enslavement was not brutalizing, "not dehumanizing"[338], but consisted of services useful to the community. It is highly significant that only the Colonel still knew about the existence of such "slaves" in Maroon communities, whereas all others who talked with me in Charlestown had never heard anything about this before, further indicating that such slaves easily merged with the rest of the community. As the Colonel summed up, "Maroon ah no slave driver" (the Maroon is no slave driver).

---

334 Tour and Reasoning with Ms. Marcia (aka Kim) Douglas; Custodian of the Maroon Museum in Charles Town, Portland, Jamaica on 17.2.2011.
335 Return of the Charles-Town Maroons 1st November 1831 CO 140/121, downloaded from http://jamaicanfamilysearch.com/Members/M/MaroonsCharles (accessed 19.2.2011).
336 Conversation with Colonel Frank Lumsden at Somerset Falls, Jamaica on 20.2.2011.
337 Telephone conversation with Colonel Frank Lumsden on 18.2.2011.
338 Ibid.

x. Summary: Marginality of African "slavery" – expansion and degradation through European imposed transatlantic enslavement

We have seen by all these examples that "slavery" in pre-Maafa Africa, and even later and in African diaspora societies, was fundamentally different from genocidal transatlantic slavery. Not only was the treatment of enslaved persons completely different and respectful of their humanity, but enslavement was also legally regulated and only legitimate if keeping within those boundaries.

In its indigenous form, slavery had functioned on the edge of society. Generally, slaves were people who had failed to pay debts, been convicted of crimes, seized in war, or transferred as compensation for damages. As in Europe (see Chapter II. 3.c.), the causes that could justify war were limited to the violation of interstate treaties which had been sealed with the respective national oaths; the harming of envoys and the failure of the violating state to make reparation for the violation; the support of an enemy during war by a hitherto friendly or tributary state; and the defence of a state against an aggressor. Some acknowledged rules for the conduct of war also existed. For example, the lives of innocents were to be spared as far as possible, and sacred groves were considered inviolable.[339]

Domestic slavery also played the role prisons serve in industrialized societies. There is ample evidence that domestic slavery was a marginal economic and social force before transatlantic slavery took off. "In fact, domestic slavery became a significant phenomenon in Africa only by the nineteenth century when it was influenced by global forces and demand."[340] One effect of transatlantic slavery was the corruption of indigenous legal institutions. Instead of resorting to traditional legal means of redress, the corrupt powerful turned to the slave "trade".[341] Many African rulers who traded slaves with Europeans acted without the constitutionally proscribed advice or consent of other gremia. Such agreements of "slave" "trading" were thus contrary to customary law and illegal.[342] Comprehensive reparations must also provide means for thorough investigation into these developments that are at the root of numerous grave problems and conflicts in African society today.

With regard to transatlantic slavery there are several broad themes discernible throughout Africa. We know that pre-Maafa African past was not all idyllic, nor free of abuses of power and authority. Otherwise it is hard to imagine how transatlantic slavery could have taken root in the first place, even with all the massive pressure put on by Europeans. However, despotic and unlimited control of the individual by the omnipotent state, such as first perfected in Europe, was unknown.

---

339   Mensah-Brown (1975), 112 et seq.
340   Bailey (2007), 11.
341   Ibid., 50.
342   Allott (1975), 80.

Though African societies in the past did not emphasize individual rights in the same way that European societies do today, they did in fact know and apply the concept of individual rights. According to the definition by Ronald Cohen, a right is an entitlement:

"At its most basic level, a human right is a safeguarded prerogative granted because a person is alive. This means that any human being granted personhood has rights by virtue of species membership. And a right is a claim to something (by the right-holder) that can be exercised and enforced under a set of grounds or justifications without interference from others. The subject of the right can be an individual or a group and the object is that which is being laid claim to as a right."[343]

Such a conception of rights did inform the notions of justice in African societies, as can be seen from a brief examination of the norms governing their legal, political and social structures in pre-Maafa times. For example, both the Akamba of East Africa who are an example of a decentralized society and the Akan of West Africa with a centralized state system endowed the person with individual rights as well as obligations. As an inherently valuable being, the individual was naturally recognized to be endowed with certain basic rights. With the Akan, the presumption of innocence was deeply embedded in social consciousness, and it was an absolute principle of Akan justice that no human being could be punished without trial. Both societies recognized a wide range of individual rights. The right of life was so valued that the power over life and death was reserved for a few elders and was exercised only after following an elaborate judicial procedure, with a system of appeals, and only in cases of murder and manslaughter.[344] Many of these Akamba and Akan norms and structures were common to other pre-Maafa societies, where respect for and protection of the individual and individuality within the family and the greater socio-political unit was fundamental. Fernyhough has outlined many of the rights protected in African pre-Maafa societies, including the rights to life, personal freedom, welfare, limited government, and free speech, conscience and association.[345]

There is abundant evidence confirming that in pre-Maafa Africa no wars were waged with the aim of procuring slaves. This resorts also from notes and testimonies by European enslavers and colonialists. For example, Dominique Harcourt Lamiral, a French commercial agent, reported that on the coasts of Africa, "no war

---

343   Cohen, Ronald (1993). "Endless Teardrops: Prolegomena to the Study of Human Rights in Africa", in: Ronald Cohen and Goran Hyden (ed.): Human Rights and Governance in Africa, Gainesville: University of Florida Press, 3-38, 3 et seq.

344   Fernyhough, Timothy (1993). "Human Rights and Precolonial Africa", in: Ronald Cohen and Goran Hyden (ed.): Human Rights and Governance in Africa, Gainesville: University of Florida Press, 39-73, 62).

345   Mutua (2002), 72 et seq.

is waged with a direct intent to make slaves"[346]. It was only war captives whose captivity was the result of wars waged for legitimate purposes who could be taken and sold.[347] With the advancement of time however, these legal and social precepts were undermined. The vast majority of those deported to the Americas were neither criminals nor war captives, but people kidnapped in raids.

There is also abundant evidence from accounts by European traders that in many African societies it was not possible to sell second generation slaves. For example, slave trader Francis Moore noted in the 1730s that along the Gambia River "(...) they think it a very wicked thing, and I never heard of but one that ever sold a Family-slave, except for such crimes as would have made them to be sold had they been free. If there are many Family Slaves and one of them commits a Crime, the master cannot sell him without the joint consent of the rest, for if he does, they will all run away, and be protected by the next kingdom to which they fly".[348] In contrast, other European observers noted that transatlantic slavers used thumbscrews on children[349], stated the "general cruelty of the system", and that "merchants, captains, officers, and crew members thought about it, worried about it, took practical action against it. Each and all assumed that the enslaved would rise up in a fury and destroy them if given half a chance"[350]. European observers recognized and testified throughout the long period of transatlantic slavery this distinct nature of indigenous African "slavery" and how it deteriorated because of the transatlantic system. Thus, the British Chief Justice Lord Denham explained in 1848 that "(...) slavery is universal among these [African] nations, but it is of mild character (...). The right to treat human beings as articles of trade was taught them (...) by the sons of civilized, Christian Europe (...)."[351]

One day a friend of mine who had grown up and always lived in Paris, France, but whose family is originally from Senegal, told me that her parents would accept only a Senegalese husband for her. Furthermore he would not just have to be Senegalese, but would also have to belong to the same ethnic group, the Peul. She said that, ideally, he would have to come from the same "caste", fisher, too, and could not be a "slave". When I asked her what exactly "slave" meant in that context, she said that in past times "slaves" were people who for one reason or another did not have access to land and labored for other people, yet they were compensated for their work. They were properly nourished, housed and taken care of. She also explained that in Africa, "slaves" were traditionally people who had transgressed the law and who had to be kept in check by putting them to slavery, and sometimes their family as well. This coincides with the academic researches

---

346   M'Bow (2002), 294 et seq.
347   Ibid.
348   Lovejoy (2000), 115 et seq.
349   Rediker (2008), 216 et seq.
350   Ibid., 292.
351   Hickling (2009), 26.

and historical sources reviewed and presented in this work so far. Thus, even though there was and is clearly a social stigma attached to the status of "slave", it is evident that African "slavery" was fundamentally different from transatlantic slavery.

Generally speaking, the fact of being a "slave" reveals a particular civil status, that of a non- or excluded citizen dependant on a master. Yet as such it tells nothing about the real treatment and socio-economic status of enslaved persons in a particular society. Throughout all the evidence that I have reviewed in the past three years, I have found no indication whatsoever that pre-Islamic or pre-Maafa African societies would have dehumanized or systematically brutalized slaves, or would have been slave societies.[352] Most authors who allege an historical existence of indigenous African slave societies, such as Flaig in Germany[353] or Pétré-Grenouilleau in France[354], base their contentions entirely on evidence about African societies from a time when Islamic jihads and/or European military conquests had already set in. These African societies had thus already been substantially altered through the pressure of foreign induced razzias and aggression.[355] Yet, the proposals of European historians such as Flaig or Pétré-Grenouilleau superficially suggest that Africa would have been a huge reservoir of slaves from time immemorial. This in turn would also imply that African societies were in a state of perpetual war against one another, yet this, again, is belied by the historically documented facts. This must be why certain European historians cite very few or no sources at all for their contentions through large parts of their oeuvres. Those sources simply do not exist. Yet unfortunately such historians sell too many books and are given prominence in mainstream media. There were conflicts of course in pre-Maafa Africa, but also enough examples of stability, security, peace and development. For example, Wagadou, founded in the early centuries CE, and reaching its apogee in the 9th century at a time when Charlemagne tried in vain to gather warring European nations in his Holy Roman German Empire, extended on a surface comparable to that of the entire Western Europe.[356]

Some people contend that they are against reparations, because "there was always slavery in different places and times. Should those who were enslaved by the Romans also be compensated? I don't think so!" Yet, that kind of view relies heavily on misinformation and ignorance of historical facts. Contrary to ancient Roman slavery, transatlantic slavery was not only illegal during the entire time span it was conducted, but it also produced a systematic legacy that is founded

352 Popo (2010), 65.
353 Flaig, Egon (2009). Weltgeschichte der Sklaverei, München: C.H. Beck.
354 Pétré-Grenouilleau, Olivier (2004). Les traites négrieres, essai d'histoire globale, Paris: Editions Gallimard.
355 Ibid., 67.
356 Popo (2010), 69.

on socially charged markers of physical appearance. This systematic legacy is global and structures the daily existence of the descendants of its original victims up to this very day. This does not only concern the African diaspora, but also continental Africa. According to the legal theory of trans-generational obligation, obligations (to repair, for example) do not hold when there has been a radical discontinuity between the community of generations. Thus, the present Greek government would have no obligation to make reparations to the descendants of ancient Anthenian slaves.[357] In contrast, descendants of the victims of the transatlantic slavery system and the Maafa, that is Africans, are still discernable, still suffer from the crime and have in a historically unbroken chain claimed reparations. Thus, we see that the argument of "if we make reparations for transatlantic slavery, Roman slaves' descendants also have to be compensated" is nonsense.

African "slavery" was not racially constructed, and did not normally involve the repugnant scope of degradation, geographical and cultural dislocation, devastation and death that was an intrinsic feature of the transatlantic experience. Every form of enslavement carries within it a germ of cruelty and degradation, yet domestic "slavery" in Africa did not embrace the dehumanization of the transatlantic system. "Palace chiefs in many parts of Africa, though slaves, enjoyed certain privileges that were envied by lower-class and poor free people. Royal slaves of the Alafin of Oyo and Ooni of Ife [direct neighbours of Benin] were highly regarded because they had privileged access to the king and could even seek favours from him. They sometimes enjoyed relative affluence and a prestigious position."[358] Such aspects need to be reflected time and again, because they allow a more balanced outlook regarding the participation of societies like the Yoruba in active process of enslavement for the transatlantic system at a later time.

Any kind of unfree personal status and forced labor is prima facie reprehensible. I love my life, and I am grateful that as an adult person I can direct it the way it seems fit to me. The imagination of being deprived of one's natural right to freedom is distressing in any way. However, when dealing with transatlantic slavery it is important to keep conscious at all times that this was something fundamentally different than other forms of slavery and unfree labor. Its basic mode of operation was mass murder and genocide. Such European and Arab enslavement and aggression of Africans over multiple centuries led to the replacement in many parts of Africa of the indigenous *jonya* system by a slave-owning system. The term *jonya* is from the Mande people, *jon* meaning "captive". The *jonya* system was found mainly in West Africa and the Niger-Chad region. A *jon* (*jaam* in Waalo; *maccuba* in Fulfulde; *bayi* in Hausa) belonged to a lineage.

---

357   Freeman, Michael (2007). Back to the Future: the Historcial Dimension of Liberal Justice", in: Max du Plessis and Stephen Peté (ed.) Repairing the Past? International Perspectives on Reparations for Gross Human Rights Abuses, Antwerpen/Oxford: Intersentia, 29-51, 45f.

358   Kolawole, Mary E. (1994). "An African View of Transatlantic Slavery and the Role of Oral Testimony in Creating a New Legacy", in: Anthony Tibbles (ed.): Transatlantic Slavery. Against Human Dignity, London: HMSO, 105-110, 106.

"He was not transferable, he owned the bulk of what he produced and, in so-cieties in which the system flourished, he belonged to a socio-political category that was part of the ruling class and thus had a share in the sovereignty of the State and its political apparatus. Both as a system and a social class *jonya* played a considerable and novel role in the States and empires of Ghana, Takrur, Ka-nem-Borno, Asante, Yoruba and Mutaoa."[359]

Some of these "slaves" belonged to the dominant ruling class in state affairs, ex-ercised some power, made fortunes and could even themselves own slaves. How-ever, increasing instability, continual warring and slave raiding for transatlantic and trans-saharan enslavement contributed first to the expansion of *jonya* in the 16th century and then to its development into harsher slave-owning systems and new colonial forms of slavery.[360] Before these social changes, European-type own-ership, understood as a right to use and transfer people like chattels, was practi-cally non-existent.[361]

It is significant to make known the fact that in most of the town centers of the transatlantic slave "trade" in Africa the majority of the population were slaves, for example 56 per cent in Saint Louis/Senegal in 1779. However, many of these slaves were slave soldiers, wives and concubines and urban, domestic slaves. Many did manual labor, for example as stevedores, carpenters, masons and ship-builders. Slaves were part of boat crews, and often traded on their own account or for their master. There were also slaves who worked the land. A questionnaire conducted by French colonialists reported the labor obligations of slaves in Saint Louis as five days a week from sunrise to early afternoon prayer (about two o'clock). The other days and the afternoons, slaves worked on their own plots, although at harvest time they may have been asked to work more. Meillassoux assessed in an-other near-by region, Gumbou, that the initial development of servile institutions probably dates to the early 18th century, thus a time when transatlantic enslave-ment had already been imposed on the people for several centuries.[362]

Transatlantic slavery also led to the emergence of an African military aristoc-racy and the development of state slavery that was devoted to the provisioning of the military and state functionaries who could not produce their own subsistence. Yet at the same time protracted warfare and constant removal of population from neighboring communities through enslavement retarded the development of di-vision of labor and inhibited the growth of trade and inter-regional specialization, through which the subsistence and needs of those state functionaries could be met. The aristocratic and militaristic elite had to be self-sufficient, and therefore

---

359   Diagne, Pathé (1992). "African political, economic and social structures during this period", in: B.A. Ogot (ed.): General History of Africa V. Africa from the Sixteenth to the Eighteenth Century, Paris: UNESCO, 23-45, 24.
360   Ibid.
361   Ibid., 28 et seq.
362   Klein (2010), 30 et seq.

a part of the captives had to be retained for this purpose. Meillassoux argued that the evidence indicates that through transatlantic slavery the dominant classes in many African societies became reliant on war and the administration of war as a means of domination. Yet the extremely low ratio of population, again a result of transatlantic enslavement, made wage labor for agricultural production largely unavailable and in turn encouraged the spreading of the use of slave labor. This became even more rampant with the growth of agricultural export production in the second half of the 19th century and direct colonialism.

"Thus, by the last quarter of the 19th century, important areas of tropical Africa had a sizeable proportion of their populations held under conditions approximating those of chattel slavery. This division of important African societies into military aristocracies and slaves, or merchants and slaves, weakened them both economically and politically. As pressure from European imperialists mounted in the late 19th century, the oppressed slaves could not be counted on to defend the exploiters against new oppressors (...). It is not for nothing that resistance to colonial conquest tended to be more protracted and more bloody in areas where these classes were little developed."[363]

Inikori concluded, speaking of Africa in general, that it
"may well be the case [that] in places like Asante, Dahomey, and the Benin kingdom of south-western Nigeria (...) a significant population of dependent people, whose socio-economic conditions approximated those of slaves, existed side by side with others, in greater numbers, whose conditions were closer to those of serfs. [It is important to remark in that regard that the consolidation of the Asante, Dahomey and Benin states was directly connected to transatlantic slavery, and that even then life conditions for slaves in those societies were significantly different from genocidal transatlantic slavery.] But there are regions in which the people described as slaves by scholars had so much freedom that it will not even be appropriate to call them serfs. Such was the case with of the Puna and Kuni societies of modern Congo. Here, the so-called slaves labored the same way as their free counterparts; they could hold any office in the society, and they were usually married to free spouses from lineages of their masters. Then we have the very interesting case of the servile warriors of Mozambique in the period from 1825 to 1920, who look more like knights of medieval Europe. They lived in their own villages, which were scattered all over the land; they had their own leaders (...)."[364]

How important a precise use of terms with regard to an accurate historical and juridical appreciation of the reparations claim is, is shown in the following statement made during of the debate on reparations in the British House of Lords.

"Slavery has occurred in many countries and people were enslaved in Europe during the past war. It is a phenomenon which is far from confined to black na-

---

363   Inikori (1992b), 38 et seq.
364   Inikori (1999), 67.

tions (...). As regards compensation, therefore, one has to ask how far it would be proposed to go back in time. (...) And who would pay compensation? Almost every country was responsible for slavery in those days, including the French, the Spanish and the blacks themselves (...)." (Lord Gisborough).[365]

Within a historical and chronological perspective, Inikori has well unmasked this kind of argumentation by representatives of (former) European enslaver and colonial states:

"Slavery in Africa was a major theme constructed by the European slave traders to defend their business against the abolitionist onslaught in the 18th century. The same theme also became very fashionable for the agents of European colonialism in the late 19th and early 20th centuries, as the abolition of slavery was presented to the moral conscience of Europeans as a part of the European 'civilizing mission' to Africa. The propaganda by the slave traders and by the agents of colonialism was so effective that it was given intellectual respectability in history textbooks."[366]

Yet today, the same artificially constructed argument is still employed to deny reparations claims and to carry on with neo-colonialism, built on the structures of transatlantic slavery. It is crucial that African people, especially the descendants of those deported, get acquainted with the information presented in this section. Too much grudge and confusion between diasporan and continental Africans is due to the dominant misrepresentations of indigenous African "slavery" and collaboration in the transatlantic system. What we need though is unity, and unity can come through truth.

xi. African collaboration and resistance

We have seen clearly over the previous pages that African "slavery" was fundamentally different from transatlantic slavery not only in terms of legitimate reasons of enslavement, but also in terms of life conditions and treatment. The question must thus be asked with regard to African collaborators if they were fully aware of what they were participating in and of what horrors awaited their victims on the slave ships and on the American plantations, since nothing comparable existed in pre-Maafa Africa.

Yet there is no denying that historical records testify to a few sporadic examples of African enslavers who had previously themselves gone through transatlantic slavery as victims. However, anyone who has familiarized him or herself even slightly with documentation about the Middle Passage will see that this journey of several months could inflict severe mental damage on any human being. Equinao wrote in his autobiography in 1789 about the experience of the Middle

---

365   House of Lords Debate on Slavery Reparations, March 14, 1996, downloaded from http://www.publications.parliament.uk/pa/ld199596/ldhansrd/vo960314/text/60314-26.htm (accessed 5.4.2012).
366   Inikori (1996), 64.

passage: "I am yet at loss to describe"[367]. The fact that not even a handful of Africans who had gone through this most traumatic experience later participated in inflicting the same barbarity on others can in no way be used to bolster an alleged "legality" of transatlantic slavery within African societies, as reparations negationists usually do.

Up to this point we have spent a great deal of energy and space in assessing the evidence about African slavery and, to some extent, African collaboration in transatlantic slavery. It is therefore now time to focus on African resistance against transatlantic slavery. When talking about African collaboration, it is important to at all times keep conscious of the fact that throughout the long centuries of transatlantic slavery, many African people and leaders fought with all their might to stop this massive crime. What is essential to retain is that, just because some individual African rulers were corrupt and participated criminally in transatlantic slavery, this does not mean that chattel slavery had been lawful in their respective countries.

That numerous Africans leaders and regents, such as kings in Jolof, Benin, or Kongo opposed transatlantic slavery is documented in the recorded evidence. Tragically, by some means or other, European slavers could always find individual Africans who would collaborate with them by making and supplying captives for personal greed for wealth and power. "It only required a few greedy or opportunistic persons, who felt they should enrich themselves rather than resist the inexorable pressures of supply and demand, to keep the slave trade alive. Those suppliers, in turn, rapidly became wealthy enough to become a focus of power to whom others had to accommodate."[368]

The available evidence suggests that especially in the first decades and centuries, kings, queens and leaders actively resisted transatlantic slavery, whereas with the advancement of time collaborators gained the upper hand, backed by European arms, material support and direction. Yet, it also resorts from the historical records that the majority of African people always resisted transatlantic slavery and applied various strategies to oppose it from the 15th to the 19th century.[369]

That African slaves were not available in abundance, only waiting to be purchased by Europeans, as often suggested or implied by reparations detractors, is supported by early eyewitness accounts of African resistance by Portuguese explorers and traders. It resorts from such documents that in both Senegal and Gambia Portuguese ship captains tried to kidnap people and so aroused the hos-

---

367   Rediker (2008), 108.

368   Manning, Patrick (1990). Slavery and African Life: occidental, oriental and African slave trades, Melksham: Redwood Press, 34.

369   Adu-Boahen, Albert (ed.) (1985). General History of Africa, Vol. VII, Africa Under Colonial Domination 1880-1935, California: Heinemann & UNESCO, 3.

tility of local communities.[370] For example in 1446, after several other captains had already kidnapped people in the lower Gambia, Nuno Tristão entered the Gambia river hoping to make more slaves, but he was greeted by several boats full of men armed with bows and poisoned arrows. He and 20 of his crew lost their lives.[371] The Portuguese soon learned that it would be wiser for them to deal with local elites.[372] Various historic sources also show that early Portuguese enslavers were only able to kidnap children because of the great popular resistance to enslavement.[373]

In the Sierra Leone region, one of the first British enslavers, John Hawkins, led raiding parties to kidnap Africans, a fact that implies that slaves were not easily obtainable through commerce. "Otherwise, European merchants would simply have bought slaves, which usually took less time and involved fewer risks than capturing slaves."[374]

In Benin, the reigning Oba, or king, from 1504 to 1550, thus at the beginning of Portuguese slaving activities in the region, was actively opposed to transatlantic slavery. Capable of raising armies from 20,000 to 100,000 men, he seized all slavers and their ships who intruded his territory.[375]

Queen Nzinga Mbandi of Angola federated the region into the United Provinces and allied them with resistance fighters in Congo in the late 16th century. She maintained the rebellion against Portuguese enslavers for about 30 years. In a first great victory the alliance took over Luanda. Tragically, as usually, resistance was finally defeated through the European strategy of identifying and arming collaborators.[376]

African resistance and attacks on transatlantic slavers and trading posts bear witness that transatlantic slavery was not considered normal and "legal" in the eyes of the African majority, but as decidedly illicit. This is the reason why, wherever possible, as in Saint-Louis and Gorée (Senegal), James (Gambia), and Bance (Sierra Leone), slave dungeons were located on islands to render escapes and attacks difficult. African people opposed transatlantic slavery to the extent that in some areas, such as Guinea-Bissau, Europeans gave instructions that as soon as people approached their ships "the crew is ordered to take up arms, the cannons are aimed, and the fuses are lighted. One must, without any hesitation, shoot at them and not spare them. The loss of the vessel and the life of the crew are at

---

370   See, e.g., eZurara, Gomes Eanes (1453). Chronique de Guinée, Paris: Editions Chandeigne (ed. 1994); see also examples cited in: Klein (2010).
371   Klein (2010), 19.
372   Ibid.
373   eZurara (1453), 186 et seq.
374   Lovejoy (2000), 43.
375   Ibid., 115.
376   Ibid.

stake"[377].

From the early 16th century onwards, it is documented that ships belonging to an African "fraternity" patrolled in the Gulf of Guinea, and that their crews of 60 and more men, armed with sparrows and shields, attacked European slave vessels. Such resistance was also put up by various chiefs and kings.[378] Until the mid-18th century the entire countryside from Sierra Leone to Cape Mount was rife with rebellions against transatlantic slavery. Not a single year passed without groups of Africans attacking some slave vessel. People succeeded in establishing free zones on the coast and attracting runaway slaves from all over the area.[379]

When Europeans commenced transatlantic slavery, the non-islamized societies of Siné and Lower Gambia were ferociously opposed to this criminal enterprise, as is indicated by the testimony of Ca Da Mosto.[380] According to Jean-Pierre Plasse, a contemporary witness in the middle of the 18th century, the people from Cape Verde to Ivory Coast had a reputation of being hostile to the European slavers.[381]

Documented evidence of resistance to transatlantic slavery is indeed very ample. "Fort-Joseph in Senegal was attacked and all commerce ceased for six years. Several conspiracies and actual revolts by captives also erupted in Gorée Island, resulting in the death of the governor and several soldiers. In Sierra Leone the people sacked the captives' quarters of an infamous trader, John Ormond. (...) Written records of the attack of 61 ships by land-based Africans (...) have already been found for the 17th and 18th centuries."[382]

In Senegal, the marabouts, Muslim teachers and leaders, staged a war against transatlantic slavery in the 17th and 18th centuries. They grounded themselves in the teachings of a Muslim scholar who had sustained that "God does not allow the kings to rob, kill and make their peoples captifs whom He has given to them so that they will maintain them and protect them from their enemies. The peoples are not made for the kings, but the kings for the peoples"[383]. The marabouts succeeded in creating a region of refuge in the Fouta, but they too were at last defeated by an alliance of a neighbouring king who had been armed by the French and their slave dealers of St. Louis.[384]

The Felupe put up fierce resistance to enslavement, and for some time they dissuaded slavers from visiting their region by attacking slave vessels. They were, Alvares wrote, "the mortal enemy of all kinds of white men. If our ships touch

---

377   Durand, Jean-Baptiste (1807). Voyage au u Sénégal fait dans les années 1785 et 1786, Paris: Dentu, 191.
378   Lara, Oruno D. (1997). Résistances et luttes, in: Diogène, No. 179, 169-170.
379   Barry (1998), 122.
380   Popo (2010), 156.
381   Ibid., 162.
382   Diouf (2003b), XII.
383   Ajavon (2005), 114.
384   Ibid., 114 et seq.

their shores, they plunder the goods and make the white crew their prisoners".[385]

On the other side of the Atlantic too, African resistance began with the first ship that landed and never stopped until today. Countless revolts throughout the Americas are recorded throughout the course of transatlantic slavery.[386] Governor Nicolás de Ovando of Hispaniola reported in 1503 that slaves escaped as soon as the first human cargo disembarked on the island. There and elsewhere, the freedom-takers (commonly referred to as "runaways") established settlements in remote areas. Many Maroon communities fought the colonists and forced them to accept truces. So did the Maroons in Mount Orizaba/Mexico, Jamaica, Guyana, Suriname, Venezuela, and elsewhere. Maroon communities existed everywhere where transatlantic slavery was practiced, such as in Lousiana, South Carolina, Georgia, Virginia, Saint-Domingue, Martinique, Guadeloupe, Saint Lucia or Barbados.[387]

Because of this well documented resistance, most contributors to the UNESCO General History of Africa editions agree that the deprivation of sovereignty through transatlantic slavery was a crime that was perpetrated against Africa very much contrary to the expressed will of the masses of African people and their rulers throughout the continent and the diaspora.[388]

Tragically, the resistance of African leaders and people did not prevail because Europeans supplied fire-arms to African rulers and individuals who were ready to enslave others. This scheme resulted in a situation where the choice for most Africans became one of being enslaved or enslaving others.[389] The seminal 1978 UNESCO Meeting of Experts unanimously stated that "European pressures in this field continued to increase from the 16th century – when they already existed for example in the Congo and in Zimbabwe – to the 18th century. In the case of some African societies the choice was often decisive. That of the Ovimbundi in Angola was described to the participants: in order to survive as an organized group, they entered into the system of the Portuguese slave-trade."[390] Thus, when contemplating on the question of African collaboration and responsibility, it is indispensable and legally significant to consider that historical documentation and analysis give unambiguous evidence to the "gun-slave-cycle/iron-slave-cycle" theory. In all regions affected by transatlantic slavery, acquisition of firearms and/or iron became a necessity for self-defence as slave raiding by others who had thus been armed by Europeans augmented. Guns and iron could only be acquired from European

---

385   Hawthorne (2003a), 98.
386   Palmer (1998), 15 et seq.
387   Ajavon (2005), 116 et seq.
388   Adu-Boahen (1985), 3.
389   Ibid., 47.
390   United Nations Educational, Scientific and Cultural Organization (ed.) (1978). Meeting of Experts on the African Slave-Trade, Final Report, Port-au-Prince, Haiti, 31 January- 4 February 1978, downloaded from http://unesdoc.unesco.org/images/0003/000333/033360eb.pdf (accessed 21.6.2012).

slave traders in exchange for slaves. "This is why the most important slave-exporting areas of the time, in particular, the Bonny trading area, were also the largest firearms importers in West Africa during this period."[391] Numerous academic researches have clearly established that for many African communities and states the only possibility to resist enslavement within the transatlantic system was to become slavers themselves.[392]

B. MUSLIM SLAVERY

Yet it is no news, often emphasized by European reparations opponents, that enslavement and "trade" of African captives initiated and operated by Arabs and Muslims had preceded transatlantic slavery by centuries. This is true; Arabs and Muslims began to enslave Africans from the first centuries CE, exporting them through the Sahara, the Red Sea and the Indian Ocean. Up to the 15th century the Muslim territories around the Mediterranean and beyond were the main slave importing regions of the world, and slaves were taken there both from Europe and from sub-Saharan Africa.[393] The slaves coming from Europe had generally become enslaved as a consequence of war captivity, legal conviction or debt pawning, thus by that time internationally accepted legal means of enslavement. Until the 13th century though, enslavement and slave trading of European slaves diminished greatly due to the consolidations of European kingdoms, the end of conquest of European territories by Muslims and the abolition of slavery in large parts of Europe.[394]

Conform to this general international legal standard, slaves in Islam were initially and legally prisoners taken in holy wars, and only those who were not Muslims were legally enslavable. This rule, however, was violated more often than not with regard to Africans.[395]

I do not wish to repeat here the debate on comparisons between transatlantic and trans-saharan slavery with its attempts to diminish guilt and responsibility by pointing to crimes committed by others. Trans-saharan slavery had been carried on for a much longer time span, but it never attained the horrific dimensions of transatlantic slavery, neither quantitatively nor qualitatively. However, from the abundant evidence gathered in the course of this research, it resorts that a large part of this "trade" was also illegal, as shall be elaborated over the next pages. Reparations may therefore also well be due to Africa from Arab countries and societies. This problematic will have to be dealt with in detail in another separate research. For the purpose of this work, it must suffice to detect that "pre-Europe-

---

391   Inikori (1982), 136 et seq.
392   Rashid (2003), 141.
393   Inikori (1982), 13.
394   Sweet, James (1998). The Iberian Roots of American Racist Thought, in: Colin A. Palmer (ed.), The worlds of unfree labour: from indentured servitude to slavery, Ashgate, NY, 143-166, 155.
395   Lovejoy (2000), 15 et seq.

an" slavery in Africa was mainly introduced through contact with Islam. This is evidenced by the available historic documents. These developments subsequently transformed the prevalence and character of already previously existent servile institutions in the concerned African societies. It is crucial to address this aspect, because reparations negationists often point to an alleged existence of savage "slavery" in Africa "since time immemorial", in order to back their contention of "legality" of transatlantic slavery. What they are referring to though, really, is Arab or Muslim enslavement of Africans.[396]

Throughout the multitude of historic studies consulted for this present work, I have not found any evidence of "slavery" sanctioning rampant brutalization and disregard for life in any African societies that had not been previously subjected to Arab or European enslavement. It is also important to consider that throughout the entire medieval period Portugal, the first European nation to illegally enslave Africans, maintained close contact with the Islamic societies of the Mediterranean, notorious enslavers of Africans.[397]

It has been argued that since the 8th century, due to the conquest of Iberia by Muslims, Iberian Christians adopted and reinforced Muslim enslavers' attitudes towards Black Africans, since they were not only not Christians, but they were perceived as the "heathen's heathen", the Muslims' slaves.[398] Sweet sustained in his research that Christians and Muslims regarded one another as infidels, but were united in their disparagement of Black Africans. Thus, Iberian literature and written testimonies by rulers testify to anti-Black racist attitudes in the 13th century, such as a story contained in King Alfonso's *Cantigas*, where he addressed interracial and interreligious adultery.

"Cantiga 186 begins by describing a happily married couple threatened by the husband's jealous mother. One day while the wife is sleeping, the mother-in-law orders her black Moorish slave to lie beside the wife, then calls her son to witness the scene. The townspeople find the two victims guilty of adultery and take them to the town square to be burned at the stake. The virgin cries for help from the Virgin Mary and is miraculously saved; the Moor is allowed to burn. The content and accompanying pictures of Cantiga 186 suggest that the Moor was punished in such a painful manner because of his color. He is 'black as pitch' and the principal panels show a very dark person with teeth resembling those of wild animals. (...) The persons with the darkest skins are consistently portrayed as posing the gravest danger to Christian purity and receive more severe punishments than those meted out to other infidels. (...) The strength of Iberian Christians' distaste

396   e.g. Flaig (2009).
397   Peabody, Sue/Grinberg, Keila (2007). Slavery, Freedom, and the Law in the Atlantic World. A Brief History with Documents, Boston/New York: Bedford, 22.
398   Sweet, James (1998). The Iberian Roots of American Racist Thought, in: Colin A. Palmer (ed.), The worlds of unfree labour: from indentured servitude to slavery, Ashgate, NY, 143-166, 149f.

for blacks appears especially in their ideas about the underworld. The demons of hell were black. (...) The association of blackness with sin was a frequent theme in religious works."[399]

It is really important to grasp these connections, even more so since it was the virtual cessation of the trade of Caucasian slaves from the east that in all probability prompted the Portuguese to look for African slaves. When the only remaining bastion of Christian control over the Black Sea fell to the Ottoman Turks at Constantinople in 1453 and Ivan rose to power in Russia in 1462, the Portuguese were cut off from slave supply because the Ottomans prohibited the sale of light-skinned Muslims from the conquered territories and the consolidation of a Russian empire ultimately translated into state protection from illegal slave raids. So the Portuguese had to find a new strategy to supply themselves with slave labor.[400] But we will come back to the Portuguese in a little while. For now, let us look some more into the history of enslavement of Africans by Arabs and Muslims.

i. Arab Muslim enslavement of Africans

The process of islamization of African societies itself is directly linked with the arrival of Arabs in the whole of North Africa, starting with Egypt and Libya. In 642 Kalidurat, King of Nubia, was militarily defeated by Muslim invaders commanded by Abd Allah ibn Saarth. A treaty was then imposed by the Muslim sovereign of Egypt on the King of Nubia. One article of this treaty stipulated that Nubia had to send 442 slaves to Cairo each year.[401] The invader also forced the Nubian ruler to accept the obligation to construct a mosque and to maintain it well.

In 666-667 Muslim troops intruded until Fezzan and Jarma and also demanded a tribute of 360 slaves annually. From there, they conquered Kawar north of Lake Tchad. These Arabs not only established themselves in the countries of Black Africa where they facilitated the penetration of Islam, but they also developed the hunt on Black Africans and their "trade" across the Sahara to the Muslim empires and later also to the Iberian peninsula. Heers retraced that these captures and slave convoys demanded a certain infrastructure, the development and maintenance of which was the responsibility of men who subsequently mingled with the native people and formed households with indigenous African women.[402] As the islamization of Africa accelerated, the exportation of Black slaves destined to serve in the Muslim empire also increased. In some cases, this subjection of the native populations was the result of military aggression such as in Nubia, Kawar and Jarma, while in other cases the Muslims preferred to align themselves peacefully with the local elites and kings. In both cases, African slaves were deported to

---

399   Sweet, James (1998). The Iberian Roots of American Racist Thought, in: Colin A. Palmer (ed.), The worlds of unfree labour: from indentured servitude to slavery, Ashgate, NY, 143-166, 152ff.

400   Sweet, James (1998). The Iberian Roots of American Racist Thought, in: Colin A. Palmer (ed.), The worlds of unfree labour: from indentured servitude to slavery, Ashgate, NY, 143-166, 155.

401   Heers, Jacques (2008). Les négriers en terres d'islam, Paris: Librairie Académique Perrin, 27.

402   Ibid., 27 et seq.

the markets of Cairo and then shipped across the Indian Ocean and the Red Sea.[403]

Just like the Europeans at a later time, the Arab enslavers also kidnapped children if they could not otherwise provision themselves with enough slaves. The *Kitab al-Ajaib al Hind*, a document written in the mid-10th century, describes the technique used by Arab abductors: "... they steal the children by attracting them with fruits. They transport them from one place to another and finally transport them in their countries."[404]

The presence of African slaves is documented for the period of the 10th to the 15th century in Arabia and the Persian Gulf, as well as in China and India in smaller numbers. Most of them probably came from the Horn of Africa. By the end of the 15th century this slave trade was a more or less established practice on the Swahili coast, but remained relatively small in numbers.[405] The enslavement of Africans in that direction took place over several centuries, and continued into the early 20th century, yet the numbers deported each year were never very great.[406] The Cairo papers dating from the 10th to the 13th century often refer to the buying and selling of slaves for use as servants or business agents, but do not mention a large-scale slave trade. The *Minhadj of al-Makhuzumi*, a detailed account of Egyptian commerce and port customs from the late 12th century, contains not a single word about the trading of slaves.[407]

The illegal enslavement of Africans by Arabs and Muslims had definitely acquired a very racist connotation by the 19th century, when al-Nasiri stated in his treatise on slavery:

"Thus will be apparent to you the heinousness of the affliction which has beset the lands of the Maghrib since ancient times in regard to the indiscriminate enslaving of the people of the Sudan and the importation of droves of them every year to be sold in the market places in town and country where men trade them as one would trade in beasts – maybe worse than that. People have become so inured to this generation after generation that many common folk believe that the reason for enslavement according to Holy Law is merely that a man should be black in colour and come from those regions. This, by Allah's life, is one of the foulest and gravest evils perpetrated upon Allah's religion, for the people of the Sudan are Muslims having the same rights and responsibilities as ourselves."[408]

---

403   Plumelle-Uribe (2008), 43 et seq.
404   Ibid., 46 (t.b.a.).
405   Vernet (2009), 39 et seq.
406   Inikori, J.E. (1992a). "Africa in world history: the export slave trade from Africa and the emergence of the Atlantic economic order", in: B.A. Ogot (ed.): General History of Africa V. Africa from the Sixteenth to the Eighteenth Century, Paris: UNESCO, 74-112, 74.
407   Davidson, Basil (1969). The African Genius.An Introduction to African Cultural and Social History, Atlantic Monthly Press Book, Boston/Toronto, 214.
408   Willis, John Ralph (1985a). "Introduction", in: John Ralph Willis (ed.): Slaves and Slavery in Muslim Africa, VolumeI. Islam and the Ideology of Enslavement,London: Frank Cass and Company, 1-15, 9.

Now, as mentioned already, Arabs did not only enslave Africans, but Europeans as well. Yet, from the available records it seems as if anti-Black-African resentments within parts of the Muslim elite had already very early influenced the manner and amplitude of enslavement of Africans. Thus, Ahmad Baba, author of the famous *fatwah* condemning as illegal most of the enslavement of Africans, thought it necessary to refute the idea of the curse of Ham. "Now the pronouncement of Nuh is in the Torah, and in it there is no mention of black colour. (...) Thus, to ascribe the blackness of Ham to that curse betrays an ignorance of the nature of heat and cold and their effect on the air, and on animals that are created therein."[409] In an effort to counter anti-Black resentments, Al-Jahiz, one of the greatest writers of the Muslim world in the 9th century, gave a list of natural things in which a dark hue is thought to be preferable in terms of quality, beauty, strength, utility and calmness: dates, certain vegetables, ebony, gems, rocks (Black Stone of the Ka'ba), lions, donkeys, cows, sheep, ambergris, musk, antimony, night. With respect to human beings he mentioned Ethiopian and other women of Sudan, and claimed that Arabs had been more inclined to marry them in the pre-Islamic than in the Islamic period. He classified Arabs as a sub-group of the Sudan, and went on to assess that the 10 children of 'Abd al-Muttalib and the family of Abu Talib, the paternal grandfather and uncle of Prophet Muhammed, were *Sudanese*, thus Black Africans.[410] Abu al-Faraij Ibn al-Jawzi of Baghdad, a specialist of great fame in the Hadiths (traditions) and jurisprudence, in the 12th century exalted dark-complexioned people in one of his works, their physical strength, bravery, generosity, good manners, harmlessness, cheerfulness, sweetness of breath, easiness of expression and fluency.[411] These defenses had apparently been necessitated by a prevailing negative attitude among elites in Muslim societies toward Africans and other minorities, as there also existed very unpleasant statements in Arab literature regarding African people.[412]

ii. Islamized African slavers

From the writings of Yakubi in the 9th and Al-Idrissi in the 12th century it appears that people from the islamized Ghana kingdom sporadically overtook villagers to the south (the region that would become Mali) by surprise to sell them to Arab merchants.[413]

Al-Idrissi wrote in the 12th century that "stealing the children of one people by another is a prevalent custom among Sudan"[414]. He substantiated that in Ghana,

---

409   Cited in: Muhammad, Akbar (1985). "The Image of Africans in Arabic Literature: Some Unpublished Manuscipts", in: John Ralph Willis (ed.): Slaves and Slavery in Muslim Africa, VolumeI. Islam and the Ideology of Enslavement, London: Frank Cass and Company, 47-74, 49.
410   Muhammad (1985), 49 et seq.
411   Ibid., 55.
412   Isaac (1985), 80.
413   Ibid.
414   Levtzion, Nehemia/Hopkins, J.F.P. (ed.) (1999). Corpus of Early Arabic Source for West African

Takrur and Silla in the Senegal River valley, "the slave trade was more important in areas further east like Kanem, which did not have gold, but even in Ghana the export of slaves was a valuable way to pay for commodities from the Mediterranean"[415]. Yet, this was not slavery as in the transatlantic system. Ghana had slave officials, and the importance of slaves was seemingly more political than economic. After Sundiata and his huge anti-slavery empire of Mali had been defeated by the Muslim invaders, slave officials were also important in Mali. The official closest to the King, the Mansa, was a slave in charge of the administration.

One son of Askia Dawud, Emperor of Songhay, claimed that it was possible for a raiding party to collect as many as 10,000 slaves. Many of these captives were exported to North Africa, others sold into the Sahara, where they tended herds, mined for salt or smelted copper. Young women were taken as concubines into the harems, and male slaves served as soldiers. Many slaves were also settled in agricultural estates where they produced rice under the direction of slave chiefs. Agriculture did not rely solely on them, but there was also a large free peasant sector. It was the dominant political, military and mercantile classes that were serviced by larger numbers of slaves. Slaves themselves were in a way part of that ruling elite as soldiers, eunuchs and mothers of future rulers.[416]

Yet, historical evidence relates that such slavery activities only began with Muslim presence in these Northern parts of Africa and that they spread with Muslim expansion.[417] In and around the northern Savannah where Islam had taken root, including Songhay, Mali, Borno and the Hausa states, slave raids were becoming common.[418] It is important to note that even though it was Africans themselves who enslaved other Africans in these North African empires, that enslavement was a consequence of their previous islamization and the Muslim doctrine of the enslavability of unbelievers in holy wars. Again, up to now I have come upon no historic sources that would indicate in any way the existence of large-scale slavery in any African society that had not previously been islamized or in later times subjected to the transatlantic slavery system.

There is no doubt that Muslim influence gave rise to the expansion of slavery in Africa, and also entailed long-term effects in that regard. A survey of slaves conducted in 1903-1905 in French West Africa comparing two cantons in the region of Kankan revealed that the proportion of slaves was higher in the predominantly Muslim area. In the canton labelled "fetishist", slaves constituted only about 5% of the population, compared to 40% in the Muslim canton. Other studies also showed that there were fewer slaves among the non-Muslim Bobo, and almost none among the non-islamized Diola of Casamance.[419]

History, Cambridge: Cambridge University Press, 119.
415   Ibid.
416   Klein (2010), 14 et seq.
417   Diop-Maes (1996), 217.
418   Lovejoy (2000), 28 et seq.
419   Levtzion (1985), 194 et seq.

But even in islamized African societies, slavery was of a different quality than in the Arab and European slave systems. Research by Boutillier showed that among the islamized Buna of northern Ivory Coast, slaves used to work in the fields together with their master and his family. They shared the same way of life and became integrated into society after a few generations. Among the Hausa, slaves were engaged in the same trades as freemen after their conversion and the Muslim naming ceremony. "Slaves practiced the same institutions and culture as their owners and, though occupying a clearly subordinate status, were members of a common society with their owners."[420]

Klein assessed for the islamized western Sudan, more precisely Masins, that enslaved persons were given land to produce for themselves and maintain their own families. They had to give their master one-sixth of the harvest as rent for the land, and a quantity of grain had to be paid in dues.[421] Other authors came to the same diagnosis for other neighboring communities.[422]

In the Fouta-Djallon (present-day Republic of Guinea), following a jihad in the 18th century led by the Fulani, the conquered Diallonke and Susu were enslaved and settled in villages where they produced for themselves on lands rented from the Fulani masters. In these villages, they were economically self-sufficient and had their own kin group. They owed the masters land rent and labor dues: "Men, women and children worked five days a week for their masters from early morning until early afternoon."[423] Thus the servile population in this region was not really "slaves", even if labelled as such.[424]

In East Africa, more precisely in Zanzibar and the island of Pemba, existed clove plantations run by Omani Arabs. Life conditions of the workers there were brutal and can indeed be approximated to chattel slavery. Yet it is important to fully realize that this institution was not indigenously African, but was introduced and maintained by Arab Muslims. Even so, the majority of the servile laborers had greater autonomy than in transatlantic slavery. In Mombasa, servile cultivators lived in villages of their own. Some of them even worked on their own account and paid their masters a monthly or annual sum called *ijara*. Others worked the fields without supervision, while a quantity of grains had to be paid periodically. People working for different masters lived together in villages, with an elected

---

420   Ibid.

421   Klein, Martin A. (1988). "Slave Resistance and Slave Emancipation in Coastal Guinea", in: Suzanne Miers and Richard Roberts (ed.): The End of Slavery in Africa, Madison: University of Wisconsin Press, 203-219, 208 et seq.

422   Johnson, Marion (1976). The Economic foundation of an Islamic Theocracy - the Case of Masina, in: Journal of African History, XVII, 4, 488-489.

423   Derman, William (1973). Serfs, Peasants, and Socialists: A Former Serf Village in the Republic of Guinea, Berkeley: University of California Press, 30.

424   Inikori (1999), 64.

headman.[425]

Scholarly description of the 19th century Sokoto Caliphate in northern Nigeria puts into evidence that enslaved populations lived in agricultural villages (rumada) with their own village chief. They worked with their families on their own farms, allotted to them by their masters, from the early hours of the morning to 9:30 a.m., at which time they went to their lords' fields. "There they worked until midday, when food was sent to them on the fields by their lords. By 2:30 p.m. work on the lords' fields was over and they were free to return to their own farms."[426] The land that they possessed for their own use was inheritable, though it could not be sold. People were also paid for any additional work, such as thatching, done for the master.[427] Hausa tradition and customary law imposed severe limitations on the possibilities of the masters to sell servile individuals living in a household.[428] Despite such facts, European scholars called these people "slaves" and their settlements "slave-villages".[429]

Mason asserted concerning the Bida emirate, which was part of the Sokoto Caliphate, that it conquered other groups (Yoruba, Afenmai, Hausa, Fulani and Nupe) and settled captives of these people in agricultural villages. However, they did not render any labor services to their lords, but rather produced entirely for themselves and paid tributes. "Both in status and economic independence, most of them were superior to the *bovarii* of 12th-century England. Many were in the category of the villein of medieval Europe", and had even greater economic independence than the villeins of medieval Europe and higher economic independence and social status than the 19th century Russian serfs. Thus, Inikori concluded that "the bulk of servile populations in the Caliphate hitherto referred to as slaves by scholars were in fact *servi casato*, that is, serfs"[430]. Hill stated concerning the same region that "unlike genuine chattel slaves in ancient Greece and Rome, in the United States, and in Brazil and Haiti, who were always totally devoid of rights, farm-slaves in rural Hausaland normally enjoyed so many rights (...) that it is reasonable to ask whether the term slave is, in fact, an appropriate translation of the Hausa *bawa*."[431]

Several researchers such as Deng and Howard have assessed that the ancestors of Northern Sudanese Arabs introduced slavery to that region, and that the

---

425   Ibid.,65.
426   Ibid., 59.
427   Hill, Polly (1976). From Slavery to Freedom: The Case of Farm-Slavery in Nigerian Hausaland, in: Comparative Studies in Society and History, Vol. 18, No.3, 418.
428   Inikori (2001), 54, 60.
429   Smith, Mary (1954). Baba of Karo: A Woman of the Muslim Hausa, London: Faber and Faber.
430   Inikori (1999), 62.
431   Hill (1976), 397.

Black African Dinka were and still are its principal victims.[432] The Dinka explicitly condemn the practice of slavery as incompatible with the universal dignity of the individual, whatever his or her race or country of origin. Thus, one Dinka elder is quoted by Deng as stating that:

"A human being created by God was never made a slave by the black man [the Dinka]; it was the Arabs who made them slaves. (...) Slavery is not known to us. (...) To capture people to become slaves among us is unknown. (...) He [the person of servile status] is not treated like a slave; he becomes a member of the family. The treatment I told you before, where people are crippled and where people's testicles are pricked, never happened among the black people."[433]

In response to the allegation that the Dinka in the past would have likewise captured Arabs, Dinka elders argued that although this may have happened on occasion, it was always a retaliatory act and its purpose was not to enslave. Furthermore, a person thus captured was adopted and became "a member of the family". Deng quotes another chief of the Dinka who commented that

"what the Arabs have written down is a lie. (...) Even our ancestors tell us they never captured Arab children. People kill themselves in war, face to face, but we do not go and capture people. (...) We have something God gave us from the ancient past, from the time our ancestors came leading the people. (...) War has always occurred [but we] have war ethics that came with us from the ancient past. We never ambush (...), we kill face to face. It is the Arabs who treat us as slaves and capture us in secrecy."[434]

Most islamized Black African societies integrated slaves into their families before transatlantic slavery and to some degree also thereafter. This was consistent with African social values, and Islamic law also accorded some practical and personal protection to slaves. After conversion, which was a necessary condition for their enslavement, the children they produced were free Muslims and not slaves (contrary to transatlantic slavery). In islamized Black African societies, slaves fulfilled a wide array of tasks, from soldiers, royal wives, to domestic aids and many more. Women and children were acquired to aggrandize the household. Masters often presented enslaved members of their households as their "children".[435]

iii. Legal status

According to Islamic law, it is legal to enslave only non-Muslims. This logic,

---

432   Deng (1990).
433   Ibid., 286.
434   Ibid., 286 et seq.
435   Miller, Joseph C. (2002). 'Stratégies de marginalité. Une approche historique de l'utilisation des êtres humains et des idéologies de l'esclavage: progéniture, piété, protection personelle et prestige - produit et profits des propriétaires', in: Isabel Castro Henriques and Louis Sala-Molins (ed.): Déraison, esclavage et droit. Les fondements idéologiques et juridiques de la traite négrière et de l'esclavage, Paris: EDITIONS Unesco, 105 - 161, 131 et seq.

however problematic in itself, was not respected with regard to Africans. Following the southwards expansion of Islam in Africa, the majority of those enslaved were Muslims at the time of their captivity, making their enslavement illegal.

Because this illegal practice was soon becoming a serious problem and a controversy within Islam, renowned Malian law scholar Ahmad Baba issued a famous *fatwah* on the question of the legality of the enslavement of Africans by Arab Muslims. In that *fatwah* he condemned trans-saharan slavery[436] and stated that "the cause of slavery is non-belief". He clarified that "the burden of proof rests upon those who buy" and that "if ownership is obscure, abstention [from possession] is a pious act".[437] Ahmad Baba's opinion was by no means a minority position; it was in fact echoed by other Muslim law scholars, such as Shehu Usuman dan Fodio, *mujahid* of the Nigerian north, who cautioned restraint in enslavement of Africans in his *Tahqiq al-'li-jami' tabaqat hadhihi l-umma*. Shaykh al-Hajj 'Umar b.Sa'id, *mujahid* of the Senegal region, also passed a harsh legal judgement on those who undermined the principles of slavery in Islam.[438] In 1391, the King of Bornu, Biri Ben Idriss, wrote a letter to Sultan al Malik Az Zahir Barquq, where he denounced that Arab slaver gangs raided his country and abducted numerous of his subjects who were Muslims themselves and thus not legally enslavable.[439] Centuries later, the Moroccan historian and man of letters Ahmad al-Nasiri al-Salawi, also echoed the admonition of Ahmad Baba and condemned his countrymen for their indiscriminate enslavement of the people of the Sudan:

"[The people of the Sudan] are among the best peoples in regard to Islam, the most religiously upright, the most avid for learning and the most devoted to men of learning. This state of affairs is to be found in most of their kingdoms bordering on the Maghrib as you are aware. (...) Even if you assume that some of them are pagans or belong to a religion other than Islam, nevertheless the majority of them today [1880] as in former times are Muslims, and judgement is made according to the majority. For the reason in Holy Law which existed in the time of the Prophet and the pious forefathers for enslaving people does not exist today; that is being taken prisoner in a jihad which has as its object to make the word of Allah supreme and to bring men to his religion."[440]

This shows that the enslavement of a majority of those captured in trans-saharan slavery was illegal (even by the standards of Islamic law), and that reparations from Arab societies may well be due to Africa as well. Albeit not as horrible as in the transatlantic system, life was a brutalizing experience for many enslaved Africans in Arab and islamized societies. They were subjected to inadequate nutrition,

---

436   Baba Kaké (1998), 26.
437   Willis (1985), 5.
438   Ki-Zerbo (1978), 158.
439   Ibid.
440   Willis (1985), 6 et seq.

sexual abuse, or castration.[441] In any case, the characteristics of Muslim slavery, with its more clearly defined distinctions between slave and free, and the occasional employment of slaves in productive activities, constituted a sharp break with the indigenous systems of servile labor of societies in Africa. The expansion of Islam led to an institutionalisation of slavery in the regions concerned. [442]

Despite the already harsh and illegal conditions of trans-saharan and Arab enslavement of Africans, they did not measure up to the genocidal brutality of what was to come with transatlantic slavery. In Muslim societies, enslaved concubines became free legally upon the death of their master and they could not be sold once they gave birth.[443] In transatlantic slavery, this was not so. Masters could, and did, force sexual relations on any female slave they wanted. Even if relations had been continuous and brought forth children, these women still remained slaves after the master's death, and they could be sold at any time, just like the children.

Contrary to transatlantic slavery, Arab/trans-saharan slavery also valued the individual skills of enslaved persons to some extent. Goldsmiths, scribes and others often continued to work in their profession for their new master. In transatlantic slavery, Africans trained as highly skilled craftsmen or scholars were treated as nothing more than plantation chattel.

In Muslim society, despite restrictions placed on admission to the merchant community and the high office, slavery was not an excluding barrier. Merchants had to be Muslims, and rulers had to have an aristocratic heritage, yet in neither case were slaves excluded. Slave women were taken as wives and concubines, and their children had legitimate claims.[444] Historians have assessed that even in islamized regions of Africa where slavery was rampant, such as Djenne and Timbuktu, slaves lived with their own families, and that their position often equalled that of serfs attached to a special domain.[445]

Finally, it is important to take note of the fact that transatlantic and trans-saharan/Arab enslavement of Africans also mutually amplified one another at all times. Thus, for example, the growth of slaving business for the transatlantic system along the Rio Geba in the 18th century was less a consequence of direct Portuguese actions than the consequence of a *jihad* in the interior of that region which produced large numbers of captives.[446]

Arab trans-saharan enslavement also expanded with the start of transatlantic slavery in the 15th century and continued to do so until the 19th century.[447] An early example of the mutually amplifying negative effects of Arab Muslim and

---

441   Lovejoy (2000), 36.
442   Ibid., 18.
443   Ibid., 17.
444   Ibid., 34.
445   Ki-Zerbo (1978), 210.
446   Hawthorne (2003a), 77.
447   Lovejoy (2000), 17.

European activity in Black Africa is the conquest of Songhay by Morocco in 1591. The thousands of captives were sold by Arab slavers to Europeans and caused a temporary increase in the volume of transatlantic deportations.[448]

C. LEGAL SITUATION IN EUROPE

We have seen so far that transatlantic slavery was abnormal and illegal by African and Muslim law standards, and that Muslim enslavement of Africans was to a large extent illegal by their own Islamic law. Establishing the contemporary historical legal situation in Europe is now the next logical step to be made in our analysis.

In the early Middle Ages, slaves were still deported from Europe on a small scale, just as from Africa. They were taken to Egypt, China or India by mostly Arab merchants. In their majority those deported were captives from wars between western European and Slavic nations. This practice reached its apogee in the 10th century. Thereafter it declined steadily. The Vatican issued prohibitions of the slave trade at several instances, beginning in 1317.[449] As seen in the last section, the Iberian Peninsula also received, on a small scale, slaves from the Caucasus und later from Africa via Muslim merchants.

Initially and up to the early Middle Ages, "slavery" was considered legitimate by European, Muslim Arab and African law, though we have seen that African slavery in treatment coincided more with European serfdom, if it resulted from captivity in a "just war". However, both Arab and transatlantic enslavement of Africans was for the most part NOT taking place in the context of such a "just war". Furthermore, the conditions of transatlantic slavery were never tolerated by any legal system. This is why Las Casas, originally in favour of the importation of African slaves to the Americas, strongly condemned it once he learned that their enslavement was both formally (no "just war") and materially (life conditions and treatment of enslaved Africans) illegal. He concluded that their captivity was as unjust as that of the indigenous people of the Americas that he had always militated against.[450]

The doctrine of "just war" in Europe can be retraced back to Roman times. Marcus Tullius Cicero, the famous Roman orator and statesman, noted in *De Re Publica* that not only were formalities to be observed in declaring war, but that it was necessary that Rome's participation in a conflict rested upon a *iusta causa*.

---

448   Ibid., 26.
449   Plumelle-Uribe (2008), 21.
450   Capdevila, Nestor (2002). "Las Casas et les Noirs: quels problèmes ?" in: Isabel Castro Henriques and Louis Sala-Molins (ed.): Déraison, esclavage et droit. Les fondements idéologiques et juridiques de la traite négrière et de l'esclavage, Paris: EDITIONS Unesco, 41-58, 42. (see: De las Casas, Bartolomé (ed. 1989). Historia de las Indias, III, Editions des Obras completas, Madrid: Alianza Editorial, 2324).

Such a just cause could only be assumed if it was to avenge a wrong suffered, or in self-defense. Cicero stated that "the only excuse (...) for going to war is that we may live in peace unharmed. (...) [N]o war is just, unless it is entered upon after an official demand for satisfaction has been submitted, or warning has been given and a formal declaration made."[451]

Roman jurist Florentius contended that slavery was "an institution of the common law of peoples (*ius gentium*) by which a person is put into the ownership (*dominium*) of somebody else, contrary to the natural order. (...) Slaves (*servi*) are so called because commanders generally sell the people they capture and therefore save (*servare*) them instead of killing them"[452]. The wording of this legal definition reflects the fact that slaves were originally prisoners of war.[453]

The existence of previously established institutions such as international treaties demanding mandatory compliance or arbitration for dispute settling, as well as the humanization of "justified" warfare was confirmed and strengthened during the Middle Ages in Europe. It was also during this period that human limits of civil power and its submission under a superior law commonly binding for all were progressively recognized by law doctrine and practice.[454] It was generally recognized in Europe that a legitimate war had to be based on a just cause and could by no means be a war with the aim to conquer. It was reglementated by strict forms of notification, rejection and a delay between rejection and the beginning of violence. Religious sites, women and children had to be spared.[455] These legal requirements do not quite fit with the image one usually associates with the Middle Ages – one of brutality and endless wars –, but as Grewe rightly highlighted, this depressing picture does not delete the effect of those regulations of war. Historical transmission is always much more silent about the observance of law than about its violation in wars.[456]

Grotius sustained that only a war declared by public authority conferred upon the belligerent parties, under *jus gentium*, the right to harm the enemy regardless of the justice of the cause. This right, however, was limited insofar as prisoners were not to be killed nor, in a war between Christians, made slaves.[457] The relevance of these elaborations with regard to transatlantic slavery may be belittled by reparations opponents, yet it is crucial to highlight that this legal opinion of Grotius was invoked for the persecution of war criminals after WWII, and cited by the United States through its Attorney General (later Supreme Court Justice)

---

451   Bederman (2001), 222.
452   Wiedemann, Thomas (ed.) (1981). Greek and Roman Slavery, London: Routledge, 13.
453   Bush, Michael L. (1996). Serfdom and Slavery: Studies in Legal Bondage, New York, Longman, 73.
454   Hummer/Neuhold/Schreuer (1997), 34.
455   Grewe (1984).
456   Ibid., 143.
457   Nussbaum (1954), 110.

Jackson in support of its discriminatory policies against Hitler's Germany before the entry into the war.[458] There is therefore no reason why it should not also be invoked in the context of transatlantic slavery.

Vitoria accorded to the "pagan" rulers a legal position similar to that of Christian princes concerning the benefits of the law of war to both belligerent parties.[459] Scholar Alberico Gentili (1552-1608) in his *Law of War* wrote that "he considers as a war only a contest between public armed forces, thus discarding the 'private' wars of old".[460]

An aspect that is often overlooked is that the law of nations or international law of the Middle Ages did not recognize a right to conquest. Such a right would have contradicted the logic of the theory of just war that bound the aim of war with a *iusta causa*. War was only legitimate if it was declared in order to avenge a legal breach and to restore the material legal position. The fact that European nations felt a persistent urge to have their conquests in Africa and America sanctioned by the Pope testifies to their deficiency of legal titles according to the accepted doctrine of just war.[461] Thus, for example, in 1493 Alexander VI issued the two papal bulls *Inter Cetera* in which he conferred the new lands "discovered and to be discovered" to the Iberian royals Isabella and Ferdinand.[462]

And transatlantic slavery was indeed a prominent and well discussed subject in contemporary European legal law doctrine. This indicates that transatlantic slavery was not seen as "normal" and unproblematic at all at the time of its realization, contrary to what reparation negationists want to make believe today. None of the renowned scholars of that time deemed slavery as legal without any restrictions, and the majority rejected it or recognized serious boundaries based on natural law.

Thus, according to Suarez, slavery was not even an institution of *ius gentium*, but admissible merely as part of positive penal law following strict legal confines, whereas he recognized liberty positively as a part of natural law.[463] Both Suarez and, earlier, Aquinas furthermore stated that unjust laws, defined as contrary to a precept of natural law, were not to be obeyed under any circumstances.[464] Since transatlantic slavery did not conform to positive national laws (as we shall see in this section) at its inception and in striking contrast to natural law, it follows that the laws that European enslaver nations issued from the 17th century onwards

---

458   Ibid., 114.
459   Ibid., 82.
460   Ibid., 95.
461   Grewe (1984), 152 et seq.
462   Watson (1989), 47.
463   Lumb, D. (1968). "Legality and Legitimacy: The Limits of the Duty of Obedience to the State", in: Charles Alexandrowicz (ed.): Studies in the history of the laws of nations, The Hague: Grotian Press Society, 52-82, 59.
464   Ibid., 63.

were not to be obeyed according to these founding fathers of the classical law of nations. The concept of international law by Grotius rested on an integrative vision composed of natural law derived by human reason as well as of norms issued by the will of the nations. Montesquieu explained that all nations knew the existence of a body of special rules to regulate their relations, the "law of the nations".134 Even when transatlantic slavery was already fully instituted, the founding fathers of European international law doctrine, such as Vitoria, Suarez, Grotius and Vattel, continued to accord an important status to the existence of a superior or natural law imperative for all men and nations. Many of the principles that they drew from natural law were also found in Roman law, which was considered by European scholars as the common legal heritage of the "civilized" world of the epoch.[465] We have already seen that Rome had maintained contacts and agreements with Africans and that, to the knowledge of Europe, Africa was "civilized". Research has furthermore established that "the natural law argument, that law derives from God or a Supreme Being has long been a substantial element in African legal philosophy (...)"[466].

Although scholars at that time did not necessarily think that "slavery" as such was contrary to natural law, it is important to investigate how they defined slavery. The influential Ulrich Huber (1636-94) of Friesland stated in his *Praelectiones Juris Civilis on the Institutes* I.3: "As we just said, slavery is not necessarily at odds with reason. For the Christians themselves only late disapproved of slavery, nor is it disapproved of in the Old or New Testament. (...) But from (...) 1212 A.D. or not much later, Christians stopped enslaving one another. (...) The result was a flood of free persons whom wantonness and need drove to wickedness or beggary. The ministrations of the enlarged family were reduced. (...) Slaughter in war became more frequent when slavery was removed, which the Romans put to the test in civil wars in which the captives were not made slaves."[467] Huber's view of slavery as a sometimes necessary consequence of legitimate warfare was by no means isolated. However, he expressed in another treatise his disapproval of slavery as it was practiced in America, because it violated those legal requirements.[468]

A veritable treasure with regard to assessing the international legal status of transatlantic slavery at its time from a European perspective is the treatise *A Just Defense of the Natural Freedom of Slaves. All Slaves Should be Free*, by Epifanio de Moirans, originally written in 1682.

De Moirans, like the more prominent scholars mentioned above, highlights the

---

465   de Frouville, Olivier (2004). L'intangibilité des droits de l'homme en droit international. Régime conventionnel des droits de l'homme et droit des traités, Paris: Editions Pédone, 13. See also: Carreau (2007), 35.

466   Nmehielle (2001), 11.

467   Watson (1989), 95.

468   See Huber, Ulrich (ed. 1722). Eumonia Romana on D.1.5.5.1, Amsterdam: unknown, 49; cited in: Watson (1989), 95.

importance of the doctrine of "just war" for the assessment of the legal status of slavery.

"Slavery pertains to the law of nations, because this law dictates that captives from hand-to-hand combat in just wars, who would be subject to execution, should be kept alive and become slaves instead. Thus it was for themselves that humans made this law, which has been enacted and adequately promulgated by the agreement of all nations, because this law is reasonable, because someone who might in all justice be executed is kept alive and becomes a slave, inasmuch as slavery flows from death, just as freedom flows from life, as we indicated above. Thus where executions are just, there also will enslavements be just; likewise, where executions aren't licit, neither are enslavements licit. But the slavery that pertains to the law of nations is what flows from the law of war, as mentioned before, when the victors do not annihilate the vanquished but keep them as slaves. On this, all of the professors, jurists, and theologians are in consensus and agreement. (...) If the innocent captured in a just war belong to a community that is to blame for the war waged against it, they may be killed in that war; in like manner, captives may be kept alive as slaves. When, therefore, the war is unjust or no war is being waged, it is never licit to make slaves by taking captives, according to the law of nations. I say, therefore, that the Blacks' enslavement runs counter to the law of nations. The proof: because the law of nations says that enslavement occurs when losers in just wars are kept alive instead of being executed by victors, who could justly kill them; but the Blacks are not captives from just wars where they might justly be killed by the victors; thus their enslavement runs counter to the law of nations."[469]

He further substantiated with regard to the reality of transatlantic slavery and international law that "all the conditions for just wars are missing in wars among the Blacks; therefore, they aren't just wars, and the Blacks aren't taken captive in just wars. Instead, all these wars are conflicts, robberies, plunder, wrongs, iniquities, and injustices. Consequently, the Blacks are slaves contrary to the law of nations."[470] At numerous instances De Moirans argued that "slavery from the law of nations arises out of just wars in which the victors who can kill the vanquished keep them as slaves; but among the Blacks, no war is just; and so slavery is illicit according to the law of nations."[471]

De Moirans provided a list of the conditions of "just war" according to the law of nations at that time, and commented on them. The first condition was that a declaration of war after peaceful means to resolve a conflict had proven futile. This condition was clearly missing in most instances of transatlantic enslavement. "The second condition is a just cause; and clearly this isn't present (...). (...) The

---

469 De Moirans, Epifanio (1682). A Just Defense of the Natural Freedom of Slaves. All Slaves Should be Free, Lewiston: Edwin Mellen Press (ed. 2006 by Edward Sunshine), 149 et seq.
470 Ibid., 157.
471 Ibid., 165.

third condition is right intention, and in this case the intention is greed."[472] For all these reasons, he assessed that "by the law of nations, as well as by divine natural and positive law, because those who are not slaves may not be bought and sold into slavery, nor may they be owned. Instead, their freedom must be restored to them and the price of their labor paid in full, because all of this follows necessarily. (…) It is the duty of slave-masters, in setting slaves free, to make restitution to them for their labours and pay them full compensation."[473] Following his detailed exegesis of the law of that time, DeMoirans came to "the clear conclusion that Blacks aren't slaves under any title – neither just war nor delinquency nor sale by fathers trapped in extreme necessity. So they are slaves unjustly, contrary to the law of nations, divine positive law, and natural law, in common and in general."[474]

De Moirans also reasoned that European enslavers not only had doubts but indeed knew that most enslaved Africans were seized unjustly, and that "it follows from this argument that the purchase of slaves is clearly illicit and buyers are obligated to make restitution to them. Therefore, this trade is in such disrepute nowadays that everyone condemns it; because the experts hold it to be illicit; because people who come from those areas confirm that the Blacks are abducted, most seized by force, trickery, and deceit and many purchased from the Blacks who abducted them; and because nobody at all is purchased with an investigation or examination or justification of a title of slavery (…)."[475]

It is indeed highly significant that it was in 1683 that De Moirans penned this assessment of the legal situation and concluded that the buying, selling and owning of African slaves was illegal, unless specifically justified by a title of "just slavery". He wrote this at a time when transatlantic slavery had previously and constantly accelerated over a period of 200 years, yet before most enslaver nations passed their laws aiming at sanctioning their crime against humanity. And the evidence that De Moirans put on the table to substantiate the claim of the fundamental illegality of transatlantic slavery is indeed very detailed:

"In Angola, Portuguese who invade African lands abduct all the inhabitants possible by force, make them slaves, and sell them. Father José Maria, a Capuchin apostolic missionary in Lisbon, told me what he had seen of this and how Capuchins resisted such great wrong doing contrary to all natural law and forced the Portuguese governor to grant them freedom and make restitution to those captured by force of arms and abduction."[476]

Elsewhere in his book, he laid down that "titles of just slavery aren't ordinarily verified or justified, either in America or in Africa. Therefore, consider this

---

472   Ibid., 169.
473   Ibid., 173.
474   Ibid., 183.
475   Ibid., 207.
476   Ibid., 55.

conclusion to have been established: No one may buy or sell any of the African slaves that are commonly called Blacks"[477]. De Moirans referred several times to the "Rule of Law" contained in the "Sixth Book" of the Decretals, promulgated by Pope Gregory IX in 1230 and constituting an important source of Canonic law:

"Those who own slaves contrary to the order of nature and bad-faith owners who can never claim titles of ownership must make restitution (...). Here we are dealing with the natural law, so no excuse due to ignorance is admissible. Thus all who don't make sure of the titles of just slavery of Blacks may neither sell them in America nor, consequently, buy and own them in America without justification and verification of true slavery, especially because hearsay says just the opposite and this business and trade are notorious and condemned in all kingdoms and denounced by theologians. Hence it is that, because of the veil rumors, abductions, frauds, and crimes that are committed, everybody must substantiate and verify with certitude the just slavery of the slave to be purchased or possessed."[478]

He proceeded to legally substantiate how children and grandchildren of illegally enslaved Africans were also unjustly and illegally held in bondage.

De Moirans continuously quoted other acknowledged law experts and scholars who had also expressed themselves attesting the illegality of transatlantic slavery.

"Those who own them unjustly must emancipate them and give them back their freedom and everything that follows from this. Such is the verdict of the theologians. Hence, Cruz has this in the *Directorium conscientiae*: 'Just as slaves fraudulently seized – like almost all Ethiopians and their descendants living among us – are masters of their freedom and enslaved unjustly, so also are they masters over what they acquire.' Therefore, owners must restore both freedom and everything following therefrom over which Blacks have dominion. (...) It is the duty of slave-masters, in setting slaves free, to make restitution to them for their labours and pay full compensation.[479] (...) This doesn't mean just damages now; because slaves are their ancestors' heirs and successors, masters must restore to them what their dead ancestors' freedom, labours, and profits are worth and compensate for all damages, in the judgement of prudent persons. Because by law all of this belongs to the Blacks who are their descendants, such as their back wages and profits and damages that followed therefrom for their children themselves, masters must make restitution for all of this when setting slaves free (...)."[480]

Another professor that De Moirans cited was Avendaño who had argued in a work called *Thesaurus indicus* (title 9, chapter 12, §8) that,

"the trade of theirs is unjust and carries the obligation of restoring freedom,

---

477   Ibid., 103.
478   Ibid., 103 et seq.
479   Ibid., 109.
480   Ibid., 395.

because the titles of slavery, generally speaking, are unjust (...). If the merchants in the trade were to examine the titles in a most careful way and discover that they were just, the trade would be licit. Nevertheless, it is a known fact that this is morally impossible and that the care they are commonly said to exercise is altogether superficial. (...) Traders who make purchases in great numbers from other traders that bring those poor souls out of Ethiopia commit a mortal sin and are under obligation to make restitution, unless a just title of captivity is established with due diligence."[481]

From his assessment of the law of nations and the legal debates at that time concerning the legal status of transatlantic slavery, De Moirans concluded that

"restitution must be made not only for the slaves' freedom but also for their labor (...). For it is manifestly necessary that there be restitution of freedom and everything that follows on freedom, as well as everything that made slave-masters richer, because slaves are enslaved unjustly, their purchase and sale are unjust, ownership of them is wicked, and their owners are in bad-faith, contrary to natural and divine positive law and the law of nations. On this all theologians agree that owners in bad faith are under obligation to restore everything; (...) because residents of the Indies and Europe have become wealthier through injustice to Blacks, contrary to the natural right of slaves, they evidently must restore all that has made them more affluent."[482]

He contended that enslavers had a duty to "make restitution for harm as well as the value of their labours", and based this assessment on legal expertise by Sylvester Prierias ("Restitution"; *Cajetan*, chapter 1), Medina (*Codex de rebus restituendis*), de Soto (book 4, *De iustitia et iure*, question 7, article 2), and Molina (*De iustitia et iure*).[483] "If those who are obliged to make restitution because of property unjustly taken have acquired it in bad faith, they are obliged to make restitution not only for that property, but also for all the loss that the true owner has suffered in the meantime from the lack of it. (...) Thus for all this and the other harm they have suffered, as well as for everything that has made masters richer, there must be restitution."[484] Linking the observation that the illegality of transatlantic slavery was well acknowledged by the scholars of that time with contemporary legal standards on violations of law and restitution, he contended that "there isn't anyone who hasn't had doubts (...) because of the rumors spread everywhere and the trade's notoriety. Thus, everybody, when setting slaves free, is bound to make restitution for slaves' labours, pay compensation for all the damages, and make restitution for the profits".[485]

It is very significant and instructive for the purpose of assessing the legal pos-

---

481   Ibid., 233.
482   Ibid., 363.
483   Ibid., 373.
484   Ibid., 387.
485   Ibid., 395.

sibilities for transatlantic slavery reparations today that we dispose of this document dating from the 17th century which explicitly and at length invoked the duty of European slavers to make reparations for the heinous crime of transatlantic slavery. The fact that De Moirans referred to and quoted numerous other legal experts shows that his was indeed not a marginal position.

De Moirans' assessment also takes account of the specifics that made transatlantic slavery genocide, although he does not use this term that had then not yet been explicitly conceptualized. He set out that all African and Black people were first of all defined as slaves by European slavers, and that their full human status as granted by natural law was generally denied them. "Thus Blacks who are discovered without masters or letters of freedom are considered to be the personal slaves of those who find them. In certain places, they belong to the king, so the governor sells them; in other places, they belong to the Holy Crusade."[486] De Moirans also recalled that any "white" person who killed any Black person was not liable for punishment, and denounced this whole situation as contrary to the order of nature, divine law, and the law of nations.[487]

An additional crucial point recalled by De Moirans that must be considered in the assessment of the legal status of transatlantic slavery is that the Rules of Law in the Sixth Book of the Decretals postulated that "what doesn't hold good in law in the beginning doesn't get established with the passage of time"[488]. This further confirms that legal questions of responsibility and reparations for transatlantic slavery must be appraised by the law in force at the time when it was forced on Africans, and not by the colonial laws that were themselves a product of the crime they are to judge.

The Decretals built to a large degree on Roman law, and Roman law was indeed the formal legal basis for European legislation on slavery at the onset of transatlantic slavery in general. Many jurists and judges of European enslaver nations relied on analogies from Roman law when no explicit national laws could be found. However, even in Rome rules concerning slavery were incomparably more reasonable than the transatlantic practice. Roman slaves could be highly skilled and earn a lot of money for their masters. There was no racial bias in slavery, and race was not an obstacle to manumission and freedom.

Slaves in Rome could own no property, but neither could sons or daughters as long as their father (or grandfather) was alive. Like sons, they were also given a fund called the *peculium*, which technically belonged to their owner but which they could use as their own within the limits laid down by the master. And it was common for masters to allow slaves to buy their freedom with the peculium.[489]

---

486   Ibid., 53
487   Ibid., 53
488   de Moirans (1682), 389.
489   Watson (1989), 24.

Contrary to transatlantic slavery, manumission was an integral feature of slavery in the Roman setting. Masters simply declared slaves free in their wills.[490] Whereas in Rome manumission became ever less formal and the master's rights to punish more restricted with the progress of time, the reverse happened in transatlantic slavery. Racism and genocide were provided for in the colonial slave laws, rendering manumission ever more difficult, allowing masters to punish harsher, and outlawing it to give financial support to free Blacks. Free Blacks were treated as being closer to slaves than freemen, as we shall see in the next section.[491]

In Rome, masters' powers to punish slaves were restricted, and outsiders, except public officials, were not allowed to interfere with a slave with impunity. It was recognized as murder to kill another's slave deliberately. From the time of Justinian's *Institutes*, masters who killed slaves without cause were also to be punished for murder.

Slaves were not granted legal personality, yet this does not necessarily imply a denial of the slave's humanity. Slaves were juridically defined as *personae* (though *personae servilis*), thus recognized as fully human.[492] To say that a slave had no legal personality was basically to deny him standing before a civil law court. Yet the slave's humanity was recognized by restraints on cruel masters.[493] Slaves still had certain rights in court. If they claimed to be free, and someone else said that they were slaves, they could appear in court on their own behalf through an indirect mechanism.[494] If a slave was ill-treated, he could flee to a shrine or an emperor's statue. A judicial inquiry would follow, and if the master was found guilty of the accusation of mistreatment, the slave would be sold to a more correct master.

If a Roman slave ran away, his capture was the master's business only. On recapture, it was the master who decided, within the limits of the law, whether and how severely the slave was to be punished. In transatlantic slavery, an enslaved African was subordinate to every "white" person. He could be stopped and questioned by any "white", and patrols were organized to recapture freedom-takers ("runaways"). The colonial enslaver states also intervened in the education of slaves by prohibiting teaching them to read or write, whereas the education of slaves was encouraged in Rome.[495]

Although slaves could not officially marry in Rome, Emperor Constantine issued a law (C.3.38.11.) in 334 CE whereby divisions of property should be made in such a way that close relations among slaves should remain with one single successor. "For who will tolerate that children be separated from parents, sisters from

---

490   Ibid., 29.
491   Ibid., 128.
492   Niort, Jean-Francois (2010). 'Homo Servilis. Un être humain sans personnalité juridique: Réflexions sur le statut de l'esclave dans le Code Noir'', in: Tanguy Le Marc'hadour and Manuel Carius (ed.): Eslavage et Droit. Du Code noir à nos jours, Arras: Artois Presses Université, 15-41, 28.
493   Watson (1989), 32.
494   Ibid., 35 et seq.
495   Watson (1989) 65 et seq.

brothers, wives from husbands?" If slaves who constituted a family were taken off to different masters, they were compelled to return them together again.[496]

Roman slaves were employed in a vast array of occupations. There were 80 different descriptions of functions for slaves, ranging from artisan, janitor, baker, agricultural laborer, herdsman, steward, hairdresser, musician, dancer, actor, teacher, midwife, librarian, stenographer, cleaner, and even medical doctor. "A fortunate slave might even inherit the master's business."[497] This clearly demonstrates that, even in Rome slaves did not categorically perform arduous and harsh tasks, but worked for and in distinct professions, and were covered by certain protective laws. Labour in mines was a consequence of punishment for rebellious slaves and did not reflect the normal condition of Roman slaves.[498]

Additionally, the Romans, often invoked by reparation opponents to claim that "slavery" would always have been a "normal" part of the human experience in all societies, never went to war with the intent of procuring slaves, but always for political motives.[499] The Roman doctrine of just war was resuscitated by St. Augustine (354-430). He sustained that war may be justly waged for the avenging of injury suffered. This was considered to be the case when one must vanquish a community or state which is unwilling to punish a bad action of its citizens, or which refuses to restore what it has unjustly taken. War was never legitimate to start out of a craving for power or revenge.[500] Thomas Aquina's *Summa Theologica* carried on this conception and stipulated that a war could only be considered "just" if the prince (sovereign) authorized the war; if there was a justa causa and if the belligerent possessed *recta intention*. During those centuries, moral theology, jurisprudence and international law were tightly knitted together. Moral theologists laid the foundation of European international law doctrine.[501] Legal doctrine recognized natural law as of divine origin, preceding and co-existing with "human" law. These two laws were not considered as being on the same level; natural law was held superior to human law. Thus, in the dominant view of the Middle Ages, statutes, judgements, decrees, and generally all legal transactions were null and void if they were violative of natural law.[502] De Vitoria and Suarez, for example, were versed in law and theology, as theology and legal science were then closely associated. Secular Spanish jurists were of lesser stature, which is why we do not even retain many prominent names among them today. But even they worked along the line of scholasticism and in conformity with the theologists.[503]

---

496   Ibid., 33.
497   Ibid., 76 et seq.
498   Flaig, Egon (2009). Weltgeschichte der Sklaverei, C.H. Beck, München, 64.
499   Ibid., 57.
500   Nussbaum (1954), 35.
501   Ibid., 36 et seq.
502   Ibid., 39.
503   Ibid., 73.

In European legal theory at the time period before and at the beginning of transatlantic slavery, captivity in "just war" was generally recognized as the most important legitimate means of enslavement. Molina wrote in 1574 that, since the Portuguese were seldom enquiring of the origin of the enslaved Africans they took, in the majority of cases, their "slave" traffic was clearly illicit and the captivity of the Africans not to be justified.[504]

Fernando Perez, rector of Evora University from 1576 to 1577 and teaching at Coimbra from 1577 to 1595, authored two commentaries containing the doctrine that was to prevail for two centuries at Evora University.[505] While principally sanctioning the legitimacy of servitude, *an unus homo possit esse dominus alterius*, the origins of which he saw covered by the law of nations and justified in the Holy Scriptures, he enumerated the legal titles of servitude, the first of which was the right of origin (*per nativitatem*) following the ancient Roman legal rule of *partus sequitur ventrem*. The second title stemmed from civil penal law, thus covering legal conviction for an offence. Thirdly, a title could be recognized if a captive was made slave in a "just war" (*Qui in bello justo capiuntur et juste retinentur juste sunt servi*). In all other cases, slavery was illegal. Thus, Perez concluded that transatlantic slavery was illicit. In this assessment he furthermore based himself on the conclusions of Domingo Soto who in his *De iustitia et de jure* had also considered the whole transatlantic "slave" "trade" illegitimate. Perez also acknowledged the humanity of the slaves as inherent in every human being, forbidding the exercise of the power of things over human beings.

Another legal scholar from the prestigious Evora University was Fernando Rebelo who succeeded Molina, and who scrutinized the theme of slavery in his *Opus de obligationibus justitiae, religionis et caritatis*.[506] Therein, he parted from the principle that all humans were naturally free. Yet he recognized that the guilt of a person for a crime may necessitate servitude as a means of punishment in accordance with the law of nations (*"Secundum intentionem secundam fuit ut supposita culpa, servitu in poenam, iure gentium, induceretur"*). He then analyzed the legitimacy of transatlantic slavery by means of the manner in which Africans generally became enslaved in the transatlantic system. Rebelo, too, concluded that this slavery was illicit and condemnable. He also recognized that the capture of people with the sole proclaimed reason of converting them to Christianity did not meet the requirements of a "just war". Furthermore he contended that the deportation of recently baptized African captives to the Americas was an insult to Christianity.

Joao Baptista Fragoso, also teaching at Evora, stuck with the argumentation of his predecessors, and vigorously condemned the trade in Africans so unjustly captured.

Thus, the position of the vast majority of law doctors was uniform in this re-

---

504   Capela (2002), 340 et seq.
505   Ibid., 340.
506   Ibid., 340 et seq.

gard and unambiguous in their condemnation of transatlantic slavery as illicit. The legal justifications for servitude and slavery that they enumerated converged with those traditionally upheld in Africa.[507]

There were also certain Jesuits who opposed transatlantic slavery in a very concrete manner, whether in Africa or in Brazil, such as Miguel Garcia and Goncalo Leite, who did not recognize any legal title justifying the captivity of Africans. The Austrian Jesuit Mauritz Thomann was, as all Jesuits, expulsed from Mozambique in 1756, and left a testimonial in which he exposed the traditionally legitimate circumstances of enslavement in that region.[508] As in Europe at the same time, slaves had to be captured in a "just war". People could also conclude a contract and voluntarily submit their service to a master in exchange for material benefits. Thomann also noted that a slave who displayed aptitude was instructed to learn a profession. Furthermore, he assessed that in African society, servile labor tasks were generally not painful or exceedingly hard. He even stated that European serfs and domestic servants worked ten times harder and were treated much harsher by their masters than these "slaves", and mentioned that African masters had to be considerate towards their slaves, who otherwise had a customary right to flee.[509]

Already on October 7, 1492, Pope Pius II had addressed a letter to the bishop of Portuguese-occupied Guinea in which he had designated the enslavement of Africans who were willing to take on Christianity as *magnum scelus*, a big crime. Though this requirement of a willingness to convert to Christianity is in itself problematic, the historical records testify that Africans had warmed up to Christianity, because in its original teachings it was compatible with what they had practiced spiritually from ancient times. In 1537, Pope Paul III interdicted the enslavement of the indigenous people of the Americas as well as of all peoples that were still to be "discovered" thereafter.[510]

After this review of the doctrinal debate and of the overall legal historical precursors to colonial slavery regulations in Europe, we will now review the hard facts of national reglementation in European enslaver states. Chattel slavery, such as practised in the transatlantic system, was not only illegal in the legal orders of African societies, but also by the national laws of the participating European nations.

In contrast to France and England whose legal systems did not tolerate slavery at all, both Spain and Portugal had legal codes, based in Roman law, which regulated slavery and favored individual manumission. Iberians had maintained

---

507   Ibid.
508   Ibid.
509   Ibid.
510   Flaig (2009), 164.

a small minority of slaves since Islamic and medieval times, and consequently also had a body of slave law regulating the status of slaves.[511] The French and the English had no positive law regarding slavery, but rather recognized legal principles that freed enslaved persons upon setting foot on their national soils. Although Portugal was the first European nation to start transatlantic slavery, it seems appropriate to begin with Spain, because Portugal had for long relevant periods of time been part of that nation and shared its legal heritage even at times of independence.

i. Spain

Slavery had a long tradition in Iberian societies. It had never totally disappeared in the Spanish kingdoms during the Middle Ages. However, there were relatively few slaves, and they were employed almost exclusively as servants.[512] Muslim traders also brought slaves from sub-saharan Africa to Spain from the 14th century onwards. By that century, slavery regulation was no longer passed by towns but left to royal legislation. After the Reconquista, which ended in 1492, slavery seems to have become mostly restricted to Moorish and African captives.[513] Now, Roman law, especially the elaborate slave laws contained in the Code of Justinian, had been recovered and assimilated into the legal systems of some medieval European kingdoms. In Iberia, slavery had become legally regulated in the body of laws known as the *Siete Partidas*, with heavy influences derived from Roman law.[514] The *Siete Partidas* were promulgated by King Alfonso X around 1265, thus at a time when Spain and Portugal were unified into one state, and were confirmed again as law in the *Leyes de Toro* of 1505.

Consistent with Roman jurisprudence, Spanish and Portuguese law considered slavery to be contrary to nature and held liberty as the natural state of man.[515] It declared that by nature all creatures were free, especially humans, who have understanding above all others.[516] Law One of the *Siete Partidas* read that "(l)iberty is the power that every man has by nature to do what he wants, except in those areas where the power of right of law restrains him"[517].

The *Siete Partidas* included regulations that protected slaves from abuse by their masters, permitted marriages, allowed the slaves ownership of property within certain limits, and provided for manumission under a variety of circumstances. Fundamentally, and in line with practically all pre-transatlantic slavery legal traditions, the *Siete Partidas* departed from the premise that freedom was in

---

511   Peabody/ Grinberg (2007), 24 et seq.
512   Ibid., 15.
513   Ki-Zerbo (1978), 211.
514   Bush (1996), 81.
515   Peabody/Grinberg (2007), 16.
516   Watson (1989), 46.
517   Peabody/Grinberg (2007), 102.

principle the right of every human being.[518] Manumission only depended on the will of the owner, in contrast to transatlantic slavery.[519]

The *Siete Partidas* also exhaustively enumerated the legitimate grounds for enslavement. They were, again, as in Africa and elsewhere, capture in war; inheritance of slave status; and voluntary self-sale. This body of laws also allowed a slave to marry against the master's will. Once married, couples were not to be separated. If they belonged to different masters, an effort had to be made to let them work and live in the same place. A slave who was badly treated could complain to a judge, and a master who killed a slave would be tried for murder.[520] An owner could punish a slave only in due measure and had no right to hit him with a stone or stick or anything else that was hard. If he contravened this law, but did not intend to kill his slave and the slave died, the owner was sentenced to banishment for five years. If the master punished the slave with the intention to kill, he was to be punished for murder.[521] A slave had direct access to courts to make his complaint and demand that he be sold to a different, correct master.[522]

Historic sources document that the *Siete Partidas* were applied to African slaves on the Iberian Peninsula up to the 16th century. African slaves in Iberia had their own principal judge from among them who represented them and was known as the "Negro count". With the passage of time, they mingled with free Iberians and lost their ethnic identity.[523] Some free Africans achieved distinction in Spanish society. Cristóbal Meneses, for example, became a prominent Dominican priest. Juàn de Pareja and Sebastian Gómez were painters. Leonardo Ortez became a renowned lawyer. Juàn Latino, after receiving two degrees from the University of Granada in 1546 and 1556, held a teaching position there.[524]

Thus, we see that traditional Iberian slavery had been qualitatively and quantitatively different from transatlantic slavery, where enslaved Africans had none of these rights and were forced into conditions that threatened their very existence and were characterized by oppression, dehumanization and brutality.

That the provisions of the *Siete Partidas* were not enforced in the Spanish and Portuguese colonies does not change the fact that they were the formally valid legal basis and what is relevant in the assessment of the international legal status of transatlantic slavery.

---

518   Palmer (1998), 11.
519   Watson (1989), 44 et seq.
520   Hugh, Thomas (1999). The Slave Trade. The Story of the Atlantic Slave Trade: 1440-1870, New York: Simon & Schuster, 40.
521   Watson (1989), 44 et seq.
522   Ibid., 46.
523   Davidson (1961), 40 et seq.
524   Harris, J.E. (1992). "The African diaspora in the Old and the New Worlds", in: B.A. Ogot (ed.): General History of Africa V. Africa from the Sixteenth to the Eighteenth Century, Paris: UNESCO, 113-136, 114.

When Spain made colonies in the Americas, these were incorporated into the kingdom of Castile, and it was unanimously held by jurists such as Bartolus, Baldus, de Afflictis or Azevedo that these territories became in law part of Castile and were governed by the same laws. This meant a complete transplant of the law of Castile to these territories, including the laws on slavery, which were derived in large measure from Roman law, and which, as we have just seen, provided slaves with a series of basic rights that were not respected in transatlantic slavery.[525]

ii. Portugal

From 1550, about one-tenth of Lisbon's population consisted of slaves.[526] For most of the time of Portugal's involvement in transatlantic slavery, its main applicable laws were the *Ordenaçoes Filipinas*, alongside the Spanish legal traditions just outlined. Those were ordinances promulgated by Philip II for Portugal under Spanish domination in 1603 and later confirmed by a law of Portuguese King João IV in 1643. They remained in force for over three centuries, even after Brazil became independent in 1882, until 1917.[527]

The *Ordenaçoes Filipinas* did not contain vast regulations on slavery, but 5.36.1 allowed owners only moderate physical punishment of slaves. In this regard, slaves were expressly placed on a level with servants, pupils, wives, or children. Similar rules were already contained in the *Siete Partidas* (7.8.9.).

Before and apart from the *Ordenaçoes Filipinas*, although leaving many gaps, there was no other law or custom used by the courts with regard to slavery. Therefore, Roman law, especially the *Corpus Juris Civilis* of Justinian, was directly relevant and was indeed the main legal source concerning slavery. If that source also did not provide a solution to a problem, recourse would be had to the *Accursian's gloss* (commentaries) of the Justinian code. If even that failed, the opinion of Bartolus would be looked after, unless the general opinion of law doctors was against him. Philip II and Phillip III, in laws of 1597 and 1612, expressly approved the writings of Bartolus, the renowned 14th century Italian law professor and one of the most prominent continental jurists of medieval Roman law. Thus, at beginning of transatlantic slavery and when the colonies were incorporated into Portugal, the existent and relevant legal corpus on slavery relied directly on Roman law.[528]

By these law standards, manumission did not require any particular formalities. However, very few (0,5-2%) slaves were actually freed in the Portuguese slave colonies. The *Ordenaçoes Filipinas* and Roman Law permitted only moderate punishment by the owner of the slave. "The owner could only punish a slave, as a father a son, or a master a servant. (...) If a master was vicious, the law authorized

---

525   Watson (1989), 47.
526   Ki-Zerbo (1978), 211.
527   Peabody/Grinberg (2007), 22.
528   Watson (1989) 91 et seq.

a slave to request that the owner sell him."[529]

In 1769, the *Ordenaçoes Filipinas* were modified by the *Lei da Boa Razão* (the Law of Sound Reason). Roman law ceased to be subsidiary law. Instead, recourse was to be taken to the "perpetual and immutable principles of natural law and the universal rules of the *ius gentium*".[530] The *Lei da Boa Razão* did not add to the substantive law on slavery.

However, even if technically the *Lei da Boa Razão* abolished the rule of Roman law, much Roman law had already been incorporated into slave law before 1769, through decisions in the courts of the Portuguese kingdoms and by long-established custom. Furthermore, natural law and the universal rules of the *ius gentium* relied heavily on Roman law. Also, little new legislation on slavery was forthcoming. The law on slavery therefore depended much on the senses attributed to natural law and the law of nations. Scholars have assessed that the *Lei da Boa Razão* departed from the premise that natural law were comprised of the rules that can be uncovered by the use of reason to enable humans to live peacefully.[531]

There are several recorded instances when Portuguese authorities on those legal bases esteemed the enslavement of certain groups of Africans illegal and ordered their return. In 1805, representatives of the Portuguese state led a series of razzias against communities between the Kwanza and Kwango rivers. A certain Portuguese by the name of Galiano had been sent on a mission to negotiate a treaty with the ruler of Kasanje, Malange a Ngonga, who was one of the biggest enslavers in the region. Upon returning, Galiano's troop attacked villages in this territory and enslaved people. After receiving complaints from several chiefs in this region, the Portuguese governor declared that the enslavements had been illegal.[532]

A similar occurrence had taken place earlier, in 1621, when the Portuguese governor Joao Correira de Sousa raided communities in Kasanze, in the periphery of Luanda and deported the captives to Brazil. The Portuguese crown decided that this had been illegal and ordered the return of the deported. Many, however, in the meanwhile had not survived the horrors of the Middle Passage.[533] Even though these decisions by the Portuguese government were in conformity with and grounded in their own and in international law, it is important to note that they related to an illegal practice that was commonplace in the transatlantic system and usually condoned or directed by that same and other European govern-

---

529   Ibid., 159.
530   Ibid., 93 et seq.
531   Ibid.
532   Curto, José C. (2002). "Un butin illegitime: razzias d'esclaves et relations luso-africaines dans la region des fleuves Kwanza et Kwango en 1805'', in: Isabel Castro Henriques and Louis Sala-Molins (ed.): Déraison, esclavage et droit. Les fondements ideologiques et juridiques de la traite negriere et de l'esclavage, Paris: EDITIONS Unesco, 314- 327, 320 et seq.
533   Ibid., 323.

ments. The main reasons why in these few instances Portugal opted to conform to the law seem to have been opportunism and pragmatism. In these two concrete cases, the actions of Portuguese state representatives had put Portugal in confrontation with important local collaborator kings and chiefs with whom it had a high interest to maintain good relations in order to secure large numbers of enslaved Africans in the long run.

Apparently the Portuguese crown had issued a directive in 1622 that wars against the populations in their colony Angola could only be led for defensive purposes, thus prohibiting engagement in violence with the aim to make slaves. This was the law, conforming to the standard of the law of nations at that time. However, the Portuguese subsequently often constructed stories to contend that their rights had been violated by African rulers (the refusal to trade; trading with European or African enemy states; the refusal to allow the construction of religious missions; or the welcoming of ambassadors of enemy nations to the Portuguese, ...) in order to continue to enslave people from those regions.[534]

So to sum up, slavery such as practised in the transatlantic system was illegal by Portuguese law standards.

iii. England

As already mentioned, there was no slave law in England prior to transatlantic slavery. There was also no reception of Roman law in that country.

Inikori retraced that slavery had at some point been brought to England by the Romans and by continental Europeans from Denmark, Germany and Holland. These Anglo-Saxons raided England for slaves and eventually took over the country in the 5th century. Many Celts, the indigenous people, were enslaved. Because the Anglo-Saxon kingdoms continued to fight among themselves and to take captives, slaves made up a large proportion of the population of Anglo-Saxon England.[535] This situation persisted until the very end of the 11th century when conquest by the Normans stopped the warring. The Westminster Council proclaimed in 1102 "that no one is henceforth to presume to carry on that shameful trading whereby heretofore men used in England to be sold like brute beasts".[536] Anglo-Saxon slaveholders then began to move their "slaves" into separate landholdings of their own, a situation which allowed them "much freedom to cater to themselves and maintain households of their own, while continuing to render labor services to the lords (...). At the same time however, the lords continued to hold other slaves directly in their estates."[537]

The common denominator for the servile populations in England from the 12th century onwards was that they possessed some land which they cultivated for

---

534   Ibid., 324 et seq.
535   Inikori (1999), 51.
536   Ibid.
537   Ibid., 52.

themselves, while owing labor services to their lords. They also suffered a lack of freedom to move.[538] Thus, by that time, they were really serfs and no longer slaves. Slavery had definitely been outlawed in England at the time when this nation became active in the transatlantic system. This has been well documented by historians and is also indicated, for example, by the report of an English captain called Jobson, dating from 1623[539], in which the author wrote that a "Mandingo trader showed unto me certain young black women (...), slaves, brought for me to buy. I made answer, 'We were a people who did not deal in any such commodities, neither did we buy or sell one another, or any that had our own shapes'"[540].

Yet, England had started to enslave and deport Africans during the reign of Elizabeth I, in 1562 even though it is documented that this queen was well aware of the unlawfulness of that practice. When Captain John Hawkins returned from his first voyage to Africa and Hispaniola, where he had carried enslaved Africans, Elizabeth sent for him, and expressed her concern "lest any of the Africans should be carried off without their free consent", declaring that "it would be detestable, and call down Heaven's vengeance upon the undertakers"[541]. Captain Hawkins promised to comply with the injunctions of Elizabeth in the future, but he failed to do so; and as soon as it became apparent that huge financial profits could be made, the queen also forgot her legal and moral concerns.[542] Hawkins' next voyage to the African coast appears to have been principally calculated to enslave Africans, in order to sell them to the Spanish who already had colonies in the Caribbean.[543] It is recorded that south of Cape Verde the native Africans took flight from Hawkins and his men. Hawkins and his crew then travelled further, and upon taking anchor sent men to burn and spoil towns and captured the inhabitants. They observed that the land was well cultivated, with plenty of grain and fruits, and towns prettily laid out. On December 25, 1564, they made an alliance to plot with some Portuguese to attack a town called Bymba, where they hoped to steal gold and take the over 140 inhabitants as slaves. However, they only managed to capture about 10 people. They then travelled down the coast and captured more Africans and took sail to the Caribbean where they sold them to the Spanish.

Queen Elizabeth, convinced by profit and greed, finally sanctioned this internationally illegal practice and granted patents for carrying on the "slave" "trade"

---

538 Ibid., 53.
539 This incident happened at a time when that region of Africa had already undergone more than a century of transatlantic enslavement at the hand of the Portuguese and Spanish, resulting in social changes and the emergence of a class of African collaborators, as analysed above.
540 Davidson (1961), 61.
541 Goodell, Rev. William (1852).Slavery and Anti-Slavery: A History of the Great Struggle In Both Hemispheres; With A View of The Slavery Question In The United States, New York: William Harned Pub, 6.
542 Ibid.
543 Benezet (1767), 30.

from the North part of the river Senegal to a hundred leagues beyond Sierra Leone. These developments then gave rise to the establishment of the Royal African Company who deported millions of Africans in genocidal conditions.[544]

However, no regulation had yet been passed concerning this "slave" "trade". There was no act of the British Parliament which would have explicitly legalized it. Quite to the contrary, the "Act for extending and improving the trade to Africa" (23 George II, chap. 81 (1749-50)) provided in its section 29 that "no commander or master of any ship trading to Africa shall by fraud, force, or violence, or by any other indirect practice whatsoever, take on board, or carry away from the coast of Africa, any negro or native of the said country, or commit, or suffer to be committed, any violence on the natives, to the prejudice of said trade"[545]. Section 28 of the same act authorized the holding of slaves at the station of the Trading Company in Africa, yet gave no authority to transport them to America or elsewhere. "Undoubtedly the secret design was to stimulate the slave trade. But a sense of shame, and a consciousness of wrong-doing, prevented the Parliament from employing the terms which, upon a strict legal construction, could give to that feature of the African trade the shelter of valid law."[546]

Indeed, the English judicature and other governmental branches sustained a somewhat ambiguous approach concerning the legal status of transatlantic slavery. The earliest as well as the majority of decisions and opinions clearly rejected slavery as contrary to English law. It was only, and it is important to fully grasp this, with the passage of time and the increasing dependence of the English economy on the genocidal transatlantic system that decisions were rendered which interpreted transatlantic slavery as compatible with law.

The first recorded case was decided in 1569, involving a certain Cartwright, who had brought a slave from Russia. We are thus dealing here with a decision about the legality of slavery in general. The court ruled unambiguously that chattel slavery was incompatible with English law.[547]

Yet in 1667, motivated by the enormous economic gains expected from transatlantic slavery, a Crown legal position was issued that declared Africans as goods ("negroes ought to be esteemed goods and commodities within the Acts of Trade and Navigation"[548]). However, it must be emphasized that such an act of legislation could not and did not change the fact that Africans were humans, and not goods. It must therefore be considered futile and void, whereas the preceding English legal reglementation that did not recognize chattel slavery remained in force. It is a general precept of law that legislative acts that are factually absurd

---

544   Ibid., 30 et seq.
545   Goodell (1852), 7.
546   Ibid.
547   Mtubani, C. D. Victor (1983). African Slaves and English Law, in: PULA Botswana Journal of African Studies, Vol. 3, No. 2, 71-75, 71.
548   Goodell (1852), 24.

are null and void. Yet, this futile governmental conceptualization of enslaved Africans as goods and chattels was maintained by a court in the common-law case of Butts v. Penny (1677) where it was ruled that since Africans were "usually bought and sold among merchants, as merchandise, and being infidels there might be a property in them to maintain trover"[549].

Most courts, however, continued to uphold the view that slavery was incompatible with English law. Thus, in 1701, Chief Justice Sir John Holt ruled that a slave became free as soon as he arrived in England: "One may be a villain in England but not a slave"[550]. Five years later, the same Chief Justice Holt ruled in Smith v. Gould (1706) that "(b)y the common law no man can have a property in another"[551].

Indeed courts had so consistently ruled in favor of Africans suing for their freedom that in 1729 slave owners who had become increasingly worried by that general position of English courts asked two senior officers of the law, the Attorney-General Philip Yorke and the Solicitor-General Charles Talbot, whether residence in England or baptism gave the slave his freedom. They declared that neither did, and stated "that a Slave by coming from the West-Indies to Great Britain, doth not become free, and that his Master's Property or Right in him is not thereby determined or varied: And that Baptism doth not bestow freedom on him, nor make any Alterations in his Temporal Condition in these Kingdoms".[552] Although this was only an opinion, contradicting precedents and expressed not by a court, but after dinner at Lincoln's Inn Hall and thus not formally disposing of any legal force, it was to have grave implications and was subsequently used by enslavers to defend their interests. This informal opinion was given the authority of a legal ruling 20 years later in another court case (Pearne v. Lisle (1749). It is important to acknowledge, though, that the ruling judge in that case was the same Philip Yorke who had co-authored the opinion in the first place. Now he relied on it under his new official appellation of Lord Chancellor Hardwicke. As such he ruled that African slaves were chattels. He overturned the 1706 ruling by Chief Justice Holt (Smith v. Gould) and held that a slave "is as much property as any other thing".[553]

However, other than some singular Crown jurists who were put into their positions only because of the royal interests in slavery profits, courts continued to uphold law and justice. In Shanley v. Hervey (1762), Lord Chancellor Henly at the Chancery court ruled that "(a)s soon as a man puts foot on English ground, he is free: a Negro may maintain an action against his master for ill-usage [which

---

549 Ibid.
550 Ibid.
551 Ibid.
552 Sammons, Diane E. (2007). "Corporate Reparations for Descendants of Enslaved African-Americans", in: Max du Plessis and Stephen Peté (ed.): Repairing the Past? International Perspectives on Reparations for Gross Human Rights Abuses, Antwerpen/Oxford: Intersentia, 315-358, 336.
553 Ibid.

may translate into a claim for reparations], and may have a *Habeas Corpus*, if restrained of his liberty".[554] Three years later, in Smith v. Brown and Cooper (1765), Chief Justice Holt remained firm in upholding the law and stated "that as soon as a negro comes into England, he becomes free: one may be a villein [serf] in England, but not a slave".[555] In a ruling in Scotland (Knight v. Wedderburn, 1778), the judge declared that "the state of slavery is not recognised by the laws of this Kingdom", and that "the law of Jamaica, being unjust, could not be supported in this country".[556] He therefore decided that the defender had no right to the African's service.[557]

Finally, in the famous Somerset case, Chief Justice William Murray, Earl of Mansfield, ruled in 1792 that "so high an act of dominion must be recognized by the country where it is used. The power of a master over his slave has been extremely different in different countries. The state of slavery is of such a nature, that it is incapable of being introduced on any reasons, moral or political; but only by positive law (...). It is so odious that nothing can be suffered to support it but positive law. Whatever inconveniences, therefore, may follow from a decision, I cannot say this case is allowed or approved by the law of England; and therefore the black man must be discharged".[558] The court recalled explicitly that from 1540 to 1771 (Somerset had escaped his master in 1771), English law had only recognized "slavish servitude", a condition the court judged as altogether different from transatlantic chattel slavery and which limited permissible physical abuse.[559]

By all this we see that in England too, transatlantic slavery was illegal.

A review of laws and legal appreciations concerning slavery in British American colonies before the American war of independence is also very instructive when it comes to assessing the state of British law on the matter. As with all European colonial slave colonies, slavery was first introduced in the English colonies without legal authorization. There were enslaved persons but no law of slavery. Judges dealing with cases concerning slavery, regularly observed that villenage in England was not slavery.[560]

Thus, for example, the first settlement in Georgia was decidedly hostile to slavery. General James Oglethorpem, a member of the British Parliament, reported in the mid-18th century that the governing trustees of that colony strictly prohibited slavery, and "declared [it] to be not only immoral, but contrary to the laws of

---

554   Goodell (1852), 24.
555   Ibid., 24.
556   Mtubani (1983).
557   Ibid.
558   Peabody/Grinberg (2007), 72 et seq.
559   Cleeve, George Van (2006).Somerset's Case Revisited: Somerset's Case and Its Antecedents in Imperial Perspective, in: Law and History Review, Vol.24 (3), 601-645, 637.
560   Watson (1989), 65 et seq.

England".[561]

The first deported Africans arrived in the territory of what would become the USA in 1621 in Virginia, and were held in slavery though there were no slavery laws at that time. Slavery laws were passed in the following decades with the slow but steady growth of transatlantic slavery for profits by any means. It was only in 1670 that life-long enslavement for "Blacks" was enacted, and in 1669 that the murder of an enslaved African by his master was no longer punishable.[562] Before these enactments, the genocidal practice had taken place without any semblance of formal legal coverage. "The practice of slave-holding grew up and was tolerated without law, till at length it acquired power to control legislation and wield it in favor of slavery."[563]

Early court cases from Massachusetts testify that, there too, slavery was at first considered a punishment for criminal conduct. Even so, slaves, who were then sometimes "white", were not generally considered to be perpetually bound.[564] In 1641, Massachusetts passed a law that read: "There shall never be any bond slav-erie, villinage or captivitie amongst us unless it be lawful captives taken on just warres, and such strangers as willingly sell themselves. And these shall have all the liberties and Christian usuages, which the law of God established in Israel concerning such persons doth morally require. This exempts none from servitude, who shall be judged thereto by authority."[565]

In 1646, the General Court in Boston issued an order to return two captured Africans to their homeland at public expense because it estimated that enslaver James Smith had acquired them by illegal means, that is, man-stealing.

"The General Court conceiving themselves (sic!) bound by the first opportu-nity to bear witness against the heinous and crying sin of man-stealing, as also to prescribe such timely redress for what is past and such a law for the future, as may sufficiently deter all others belonging to us to have to do in such vile and odious courses, justly abhorred of all good and just men, do order that the negro interpreter with others unlawfully taken, by the first opportunity at the charge of the country for the present, sent to his native country (Guinea) and a letter with him of the indignation of the Court thereabouts, and justice thereof desiring our honoured Governor would please put this order to executions."[566]

Please consider in that context that a great part of the millions and millions of victims of transatlantic slavery had been enslaved or killed through man-stealing.

Other colonies had passed similar laws. For instance, the Connecticut Code,

561   Goodell (1852), 24.
562   Slavery and the Law in Virginia; downloaded from http://www.history.org/history/teaching/slavelaw.cfm (accessed 20.3.2011).
563   Goodell (1852), 17.
564   Brooks (2004), 23.
565   Dass, Sujan (ed.) (2010). Black Rebellion. Eyewitness Accounts of Major Slave Revolts, Atlanta: Supreme Design, 139 et seq.
566   Ibid., 140.

enacted in 1650, contained the following section: "If any man stealeth man or mankind, he shall be put to death". The New Haven Code (1656) also contained an article (II.Capital Laws. 10) that stated that "(i)f any person steale a man, or mankind, that person shall surely be put to death"[567].

Most, if not all of the colonial enactments sanctioning slavery were passed many years after transatlantic slavery had been introduced. It appears thus "evident that the usages of slavery grew up first, and that the colonial legislation came in, to sanction and shelter them, afterwards, indicating the fact of a previously existing slavery without statute, and consequently ILLEGAL, since no one maintains that it could have originated in natural right, or in the principles of common law"[568].

US courts' decisions throughout the entire centuries long period that transatlantic slavery was conducted, confirmed its fundamental illegality by English, early colonial and international law. A 1836 court decision (Commonwealth v. Aves) cited a 1640 precedent on returning slaves as victims of kidnapping, and stated that "by the constitution and laws of this Commonwealth, before the adoption of the constitution of the United States, in 1789, slavery was abolished, as being contrary to the provisions of the declaration of rights. (...) By a very early colonial ordinance (1641) it was ordered that there should be no bond slavery, villenage, or captivity. (...) The law of this State is analogous to the law of England, in this respect; that (...) slavery is considered as unlawful and inadmissible in both (...) because contrary to natural right and to laws designed for the security of personal liberty".[569]

A Virginia court assessed in 1827 (Commonwealth v. Turner) that "(...) when slavery, a wholly new condition, was introduced, the common law could not operate on it. The rules were to be established, either by the positive enactments of the law-making power, or to be deduced from the Codes of other countries, where that condition of man was tolerated".[570] As we have seen so far, nowhere was it legally tolerated.

Also just before the Civil War, US courts had occasionally recognized that participation in transatlantic slavery and slave trading constituted a fundamental violation of international law norms. In United States v. The Schooner Amistad (1841), the concerned tribunals, up to the Supreme Court, ordered the release of the deported Africans from the Schooner Amistad and recognized the Africans' right to resist "unlawful slavery", because they estimated that the Africans were not convicted criminals, but had been illegally kidnapped.[571] Please bear in mind

---

567   Goodell (1852), 11.
568   Ibid., 24.
569   Ibid.
570   Watson (1989), 11.
571   Van Dyke, Jon M. (2003). "Reparations for the Descendants of American Slaves Under International Law", in: Raymond A. Winbush (ed.): Should America pay? Slavery and the raging debate on

once again that this was equally the case for the vast majority of the millions and millions of Africans deported in the transatlantic system. It is also noteworthy that President John Tyler on December 6, 1842 quoted from the Tenth Article of the Treaty of Ghent, which had been signed by the US and Great Britain to end the war of 1812, a passage stating that "(t)he traffic in slaves is irreconcilable with the principles of humanity and justice".[572]

All of this confirms that transatlantic slavery had clearly been illegal by English law, and that it was also illegal by the foundational laws of English colonies in North America.

iv. France

France, historically another big enslaver nation next to England, Spain, Portugal and the United States specifically condemned slavery. Several royal proclamations, legal dictums and numerous court decisions clearly declared and confirmed this.

The reception of Roman law in France had come about in a different manner than in Spain. France had developed no equivalent to the *Siete Partidas*. Furthermore, it had no unitary law. The *pays de droit écrit* of the Burgundians and the Visigoths relied on Roman law as custom. Justinian's *Corpus Juris Civilis* was considered law except when there were derogations by later custom or legislation. In the *pays de droit coutumier*, gaps in the law were filled by taking recourse to Roman law. There was no other slavery law, except for what could be derived from these two traditions of Roman law reception. Jean Domat's *Les Loix civiles dans leur ordre naturel* (1689), which remained one of the most influential French law books for several centuries, sustained that Roman law contained rules of justice and equity, called "written reason".[573] Thus once again, we see that natural law was considered part of the valid and applicable law at that time.

It has been pertinently established by academic research that France had no slaves and no law of slavery before transatlantic slavery. In fact, France deported and kept Africans as slaves for centuries in the transatlantic system before promulgating regulation on that practice.

As early as 1315 and 1318, the Kings of France, Louis X and his brother Philip V had issued ordinances, declaring that all men were free-born by nature. Since their kingdom was called the kingdom of *Franks*[574], they had determined that reality should measure up to that name. They therefore ordered the emancipation of slaves and serfs in the whole kingdom, "upon just and reasonable conditions".

---

reparations, New York: Amistad, 57-78, 60.

572   Winbush, Ray (2009). Belinda's Petition. A Concise History of Reparations for the Transatlantic Slave Trade, Bloomington: Xlibris, 23 et seq.

573   Peabody (2007), 51.

574   The Franks, a germanic people, orginally derived their name from a type of axe they used, meaning "free man" (http://en.wikipedia.org/wiki/Frank_%28given_name%29).

[575] Thus, although the term "constitution" as such seems to only have emerged in the early 17th century, in essence this Principle of Freedom was part of that kingdom's unwritten constitution, upon which the creation of France was indeed founded. The edicts carrying this constitutional Freedom Principle were also carried into immediate execution within the royal domain. Another royal proclamation of 1517 stated that France, mother of liberty, permitted no slaves. During the siege of Metz in 1552, the general of the Spanish Cavalry, Dom Louis Davilla, requested of the Duke of Guise that a slave who had been taken be returned to him. The Duke responded that according to French law and custom, he could not return the slave who had acquired his freedom by reaching the city of Metz.[576]

Charondas, a renowned jurist at the Parliament of Paris, recorded another similar case that took place in 1538, when "(a)n Italian brought into France a slave who was Greek by origin. The Italian then dies, and his heirs brought an action claiming the Greek (...). The Greek was declared free in accordance with the common law of France".[577]

Jean Bodin, a scholar of highest importance for the historical development of European international law doctrine, mentioned in the previous section about the sovereignty of African states, declared that slavery had become extinct in his country four centuries earlier, and that "a slave became free merely by touching French soil".[578] He stated in *Les six livres de la république* (first published in 1579) that

"(...) in France, although there may be some remembrance of old servitude, yet it is unlawful there to make any slave, or to buy any of others; In so much that the slaves of strangers as soon as they set their foot within France become franke and free; as was by an old decree of the court of Paris determined against an ambassador of Spain, who had brought a slave with him into France".[579]

This precept that slaves became free upon touching French soil was known as the Freedom Principle. Although in existence before, in 1607 a legal dictum was issued that declared that "(a)ll persons are free in this kingdom: as soon as a slave has reached those frontiers, and becomes baptised, he is free".[580] When France started to engage in transatlantic slavery, the law of the French overseas colonies was basically the *Coutume de Paris*, the law of Paris, which contained nothing on slaves. Neither did other French *coutumes* deal with slavery law.[581] The Freedom Principle extended to the entire kingdom as the maxim that "all persons are free

---

575   Benezet (1767), 34.
576   Peabody, Sue (1996). "There Are No Slaves in France". The Political Culture of Race and Slavery in the Ancien Régime, New York/Oxford: Oxford University Press, 30.
577   Watson (1989), 124.
578   Brooks (2004), 186.
579   Watson (1989), 123.
580   Davidson (1961), 62.
581   Peabody/Grinberg (2007). 51.

in this kingdom, and as soon as a slave has arrived at the borders of this place, the slave is free".[582] Several French cities and regions, including Toulouse and Bordeaux, had legal rules providing that slaves who entered their jurisdiction would be free. The Freedom Principle was anchored so deeply that the *Parlament de Paris*, France's most important court, refused to register the colonial slave laws that the government issued in the 17th and 18th centuries. Its judges esteemed those laws to be contrary to French legal traditions and the nation's unwritten constitution. Lower courts continuously refused to acknowledge a master's control over a slave and freed slaves in many cases.

The validity of the Freedom Principle was indeed confirmed in a multitude of court cases, even in jurisdictions that were later to become important ports for the transatlantic slavery system. In Bordeaux, a Normand slaver arrived in 1571 with a group of captive Africans he wanted to sell. The Parliament of Bordeaux not only refused to allow him to sell them, it also set them free, because of its conviction that slavery was illegal and that everyone who touched French soil became free.[583]

The Parliament of Guyenne also decided in a case in 1571, when slave holders had tried to bring their domestic slaves into France, that "France, mother of liberty" did not tolerate slavery in any form.[584]

Lawyer Antoine Loysel endorsed in 1608 in his collection of French customary law, *Institutes coutumières*, that "all persons are free in this kingdom, and as soon as a slave reaches its borders and is baptised, he is free".[585] However, access to liberty through baptism was also systematically refused to Africans.[586]

Despite those legal standards, the French started to deport Africans to their Caribbean colonies of Martinique, Guadeloupe, and Saint Christophe to grow tobacco from the early 17th century. At first people were brought there as indentured servants, not slaves. After a while however, following the example of the Portuguese, Spanish and British, France began to invest in the more labor intensive but potentially more lucrative product sugar, and started to engage in genocidal transatlantic slavery.[587]

Just like Queen Elizabeth in England, Louis XIII (1601-1643) harboured grave concerns and was very uneasy when he was to sanction transatlantic slavery at first. He demanded that Africans were only to be brought into the colonies on

---

582   Ibid., 6 et seq.
583   Pétré-Grenouilleau, Olivier (1998). Nantes au temps de la traite des Noirs, Paris: Hachette Litératures, 132.
584   Flaig (2009), 182 et seq.
585   Ibid. (t.b.a.).
586   Castaldo, André (2006). Codes Noirs de l'esclavage aux abolitions, Paris: Editions Dalloz, 5.
587   Peabody (1996), 11 et seq.

their own consent and that they were to be educated in the Christian religion.[588] This is further evidence not only of the illegal status of transatlantic slavery, but also evidence of the knowledge of European sovereigns that their dealings were fundamentally and grossly illegal.

Because of the increased demand for labor, Louis XIV's minister Colbert granted the *Compagnie des Indes Occidentales* (1664) and its successors, the *Compagnie du Senegal* (1674) and the *Compagnie de Guinée* (1683) exclusive permission to transport slaves from Africa to the French colonies. This was done in spite of the Freedom Principle and the interdiction of slavery in France. In 1685, the French government sought to legally regulate the criminal oppression of Africans for all French colonies in an elaborate royal decree known as the *Code Noir*.[589] However, just like the later slavery edicts of 1716 and 1738, the *Code Noir* was refused registration by the Parliament of Paris, because it violated the Freedom Principle. Thus, it never obtained formal legal validity.

Already prior to transatlantic slavery French courts and public authorities had freed slaves upon arrival in their jurisdiction. In 1402, for example, four slaves escaped to Toulouse and when their owners attempted to reclaim them, the city's syndic ruled that by the privilege of that city, any slave who set foot within its territory was free.[590]

Such cases of slaves arriving in France and being freed were quite isolated and infrequent until the late 17th century, when French involvement in the transatlantic system produced more slaves and brought them to France. This created a dilemma. Slavery was encouraged by the state in the colonies and in Africa, yet in the early decades the king, his ministers, and the parliaments officially upheld the traditional legal position of France not allowing slavery. Yet, so many court rulings, such as another one in 1691, under the regency of Louis XIV., confirmed the standard of the Freedom Principle and set the concerned enslaved Africans free.[591]

There is also ample documentation of contemporary legal appreciation by French government authorities that leave no doubt that slavery was illegal by the law of France. When in 1691, for example, two enslaved Africans managed to cross over to France from Martinique as stowaways, Pontchartrain, secretary of state for the marine, issued to following instructions and outlined Louis XIV's response to a certain worry the authorities and planter made.

"The king has been informed that two negroes from Martinique crossed on the ship l'Oiseau. His Majesty, to punish Monsieur Chevalier de Here, who commanded the ship, for not having paid enough attention to prevent them from embarking, gives order to Monsieur Ceberet to withhold the price of them from

---

588   Goodell (1852), 7.
589   Peabody (1996), 11 et seq.
590   Ibid.
591   Ibid.

his salary, at the cost of 300 livres for each one, and to remit it to the writer of the ship *le Vaillant* to pay, following your orders, the owners of the negroes. He has not judged it apropos to return them to the isles, their liberty being acquired by the laws of the kingdom concerning slaves, as soon as they touch the soil."[592]

We see that the French government's legal appraisal was unambiguous and clear. The enslaved Africans had reached France, and were thus free because France deemed slavery illegal by its most fundamental law standards. Pontchartain, concerned by the demand of colonial slaver holders to bring slaves with them on their journeys to France, therefore wrote to the intendant of Martinique in 1696: "I have not found any ordinance which permits colonists to keep their negro slaves in France when they [the slaves] want to serve themselves of the liberty acquired by all who touch its soil".[593] A later ministerial letter to the intendant confirmed such automatic recognition of freedom upon arrival in France, and also assessed that the government could not force such formerly enslaved Africans to return to the colonies against their will.[594] This, however, is what was actually done and also decreed a little later by the French government.

Lawyer J.B. Denisart stated in 1754 in his collection of legal decisions that the royal slave decrees were in contradiction to the law of the kingdom, according to which every human being was free when staying in countries that belong to France's kings.[595] It is for this reason that, as mentioned, the Parliament of Paris never registered the Code Noir and the edicts of 1716 and 1738. The Parliament of Paris, whose jurisdiction comprised one-third of France, and appellate Admiralty courts also consistently ruled in favor of Africans seeking their freedom up to the French Revolution.

Yet, with the expansion of transatlantic slavery, more slave owners began to travel to France with their domestic slaves in the late 17th century. Because, as just mentioned above, the courts consistently ruled in favour of the freedom of African plaintiffs, the king and his government were called upon to set policy regarding this situation which began to seriously worry the rich and powerful planters. Louis XIV's first response was to uphold the valid law, that is the Freedom Principle, by fiat. Individual enslaved persons continued to regain their freedom when petitioning for it upon their arrival in France. However, some French provincial administrations, notably that of Nantes, which was the most important port for selling and shipping Africans in France, were by the early 18th century pressing for legislation that would unambiguously resolve the status of slaves in France in their interest.

The Parliament of Paris and other courts in districts which were not directly

---

592   Ibid., 13.
593   Ibid.
594   Ibid.
595   Flaig (2009), 182 et seq.

involved in slave trading, remained firm in upholding of the Freedom Principle. But even courts in districts that were heavily involved in the transatlantic system also decided in that manner in cases. For example, in 1715 a young enslaved African woman was brought to France from the colonies and placed with the nuns of Calvary in Nantes for the time that her mistress made a trip to Paris. When the mistress returned, the nuns refused to deliver the African woman. The Admiralty Court of Nantes decided that the woman was free, because the owner had failed to declare her as a slave when entering France and had thus violated the remnants of the Freedom Principle. G. Mellier, mayor of Nantes, stated that the lawyers had searched diligently for some positive law regulation on the issue in order to give the mistress back her slave, but had found none. Mellier, fearing that decisions such as this one could put Nantes' high profits from participation in genocidal transatlantic slavery at risk, subsequently urged the king's ministers to draw up definitive legislation to which judges could turn in order to maintain Africans in slavery. [596] It was only then that the French state issued the royal Edict of October 1716 which stated that colonial property owners and military officers could temporarily bring slaves to France without fear of losing their property rights under the condition that they gain permission from the colonial governor before departure, and that they registered the slaves with the clerk of the Admiralty upon arrival in France. A further condition was that the enslaved person learned a trade or received instruction in the Catholic faith. If an owner should fail to meet these legal requirements, the enslaved person would be recognized as free still. Hence, the Freedom Principle was not yet totally abolished. The 1716 edict also contained stipulations prohibiting the sale or trade of slaves in France.[597]

Yet, the legal situation remained ambiguous. The 1716 edict created a disruption in the French legal system. Because transatlantic slavery profits had become tremendous and very important for French royalty and capitalists, more legislation was passed two decades later in an effort to restrict the flow of enslaved persons – that is Africans – entering France. The Declaration of December 1738 reiterated the provisions of the 1716 edict that required the governor's permission and registration with French Admiralty clerks. A limit of three years was set on the slaves' stay in France. Most importantly, it stipulated that enslaved persons held in violation of these conditions would no longer be free, but confiscated in the name of the king and returned as slaves to the colonies. Thus, the royal declaration of 1738 aimed to abrogate the Freedom Principle in its entirety. However, the Parliament of Paris refused to register both the 1716 edict and the 1738 declaration. They were not ratified and could, according to the law of the land, be overlooked by the courts, which is exactly what happened.

In fact, France's legal system was rather complex, with overlapping jurisdic-

---

596   Peabody (1996), 15.
597   Ibid., 16 et seq.

tions and systems of appeal. The highest level courts were 12 regional *Parlements* and two sovereign courts that presided over specific regional districts. The most important court was the Parliament of Paris, whose jurisdiction covered about one-third of the territory of France.[598]

Acts of legislation, such as the Edicts of 1716 and 1738, once issued by the government were sent to the Parliament of Paris and the other regional *Parlements* where they had to be registered. The *Parlements'* parquets' senior officers reviewed and checked the laws to assess whether they were sound and consistent with the fundamental laws of the country. If they objected to a law or aspects of it, they recommended changes or refused outright to register it, which is what most *Parlements* did with the royal slavery decrees.[599] Courts in consequence and in adherence to the constitutional Freedom Principle refused to apply these slavery laws.

Regional Parliaments of minor significance like the ones of Dijon and Rennes did register the Edict of October 1716, but the majority, among them the Parliament of Paris, did not. The only available document that gives some direct insight concerning the reasons for this refusal is the recollection of Guillaume Francois Joly de Fleury, who was the *avocat général* of the *Parlement's* parquet chamber, as recorded by his son in 1756. The *avocat general* was responsible for offering his opinion on legislation before it was registered by the court. After the royal government issued the edict on October 23, 1716, it was sent to de Fleury for legal review and to be registered. Joly de Fleury solicited the opinion of an ecclesiastical lawyer, Pierre Lemerre the younger, barrister of the clergy at the Parliament of Paris.[600] Lemerre presented an extensive report on the legal traditions that underlay the maxim that all slaves were free upon arrival in France. He started his review with the ancient Hebrew slave laws and the church's teachings on slavery and manumission, and concluded that "one cannot have recourse to roman civil law nor to canonical constitutions to establish French liberty".[601] Rather, he affiliated the Freedom Principle with three elements. First, Henry II had issued an edict in 1556, which had enfranchised all serfs on the grounds that previous kings had already not tolerated that their subjects be held in a servile condition. Second, natural law recognized all men as equal. Third, Christianity held that man was created in God's image. Therefore man could not be treated like a beast under the domination of other men.[602] It was on the basis of Lemerre's report that de Fleury and de Chauvelin, the keeper of the seals of the Parliament of Paris, decided that the Edict of 1716 could not be registered. The count of Toulouse, drafter of the Edict, was informed of this decision. He did not insist on its registration.[603]

---

598   Peabody (1996), 15.
599   Ibid., 18 et seq.
600   Ibid.
601   Ibid.
602   Ibid., 21.
603   Ibid., 22.

Numerous cases involving claims of freedom by enslaved Africans continued to reach the courts of France. In June 1738, the Admiralty Court of Paris heard two petitions for freedom. At these occasions, the 1716 edict's lack of registration was first discussed by the court. One claim was brought in by Jean Boucaux, an enslaved African from Saint Domingue, and was to become a landmark case laying down the arguments that would constitute the basis for all such future cases. His lawyers relied on the national maxim that any slave who set foot on French soil was free.[604] They started their argument by recalling how according to natural law all men were born free. In wars, the winners spared the lives of their adversaries by making them slaves. They further retraced that the Romans had brought slavery to France, conquering and enslaving the Gauls.[605] However, by the 14th century, slavery had again disappeared from France, and Louis X had issued an ordinance on July 3, 1315, confirming this. The lawyers quoted from this royal ordinance: "We, considering that out Kingdom is called and named the Kingdom of Francs, and wishing that the thing be in truth according with its name, (...) have ordained and do ordain that generally, throughout our kingdom, as much as it can be shared by us and our successors, such servitude will be restored to freedom, (...) at good and suitable conditions".[606]

What is also highly significant is that the slave owner's lawyer Tribard did not at all challenge the uncodified maxim of the Freedom Principle. Quite the contrary, he seemed to affirm it four times. He based his argumentation entirely on the *Code Noir* of 1685 and the Edict of 1716. He also affirmed the notion that in their original state, humans were free, and slavery a consequence of war captivity. He supported the opposing lawyers' view that Christianity was responsible for the abolition of Roman slavery in France. The slave owner's lawyer only dwelt on varieties of serfdom, aiming at emphasizing that unfree relations were a persistent feature of French society.[607] Yet, serfdom was a condition altogether different from genocidal transatlantic slavery. Even the Crown persecutor, whose role was to represent the interest of the state, challenged many of slave owner's lawyer's points, and sustained that "(...) corporal serfdom no longer exists"[608], and emphasized that the ownership of a person by another had totally been eradicated in France. Furthermore, he refuted the slave owner's central thesis that the *Code Noir* and the Edict of 1716 authorized slavery under certain conditions, by pointing out that neither law had been registered by the Parliament of Paris and therefore had no standing in the Admiralty Courts.[609]

Considerate of these legal arguments, the Admiralty Court of France, maintain-

---

604   Ibid., 23 et seq.
605   Ibid., 26 et seq.
606   Ibid.,28 et seq.
607   Ibid., 32 et seq.
608   Ibid., 34.
609   Ibid.

ing appellate jurisdiction from provincial admiralty courts and thus the juridical authority over colonial affairs, issued its ruling in favor of Boucaux on August 29 and September 10, 1738. Boucaux was freed, but keeping with an old French tradition, no grounds were revealed.[610] This case constituted an important precedent for future decisions in the Admiralty Court of France.[611]

It was only three months after that decision that the French King issued a declaration "concerning the enslaved negroes of the colonies" that would become known as the Declaration of December 15, 1738.[612] It followed the general provisions of the Edict of October 1716 but attempted to eliminate many of the loopholes that favored the proliferation of Black slaves in France. If slave owners neglected to conform to the formalities of the law and did not register their slaves before and upon arrival in France, the slaves were no longer freed but confiscated at the profit of the King and returned to the colonies. This Declaration was registered by every court of France except that of Paris. This refusal by the Parliament of Paris, due to its incompatibility with the unwritten constitutional Freedom Principle, set the stage for a series of lawsuits that began in the 1750s and continued up to the Revolution.[613]

The Parliament of Paris and the Admiralty Court of France not only refused to register the illegal Edicts of 1716 and 1738, but also to confiscate slaves. Instead they freed them.[614] In the case of Jean Baptiste, the judges of the Admiralty Court of France did not order his confiscation, as provided by article 4 of the Declaration of 1738, but instead awarded him his freedom, in direct opposition to the royal decree. Apparently, the judges considered that the Declaration of 1738 was invalid, because unregistered and unconstitutional.[615] Indeed, only a few regional courts of Brittany, being at the center of the French transatlantic enslavement, enforced the Declaration of 1738 to the letter because it suited their interests, such as is illustrated by the case of Catherine Morgan who was brought to Nantes by her master in 1746. Catherine was ordered by the Admiralty Court of Nantes to be confiscated and returned to the colonies to perform labor in the public works.[616]

It is also significant that in 1848 Article 7 of the decree that abolished slavery still made reference to the maxim of the "common law" of the Freedom Principle.[617]

In 1755, the Admiralty Court of France in Paris awarded a certain Corinne her

---

610   Ibid., 36 et seq.
611   Ibid., 23 et seq.
612   Ibid., 38 et seq.
613   Ibid.
614   Ibid., 41.
615   Ibid., 52.
616   Ibid., 41.
617   Harris (1992), 115.

unconditional freedom and 500 livres in wages and expenses. Thus, the court recognized her right to reparations. Five other enslaved Africans were also granted their freedom by the same court that year. In fact, each and every slave, in total 154, who sued for freedom within the Admiralty Court of France over the next 45 years, won their case.[618]

However, tragically for Corinne and several other Africans who had won their cases in 1755, the royal administration intervened by fiat, as in the case of Jean Boucaux in 1738. The French King ordered their arrest and transfer to the port of Le Havre, from where they were returned to Saint Domingue at the expense of their masters.

These contradicting developments called for a clarifying ruling by the highest court of France, the Parliament of Paris.[619] In the case of Francisque, the *Parlement* rendered a landmark decision in 1759 that established once and for all the status of slaves who sued for their freedom within the jurisdiction of this court and all the Admiralty Courts within its domain. Although the judges of the *Parlement de Paris* ruled again in favor of freedom, it is difficult to retrace their decision's legal reasoning, because no grounds were given.[620] The lawyers in this case argued that Francisque, an Indian, was not a "nègre", and thus not subject to the laws of 1716 and 1738.[621] They also maintained that vestiges of ancient servitude, that is serfdom, were not the same as slavery. The lawyers argued that "Indians are a free people", and that "though the Hindus practice an idolatrous religion, they are ruled by laws, subject to monarchs, rich by the fertility of their lands"[622]. The same was true for Africa at that time.

In a later case that cited Francisque's case as a precedent, the laws' lack of registration was the focus rather than the debate over Francsique's questionable status as a "nègre", thus further pointing to the general illegality of transaltantic slavery as the decisive legal ground behind the court's decisions.[623] In another such claim for freedom, the court stated that "(...) in France, where only criminals are used as galley slaves, it was held that they acquired their liberty".[624]

So, despite determined state efforts to sanction transatlantic slavery through the Code Noir and the 1716 and 1738 edicts, over 150 enslaved Africans won their freedom in Paris's Admiralty Court in the 1750s, 60s and 70s. The lawyers argued that the unregistered laws were not valid and that the Freedom Principle, a fundamental maxim of the kingdom, guaranteed freedom to all who set foot on French soil. In all of the cases that were contemplated by the Admiralty courts of France after the Francisque case, the Africans were recognized as free. Sometimes

---

618   Peabody (1996), 55 et seq.
619   Ibid.
620   Peabody/Grinberg (2007), 51.
621   Ibid., 57.
622   Ibid., 62.
623   Ibid., 69 et seq.
624   Ibid., 29.

back wages for services rendered were awarded.[625] Thus the courts recognized the right to reparations of illegally enslaved Africans! It is important for the present-day reparation struggle to disseminate knowledge about this fact that even in the times of transatlantic slavery reparations were granted by courts in order to disperse the attitude of too many people that reparations would just be a big illusion that will never be attained anyway.

Thus, in 1762, the Admiralty Court of France rendered another important judgement in favor of an enslaved person called Louis. Louis was declared free since his arrival in France seven and a half years earlier, and his former master Le Fèvre was ordered to pay him 750 livres, plus interest, for back wages.[626] Thus, even against huge economic and political pressure from national slave holding interests, the Admiralty Courts of France and the Parliament of Paris held firm in their assessment of the invalidity of both the Edict of 1716 and the Declaration of 1738, because they had not been registered by the Parlement of Paris and violated the maxim that any slave who entered France was free.[627]

The number of lawsuits for freedom brought before the Admiralty courts in France in the 1760s increased six-fold compared to previous decades. One reason was simply that transatlantic slavery was expanding. As those lawsuits became more common, the judicial procedure became standardized. In all cases assessed during the 18th century, the rulings recognized the petitioner's freedom, even when they previously had journeyed through jurisdictions that had registered the 1738 edict, such as Britanny or Guyenne. This indicates that the highest judges of France never swerved from their conviction that the royal declarations violated the constitutional Freedom Principle, and were not valid even when registered by some provincial parliaments. When monetary awards and back wages – that is reparations – were sought, the provisional sentence awarded the petitioner the right to a hearing before the Admiralty Court of France's Chambre. Although the readily available documents do not indicate how the Chamber ruled in these cases, it is already significant that in principle the right to reparations was legally recognized here, something which is denied to descendants of the enslaved Africans today. In not one single case did a slave owner win a final decision against a slave in the Admiralty Court of France from 1730 to 1790.[628]

However, given the importance of transatlantic slavery profits for the French economy, these court decisions spurred the king's administrators to develop new legislation that would end this situation. It was passed on August 9, 1777. The *Déclaration pour la police des Noirs* finally sidestepped the Freedom Principle by declaring that all non-"whites" had to be quarantined upon their arrival in France

---

625   Peabody (1996), 5 et seq.
626   Ibid., 73.
627   Ibid., 54 et seq.
628   Ibid., 88 et seq.

and shipped back to the colony from which they came on the next available boat.[629]

It is thus clearly documented that in France, just like in other European enslaver nations, legislation aiming to sanction transatlantic slavery was passed only in the early 18th century, after it had been practised for a long time. The royal edicts of 1685, 1716, 1738 and 1777 stood in sharp contrast to the Freedom Principle[630] and international law. Transatlantic slavery was illegal and remained so by French law.

v. The Netherlands / United Provinces

Like France and England, the United Provinces had no slavery law. The lands they occupied in the Americas were defined as "territories" and not officially as colonies. The Dutch government, via its States-General, never created such law, but put the territories under the control of a trading company. This company was primarily interested in making the highest profits possible, with little concern otherwise in controlling the behavior of enslavers and colonists.[631] The founding Charter of the Dutch West India Company was granted by the States-General of the Netherlands on June 3, 1621. It did not confer power to legislate to the Company and remained mute on what law was to be applied in the territories the company colonized. A *placaat* of October 13, 1629 (*Ordre van Regieringe in West-Indien*) provided explicitly in its article 56 that in private law actions in the colonies the law to be applied was the common law of the United Provinces. The company was given power to refuse to apply part of that law. It was, however, never given power to legislate. In practice though, the company did issue numerous *placaaten*, alongside and under the supervision of the States-General.[632]

Thus, as for France and England, transatlantic slavery was introduced into the Dutch American colonies without a law of slavery. The colonial administration never issued systematic or comprehensive legislation.[633]

Roman law in general and Roman slavery law in particular had not been received in the United Provinces until the 15th century. Even when some Roman law became relevant, slavery was not accepted.[634] Law in general and Roman law perceptions were slightly different in the various Provinces. However, what they all had in common was an absence of slavery and of slavery law.[635] In 1629, a legal manipulation of an article (61) of the just mentioned *placaat* dating of October 13 was used to take recourse to Roman slave law as a legal basis for transatlantic enslavement. Article 61 ordered that for "other matters of contracts of all kinds

---

629   Ibid., 5 et seq.
630   Watson (1989), 171.
631   Ibid.,102 et seq.
632   Ibid.
633   Ibid.,102 et seq.
634   Ibid., 114.
635   Ibid.,102 et seq.

and trading the common written laws should be followed", but since Roman slave law had never been adopted by Dutch legal tradition, there was no justification to do so now only because it had become opportune. Scholars have sustained that this misuse of article 61 was probably deliberate, because the mighty by then had a need for slave law in view of their practice of transatlantic slavery.[636]

Later, when transatlantic slavery had financially become highly profitable, the West India Company issued *placaaten* on slavery itself, with the approval of the Dutch government. It is questionable whether they can really be considered law, since they were not issued by a state agency. However, the local courts of the Dutch de-facto-colony applied them. They prohibited enslaved Africans to drum, dance and move around, established penalties (including death), and regulated behavior of slaves and also of free Blacks by restricting their access to certain places or requiring written passes.[637]

Yet, despite all of this and because slavery was contrary to Dutch law, Flemish and Dutch courts, just as French and British, in their vast majority ruled that enslaved Africans suing for their freedom were free throughout the long centuries of transatlantic slavery.[638]

vi. Conclusion – chattel slavery illegal by European law at the time in question

We have seen that the review of European enslaver nations' laws on slavery leads to the unambiguous conclusion that transatlantic slavery was illegal by the legal orders of all these states at the time they engaged in it.

In 1825, US Chief Justice Marshall reasoned in the Antelope Case that US slave-trading was lawful since it would then have been "sanctioned by the laws of all nations who possess distant colonies".[639] We have just seen that this was really not the case, but that transatlantic slavery was illegal by the laws of all these nations. *Argumentum e contrario*, the obvious conclusion is that the colonial slave laws passed in the 17th and 18th centuries were illicit and void. Personal, group or even national behavior, what some people do, is not the standard of what is lawful and constitutional.[640] The legal standard is what the law says. A genocidal and fundamentally illegal practice cannot be rendered legal by the perpetrators, simply by maintaining it over a long period of 400 years and thereafter declaring that it would have been licit from the start. Not only logic and justice command this, but it has also been a legal standard from ancient times. *Quod ab initio non valet in tractu temporis non convalescet* (That which is bad in its commencement improves

---

636   Ibid., 104 et seq.
637   Ibid., 105 et seq.
638   Flaig (2009), 182 et seq.
639   US Chief Justice Marshall cited in: Peté/Du Plessis (2007), 21.
640   What Lincoln and Other Yankees Knew: The evidence that pre-civil war U.S. slavery was illegal, downloaded from http://medicolegal.tripod.com/slaveryillegal.htm#2 (accessed 14.10.2010).

not by lapse of time)[641], or *Quod initio non valet, tractu temporis non valet* (A thing void in the beginning does not become valid by lapse of time).[642] Indeed, "mere passage of time does not turn the illegal into legal. Every bank robber knows that: delay in apprehension does not thereby make the robbery legal and the loot his legal possession or property!" [643] Or, as DeMoirans recalled in the 17th century with special regard to transatlantic slavery, what "is instituted secretly or forcefully or otherwise illicitly shall have no firm reason to remain in existence".[644]

D. HISTORICAL SLAVERY IN THE LEGAL ORDERS OF OTHER PARTS OF THE WORLD

Before we go on to assess the legal qualification of transatlantic slavery as genocide and the legal responsibility of European enslaver states, a quick look at the legal situation regarding slavery in other regions and times seems warranted in order to substantiate the appraisal of the legal status of transatlantic slavery more deeply.

It is interesting to review the legal situation in my birth country, Austria, because that nation was for a long time connected through the Habsburger lineage (for example Charles V) with one of the first enslaver states, Spain, which was also the last to abolish slavery. Until the mid-18th century, a legal definition based on a decree from 1595 and delimiting slavery from villeinage remained valid in Austria. Again, we find that the principal legal justification for enslavement was captivity in a just war. Captured turks could be sold, given as gifts, exchanged, etc. In 1758, the (never ratified) Codex Theresianus abolished villeinage among Christians, although still providing for the enslavement of "heathens" in "just wars". Several cases are documented where Africans were treated as saleable goods in Austria. In 1704 Marcus Moro was sold by a certain field marshal Conte di St. Felice. Some 20 years later an enslaved African whose name is unknown was sold by the Prince of Liechtenstein. The autobiographies of the enslaved Africans Angelo Soliman and Reiske conject that a small-scale trade of enslaved Africans was going on between different Austrian and other European aristocrats. What is important is that, although the enslavement of those captured in war was considered legal, slave status was not inheritable in Austria.[645]

It is also significant that Soliman, the most prominent African slave who reached Austria via the transatlantic system, achieved some distinction and a fairly high living standard, even when compared to most of his Austrian contemporaries

---

641   Black's Law Dictionary (1979). 5th edition, St. Paul: West Publishing, 1126 et seq.
642   Ibid.
643   What Lincoln and Other Yankees Knew (2010).
644   De Moirans (1682), 227.
645   Sauer, Walter/Wiesböck, Andrea (2007). "Sklaven, Freie, Fremde. Wiener" Mohren "des 17. und 18. Jahrhunderts", in: Walter Sauer (ed.): Von Soliman zu Omofuma. Afrikanische Diaspora in Österreich 17. bis 20. Jahrhundert, Innsbruck/Wien: Studienverlag, 23- 56, 47 et seq.

in material regards. He was appointed educator of Prince Alois of Lichtenstein, and later managed to put himself in the position to negotiate a higher salary (!) from his master.[646] Although enslaved Africans arriving in Austria generally went through some of the channels of the transatlantic system and were enslaved in the same illegal manner of kidnapping or man-stealing as many of their brothers and sisters who ended up as plantation chattel in the Americas, they were not treated as chattel, because such slavery was not recognized as legal in Austria. Their status was unfree, and could probably be subsumized under villeinage, although their material well-being in some cases was at a much higher level than that of ordinary villeins. My direct ancestors on my mother's side were villeins who labored hard in the fields, yet they were no chattel and managed to create and accumulate some fortune through hard work over the centuries, something that was categorically denied to Africans in the transatlantic system. All of this indicates that in one more European country, Austria, genocidal and dehumanizing slavery was abnormal and not recognized by law or society. Nonetheless, the mode of enslavement of these Africans may have been illegal, if based on man-stealing, and part of the transatlantic system. They were also victims of racism. Although Angelo Soliman received some distinctions in Austrian society, upon his death he was stuffed and exposed alongside animals in a museum, adorned with a "traditional African" feather loin-cloth like he had never worn in his lifetime. The long legal battle that his daughter Josephine led to stop this objectification and humiliation and to bury her father in dignity proved futile. Additionally, it is important to keep in mind that Angelo Soliman was one individual with an exceptional fate and "luck" in some regards. We do not have much evidence about the life conditions of other enslaved Africans brought to Austria. They might have been much worse off.

According to Watson, slavery did not exist in Germany before and during transatlantic slavery.[647]

In Goa, India, if we are to trust contemporary Portuguese sources, existed a practice of "selling one's body". This, however, consisted of selling oneself to a person of authority, by necessity, especially in times of famine or following a condemnation for a criminal offense. One Portuguese chronicler attested that no master could claim to be of good faith in that region if he had not obtained his slave through the only legitimate means for "slavery", namely through capture in a "just war". This, again, corresponds with the detected legal standard of legitimate enslavement throughout Europe and Africa.[648]

---

646   Blom, Philipp/ Kos, Wolfgang (ed.) (2011). Angelo Soliman. Ein Afrikaner in Wien, Wien: Wien Museum/Christian Brandstätter Verlag, 98.
647   Watson (1989), 93 et seq.
648   Capela (2002), 332 et seq.

In ancient China, recorded from the Han dynasty upwards, the only reasons for legal enslavement were punishment for crime, self-sale to pay debts, and war captivity, although people were reportedly also forced into enslavement illegally. That difference between legal and illegal enslavement was recognized though. Convicts guilty of certain crimes were made government slaves, as well as their families and relatives. Slaves worked as household servants, in agriculture and construction, and as government officials. Slave status was hereditary for both private and government slaves, but slaves could pay for their freedom or be grant- ed freedom by their masters. Social fluidity was high at the time, and a few more fortunate slaves moved up the social ladder very quickly. Specific slaves were sold in the market, but trade of people who had been free up to that time was illegal. Slave raiding occurred although it was illegal. Yet there were strict laws against kidnapping and selling kidnapped people. As for the common treatment of slaves, Nurhachi, the founding father of the Manchu state, stated that "the Master should love the slaves and eat the same food as him"[649].

It is of no interest for the purpose of this work to enter the debate about the val- ue of the Bible as a historical document. Yet, it has been maintained that the state of servitude to which the Canaanites were reduced according to Bible descrip- tions was in many respects not worse than that of poor laboring people in other countries. They were made hewers of wood and drawers of water, yet were paid for this arduous labor "in such a manner as the nature of their service required, and were supplied with abundance of such necessaries of life as they and their families had need of".[650] Equiano argued that they were often employed in honor- able service. He also assessed that nothing in the Law of Moses could warrant the practice of transatlantic slavery. "But, on the contrary, and what was principally intended thereby, and in the most particular manner, as respecting Christians, that it contains the strictest prohibitions against it."[651]

In ancient Kemet (Egypt), people who are commonly referred to as "slaves" in today's historical discourse had vacation days off and received remuneration, paid in naturalia, fixed in apprenticeship contracts.[652] It has been sustained that docu- ments show that some even went on strike for better wages. What is important here is that there are no original ancient documents relating to the existence of "slavery" in Kemet. Apparently, there was not even a Kamêw word for "slave".[653] Recent trends in Egyptology tend to sustain that Kemet was not a slave civiliza-

---

649   Kim, Young Yoon (2009). Slavery in Imperial China, KoreanMinjokLeadershipAcademy, down- loaded from http://www.zum.de/whkmla/sp/0910/hersheys/hersheys5.html#ii (accessed 2.3.2011).
650   Cugoano (1787), 38.
651   Ibid.
652   Flaig (2009), 54.
653   Popo (2010), 25.

tion.[654]

Egyptologist Robert-Jacques Thibaud also pointed out that, contrary to standard representations, no slaves were employed to build the great African pyramids. This was confirmed later by research by renowned archaeologists Zahi Hawasss and Mark Lehner.[655] They showed that the construction of these architectural marvels was conceptualized and orchestrated by professionals. The workers who labored under the responsibility of these intellectual elite were partly professional artisans, partly peasants who voluntarily came out in the agricultural off-season to work for the erection of these holy monuments out of piety and devotion for the spiritual system that was the background for these monumental works.[656] The Ancient Egyptians responsible for the most stunning and phenomenal structures ever built by humans were Africans, and apparently they succeeded to do so without resorting to means of forced labor.

These random examples of societies of different times and regions further substantiate the conclusion that transatlantic slavery was fundamentally abnormal and illegal by common legal standards. Since legal principles common to a large number of systems of national or municipal law are recognized as general principles of international law, transatlantic slavery was clearly illegal by the international law standards of its time.

The International Court of Justice ruled in the Indo-Portuguese dispute over a 1779 treaty concluded between Portugal and the Maratha state that it was established that this treaty was "an international agreement fully valid according to the law in force at the time of its conclusion"[657]. The Court further sustained that the treaty must not be judged by *ex post facto* law, and thus condemned the fallacy of projecting contemporary international law into the past. It is of highest importance for our purpose that the Court stated that the case had to be evaluated "on the basis of the fundamental principles of pre-nineteenth century law of nations common to all sovereign entities irrespective of religion, civilisation or geographical location".[658] Transferred to the case of transatlantic slavery, the logic of the reasoning of the ICJ commands that responsibility for transatlantic slavery has to be evaluated by means of the laws that were analyzed in this chapter and by which transatlantic slavery was clearly illegal. In 1814, Sweden, Russia, Prussia, Austria, France, Britain and Portugal also confirmed this by stating in their declaration of European Nations that the slave trade was "contrary to the general

---

654 Menu, Bernadette (2006). Egypte pharaonique. Nouvelles recherches sur l'histoire juridique, économique et sociale de l'ancienne Egypte, Paris: L'Harmattan.
655 Morell, Virginia (2001). The Pyramid Builders, downloaded from http://ngm.nationalgeographic.com/ngm/data/2001/11/01/html/ft_20011101.5.fulltext.html (accessed 11.3.2012).
656 Ajavon (2005), 17.
657 Case concerning Right of Passage over Indian Territory (Merits), Judgment of 12 April 1960, ICJ Reports 1960, p. 6.
658 Schulte-Tenckhoff (1998), 11 et seq.

principles of morality and humanity" at the Congress of Vienna.

E. CONCLUSION: TRANSATLANTIC SLAVERY VIOLATED GENERAL PRINCIPLES OF INTERNATIONAL LAW

The review presented over the preceding pages shows clearly that transatlantic slavery violated general principles of international law, such as derived from the vast majority of national, regional and communitarian legal systems. Both the typical modes of enslavement – that is kidnapping, slave razzias and fraudulent criminal administration – and the genocidal treatment that enslaved Africans were subjected to violated these general principles of law. Virtually all legal systems restricted the legality of enslavement to cases of captivity in "just wars" – and what was considered a "just war" was again legally reglemented – criminal conviction, and self- or debt-bondage. In all legal systems, enslaved persons retained some rights, such as the right to life and rights to seek protection from gross abuse. So, indeed, in view of documentation, evaluated in this work, no room for doubt remains that transatlantic slavery violated general principles of law.

The current legal ostracism of genocide and crimes against humanity is explicitly grounded in the historical existence of general principles of law and general principles of humanity, and this reprehension of genocide and crimes against humanity makes up a large part of the most compelling category of international law rules today. The International Military Tribunal judging Nazi atrocities contended that it was persecuting crimes that were "criminal according to the general principles of law recognized by the community of nations".[659] Just a page above, we have seen that European powers built their condemnation of the "slave trade" at the Congress of Vienna in 1814 on the recognition that it was "contrary to the general principles of morality and humanity".

During the centuries of transatlantic slavery, slavery remained illegal inside all European nations, and even concerning the colonies the vast majority of courts in Europe persistently upheld the illegality of genocidal transatlantic slavery. Transatlantic enslavement and slavery also remained illegal in African states and societies, such as retraced in this chapter, even if due to the systematic imposition of violence on the continent on parts of European slavers, the practice of some states and societies changed. But the fact remains that the legal precepts outlawing transatlantic enslavement remained in force and the treatment meted out to enslaved Africans in the transatlantic system stayed illegal in the legal systems of European, African and other states, and thus constituted general principles of law. Such general principles of law, rooted in natural law yet recognized as positive law at the time of transatlantic slavery, remained in effect throughout the transatlantic system and are concretized today in the form of the explicit prohibition of

---

659   Jos (2000), 141.

genocide and crimes against humanity. By these general principles, transatlantic slavery clearly was and remained illegal by general principles of international law throughout the long centuries it was perpetrated.

III. Transatlantic Slavery and the Legal Concepts of *Genocide* and *Crime Against Humanity*

Following our assessment of the illegality of transatlantic slavery at its time and before proceeding to assess the attribution of legal responsibility of states, it seems expedient to recapitulate some general features and facts of transatlantic slavery in light of the legal concepts of genocide and crime against humanity. The disturbing examples of atrocities presented in this chapter put it beyond doubt that transatlantic slavery was fundamentally different, qualitatively and quantitatively, from other forms of forced labor and "slavery", such as discussed in the previous chapter.

Genocide is generally acknowledged as a particular form of crime against humanity.[660] Both terms, "genocide" and "crime against humanity", were new in 1944, yet a year later they were already used in the indictment by the International Military Tribunal that judged Nazi criminals. Within two years, "genocide" was the subject of an UN General Assembly resolution.[661] That was possible because only the explicit terms "genocide" and "crime against humanity" were innovations in international law growing from the Nuremberg tribunals, while the content prohibitions of outlawed conduct they circumscribed was not.[662]

At that time after WW II, with regard to the Charter of the International Military Tribunal, crimes against humanity and genocide, the crucial question "was whether the laws under which these crimes, positively defined by the Charter after the fact, were only the positive embodiment of pre-existing unwritten law, and thus legally valid, or simply an exercise in ex post facto victor's vengeance, which would be legally invalid".[663] The view prevailed that a higher law did exist under which the committed atrocities were indisputably prohibited at the time of

---

660   Schabas (2000), 253.
661   Ibid., 4.
662   Schabas, William A. (2008). "Origins of the Genocide Convention: from Nuremberg to Paris", in: Case Western Reserve Journal of International Law Vol. 40, 35-55.
663   Bassiouni (1992), 64.

their commission, thus before the explicit conceptualization of the terms. "Such a naturalist view could also find support in positive law, namely the 1907 Hague Convention which posits the prohibition of the conduct which is contrary to 'laws of humanity' (...)."[664]

When the IMT Charter was drafted and applied, reference was often made to principles of equity to reach legal conclusions. "The equity principle reflected in the formulation of the Charter derives in part from the Roman Law maxim of *ex injuris ius non oritur*. The rationale of the equity principle is as follows: can one who participated in the subversion of the law benefit from it, or as the equity maxim would have it, those with unclean hands cannot seek the benefits of equity."[665]

Scholars pertinently retraced how the content of the prohibition of crimes against humanity and genocide goes back to distant times: "Because these crimes have been anti-social since time immemorial, in a sense there is nothing new in prosecution of genocide to the extent that it overlaps with the crimes of homicide and assault. Yet genocide almost invariably escaped prosecution because it was virtually always committed at the behest and with the complicity of those in power. (...) International law's role in the protection of national, racial, ethnic and religious groups from persecution can be traced to the Peace of Westphalia of 1648 (...)."[666] Schabas recalled in that regard that, in 1919, Britain had sustained that prosecution for the Armenian genocide could be based on "the common law of war" or "the customs of war and rules of international law".[667]

Grotius had already asserted three centuries before that *crimen grave non potest non essere punible*, that is, gross crimes cannot be non-punishable.[668] Now, the drafters of the Charter of the Nuremberg Tribunal "reflected a laicized naturalist philosophy in the Grotian tradition".[669] Thus again, we see that there is indeed a continuing thread spanning from before and during transatlantic slavery up to our days in the condemnation of conduct constituting, in today's terms, genocide and crimes against humanity. As the Nuremberg Tribunal concluded in a judgement about a Nazi criminal, "so far from it being unjust to punish him, it would be unjust if his wrongs were allowed to go unpunished"[670]. Schabas thus assessed that "certain basic truths like this remain immutable throughout the course of time, and spring naturally to the minds of rational and thoughtful persons".[671] Justice Jackson highlighted in his opening statement of the Nuremberg trial that

---

664 Ibid.
665 Ibid., 72.
666 Schabas (2000),15.
667 Ibid., 20 et seq.
668 Bassiouni (1992), 64.
669 Ibid., 70 et seq.
670 International Military Tribunal, cited in: ibid., 64.
671 Ibid., 64.

"I cannot, of course, deny that these men are surprised that this is the law; they really are surprised that there is any such thing as law. These defendants did not rely on any law at all. Their program ignored and defied all law. German law, any law at all was to these men simply a propaganda devise to be invoked when it helped and to be ignored when it would condemn what they wanted to do. That men may be protected in relying upon the law at the time they act is the reason we find laws of retrospective operation unjust. But these men cannot bring themselves within the reason of the rule which in some systems of jurisprudence prohibits *ex post facto* laws. They cannot show that they ever relied upon International Law in any state or paid it the slightest regard."[672]

The same reasoning is applicable to transatlantic slavery, just as the maxim that those who seek equity must do equity. "Those who shaped the laws that permitted them to do their misdeeds should not, therefore, be able to claim the protection of legal defenses that they established for their benefit prior to the commission of their misdeeds."[673] Likewise, the colonial slave laws cannot serve to exonerate European slaver nations from their responsibility. Equity, being a general principle of international law, is recognized as applicable international law in the inventory of sources of international law – that is Article 38 of the Statute of the International Court of Justice.[674]

There are some disagreements as to the precise legal theoretical entrenchment of the validity of the principles enshrined in the Nuremberg Charter, but the general consensus is that they were in existence and valid before the Charter, and that consensus is virtually undisputed. Naturalists viewed the Charter as the legally valid embodiment of a compelling higher law, and even pragmatists and utilitarians saw it as the enunciation of a positive norm that was "grounded in a variety of historical legal precedents whose evolution was justified by moral-ethical considerations and by legal policy".[675]

United Nations law specialist Bassiouni highlighted that

"(p)rinciples of justice are necessarily unbound by space and time (...). Crimes do not disappear merely in time, or through a lack of prosecution – these are prosecutorial and punishment policy decisions which arise after the criminal fact. Above all, they have no bearing on the harmful results and victimization produced by the crime, even when for policy reasons they may no longer be prosecutable or punishable. (...) Only rigid positivists would uphold the validity of these Nazi German laws according to which 'crimes against humanity' had been committed. All other philosophical views would invalidate the national laws of Nazi Germany which mandated or permitted the commission of those acts falling

---

672   Ibid., 72.
673   Ibid., 110.
674   Ibid., 70 et seq.
675   Ibid., 79.

within the meaning of Article 6(c). But the logical conclusion to the rejection of such post-1935 Nazi laws would have been to apply German criminal law as it existed before the Nazi changes instead of the Law of the Charter, which enacted an alternative normative basis for the accountability of those charged with 'crimes against humanity'."[676]

Two things are especially important to keep in mind in that regard when it comes to transatlantic slavery. "Rigid positivists" hold a minority position among global international lawyers, and adherents of all other philosophical views in consequence of their quasi-unanimous legal condemnation of Nazi crimes would have to also condemn in the same way the slavery laws that enslaver states passed after they had gained enough power to do so through the crime itself. And the second logical conclusion from this assessment of the Nuremberg Trial is that the law that has to be applied is the law that was in place before transatlantic slavery, and by which the kind of slavery and enslavement that were constitutive of the transatlantic system were illegal.

Hannah Arendt remarked once on the Nazi claim that their rule was consonant with the rule of law, that South Africa's legal apartheid discourse was also qualified by its claim of being a rule of law. Now, South Africa's apartheid laws and the laws promulgated by European nations to sanction transatlantic enslavement really sprang from the same root, that is, genocidal oppression of Africans and the violation of African sovereignty, and had indeed many systematic and explicit resemblances. Bassiouni stressed that

"crimes against humanity by virtue of their nature and scale require the use of governmental institutions, structures (...). All too frequently, however, governments have managed to co-opt the legal process which produces positive law, thereby claiming 'legitimacy' or 'lawfulness' for that which would otherwise be illegitimate or unlawful. By sustaining an absolutist positivist law approach to law, totalitarian governments claim the legitimacy and authority of the positive law, which they are able to fashion as they please in order to provide apparent 'lawfulness' to their otherwise unlawful conduct. Thus, 'state action or policy' frequently relies on positive law to carry out its otherwise violative conduct (...). It is interesting to note that throughout the 20th century most 'state action or policy' resulting in mass killings and other mass human rights violations have been committed in reliance on three interactive factors: ideology, terror, and positive law. The latter being the instrument of the other two. (...) In totalitarianism and similar regimes, law is transformed from being the embodiment of legitimate *consensus iuris* to an instrument of socio-political change devoid of historical legitimacy and legal validity. Such type of 'law' fluctuates without certainty, predictability or boundary as it follows the motions of the power it serves."[677]

Transatlantic slavery is indeed a prototype of this described situation. All of

---

676 Ibid., 81 et seq.
677 Bassiouni (1992), 242.

the elements pointed out by Bassiouni were perpetrated over more than four centuries.

1. CRIME AGAINST HUMANITY

Article 6 of the Statute of the Nuremberg Tribunal considers as crimes against humanity "murder, extermination, enslavement, deportation, and other inhumane acts committed against any civilian population, before or during the war; or persecutions on political, racial or religious grounds in execution of or in connection with any crime (...), whether or not in violation of the domestic law of the country where perpetrated".[678] This definition was taken up by UN General Assembly resolution (95) in 1946.

The specific crimes against humanity enumerated in that IMT Charter article can be found in the criminal systems of the vast majority of the world's legal systems. That does not automatically make them international *crimes*, yet it makes their prohibition a general principle of international law. What makes specific conduct a crime against humanity is its nexus to an international element. For this to be given, it is enough that the conduct is "state action or policy". That is the case if the specified crimes are committed as part of "state action of policy" ("also when committed with the connivance or knowledge of higher-ranking public officials, or when such higher-ranking officials fail to carry out their obligation to prevent the conduct in question or fail to punish the perpetrators when the conduct is discovered or reasonably discoverable"[679]), or if the action or policy is based on discrimination and persecution against an identifiable group, and if the acts committed are otherwise crimes in the national criminal laws of that state.[680] Considering the evidence presented so far, transatlantic slavery undoubtedly fulfilled these elements.

As stated, the concepts of genocide and crime against humanity in the Charter of the IMT, the UN Resolution and the Genocide Convention did not create new law. The notion of offenses against the law of nations, *delicti ius gentium*, had pre-existed the Charter by centuries.[681] Historical evolution demonstrates that what became conceptualized as "crime against humanity" had existed as "general principles of law recognized by civilized nations" long before the IMT Charter's formulation in 1945.[682]

Bassiousini assessed that "(f)or over seven thousand years, humanitarian prin-

---

678   Charter of the International Military Tribunal, downloaded from http://avalon.law.yale.edu/imt/imtconst.asp (accessed 29.6.2012).
679   Ibid.
680   Bassiouni (1992), 250 et seq.
681   Ibid., 147.
682   Ibid., 168.

ciples regulating armed conflicts evolved gradually in different civilizations. In time, these humanitarian principles formed a protective fabric of norms and rules designed to prevent certain forms of physical harm and hardships from befalling innocent civilian non-combatants, as well as certain categories of combatants such as the sick, the wounded, shipwrecked and prisoners of war."[683] The development of the concept of crime against humanity is grounded on the basic elements of the scholastic tradition's definition of *lex* or "willed law" as subordinated to a common law of mankind, or *ius gentium*. "Thus the crime against humanity is essentially a concept which involves reference to the common dictate of humanity extending beyond a particular national framework."[684]

Evidence of international criminal law norms can be found in historical records of, for example, the Chinese, the Mayas and the ancient Greeks.[685] Deuteronomy contains some very old written canons of warfare prohibiting the killing of women and children, among others.[686] Indeed, a historical review of the humanization of armed conflict

"reveals that various civilizations, dating back several thousand years, have either specifically prohibited or at least condemned unnecessary use of force and violence against civilians. This historical process, spanning several millennia, reveals the convergence of basic human values in diverse civilizations (...). In ancient Greece, there was awareness that certain acts were contrary to traditional usages and principles spontaneously enforced by human conscience. Herodotus recounts that as early as the fifth century BCE certain conduct was prohibited: "The slaughter of the Persian envoys by the Athenians and Spartans was confessedly a transgression of the [laws of men], as a law of the human race generally, and not merely as a law applicable exclusively to the barbarians. And Xerxes recognized and submitted to such general law, when he answered on suggestions being made to him that he should resort to similar retaliation; that he would not be like Lacadaemonians, for they had violated the law of all nations, by murdering his heralds, and that he would not do the very thing which he blamed in them."[687]

The Chinese scholar Sun Tzu asserted in the same century, though continents apart, that it is important to "treat captives well, and care for them".[688] Chinese, Hindu, Egyptian and Assyrian civilization all likewise devised principles of legitimacy for resorting to war and particular rules for its conduct. St. Thomas Aquinas, frequently quoting St. Augustine in his *Summa Theologica*, refers to these basic laws of humanity in the treatment of civilian non-combatants, sick, wounded and

---

683 Bassiouni (1992), 150.
684 Lumb (1968), 81.
685 O'Shea, Andreas (2007). "Reparations Under International Criminal Law", in: Max duPlessis and Stephen Peté (ed.): Repairing the Past? International Perspectives on Reparations for Gross Human Rights Abuses, Antwerpen/Oxford: Intersentia, 179-196, 179.
686 Nussbaum (1954), 2 et seq.
687 Cited in: Bassiouni (1992), 154.
688 Bassiouni (1992), 155 et seq.

prisoners of war; "these rules belong to the *ius gentium* which are deduced from natural law as conclusion principles".[689]

That there was a law of arms during the Middle Ages in Europe as well as a code of chivalry is testified by records such as that about the siege of Limoges in 1370, which mentions three French knights surrendering to the Earl of Cambridge and asking him to "act therefore to the law of arms" and to show mercy, a request that was granted.[690]

After the Middle Ages in Europe, such basic principles of humanity were further strengthened. The bilateral and multilateral treaties after the Treaty of Westphalia in 1648 are an expression of these values.[691] An example of early persecution of crimes against humanity is the execution of Conradin von Hohenstaufen in Naples in 1268, who was put to death for committing such crimes.[692]

Another crucial event in international legal history that immensely abets the qualification of transatlantic slavery as a crime against humanity at the time of facts was the trial against Peter von Hagenbach that took place in 1474. It is commonly considered as one of the first, recorded, international war crime tribunals. The antecedent to it was that Duke Charles of Burgundy got possessions on Upper Rhine from the Archduke of Austria as pledge in 1469, and nominated Peter von Hagenbach as governor. Hagenbach subsequently installed a "regime of arbitrariness and terror, extended to murder, rape, illegal taxation and wanton confiscation of private property"[693], until he was stopped by an alliance of Austria, Berne, France and the towns of Upper Rhine in 1476 and put before an *ad-hoc* tribunal, consisting of 28 judges from the Allied towns. He was accused of having "trampled underfoot the laws of God and man" and "was charged with murder, rape, perjury and other *malefacta*, including orders to the non-German mercenaries he had brought (...), to kill the men in the houses where they were quartered so that the women and children would be completely at their mercy"[694]. Though the defendant and his attorney invoked the defence of superior orders, the Tribunal refused this request on the grounds that to accept it would be contrary to the laws of God. Hagenbach was found guilty and condemned to death. It is very important to note that the condemned acts had been committed before the outbreak of open war between Burgundy and her enemies, and were thus not war crimes in a strict legal sense, but must rather be subsumed under the category of *t*.[695] The

---

689   Ibid.
690   Ibid., 158.
691   Ibid., 159.
692   Ibid., 197.
693   Schwarzenberger, Georg (1968). "Breisach Revisited. The Hagenbach Trial of 1474", in: Charles H. Alexandrowicz (ed.): Studies in the history of the law of nations, The Hague: Grotian Press Society, 46-51, 46 et seq.
694   Ibid., 47 et seq.
695   Ibid., 50 et seq.

"a coordinated plan or different actions aiming at the destruction of essential foundations of the life of national groups, with the aim of annihilating the groups themselves. The objective of such a plan would be disintegration of the political and social institutions of culture, language, national feelings, religion, and the economic existence of national groups and the destruction of the personal security, liberty, health, dignity and even the lives of the individuals belonging to such groups. Genocide is directed against the national group as an entity, and the actions involved are directed against individuals, not in their individual capacity, but as members of the national group"[703].

Lemkin concretized that the crime of genocide transpired, for example, through racial discrimination in feeding, the destruction and endangering of health, or outright mass killings. If we were to bring this definition, which was at the very basis of the contemporary international legal repression of genocide, together with the evidence of transatlantic slavery, with little doubt it would be accounted as genocide.

Shortly thereafter, and building on Lemkin's works, the resolution unanimously adopted by the General Assembly on December 11, 1946 (96(I)) declared that "[g]enocide is a denial of the right of existence of entire human groups, as homicide is the denial of the right to live of individual human beings; such denial of the right of existence shocks the conscience of mankind, results in great losses to humanity in the form of cultural and other contributions represented by these human groups, and is contrary to moral law and to the spirit and aims of the United Nations. Many instances of such crimes of genocide have occurred when racial, religious, political, and other groups have been destroyed, entirely or in part."[704]

Formally, resolutions of the General Assembly are not binding sources of law. Nevertheless, the International Court noted in 1996 that General Assembly resolutions, even if they are not binding as such, may sometimes have normative value.

"They can, in certain circumstances, provide evidence important for establishing the existence of a rule or the emergence of an opinion juris. To establish whether this is true of a given General Assembly resolution, it is necessary to look at its content and the conditions of its adoption; it is also necessary to see whether an opinion juris exists as to its normative character. Or a series of resolutions may show the gradual evolution of the opinion juris required for the establishment of a new rule."[705]

Genocide Resolution 96(I) was adopted unanimously, and additionally it is gen-

Press, 27 et seq.

703   Ibid., 25.

704   UN General Assembly (1946). Resolution 96 (I), U.N. Doc. A/63/Add.1.

705   Legality of the Threat or Use of Nuclear Weapons, Advisory Opinion of 8 July 1996, ICJ Reports 1996, 70.

occurrence of the Hagenbach tribunal bears evidence that war crimes and crimes against humanity were recognized and reprehended in international law at the time of transatlantic slavery, and that principles of natural law and humanity were considered positive law and were actually relied upon in international judicial decisions.[696]

In the 18th century, Martens, an international law scholar, asserted that "our right to wound and kill, being founded on self-defence, or on the resistance opposed to us, we can, with justice wound or take the life of none except those who take an active part in the war. (...) Children, old men, women, and in general all of those who cannot carry arms, (...), are safe under the protection of the laws of nations, unless they have exercised violence against the enemy".[697]

The appeal court in the Barbie case estimated that the crime against humanity is defined by the will to deny the humanity of an individual through inhumane treatment or through racially or religiously motivated persecutions whereby these treatments and persecutions are exercised against civil populations and the will is exercised in the political setting of a state to this end.[698] All of this happened systematically throughout the centuries of transatlantic slavery, such as seen by means of a multitude of examples presented throughout this work.

Indeed, that transatlantic slavery was a crime against humanity has lost much of its former controversiality even among Europeans in recent times. Even if couched in ambiguous terms, such as "(...) are crimes against humanity, and should have always been so" or "constitute crimes against humanity", this has been recognized in the Durban Declaration and a French law brought in by French Guianese deputy Christiane Taubira and passed in 2001. These restrictive formulations – aiming at restricting the legal qualification as crime against humanity to the present and implying that at the time of transatlantic slavery the legal concept of crime against humanity would not yet have existed, in order to avoid reparation claims that could be based on a historical legal recognition – have little effect though in that regard, since we have seen that crimes against humanity were in fact legally reprehended from before transatlantic slavery. The Inquisition, shedding so much innocent blood in Europe, was undoubtedly a crime against humanity too, yet never legally addressed because of the factual power constellations at that time. However, the fact that violations of law are not reprehended does not make them right or legal. It is also important to keep in mind that one fundamental difference of transatlantic slavery to other historical crimes against humanity, such as Inqui-

---

696   Schabas (2000), 4.

697   Ibid., 155 et seq.

698   Jos, Emmanuel (2000). "Esclavages et crime contre l'humanité", in: Serge Chalons, Christian Jean-Etienne, Suzy Landau and Andre Yebakima (ed.): De l'esclavage aux reparations, Paris: Editions Karthala, 135-148, 136 et seq.

sition, with regard to responsibility and reparations is that the descendants of the direct victims of transatlantic slavery are still identifiable as a consequence of the crime from which they, in general terms, continue to suffer up to this day and are themselves victims of the continuing crime of the Maafa.

In 1973, the International Convention on the Suppression and Punishment of the Crime of Apartheid declared apartheid as a crime against humanity. It stipulated that the expression apartheid covers "inhuman acts committed for the purpose of establishing and maintaining domination by one racial group of persons over any other racial group of persons and systematically oppressing them".[699] As will be demonstrated shortly in Chapter V, social scientists and activists have pertinently argued that the present world situation and relationship of Black and "white" people is characterized by global apartheid. Experts and institutions generally consider apartheid as either genocide or crime against humanity, depending in the facts of a case.[700] But then again, most define genocide as a special category of crime against humanity.

2. TRANSATLANTIC SLAVERY AND THE MAAFA: GENOCIDE

Thus, the question arises of whether it is possible to sustain that, legally speaking and as sustained by reparation activists, transatlantic slavery and the larger, continuing crime of the Maafa constitute genocide above this rather unproblematic and uncontested qualification as crime against humanity. It is to be answered affirmatively, and this section will retrace why.

A. GENOCIDE IN CONTEMPORARY INTERNATIONAL LEGAL PRACTICE

The term "genocide" was coined by Raphael Lemkin in 1944[701], who created it from the two words "genos" (race, nation or tribe in ancient Greek) and "caedere" (kill in Latin). He proposed to define genocide as "not necessarily imply[ing] the immediate destruction of a national or ethnic group"[702], yet as

---

699 International Convention on the Suppression and Punishment of the Crime of Apartheid, downloaded from http://www.hrea.org/index.php?base_id=104&language_id=1&erc_doc_id=930&-category_id=35&category_type=3&group= (accessed 16.11.2009).

700 Schabas (2000), 201f

701 Lemkin, Raphael (1944). Axis Rule in Occupied Europe. Laws Of Occupation, Analysis Of Government, Proposals For Redress, Washington: Carnegie Endowment for International Peace, Division of International Law.

702 Schabas, William A. (2000). Genocide in International Law, Cambridge: Cambridge University

erally accepted that its content precises pre-existing law.

Only five years later, in 1951, the International Court of Justice associated Resolution 96(I) with the Genocide Convention in order to conclude "that the principles underlying the Convention are principles which are recognized by civilized nations as binding on States, even without any conventional obligation".[706]

Finally, in the Genocide Convention's Art. 2, adopted two years after the UN Resolution by the General Assembly, genocide was defined as "any of the following acts committed with the intent to destroy, in whole or in part, a national, ethnical, racial or religious group, as such:

a) Killing members of the group;
b) Causing serious bodily or mental harm to members of the group;
c) Deliberately inflicting on the group conditions of life calculated to bring about its physical destruction in whole or in part;
d) Imposing measures intended to prevent births within the group;
e) Forcibly transferring children of the group to another group".[707]

Although we have read much by now about post-'45 law developments, it is generally accepted by international lawyers that the content of the prohibition of genocide was nothing new. "There is no real disagreement with reference to the historical basis of the crime of genocide, and recognition that it had existed long before the adoption of the Convention or of General Assembly Resolution 96(I)."[708]
As Koskenniemi writes,

"Once the idea of natural law is discarded, it seems difficult to justify an obligation that is not voluntarily assumed. (...) The matter is particularly important in regard to norms intended to safeguard basic human rights and fundamental freedoms. If the only States bound to respect such rights and freedoms are the States that have formally become parties to the relevant instruments – and even then only within the scope of their often compromised wordings and multiple reservations – then many important political values would seem to lack adequate protection. It is inherently difficult to accept the notion that States are legally bound not to engage in genocide, for example, only if they have ratified and not formally denounced the 1948 Genocide Convention."[709]

In the *Reservations to the Genocide Convention case* (1951 (!), thus only two years after the entry into force of the Convention), the International Court of Justice precised that genocide is the "denial of the right of existence of entire human groups, a denial which shocks the conscience of mankind and results in great losses to humanity" and "is contrary to moral law and to the spirit and aims

---

706   Schabas (2000), 45 et seq.
707   UN General Assembly, Convention on the Prevention and Punishment of the Crime of Genocide, resolution adopted by the General Assembly, 9 December 1948, 260 A (III).
708   Ibid., 78.
709   Cited in: Peté/Du Plessis (2007), 26.

of the United Nations"[710]. The Court furthermore stated that the principles listed in the Convention and recognized by the "civilized" nations created binding obligations for states even without contractual link.[711] It is highly significant that the Court explicitly referred to "moral law" and substantiated that these binding principles antedate the Genocide Convention. "Moral law" was also recognized and referred to by both African states and people and European law scholars and jurisprudence (see, for example, the Hagenbach trial) before and during the time of transatlantic slavery, as recalled at several instances throughout this work.

With regard to transatlantic slavery, paragraphs (a)-(c) and (e) of the Genocide Convention seem most relevant. "Killing members of the group", "causing serious bodily or mental harm to members of the group", "deliberately inflicting on the group conditions of life calculated to bring about its physical destruction in whole or in part", and "forcibly transferring children of the group to another group" were all acts committed systematically against African people throughout the long centuries of transatlantic slavery. The following examples gathered from research by historians and social scientists show that the material facts of transatlantic slavery clearly fulfil the material requirements of the Genocide Convention.

B. TRANSATLANTIC SLAVERY AND THE LEGAL REQUIREMENTS FOR QUALIFICATION AS GENOCIDE

The most pertinent assessments by historians come to the conclusion that enslavement and transatlantic deportation made about 100 to 210 million direct victims, whereby they estimate that for every African who made it to the Americas and was sold there, four to five had died in Africa or during the Middle Passage through violent action associated with the transatlantic slavery system.[712] Diop-Maes estimates that Africa's population of 600 million inhabitants in the 14th century had been reduced to 200 million by the mid-19th, because of transatlantic slavery.[713]

An African who was later renamed Charles Ball recounted the following testimony of his enslavement:

"About 20 persons were seized in our village at the time I was; and amongst these were three children so young that they were not able to walk or to eat any hard substance. The mothers of these children had brought them all the way with them and had them in their arms when we were taken on board this ship. When they put us in irons to be sent to our place of confinement in the ship, the men

---

710   Reservations to the Convention on Genocide, Advisory Opinion of May 28, 1951, ICJ Reports 1951, 12.
711   Carreau (2007), 95.
712   Ki-Zerbo (1978), 218.
713   Diop-Maes (1996), 270.

fastened the irons on these mothers, took the children out of their hands and threw them over the side of the ship into the water. When this was done, two of the women leaped overboard after the children – the third was already confined by a chain to another woman and could not get into the water, but in struggling to disengage herself, she broke her arm and died a few days after of a fever. One of the two women who were in the river was carried down by the weight of her irons before she could be rescued; but the other was taken up by some men in a boat and brought on board. This woman threw herself overboard one night when we were at sea.

We had nothing to eat but yams, which were thrown amongst us at random – and of these we had scarcely enough to support life. More than one third among us died on the passage and when we arrived at Charleston, I was not able to stand. It was more than a week after I left the ship before I could straighten my limbs."[714]

The crewmen who effectuated these barbarities were employees of European state-licensed or chartered companies. Human beings, targeted on group criteria – in this case Africaness – cannot be subjected to such atrocities if the continuation of their existence is intended. Africans, enslaved and considered enslavable by European slavers and slaver states, as a group, were treated as labor commodities and no longer as human beings.

Pertaining to the forced mass removal of Africans from the continent, an UN commentary on genocide (UN doc. A/C.6/234) clearly stated that "[m]ass displacement of populations from one region to another does not constitute genocide. It would, however, become genocide if the occupation were attended by such circumstances as to lead to the death of the whole or part of the displaced population (if, for example, people were driven from their homes and forced to travel long distances in a country where they were exposed to starvation, thirst, heat, cold and epidemics). (...)"[715]. The mortality rate during the Middle Passage was between 20 and 80 per cent of the enslaved Africans on any given ship.[716]

Sugar was a very labor intensive crop, and the huge profits it yielded made the wastage of human life worthwhile to the plantocracy and European states in financial terms. It was only in very few plantation jurisdictions in the Americas (notably in the Southern United States) that enslaved Africans did reproduce demographically over the almost 400 years that transatlantic slavery lasted.[717] When the importation of slaves more or less stopped with the abolition of the "slave" "trade", the slave population declined everywhere but in continental English America.[718] Beyond the fact that many Africans were directly killed in

---

714   Brooks (2004), 28 et seq.
715   Schabas (2000), 196.
716   Crawford/Nobles/DeGruy Leary (2003), 254.
717   Thompson (2006), 100.
718   Watson (1989), 59 et seq.

transatlantic slavery, this situation fulfils the conditions of the Genocide Convention of "causing serious bodily or mental harm to members of the group" and of "deliberately inflicting on the group conditions of life calculated to bring about its physical destruction in whole or in part".

"Clothing was generally limited to a ration of one to three outfits per year, with one pair of shoes a year on the average. Presumably, it was difficult to launder the clothes if one had only one outfit that was likely worn, especially in the winter months, for twenty-four hours a day. (...) Childbearing during slavery became a prominent issue with the official end of the African slave trade in 1808. The fertility of Black women, who were referred to by slaveholders as breeders, was crucial to the economy of the United States, as its growth was based on slave labor. Black women were subjected to every type of sexual abuse imaginable. They were expected to be sexually available to the master, his friends and relatives, or Black male 'studs' assigned to impregnate them regardless of whether they had a relationship or not. This was at the discretion of the owners, some of whom allowed their Black slaves some semblance of marriage and family. These owners were the exception, however. High rates of maternal and infant mortality reflected the overwork and poor nutrition of enslaved pregnant women, who often worked on the fields up until delivery and returned to work shortly afterward. This allowed very little time for breast-feeding. In addition, midwives attending deliveries were poorly trained. Once purchased by a slaveholder, enslaved Black people could be used for any purpose their owners saw fit, including, in the case of some white science researchers, for experimentation. J. Marion Sims, M.D. (1813-1883), considered the Father of Gynaecology in medical schools throughout the United States, purchased Black female slaves to perform experimental operations on them or to use them for teaching purposes. During presumed didactic sessions, he exposed their genitals to the public. He admitted to operating on one slave woman thirty agonizing times before achieving the results he desired. Sims performed surgical procedures on these women without using anaesthesia, as, purportedly, Black people did not feel pain."[719]

From these few examples and many more presented throughout this work, one comprehends without difficulty that the material conditions of the legal definition of genocide are fulfilled. Yet, what is often considered problematic with regard to transatlantic slavery are less the material conditions of committed acts, but the mental aspect also required by the legal definition. The dominant opinion denies the qualification of transatlantic slavery as genocide on the grounds that the intent to exterminate a group would not have been given. The legally required mental aspect of genocide is composed of two elements, knowledge and intent. With regard to knowledge, the Rome Statute of the International Criminal Court

---

719 Crawford/Nobles/DeGruy Leary (2003), 255 et seq.

defines it as "awareness that a circumstance exists or a consequence will occur in the ordinary course of events" (Art 30); this definitional element is also rather unproblematic with regard to transatlantic slavery, since the system of utmost brutalization and killings could not possibly have had any other outcome than the destruction of African society and particular African groups. Genocide is an organized and not a spontaneous crime. It must typically be planned or organized by a state or by a clique associated with it, all of which was the case in transatlantic slavery. In this context the International Criminal Tribunal for Ex-Yugoslavia spoke of a "project" or "plan" to be given on the part of a perpetrator. The International Criminal Tribunal for Rwanda stated that crimes had to be "widespread and systematic", defining systematic as involving "some kind of preconceived plan or policy". In the case of transatlantic slavery, there was a plan that arguably not only accepted but indeed calculated the death of millions and millions of Africans for profits. And millions and millions actually did die.

Because our case concerns the realm of state responsibility and not individual criminal liability, it suffices to demonstrate that systematic policy, with the aim to destroy the target groups, in that case African societies, existed. "Individual offenders need not participate in devising of the plan. If they commit acts of genocide with knowledge of the plan, then the requirements of the Convention are met."[720] As the International Criminal Tribunal for Ex-Yugoslavia stated, "it would not be necessary to establish that the accused knew that his actions were inhumane"[721]. It has been assessed that "it may also be sufficient for the prosecution to demonstrate that the accused was reckless as to the consequences (...)"[722].

Yet, even if it is not necessary that individual perpetrators had full knowledge of the consequences of their actions, the required intent "to destroy, in whole or in part" a group when committing such acts, remains the critical point in the qualification of transatlantic slavery as genocide. The rest of this section will therefore be dedicated to illuminate this aspect.

When doubt remained as to whether a special intention to exterminate was given in a specific case, as required by the definition of genocide, courts usually judged inhuman acts as crimes against humanity rather than genocide and the acts remain reprimanded as such. Thus, Eichmann was acquitted of genocide for acts prior to August 1941, when the "final solution" emerged.[723] In any case, the atrocities remain illegal and entail the responsibility of the perpetrators.

According to the International Law Commission, the "intention to destroy the group 'as such'" means to destroy it "as a separate and distinct entity, and not merely some individuals because of their membership in a particular group"[724].

720   Schabas (2000), 206 et seq.
721   Prosecutor v. Dusko Tadic, ICTY, Appeals Chamber, Decision on the Defence Motion for Interlocutory Appeal onJurisdiction of 2October 1995, Case No.IT-94-1, 656-57.
722   Schabas (2000), 206 et seq.
723   Ibid., 201f.
724   International Law Commission (1996). Report of the International Law Commission on the

Perpetrators must select victims on the basis of their group identity and aim at the destruction of the group as a group. There is no doubt that in transatlantic slavery, European private slavers and the governments that stood behind them and controlled and directed the crime, selected their victims based on the fact that they were Africans in general, and that they were members of specific African groups that slavers aimed at at one time or another. And indeed, it was only through the destruction of African society at large and specific groups of Africans as such that this massive enslavement was rendered possible. European states have displayed, and also put into their records, their intent to destroy in that regard.

It is true that at the beginning of transatlantic slavery, indentured European laborers also came to the colonies, yet the following occurrence exemplifies that European administrations even then introduced and maintained a racialized system that oppressed, brutalized and killed African people because of their Africaness, with grave implications for their right to life, individually and collectively.

In 1640, three indentured servants (sic!), one African and two Europeans fled from their servitude from Virginia to Maryland. They were caught and returned. The General Court decided on identical "crimes" that "the third being a negro named John Punch shall serve his master or his assigns for the time of his natural Life here or elsewhere", whereas the "white" servants only received an additional year of servitude[725], marking the first recorded legal distinction between Africans and Europeans in what would become the US.[726]

"While white indentured servants also were forced to work on plantations in the 1700s, racism was legally sanctioned in statuses prohibiting public beatings of white indentured servants. In 1705 the law stated: In addition to the prohibition against publicly whipping a naked white Christian servant, masters were admonished to find and provide for their servants wholesome and competent diet, clothing and lodging, by the discretion of the county court. In contrast, with regard to enslaved Africans: Masters were allowed to feed, clothe, and nurse their slaves in whatever manner they saw fit."[727]

The International Law Commission assessed in the Report on the Work of its Forty-Eighth Session in 1996 that "[i]t is the membership of the individual in a particular group rather than the identity of the individual that is the decisive criterion in determining the immediate victims of the crime of genocide. The group itself is the ultimate target or intended victim of this type of massive criminal conduct."[728]

Works of Its Forty-Eighth Session, U.N. GAOR, 51st Sess., Supplement No. 10 (A/51/10).

725   Winbush (2009), 17.
726   Ibid., 18.
727   Crawford/Nobles/DeGruy Leary (2003), 255.
728   Schabas (2000), 236.

It is sometimes contended that "those times were different", and that European slavers would not have known that Africans were full human beings. If not placed in the context of such a catastrophic crime, such contentions could be ridiculous at best. Inborn knowledge tells one imperatively that the next man is a human like oneself, no matter the skin color. Moreover, "slaves were useful to slave master precisely because they were men and women like him who could execute complex orders. (...)The baseline of this system of racial classification was simply pigmentation. (...) Not every black was a slave, but most blacks were, and on this assumption every black could be treated like a slave unless they could prove free status".[729]

Since slaves were a valuable asset, free Blacks in the colonies were not safe from kidnapping. Slave-hunters in the colonies specialized in tracking down Africans who generally did not have the protection of the society or its laws. "Africans were frequently picked up and claimed by Europeans on the basis of colour. (...) Colour made Africans targets for enslavement in Europe as in Africa; and the psychological effects of this control by whites over blacks cannot be overestimated. The process of dehumanising the African was thus well in practice by the eighteenth century."[730] The genocidal transatlantic slavery system worked against all Black people, even those not enslaved. Especially when they sought to bond with Maroons or other freedom-takers, they got to feel the full ferocity of this system.

"Even when Africans had found their freedom through various behaviours such as willingness to betray slave revolts [or] willingness to have sexual relations with overlords, (...) [f]reedom could be revoked any time the White authorities felt that the freed persons constituted a burden on White society, (...) or engaged in activities that the authoritarian State considered inimical to its interests. In 1731 the Jamaican legislature passed a law imposing loss of freedom on any free Black or free Coloured person who refused to serve in the militia against runaways. In 1754 the Viceroy of Mexico proclaimed that any freed Black person caught fraternizing with Maroons would lose his freedom. In 1769 Laurent Macé, a free Black of Haiti, convicted of giving shelter to two Maroons, was reduced once again to slavery, as was his wife, another free Black, in accordance with a colonial law of 1705. A French decree of 1802 reiterated the earlier law that free Blacks caught harboring runaways could lose their freedom, and that the same would happen to their families. Viewed from this standpoint, at no time were freed persons really free while living within White slave society."[731]

Baltimore legislated in 1832 that free Black people were to be subject in every respect to the same treatment and penalties as enslaved Africans, and could to be convicted of any offence of which enslaved persons could be found guilty. Among

---

729   Blackburn (1998), 14.
730   Harris (1992), 115.
731   Thompson (2006), 32 et seq.

the common restrictions imposed indiscriminately in most jurisdictions on free Blacks were testifying against "white" persons; carrying arms, except when recruited into the colonial militia to hunt Maroons; wearing certain kinds of clothing; sitting in certain parts of the church; frequenting certain areas; and engaging in certain kinds of employment. In all southern states of North America, Black people were required to carry passes at all times. In Florida, Georgia and other states they were also forced by law to have "white" persons as guardians. Failure to comply with these laws could lead to reduction to slavery. The list of such laws was very long. "Franklin declares that a large majority of free Blacks lived in daily dread of losing the little freedom they enjoyed. Jordan adds the White attitudes were based on the assumption that 'free Negroes were essentially more Negro than free'. (...) The ultimate in absurdity was a law passed in Arkansas in 1859 requiring all free Blacks and free Coloureds who chose to remain in the state for more than a year to select guardians who had to post bond guaranteeing not to allow them to act as free persons."[732]

Black people were prohibited from wearing jewellery, silk, or "any kind of fine clothing and bombazine" in most colonies.[733] "That's why 'some free persons actually decided to take to the bush, far away from all White settlements. Some of them even joined Maroon groups, as was the case with Manuel José Alves da Costa (...) in Brazil in the early nineteenth century". Similar occurrences are documented from Colombia and Jamaica, "because they desired freedom from [colonial] authority, domination and law".[734] This clearly testifies of the systematic persecution and destruction of Black people on a racial basis, indicating intent to destroy them as a group.

The International Criminal Tribunal for Rwanda sustained that genocidal intent can be inferred from physical acts, and specifically "their massive and/or systematic nature or their atrocity". "Other factors, such as the scale of atrocities committed, their general nature, in a region or a country, or furthermore, the fact of deliberately and systematically targeting victims on account of their membership of a particular group, while excluding the members of other groups, can enable the Chamber to infer the genodical intent of a particular act."[735]

Dolus eventualis, located at the low end of recklessness, is insufficient to qualify for the crime of genocide, but as recklessness moves closer to a virtual certainty, the knowledge requirement of the *mea rea* becomes fulfilled. The actions that European governments consistently took and condoned over centuries could, with utmost certainty, not have had any other outcome than the destruction of many

---

732   Ibid., 33 et seq.
733   Ibid., 34.
734   Ibid., 36 et seq.
735   The Prosecutor v. Jean-Paul Akayesu, Judgement of September 2, 1998, International Criminal Tribunal for Rwanda, Case No. ICTR-96-4-T; cited in Ibid., 222.

African groups and African society as such. Some African communities and states were actually wiped out through the violence of transatlantic enslavement, for which, as we shall see in the next chapter, European slaver states are legally responsible.

In the Akayesu judgement, the ICTR stated that genocidal intent "is a mental factor which is difficult, even impossible, to determine", and therefore sustained that "it is possible to deduce the genocidal intent inherent in a particular act charged from the general context of the perpetration of other culpable acts systematically directed against that same group, whether these acts were committed by the same offender or by others"[736]. In the case of transatlantic slavery, in which the genocidal facts mount back up to 400 years, it is even more difficult to determine genocidal intent on part of the responsible heads of states and individual perpetrators. Thus, the loosened evidence requirement concerning intent that was employed in the Akayesu judgement must also be utilized in the legal assessment of transatlantic slavery. And since the countless acts that fulfil the material requirements of genocide were clearly systematic, it must be qualified as genocide.

Both apartheid and the mass removal and killings of the Herero by colonial Germany are generally considered genocide. Yet, very similar criminal acts were also committed during transatlantic slavery, where whole villages and groups were exterminated and wiped out. This is taken note of in a UNESCO report, where the necessity for more pertinent research to assess the details and amplitude of such extinction was highlighted.[737] The succession of criminal and genocidal conduct also exemplifies the continued character of the violation of law that transatlantic slavery, colonialism and apartheid constitute in the overall crime of the Maafa.

Before the late 18th century, most enslavers felt that it was cheaper to buy than to "breed" working hands, so mothers and pregnant women were allowed little or no special attention.

"Pregnant women were often worked in the fields up to the last day or two before the expected date of childbirth, and were sent back into the fields shortly after delivery. When they were whipped, their distended bellies were placed in a special hole in the ground. Stedman recorded an almost unbelievable instance of brutality in Suriname on a woman who had broken a crystal tumbler. Although she was eight months pregnant, her overlord caused her to be whipped until her intestines protruded through her body. Many miscarriages occurred because pregnant women were whipped severely, placed in stocks, kicked in their bellies and subjected to other brutalities."[738]

---

736 The Prosecutor v. Jean-Paul Akayesu, Judgement of September 2, 1998, International Criminal Tribunal for Rwanda, Case No. ICTR-96-4-T.
737 United Nations Educational, Scientific and Cultural Organization (ed.) (1978). Meeting of Experts on the African Slave-Trade, Final Report, Port-au-Prince, Haiti, 31 January-4 February 1978, downloaded fromhttp://unesdoc.unesco.org/images/0003/000333/033360eb.pdf (accessed 21.6.2012).
738 Thompson (2006), 95.

Generally speaking, "the black slaves of the Americas were also often denied conditions for raising children, their owners sometimes deeming it cheaper to replenish their crews by buying slaves from the traders rather than by encouraging their slaves to bring up children."[739]

One Pruneau de Pommegorge who was an employee of the *Compagnie des Indes* on the African West Coast, related how one day he went to a trader where several captives were presented to him, among them a woman of about 24 years who looked immensely sad. "I insisted to say that she had a child. Impatient with my interjecting, he told me that this should not keep me from buying the woman, because her child would be thrown to the wolves in the evening." Pommegorge then bought the woman with the child, but noted that "since this crime is repeated almost every day, I felt obliged to abstain from going to the traders because my wealth would not be sufficient for such good deeds".[740]

Babies often had to be taken to the field, so that no working time would be wasted with going back and forth for nursing, and were put into a long trough instead of a cradle. "Yet sometimes it is recorded that heavy rain fell, yet no one was allowed to care for the babies and by the time they reached there all of them were drowned and dead."[741]

During the Middle Passage, not only the sick but also the new-borns were often thrown overboard because they were particularly weak and prone to sickness and their lives were economically worthless to the slavers.[742]

In Brazil, for example, the rate of precocious child death was very high. Children who made it to adulthood were a rare exception. According to the archives, one out of ten children was an orphan before turning one. At five, half of the children were orphans. This kind of demographics is otherwise only found in communities ravaged by prolonged states of war or epidemics.[743]

With regard to the legal sense of "destroy", it has been specified in legal doctrine that it comprises the profound and violent altering in an organised manner of a people in a way that annihilates essential aspects and characteristics of the group. Not only did transatlantic slavery violently and intentionally destroy African societies, as elaborated on proceeding and following sections of the present work, but life conditions imposed on enslaved Africans in the Americas were so exhausting that they often were not able to reproduce. Thus, on the Fontezuela

---

739 Blackburn Robin (1996). "Slave exploitation and the elementary structures of enslavement", in Bush, M.L. (ed.): Serfdom and slavery: studies in legal bondage, New York: Longman, 158-180, 158.
740 de Pommegorge (1789), 210f (t.b.a.).
741 Brooks (2004), 31.
742 Ki-Zerbo (1978), 216.
743 Florentino, Manolo/de Goes, Jose Roberto (2002). 'L'enfance asservie: les esclaves du Brésil aux XVIIIe et XIXe siècles', in: Isabel Castro Henriques and Louis Sala-Molins (ed.): Déraison, esclavage et droit. Les fondements idéologiques et juridiques de la traite négrière et de l'esclavage, Paris: EDITIONS Unesco, 349- 363, 352.

plantation in Brazil, owned by the Betlemitas Order, only eight babies were born in fifty years, six of whom died before their first birthday.[744]

Extreme cynics may still sustain that such actions were not committed with the intention to destroy Africans, or groups of Africans, as such. Yet, it seems incontestable that, even if the perpetrators, states and private enslavers had a will to keep some Africans as a group of labor chattel, their systematic acts of ferocity testify of an intention to destroy them as a human group culturally, socially and also physically.

Hans Sloane, author of a renowned book on the natural history of Jamaica reported that slaves were permanently underfed to the extent that they perished.

"[T]heir owners, from a desire of making the greatest gain by the labour of their slaves, lay heavy burdens on them, and yet feed and clothe them very sparingly, and some scarce feed and clothe them at all. (...) In Jamaica, if six in ten of the new imported Negroes survive the seasoning, it is looked upon as a gaining purchase. And in most of the other plantations, if the Negroes live eight or nine years, their labour is reckoned a sufficient compensation for their cost. (...) It is a dreadful consideration, as a late author remarks, that out of the stock of eighty thousand negroes in Barbados, there die every year five thousand more than are born in that island; which failure is probably in the same proportion in other islands. In effect, this people is under a necessity of being entirely renewed every sixteen years."[745] (emphasis added)

Such policy, which was systematic in transatlantic slavery, shows that the destruction of Africans as a group, or of part of that group, was not only accepted but was calculated with cold and utilitarian logic. Many died because they fell into the boiling sugar cane or came between the millstones. The occurrence of such accidents was expedited by the fact that slaves generally only got about three to four hours of sleep a day. It is generally agreed among historians that field slaves on sugar plantations in the Americas lived only between five and ten years from when they were forced to begin to labor.[746]

Sloane further recollected the treatment that he witnessed Africans to suffer.

"For rebellion, the punishment is burning them, by nailing them down to the ground with crooked sticks on every limb, and then applying the fire, by degrees, from the feet and hands, burning them gradually up to the head, whereby their pains are extravagant. For crimes of a less nature, gelding or chopping off half the foot with an axe. – For negligence, they are usually whipped by the overseers with lance-wood switches. – After they are whipped till they are raw, some put on their skins pepper and salt, to make them smart; at other times, their masters

---

744   Benezet (1767). 97.

745   Ibid., 44.

746   Coco (2005), 55et seq; see also Ki-Zerbo (1978), 216.

will drop melted wax on their skins, and use several very exquisite torments."[747]

The fact that enslaved Africans who participated in rebellions received the harshest and most brutal punishments is hardly surprising, yet it abets the claim that transatlantic slavery was genocide since it was through rebellions that Africans affirmed themselves as a group and were intentionally and ferociously killed and brutalized for this precise reason. Yet still, many of those who joined the Maroons calculated that they were likely to live longer than as plantation slaves, even though Maroons lived in a permanent state of war with the colonists in most areas of the transatlantic system. One Sebastião Ferreira Soares wrote in 1860 that he had been informed that a planter had calculated that of every one hundred slaves introduced into the plantation system, only about twenty-five were likely to be alive at the end of three years. In contrast, Louis, a captive from the Maroon settlement André in French Guiana testified in 1748 that none of André's inhabitants had died in the previous two years.[748]

The intent requirement is also fulfilled if it extends only to the destruction of a part of a victim group. Taking account of the historical facts, there can remain no serious doubt that European enslaver states disposed of such intent with regard to the Maroons, the communities of self-liberated Africans who had succeeded to escape from the plantations and reconstituted their communities from elements of their African home-societies. It is crucial in that context to fully comprehend that Maroons were determined to uphold their identity as Africans, and that it was also because of this determination that the colonial states persecuted them with such utmost ferocity. They thereby testified their intent to destroy the Maroon part of African society precisely because of their unrelenting free Africaness, which was incompatible with the slave status that European slavers aimed to impose on all Black people.

Colonial powers trained dogs to lacerate Black people. One example of this is documented from mid-16th century Panama, where the Spanish loosened dogs on a group of Maroons who had refused to give up their spirituality and accept conversion to Catholicism. The dogs had been trained to tear at the flesh of Black people. The Maroons had only thin rods to defend themselves with. "[T]hat in fact enraged the animals only further, who sank their teeth in the flesh of their victims and tore large pieces of flesh."[749] The following description of this kind of dog training effectuated in Haiti is more than shocking:

"As they approached maturity, their keepers procured a figure roughly formed as a Negro in wicker work, in the body of which were contained the blood and entrails of beasts. This was exhibited before an upper part of the cage, and the

---

747   Benezet (1767). 43.
748   Thompson (2006), 45f; see also Ki-Zerbo (1978), 222.
749   Thompson. (2006), 152 et seq.

food occasionally exposed as a temptation, which attracted the attention of the dogs to it as a source of the food they wanted. This was repeated so often, so that the animals with redoubled ferocity struggled against their confinement while in proportion to their impatience the figure was brought nearer, though yet out of their reach, and their food decreased till, at the last extremity of desperation, the keeper resigned the figure, well charged with the nauseous food before described, to their wishes. While they gorged themselves with the dreadful meat, he and his colleagues caressed and encouraged them. By these means the whites ingratiated themselves so much with the animals, as to produce an effect directly opposite to that perceivable in them towards the black figure; and, when they were employed in the pursuit for which they were intended, afforded the protection so necessary to their employers."[750]

Such dogs were used by state-operated militia sent out against Maroons and freedom-takers. They were trained to kill Black people only in the most bestial manner.

When Amsterdam, leader of a Maroon settlement in Demerara, was captured in 1795 "[h]e was sentenced to be burnt alive, first having the flesh torn from his limbs with red-hot pincers; and in order to render his punishment still more terrible, he was compelled to sit by, and see thirteen others broken and hung; and then, in being conducted to execution, was made to walk over the thirteen dead bodies of his comrades. Being fastened to an iron-stake, surrounded with the con-suming pile, which was about to be illuminated, he regarded bystanders with all the complacency of heroic fortitude, and exhibiting the most unyielding courage, resolved that all the torture ingenuity or cruelty might invent should not extort from him a single groan."[751]

In 1749, a captured Maroon couple was executed publicly in Cayenne, "French" Guiana. "Copena is sentenced to having his arms, legs, thighs, and back broken on a scaffold to be erected in the Place du Port. He shall then be placed on a wheel, face toward the sky, to finish his days, and his corpse shall be exposed. Claire, con-victed of the crime of maroonage and of complicity with maroon Negroes, shall be hanged till dead at the gallows in the Place du Port. Her two young children Paul and Pascal, belonging to M. Coutard, and other children – Francois and Batilde, Martin and Baptiste – all accused of maroonage, are condemned to witness the torture of Copena and Claire."[752] The genocidal plantation system not only kept the enslaved adults in check by the omnipresent reality of bestial punishment for captured freedom-takers and the constant threat it implied for every enslaved African, but also by keeping of the same threat for the children of those who dared to break free. "Captured women with small children ran the risk of seeing

---

750   Ibid., 152 et seq.
751   Ibid., 170.
752   Ibid., 168.

heavy chains being placed around the necks or feet of their infants, some only six years old, which weighed them down and, in the view of one government official, always left severe bruising." In 1832 Xavier Tanc, a magistrate in Guadeloupe observed "a little girl about six years old dragging this heavy and irksome burden with torment as if the crime (...) of the mother was justification for punishing this young child in such barbarous manner. At that age, her fragile frame and delicate flesh were all battered."[753]

This continued policy against the Maroons, one portion of deported Africans and their descendants, clearly aimed at exterminating them and at the same time pursued to turn the rest of captured Africans into "slaves" while violently stripping them of their African identity, and particular African group identities. This policy testifies of the intent to destroy Africans as such, and particular groups of Africans, the Maroons.

Another tragic example that illustrates well the intent to destroy can be found throughout the history of Haiti since transatlantic slavery was introduced there. In 1801, in the middle of the Haitian Revolution by which the enslaved Africans had started to liberate themselves in 1791, Napoleon Bonaparte stated in an order to his foreign minister that "[m]y decision to destroy the authority of Haiti is not so much based on considerations of commerce and money, as on the need to block forever the march of blacks in the world"[754]. Although money was without question a considerable factor for the continued "interest" of France in that island, since the French economy depended to a large degree on its sugar colonies and Haiti was its "jewel" in that regard, this statement in combination with the factual actions of European slaver nations, abets the qualification of transatlantic slavery as genocide.

The united experts of a UNESCO conference concluded that the "premise of the 'superiority' of the white man, which was 'demonstrated' by his economic success, proved the 'inferiority' of the Blackman, which was 'demonstrated' by the fact of his capture and enslavement. The Blacks were made to feel radically inferior in their dependent situation, thus breaking the individual and collective capacity to put up any resistance. They were only able to regain that capacity when they had faith in the values of their own society, values which the enslavement process sought to make them forget as rapidly and completely as possible"[755]. The Haitian revolution departed from the spiritual practice of voodoo and relied on the strength of this and other African cultural practices for its eventual success.

Yet after the accomplished revolution, Haiti was forced by France to pay an

---

753   Ibid., 168.
754   Ifa, Kamau Cush (2010).A tale of two countries, in: New African No. 499, London: IC Publications, 26-27, 26.
755   United Nations Educational, Scientific and Cultural Organization (ed.) (1978).Meeting of Experts on the African Slave-Trade, Final Report, Port-au-Prince, Haiti, 31 January-4 February 1978, downloaded fromhttp://unesdoc.unesco.org/images/0003/000333/033360eb.pdf (accessed 21.6.2012).

extra-ordinarily large amount of money in order to remain free from aggression. This will be dealt with in detail in the next chapter. Hilary Beckles, pro-vice-chancellor of the University of the West Indies, sustained in that respect that

"[t]he French government bled the nation and rendered it a failed State. It was a merciless exploitation that was designed and guaranteed to collapse the Haitian economy and society. Haiti was forced to pay this sum until 1922 when the last instalment was made. During the long 19th century, the payment to France amounted to up to 70 per cent of the country's foreign exchange earnings. Haiti was crushed by this debt payment. It descended into financial and social chaos. Haitian governments borrowed on the French money market at double the going interest rate in order to repay the French government. When the Americans invaded the country in the early 20th century, one of the reasons offered was to assist the French in collecting its reparations. Haiti did not fail. It was destroyed by two of the most powerful nations on earth, both of which continue to have a primary interest in its current condition. The value of this amount was estimated by financial actuaries as US$21 billion. This sum of capital could rebuild Haiti and place it in a position to re-engage the modern world. It was illegally extracted from the Haitian people and should be repaid."[756]

In 2003, Haiti's President Jean-Bertrand Aristide announced the findings of a restitution commission that had been formed by his government and that had determined that France owed Haiti $21 billion, the current dollars value of the money France had extorted from Haiti. "On October 12, 2003, the President convened a four-day international conference of experts (...) to further discuss Haiti's restitution claim against France for repayment of the debt. Among the participants were French historian, human rights commissioner, and author of The Crime of Napoleon, Claube Ribbe, and Tulane law school professor Gunther Handl, a respected authority on international law. (...) One month after the conference, in December 2003, French foreign minister Dominique de Villepin sent his sister to Port-au-Prince to tell Jean-Bertrand Aristide, the democratically elected president, that it was time for him to step down."[757] Yet, the same Villepin, at that time Minister of Foreign Affairs, had declared in a speech years earlier that "[i]nternational criminal justice is not a recent phenomenon, as is shown by the tribunal set up in 1474 to try Peter de Hagenbach, the Duke of Burgundy's governor (...)"[758], and at another occasion before the International Law Academy in The Hague that the "aim (...) is no longer for the victors to sit in judgement on the vanquished, but to enforce a principle: those guilty of crimes that shock the conscience of humanity must be aware that sooner or later they will answer for their actions. This is a moral

---

756   Beckles, Sir Hilary (2010).Haiti destroyed by design, downloaded from http://rastareason.word-press.com/tag/sir-hilary-beckles (accessed 3.2.2010).
757   Ibid.
758   Visit to the Netherlands - Speech by M. Dominique de Villepin to the International Law Academy, The Hague 11.03.2004, downloaded from http://www.ambafrance-uk.org/Visit-to-the-Netherlands-Speech-by.html (accessed 7.3.2010).

requirement, which alone can restore the victims to their full humanity."[759] Thus, the question poses itself if we are dealing with a case of serious schizophrenia or of deeply embedded anti-African racism here.

If European powers, and especially France, had not wrecked Haiti so much over the centuries, the infrastructure and material housing conditions of that country would have been much more stable during the 2010 earthquake, and much less than 200,000 people would most probably have died. At one of the sittings of the Jamaica Reparations Commission to which I was invited and which took place shortly after the earthquake, the then Mayor of May Pen M. Brown said that the extent of the catastrophe in Haiti at that moment was definitely linked to slavery.[760]

The fact that France called its illegal kidnapping of President Aristide in order to prevent him from claiming reparations, *Opération Bonaparte-Opération Rochambeau*[761] – after their former Head of State who uttered the just mentioned hateful statement against Black people and his butcher general Rochambeau who had sustained that France should "destroy at least 30,000 negroes"[762] and under whose commands the most barbaric atrocities were realized–further abets the claim that we are really dealing with a still continuing violation of law, that is the Maafa, of which transatlantic slavery was indeed only one stage and component and which is charaterized by genocide.

Generally, it is important to point out concerning the legal requirement of intending the "whole or partial destruction of a protected group" that to be able to maintain transatlantic slavery over more than 400 years, it was intrinsically necessary to destroy Africans as a group, and particular groups of Africans. European enslaver states were well aware of this, and pursued it as policy, as will be elaborated in detail in the section about the gun-slave-cycle in the next chapter. It simply would not have been possible to maintain this cycle of violence without assaults directed at African group identities and the existence of groups of Africans as such.

It was also in and through the laws and legal orders passed by European enslaver nations that the genocidal character of transatlantic slavery manifested, since they denied the humanity of Africans.

The law that became known as *Police des noirs*, promulgated by Louis XV, aimed at keeping Black people out of France (that is, except those detained in slave ship

---

759   Ibid.
760   JamaicaNational Commission on Reparations, May Pen Sitting, 25.9.2009.
761   Haïti, les récentes Opération "Bonaparte", Opération "Rochambeau". Ou quand la France insiste pour se venger, downloaded from http://www.bworldconnection.tv/index.php/Articles/Caraibe/Haiumlti-les-reacutecentes-Opeacuteration-quotBonapartequot-Opeacuteration-quotRochambeau-quot.-Ou-quand-la-France-insiste-pour-se-venger.html (accessed 24.5.2012); see also other documents on file with author.
762   James (1938), 360.

dungeons at the ports of Nantes, Bordeaux, etc., from whose lives France made huge revenues). The next-to-last provision of that law's proposal spelled out its ultimate aim, that is, "in the end, the race of negroes will be extinguished in the kingdom as soon as the transport of them is forbidden". Noting that it was impossible to prevent African people from marrying one another and reproducing, a French commissioner suggested that, "one can render the act of marriage difficult, without ever invoking the power of the king to render them null (...) by these difficulties they will be extinguished".[763]

The legislated denial of the humanity of the victims as a group in codices such as this one bears evidence to the intent to destroy the victim group as required by the legal definition of genocide. That legislated and codified denial of humanity to African people is one of the exclusivities of transatlantic slavery that has no precedent in history and is one of the features that also distinguishes it from Arab slavery.[764]

In the racialized context of transatlantic slavery, it was not only "the number of victims (...) that determines (...) genocide than what ultimately gives rise to the casualties, namely the fact of denying (...) the human status", such as it happened in the *Code Noir* (1685) or the *Codigo negro carolino* (1784). "It is in the very existence and content of such legislation that the genocidal character of slavery is clearly evident. (...) Legislation on [transatlantic] slavery contains in itself what determines genocide: namely, the way and will to deny another's humanity"[765]. The negation of the humanity of a victim group, implying the intent to destroy it, is at the very core of the crime of genocide, and exactly what the European enslaver states explicitly provided for in their laws and sustained in their policies.[766] Thus, an official communication dating from 1522 uses the term "peça" (piece) for slave. "There was found dead a piece which had died of corromica and which belonged to our lord the King; it was cast into the sea (...)."[767]

Beyond legislation and as shown already to some extent above, the practice of transatlantic slavery also drastically testified of a specific intent to destroy Africans for profits on part of European slavers and states. Even if the prime motivation may not have been to destroy African peoples as an end in itself, their destruction, or the destruction of part of African society and particular African groups in their entirety, was calculated and intended in order to generate economic profits. The underlying principle was that African slave labor had to be obtained by any means and at the lowest cost possible, irrelevant of the con-

---

763   Peabody (1996), 117.
764   Plumelle-Uribe (2008), 115 et seq.
765   Somé, Roger (2001). "Slavery, Genocide or Holocaust?" in: Doudou Diène (ed.): From Chains to Bonds. The Slave Trade Revisited, Paris: Unesco/Berghahn Books, 416-430, 418.
766   Jos (2000), 144.
767   Fragments of the ship's book of the Sao Miguel trading to Benin in the year 1522 (A.T.T. Corpo Cronológico II, maço 149, no.29)

sequences for Africans, individually and collectively. Yet, beyond that economic motive that underlied the systematic policy of European enslaver states, it is clear from the abundant evidence of utmost brutality that transatlantic slavery could only take place in that ferocious way in which it was operated because the enslavers, both individually and collectively, also disposed of hateful intent towards Africans as such.

In essence, "[t]he organizers and planners must necessarily have a racist or discriminatory motive, that is, a genocidal motive, taken as a whole. Where this is lacking, the crime cannot be genocide. Evidence of hateful motive will constitute an integral part of the proof of existence of a genocidal plan, and therefore of a genocidal intent. At the same time, individual participants may be motivated by a range of factors, including financial gain, jealousy and political ambition. (...) In conclusion, it should be necessary for the prosecution to establish that genocide, taken in its collective dimension, was committed 'on the grounds of nationality, race, ethnicity, or religion'. The crime must, in other words, be motivated by hatred of the group."[768] The documented facts of transatlantic slavery speak for themselves. If it would not have been for the hatred of African people as such, it is unconceivable that it would have been possible to brutalize and murder them to this extent over centuries. That individual participants, be they kings, merchants or plantation owners, were additionally motivated in their intent to destroy Africans by financial gain does not hinder the legal qualification as genocide.

C. "INTENT TO DESTROY" – REVISITED FROM A LEGAL HISTORICAL PERSPECTIVE

Not only with regard to transatlantic slavery and the Maafa, but in general terms it is highly problematic if, without *proof* of a specific intent to destroy a group just for the sake of destroying it, "accepting" large numbers of deaths of members of a targeted group is considered as not fulfilling the international legal definition of genocide on grounds that it would not specifically aim at destroying the group as such. In reality, in each and every genocide do the perpetrators have an underlying motive – as insane and illogical as it might be – for persecuting members of their target group that goes beyond wanting to exterminate just for the sake of exterminating as such. Even the Nazi arguably aimed at exterminating the Jews because of economic envy and to pursue their delusion of "cleaning" the "German race". In the case of transatlantic slavery, Africans were indiscriminately and intentionally killed or purposefully exposed to life-threatening situations because of their Africaness, even if the underlying motive was also economic. The massive enslavement was indeed only possible through the intentional destruction of African group identity and culture, accompanied by mass killings and

---

768   Schabas (2000), 253 et seq.

enslavement. The currently dominant requirement standard for intent as the aim to destroy a group qua group is highly problematic, for in practically all cases of genocide is it possible to argue that the perpetrators followed a motive above the simple desire to destroy a group as such. "Although members of one of Cambodia's ethnic groups, the Muslim Chams, were particularly targeted by the terror, the fact that the campaign was committed in the name of communist ideology makes it difficult to fit this destruction within the model of a purpose to destroy a group qua group. Similarly, between 1962 and 1972 as many as fifty per cent of Paraguay's Northern Aché Indians were killed as part of an effort to free Aché territory for economic development. When asked about these events, the Paraguayan Defense Minister admitted the attacks but denied that the requisite genocidal intent existed since the purpose of the campaign was to further economic development (...)."[769] Indeed, if the intent requirement is interpreted as narrowly as to cover only situations where the perpetrator had no other motive than a completely abstract hatred – and hatred is hardly ever totally abstract – for the victim group, then it might even be possible to "exonerate Hitler on the grounds that his purpose was the pursuit, for example, of 'German purity' [and economic grudge] and that the destruction of Jews was merely a means to this end"[770].

The approach of the International Law Commission that the specific intent to genocide requires more than discriminatory selection accompanied by knowledge of the consequences of those actions, but that "the intention must be to destroy the group ... as a separate and distinct entity, and not merely some individuals because of their membership in a particular group"[771], covering all situations that fall between these limits, might help to resolve this problem. Such an approach also covers transatlantic slavery where the attainment of the underlying motive of economic greed was only possible through the purposeful destruction of particular African groups and African society as such.

The inclusion of the wording "in part" in the text of the Genocide Convention clearly expresses that genocide can take place when the relevant intent extends only to the destruction of some but not to all of a certain group.[772] This conception was further substantiated by the UN's International Law Commission when it sustained that it "is not necessary to intend to achieve the complete annihilation of a group from every corner of the globe. Nonetheless, the crime of genocide by its very nature requires the intention to destroy at least a substantial part of a particular group"[773]. However, any intent that does not aim at the complete

---

769   Greenawalt, Alexander K.A. (1999). Rethinking Genocidal Intent: The Case for a Knowledge-Based Interpretation, in: Columbia Law Review, Vol. 99, 2258-2294, 2285.
770   Ibid., 2286.
771   International Law Commission (1996). Report of the International Law Commission on the Works of Its Forty-Eighth Session, UN GAOR, 51st Sess., Supplement No. 10 (A/51/10).
772   Greenawalt (1999), 2259.
773   International Law Commission (1996). Report of the International Law Commission on the

destruction of a group but is limited to the destruction of parts of a group must logically incorporate another motive that goes beyond the aim to destroy a group qua group. If intent to destroy is based only on abstract hate, without any other underlying motive, it *must* logically extend to the destruction of the target group from every corner of the globe. The text of the Genocide Convention itself therefore unambiguously includes situations where a motive other than abstract hatred, such as economic greed, joins in the intent. Such a motive going beyond the intention to destroy for the sake of destroying as such can be the only logical reason why only specific segments of a group are targeted.

Historically, the international legal reprehension of atrocities and crimes against humanity reposed to a large extent on individual criminal responsibility (see, for example, the Hagenbach tribunal). Thus, as argued by Greenawalt, "the word 'intent' [should be read] in light of traditional criminal law doctrine and the drafting history of the Convention"[774]. Now, according to "traditional common-law doctrine, criminal perpetrators intended the consequences of their actions if they knew to a practical certainty what the consequences of those actions would be, regardless of whether or not they deliberately sought to realize those consequences"[775]. Since the crime of transatlantic slavery and the continuing violation of the Maafa extended over such a long period, transitions between the precise requirements of the concrete details of the legal prohibitions of the ferocious conduct are blurred and difficult to reconstruct. Given the looser bar of criminal intent that appears to have been legal standard for individual criminal responsibility in the times of transatlantic slavery, the strict *mens rea* requirement of today may not necessarily be the one that has to be applied in this case.

The argument for a looser standard of intent, covering also situations of an underlying motive and not just of destructing a group qua group because of abstract hatred, is further abetted by the debates that preceded the adoption of the Genocide Convention. It is uncontested that the prohibition of the crime of genocide goes back to long before the adoption of the Convention, yet these debates clearly indicate that the intent requirement had not always been as strict as after the adoption of the Convention. Therefore, the strict requirement of intent does not necessarily apply to situations that began before the adoption, even though the prohibition of genocide itself does. Thus, Art. 1 of the UN Secretariat's draft for the Genocide Convention had defined genocide as a "criminal act directed against any one of the aforesaid groups of human beings [racial, national, linguistic, religious, or political] with the purpose of destroying it in whole or in part, or of preventing its preservation or development"[776]. The legal principles that

---

Works of Its Forty-Eighth Session, UN GAOR, 51st Sess., Supplement No. 10 (A/51/10).

774   Greenawalt (1999), 2289.

775   Ibid., 2266.

776   UN ESCOR (1947). Draft Convention on the Crime of Genocide, UN ESCOR, 5th Session, UN

antedate the Convention thus even covered the intent to prevent the preservation or development of a group, an intent that was undoubtedly present on parts of European state perpetrators throughout transatlantic slavery. Maktos, Chairman of the Ad Hoc Committee on Genocide to the Economic and Social Council and representative of the USA in preparation of the Genocide Convention, proposed a loose standard of intent and argued that "political groups, for instance might be eliminated on economic grounds", that such situations might be genocide and should not be categorically eliminated from the reach of the Convention.[777]

At the beginning of the process that expatiated the term "genocide" during and after WW II and that finally culminated in the Genocide Convention, Lemkin wrote that "the world represents only so much culture and intellectual vigor as are created by its component national groups. Essentially the idea of a nation signifies constructive cooperation and original contributions, based upon genuine traditions, genuine culture, and a well-developed national psychology. The destruction of a nation, therefore, results in the loss of its future contributions to the world"[778]. This conception was echoed by the General Assembly in the preamble of Resolution (96) where it is spoken of the "great losses to humanity in the form of cultural and other contributions" wrought by the "denial of the right of existence of entire human groups" and also stated that "many instances of such crimes have occurred when racial, religious, political and other groups have been destroyed, entirely or in part"[779]. No doubt, this is what happened on a gigantic scale through transatlantic slavery where enormous cultural contributions by African societies were destroyed and lost, as were many African groups themselves, through the denial of the right to existence of African groups by European enslavers and their African collaborators. Furthermore, according to Article 31 of the Vienna Convention on the Law of Treaties, the principal rule of interpretation of international treaties – and the Genocide Convention is one – is "the ordinary meaning given to the terms of the treaty in their context and in the light of its object and purpose"[780]. This suggests that in the case of transatlantic slavery a direct and retroactive application of the text of the Genocide Convention may be appropriate.

Throughout this work and especially in the upcoming next chapter it is unambiguously shown that the genocidal conditions imposed on Africans during the Middle Passage and the entire process of dehumanization taking place in the Americas reposed on the sole moral and legal responsibility of the European pow-

---

Doc E/447.
777   Greenawalt (1999), 2276.
778   Lemkin (1944), 91.
779   UN General Assembly (1946). Resolution 96 (I), UN Doc. A/63/Add.1.
780   United Nations, Vienna Convention on the Law of Treaties, 23 May 1969, United Nations, Treaty Series, Vol. 1155, 331.

ers.[781] Descendants of enslaved Africans who still suffer today from the legacy of transatlantic slavery, resulting in a situation of global apartheid, claim genocide as a basis for their reparation claims, such as resorts from a letter by the "All Mansion's Secretariat of the Ethiopian Peace Foundation, Jamaica Branch, International Rastafari Community" to "Her Royal Majesty Queen Elizabeth II" via the Deputy British High Commissioner, dating of 15 January 2003, in which they qualify the primary international violation committed during the period of racial commercial chattel slavery as genocide.

Before we go on to discuss attribution of legal responsibility to states for the illegal and genocidal conduct that constituted transatlantic slavery, it should be pointed out that in *Barcelona Traction* the International Court of Justice made an "essential distinction between the obligations of a State towards the international community as a whole, and those arising vis-à-vis another State in the field of diplomatic protection. By their very nature the former are the concern of all States. In view of the importance of the rights involved, all States can be held to have a legal interest in their protection; they are obligations erga omnes." Among these, the Court cited "the outlawing acts of aggression, and of genocide" and "the principles and rules concerning the basic rights of the human persons, including protection from slavery and racial discrimination"[782]. Thus, every state could today take up the legal claim for responsibility and reparations for transatlantic slavery.

In view of the historical and present-day facts and their legal qualification as genocide, the international community must urgently engage legal mechanisms to deal with the contemporary global situation, resulting from what was arguably the greatest genocide ever and which continues to produce fatal consequences for the descendants of the original victims. However and considerate of the discussions leading up to the passing of the Genocide Convention, it would not seem to be far-fetched to think that nowadays the requirement of intent is kept at such a restrictive and rigid level because Western European lifestyle in essence is genocide, and the broadening of intent to include situations where the destruction of groups of people is calculated for economic profits would open the gate for a flood of claims of genocide against western enterprises and politicians. Western European lifestyle is only maintainable because massive exploitation is outsourced to Congo or Bangladesh, for example, so that Europeans and North Americans can shop for a new mobile phone and a stylish wardrobe every season. It also means the destruction and death of thousands and indeed millions of people who get poisoned and drained by systematic practice. Western governments, authorities and multinational enterprises know this and intentionally uphold this system with their policies, in the name of capitalism and profits. Yet, a legally more appropriate standard of intent, such as sustained during the preparation of the Genocide

---

781   Plumelle-Uribe (2008), 117 et seq.
782   Barcelona Traction, Light and Power Company, Limited, Second Phase (Belgium v. Spain), Judgement of 5 February 1970, ICJ reports 1970, 3, para.33.

Convention, might cover such situations and make them legally reprehensible as genocide.

IV. International Legal Responsibility for Transatlantic Slavery

"Twenty-two people were sleeping. I herded them as if they had been cattle towards the boats" - Diego Gomes, knight, magistrate and envoy of Prince Henry of Spain, on the River Gambia [783]

"One day the white men arrived in ships with wings, which shone in the sun like knives. They fought hard battles with the Ngola [king] and spat fire at him. They conquered his saltpans and the Ngola fled inland to the Lukala River" - Pende oral tradition (Congo) [784]

European states insist that reparations are not due legally because genocidal transatlantic slavery would have been "legal", but we have seen so far that this was not at all the case and that transatlantic slavery was illegal from the beginning and remained so. The main argument of reparations opponents is thus pertinently deconstructed and the factually incorrect contention that this kind of slavery and genocide would have been legal can thus no longer be employed to deny African reparation claims. As an ancient legal maxim states, ignorance of the law does not constitute an excuse or defence for its violation.

Unfree labor was not illegal per se at that time, and neither is today as exemplified by the US prison industrial complex, but the fundamental and defining elements of transatlantic slavery were illegal at all times and constituted genocide. There is no statute of limitations in law for the crimes of murder, genocide and enslavement. The Rastafari movement, in a communication to the Queen of England, took reference to these particular conditions of transatlantic slavery as the basis of the claim for reparations: "They captured men, women and children from their various villages by force, then shackled them together and loaded them on to cargo ships. The conditions on board these ships were horrible and inhumane. The

---

783 Adibe, Patrick/Boateng, Osei (2000). Portugal, the mother of all slavers:Part 1, in: New African, March 2000, downloaded from http://findarticles.com/p/articles/mi_qa5391/is_200003/ai_n21452668/ (accessed 18.7.2011).
784 Ibid.

journey to the west took many months and lost many lives. We will not elaborate further as to the situation we were faced with, as we are all sure Her Majesty is knowledgeable of. (...) Governments today (must) take responsibility for what has happened over one hundred and fifty years ago and beyond; according to the demands of international morality and the evolution of international law"[785].

On the basis of having established that transatlantic slavery was illegal by the relevant law of its time, the following chapter traces whether legal responsibility can be attributed by international law to former enslaver states for their conduct in transatlantic slavery. Such a successful attribution of responsibility would put them into an obligation to make reparations. The establishment of legal responsibility is the essential precondition to anchor an obligation to make reparations in international law. Generally speaking, the term "international responsibility" covers the new legal relations which arise under international law by reason of the internationally wrongful act of a State."[786] Now, private slavers and European states realized transatlantic slavery through a multitude of illegal acts and conduct. To give a general impression of the different modalities of European state involvement, a brief historical account of some exemplary vertices of conduct seems expedient before proceeding to assess legal responsibility in a more concrete manner.

Transatlantic slavery, for all involved European nations, started as a royal enterprise. It all began with kidnapping free Africans, a practice condemned by the laws of nations at that time as seen in previous chapters. As early as 1434, Alonzo Gonzales, the first recorded European explorer on the West African Coast, pursued and attacked a number of Africans. Six years later, Gonzales attacked indigenous people again, and took twelve prisoners. This time however, the Portuguese were met with the resistance of the African people there and took sail. However, they continued to send vessels on the West African Coast. One documented example is their falling upon a village, "whence the inhabitants fled, and being pursued, twenty-five were taken".[787] On their way back to the ship, they killed some Africans, and took fifty-five more as slaves. The first sale of African captives is recorded to have taken place in 1444 in Lagos, Portugal, and was followed by organized razzias on the African coast by Lancarote, sent on this mission by Dom Henrique (Prince Henry), of Spain.[788] Dinisanes Dagrama subsequently landed on the island of Arguin, and "took" fifty-four more Africans, and then "running along the coast

---

785   Letter of January 15, 2003 by the All Mansion's Secretariat of the Ethiopian Peace Foundation, Jamaica Branch, International Rastafari Community, Rastafari Brethren of Jamaica, to Her Royal Majesty Queen Elizabeth II, Buckingham Palace, Attention: Mrs. Kay Brock, Assistant Private Secretary, c/o Mr. Gavin Tech, Deputy British High Commissioner, Kingston.

786   Crawford, James (2002). The International Law Commission's Articles on State Responsibility. Introduction, Text and Commentaries, Cambridge: CambridgeUniversity Press, 77.

787   Benezet (1767), 26 et seq.

788   Popo (2010), 71.

eighty leagues farther"[789] another fifty people. Again, the Portuguese enslavers met resistance and seven of them got killed. The historic documents relate many more captures of this kind on the coast of Barbary and Guinea made in those early times by the Portuguese.[790] The reports of Nuno Tristão and Gomes Eanes eZurara (~ 1440) contain nothing indicating an abundant availability of slaves for sale, but rather tells of attacks and raids by the Portuguese.[791]

Indeed, Eanes eZurara reported that he and his crew pursued and captured people on several occasions in the "land of Blacks".[792] Some areas on the coast of Guinea were accessed with the help of Portuguese canons, and he reported of several instances of people resisting capture.[793] Because of this resistance and physical strength of the encountered Africans, the Portuguese were only able to capture and enslave mostly children at the beginning.[794] That Portuguese mission and countless others employed all sorts of tricks and deceit to lure Africans near to their boats and then attack them once they were far from the coast. Fortunately, some Africans swam so well, "like cormorants", that they could escape by abandoning their boats for the water.[795]

In another incident, Eanes eZurara's crew wanted to overtake a village and enslave the approximately eighty inhabitants, but these were not taken by surprise but had prepared and armed themselves. They shot the Portuguese with empoisoned arrows and forced them to retreat in such a hurry that they could not aweigh anchor, but had to cut the ship's ropes.[796] The Portuguese also encountered other African navals, highly armed for defense, at several instances, and chose not to confront them, given the "great superiority" of these Africans and fearing the potential poison in their arrows.[797] Faced with such resistances, the Portuguese thus soon began to also purchase enslaved Africans from Moors at Arguin and in Mauretania:

"From the foregoing accounts, it is undoubted that the practice of making slaves of the Negroes, owes its origin to the early incursions of the Portugueze on the coast of Africa, solely from an inordinate desire of gain. This is clearly evidenced from their own historians, particularly Cada Mosto, about the year 1455, who writes, 'that before the trade was settled for purchasing slaves from the Moors at Arguin, sometimes four, and sometimes more Portugueze vessels, were used to come (...) well-armed; and landing by night, would surprise some fishermen's villages: (...) entered into the country, and carried off [people] of both

---

789   Benezet (1767), 26 et seq.
790   Ibid.
791   Popo (2010), 122.
792   e Zurara (1453), 108.
793   Ibid., 134 et seq.
794   Ibid.,186 et seq.
795   Ibid., 220.
796   Ibid., 241.
797   Ibid.,246.

sexes, whom they sold in Portugal. (...) The Portugueze and Spaniards, settled on four of the Canary islands, would go to the other island by night, and seize some of the natives of both sexes, whom they sent to be sold in Spain."[798]

It is crucial to grasp the fact that besides kidnapping, the Portuguese came to rely on purchasing Africans from light skinned Moors in Mauretania in the initial phases of transatlantic slavery. Light skinned Moors and Arabs were the ones who had illegally enslaved Africans for a long time, as we shall elaborate further shortly. And they continue to do so up to this day. As I am writing this, several Black activists are jailed and tortured in Mauretania because they burned copies of the black codes of the Maliki School of Islamic law which aim at legitimizing the enslavement of Black people.

Yet to come back to the beginning of Portuguese slaving activities in Africa, shortly after their linking up with the Moors in Mauretania, the Portuguese started to occupy Sao Tomé, an island off the West Coast of Africa, lacking an indigenous population. Captives in large numbers were therefore brought in as a labor force from the mainland. What is also essential to grasp in that regard is that in the first decades of transatlantic slavery and even before their arrival in the Americas, Europeans established their first slavery plantations on islands, such as Sao Tomé and also the Canaries. The reason for this was that they were confronted with massive resistance against their illegal activities in mainland Africa, and that is also why they shipped hundreds of millions to the Americas. They were not able to exploit their labor in Africa because of this resistance. Africa is huge, and if they could have exploited African labor there, they would have had no reason to take up the expenses and cost to carry them around half the globe. But they could not because what they were doing was illegal and they met massive resistance in Africa.

So, in 1493 John II of Portugal gave the captain of the island a license to import 1,080 slaves from mainland Africa to Sao Tomé over a period of five years. Subsequent years saw a number of about 500 captives brought to this island annually. It has been estimated that about half of them came from Benin.[799] We are left with contemporary reports of Portuguese complaints about not receiving enough slaves from Benin, indicating that African slaves were not available in abundance but came from the limited legitimate means of enslavement such as criminal conviction or war captivity. "It was in these circumstances that King Manuel decided in 1514 to grant a four-year lease of the Benin trade to Antonio Carneiro, the lord of Principe, with the provision that Carneiro should supply all the slaves needed for the gold trade."[800] Analysis of settlement patterns and the consolidation of those material records with other documentary sources allow to retrace how armed incursions by the Portuguese at the beginning of the 16th century caused

---

798   Benezet (1767), 26 et seq.
799   Ryder, Alan (1969). Benin and the Europeans 1485-1897, London: Longman, 35 et seq.
800   Ibid., 43 et seq.

a mass exodus of coastal peoples to the hinterland, so that "out of the more than four hundred coastal settlements, including many highly developed city-states, only a handful were inhabited by the 17th century".[801] The Portuguese seemed to have been determined to get their African slaves by any means necessary, and since they could not acquire sufficient numbers from trad they did not hesitate to make captifs. At this point, we should thus retain that the very beginnings of transatlantic slavery were conducted and controlled by the Portuguese Crown, that most of these enslavements were illegal and that these violations of law can be attributed to Portugal, establishing its legal responsibility.

Soon, the Portuguese also reached the Congo kingdom in their search of enslavable Africans. At the time of their arrival in 1482, the Congo kingdom covered an area of over 2 million km^2, and was thus larger than the whole of Europe. It had been founded in the 14th century, following a progressive consolidation of political and economic structures of the territory. Its provinces were administrated by governors installed by the king or by an assembly of notables.[802]

Agriculture, palm oil production and cattle rearing assured a comfortable alimentary security. The production of jewellery, crafts and rapphia velours also constituted another prospering branch of their economy and trade. There existed a small-scale slave trade. A few people had become slaves by one of the legitimate means of enslavement, that is criminal conviction, war captivity or pawning, and this slavery at no point constituted an important part of the economy.[803] Portuguese sources testify of their authors' astonishment at the discovery of the greatness of this empire and its numerous natural riches, such as iron, copper, ivory and exotic animals. The country played an important role in continental trade networks.

Official relations between Congo and Portugal became closer from 1491. The people of Congo, however, rose up early and at several occasions against their first christianized king Mwene Nzinga Nkuwu, by then baptized João I, because of his illegal slave dealings with the Portuguese from the late 15th century onwards. Tragically, he could always suppress the uprisings with the armed help of the Portuguese, notably Luiz da Souza, one of the first enslaver captains dispatched by the Portuguese crown. After the death of their christianized puppy ally João I, the Portuguese continued to infer directly with Congolese politics for illegal enslave-

---

801   Ogundiran, Akinwumi/Falola, Toyin (2010). "Pathways in the Archaeology of Transatlantic Africa", in: Akinwumi Ogundiran/Toyin Falola (ed.): Archaeology of Atlantic Africa and the African Diaspora, Bloomington/Indianapolis: IndianaUniversity Press, 3-45, 17.

802   Ballong-Wen-Mewuda, Joseph B. (2002). 'L'esclavage et la traite négrière dans la correspondance de Nzinga Mbemba (dom Afonso I), roi du Congo (1506-1543): la vision idéologique de l'autre', in: Isabel Castro Henriques and Louis Sala-Molins (ed.): Déraison, esclavage et droit. Les fondements idéologiques et juridiques de la traite négrière et de l'esclavage, Paris: EDITIONS Unesco, 301- 314, 302 et seq.

803   Plumelle-Uribe (2008), 59.

ment purposes.[804] This culminated in the ascension to the throne of Nzinga Mbemba, baptised Afonso I (1506-1543), following a secession war between him and his brother Mpanzu A Nzinga, who was the leader of a group of notables faithful to the spiritual traditions of the ancestors. With the help of the Portuguese, Afonso took victory and power. He remained in power until 1546 and became one of the first important African collaborators of the Europeans in transatlantic slavery, albeit a somewhat unfortunate and maybe naïve one.

In 1512, he entered into alliance with the King of Portugal and Portugal sent him a "resident counsellor". Afonso gave 300 slaves as a gesture that was customary between allied monarchs at that time. It has been sustained that, in view of the Christian religious teaching that he was presented with, Alfonso would not have imagined that the people he gave to the Portuguese could be treated any worse than they were with him.[805] In Congo language, the same word was used to designate both "slave" and "war captive", thus indicating the source of slaves and providing further evidence that war captivity was indeed a globally recognized reason of legitimate enslavement.[806]

The Portuguese soon started to cause Afonso serious problems. As early as 1513, Afonso informed the King of Portugal through his ambassador Ndo Mpêtelo Kinsunsa that he was in the process of subduing a chief in the south, Mpanzu'a Lungu, who had been incited to rebel against him by the Portuguese.[807] Afonso also protested the illegal and massive enslavement of his people by Portuguese slavers in letters. But because he was so dependent, indeed in power only because of them, Afonso I was not able to render effective the legal restrictions on enslavement that he officially communicated to the Portuguese crown and merchants. Portugal demanded only more slaves in return for sending its priests. In one of the early letters, the Congolese King pleaded "for the love of our Lord, to buy only real slaves and no woman".[808] Afonso asked for technical assistance, reportedly artisans and instructors to develop his Christian state. He did not receive any such assistance though, only enslavers and a few priests. The Portuguese, in exchange for their support of him, demanded slaves.[809] This "cooperation" between Portugal and Congo is recorded in twenty-nine letters between Afonso and Portugal between 1514 and 1539.[810]

In the ensuing years, rulers of the different regions of the empire, armed by the Portuguese, started to chase other Africans and trade them to the Europeans

---

804   Popo (2010), 139.
805   Plumelle-Uribe (2008), 62 et seq.
806   Vasina, J. (1992). The Kongo kingdom and its neighbours, in: B.A. Ogot (ed.): General History of Africa V. Africa from the Sixteenth to the Eighteenth Century, Paris: UNESCO, 546-587, 550.
807   Batsikama ba Mampuya ma Ndawla, Raphaël (1999). L'Ancien royaume du Congo et les baKongo, Paris: L'Harmattan, 110.
808   Ballong-Wen-Mewuda (2002), 312.
809   Popo (2010), 140.
810   Ballong-Wen-Mewuda (2002), 302 et seq.

for luxury goods and more arms. Afonso could no longer do a thing about this, because the fire arms were already in, causing his empire to disintegrate. Backed by the might of these arms, the renegade rulers refused to pay taxes to the Ma-ni-Congo, the King of Congo, and rejected his suzerenity. Slave raids were mul-tiplying at an ever faster speed. The brutality of this situation surpassed anything known before and provoked a fast disorganization of society. Afonso continued to send protest letters to his Portuguese homologue about the man-chasing in-stigated by representatives of that King. From these letters, it appears that Afonso seemed to believe that the Portuguese king was not aware of the banditry of his agents.[811] Meanwhile, the highest representatives of that Portuguese king were expressing their ideas about Afonso rather unambiguously. Simão da Silva, am-bassador of Portugal in Congo, proclaimed that the King of Congo "were a man of nothing, merits nothing of what the Portuguese king sends him". Fernão de Melo, another royal agent and instigator of intrigues against Afonso who nevertheless remained generous with him, spoke of him as a "pagan dog".[812] The Mani-Congo finally prohibited slave trading in his empire, but it was too late.[813]

Like many rulers around the world, King Afonso had initially understood slav-ery as a condition befalling prisoners of war, criminals, and debtors, out of which slaves could earn or marry their way, and which was generally not hereditary. "This was nothing like seeing this wholly new and brutal commercial practice of slavery where tens of thousands of his subjects were dragged off in chains. When the king sent emissaries on a long and arduous sea voyage to appeal to the pope in Rome, the emissaries were arrested upon their arrival in Lisbon."[814]

When Portuguese slaving activities first began in Congo, they had been based on a mutual agreement with the Congo king, and were conform with the custom-ary act of one monarch turning over to another, his ally, a quantity of captives. This custom was common in both Africa and Europe. However, the Portuguese did not honor the agreement concluded with the Congolese King. It was in these circumstances that King Afonso I, in 1526, sent another letter to his Portuguese homologue John III, stating that,

"We cannot reckon how great the damage is, since the above-mentioned mer-chants daily seize our subjects, sons of the land and sons of our noblemen and vassals and our relatives. Thieves and men of evil conscience take them (...). They grab them and cause them to be sold: and so great, Sir, is their corruption and li-centiousness that our country is utterly depopulated. The king of Portugal should not countenance such practices. (...) we need from your Kingdom no other than

---

811   Ballong-Wen-Mewuda (2002), 312.
812   Ibid.
813   Plumelle-Uribe (2008), 62 et seq.
814   Robinson, Randall (2000). The Debt. What America Owes to Blacks, New York: Penguin Group, 26.

priests and people to teach in schools, and no other goods but wine and flour for the holy sacrament: that is why we ask of Your Highness to (...) assist us in this matter, commanding your factors that they should send here neither merchants nor wares, because it is our will that in these kingdoms [of Kongo] there should not be any trade in slaves nor market for slaves."[815]

This and other letters of protest by King Afonso I of Congo to the King of Portugal and the pope are kept in the archives of Lisbon and the Vatican. The European addressees ignored these notes of protestation and continued to breach their initial agreements with the Congolese sovereign. Yet he persisted to protest, so Portuguese slavers tried to kill him on Easter Day in 1540 in the church if Sao Salvador de Mbanza Kongo. They also directed another focus of activity to the Congolese province of Luanda, where they were to create the "contract of Angola" with the official backing of the Portuguese king, in order to distract themselves from control by the Congolese authorities, and goaded the secession of that region.[816] But before that and after Afonso's death a few years earlier, a dozen of his family members were intercepted during a voyage destined to Portugal and enslaved to Brazil.[817]

Still, all of this did not completely destroy Congolese resistance to enslavement. In 1556, the ruler of Ndongo, one of the provinces of the Congo Empire, was counselled by Portuguese slavers into resigning his submission to the Mani-Congo. In the ensuing war, the Ngola (ruler) of Ndongo, armed and aided by the Portuguese, took victory, thus further destabilizing the King of Congo's power to halt slaving. The lesson for future rulers was that they would need to comply with Portuguese interests if they wanted to maintain their positions. Survivors of the Congolese army fled to the forest and continued to put up military resistance against the Portuguese for another century.[818]

Then, on May 3, 1560, Pablo Diaz de Novais, grandson of Bartolomeu Diaz, arrived in Congo with three vessels, with the explicit goal of encouraging a rebellion that should lead to Portuguese control over another large part of the Congo basin. The plan was discovered and he was arrested by local authorities and kept imprisoned for seven years. Upon regaining his freedom, he returned to Portugal and obtained from his king, then Dom Sebastien, a concession to subdue "all people from Coanza Bay to the 15th degree north"[819]. That region was to become the colony of Angola. In 1575, stimulated by its activities in Brazil, the Portuguese crown accorded a charter to Diaz de Novais, and authorized him to conquer around 200 km along the coast south of Cuanza and also to the interior thereof. Between

---

815   Davidson (1961), 158 et seq.
816   Popo (2010), 140.
817   Ajavon (2005), 77.
818   Plumelle-Uribe (2008), 63 et seq.
819   Popo (2010), 141.

1578 and 1587, Diaz de Novais also received five times royal material support in men and goods.[820] He was equipped financially, materially and militarily by the Portuguese crown, and arrived back in Congo in 1575 and instantly began to engage in activities to foster secessions in the region.[821] Meanwhile, Mpanzu-a-Nzinga IV aka Alvaro I had been enthroned illegitimately, backed by Portuguese arms, in 1568. This move had become necessary because the Portuguese were encountering increasing resistance to slaving operations. The previous ruler of the region of Angola had thirty Portuguese killed because he had been informed of their true motives of procuring slaves and taking over the silver and other mines. In the following years and decades the Portuguese engaged in numerous wars that produced plenty of slaves for them. Finally, the sobas, the indigenous rulers, were placed under the authority of white missionaries or military officials. A system was imposed where tribute in slaves and natural produce such as raphia was versed directly to the royal treasury kept by the governor of the Portuguese colony Angola.

But because of the illegitimacy of his ascension to power, the new Mani Congo was soon obliged to flee the capital for the river island of Nzadi. He could only return to the throne because of massive military assistance by the Portuguese.[822] Yet despite this, in pursuit of their divide-and-rule strategy, Diaz de Nova was offered the title of "king" to the ruler of Kilwângu in exchange for his loyalty to Portuguese enslavement activity. This ruler, however, chose to remain loyal to the Mani Congo, and confronted the Portuguese militarily. Due to their canons and the aid of other corrupt local rulers, the Portuguese took victory once again.[823] Similar happenings have been recorded by European witnesses throughout the 17th century, of the Portuguese conducting numerous wars without any provocation on the part of Africans, with the unique aim of making slaves.[824]

In the midst of all of this, a whole heap of confusion still prevails in historic analysis about a group, or groups, that appeared in the 16th and 17th centuries in the Congo, and which have been named Jaga, and/or Imbangala. Cannibalism, slave raiding and generalized infanticide have been ascribed to them. However, it has been suggested by researchers that this term in contemporary Portuguese documents may in fact have referred to a wide range of different warrior groups that were at one time or another involved in the havoc that was brought to the country by the Portuguese invasion and policy of pitting one group against the other. What seems to be certain is that the first mention of the Jaga is associated with the Congo-Tio wars and the subsequent complete cessation of the "slave"

---

820   Randles, W. G. L. (1969). De la traite à la colonisation: les Portugais en Angola, in: Annales Économies, Sociétés, Civilisations 24 (2), Paris, 289-304.
821   Batsikama ba Mampuya ma Ndawla (1999), 81.
822   Popo (2010), 141.
823   Ibid., 141.
824   Randles (1969), 289 et seq.

"trade" in 1561. Other documents speak of an invasion from the interior in 1568. The rebels occupied São Salvador until a combined Portuguese-Congolese expedition drove them out of the capital again.[825] Some evidence suggests that the ranks of the Jaga were swollen by many villagers who were weary of being exploited and slave-raided.

"In the Battle of Lukala the Portuguese were defeated by a coalition of Kingdoms of Matamba and Ndongo on December 29, 1589. (...) This halted the Portuguese advance in the region until they made alliance with the 'Imbangala' who were African mercenaries. The most important military and enslavement operations were the large and complex military campaigns waged in 1618-1620 under Portuguese leadership against the Kingdom of Ndongo, during which thousands of its inhabitants were captured and deported."[826] As for the international reparation claim, it is important to acknowledge that the driving force behind this violence, effectuated to produce slaves, was not private Portuguese criminals, but the Portuguese state and its agents. "It was the Portuguese Luis Mendes de Vasconqelos, who arrived in the colony of Angola in 1617 and served as governor until 1621 who led the campaigns. In these three years of his office, Angola exported about 50,000 slaves, far more than were exported before."[827] Thus, Portuguese royal involvement was directly responsible for the massive onset of transatlantic enslavement of Africans.

Other reports also speak of the Jaga (or Mbangala or Imbangala) communities of nomadic warriors who were mercenaries for the Portuguese, aiding them to subdue a large part of the kingdom from 1617 to 1621.[828] The evidence regarding the group(s) is somewhat clouded, and it is not clear whether ethnic groups with these names actually ever existed.

Be that as it may, resistance in the Congo region continued. For example, in 1704, thus at a time when Congo had been plunged into chaos for over two centuries of massive slave raiding and warfare, a young woman named Kimpa Vita alias Dona Beatrice called to fight the Europeans to give back to Congo its sovereignty, while proclaiming an emancipatory and Congo-nationalist Christian faith. Captured in 1706, she was burned alive with her baby at the age of 22 by the Portuguese.[829]

In 1555, the Englishman William Towerson who, according to the law of his home country deemed slavery illicit and traded in a peaceable manner with the Africans, had reported that they made complaint to him of the Portuguese, "who were then settled in their castle at D'Elmina, saying, 'They were bad men, who

---

825   Lovejoy (2000), 41.
826   Thornton, John (1998). The African Experience of the '20. and Odd Negroes' Arriving in Virginia in 1619, in: William and Mary Quarterly, Third Series, Vol. 55 (3), Williamsburg, 421-434, 424 et seq.
827   Ibid.
828   Vasina (1992), 558 et seq.
829   Ajavon (2005), 114.

made them slaves if they could take them, putting irons on their legs'"[830]. As we have seen in the previous chapter, man-stealing was explicitly condemned by European monarchs such as Queen Elizabeth of England. However, the immense material profits made the governments of European nations, including England, soon abandon their initial respect for the law. They started to engage in illegal man-stealing, following the Portuguese example.

Early "traders", like Sir John Hawkins, pillaged villages and engaged in kidnapping. Later on, European enslavers developed a system where they relied to a large extent on African collaborators. Yet kidnapping, also directly by Europeans, always remained one of the most important means of acquiring slaves for the transatlantic system. "Also, as the African oral histories and narratives of ex-slaves reveal, deception and guile were sometimes used to lure Africans into ships"[831].

As late as 1930-1938, the Federal Writers' Project (FWP) sought to speak with and record the testimonies of former slaves. These records reveal that the methods in the context of which most Africans were enslaved within the transatlantic system were kidnapping and "tribal wars". It also revealed explicit memories of how some "tribal wars" were staged for the sole purpose of enslaving, at the instigation of European slavers and slaver states.[832]

Boyereau Brinch ("The Story of the Blind African Slave, or, Memoirs of Boyereau Brinch"), who had managed to free himself in the United States, wrote a report in 1758 of his enslavement. He wrote that as children, he and his companions went to bath in the Niger River after a day of festivities, but were

"waylayed by thirty or forty more of the same pale race of white *Vultures*, whom to pass was impossible, we attempted without deliberation to force their ranks. (...) Eleven out of fourteen were made captives, bound instantly, and notwithstanding our unintelligible intreaties, cries and lamentations, were hurried to their boat, and within five minutes were in board, gagged, and carried down the stream like a sluice; fastened down in the boat with cramped jaws, added to the horrid stench occasioned by filth and stinking fist; while all we were groaning, crying and praying, but poor creatures to no effect"[833].

After a few days, the gaged captives down in the ship dungeons witnessed the realization of another perfidious plan by their captors. The ship crew was staging a grand feast on board of the ship and all the inhabitants of the coast town were to attend. "This was considered as a civility due from that deluded people, to the officers of the vessel, while (...) perfidy rankled in the hearts of those traitorous vil-

---

830   Benezet (1767), 29.
831   Bailey (2007), 126.
832   Brooks (2004), 27.
833   Bailey (2007), 103 et seq.

lains, who conceived and executed the plot!"[834] Following the general invitation, practically all inhabitants came to attend and were brought on board their ship by boats. Only the sick, lame, aged, and children remained in town. The Africans were given a festive meal and drinks, with laudinum secretly conveyed into their liquor. As soon as a general intoxication set in and everyone had fallen asleep, the ship took sail for America.[835] "These dexterous dealers in iniquity seized upon the moment, fastened with implements already prepared, each individual down upon their backs, with poles across their breasts and legs, with hands and feet drawn up by cords to certain loop holes therein."[836]

Similar incidences where inhabitants of whole towns were lured into ships to attend a "feast", have happened elsewhere, such as in Atakor. Ayi Kwei Armah also incorporates such oral history traditions of similar content in one of his novels, *Two Thousand Seasons*. Since kidnapping was at all times an important means of procurement of Africans for transatlantic slavery, this part of the crime should not be conceptualized and thought of as a "trade", as trade generally involves a mutually consented transaction. In the case of transatlantic enslavement and slavery, most enslaved Africans had previously been free and were enslaved by criminal individuals and groups who thereafter "traded" them with equally criminal other individuals and groups.

At about the same time of the Atakor incident, one William Smith, captain of a slave ship reported from the Ivory Coast that they lay before several towns and "fired guns" as an invitation for people to come near, but no one ever turned up. Upon going onshore to find out why, they learnt that "the natives came seldom on board an English ship, for fear of being detained or carried off"[837]. The African people there also held one Englishman, Benjamin Cross, mate of a vessel, hostage as reprisal for some of their own men, who had been carried away by some English ship. Other contemporary documents testify with regard to kidnapping that "[t]his villainous custom is too often practised, chiefly by the Bristol and Liverpool ships"[838]. A certain John Snock, reported of the same problem of "not one Negro coming on board", and of being informed upon inquiry that "two months before, the English had been there with two large vessels, and had ravaged the country, destroyed all their canoes, plundered their houses, and carried off some of their people, upon which the remainder fled to the inland country".[839]

It is therefore accurate and important to stop speaking of "slaves" concerning the transatlantic system, and to use the more appropriate term "captive", "because

---

834 Ibid.
835 Ibid.
836 Cited in: Bailey, Anne C. (2007). African Voices of the Atlantic Slave Trade, Kingston/Miami: Ian Randle Publishers, 103ff.
837 Benezet (1767), 15et seq.
838 Ibid.
839 Ibid.

the vast majority of the people sold and exported were free individuals seized by force. This forceful seizure took a number of forms: kidnapping by one or more individuals; raids by well-organized private groups; raids organized by the state; inter-territorial war (war between kingdoms or communities)".[840] The use of "captive" or "enslaved African" acknowledges and reflects the reality of the fundamental illegality of transatlantic slavery, whereas the use of "slave" serves to bolster the hegemonic fiction of a traditional and savage African slavery.

North American abolitionist Anthony Benezet claimed in his 1771 work *Some Historical Account of Guinea* that a study of early European accounts of Africa shows that at the time of the first European contacts with sub-Saharan Africa, its inhabitants generally lived in peace amongst themselves, with only rare references to wars, or to the sale of captives. He thus inferred that the prevalence of war in more recent times was due to the transatlantic slavery system.[841] Eventually, practically no community in large parts of Africa was free from involvement in these hostilities:

"Some did not take an aggressive stand, but were liable to attack from other tribes: the Nalus from the Beafadas, Papels, and Bijagos; the Balantas from the Papels and Bijagos; and the Djolas from the Mandingas. (...) At first, the Djolas were taken unawares, but obviously they soon began to prepare for these attacks, and many Mandingas were in turn made captive."[842]

These "wars" were not fought to gain territory or political dominance or for inter-communal animosities, but were directly connected and fomented by the transatlantic system which was controlled by European states.

"This was the view consistently maintained by observers like de Mercado in 1569, the Bishop of Cape Verde at the end of the sixteenth century, and the Jesuits in the early seventeenth century. (...) One of the things about which the Capuchins were quite definite in their reports was that all of the conflicts which they heard termed 'wars' were nothing more than robberies and manhunts (...)."[843]

Historical evidence accounts for the fact that Europeans continuously armed African groups with the explicit intent to procure slaves, such as in the Sagbadre War.[844] We will soon come back to this in more detail.

Yet, part of the strategy that was necessary to carry on transatlantic slavery for so long was the persistent dispersion of false propaganda that suggested that slaves were available in abundance in Africa. For example, John Matthews, a spokesman for Liverpool (one of the main slave ports on England) interests, stressed that captives who were purchased by European ships were mainly the

---

840   Inikori (1992b), 25.
841   Law, Robin (2008). The Impact of the Atlantic Slave Trade upon Africa, Wien: Lit Verlag, 9.
842   Rodney (1970), 104 et seq.
843   Ibid.
844   Bailey (2007), 169.

result of Muslim jihads. Though transatlantic and trans-saharan enslavement of Africans did reinforce one another, it is imperative to acknowledge that

"it was orthodox proslavery propaganda that captives were victims of African wars whose origin and development were quite unconnected with the slave trade. However, not long after Matthews wrote, Thomas Watt penetrated to Timbo and reported that he was told by the Almami's deputy 'with a shocking degree of openness, that the sole object of their wars was to procure slaves, and they could not get slaves without fighting for them'."[845]

And exactly the same argument that was employed then in order to carry out genocidal transatlantic slavery in the first place, that enslaving and selling one another would have been a normal feature of African life, is still used today to deny reparation claims for the crime. It is essential to grasp this fully and to disseminate the truth so that reparation opponents can no longer fool the people.

From 1513 onwards, the Spanish crown had instituted a system of licences or *asientos* that transferred the monopoly of importing slaves to private parties.[846] King Carlos V signed an *asiento* in 1517, authorizing the exportation of 4,000 Africans from Guinea to the Spanish possessions in the Americas.[847] European governments profited from the granting of trade company charters as well as from direct investment in enslavement. In a formal perspective, transatlantic slavery was started as a royal enterprise based on state-monopoly by Portugal, Spain, England and France.[848] There is no way to deny this historic truth.

Though direct royal and state involvement decreased, transatlantic slavery was still dominated by state-chartered European companies throughout the 17th and 18th centuries. Portugal, Spain, England, France, Sweden, Denmark, the United Provinces, Brandenburg and Scotland were all involved in this manner. Additionally, private traders worked within a framework of royal/governmental regulations, and British royal officials, for example, were appointed to reside on the African coast to ensure the smooth running of transatlantic slavery.[849] Up to 1790, the majority of Danish commercial slavery activities were in the hands of Charter Companies who had received a royal monopoly on the commerce in certain regions. In 1790, the Danish government authorized traders to engage in private slaving commerce.[850]

---

845   Rodney (1970), 236.
846   ZeBelinga, Martial (1999). 'Productions, Impossibilités et renouvellements des asservissements du Noir', in: Esclavages et servitudes d'hier et aujourd'hui, Actes du colloque de Strasbourg des 29 et 30 mai 1998, Strasbourg: Histoire et Anthropologie, 234.
847   Andrade, Elisa Silva (1995). 'Le Cap-Vert dans l'expansion européenne', in: Elikia M'Bokolo (ed.): L'Afrique entre l'Europe et l'Amerique. Le rôle de l'Afrique dans la rencontre de deux mondes 1492-1992, Paris: UNESCO, 69-79, 76.
848   Davidson (1961), 58.
849   Bailey (2007), 115.
850   Hernaes, Per (2001). "Les forts danois de la Côte de l'Or et leurs habitants à l'époque de la traite des esclaves", in: Djibril Tamsir Niane (ed.): Tradition orale et archives de la traite négrière, Paris:

Generally speaking, it is important to keep in mind that without European demand for African slaves, millions of millions of Africans would not have been turned into chattel slaves, murdered, tortured and exploited. Many features of this crime against humanity were the exclusive responsibility of the involved Europeans.[851] The main aspects were planned in Europe where everything from the investor's potential profit to the insurance premiums on slaves was calculated.[852] Little was left to chance in this for Europe economically highly profitable "enterprise". Conditions on slave ships were truly hellish and, in a ruthlessly efficient system, closely linked to existing European knowledge about slave mortality, technological advances in the European shipping industry, and European legislation. Thus, in the earlier phases of the transatlantic system, slavers aimed at packing as many slaves as possible into a ship without any regard at all for ventilation or physical space. Then, from the mid-18th century, traders and legislators acknowledged the high mortality of such voyages and gradual changes in the kinds of ships that were built were the consequence.[853] Again, such constitutive aspects of the transatlantic slavery genocide were the sole responsibility of Europeans.

A first-hand testimony of Alexander Falconbridge, a slave ship doctor, illustrates the horrible conditions of the Middle Passage:

"One instance will serve to convey some idea, though a very faint one, of their terrible sufferings. (...) Their rooms became so extremely hot as to be only bearable for a very short time. But the excessive heat was not the only thing that rendered their situation intolerable. The deck, that is, the floor of their rooms was so covered with blood and mucus which had proceeded from them in consequence of the flux, that it resembled a slaughterhouse. It is not in the power of the human imagination to picture a situation more dreadful or disgusting."[854]

Slave ships took up to nine months for the Middle Passage, in general three. Equiano reported in his autobiography that

"the apartments were 'so crowded that each had scarcely room to turn himself.' The enslaved were spooned together in close quarters, each with about as much room as a corpse in a coffin. The galling of the chains rubbed raw the soft flesh of wrists, ankles, and necks. The enslaved suffered extreme heat and poor ventilation, copious perspirations, and sea-sickness. The stench, which was already 'loathsome', became 'absolutely pestilential' as the sweat, the vomit, the blood, and the 'necessary tubs' full of excrement 'almost suffocated us'. The shrieks of the terrified mingled in cacophony with the groans of the dying."[855]

Greed was so unsatisfiable that "no place capable of holding a single person,

---

UNESCO, 112-119, 114.
851   Bailey (2007), 112.
852   Ibid., 116 et seq.
853   Ibid., 130.
854   Ibid., 132.
855   Rediker (2008), 120.

from the one end of the vessel to the other, [was] left unoccupied".[856] The merchants, sent or commissioned by their European governments, built death into the planning of each and every voyage.

The above-mentioned doctor also evidenced that transatlantic slavery was the cause for many social troubles and warfare in Africa, and not the fruit of pre-existing violent conflicts between Africans, as often contended. He wrote that after two incidents had led to a temporary suspension of the "trade" for a few years in the region of the River Ambris in Angola, peace and confidence among the natives was restored, "which upon arrival of the ships, is immediately destroyed by the inducement then held forth in the purchase of slaves".[857]

Last but not least, European sovereigns promulgated the law codes that aimed to legitimize the extreme brutalization and the denial of the humanity of Africans[858], such as the *Code Noir* enacted by Louis XIV in 1685 or the Spanish *Codigo Negro* of 1784.[859]

I hope that the past pages have given a general impression of the kind and extent of involvement in, and hence responsibility – moral and legal – of European states for transatlantic slavery. In the next section, we will deal with the details of legal responsibility, by means of the Articles on State Responsibility adopted by the International Law Commission in 2001 as a guiding instrument. Guiding instrument because the Articles stem from very recent present-day international law developments, whereas the criminal facts that we are concerned with, began over 500 years ago. But since we are really dealing with a continuing violation of law – the Maafa t– and since the basic structures and principle of the international reparations regime go back far in history and also are still found today in the Articles, it seems appropriate to see what they provide.

1. ATTRIBUTION OF RESPONSIBILITY BY PRESENT-DAY INTERNATIONAL LAW AND THE ILC ARTICLES

It was in 1948 that the United Nations General Assembly, in fulfilment of its mandate of "encouraging the progressive development of international law and its codification", stipulated in the Charter of the United Nations, established the International Law Commission (ILC). State responsibility was one of fourteen topics

---

856   Ibid., 339.
857   Ibid., 112.
858   Sala-Molins, Louis (1998). "L'esclavage en codes", in: Doudou Diène (ed.): La chaine et le lien. Une vision de la traite négrière, Paris: UNESCO, 288-293, 291.
859   Somé, Roger (1998). "Esclavage, génocide ou holocauste?", in: Doudou Diène (ed.): La chaine et le lien. Une vision de la traite négrière, Paris: UNESCO, 527-542, 531.

that the Commission should particularly deal with. Following many debates and changes of rapporteurs[860], the ILC presented the Draft Articles on Responsibility of States for Internationally Wrongful Acts to the General Assembly in 1996. They were subsequently referred to and cited by courts as well as discussed in the academic literature even before their final adoption by the ILC in 2001.[861]

In the years leading up to 2001, detailed commentaries by governments were received and a final round of written comments took place in 2000, based on the complete provisional text as well as on assessments made by a study group of the International Law Association. That study sustained that the comments by governments and others on the provisional text suggested that, overall, its basic structure and most of its individual provisions were accepted by states.[862] Thus, the ILC Articles constitute a codification of the international law of state responsibility, such as considered law today by the vast majority of states.

Subsequently, the Articles were adopted in 2001 by General Assembly resolution 56/83. General Assembly resolutions are generally considered "non-binding". However, the content of the Articles has in large parts already been contained in binding customary international law, such as indicated by the affirmative commentaries by governments during the codification process. Adopted without a vote and with consensus on virtually all points, they "reflect the balance of opinion within the ILC, following prolonged discussion and debate over several decades" as well as a balance of opinion of governments.[863] On a number of occasions, the International Court of Justice and other tribunals have also referred to these Articles that deal with the law of state responsibility for internationally illicit acts.[864]

According to Article 1, every internationally wrongful act of a state entails its responsibility. Article 2 defines an internationally wrongful act by two elements only: conduct (act or omission) is (a) attributable to a state by international law, and (b) constitutes a breach with the international obligations of that state. There is no requirement for fault, wrongful intent or any mental element at all.[865] Thus, in the case of transatlantic slavery, it would suffice that it was illegal and that it is attributable to states by international law. The first requirement has already been assessed and confirmed above. The second condition, attribution, is what this chapter will deal with. Generally speaking, "(i)n every case, it is by comparing the conduct in fact engaged in by the State with the conduct legally prescribed by the international obligation that one can determine whether or not there is a breach of that obligation. The phrase 'is not in conformity with' is flexible enough

---

860   Crawford (2002), 1 et seq.
861   Ibid., 11.
862   Ibid., 26 et seq.
863   Ibid., 60.
864   Crawford (2002), 58 et seq.
865   Ibid., 12; see also 84.

to cover the many different ways in which an obligation can be expressed, as well as the various forms which a breach may take (...)."[866] That principle of state responsibility is also expressed in the ILC Articles with the formulation "regardless of its origin" (Art 12). "They apply to all international obligations of States, whatever their origin may be"[867], and thus include natural law and the law of nations, such as in force at the time of transatlantic slavery and retraced in Chapter II. The International Court of Justice had stressed this earlier in *Gabĉikovo-Nagymaros* when it stated that it is "well established that, when a State has committed an internationally wrongful act, its international responsibility is likely to be involved whatever the nature of the obligation it has failed to respect"[868]. Obligations imposed on states by peremptory norms, such as the prohibition of genocide, "necessarily affect the vital interests of the international community as a whole" and may even entail a stricter regime of responsibility than that applied to other internationally wrongful acts.[869] In the past chapter, we have already seen that during the long centuries of genocidal transatlantic slavery, states engaged in conduct which contravened both treaty obligations to African states and sovereigns, natural law, national law and general principles of international law.

The principle maintained in Art. 1, that every internationally wrongful act entails the responsibility of the committing state, was drawn upon by international courts in numerous cases both before and after the passing of the Articles, some of the most prominent of which are *Phosphates in Morocco*[870](PCIJ); *Corfu Channel*[871]; *Military and Paramilitary Activities*[872]; *Gabĉikovo-Nagymaros*[873]; *Reparation for Injuries*[874]; *Interpretation of Peace Treaties, Second Phase*[875] (ICJ), as well as by many arbitral tribunals.[876] Thus, "every internationally wrongful act of a State entails the international responsibility of that State, and thus gives rise to new international legal relations additional to those which existed before the act took place, has been widely recognised, both before and since Article 1 was first formulated by

---

866   Crawford (2002), 126 et seq.
867   Ibid.
868   Gabĉikovo-NagymarosProject (Hungary v. Slovakia), Judgement of September 25, 1997, ICJ Reports 1997, 7.
869   Crawford (2002), 126.
870   Phosphates in Morocco (Italy v. Fr.), Judgement of June 14, 1938, PCIJ, Series A/B, No. 74.
871   Corfu Channel case (UK and Northern Ireland v. Albania), Judgement of April 4, 1949, ICJ Reports 1949, 4.
872   Military and Paramilitary Activities in and against Nicaragua (Nicaragua v. United States of America), Judgement of June 27, 1986, ICJ reports 1986, 14.
873   Gabĉikovo-NagymarosProject (Hungary v. Slovakia), Judgement of September 25, 1997, ICJ Reports 1997, 7.
874   Reparation for injuries suffered in the service of the United Nations, Advisory Opinion of April 11, 1949, ICJ Reports 1949, 174.
875   Interpretation of Peace Treaties (second phase), Advisory Opinion of July 18, 1950, ICJ Reports 1950, 221.
876   Crawford (2002), 78.

the Commission."[877]

Both criteria, attribution and qualification as wrongful, have to be assessed by means of international law only. That means that "attribution of conduct to the State as a subject of international law is based on criteria determined by international law and not on the mere recognition of a link of factual causality."[878] That means that even if transatlantic slavery were imputable to European states on a moral level because they profited from this illegal practice and condoned it, this alone would not suffice to see their responsibility to make reparations engaged, legally speaking. What is needed for legal attribution is a link to the state of those acting. However, "in determining what constitutes an organ of a State for the purposes of responsibility, the internal law and practice of each State are of prime importance. The structure of the State and the functions (...) are not, in general, governed by international law. (...) For example, the conduct of certain institutions performing public functions and exercising public powers (...) is attributed to the State even if those institutions are regarded in internal law as autonomous and independent of the executive government".[879]

Thus, the ICJ deemed it a sufficient basis for Albanian responsibility that the Albanian state knew, or must have known, of the presence of the mines in its territorial waters and did nothing to warn third states. In the *Diplomatic and Consular Staff* case, the Court concluded that the responsibility of Iran was a result of the "'inaction' of its authorities which 'failed to take appropriate steps', in circumstances where such steps were evidently called for. In other cases it may be the combination of an action and an omission which is the basis of responsibility".[880] As we shall see in this chapter, legal responsibility of European states can clearly be established along these lines.

According to international customary law and Art. 3, "the characterization of an act of a State as internationally wrongful is governed by international law. Such characterization is not affected by the characterization of the same act as lawful by internal law." That the qualification as internationally wrongful is not altered by differing internal law is again highlighted in Art. 32, where it is stated that "(t)he responsible State may not rely on the provisions of its internal law as justification for failure to comply with its obligations under this Part." Thus, European states cannot rely in the least on their colonial slavery codes to sustain that genocidal transatlantic slavery would have been legal.

That legal tenet had been reaffirmed many times before, such as by the Permanent Court of International Justice in the *S.S. Wimbledon* case. The PCIJ also held in the 1930s in *Greco-Bulgarian Communities* that "it is a generally accepted

---

877   Ibid.
878   Ibid., 92.
879   Ibid.
880   Ibid., 82.

principle of international law that in relations between Powers who are contracting Parties to a treaty, the provisions of municipal law cannot prevail over those of the treaty".[881] In *Free Zones of Upper Savoy and the District of Gext*, the Court reasoned that "it is certain that France cannot rely on her own legislation to limit the scope of her international obligations".[882] In *Treatment of Polish Nationals*, it sustained that "a State cannot adduce as against another State its own Constitution with a view of evading obligations incumbent upon it under international law of treaties in force".[883]

A few years after that last judgement, Hermann Goering challenged the prosecution at the Nuremberg tribunal, stating "(b)ut that was our right! We were a sovereign State and that was strictly our business"[884]. This defense was rightfully rejected since the definition of what is internationally wrongful depends exclusively on international law standards, and states cannot rely on their national laws as a defense. In the case of transatlantic slavery, what is thus decisive is the law of nations at that time, and not the national laws that enslaver states issued a few centuries after they had started to engage in their wrongful conduct.

It is somewhat ironic that the same European ex-enslaver states who deny reparations claims by pointing to their internal criminal slavery legislations, today claim that it is them who would be holding this legal principle in the highest respect. For example, the UK Crimes Against Humanity and War Crimes Bill also states in section 10 that it "is not a justification, excuse or defence with respect to an offence under this Act that the offence was committed in obedience to or in conformity with the law in force at the time and in the place of its commission".[885] Everybody should easily detect the double-standard when it comes to crimes against humanity against Africans.

Transatlantic slavery was the most massive crime with many protagonists that extended over five centuries and was as such composed of countless individual acts. The ILC Articles that seem most appropriate are Art. 4, 5, 8 and 11. At this point, it is also not really essential to determine rigorously under which one of those Articles an individual act by an individual enslaver government is to be subsumed. The principles underlying the ILC Articles are really part of a much older legal tradition. It is only the formal organization and details of the Articles,

---

881   Greco-Bulgarian Communities (Bulgaria v. Greece), Advisory Opinion of July 31, 1930, PCIJ, Series B, No.17, 32.

882   Free Zones of Upper Savoy and the District of Gex (France v. Switzerland), Order of August 6, 1930, PCIJ, Series A, No.24, 12.

883   Treatment of Polish Nationals (Poland v. Danzig), Advisory Opinion of February 4, 1932, PCIJ, Series A/B, No.44, 4, para. 24.

884   Hajjar, Lisa (2004). "Human Rights", in: Austin Sarat (ed.): The Blackwell Companion to Law and Society, Oxford: Blackwell Publishing, 589-604, 591.

885   Crimes Against Humanity and War Crimes Bill 2000, downloaded from http://www.parliament. the-stationery-office.co.uk/pa/cm199900/cmbills/166/00166--a.htm#10 (accessed 15.11.2010).

including the repartition of attribution criteria in Articles 4-11, that stem from recent international law developments and may serve us as a guideline in the establishment of international legal responsibility for transatlantic slavery. Generally speaking, what is decisive for attribution of conduct is whether a person acts in an apparently official capacity or under the colour of authority. "The case of purely private conduct should not be confused with that of an organ functioning as such but acting *ultra vires* or in breach of the rules governing its operation. In this latter case, the organ is nevertheless acting in the name of the State; this principle is affirmed in article 7".[886]

Most illegally enslaved Africans were deported from forts that were built and maintained by European states. European states also forcibly wrenched such forts from one another. This indicates subsumption under Article 4 (Conduct of organs of a state). Yet most ships, though sailing under governmental regulations, belonged and were staffed by state-chartered (Art. 5; Conduct of persons or entities exercising elements of governmental authority), and later private, companies. From the moment the captives left the forts for the brutal Middle Passage which cost so many lives, state responsibility can be established under Art. 8 (Conduct directed or controlled by a state). Plantations were in most cases not run by states, and enslaved Africans were not brutalized and murdered directly by the colonial enslaver states that controlled, directed and profited from this system. However, states also acknowledged and adopted the criminal conduct of private slavers for themselves (Art. 11) by proscribing taxes and pocketing huge financial gains through it, as part of a larger setting that the states controlled through legislation and policy.

The diagnosis sustained by the reparations movement and indeed in substance by many African people globally, of transatlantic slavery as constituting only one component of the continuing violation of law that constitutes the Maafa (transatlantic slavery, colonialism, and neo-colonialism), renders the direct application of concrete norms and legal decisions of current international law possible. Thus, it would seem entirely legitimate to establish state responsibility for this most massive genocide by means of the ILC Articles.

A. ART. 4 - CONDUCT OF ORGANS OF A STATE

According to Art. 4, the "conduct of any State organ shall be considered an act of that State under international law, whether the organ exercises legislative, executive, judicial or any other functions, whatever position it holds in the organization of the State, and whatever its character as an organ of the central government or of a territorial unit of the State". The reference to "State organ" covers all

---

886   Crawford (2002), 99.

the individual or collective entities which make up the organization of the state and act on its behalf.[887]

Already in 1999, the International Court of Justice acknowledged in *Difference Relating to Immunity from Legal Process of a Special Rapporteur of the Commission on Human Rights that* "(a)ccording to a well-established rule of international law, the conduct of any organ of a State must be regarded as an act of that State. This rule (…) is of a customary character".[888]

As we have seen and shall see again later, transatlantic slavery was initially a European royal undertaking. The agents were either direct royal envoys or employees and they travelled on behalf of their king, queen or government.

i. Examples of attribution to Portugal and Spain

That was the case not only in West and Central Africa, but also in East Africa, where city-states and urban polities had been developing between 100 and 1500 CE. By the time of the arrival of the first Portuguese, several large capitals with 10,000 and 25,000 inhabitants existed in that region. The first coastal town to fall to the Portuguese was Kilwa in 1505. That raid was organized by Francisco d'Almeida (appointed Viceroy of "Portuguese India" by King Manuel I earlier in that year) after the city defaulted on a tribute promised to Vasco da Gama (Admiral of King Manuel I). A conversation between da Gama and King Ibrahim of Kilwa was recorded by Gaspar Corrêa in *Lendas Indias*, and illustrates how the Portuguese were determined to conquer and acquire Kilwa in order to secure access to and control of trade with Zambezia, a source of much gold and ivory. They reasoned that because of Kilwa's importance in long-distance trade, whoever controlled it would inevitably control the whole Swahili coast. So they demanded that King Ibrahim pay them tribute each year in money or jewellery as a sign of friendship, to which the king replied, not surprisingly, that that was not friendship but tributary subjugation which he did not want. "It would be like to be a captive." Vasco da Gama responded, "take it for certain that if I so decide your city would be grounded by fire in one single hour, and if your people wanted to extinguish the fire in town, they would all be burned, and when you see all this happen, you will regret all you are telling me now, and you will give much more than what I am asking you now, it will be too late for you. If you are still in doubt, it is up to you to see it".[889] King Ibrahim, wanting to get rid of the intruder told him, "Sir, if I had known that you wanted to enslave me, I would not have come, and I would have fled into the forest, for it is better for me to be a fox but free, than a dog locked

---

887   Ibid., 94.
888   Difference Relating to Immunity from Legal Process of a Special Rapporteur of the Commission on Human Rights, Advisory Opinion of 29 April 1999, ICJ Reports 1999, 62; cited in: Crawford (2002), 95.
889   Cited in: Kusimba, Chapurukha M. (2010). "The Collapse of Coastal City-States of East Africa", in: Akinwumi Ogundiran/Toyin Falola (ed.): Archaeology of Atlantic Africa and the African Diaspora, Bloomington/Indianapolis: Indiana University Press, 160- 184, 174 et seq.

up in a golden chain"[890]. To save his city, he consented to paying the tribute. But he only salvaged his city for a short time, because the Portuguese returned three years later, plundered Kilwa and installed a puppet ruler. Similar happenings are recorded for other city-states on that coast. The inhabitants of some towns refused to pay the tribute, and saw their cities burned in consequence. Many were slain or enslaved. Testimonies by Portuguese eye-witnesses recorded the extreme brutality of the Portuguese. They cut off many women's arms to rob them of the rich jewellery.[891]

Vasco da Gama was the Admiral of King Manuel I of Portugal, and commissioned by him for this voyage. Many structurally similar occurrences took place in other regions of Africa, such as in Congo at about the same time, as we have seen above. Such conduct is attributable to the Portuguese state via Art. 4, since these missions were carried out by state officials sent by the government.

From 1516 onwards, the Portuguese organized a round-traffic of slaves from Benin to their first sugar colony of Sao Tomé and Principe. Their ships carried about 600 enslaved Africans per year. The Portuguese Crown however was soon dissatisfied with this number and, fearing the loss of potential gains, withdrew the concession from the company handling the "slave" "trade". The Crown reverted to its previous policy of engaging directly in the slave trade, with the important modification that Sao Tomé was henceforth the base for the Crown's operations. They launched campaigns in Benin, which led to an inflow of captives to put to work in Principe:

"Instructions reorganising trade on these lines were issued in February 1519 to come into operation at the end of that year. (...) Care was to be taken that no slave cost more than 40 manillas, and that those bought at this price were young and healthy. (...) Immediately a slave had been purchased a cross was branded on his or her right arm to mark him as the property of the king of Portugal, and he was to be kept under close guard aboard the ship while it lay in the Benin River. (...) Unless suited for employment as an overseer on the plantations, no slave was to be kept long on the island, for fear that he might run away to join the growing number of fugitives who had already constituted a serious menace to Portuguese authority. Hence the royal sugar plantations relied upon a continuous flow of slaves from the mainland."[892]

From 1525 to 1527 the royal factor in Sao Tomé received a total of 6,300 enslaved Africans from the mainland. Benin is often brought up by reparation negationists as an example of African societies which would have unscrupulously enslaved and sold another. However, in 1526 Benin supplied only 274 slaves. Benin at that time also refused to sell male slaves. These facts "must lead us to consider the apparent lack of enthusiasm for the slave trade displayed by the rulers of Benin

---

890   Ibid.
891   Ibid.
892   Ryder (1969), 54 et seq.

and their principal advisers. Either they had few slaves to sell, which would seem improbable in a period when the kingdom was engaged in constant and successful wars of expansion, or else the services and prestige accruing to the great men of Benin from the possession of many slaves outweighed the value of the manilas and cowries for which they could be exchanged".[893] Though it is true that at later times, the rulers of Benin were some of the greatest collaborators in transatlantic slavery, their ascension to power, the manipulation of legal standards for enslavement and the wars that produced the slaves were direct consequences of continuous and purposive European intervention. Thus, responsibility for the onset of illegal transatlantic slavery can be legally attributed to Portugal via Art. 4.

After a short interval when Sao Tomé's slave shipping was once more handled by a company, the Portuguese crown in 1532 resorted again to handling this business itself on the grounds that direct administration would yield a higher income, "and also so that the Mina may be better supplied with slaves"[894]. Apparently the company had failed to deliver the 500 slaves now required every year for the gold trade at the Costa da Mina. More slaves were also needed because a growing number of African slaves had been reaching the Spanish colonies in the Caribbean during the 1520s. They had come by way of the Lisbon slave market, but it had been agreed in 1528 with two Dutch who already held a contract to supply slaves to the islands occupied by the Spanish who they would transport slaves directly from El Mina to Portuguese colonies in the Americas. "Elmina was a self-consciously royal establishment: private merchants were not allowed near it. (...) There was now a town beneath its walls: inhabited by half-Europeanised Africans, 'the Mina blacks', it became a self-governing republic at the disposal of the Portuguese governors."[895] Sao Tomé also remained one base for these operations. In November 1532, the Portuguese vessel *Santo Antonio* carried the first cargo of 201 enslaved Africans from Sao Tomé to Santo Domingo and San Juan. [896]

The Portuguese monarchs promoted and licensed "slave" "trading" in Africa from the 15th century onwards. The Spanish authorities formally regulated the slave traffic via the asiento system from the 16th to the 18th century. The Dutch, the British and the French all set up state-sponsored slave trading companies, with forts and trading posts in Africa, in the 17th century. Once the captives arrived in the Americas, their life conditions were regulated by public policy. Governments also regulated and profited from the commerce in slave produce.[897]

---

893   Ibid., 65.
894   Patric, Adibe/Boateng, Osei (2000). "Portugal, the mother of all slavers", in: New African, No. 385, London: IC Publications, 20.
895   Ibid.
896   Ryder (1969), 66 et seq.
897   Blackburn, Robin (1998). The Making of New World Slavery. From the Baroque to the Modern 1492-1800, London/New York: Verso, 6.

A contemporary European eye-witness reported concerning Nueva Andalucía, a territory in present-day Venezuela records that "I witnessed the enslavement of Blacks who had come to this region as free persons out of zeal for the faith, in order to be instructed in it. But because they were Blacks, the governor sold them as if they were royal property, for his own enrichment. (...) So embedded have error and perverse custom become that any Black whatsoever is obliged to be a slave, like a horse or a cow, or acquired, sold, ground down, and crushed, like a dog, even as wild beasts are taken, hunted, and seized."[898]

Thus, just by means of these few examples it already becomes manifest that much of the conduct that constituted transatlantic slavery can be attributed to European governments, such as Portugal and Spain, via Art. 4.

ii. Excursus: Art. 7 (Excess of authority or contravention of instructions)

Of course, as with the last example, it may not always be possible to prove for certain from the available historical evidence if a governor was exceeding his competences or contravening instructions or if the details of his conduct were indeed ordered by the Spanish government. That question is practically of little importance though, because responsibility could be established in both cases, via Art. 4 (Conduct of organs of a state) or Art. 7 (Excess of authority or contravention of instructions). Art. 7 holds that "(t)he conduct of an organ of a State or of a person or entity empowered to exercise elements of the governmental authority shall be considered an act of the State under international law if the organ, person or entity acts in that capacity, even if it exceeds its authority or contravenes instructions". Thus, even if the behavior of Nueva Andalucía's governor was indeed an "unauthorized *ultra vires* act", it would still remain attributable to Spain.

This approach is also covered by international law practice antedating the Articles on state responsibility. In 1930, a majority of states responding to the Preparatory Committee of the Hague Codification Conference's request for information were clearly in favour of the broadest formulation of the rule that provides for attribution of conduct to states in the case of "acts of officials in the national territory in their public capacity (*actes de fonction*) but exceeding their authority".[899] In the *Caire case*, the concerned Commission held in 1929 "that the two officers, even if they are deemed to have acted outside their competence (...) and even if their superiors countermanded an order, have involved the responsibility of the State, since they acted under cover of their status as officers and used means placed at their disposal of that status" [900]. This case concerned the murder of a French national by two Mexican officers who, after failing to extort money, shot him.

Thus, Crawford sustained that "(...) the central issue to be addressed in deter-

---

898   De Moirans (1682), 57 et seq. (emphasis added).
899   Crawford (2002), 107 et seq.
900   Ibid.

mining the applicability of Article 7 to unauthorized conduct of official bodies is whether the conduct was performed by the body in an official capacity or not. (...) The problem of drawing the line between unauthorized but still 'official' conduct, on the one hand, and 'private' conduct on the other, may be avoided if the conduct complained of is systematic or recurrent, such that the State knew or ought to have known of it and should have taken steps to prevent it"[901]. Now, the conduct of European state officials, whether entirely covered by instructions or formally exceeding them, was without doubt cause and driving force that made transatlantic slavery the genocidal system that it was, encompassing large parts of the globe. Illegal and genocidal conduct by European states was systematic and recurrent, such as evidenced by the examples mentioned so far and those that will be recalled in the upcoming pages. As seen in Chapter II. 3. c., the involved European states were also aware of the illegality of this systematic conduct, and thus "should have taken steps to prevent" acts of their officials if they constituted excesses of authority or if the state agents contravened instructions.

Yet, involved European governments not only took no steps to prevent the conduct that made transatlantic slavery a systematic reality, but they actually set it up, and explicitly permitted owners to mutilate slaves in later colonial laws, such as Portugal until 1824.[902] The use of the whip was abolished only in 1886. By law, freedom-takers were to be cruelly tortured. Rules introduced in the 18th century allowed branding with a hot iron. All of this happened although in the imperial constitution of 1824 torture, branding, and cruel punishments in general were prohibited. Public rights of freed Africans were also severely limited. This has already been exposed in the chapter on the legal qualification of transatlantic slavery as genocide.[903]

So, when representatives of the Portuguese Crown periodically organized razzias and *coup d'états* in Congo and in what would become Angola, this is generally attributable to Portugal via Art. 4. Yet, even in case that it should be established that the acting officials contravened instructions, attribution to Portugal via Art.7 would still catch on. [904]

iii. Examples of attribution to England

After this brief excursion into Art. 7 on the basis of examples of conduct of Portuguese organs, which may – after pertinent clarification of the historical facts – also well remain attributable via Art. 4, a few more words should be said on this Article and the conduct of other enslaver states, such as Britain.

---

901 Ibid., 107f (emphasis added).
902 Watson (1989), 159.
903 Ibid., 100 et seq.
904 Curto, José C. (2002). 'Un butin illegitime: razzias d'esclaves et relations luso-africaines dans la région des fleuves Kwanza et Kwango en 1805', in: Isabel Castro Henriques and Louis Sala-Molins (ed.): Déraison, esclavage et droit. Les fondements ideologiques et juridiques de la traite negriere et de l'esclavage, Paris: EDITIONS Unesco, 314- 327, 314 et seq.

A good example of conduct that is attributable via Art. 4 is the passing of a legal opinion by law officers of the British Crown that was issued as a means to counter abolitionist efforts and to continue to carry on with illegal chattel slavery. In 1729, slave owners had become very worried over the consistent position of English courts, which in a series of decisions, had upheld the Freedom Principle and set formerly enslaved Africans free. Slave owners asked the British Attorney-General Philip Yorke and the Solicitor-General Charles Talbot to render an opinion on this question. Yorke and Talbot declared "that a Slave by coming from the West-Indies to Great Britain, doth not become free, and that his Master's Property or Right in him is not thereby determined or varied: And that Baptism doth not bestow freedom on him, nor make any Alterations in his Temporal Condition in these Kingdoms".[905] This so-called Yorke-Talbot opinion subsequently became an important argument for the "legality" of slavery, and against the mounting pressure to abolish the institution. Yorke and Talbot were both elevated to the rank of Lord Chancellor as Lord Hardwicke and Lord Talbot, respectively, by the Crown soon after. The opinion, delivered in a pub, was given the full respect and authority of a legal ruling twenty years later, when the same Philip Yorke who had issued it, by then Lord Chancellor Hardwicke, ruled that African slaves were chattels as far as English law was concerned in the Pearne v. Lisle (1749) case. [906] He was clearly contravening the Freedom Principle that had been constantly recognized and confirmed as a centuries-long tradition in court rulings, as well as the general principles of international law. "Nevertheless, the opinion was taken by slave owners as establishing the legitimacy of slavery in England, despite its lack of support from precedent."[907] Since Art. 4 covers conduct by every branch of the state, including the judicative and legislative, this is a case for its application and the responsibility of England is thus engaged.

iv. Examples of attribution to France

In 1685, the French government began to establish rules that would regulate the relationship between masters and slaves for all the French colonies in the royal decree known as the Code Noir. It was the first such piece of European legislation.[908] Although legislation itself belongs to the realm of application of Art. 8 (Conduct directed or controlled by the state), and will be treated in more detail in the section dealing specifically with that Article, the conduct of French state officials, such as judges and governors, who based their conduct on that legislation, are cases for application of Art. 4.

---

905   Sammons (2007), 336.
906   Ibid.
907   Yorke–Talbot slavery opinion, downloaded from http://en.wikipedia.org/wiki/Yorke%E2%80%93Talbot_slavery_opinion (accessed 19.10.2010).
908   Peabody (1996), 11 et seq.

Art. 44 of the *Code Noir* considered slaves as *biens meubles* or chattel.[909] The Code aimed to give a legal basis to physical abuse and punishments such as branding, the cutting off of ears, hamstringing, and death, as provided in Articles 34 to 38 or 42 to 58.[910] It also contained provisions to protect slaves from masters' arbitrariness to a certain extent. Shackling, beating and whipping were permitted, whereas deliberate mutilation and killing were not (Art 42-43). Husbands, wives and children were not to be sold separately. These provisions of protection, however, were not observed and largely remained *lettre mort*.[911] This state of affairs is highlighted by various scholars and is testified by the great number of acquittals of masters by French judges, even when it was uncontested that masters had brutalized and murdered enslaved persons. Even when condemned, punishment was light, such as simple advertisement of conviction or the imposition of small fines.[912] In reality, it was the enslaved person who was punished when taking legal action against mistreatment, such as in the case of Babet Binture. When she sued for her freedom in Martinique in 1705, the judge found it appropriate that to "punish her temerity to start inappropriate and groundless proceedings against the said Miss Pallu, her mistress, we have condemned and do condemn her to submit to a month in prison, feet in chains, in the royal prisons of this island".[913] Such conduct of French judges and state officials violated both constitutional French law (see Chapter II. 3. c. iv. on the Freedom Principle) and international legal standards.

This disrespect for the fundamental laws prohibiting the kind of slavery practised in the transatlantic system, by the executive and legislative branches of the French state was crucial for the whole functioning of the transatlantic slavery system. The illegal actions of these judges are attributable to France per Art. 4.

v. Less prominently involved European states

Attribution of conduct to other, less prominently involved states, such as my birth country Austria, still necessitates much further research. It is documented that a number of enslaved Africans came to Austria, by means of the connections of the Austrian Habsburger lineage with the royal families of Portugal and Spain as well as through the slave port of Messina.[914] Although life conditions of these Africans were, for the few records that we have, far superior to those of transat-

---

909   Richard, Jérémy (2010). "Du Code Noir de 1685 au projet de 1829: De la semi-réification à l'humanisation de l'esclave noir", in: Tanguy Le Marc'hadour and Manuel Carius (ed.): Eslavage et Droit. Du Code noir à nos jours, Arras: Artois Presses Université, 15-41, 60 et seq.

910   Ibid.

911   Peabody/Grinberg (2007), 52; see also Castaldo (2006), 11.

912   Benoiton, Laurent (2010). 'Le droit de l'esclave d'ester en justice contre son maître. Réflexions sur une disposition du Code noir protectrice de l'esclave', in: Tanguy Le Marc'hadour and Manuel Carius (ed.): Eslavage et Droit. Du Code noir à nos jours, Arras: Artois Presses Université, 15-41, 49 et seq.

913   Peabody/Grinberg (2007), 38.

914   Sauer/Wiesböck (2007), 37.

lantic plantation slavery, their enslavement was still presumably illegal and they were put through the horrors of parts of the Middle Passage. Since the aristocrats and state officials held these potentially illegally enslaved Africans in bondage in their function as state representatives, responsibility may be attributable to Austria via Art. 4 for the illegal subjection to slavery of these Africans.

The Austrian *East Indian Company* held profitable trading posts on the coast of Mozambique and on the Nicobares from 1777 to 1781, though it is not clear from the materials accessible so far to what extent it was implicated in transatlantic slavery, and what was its destiny after 1781.

One enslaved African named Jacob Bock was put to death by hanging in Vienna on August 23, 1704. The man reportedly came from the kingdom of "Chongo", and had been taken by the police after a bar fight. Although not more involved in the tumult than dozens of others, he was easily identifiable because of his colour and the only one arrested and charged. Bock had probably reached Austria via Portugal.[915]

There are four documented instances when the bodies of deceased Africans (Anjou, Arcate, Soliman and Hammar) were withheld from their families and not allowed to be buried. They were, on order or with acknowledgement of the highest authorities of the state, used for research and exposed alongside stuffed animals.[916] These occurrences provide lines of reflection that may be worth further investigation for establishing legal responsibility.

B. ART. 5 - CONDUCT OF PERSONS OR ENTITIES EXERCISING ELEMENTS OF GOVERNMENTAL AUTHORITY

Art. 5 relates to conduct performed not by state organs in the sense of Art. 4, but by entities and persons which although formally not state organs are nonetheless authorized to exercise governmental authority. This constellation covers parastatal entities which retain certain public or regulatory functions, and which may be empowered by the law of a state to exercise elements of governmental authority. Public corporations, semi-public entities, public agencies, and even private companies are all covered by this, provided that in each case the entity is empowered by the law of the state and exercises functions of a public character normally exercised by state organs. [917] Although crimes against humanity should never be a "function of a public character normally exercised by State organs", they are by their very nature normally committed in a state setting. The whole enterprise of transatlantic slavery took place in a setting which was directed and guided by European states.

Crawford explains in his commentary that

---

915   Sauer/Wiesböck (2007), 26 et seq.
916   Ibid., 47.
917   Crawford (2002), 100 et seq.

"(i)f it is to be regarded as an act of the State for purposes of international responsibility, the conduct of an entity must accordingly concern governmental activity and not other private or commercial activity in which the entity may engage. Thus, for example, the conduct of a railway company to which certain police powers have been granted will be regarded as an act of the State under international law if it concerns the exercise of those powers, but not if it concerns other activities." [918]

Transatlantic slavery did not involve a railway company, but it did involve mass transportation, although not on a voluntary basis, and the companies were granted coercive powers by the European states. The British state, for example, established the Royal African Company and endowed it with a royal monopoly patent vested with the Great Seal of England, dated September 27, 1672. The Charter of the Company was signed by King Charles II and early British slave trading ventures were conducted by the Royal African Company. This "trade" was sanctioned by British law and tenaciously supported by the British Parliament until its abolition in 1807.[919]

Generally speaking, "(w)hat is regarded as 'governmental' depends on the particular society, its history and traditions. Of particular importance will be not just the content of the powers, but the way they are conferred on an entity, the purposes for which they are to be exercised and the extent to which the entity is accountable to government for their exercise."[920] Royal slavery companies were at all times accountable to their national governments, and their conduct was directed and concretized by government activity, to varying degrees at different times. What makes attribution even less difficult is that under Art. 5, "(...) there is no need to show that the conduct was in fact carried out under the control of the State" once the state has vested the entity with the mentioned powers. [921] This was clearly the case with European enslaver states and their Royal Companies they founded and regulated.

i. Examples of attribution to England

The Royal African Company directed the way in which the genocidal ship dungeons in which millions of captured Africans were transported and died, were laid out:

"In addition to shackles and bolts, material for constructing platforms was among the items the Royal African Company required ship owners to provide before their departure for the African coast. The Company's agreement regarding Bingham's ship stipulated, for example: 'The owners [are] to provide ye s.d. ship w.th (sic!) a sufficient Quantity of Deals for platforms for ye Negroes, Shackles,

---

918   Ibid., 100 et seq.
919   Gifford (2007), 259 et seq.
920   Crawford (2002), 101.
921   Ibid.

bolts, firewood, a bean room large enough to stow such a quantity of beans as is sufficient (...)'."[922]

Such action of that state-chartered entity the conduct of which is attributable to the British state via Art. 5 in the conditions just laid down, was directly causal for the brutal death and sufferings of millions of illegally enslaved Africans.

On August 15, 1706, the Royal African Company's secretary further notified the said Bingham that "[the company officials] have considered your last proposal and are come to a Resolution that your Ship shall take in 450 Negroes and no more by reason she is a Crank [top-heavy] Ship"[923]. This represented one hundred enslaved Africans more than originally agreed. According to historians this crass over-packing became routine. "Whatever the number of captives a ship was allowed to carry, it was routine to permit and indeed to encourage ship owners and their captains to squeeze more bodies into their human cargoes. Though the Spanish Merchant was 'freighted' to carry 550, the company agents at Whydah had leave to put ten to 20 more persons aboard if they thought it 'convenient' to do so. The company's instructions regarding the William & Jane likewise noted that the ship was 'contracted to take in 230 slaves and 20 more if you can conveniently put them aboard'. And it was with approval that officials in London noted the use of children as filler to top off the cargoes put aboard the company's ships. 'We like well yo.r method (...) of putting some small boys & girls of 10 years of age and upwards abd. our own ships over and above ye complement we intended them for'"[924], one British official wrote to a ship captain.

The Forts that the Royal African Company entertained in, for example, James Island (Gambia), Bunce Island (Sierra Leone), Cape Coast, Dixcove, Winneba, Anomabu, Accra (Ghana) or Whydah (Benin) were truly dungeons that today remain material reminders of the genocide that transatlantic slavery was. I visited Cape Coast "Castle" for the first time about ten years ago, and I remember vividly my absolute shock, incomprehension and deep sadness about how humans could do this to other humans. The subterranean dungeons held about 250 people or more at any moment. They were kept there for weeks or even months, with one small hatch for light and through which food was thrown in. The dead and sick were there together with the living, like in the ships during the Middle Passage. Most times, the dungeons were so crowded that people did not even have space to lie down. One can still see today on the walls how over the decades and centuries the floor level raised about 1,5 metres from excrements, blood and decomposing human matter. All of this is attributable to the British state via Articles 4 and 5 and can be lodged in a legal reparations claim against that state.

---

922   Crawford, Jewel/Nobles, Wade W./DeGruy Leary, Joy (2003). "Reparations and Health Care for African Americans", in: Raymond A. Winbush (ed.): Should America pay? Slavery and the raging debate on reparations, New York: Amistad, 251-281, 254.
923   Ibid.
924   Smallwood, Stephanie E. (2007). Saltwater Slavery. A Middle Passage from Africa to American Diaspora, Cambridge: Harvard University Press, 69 et seq.

The following assessment of the Middle Passage, such as effectuated by the Royal African Company and other European state-chartered companies is not less disturbing:

"Human beings were chained together, and then piled on top of each other, where they had to lie and sleep in their own waste as well as that of the persons crowded next to them for weeks on end. A vicious cycle of disease ensued as African people huddled together crying, screaming, vomiting, and defecating uncontrollably. Along this human chain of misery, some were dead and some alive, the waft of rotting bodies adding to the stench. There was no escape from disease. The captives suffered from dysentery, diarrhea, eye infections, malaria, malnutrition, scurvy, worms, yaws, and typhoid fever. Slaves also suffered from friction sores, ulcers, injuries and wounds resulting from accidents, fights, and whippings. By far the greatest killer disease during the Middle Passage was the bloody flux: amoebic dysentery. Many succumbed to this bloody diarrhea, which alone resulted in a mortality rate of anywhere between 20 and 80 per cent. (...) [T]he three hundred years of the Transatlantic Slave Trade amounted to a massive Maafa (system of death and destruction beyond human comprehension and convention) unparalleled in the annals of history."[925]

Further research still needs to assess the details in the organization of the royal companies and their place within the various national European state systems, but in any case, given the mentioned historical facts, these crimes are attributable to England and other European states without much difficulty through either Art. 4 (Conduct of organs of a state), 5 (Conduct of persons or entities exercising elements of governmental authority), 8 (Conduct directed or controlled by a state) or 11 (Conduct acknowledged and adopted by a state as its own).

ii. Examples of attribution to the Netherlands

Suriname and other countries occupied by the Dutch, in whose home country slavery had no legal basis, were not officially colonies of that government, but were considered territories under the control of the Dutch West India Company, with local governors and councils. Slavery in Suriname has been described as particularly brutal, with that company having been primarily interested in looking after its financial gain with little concern otherwise in controlling the behavior of colonists and slave-holders.[926] Even though the Dutch state did not make that territory an "official" colony, the entire structures of transatlantic slavery in that territory and the acting company entity were the creations of the Dutch state, making Art. 5 fully applicable.

The Charter to the Dutch West India Company was granted by the states-general of the Netherlands on June 3, 1621. It did not grant the company power to legislate. A *placaat* of October 13, 1629, *Ordre van Regieringe in West-Indien*, provided

---

925   Crawford/Nobles/DeGruy Leary (2003), 254.
926   Watson (1989), 102 et seq.

in article 56 that in private law actions, personal or real, the law to be applied was the common law of the United Provinces. The company was given power to refuse to apply part of that law. Though not expressly given power to legislate, the company in practice issued numerous *placaaten*, as did the states-general, relating to the company's territories. [927] Theoretically, these *placaaten* were not law, but in practice the local courts gave them validity in matters such as restricting slaves from drumming, dancing or going out or in establishing penalties for freedom-takers. They regulated "decent and respectable behaviour of slaves" and even of free Blacks by restricting their access to certain places or requiring them to carry written passes wherever they went.[928]

In the 1750s, the public in Holland started to get more knowledge of the torture and hellish conditions of the Black people in Suriname, and the government saw itself obliged to take some steps to disassociate itself from those genocidal practices. The directors of the Society of Suriname thus advised their employees in 1760

"to watch with all vigilance, and have the Fiscals watch, the behavior and conduct of the Patrons and Owners there, in dealing with their slaves, but to treat them as humans and not as animals; castigating them moderately and in case they have committed crimes that merit a more severe punishment than a moderate beating they will have to turn them over to the [Court of] Justice to be punished by them with a proper Punishment as an example to the others: and insofar whites have overacted by cutting off the ears and noses of their slaves, or mutilated them in any other way and have punished them unreasonably or have mistreated them grossly or have even killed them such whites shall be responsible for this before the law, as will be decided according to the exigency of the matter"[929].

These "advices" were largely ignored by the planters of Suriname and even by the representatives of the Society. "Until far into the 18th century, the government did very little to combat the mistreatment of slaves (...)."[930]

These facts make attribution of legal responsibility to the Dutch state per Art. 5 possible, because it was that state that vested the Company with the powers to realize genocidal conduct.

iii. Examples of attribution to France

France became engaged in transatlantic slavery in the early 17th century after it had already started tobacco cultivation with indentured servants in Martinique, Guadeloupe and Saint Christophe. The change for the more labor intensive but potentially more lucrative sugar increased the demand for labor. Therefore in

---

927   Ibid.
928   Ibid., 105 et seq.
929   Wink, Marcus (2003). The World's Oldest Trade: Dutch Slavery and Slave Trade in the Indian Ocean in the Seventeenth Century, downloaded from http://www.historycooperative.org/cgi-bin/justtop.cgi?act=justtop&url=http://www.historycooperative.org/journals/jwh/14.2/vink.html   (accessed 28.4.2011).
930   Ibid.

1664, Louis XIV's minister Colbert granted the *Compagnie des Indes Occidentales* and its successors, the *Compagnie du Senegal* (1674), and the *Compagnie de Guinee* (1683), exclusive permission to bring slaves from Africa to the French colonies.[931] What has been sustained concerning the British and the Dutch state-chartered companies which transported millions of enslaved Africans in illegal and genocidal conditions, is equally valid for these French companies, thus engaging the legal responsibility of the French state through attribution via Art. 5.

C. ART. 8 - CONDUCT DIRECTED OR CONTROLLED BY THE STATE

Many of the facts just described in the section on Art. 4 contain elements that also may render attribution via Art. 8 possible. Art. 8 holds that "[t]he conduct of a person or group of persons shall be considered an act of a State under international law if the person or group of persons is in fact acting on the instructions of, or under the direction or control of, that State in carrying out the conduct". States themselves may not have run plantations and worked and tortured many millions of African people to death, but they surely planned, controlled and realized the whole setting of it. They made huge financial profits, drew up legislation, enforced (and intentionally mis-enforced) policy, and effectuated military interventions in Africa to produce slaves. The criterion of "direction or control" required by this article and customary international law poses no problem at all for attribution of illegal transatlantic slavery to European states.

As a general principle, the conduct of private persons or entities is not attributable to the state under international law. However, and logically so, when there exists a specific factual relationship between a person or entity engaging in an unlawful conduct and the state, it must of course be possible to attribute the conduct to the state under certain circumstances. Art. 8 deals with this constellation. In order that it may take effect, conduct must have taken place on the instructions of the state (officials); or it must have occurred under the state's direction or control. Following the principle of effectiveness in international law, the existence of a real link between the person or entity and the state machinery is necessary. Yet it does not matter whether the private actors' conduct involves "governmental activity" or not.

As for the degree of control which must be exercised by a state in order for the conduct to be attributable to it, some quite important court decisions have been rendered which clarified that aspect which was one of the key issues in the famous *Military and Paramilitary Activities* case. The International Court of Justice then ruled concerning the attribution of the acts of paramilitary groups that

---

931   Peabody (1996), 11 et seq.

"even the general control by the respondent State over a force with a high degree of dependency on it, would not in themselves mean, without further evidence, that the United States directed or enforced the perpetration of the acts contrary to human rights and humanitarian law alleged by the applicant State. Such acts could well be committed by members of the contras without the control of the United States. For this conduct to give rise to legal responsibility of the United States, it would in principle have to be proved that that State had effective control of the military or paramilitary operations in the course of which the alleged violations were committed."[932]

The Court sustained that the United States was responsible for its own support for the contras, but above that were the acts of the contras themselves judged attributable to the United States only in certain individual instances, depending on actual participation of and directions given by them.[933] Contrary to the situation of the Nicaragua case, however, where the United States supported the contras in a war that was taking place not solely on instigation by the United States, European enslaver states were at the very root of the transatlantic slavery system which would not have exited at all without their purposeful actions, direction and control. It is a historical fact that without their conduct, transatlantic slavery would not have happened at all. It was only by the framework that the states brought into existence (through legislation, conduct of state officials, the maintenance of slave plantation colonies, the chartering of shipping companies operating genocidal voyages, ...), that private individual enslavers and enslaver entities could carry out their individual yet systematic, murderous actions. Thus, even when judged by that rather restrictive perspective of the necessary degree of control and direction upheld by the International Court of Justice in the *Nicaragua Case*, attribution is possible in the case of transatlantic slavery since it was in its entirety set up and controlled by European states, and depended in its very foundations on brutality, barbarity and genocide.

This assessment of direction and control is of general validity for the millions and millions of single acts by private slavers. It was a decisive point for the ICJ to deny responsibility of the United States in the Nicaragua case that "such acts could well be committed by members of the contras without control of the United States"[934]. But contrary to that situation, for transatlantic slavery we dispose of an abundance of evidence about individual acts, a small abridgment of which has been mentioned in this work, which would and could never ever have happened without the direction or control of European enslaver governments.

---

932   Military and Paramilitary Activities in and against Nicaragua (Nicaragua v. United States of America), Judgement of 27 June 1986, ICJ reports 1986, 14.
933   Crawford (2002), 111.
934   Military and Paramilitary Activities in and against Nicaragua (Nicaragua v. United States of America), Judgement of 27 June 1986, ICJ reports 1986, 14.

The Appeals Chamber of the International Criminal Tribuna for Ex-Yugoslavia confirmed the standard set out in the *Nicaragua Case* and found that "overall control going beyond the mere financing and equipping of such forces and involving also participation in the planning and supervision of military operations" was necessary to attribute concrete behaviour conducted by private actors to a state. But where there was evidence that a private entity was exercising public powers, or that the state was using its ownership interest in or control of an entity specifically in order to achieve a particular result, the conduct in question has been attributed to the state. This was the case, for example, with the charter companies that effectuated the genocidal Middle Passage. According to jurisprudence, each case will depend on its own facts, and "the instructions, direction or control must relate to the conduct which is said to have amounted to an internationally wrongful act".[935]

Recently, in *Hasan Nuhanovic v. Netherlands*, the Court of Appeal in The Hague confirmed that "the decisive criterion for attribution is not who exercised 'command and control', but who actually was in possession of 'effective control'"[936]. Thus, we need not to concern ourselves with questions of which organ of European enslaver states gave specific instructions of command in occurrences that happened up to 500 years ago, but it suffices that it is historically well documented that these states exercised "effective control" over the transatlantic slavery system in its entirety and over instances of individual conduct which, cumulatively, made up that system. The Court explicitly stated that for assessing if such "effective control" took place, "the background" of a situation has to be considered, and that participation of a government in the "decision-making" about a certain conduct, has to be taken into account. "Allegations" of conduct brought against a state need to be "related" to governmental "decisions and instructions".[937]

Alongside colonial slavery legislation, the fact that European enslaver governments purposefully armed and manipulated African rulers and groups to war with one another with the aim of producing slaves for their plantation colonies makes much of such conduct which was constitutive for the crime of transatlantic slavery attributable to those states via Art. 8. European slavers left some clear evidence of their direct responsibility for wars for slave-making. One such striking example is the case of one M. Poncet, then governor of Gorée (Senegal), who in 1764 informed the French minister of his intentions to embroil the Damel Madior and Bourba Yoloff in a savage war in order to weaken both sovereigns so that they were no longer in a position to oppose French penetration of the country. "As for the king by the name Bourba Yoloff (...) if he does not want to arrange himself

---

935   Ibid., 112 et seq.
936   Hasan Nuhanovic v. Netherlands, Appeal Judgement of July 5, 2011, Gerechtshof's Gravenhage (Court of Appeal), The Hague.
937   Ibid.

with me, I will make him war with the Damel. (...) I will make him feel where his interest lies and I will give the Damel gifts of gun powder and bullets [and] I could even send him a detachment and a canon so that he will attack Bourba Yoloff."[938] Thus, even when the French did not do the dirty work of capturing Africans to enslave them with their own physical strength, the illegal enslavement is attributable to them through Art. 8.

Indeed, the regions for which we have most documents evidencing European's intervention through direction and control, such as the Niger Delta (Dahomey and Benin) and the Congo basin, are at the same time the regions where more than two-thirds of all deported Africans were taken from. We have already seen above how the Portuguese controlled deportations from the coastal area around the Niger Delta from the 15th century in order to supply Sao Tomé and later Brazil with slave labor.[939]

In the Americas, enslaved African people had only two routes to freedom – being given it by their oppressors or taking it themselves. In the first case, the granting of freedom was always dependent on the legal framework of the enslaver state. Most often, manumission could take place only with the consent of the authoritarian state and was granted mostly for "exemplary national service", which usually meant betraying revolts or Maroon hideouts.[940] This is a further proof that European states, through legislation and policy making, exercised "effective control" and directed the entire system of illegal transatlantic slavery, giving way to attribution of the genocidal conduct of private slavers to European enslaver states by means of Art. 8.

Since the evolution of transatlantic slavery, with all its contradictions, can only be retraced meaningfully – on a legal as well as moral level – in a historically chronological perspective, it seems expedient to start the pertinent assessment of possible attribution via. Art. 8 from the very beginning.

i. Examples of attribution to Portugal

It was in 1441 that the Portuguese Antão Gonçalves and Nuno Tristão captured and brought 12 Africans to Portugal, on order of Henry the Navigator. Soon after, on August 8, 1444, another 235 kidnapped Africans were landed by Lançarote de Freitas, who was an appointed customs official for Henry, near Lagos on the south-west point of the Algarve. Subsequently the Portuguese continued to capture more and more Africans as slaves. Cada Mosto, a Venetian adventurer who travelled with the Portuguese, noted that: "The Portuguese caravels, sometimes four, sometimes more, used to come to the Gulf of Arguin, [northern Mauritania],

---

938 Omotunde, Jean-Philippe (2004). La traite négrière européenne: vérité et mensonge, Paris: Editions Menaibuc, 95 (t.b.a.).
939 Popo (2010), 111.
940 Thompson (2006), 91.

well armed, and, landing by night, surprised some fishermen's villages."[941] For the purpose of attributing legal responsibility in view of reparations, it is important to acknowledge that the captains who led these kidnapping raids had to obtain a license to do so from Prince Henry the Navigator, son of King John I of Portugal, who always received a "fifth of the booty". The fact alone that these regular and illegal kidnapping raids had to be covered by such a royal license has the effect that the requirement of "effective control" is fulfilled, such as outlined above and recently confirmed by the Court of Appeals in The Hague (participation of a government in the "decision-making" about a certain conduct).

The raids soon became so lucrative that the bishop of the Algarve sent his own ship on such expeditions. Slaving was so profitable that the Portuguese sailed more unchartered seas further down the West African coast. Several of Prince Henry's protégés, such as Goncalo de Sintra, Nuno Tristão or the Danish nobleman Vallarte who had joined Henry's court, were killed while attempting to enslave Africans there. As the Portuguese death toll rose, Henry was compelled to change his tactics somewhat and thus commissioned Joao Fernandes, one of his slaving captains, to "buy" Africans instead of kidnapping them.[942] But as we have seen from evidence cited in abundance above, especially in Chapter IV, governors and other Portuguese state officials intentionally fostered wars to produce slaves whom they could then "buy" from collaborators, and also continued to engage in slave raiding themselves through the centuries of transatlantic slavery.

In 1468 and 1518, the Portuguese crown proclaimed the *Asiento do Negroes* (monopoly on the trade in slaves) in order to accelerate its provisions with African slaves.[943] In 1600, at a time when Portugal was part of Spain, it established a virtual monopoly of the slave trade by securing from the Spanish Crown a contract to supply the Spanish colonies with African slaves.[944] By all of this and other actions mentioned above and below, the Portuguese state spun a tight web through which it, as such and together with other European enslaver governments, directed and controlled illegal transatlantic enslavement and slavery, making even the illegal conduct of private slavers and collaborators attributable to Portugal.

ii. Examples of attribution to Spain

As early as 1476, Carlos de Valera had brought 400 enslaved Africans to Spain. In 1510, King Ferdinand of Spain had authorized a shipment of 50 slaves to be sent to the occupied territory of Santo Domingo.

Charles V, who was also the ruler of Germany and the Netherlands at that time, granted an exclusive patent to members of Flemish nobility to import 4,000 Africans annually, for the supply of Hispaniola, Cuba, Jamaica, and Puerto Rico

---

941   Patric/Boateng (2000), 20.
942   Ibid.
943   Harris (1992), 113.
944   Ibid., 114.

in 1517. It has been sustained that "(t)his great prince was not, in all probability, aware of the dreadful evils attending this horrible traffic, nor of the crying injustice of permitting it; for in 1542, when he made a code of laws for his Indian subjects, he liberated all the Negroes, and by a word put an end to their slavery" [945]. Unfortunately, I was not able to locate more evidence to verify this.

Be that as it may, what is sure is that the Spanish Crown subsequently organized in a very official manner the transatlantic "slave" "trade" with other European slaver nations.[946] Spain claimed to be in a position to do so, because it had been given the right to subdue that part of the world by the pope. This was realized via the just mentioned *asiento* system, by which Spain authorized private persons or entities to take a certain number of enslaved Africans to the Spanish colonies during a determined time period. This monopoly was given to the highest bidder, and was detained at various times by Portuguese, Flemish, Dutch, French or English entities. [947]

We have seen in a previous chapter that Spain and Portugal were the only European enslaver states who had had some slave law before transatlantic slavery. Transatlantic slavery was, however, not compatible with these laws, as they contained many protection clauses (prohibition of excessive punishment, manumission favored, care-taking of old or infirm slaves, etc....) and did not tolerate illegal means of enslavement such as kidnapping. Excessive punishment was to lead to the sale of a slave to another owner, and if he could not be sold, the owner was even responsible to provide for his keep without the slave returning to him. No other person had the right to punish slaves.[948]

However, in transatlantic slavery, these laws were always interpreted restrictively and eroded by colonial tribunals and administrators. It was, for example, argued that children of a former slave woman who had bought her freedom were not free. This was contrary to traditional legal practice in Spain. It was justified by the royal government on the sole basis that a different decision would reduce the number of slaves and significantly diminish royal tax revenues on the sale of slaves. "The king accepted this opinion. (...) The Spanish monarchy was in line with other governments charged with making private law: it showed little interest apart from peacekeeping and, as here, raising money."[949] To cement the subordination of African people even further, a royal colonial *ordenanza* of April 2, 1612 contained an interdiction for more than three Black people to come together in a public or concealed place for any reason.[950]

In the *Codigo Negro Carolino* for Santo Domingo, issued on March 14, 1785,

---

945   Goodell (1852), 5 et seq.
946   Tardieu, Jean-Pierre (1984). Le destin des Noirs aux Indes de Castille XVIe-XVIIe siècles, Paris: L'Harmattan, 7 et seq.
947   Plumelle-Uribe (2008), 82 et seq.
948   Watson (1989), 50.
949   Ibid., 51.
950   Ibid., 111.

manumission was further severely restricted. It was no longer possible only by the will and act of an owner, but permission of the governor was now necessary, among other additional new requirements.[951] This body of law had its origins in the Royal Order of December 23, 1783 which had ordered the formation of "rules for the economic, political, and moral governing of the blacks of the island to conform to those in the French Code Noir"[952]. The Spanish part of the island had been in economic decline for more than a century, in sharp contrast to the prosperity of the other part, Haiti, occupied by France. One of the reasons was identified as laying in the "strict", ruthless and brutal control of slaves by the French. "In contrast to the legislation emanating from Spain, this Codigo, which was far more severe toward slaves, was the result of attitudes on the spot."[953] Law 5 enacted that every Black person, slave or free, "*primerizo or terceron* and on up will be as submissive and respectful to every white person, as if each of them was his owner or master"[954]. Law 6 closed public schools to all Black people "because they are destined to work in agriculture and must not mix with whites, tercerones, and so on"[955]. Under law 7, a Black person who failed in some way to respect a "white" was to be placed in the pillory or iron ring and given 25 lashes. Law 8 punished any Black person who raised his hand, stick, or stone against any "white" for any reason with 100 lashes and two years of imprisonment on short rations, with fetters on the feet. Law 11 laid down that no Black person (including "mulatto, cuarteron or mestizo") had the right to reproach or contradict "white" people, except in very submissive terms, even if he or she knew they were right, or to raise their voices elatedly or arrogantly, or to complain to superiors of any injury they had done to them.[956]

In 1785, the Spanish Crown released a law titled *Real Instrucción or Real Cédula*. It held that slaves could buy their freedom at a fixed price. Most enslaved persons however, did not know of the existence of that law. This situation of ignorance was intentionally maintained by royal policy, because when the *Real Cédula* reached Caracas, Havana, Luisiana and Santo Domingo, "the very places where slaves were common", petitions were brought in about the very grave injuries that would follow its publication and putting it into effect. "It was maintained that the Cédula was nothing but a repetition and amplification of existing Spanish laws, which were founded on natural law, in the bonds of Christian charity and in the immutable rules of humanity."[957] However, because of "differences in climate, customs, and persons in the colonies", it was argued that the law should not be

---

951   Ibid., 52 et seq.
952   Ibid., 59 et seq.
953   Ibid.
954   Ibid.
955   Ibid.
956   Ibid.
957   Ibid.

applied. The municipal councils of New Orleans and Santo Domingo, that is Spanish administration, came up with examples of thefts and murders that would have been committed by Black people "who were only controlled by a prudent rigor" [958]. The Spanish King therefore suspended the law from application in the colonies so that genocidal slavery could go on undisturbed.

After abolition in 1886, the Spanish state set in place the *patronato* system, which was based on forced apprenticeship and retained most features of slavery, though under another name.[959] It does not necessitate any big explanations to see that by these actions Spain did direct and control the transatlantic slavery system, together with the other European enslaver states. Their responsibility to make reparations is therefore established per Art. 8.

iii. Examples of attribution to the Netherlands

Dutch colonization and slavery started with the creation of the West India Company in 1621. Its purpose was oriented towards the conquest of territories that were under occupation of other Europeans. Thus, the Dutch wrenched Luanda from the Portuguese from 1641 until 1648, and took over a part of Brazil in 1654. By 1648 they also had "colonies" in North America, on the coasts of Brazil and in the Caribbean. [960]

As already mentioned, these territories were not officially "colonies", but under the governance of the Company. But it was the Dutch state who set it up in that way in order to derive huge profits; by the establishment of the Company as such, the state exercised direction and control. Brutality and torture were abundant. In Berbice, on the north coast of South America, for example, a plantation manager in the mid-18th century brutalized a seven-year-old girl for trifling "offences". He gave her 250 lashes, had her placed in the stocks without food, except what friends and relatives smuggled to her, and kept her that way for three weeks.

A plantation overseer in Suriname had a young woman of eighteen years stripped naked and tied her up to a tree branch with her hands suspended, giving her 200 lashes because she had refused to allow him to invade her body sexually. Stedman, who was in Suriname as a mercenary to hunt down Maroons, recorded this incident and wrote that the woman had been "skinned alive". When he intervened on her behalf, the overseer was so furious that he gave her another 200 lashes. Stedman wrote that after the first whipping she had been dyed in blood from her neck to her ankles.[961] Nobel literature laureate Vidiadhar Naipaul described "Stedman's account of slave life in Suriname as a terrifying catalogue of atrocities reminiscent of the German concentration camps – with the important difference that visitors to Suriname were allowed to survey the scene and make

---

958   Ibid.
959   Peabody/Grinberg (2007), 20.
960   Plumelle-Uribe (2008), 82 et seq.
961   Thompson (2006), 25.

notes and sketches".[962] Because they set up the whole system of transatlantic slavery and controlled all these atrocities in a systematic manner, such atrocities are attributable to European enslaver states, in that case the Netherlands, via Art. 8 and engage their legal responsibility to make reparations.

iv. Examples of attribution to France

By chance, the materials I was able to gather contain much evidence concerning France, and that constitutes the sole and only reason why the following section about French responsibility will be lengthier than the previous ones about other states' responsibility. This, however, does not mean that other enslaver states were less involved and would have incurred less responsibility.

The French started their colonizing enterprise in the 16th century in North America and continued to occupy several islands and territories in the 17th century.[963] From the start, it was the French government that promoted transatlantic slavery. The French state sustained a coordinated effort to build its colonial sugar export centers with capital, credit, technology and slaves after the example of the Dutch. By 1670, there were 300 sugar plantations in Martinique, Guadeloupe and St. Christophe.[964]

The state financed the *Compagnie des Indes Occidentales* in 1664 which held a monopoly on slave deportations for quite some time. A French fleet then wrenched many factories from the Dutch in Senegambia. "In 1672, the French government offered a bounty of 10 livres per slave transported to the French West Indies. This spurred the formation of a second monopoly company, *Compagnie du Sénégal*, founded in 1673. By 1679, it had 21 ships in operation. During the 1730s alone, the French shipped probably more than 100,000 slaves from Africa. The government raised the bounty per slave delivered to 100 livres, and in 1787 upped it again to 160." [965]

Slave ship construction was also under direct governmental control. With ever more Africans being swallowed into transatlantic slavery, the ships grew bigger, and the attendant horrors of the Middle Passage were multiplied in the bigger ships. The French overtook the British in sugar production for the first time in 1767. "To keep the supply of African captives flowing, the French government had permanent establishments at the Senegal River and Whydah on the Gold Coast."[966] French slavers were also active in East Africa, shipping Africans to the French Indian Ocean island colonies, which were also thriving on sugar exports.[967]

---

962   Ibid., 27.
963   Plumelle-Uribe (2008), 82 et seq.
964   French Slavery, downloaded from http://etymonline.com/columns/frenchslavery.htm (accessed 29.5.2010).
965   Ibid.
966   Ibid.
967   Ibid.

Because of the increased demand for labor, Louis XIV's minister Colbert grant-ed the *Compagnie des Indes Occidentales* (1664) and its successors, the *Compagnie du Senegal* (1674) and the *Compagnie de Guinee* (1683), exclusive permission to transport slaves from Africa to the French colonies. This was done in spite of the Freedom Principle and the interdiction of slavery in France, retraced above. Then in 1685, the French government began to regulate the criminal oppression of Af-ricans in the Code Noir. [968]

However, as we have seen in Chapter II. 3. c. iv, no laws initially specified what should happen when an enslaved person made his or her way to France.[969] France found itself confronted with a series of law suits in which enslaved Africans upon arrival in France claimed their freedom based on the illegality of slavery and the constitutionality of the Freedom Principle in France. To tackle this contradict-ing situation, the government tried to simply keep African people from reaching France, such as in 1694 by introducing a penalty of "400 livres for each negro, whatever age and strength he may be", if a captain wittingly or unwittingly trans-ported him to France.[970]

In 1704, Mithon, *Conseilleur of Martinique*, wrote to the minister of the marine to "seek advice regarding slaves who travelled to France and then returned to the colonies with their masters"[971]. In this request, Mithon acknowledged a decision of the King of 1696 whereby slaves setting foot on French soil were free and un-der no obligation to accompany their masters back to the colonies. "In practice, however, Mithon noted that the former slaves who returned to Martinique were treated as freedmen (*t*), rather than men of free birth, and consequently owed a life time of service to their former masters." [972] Thus, we see that the prohibition of genocidal chattel slavery was systematically disregarded by French authorities. This intentional and purposeful disregard served to direct and control the course of transatlantic slavery. A general royal ordinance of October 24, 1713 forbade masters to free their slaves without written permission from the governors. Man-umission without such permission was void and freed Africans were to be re-sold at the profit of the French King. [973]

The first Code Noir of 1685 was complemented by further edicts in 1723 (for Réunion) and 1724 (for Louisiane). These laws contained similar provisions, such as a repetition of the declaration of slaves as movables and chattels. [974] Sometimes all of them are referred to as Code Noir[975] , since they were all eventually brought

---

968   Peabody (1996), 11 et seq.
969   Ibid.
970   Ibid., 13.
971   Ibid., 14.
972   Ibid.
973   Watson (1989), 88 et seq.
974   Ibid., 90.
975   Niort (2010), 16.

together and published in 1742 in Paris under that official designation.[976]

The *Code Jaune*, issued for Maurice and Madagascar in 1777 also stipulated that a written permission of the governor was obligatory for every manumission of a slave. Otherwise manumissions were void and could entail a penalty for the owner, and the seizure and sale of the concerned African for the profit of the King. This law also prohibited marriages between Black and "white" people. Children from such unions, or from relations between "whites" or free Blacks with slaves would be confiscated and were to labor as slaves for the Crown without any possibility of manumission.[977]

France had already issued a general interdiction of marriages between "white" and Black people in 1724. In 1764, more laws were passed that kept free Black people from medical, pharmaceutical, notarial and legal professions; from assembling; from property accumulation through inheritance; from taking on the name of their "white" fathers and so forth.[978] From 1763, many new legal measures were issued to prevent African people from "flaunting any signs of elevated status (...)". Former slaves and their descendants were pressed into a mandatory military service that was not required for "whites". The use of Madame and Monsieur was prohibited to them, and in 1779 a law "forbade to dress or wear hair in the manner of whites".[979] By such actions France both directly realized illegal conduct attributable via Art. 4, and, above that, directed and controlled genocidal behavior of private slavers, making attribution of the conduct of such private individuals and entities via Art. 8 possible.

By the late 1780s, France's colonies in the Caribbean produced more than two-fifths of Europe's sugar and coffee, and the French government was increasingly dependent on slavery as a source of revenue. [980] However, the wave of lawsuits caused those who profited most from slavery considerable worries and spurred the royal administrators to develop new legislation that would halt the flow of Africans to the French mainland. These royal efforts culminated in the *Declaration pour la police des Noirs*, issued in 1777. This law generally prohibited the entry of all "blacks, mulattoes, and other people of color" into the kingdom. So that colonists could still take personal slaves during their voyage, this new law established depots at France's ports where all "non-whites" (free or enslaved) would be de-

976   Watson (1989), 83 et seq.

977   Benoit, Norbert (2002). "L'esclavage dans le Code jaune ou code Delaleu", in: Isabel Castro Henriques and Louis Sala-Molins (ed.): Déraison, esclavage et droit. Les fondements idéologiques et juridiques de la traite négrière et de l'esclavage, Paris: EDITIONS Unesco, 95- 104, 100 et seq.

978   Giradin, Jean-Claude (2002). "De la liberte politique des Noirs: Sonthonax et Toussaint Louverture", in: Isabel Castro Henriques and Louis Sala-Molins (ed.): Déraison, esclavage et droit. Les fondements idéologiques et juridiques de la traite négrière et de l'esclavage, Paris, EDITIONS Unesco, 213-237, 224 et seq.

979   Peabody/Grinberg (2007), 6 et seq.

980   Peabody (1996), 3.

tained until they could be sent back to the colonies on the next available ship. That law prescribed policy based on skin color alone, rather than on slave status. This was done to prevent what had happened with the previous *Codes Noirs* that the *Parlement* of Paris had refused to register because of their violation of the Freedom Principle.[981] Now, the *Police des Noirs* was indeed registered by the Parlement of Paris. The Minister of the Marine Sartine had "deliberately advocated the use of racial language as a way to circumvent the *Parlement's* opposition to legislation containing the word "slave". As the Codes Noirs and previous legislation, the *Police des Noirs* had been ad-hoc legislation prompted by a series of court cases in which slaves had sued successfully for their freedom.[982]

Yet, even the *Police des Noirs* could not stop enslaved persons from suing for their freedom. "The tension between France's economic dependence on colonial slavery and its celebration of liberty is manifest in hundreds of court cases in which slaves who were brought to France as servants by their colonial masters sought to escape slavery in the final century of the Ancient Regime. On the basis of the Freedom Principle, nearly all of them obtained their freedom, particularly in the jurisdiction of the Parliament of Paris."[983] New cases prompted the Marquis de Castries, who had replaced Sartine as Minister of the marine in 1780, to issue a new decree that prohibited Black people from adopting the titles of *Sieur* and *Dame*. He also ordered all tribunals to refuse all petitions for freedom. De Castries promulgated a law requiring Black people to carry identification papers at all times. Failure to comply led to arrest and being sent to the colonies.[984]

We have already discussed some of the general outset and details of the *Code Noir* above. Let us recall that while the *Code Noir* prohibited the killing of an enslaved person, this remained systematically unenforced until the last days of slavery. According to Fouchard, l'Arada, a slave holder in Saint Martin, assassinated 200 of his slaves, while another by the name of Caradeux buried alive several enslaved people. Both were protected by the state's systematic and intentional failure to execute the law. Fouchard lists several other slavers who gained notoriety for their cruelty and gives a long detailed list of punishments meted out to enslaved persons in Haiti, some of which "indicated sadism that surpassed the imagination".[985] There are descriptions of the throwing of living people into ovens; suspending them over spits like barbecuing meat; burning or mutilating men's genitalia and women's genitalia and breasts; priming their anuses with gunpowder which was then set alight; burying them up to the neck and pouring sugar over them so that they were consumed by flies or ants; making them eat

---

981   Ibid., 5 et seq.
982   Ibid., 106.
983   Ibid., 3.
984   Ibid., 134 et seq.
985   Fouchard, Jean (1972). Les marrons de la liberté, Paris: Editions de l'Ecole, 116-117.

their own faeces and drink their own urine; sewing their lips together with wire; raping women in front of their husbands and children; or cutting up children in front of their parents.[986]

All of this happened systematically while the French sovereign councils of Haiti, Martinique, Guadeloupe, Saint-Christophe, Saint Domingue, Guyane and other colonies were responsible for enforcing the law and thus, undoubtedly, exercised "effective control" such as required by international jurisprudence over the genocidal situation that reigned there. As the French empire grew, the political bureaucracy of the overseas colonies had been standardized, with the king at the top. Immediately beneath him was the secretary of state for the marine. The king also appointed two royal officials for each colony. They were the governor, who was invariably a military officer from an old aristocratic family, and the intendant, who had financial and administrative oversight. Superior Councils, consisting of six of the most prominent colonists and slavers, were the highest judicial courts of appeal. "French law emanated from the king's edicts and also from colonial councils"[987], and this general setting was enacted by the French state.

The slaves received the harshest punishment for the least faults. The Code Noir both authorized and regulated whipping,

"but the colonists paid no attention to these regulations and slaves were not infrequently whipped to death. The whip was not always an ordinary cane or woven cord, as the code demanded. Sometimes it was replaced by the rigoise or thick thong of cow-hide, or by the lianes – local growth of reeds, supple and pliant like whalebone. (...) It was the incentive to work and the guardian of discipline. But there was no ingenuity that fear or a depraved imagination could devise which was not employed to break their spirit and satisfy the lusts and resentment of their owners and guardians – irons on the hands and feet, blocks of wood that the slaves had to drag behind them wherever they went. The tin-plate mask designed to prevent the slaves from eating the sugar-cane, the iron collar. Whipping was interrupted in order to pass a piece of hot wood on the buttocks of the victim; salt, pepper, citron, cinders, aloes, and hot ashes were poured on the bleeding wounds. Mutilations were common on limbs, ears, and sometimes the private parts, to deprive them of the pleasures which they could indulge in without expense. Their masters poured burning wax on their arms and hands and shoulders, emptied the boiling cane sugar over their heads, burned them alive, roasted them on slow fires, filled them with gunpowder and blew them up with a match; buried them up to the neck and smeared their heads with sugar that the flies might devour them; fastened them near to nests of ants or wasps; made them eat their excrements, drink their urine, and lick saliva of other slaves." [988]

Acts of legislation, such as the *Code Noir* and other mentioned royal edicts, are

---

986   Ibid.
987   Peabody/Grinberg (2007), 5.
988   James, C.L.R. (1938). The Black Jacobins, London: Penguin Books (2001), 10.

a case for attribution via Art. 8 rather than Art. 4, because even though they may have violated national law and constitutional principles, such as in the case of France and Britain, it may be complicated to argue that such legislation in itself violated international law of that time. Yet what is sure, as pertinently demonstrated throughout this work, is that the practical consequences intentionally engendered by these pieces of legislation violated "fundamental legal principles of civilized nations [that are] (...) considered as rules of customary international law that have universal validity and by which the State is bound"[989]. Legislative conduct of enslaver states directed and controlled the practice of transatlantic slavery, and is thus relevant for attribution of the genocidal conduct of private slavers to the French state under Art. 8. It is important not to forget that the *Code Noir* never limited the powers of masters over slaves, because previously such powers of mistreatment had not legally existed at all, as France adhered to its constitutional Freedom Principle and general principles of international law prohibited transatlantic slavery. Such maltreatment and horror had not been recognized by any law before the 1685 edict; it was the French Crown who authorized "whites" to treat Africans like chattel or things.[990]

Evidence clearly shows that the described bestial practices were integral and essential for the maintenance of transatlantic slavery and the profits that European governments reaped from it. They were the "normal" features of slave life, and not sporadic events. The horror was so routine that special names developed for the barbarities, such as the "four-post" (hands and arms were tied unto four posts on the ground for whipping); "the torture of the ladder" (tied to a ladder); or "the hammock" (a person was suspended by his four limbs). Women suspected of abortion were forced to wear an iron collar around the neck until they produced a new child. To "burn up a little powder in the arse of a nigger" was "no freak but a recognized practice".[991] Slaves were suffering a permanent experience of overwork, under-nourishment and the whip. Conditions in Haiti were so ferocious that enslaved Africans did not replenish their number by reproduction. "After the dreaded journey across the ocean a woman was usually sterile for two years. The life in San Domingo killed them off fast. The planters deliberately worked them to death rather than wait for children to grow up."[992] Again, this happened systematically under the direction and control of the European enslaver governments.

In 1788, coffee planter and slave holder LeJeune of Plaisance (Martinique) suspected that increased mortality among his slaves was due to poison. Enraged by how his property was diminishing so fast, he murdered four and attempted

---

989   Hasan Nuhanovic v. Netherlands, Appeal Judgement of July 5, 2011, Gerechtshof's Gravenhage (Court of Appeal), The Hague.
990   Popo (2010), 297.
991   Ibid.
992   Ibid., 11.

to extort information from two women by torture. This he did by roasting their feet, legs, and elbows while gagging them. He then threatened all his remaining slaves that he would kill them all if they dared to denounce him. Fourteen of the slaves still went and charged him before the law. The colonial tribunal had to accept the charges and appointed a commission which made an investigation at the plantation, thereby confirming the testimonies of the slaves. They found the two women chained, with their elbows and knees decomposing. When two women died, LeJeune was arrested, and the fourteen slaves repeated their testimonies in court. However, seven "white" witnesses came up to testify in favour of LeJeune. The planters of Plaisance petitioned, and the Chamber of Agriculture and others intervened for him as well. Both governor and intendant wrote the minister that "it seems that the safety of the colony depends on the acquittal of LeJeune". This mass murderer was acquitted by the French authorities, and charges against him declared null and void.[993] Two years later, in 1790, a certain de Wimpffen stated that not one article of the Code Noir was obeyed. "He himself had sat at a table with a woman, beautiful, rich and very much admired, who had had a careless cook thrown into the oven."[994]

At the same time, as seen in Chapter II. 3. c. iv, French courts in their quasi totality granted freedom to Africans who sued for it because of the illegality of slavery in that country. In 1755, the Admiralty Court of France in Paris awarded six Africans their unconditional freedom, plus back wages and expenses – that is reparations. In fact, 154 Africans who sued for freedom over the next fifty years won their case. Yet royal administration intervened by fiat and ordered the arrest and transfer to the colonies of some of these Africans, thus directly subjecting them to the barbaric conditions just outlined.[995]

The French state then drew up legislation to prevent the liberation of Africans by its own courts, thereby once again asserting its "effective control" over the conduct of slavers that constituted genocidal transatlantic slavery. In 1677, an enslaved woman who had travelled to France returned to the colonies and never claimed her freedom, possibly because she did not know of the law. When thirty years later, her children and grandchildren demanded their freedom, based on the French legal tradition that children followed the status of their mother, and on the fact that their mother had acquired her freedom through her stay in France, the royal minister rejected this claim. He thereby directly condemned this family to stay in chattel slavery.[996] This incident not only confirms the extent to which European governments controlled and directed the general setting of transatlantic slavery, but also how they were directly responsible for the submission of concrete

---

993   Ibid., 18 et seq.
994   Ibid., 45.
995   Peabody (1996), 55 et seq.
996   Ibid., 14.

individuals to ferocious and barbaric treatment. This incident also demonstrates the importance of access to information about one's rights, a lesson that needs to be stressed with regard to the present situation of legal reparation consciousness and the prospects of claiming and taking reparations (see Chapter VIII.).

v. Examples of attribution to England

In the 16th and 17th centuries, the British, by then ascended to a serious maritime power, started to chase and take over Spanish slave ships and to occupy colonies. By the 17th century, the British had colonies on the American North East coast and in the Caribbean.

Charles II chartered the Royal African Company in 1682, and empowered it to trade from Salle in South Barbary to the Cape of Good Hope, and to erect forts and factories on the western coast of Africa. Then in 1697, this trade was laid open by an act of parliament, permitting every private merchant to trade upon paying the sum of ten pounds for maintenance of the forts and garrisons. Some of the factories that the Royal African Company erected were in Guinea, River Gambia, Sierra Leone, Sherbro, Gold Coast, Dick's Cove, Succunda, Commenda, Cape Coast, Annamabo, Winebah, Shidoe and Accra.[997]

In order for the slaving business to run smoothly, a Crown legal position had been issued in 1667 that declared Africans goods under Navigation Acts. The British state also exercised control over the transatlantic slavery system by sanctioning insurance agreements for slave owners. Big slave markets existed in Liverpool, Bristol, London, and Glasgow. Constitutive for transatlantic slavery, they were regulated by the British state.

A law of 1690 for the British colony South Carolina provided that everyone allowing Black people to leave an estate without a ticket was to pay a fine. Anyone who did not attempt to apprehend any Black person without a ticket or did not punish him for not having a ticket was also subject to pay a fine. Owners were *obliged* to punish slaves for taking flight. The punishment was determined too; freedom-takers were to be publicly and severely whipped.[998] At second flight, owners were obliged under the threat of a fine of ten pounds to brand "R" (for "runaway") on the African's right cheek. At the third escape a severe whipping had to be complemented by cutting off of one ear. Men who were still determined to take their freedom were to be castrated. If the enslaved person should die in consequence, the owner was to be compensated from the public treasury.[999] Section 2 of that law described slaves as chattels. That such policy constituted "effective control" and was issued for that precise purpose seems evident, thus making the barbaric conduct of private slavers attributable to the British state through

---

997 Cugoano (1787), 73.
998 Watson (1989), 69 et seq.
999 Ibid., 70.

Art. 8.

Sometimes slaves were condemned to wear iron mask and collar because it was thought that "their misery caused them to eat earth to end their lives", and that would have meant the loss of a valued property. Later medical research revealed that the cause for eating earth was not a suicidal tendency, but a response to nutritional deficiencies. In any case, such devices testify of the utmost brutality of the slavery system that was controlled and directed by European states.[1000]

Also, "in several regards for criminal law free blacks were treated in the same way as slaves". [1001] If "white" men in the American British colonies met a free Black person on the road, they commonly demanded his freedom certificate, tore it to pieces, tied him to a horse, and hurried off to the next jail as fast as their horses could travel, dragging the Black person along. Such captives were then sold as slaves, and there was nothing they could do against it.[1002] Again, this was part of a genocidal system that was set up and defined by laws passed by British administration and that of other European slaver states.

Laws in most British colonies provided that no slaves could be freed without an act of approval by the state.[1003] There were cases where slave owners willed to emancipate their slaves, but manumission failed because of such laws. This was sometimes the case with old enslavers who had held slave concubines and wanted to set them and their common children free for fear of damnation after death. The British colonial judge in one such exemplary case wrote that "superstitious weakness of dying men, proceeding from an astonishing ignorance of the solid moral and scriptural foundations upon which the institution of slavery rests, and from a total inattention to the shock which their conduct is calculated to give to the whole frame of our social policy, induces them, in their last moments, to emancipate their slaves, in fraud of the indubitable and declared policy of the state (...)" and rejected the manumission on grounds of the "wise and necessary policy of the State, embodied in the Act of 1820".[1004]

After the official abolition of slavery in 1833, the British, like other European enslaver states, instituted a five-year period of "forced apprenticeship" for ex-slaves in their Caribbean colonies. Researchers assessed that this had "all the violent and exploitive characteristics of previously legal slavery". Anti-slavery activists at that time however "found it difficult to mobilize public opinion around an issue that was now seen as solved. In that case, real slavery was hidden behind another name. Today it is equally likely that something that is not slavery will hide behind that name."[1005]

1000 Peabody/Grinberg (2007), 145.
1001 Ibid., 72 et seq.
1002 Peabody/Grinberg (2007), 86.
1003 Watson (1989), 75.
1004 Winbush (2009), 17.
1005 Quirk, Joel (2009). Unfinished Business: A Comparative Survey of Historical and Contemporary

All of this constituted "effective control" and "direction and control", testified by the simple fact that without this purposeful and systematic setting of policy, the violations of law, constituting genocide, could not and would not have taken place at all.

vi. "Effective control" and the "gun-slave-cycle"

As retraced above, there has been much debate about the so-called "gun-slave-cycle". Most authors, from Rodney to Law to Inikori have convincingly argued how "[f]rom early on, there is evidence that the [European] nations would invest their money and guns in support of one group over the other. (...) More often than not (...), it was done to assist in the process of obtaining captives who would later be sold as slaves. This appears to have been an important mode of operation throughout the slave trade era."[1006] In a situation that was, from its very inception, characterized by systematic and effective control by European enslaver states through legislation and policy, this gives further substance for attribution of responsibility via Art. 8, to all participating states. One graphic example of French governor Poncet embroiling two African rulers in a war for which he had armed both of them, with the explicit aim to produce slaves for the French plantation colonies, has been mentioned at the beginning of this chapter.

Violations of African sovereignty by European states, aiming at producing slaves, started even before the massive onset of the transatlantic system. Historic documents relate that as early as in the mid-15th century, the Mali federation empire, which had issued the world's first declaration of human rights, the *Dunya Makilikan*, was on the decline because some of its provinces, particularly those in the South-West, sought secession, incited by the Portuguese by means of economic and military manipulation.[1007]

Benin and Ijon traditions relate how at the time of one Oba (king)'s violent death at the beginning of the 16th century in the Uromi war, that king had become very unpopular with his subjects, and in particular with his war-weary soldiers who brought about his death.[1008] At that time, Benin was already entangled in the European state controlled transatlantic slavery system. It is therefore more than probable that the mentioned war had to do with Portuguese slaving activities.

Indeed, a missionary priest in Benin sent a report to the *Sacra Congregatio* in 1696 and therein related that "(i)n the kingdom of Benin no good can be done for the moment, since it has been almost destroyed by the wars which have been waged among those negroes: for more than seven years they have been destroy-

---

Slavery, Paris: UNESCO, 10.

1006 Bailey (2007), 128.

1007 Popo (2010), 155.

1008 Ryder (1969), 50; see also Egharevba, Jakob U. (1968). A Short History of Benin, Ibadan: Ibadan University Press, 26.

ing each other. (...)"[1009]. Benin tradition however retains no clear memory of a major war at that time, but of a large-scale rebellion of the chiefs and people against the Oba Ewuakpe in the years around the end of the 17th century. Thus, what is described as "wars of negroes" in European documents may really have been a large-scale rebellion against continuous enslavement engendered through massive interventions by the Portuguese and the collaboration of a puppet ruler.[1010] Documents are cited by historians that hold that the "sympathies of the river people" lay with the rebels, and that the civil war or rebellion was undermining the Oba's authority.[1011] "At the end of the 17th century, the Ijos also began to hinder slave traffic on the Benin River."[1012] Some time later, an enslaver named Jacob Munnickhoven left a written testimony in 1721 in which he described the inability of Benin to quickly enough supply slaves. "Benin could not supply a full cargo in less than two or three months, and it was physically impossible to hold a large number of them at the factory in anticipation of the arrival of the ship."[1013] Thus, Europeans felt they had to help themselves in that.

Generally, the conduct of European enslavers was a direct, and most often intentional, stimulus of inter-community warfare in much of Africa since they armed various groups against each other with the intent of "producing" slaves for deportation and profit. This fanned the flames of pre-existing conflicts and created new ones. "While raiders often became raiders in order to acquire weapons, almost all raided societies learned how to defend themselves. The effectiveness of their defenses forced slavers to reach deeper and deeper into the interior (...) [and] to develop increasingly complex strategies. Almost everywhere we see that ambition and greed led some men within the communities to ally themselves to predatory enemies."[1014]

Dahomey, for example, initially exported only slaves taken in its occasional wars, but this was to change with the Portuguese arming certain kings within the Empire and inciting them to disobey the Oba. In 1795, the Oba of Dahomey swore to the name of his ancestors and his own that Dahomeans had never engaged in warlike expeditions with the aim to make slaves. He stated that "what vexes me most is that some of you unfortunately write in books that never die that we would sell our women and children to buy our brandy. We are shamefully slandered and I hope that upon my speech you will contradict these scandalous lies that are fabricated about us and that you will show the posterity that these

1009 Ibid., 114 et seq.
1010 Ibid., 118.
1011 Ibid., 135.
1012 Ibid., 146.
1013 Ibid., 169 et seq.
1014 Klein, Martin A. (2003). 'Defensive Strategies – Wasulu, Masina, and the Slave Trade', in: Sylvaine A. Diouf (ed.): Fighting the Slave Trade. West African Strategies, Athens: Ohio University Press, 62-78, 62.

imputations are false".[1015]

In 1679, Heerman Abramsz, Director-General of the Dutch West India Company on the Gold Coast, from whence a large share of captives debarked as well, admitted that since the introduction of firearms, "the whole Coast has come into a kind of state of war. This started in the year 1658, and gradually this has gone so far, that none of the passages could anymore be used, and none of the traders could come through."[1016]

In 1703, the Dutch West Indian Company (which was chartered and financed by and permanently subjected to policy of the states-general of the United Provinces) supplied the state of Akwamu on the Gold Coast with 100 soldiers and firearms to wage war against its neighbors, the resulting slaves going to the Dutch. "Warfare for slaves encouraged retaliation and set off a cycle of violence."[1017]

Indeed and contrary to what reparation opponents want to make believe, "most of the slaves sold to Europeans were acquired through wars and raids. [W]hat were often called wars were in fact slave raids. Wars to acquire slaves expanded as the external demand increased. (...) European slave traders encouraged wars through the sale of guns and gunpowder. They were active participants in the wars and conflicts that produced slaves. A slave-ship captain wrote: 'I verily believe, that the far greater part of the wars in Africa would cease, if the Europeans would cease, to tempt them with goods for slaves.'" [1018]

The gun-slave-cycle theory has been criticized by historians such as Fage and Thornton, on grounds that guns at that time would have been unreliable, often broke down and were difficult to repair.[1019] They argue that this would prove that guns provided by Europeans had no significant impact on enslavement. This critique has been pertinently refuted by other historians, however. Common sense also indicates that Europeans did not ship millions of guns – and that they did so is a documented fact – into Africa during centuries just for the fun of it. Inikori therefore assessed that

"[t]he firm preference of the slave sellers for guns indicates very strongly the connection between firearms and the acquisition of slaves. It reinforces the slave-gun circle theory according to which the states and individual or groups of individual slave gatherers bought more firearms to capture more slaves to buy more firearms. (...) For some states the necessity may have been imposed by defence requirements. (...) The commodity preference of foodstuff sellers fails to support the thesis that firearms were used primarily for crop production. If this were true one

---

1015 Ibid., 67.
1016 Inikori (1992a), 106.
1017 Reynolds, Edward (1994). "Human Cargoes: Enslavement and the Middle Passage", in: Anthony Tibbles (ed.): Transatlantic Slavery. Against Human Dignity, London: Merrell Holberton Publishers, 29-34, 30.
1018 Ibid.
1019 Hawthorne (2003a), 109 et seq.

should find sellers of yams, corn, plantain (...) demanding firearms in payment. This is not borne out by the evidence. (...) The implication of all of this is that the firearms imported into West (...) were used mainly for slave gathering and the wars largely stimulated by the latter. This is why the most important slave-exporting areas of the time, in particular, the Bonny trading area, were also the largest firearms importers in West Africa during this period."[1020]

Europeans not only supplied firearms, but also iron for local weapons' production. Iron was imported into Dahomey from the early 17th century at a large scale.[1021] Also, for example, in "Guinea-Bissau, warriors used few guns when staging attacks. Iron weapons and iron-reinforced weapons (...) were ubiquitous."[1022] In that region,

"coastal people used imported guns only to a limited extent. (...) Iron knives, spears, and swords were the weapons of choice. (...) In sum, the need to obtain European weapons for defensive purposes may not have compelled Africans to conduct slave raids, but the need to obtain iron from which to forge practical defence (...) weapons (...) did compel coastal Africans in Guinea-Bissau to produce and market captives. (...) Written sources make clear that iron was in high demand in Guinea-Bissau's coastal zones. (...) Shipping records from the late 17th century indicate that iron made up the bulk of imports into the Guinea-Bissau region. Imports continued to have much the same composition in the 18th century, though rum and gunpowder at times filled most of ships' hulls."[1023]

Under the pressure of the general transatlantic system, decentralized populations, such as in Guinea-Bissau, had increasingly found that they had to participate in the "slave" "trade" so that they could procure the iron necessary to defend themselves against attack and which European merchants only offered in exchange for slaves. The presence and actions of the Europeans did "bring a military revolution, one that compelled participation in the slave trade as a price for survival." [1024]

Although iron and iron-core were not excavated in abundance in that region, people had traded for it along routes to the east before the arrival of European slavers. The arrival of the latter however changed the constellation in trade and superseded previous traders. All of a sudden, Guinea-Bissau people "were forced to deal with new trading partners who had no interest in salt, but demanded slaves or ivory". [1025]

1020 Inikori (1982), 136 et seq.
1021 Ogundiran/Falola (2010), 26.
1022 Hawthorne (2003b). "Strategies of the Decentralized. Defending Communities from Slave Raiders in Coastal Guinea-Bissau, 1450-1815", in: Sylvaine A. Diouf (ed.): Fighting the Slave Trade. West African Strategies, Athens: Ohio University Press, 152-169, 161.
1023 Hawthorne (2003a), 98.
1024 Ibid., 109 et seq.
1025 Ibid.

Maes-Diop analysed archeological evidence which traces iron smelting traditions in large parts of Africa to the ancient iron industries in the vast Nile zone. Davidson also attested to the existence of metallurgy in Nigeria for as early as 3500 BCE.[1026] In some languages, such as those of the Bantu linguistic group, the multiplicity of terms relating to metallurgy points to an indigenous tradition.[1027] All of this indicates that African people had the knowledge and skills to work iron, and the documented evidence shows that Europeans brought large quantities of iron to Africa that were transformed into weapons used for slave raiding.

In addition to the iron aspect, another point that is disregarded by those arguing that European presence and intervention had nothing to do with the massive rise of enslavement and wars is that the financial gains made through the enslavement business with Europeans enabled kingdoms such as Hueda (the predecessor of Dahomey in Ouidah) to hire mercenary soldiers from other African communities for the wars they led against their immediate neighbors.[1028]

We have seen in previous parts of this work, especially in Chapter II. 3. a. xi, that the resistance of African people and communities was omnipresent and enduring. Tragically, it did not prevail because Europeans supplied fire-arms, iron and material profits to African rulers and individuals who were ready to collaborate and enslave others. Only a few corrupted individuals, to whom European slavers could give material and military support, would have sufficed to change power constellations in a region. This scheme resulted in a situation where the choice for most Africans became one of being enslaved or to enslave others.[1029]

In view of that situation, a statement by Law, one of the most acknowledged scholars on slavery who worked extensively on the history of Dahomey (one of the few African kingdoms that were undoubtedly actively participating in the making of slaves from the 17th century onwards), must be taken into consideration when contemplating on the question of African and European responsibility. Law wrote that he does not

"(...) subscribe to the view that the involvement of some Africans in the operation of the slave trade serves to exonerate either the European societies or the individual Europeans who engaged in it. In part, this is because it implicitly assumes a sort of moral calculus, positions a fixes quantum of responsibility available for distribution, which would seem bizarre if applied in other contexts – in a case of murder, for example, where contributory responsibility assigned to others would not, I think, normally be thought to cancel or even diminish the guilt of the murderer."[1030]

1026 Diop-Maes (1996), 53.
1027 Ibid., 60.
1028 Law (2004), 48 et seq.
1029 Ibid., 47.
1030 Ibid., 12 et seq.

Manning, another renowned scholar on slavery, sustained that

"(o)ne way or another, European slave buyers could always find an African who would supply them with slaves. It only required a few greedy or opportunistic persons, who felt they should enrich themselves rather than resist the inexorable pressures of supply and demand, to keep the slave trade alive. Those suppliers, in turn, rapidly became wealthy enough to become a focus of power to whom others had to accommodate."[1031]

It was stated by the Nuremberg Tribunal that "necessity is a defence when it is shown that the act charged was done to avoid an evil both serious and irreparable; that there was no other adequate means of escape; and that the remedy was not disproportionate to the evil"[1032]. In the Farben Trial, the Tribunal specified that the plea of necessity has to be evaluated in the light of whether moral choice was possible. The majority of the defendants were acquitted on this ground.[1033] Now, for numerous African societies the only possibility to prevent their own imminent enslavement was to defend themselves against slave raids. Since raiders were armed by Europeans, communities and states had to see that they equipped themselves with these defense materials. The sole source of supply was the Europeans who only gave arms and iron for slaves. Thus, "moral choice" in many instances, was not possible. It is documented that, at the same time, gun manufacturers in England, for example, were constantly pressured to produce more guns. A total of 1,615,309 guns were imported into Africa from England alone and the bulk of these were exchanged for slaves in the 18th century.[1034] Concerning one community, the Anlos from by the Volta River, it has been assessed that "before the Europeans their fights with outside groups were 'fights, not wars'"[1035].

In the 18th century alone, between 283,000 and 394,000 guns were imported into Africa each year by European traders.[1036] At least 20 million guns were sold to African merchants in total during the time of transatlantic slavery. Between 1750 and 1807, England sold over 22,000 metric tons of gunpowder (384,000 kg) and 91,000 kg of lead annually.[1037] "It is clear that the actions of European nations were a direct stimulus of interethnic warfare on the coast in that they armed various groups when it suited their purposes. This only served to fan the flames of pre-existing conflicts and to create new ones where they would not otherwise have existed".[1038] These arms exports were controlled by European states, as can be seen by means of the many examples cited here. Wars were oftentimes directly

---

1031 Manning (1990), 34.
1032 Lumb (1968), 78.
1033 Ibid.
1034 Bailey (2007), 165.
1035 Ibid., 166.
1036 Ibid., 121.
1037 Lovejoy (2000), 109.
1038 Bailey (2007), 121.

stimulated by European states in order to produce slaves for their use. For many regions, the relationship between gun importation by Europeans and the expansion of transatlantic slavery has been clearly established.[1039] Such conduct by European states, constitutive for transatlantic slavery in its entirety, taken together with other essential elements of the transatlantic slavery system for which those European states were the sole responsible – such as slavery legislation and setting of policy for the Middle Passage and on the colonies – engages the legal responsibility of European enslaver states via Art. 8.

In that regard, the recent judgement in *Hasan Nuhanovic v. Netherlands* is instructive in which the Court of Appeal at The Hague specifically sustained that whether a "State has 'effective control' over (...) conduct (...), must be answered in view of the circumstances of the case. This does not only imply that significance should be given to the question whether that conduct constituted the execution of a specific instruction, issued by (...) the State, but also to the question whether, if there was no such specific instruction, (...) the State had the power to prevent the conduct concerned."[1040] Thus, European enslaver states are legally responsible for the illegal enslavement and mass killings in the course of enslavement operations on the African continent, because they had not prevented these massive arms exports to Africa, in light of the general circumstances of transatlantic slavery which they controlled and directed and of the fact that these arms exports were effectuated for the sole purpose of providing the states' genocidal plantation colonies with deported and enslaved Africans. The Court explicitly stated that for assessing if such "effective control" took place, "the background" of a situation has to be considered.[1041] If we apply this to transatlantic slavery, effective control by European states was definitely given.

Also, there was generally no long-term stability in the role of specific African societies in transatlantic slavery. A community could be a source of slaves at one time and later have played a middleman role.[1042] In any case, the participation of African collaborators does not erase the legal responsibility of the mastermind. This has also been confirmed recently in *Hasan Nuhanović v. Netherlands* where the Court confirmed the "possibility of attribution to more than one party".[1043]

Additionally, documents show that in some instances, if manipulation of African states and communities through the arming of rivalling factions and individuals failed, Europeans did not hesitate to get rid of African rulers who were acting

---

1039 Hawthorne (2003a), 109 et seq.
1040 Hasan Nuhanovic v. Netherlands, Appeal Judgement of July 5, 2011, Gerechtshof's Gravenhage (Court of Appeal), The Hague.
1041 Ibid.
1042 Browner Stahl, Ann (2010). 'Entangled Lives: The Archaeology of Daily Life in the Gold Coast Hinterlands, AD 1400-1900', in: Akinwumi Ogundiran and Toyin Falola (ed.): Archaeology of Atlantic Africa and the African Diaspora, Bloomington/Indianapolis: Indiana University Press, 49-76, 68.
1043 Hasan Nuhanovic v. Netherlands, Appeal Judgement of July 5, 2011, Gerechtshof's Gravenhage (Court of Appeal), The Hague.

contrary to their interests, by shipping them away.[1044] One example of this is the already mentioned Atarkor incident. African oral history from other regions too reveals that deception and guile were used to lure Africans into ships, which then sailed away and deported them to the plantation colonies.[1045]

Many authors have pertinently shown that the high incidence of warfare that prevailed throughout the period from the middle of the 17th century to the 19th century was created and fuelled by the exigencies of transatlantic slavery. The increase in the supply of firearms and iron core for weapons production, caused by the extreme financial profitability of this system for the involved Europeans and African collaborators, provided additional incentives for warfare. Slave raiding and kidnapping had become an established occupation in some parts.[1046] Scholars have shown how famines in Senegambia, Cape Verde and Angola led families to sell children as slaves. These famines, however, most often had their roots in the disruption of economic and social structures brought about by the havoc caused by the European instigators of the transatlantic slavery system and the intentional manipulation and intervention by European states. This permanent state of insecurity and violence led to the dispersal of many towns and the abandonment of farming lands.[1047] Since European states brought about this situation through direct intervention or manipulation, that is, "effective control", responsibility for all of this is legally attributable to them as well.

Transatlantic slavery also had the effect of making the administration of justice in indigenous African courts harsh and corrupted as enslavement became the standard punishment for many offences which hitherto had attracted only fines.[1048]

While kidnapping was increasing, individuals were enslaved by the elites for all kinds of alleged crimes. By the 17th century, the law practice of some societies "functioned as a handmaiden to the trade". A contemporary report states that "the Kings are so absolute, that upon any slight pretense of offense committed by their subjects, they order them to be sold for slaves without regard to rank or profession".[1049] Another holds that "some of the negroe rulers, corrupted by the Europeans, violently infringe the law of Guinea".[1050]

1044 Diouf, Sylvaine A. (2003c). "The Last Resort. Redeeming Family and Friends", in: Sylvaine A. Diouf (ed.): Fighting the Slave Trade. West African Strategies, Athens: Ohio University Press, 81-100, 87 et seq.
1045 Bailey (2007), 126.
1046 Perbi (2004), 36 et seq.
1047 Manning, Patrick (1998). "La traite négrière et l'évolution démographique de l'Afrique", in: Doudou Diène (ed.): La chaine et le lien. Une vision de la traite négrière, Paris: UNESCO, 153-173, 156.
1048 Ibid., 66.
1049 Reynolds (1994), 30.
1050 Ibid.

Witchcraft accusations were also on the high rise throughout this long period, and led to many cases of enslavement. Law practice became fraught in many societies, and remained so over centuries, leaving deep wounds that manifest themselves today in deeply corrupted judicial institutions and the non-availability of justice through their domestic legal institutions for the people of many African states.[1051]

The fact is that, directly and indirectly, the transatlantic system stimulated frequent wars which distorted the political and social structures of African societies. One such major distortion was the rise of military aristocracies that became so influential that they determined the direction of state policy in virtually all major African states.[1052] Under the structural impact of export enslavement, first in Arab and then in transatlantic slavery, forms of personal dependence that had previously existed in Africa worsened to the extreme and were transformed into institutions that approximated chattel slavery.

"The traditionally organized authorities (...) all suffered immediate defeat, or such transformation of their relations with the societies that they represented that they became either the forced instruments of the traders or the victims of less scrupulous political rivals. The slave trade had an indisputably destructive effect on the oldest African authorities; on the other hand, new forms of authority arose more or less directly out of the slave trade. There were some kings who sought, through the formation of docile groups of slaves, a means of domination without opposition, contrary to traditional customs. Their domination was found to have taken on increasingly tyrannical forms."[1053]

Large proportions of the people of some major African societies became oppressed by an elite that was connected directly or indirectly with export slavery, as merchants or as state functionaries. The structures so developed had become deeply entrenched when direct labor and resource exploitation in Africa itself was becoming increasingly profitable for European states, which then proceeded to instigate official colonialism on these same structures they had set up through centuries of transatlantic enslavement. "In combination with the forced labor regime the colonial powers upheld in Africa, they further provoked the expansion of the slave mode of production in Africa."[1054]

After the end of enslavement deportations to the Americas and at the beginning of official colonialism, Africa was left with shattered internal markets, agricultural and industrial sectors and with small-scale states dominated by merchants and warriors who had risen to power through collaboration in enslavement. The

---

1051 Ibid.
1052 Inikori (1992a), 107.
1053 United Nations Educational, Scientific and Cultural Organization (ed.) (1978). Meeting of Experts on the African Slave-Trade, Final Report, Port-au-Prince, Haiti, 31 January-4 February 1978, downloaded from http://unesdoc.unesco.org/images/0003/000333/033360eb.pdf (accessed 21.6.2012).
1054 Ibid., 108.

foundation was thus firmly laid for direct colonial rule and exploitation.[1055] Given these changes in internal African governance imposed in the transatlantic slavery system, a few more words should now be said on what concerns the conduct of African collaborators in this general setting of direction and control exercised by European enslaver states.

D. RESPONSIBILITY OF OTHER STATES IN CONNECTION WITH THE ACTS OF EUROPEAN ENSLAVER GOVERNMENTS

The ILC Articles, in Part IV, also deal with the responsibility of a state in connection with the wrongful act of another state. Articles in this Part require that the assisting or contributing state is aware of the circumstances of the internationally wrongful act in question. A specific causal link must be established between that act and the conduct of the assisting state.

i. African collaboration and responsibility

Article 17 (Direction and control exercised over the commission of an internationally wrongful act) is relevant in particular when contemplating African collaboration and responsibility, and holds that "a State which directs and controls another State in the commission of an internationally wrongful act by the latter is internationally responsible for the act if: (a) that State does so with knowledge of the circumstances of the internationally wrongful act; and (b) the act would be internationally wrongful if committed by that State".

With regard to customary international law to the same effect, the Holy See asserted in respect of wrongful acts committed by Italian police who forcibly entered the Basilica of St.Paul in Rome in February 1944 the responsibility of the German authorities. "In such cases the occupying State is responsible for acts of the occupied State which it directs and controls."[1056]

Following the logic of Art. 17 and international legal tradition, European states are thus responsible for the acts of the African states that they manipulated and, sometimes indeed forced into enslaving others. As pertinently shown in Chapter IV 1. c., there remains no doubt that the European enslaver powers directed and exercised effective control over the process of enslavement for the transatlantic system in Africa, and that this situation of control made it a necessity for many African states to engage in illegal enslavement of free Africans in order to save themselves, at least for a little while, from falling victim to enslavement.

International tribunals have concretized that Article 17 is limited to cases where a dominant state actually directs and controls conduct that would as such

---

1055 Ibid., 110.
1056 Crawford (2002), 153 et seq.

constitute a breach of an obligation of the dependent and assisting state, and have refused to infer responsibility merely because the dominant state may have had the power to interfere if that it was not exercised in the particular case. Now, we have seen that transatlantic slavery violated African and international law, by both of which African states were bound, and that European states exercised their power consistently and systematically to direct and control the course and amplitude of enslavement on the continent. "(T)he word 'directs' does not encompass mere incitement or suggestion but rather connotes actual direction of an operative kind. Both direction and control must be exercised over the wrongful conduct in order for a dominant State to incur responsibility."[1057] There are countless such instances of wrongful conduct over which European states exercised direction and control, of which only a little fraction could be accounted for in this work, but which nonetheless engage their legal responsibility.

We have seen that a review of pertinent historical studies on slavery in Africa and in the transatlantic system leads unmistakably to the conclusion that there was no indigenous pre-European and pre-Islamic African system of chattel slavery, or even "slavery" as such on a larger scale. The documented incidences of indigenous African "slavery" that do exist highlight the role of this social institution to keep war captives and criminal convicts or their descendants in the society, conform to the standard of the law of nations at that time. Historical evidence also shows that those African societies that eventually participated actively in the transatlantic system as capturers and providers of slaves, such as Dahomey and Ashanti, came into existence only during the 18th century and were themselves products of the transatlantic slavery system set up by European states.[1058]

"The majority of the slave-trading African kingdoms were a product of the historic enslavement by Europeans. (...) The high point of these formations often coincided with the height of Atlantic deportations and their decline with the rising of abolitionism."[1059] Some African collaborators, once risen to power, styled themselves with titles such as king or vice-king and also entered historiography as such.[1060] This was the case, for example, with Jack Ormond alias Mongo John in Dahomey who was the son of an English slaver and local woman, and was called "king" by himself and other slavers. Just because such corrupted individuals entered European records as "kings" does not mean, however, that their illegal actions would have been licit in African societies. It was in general often the offspring of European enslavers and local women who established themselves on the African coast and reigned like mafia dons over the illegal economy of slavery. Most times they did not raid themselves, but financed and equipped African col-

---

1057   Ibid.
1058   Popo (2010), 147.
1059   Ibid., 183.
1060   Ibid., 169.

laborators.[1061]

Law stated that "(c)ertainly, the militarism of the Dahomian state was not an ancient condition (...), but something new, which developed only from the late seventeenth century, in parallel with the increase of slave exports, and arguably in consequence of it."[1062] Generally speaking, historians have pointed out that the increasing volume of slave exports went hand in hand in time with rising prices for slaves from the mid-17th century, further indicating the primacy of European demand rather than African supply. This violent demand increased the incidence of warfare and violence in Africa.[1063]

In the period that saw the highest numbers of deportations, from the mid-late 17th century to the abolition of the slave trade in the mid-19th century, the majority of captives came from the Bight of Benin (e.g. Dahomey) and Angola (Kongo).[1064] Ports in both regions and their hinterlands were direct products of European intervention, and only came into existence after the European powers present had been active in enslaving for almost 200 years. Dahomey integrated and took control of Ouidah in 1727, and Angola had become a direct Portuguese colony already in the 16th century. And of course, this had happened not by accident, but the Portuguese had directed an aggression war with the aim of enslaving Africans for deportation.

The Benin Coast had come into sporadic contact with Europeans as early as the 14th century.[1065] Dahomey was a major supplier of slaves for sale at the coast since at least the 1680s and its forces were equipped with imported European firearms obtained in exchange for slave exports. European intervention was a necessary condition for the development of militarization of Dahomian society. Thus, this kingdom that was to take over Ouidah in 1727 was in itself a consequence of the impact of transatlantic slavery. [1066]

Thus, it is fundamental to acknowledge that,

"Africans did not enslave themselves in the Americas. The European slave trade was not an African venture, it was pre-eminently a European enterprise in all of its dimensions: conception, insurance, outfitting of ships, sailors, factories, shackles, weapons, and the selling and buying of people in the Americas. (...) The closest any scholar has ever been able to arrive at a description of a slave society is the Dahomey kingdom of the nineteenth century that had become so debauched by

---

1061 Popo (2010), 176 et seq.
1062 Law (2008), 11.
1063 Ibid., 12.
1064 Law (2004), 1 et seq.
1065 THE SLAVE TRADE ARCHIVES PROJECT, Restricted Final Report 516INT5061, Paris, February 2005, downloaded from http://portal.unesco.org/ci/en/files/18318/11159056237Slave_trade_archives_-_Final_Report.doc/Slave%2Btrade%2Barchives%2B-%2BFinal%2BReport.doc (accessed 14.3.2010), 6.
1066 Law (2004), 48 et seq.

slavery due to European influence that it was virtually a hostage of the nefarious enterprise. However, even in Dahomey we do not see the complete denial of the humanity of Africans as we see in the American colonies. (...) No laws protected the African from any cruelty the white master could conceive. The man, woman, or child was at the complete mercy of the most brutish of people. For looking a white man in the eye the enslaved person could have his or her eyes blinded with hot irons. For speaking up in defense of a wife or woman a man could have his right hand severed. For defending his right to speak against oppression, an African could have half his tongue cut out. For running away and being caught an enslaved African could have his or her Achilles tendon cut. (...) The enslaved person could be roasted over a slow-burning fire, left to die after having both legs and arms broken, oiled and greased and then set afire while hanging from a tree's limb, or being killed slowly as the slave owner cut the enslaved person's phallus or breasts. A person could be placed on the ground, stomach first, stretched so that each hand was tied to a pole and each foot was tied to a pole. Then the slave master would beat the person's naked body until the flesh was torn off the buttocks and the blood ran down to the ground."[1067]

It has been argued by some that there must have been an informed understanding of the fate that awaited their victims within the Dahomian ruling elite, because there were Dahomian officials who had been to America and Europe on diplomatic missions. This argument is not conclusive because the experience of a diplomatic mission did not necessarily give insight into the conditions of transatlantic slavery. The conditions of voyage of these ambassadors and emissaries were most probably very different from the common horrific experience of the captured Africans during the Middle Passage.

In this regard it is essential to also remember that it was the information that the abolitionist movement provided to the European public regarding conditions on slave ships and plantations which led to a change in public attitude. "Black and white abolitionists alike publicized the physical horrors of the Middle Passage in such graphic detail that legislators, shipbuilders, and others were forced to respond in some definitive way"[1068]. In a similar vein, African collaborators cannot be expected to have known more about the cruel details of transatlantic slavery than did the general public in Europe.

This perception is backed by testimonies such as that by Quobna Ottobah Cugoano who was kidnapped in 1770, when he was about 13 years old. His father and other relatives were "chief men in the kingdom of Agimaque and Assinee", thus pertaining to the Fantee, a nation of the same region as Ashanti.[1069] The description of his kidnapping and journey to the coast is not positive, but becomes

1067 Asante (2003), 7 et seq.
1068 Bailey, 130.
1069 Cugoano (1787), 7.

significantly more dreadful upon arrival at a European slave "castle" on the coast. "(...) I was soon conducted to a prison for three days, where I heard the groans and cries of many, and saw some of my fellow-captives. But when a vessel arrived to conduct us away to the ship, it was a most horrible scene; there was nothing to be heard but rattling of chains, smacking of whips, and the groans and cries of our fellow-men. "[1070] On the plantation in the Caribbean to where he was deported, "for eating a piece of sugarcane, some were cruelly lashed, or struck over the face to knock their teeth out. Some of the stouter ones, I suppose often reproved, and grown hardened and stupid with many cruel beatings and lashings, or perhaps faint and pressed with hunger and hard labour, were often committing trespasses of this kind, and when detected, they met with exemplary punishment. Some told me that they had their teeth pulled out to deter others, and to prevent them from eating any cane in the future (...)"[1071]. He made an explicit comparison between the two kinds of "slavery", from a perspective of someone who had known both first-hand:

"I was first kid-napped and betrayed by some of my own complexion, who were the first cause of my exile and slavery; but if there were no buyers there would be no sellers. So far as I can remember, some of the Africans in my country keep slaves, which they take in war, or for debt; but those which they keep are well fed, and good care taken of them, and treated well; and, as to their clothing, they differ according to the custom of the country. But I may safely say, that all the poverty and misery that any of the inhabitants of Africa meet with among themselves, is far inferior to those inhospitable regions of misery which they meet with in the West-Indies, where their hard-hearted overseers have neither regard to the laws of God, nor to the life of their fellow-men."[1072]

Cuguano stated that "these kidnappers and slave-procurers, called merchants, are a species of African villains, which are greatly corrupted (...). (W)icked and barbarous as they certainly are, I can hardly think, if they knew what horrible barbarity they were sending their fellow-creatures to, that they would do it. (...) The Europeans, at their factories (...) have always kept some as servants to them, and with gaudy cloaths, in a gay manner, as decoy ducks to deceive others, and to tell them that they want more to go over the sea, and be as they are. So in that respect, wherein it may be said that they will sell one another, they are only ensnared and enlisted to be servants, kept like some of those which they see at the factories (...)."[1073] Cuguano's testimony gives us the opportunity for a better appreciation of the true state of awareness of African collaborators about the cruelties they were delivering their victims into.

1070 Ibid., 14 et seq.
1071 Ibid., 16 et seq.
1072 Ibid.
1073 Ibid., 26.

Now, there is documented evidence of a less-than-handful number of individuals who had been enslaved to the Americas, managed to return to the motherland and thereupon became involved in the transatlantic slavery business, this time as an oppressor. Irookoo *alias* Dom Jeronimo was a prince of the Dahomian royal family who had been sold into slavery in Brazil by a ruler, but was redeemed and returned to Dahomey by another. He became a prominent slave-dealer in Ouidah in the 1780s.[1074]

Africa-born Antonio d'Almeida had also been enslaved to Brazil and managed to return to Africa. Although he did not engage in transatlantic slavery business, but bequeathed in his will of 1864 several domestic slaves to various members of his family and provided for the continuation of two senior slaves in their positions within his household. [1075]

Several things need to be clarified regarding this aspect that is often amplified and exploited by reparation negationists. First, the human psyche is a complex phenomenon. The genocidal horrors of both the Middle Passage and plantation life in the Americas could and did trigger numerous mental health problems with grave consequences. It is more than imaginable that the horrors that these collaborators had experienced personally would have made them crazy. Second, a few wicked and corrupted individuals can be found anywhere at any time. Third, their existence does not lead to the exemption of legal responsibility of the directing and controlling states. Otherwise, the presence of the very few Jewish collaborators in the nazi terror would have been enough to topple Jewish reparation claims against Germany and Austria, an idea that would seem very unjust and indeed scandalous to most. "The fact is that European and American nationals played a critical role in the operations of the Atlantic slave trade on four continents (...), including the persistent demand for labor in the New World and the willingness to meet this demand by any means."[1076]

Thus, Benezet wrote in the mid-18th century that "(b)y the most authentic relations of those early times, the natives were an inoffensive people, who, when civilly used, traded amicably with the Europeans. (...) It was long after the Portugueze had made a practice of violently forcing the natives of Africa into slavery, that we read of the different Negroe nations making war upon each other, and selling their captives. And probably this was not the case, till those bordering the coast, who had been used to supply the vessels with necessaries, had become corrupted by their intercourse with the Europeans, and were excited by drunkenness and avarice to join then in carrying on those wicked schemes, by which those unnatural wars were perpetrated; the inhabitants kept in continual alarms; the country laid waste; and as William Moor expresses it, *Infinite numbers sold*

1074 Law (2004), 117.
1075 Ibid., 77 et seq.
1076 Bailey (2007), 58.

into slavery."[1077]

One William Smith, sent in 1726 by the Royal African Company to survey their settlements, said that "(t)hat the discerning natives account it their greatest unhappiness, that they were ever visited by the Europeans. (...) That we Christians introduced the traffik of slaves; and that before our coming they lived in peace".[1078]

In 1720, Tamba, king in the Rio Nunez region (Guinea), organized his people against European and African slavers. He obstructed their trade and executed captured middlemen. However, due to the might of European firearms, he was caught, sold, and enslaved but still organized a revolt among the captives on the ship. It was brutally put down, and Tamba was killed and his liver fed to his supporters, who were subsequently executed.[1079]

A union of *marabouts* succeeded in creating a region of refuge in the Fouta in the late 17th and 18th centuries, but they too were at last defeated by an alliance of a neighbouring king who had been armed by the French and slave dealers of St. Louis.[1080]

In 1787, a Swedish observer noted the fate of a king in the Senegal region who promulgated a law that let no slave convoy pass his territory. At that moment, several French slave ships were waiting for human cargo at the Senegal river. This policy kept the French from filling their ships, so they made presentations before the king, but could not make him change his mind. He refused their gifts and told them that all the riches of the *Compagnie du Senegal* could not make him change position. Therefore the French went to link up with their old auxiliaries, the Arab Moors who had already done much enslavement business for them before. Armed by the French, the Moors overtook the kingdom of the resistant king by surprise. [1081]

As mentioned already earlier, in an incident in Atorkor (Ghana) European enslavers tricked drummers of the chief and members of his family with repeated feasts and gifts onto their ship. Once the Africans has gotten accustomed to this and abandoned caution, on one occasion the Europeans took sail with all of them. From this we see that even in the 19th century transatlantic slavery was not a "trade", but involved theft, trickery, and kidnapping.[1082]

Atorkor and other kidnapping incidents of the 19th century also reveal that many African collaborators came to find themselves, "like their captives, in insecure and precarious positions".[1083] Such methods of getting rid of governments

1077 Benezet (1767), 31.
1078 Ibid., 32.
1079 Rashid, Ismael (2003). A Devotion to the Idea of Liberty at any Price. Rebellion and Anti-Slavery in the Upper Guinea Coast in the Eighteenth and Nineteenth Centuries, in: Sylvaine A. Diouf (ed.), Fighting the Slave Trade. West African Strategies, Athens: Ohio University Press, 132-151, 137.
1080 Ajavon (2005), 114 et seq.
1081 Davidson (1961), 217.
1082 Bailey (2007), 49.
1083 Ibid., 55.

and leaders who were not docile enough have been continuously employed by European powers in Africa throughout the centuries from the earliest times of transatlantic slavery to Lumumba and Sankara to their more recent military interventions in Haiti and Ivory Coast.[1084] It is also important to acknowledge that, now and then, even if some rulers were and are collaborating, the people fought the enslavers.

Most of the African contributors to the UNESCO General History of Africa agreed that the deprivation of sovereignty was a crime that was perpetrated against Africa very much contrary to the expressed will of the masses of African people and their rulers throughout the continent and even in the diaspora. Adu-Boahen wrote that "(...) an overwhelming majority of African authorities and leaders were vehemently opposed to this change and expressed their determination to maintain the status quo and, above all, to retain their sovereignty and independence, an issue on which virtually all of them were not in any way prepared to compromise. This answer can be documented from the very words of the contemporary African leaders themselves"[1085]. Niane assessed in another UNESCO publication that "(...) the Africans were forced partners. Could one escape this trade? No, one has to tell this loud and strong. Colonization, after military conquest imposed us peanut culture, coffee or cacao. The mines were exploited without us being able to escape from exploitation. Mutatis Mutandis, through the power of events the supply of slaves was imposed on us, against our free will. The great responsible, the only definite responsible, remains Europe. The African demography was strongly affected; entire regions were voided of their inhabitants. To speak of reparation is not a vain reclamation"[1086].

Legal scholars have sustained with regard to reparations in general that "prior to or concurrent with designing a reparations process, it is critical to situate and characterize the violence that has occurred, including who was or is responsible for it, in order to assess its effects, as well as to begin to visualize the categories of victims and perpetrators, and the often very complex relationships between them".[1087] It is crucial to distinguish "between vertical violence, that is, violence exercised directly by a powerful state against its opponents (...) and horizontal violence, that is, violence exercised by one social group against another", while recognising that both forms often occur simultaneously, whereby the latter is often a consequence of the first. "Thus the analysis of the types of violence should be comprehensive, taking these complex forms into account, while avoiding fre-

---

1084 Plumelle-Uribe (2008), 152.

1085 Adu-Boahen (1985), 3.

1086 Niane, Djibril Tamsir (ed.) (2001). Tradition orale et archives de la traite négrière, Paris: UNESCO, 12 (t.b.a.).

1087 Lykes, M. Brinton/Mersky, Marcie (2006). "Reparations and Mental Health: Psychosocial Interventions Towards Healing, Human Agency, and Rethreading Social Realities", in: Pablo de Greiff (ed.): The Handbook of Reparations, Oxford: Oxford University Press, 589-622, 608.

quent pitfalls characteristic of some truth-seeking and reparations processes, that is, that of equating all forms of violence."[1088]

Oral African traditions recorded in the course of a UNESCO research project revealed that African populations make a clear distinction between the time of the stable kingdoms and empires and the times of insecurity created by transatlantic slavery. The multiple researchers pointed out that field research pertinently brought fourth this fact. [1089] Even today in the Upper Guinea region, the period of slave raiding is still remembered and referred to as *Téguéré* or *Teré Télé* in Mandingue language, which means the "time of robbers" and does not invoke any voluntary economic business.[1090] Another point brought to light by this project was that oral tradition in the Congo region relates that Europeans first came to this region around 1491 and acquired the name "Mindele", meaning invader, a term that is still used today to refer to "white" people.[1091] An essential distinction was made by the keepers of traditional knowledge in those societies between the slavery that had previously been practiced in Africa, where "slaves" were not deprived of human rights, and slavery for the transatlantic system.[1092]

The contributors and the editors of the just mentioned UNESCO publication on oral traditions also concluded that transatlantic slavery constituted a tightly knitted system that with the advancement of time touched all Africans without exception.[1093] They expressly affirmed that the "game master" was Europe.[1094]

"Scholars have too often referred to reservoirs of people, who were tapped by the trade, as if to say that there were people waiting to be swept up (...). We have too often divided Africans into victors and victims. Life was certainly safest at the heart of the great slaving kingdoms, but those who lived in areas widely raided did not go willingly. They created defences – not only walls, but alarm systems – just as Maroon communities did. They changed the structure of their community, the crops they grew, the ways they related to strangers and to each other, all in the interest of protection. Their successes drove the slave traders deeper into the interior and pushed them to develop methods of commercial penetration, which played off people and groups within these communities. Ironically, the very egalitarian democratic nature of these societies often opened them up to the more subtle mechanisms of market-driven forces. Often, in protecting themselves, they became part of the system, enslaving others to better protect themselves."[1095]

The Genyi kingdom on the coast of Guinea is one example of how structures were profoundly changed by the transatlantic system and of the kind of wars it

---

1088 Ibid.
1089 Niane (2001), 9.
1090 Popo (2010), 301.
1091 Ibid., 301.
1092 Niane (2001), 10.
1093 Ibid., 8.
1094 Ibid., 9.
1095 Klein (2003), 73.

fostered between neighbors. Genyi only emerged in the 18th century, after the people of this region had for quite some time resisted engaging in active enslaving, but found themselves increasingly threatened by extinction due to the pressure and violence engendered by the transatlantic system. At one point then, they too found themselves obliged to join the slave catchers. [1096]

The enslaver Théodore Canot confided in his *mémoires* that 75% of the embarked African captives came from wars that were fomented through the "cupidity of whites" because local supply could not satisfy European demand.[1097] Both African private merchants and official state agents were involved as pro-active participators in the illegal mass enslavements. However, and that is important, these two categories cannot clearly be distinguished from one another, because the chaos and violence caused by the transatlantic system made it possible for traders to transform into a political elite. While traditional political systems were destroyed, these developments resulted in corrupted political and social systems in Africa. Seriously assessing these impacts and redressing them holistically would be one field of application for reparations. It is essential to highlight this disastrous impact of the transatlantic slavery system on societies on the African continent, because one prominent argument of reparation negationists is that the descendants of those deported to the Americas would be much better off today than those who remained in the motherland.

Much research of original documents still needs to be done in order to clarify the roots and extent of African collaboration, in order to make healing and true reparation possible. However, a lot of documentation was destroyed or scattered by colonial powers at the eve of independence, such as in Benin, in an effort to destroy incriminating evidence.[1098] Most documents concerning the first decades and centuries of transatlantic enslavement were transferred from Cape Verde to Portuguese archives.[1099] Part of the reparation process must also be the freeing up of access to these documents by responsible perpetrator states, as well as the funding of research.

ii. Responsibility of other European states

Article 16 (Aid or assistance in the commission of an internationally wrongful act) holds that a state that aids or assists another state in the commission of an internationally wrongful act by the latter is internationally responsible for doing so if: (a) that state does so with knowledge of the circumstances of the internationally wrongful act; and (b) the act would be internationally wrongful if committed

---

1096 Gayibor, N.L. (1990). Le Genyi, un royaume oublié de la coté de Guinée au temps de la traite de Noirs, Lomé: Editions Haho, 3 et seq.
1097 Popo (2010), 175.
1098 THE SLAVE TRADE ARCHIVES PROJECT (2005), 6.
1099 Ibid., 7.

by that state. The assisting state is responsible only to the extent that its own conduct has caused or contributed to the internationally wrongful act. Also, the state organ or agency providing aid or assistance must be aware of the circumstances making the conduct of the assisted state internationally wrongful. The aid or assistance must be given with a view to facilitating the commission of that act, and must actually do so. The completed conduct must be such that it would have been wrongful had it been committed by the assisting state itself.[1100]

This article is especially relevant with regard to what was done to Haiti. After the enslaved people there had taken their freedom in a revolution, Haiti was refused and boycotted by all European powers. The new state, just emerging from slavery and already having enough troubles due to that, could thus participate neither in commerce, nor establish embassies, nor officially defend its citizens. In this situation, it was forced to agree to pay France "reparations" in order to stay free from attack by that enslaver state and its allies. The extraction of these payments was definitely illegal and not covered by law. Haiti paid them until the 1950s. This extortion, along with further policy systematically maintained by France and the United States, firmly cemented the economic and political misery of Haiti up until today. As shown throughout this work, all European governments were aware that transatlantic slavery was illegal, and their assistance facilitated the illegal oppression of Haiti within the context of the genocidal transatlantic slavery system. Extortion for staying free from slavery would certainly have been considered wrongful if any European state had been its victim. Attribution to all assisting European states is thus possible, because there exists a causal link between the illegal aggression against Haiti by France and the collaboration of the collectivity of other European states, without which France could not have realized its malicious scheme. This shared legal responsibility of numerous European states however does not preclude the main responsibility of the acting state France. [1101]

E. CONDUCT ACKNOWLEDGED AND ADOPTED BY A STATE AS ITS OWN - ART. 11

Many of the already mentioned acts show the, sometimes smooth, transitions and over-crossings between the various means of attribution that the ILC Articles provide, such as Articles 8 and 11. We have dealt with Article 8 just above. Now, according to Article 11, "[c]onduct which is not attributable to a State under the preceding articles shall nevertheless be considered an act of that State under international law if and to the extent that the State acknowledges and adopts the conduct in question as its own." What is to be understood by "acknowledges and adopts the conduct in question as its own", has been concretized by international jurisprudence.

1100 Crawford (2002), 148 et seq.
1101 Crawford (2002), 159.

In 1980, in *United States Diplomatic and Consular Staff in Tehran*, the International Court of Justice sustained that "[t]he result of that policy [announced by the Ayatollah Khomeini of maintaining the occupation of the Embassy (...) for the purpose of exerting pressure on the United States government (...)] was fundamentally to transform the legal nature of the situation created by the occupation of the Embassy and the detention of its diplomatic and consular staff as hostages. The approval given to these facts by the Ayatollah Khomeini and other organs of the Iranian State, and the decision to perpetuate them, translated in continuing occupation of the Embassy and detention of the hostages into acts of that State"[1102] (emphasis added). If we apply the reasoning of the Court to the facts of transatlantic slavery, responsibility of all European enslaver states may be established via Art. 11 for an uncountable number of acts. Paraphrasing the words of the Court, "the approval given to these facts (through the passing of legislation endorsing the brutalization and murder of Africans by slave masters; through the proscription and encashing of taxes and revenues from slavery, for example) by European states and their organs of states, and the decision to perpetuate them, translated continuing genocidal and illegal slavery into acts of those States".

Generally in international practice, states often take positions which amount to "approval" or "endorsement" of conduct in a general sense but do not involve any assumption of responsibility. "The language of 'adoption', on the other hand, carries with it the idea that the conduct is acknowledged by the State as, in effect, its own conduct. (...) The conditions of acknowledgement and adoption are cumulative, as indicated by the word 'and'. (...) Acknowledgement and adoption of conduct by a State might be express (as for example in the Diplomatic and Consular Staff case), or it might be inferred from the conduct of the State in question."[1103] Over the centuries of transatlantic slavery, acknowledgement and adoption of the genocidal conduct of slavers were given both explicitly and implicitly by European states.

The highest European statesmen expressed their acknowledgment and approval of slavery. In 1768, Louis XV expressed his pleasure at the way "the traders of Bordeaux dedicated themselves with much enthusiasm to the trade of negroes"[1104]. From the beginning, John Hawkins, the first British enslaver, kidnapped Africans and also occasionally seized African kings and had them, their wives and courts shipped across the Atlantic. He quickly became one of the richest men in England and was appointed treasurer of the Royal Navy and dubbed knight by Elizabeth I. Elizabeth who had initially displayed legal retention, soon started to engage the

---

1102   United States Diplomatic and Consular Staff in Tehran (USA v. Iran), Judgement of May 24, 1980, ICJ Reports 1980, 3.

1103   Crawford (2002), 122 et seq.

1104   French Slavery, downloaded from http://etymonline.com/columns/frenchslavery.htm (accessed 29.5.2010) (t.b.a.).

British state in transatlantic slavery, following recommendation by Hawkins.[1105]

Free and free-born Black people were often times referred to as "slaves" in official state documents, another indication of how pervasive the racialized genocidal system was, and of how the genocidal perception of all Africans as chattel slaves denied in their full humanity was "adopted and acknowledged" by European colonial states. [1106]

In Virginia it was provided for by law that "after proclamation is issued against slaves that run away and lie out, it is lawful for any person whatsoever, to kill and destroy such slaves, by such ways and means as he, she, or they, shall think fit, without accusation or impeachment of any crime for the same (...). And lest private interest should incline the planter to mercy", the law provided "that for every slave killed, in pursuance of this act, or put to death by law, the master or owner of such slave shall be paid by the public".[1107]

Another important issue when discussing attribution due to acknowledgement and adoption of conduct, to be evaluated in the context of all other elements of evidence such as legislation and policy, is that enslaver nations extracted massive profits and revenues. Slave traders were required to pay 10 per cent of their profits for the provision of forts and factories on the coast to the British government. Ships sailed under European national flags and had to pay for this.[1108]

Spain, as other enslaver states, imposed a 20 per cent tax on slaver voyages in the late 15th century. Thus, the Spanish King made cash from slaving even before the first big licence for the deportation of Africans was given in 1510. In 1513 a royal tax was promulgated which made every licence cost two ducats, whereby a licence was understood as the permit for shipping one single slave. Additionally, there was an export tax to be paid to the European governments.[1109] The price of the licence rose steadily as the demand for slaves grew. The Spanish Crown, for example, willingly granted import licences for huge numbers of slaves because the larger the number the higher the fee; yet, the bigger a ship, the more horrendous the barbarity of the Middle Passage generally was too. Thus, European slaver governments were directly responsible for the agony and death of Africans in ships that were intentionally overcrowded. The first to obtain licences included aristocrats close to the throne. [1110]

The Dutch West India Company, established in 1621, paid a dividend to each of the town councils then comprising the Netherlands. All other European coun-

---

1105 Ki-Zerbo (1978), 211.

1106 Thompson, (2006), 10.

1107 Benezet (1767), 79.

1108 Bailey (2007), 115.

1109 Davidson (1961), 65.

1110 Malowist, M. (1992). "The Struggle for International Trade and its Implications for Africa", in: B.A. Ogot (ed.): General History of Africa V. Africa from the Sixteenth to the Eighteenth Century, Paris: UNESCO, 1-22, 9.

tries that joined in the transatlantic slavery system, such as England, Denmark, Sweden, France, and Germany, directly or through chartered companies, also captured significant tax revenues.[1111]

In the 1830s, cotton cultivated by slaves made up 50% of the trade surplus balance in the USA. [1112] "Slaves and slavery were crucial to public revenue. Their labor gave value to the land, as public domain was converted to private farms and public funds. Moreover, taxes on slaves constituted nearly half of all the tax revenue of antebellum Georgia's state and local governments, and much of the rest of tax revenue came from land recently acquired from Indians."[1113]

The sugar that the enslaved people in Haiti produced accounted for 40 per cent of France's foreign trade at a time when France was the dominant economy of Europe. The French state not only made huge profits from slavery, but also subventioned the "slave" "trade" through subsidies and primes granted to slavers depending on their tonnage and the number of deported Africans.[1114]

These acts of taxing and licensings may, by themselves, seem insufficient for attributing responsibility via Art. 11 to the concerned states, yet culminated with their conduct in the domains of legislation and determining policy without which transatlantic slavery could have taken place at all, permit to apply Art. 11. Thus, responsibility for the genodical Middle Passage and for the genocidal working and life conditions through which the taxed agricultural products were produced is attributable to states by this Article.

Article 11 seems also very suitable for a reflection on the possibility of attribution of unlawful conduct in transatlantic slavery to European countries other than those who maintained slave plantation colonies. A national of Austria commanded the slave ship *Charmante Louise*, owned by a trader from Nantes, to Benin in 1783 in order that it might sail under the Austrian flag to escape attack from British ships (France and Britain were at odds with each other at that time).[1115] Practically all western European states and/or some of their citizens were at some time and to some extent involved in transatlantic slavery. In Switzerland, a debate was brought up by a member of the National Council and a parliamentary deputy in 2003 and 2006 about the role of Swiss traders, army officials and scientists in transatlantic slavery. It was shown that Swiss firms and individuals participated through investments in slave dealing companies, were slave traders and gave ideological and military support. Even certain departments of Switzerland were engaged in state- or semi-state-organisms that were active in transatlantic slavery. Thus, the canton of Berne was a shareholder with the South Sea Company to

---

1111 Outterson, Kevin (2003). "Slave Taxes", in: Ray Winbush (ed.): Should America pay? Slavery and the raging debate on reparations, New York: Amistad, 135-149, 137.
1112 Ajavon (2005), 156.
1113 Outterson (2003), 142 et seq.
1114 Pétré-Grenouilleau (1998), 136.
1115 Ryder (1969), 214.

which Britain at one time sold the monopoly of slave shipping.[1116]

The Portuguese Kings and great enslavers John II and Manuel sought support for their activities among influential financiers of Italy and South Germany. Italians put large sums in cash or goods at the disposal of Portuguese rulers, and from the 1480s bankers, such as Bartolomeo Mar-Chioni, Sernigi and others, become actively engaged in the deportation trade of Africans. Portuguese documents reveal strong financial links between the Crown and major firms such as those of Frescobaldi, Affaitati and Fuggers.[1117]

A Brandenburger man established a slave factory in Ouidah in 1682 for the *Compagnie des Indes Occidentales Francaises* and administered a part of transatlantic slavery from there. A German connection is also documented in 1892 when some local kings exchanged slaves for firearms produced by German enterprises.[1118]

These elements alone may not suffice to attribute legal responsibility to any of those states, yet they constitute points of reference for further research, which might bring to light more details and evidence that might make it possible to attribute responsibility to European states other than those who had plantation colonies and are readily identified as colonial enslaver states. To do so might also be expedient and indeed necessary in that African reparations really concern all "white" people since the whole western European lifestyle is rooted in the capital accumulation and structures of exploitation set in place and firmly anchored with transatlantic slavery. African culture has also significantly impacted popular culture everywhere. Most young people in European societies listen to some kind of rock or pop music, not even to speak of hip hop and reggae. Yet all of these musical styles go to one extent or another back to forms of cultural expressions of enslaved Africans and their descendants. The combination of these facts that on one hand western European societies and culture in their entirety have been connected to and have been economically thriving on colonial exploitation that was firmly entrenched with transatlantic slavery, and that on the other they are today also still profiting culturally and materially so much from Africa, highlights Europeans' obligation to facilitate reparation for a continent and people who have given them so much.

Before closing this chapter, it is crucial to highlight that the concrete examples of conduct for which legal responsibility of European enslaver states has been attributed here are only that – examples – and do not at all constitute a conclusive enumeration.

1116 Plumelle-Uribe (2008), 104.
1117 Malowist (1992), 5 et seq.
1118 Kordes, Hagen (1998). "De la traite négrière au 'tri' des immigrants", in: Doudou Diène (ed.): La chaine et le lien. Une vision de la traite négrière, Paris: UNESCO, 313-325, 313.

2. RESPONSIBILITY OF THE HOLY SEE / ROMAN CATHOLIC CHURCH

A special case that deserves some extra attention with regard to responsibility is the conduct of the Papacy and the Catholic Church in transatlantic slavery in which they were directly and indirectly implicated from the very start.

In 1441, when the first convoy of African slaves was shipped to Portugal, Pope Eugene IV benefited from the "best elements of the cargo". [1119] One year later, in 1442, the *Illius qui* edict promised all those who would join slave raiding spiritual reward and eternal salvation. Pope Nicolas V empowered the Portuguese King in the bull *Dum diversas* of June 18, 1452 to conquer and reduce to "perpetual slavery" all "Saracens and pagans and other infidels and enemies of Christ" and to usurp their land and property. In 1455, the same Pope issued *Romanus Pontifex* upon Portuguese request, where he confirmed the first bull and denominated the territory to be conquered from Ceuta to Cap Bojador and Cap Nao *usque per totam Guineam et ultra versus illam meridionalem plagam*[1120]. Calixtus III established Portugal's expansion into Africa as a crusade to christianize in 1456, thus aiming at establishing a justification for slavery.[1121] The *Sacra Congregazione di Propaganda Fide* was founded by the Papacy in 1622 to direct missionary activities and, at least indirectly, fuelled colonial and slavery activities.[1122]

All of this indicates that attribution of responsibility to the Catholic Church via Art. 11 (Conduct acknowledged and adopted by a state as its own) may well be possible.

However, as transatlantic slavery and its horrors gained amplitude, and it became impossible to ignore its fundamental illegality by the law of nations, several popes condemned it. In a letter of October 7, 1462, Pie II denounced the "slave" "trade" as a great crime and ordered bishops to impose ecclesiastic sanctions on those practising it. Urban VIII condemned slavery in a letter to the Portuguese representant at the Vatican in 1639 and threatened all those engaged in it with excommunication. In 1741, Benedict XVI condemned slavery in *Immensa*.[1123]

In practice, though, Franciscan priests in Cuba who denied absolution through confession to slave masters and their wives, as long as they would not free their slaves and compensate them, were excommunicated, imprisoned and deported to

---

1119   Ajavon (2005), 13.

1120   Grewe (1984), 271.

1121   Harris (1992), 113.

1122   Ryder (1969), 100.

1123   Quenum, Alphonse (2002). "Regard chretien sur l'esclavage et la traite négrière: l'action des papes au XIX siècle", in: Isabel Castro Henriques and Louis Sala-Molins (ed.): Déraison, esclavage et droit. Les fondements idéologiques et juridiques de la traite négrière et de l'esclavage, Paris: EDITIONS Unesco, 203- 211, 204 et seq.

Spain.[1124]

The Catholic Church, or rather some of its orders, also owned plantations and slaves all over the American continent and the Caribbean.[1125] Jesuits, for example, owned and ran two sugar and one cocoa plantation in French Guiana, where at least 900 Africans were held captive at any given time.[1126] In Martinique, Father Jean-Baptiste Labat, procurator-general of all Dominican convents in the Antilles and himself a plantation owner, was occupied with the conversion of slaves from 1693 to 1705, a duty he approached with utmost barbarity.[1127] He wrote:

"I had the sorcer attached and let him have about 300 lashes which skinned him from the shoulders to the knees. He cried like in despair, and our negroes asked mercy for him, but I told them that sorcers felt no pain and that with his cries he fooled me. I had a seat brought and put an idol on it and told him to pray the devil to take it from my hands (...). Since the devil did neither one nor the other, I let him have another good whipping. (...) I had the sorcer put in irons, after having him washed with a marinade made of crushed hot pepper and limes. This causes horrible pain to those skinned by the whip, but it is a sure remedy against gangrene that will come on the wounds. I also tore all those apart who had been assembled [with the "sorcer"] to teach them not to be so curious a next time. The next day, I returned the negroe sorcer to his master (...), he thanked me for the punishment and let him have another nice whipping."[1128]

In 1700, the same Father Labat travelled to Barbados to learn British methods of fighting rebels and Maroons. From there he reported that

"those taken (...) are condemned to be passed in the millstone [grinding Negroes in the millstone; a punishment consisting in reducing them to pieces by the crushing of bones], burnt alive; or exposed in iron cages that pinch them so that they can make no movement at all and in this condition they are attached to a tree or they are left to die from hunger and rage. This is called drying a man. I confess that these means are cruel, but it has to be considered before condemning the inhabitants of this island (...) that they are often forced to neglect bounds of moderation in the punishment of their slaves to intimidate them, to imprint fear and respect on them, and to prevent themselves from becoming victims of the rage of these kind of people who being generally ten for one white, are ever ready to revolt and to undertake everything, to commit the most horrible crimes to set themselves free."[1129]

1124 Coco, Lémy Lémane (2005). Regards sur l'esclavage dans les colonies françaises, Paris: Menaibuc, 24.
1125 Plumelle-Uribe (2008), 87.
1126 Gisler, Antoine (1981). L'esclavage aux Antilles francaises (XVIIe-XIXe siècle), Paris: Karthala, 151.
1127 Ibid., 196.
1128 Cited in: Gisler (1981), 196 (t.b.a.).
1129 Ibid., 197 (t.b.a.).

The life conditions imposed in transatlantic slavery on African people were so horrendous that they often did not reproduce in numbers. For example, on the Fontezuela plantation in Brazil, belonging to the Betlemitas order (Orden de los Hermanos de Nuestra Senora de Bethelem), there were only eight babies born in 50 years, six of whom died before their first birthday. [1130]

The Holy See, episcopal jurisdiction and head organ of the Catholic Church, has been a subject of international law since, at least, the Middle Ages.[1131] For the purpose of attributing responsibility for the conduct of members of its various orders such as Father Labat, it still remains to be clarified through research of historical documents if they engaged in their criminal conduct towards enslaved Africans in their function as members of their order and the church. If that question can be answered in the affirmative, it should well be possible to attribute responsibility to the Holy See and the Catholic Church via Art.4. Generally speaking, priests are office holders of the Catholic Church, and orders are parts of its structure.[1132] Since international law stipulates that it is not sufficient to refer to internal law for determining the status of state organs, but that the status is also determined by practice, it is not really essential to assess here with absolute certainty whether they were to be considered "organs" by the internal law of the Church. Even if not, that would constitute no barrier to responsibility. "The internal law of a State may not classify, exhaustively or at all, which entities have the status of 'organs'. (...) Accordingly, a State cannot avoid responsibility for the conduct of a body which does in truth act as one of its organs merely be denying it that status under its own law."[1133]

Yet, the fact that the Holy See is in the position to excommunicate priests and monks and to suspend orders, such as done with the Jesuits in 1773, advocates the qualification of orders and priests as organs of the Holy See and the Catholic Church in international law. This seems even more appropriate on the background of the principle of effectiveness in international law.[1134] Thus, genocidal conduct such as described in the above examples, is attributable to the Holy See and the Catholic Church per Art. 4. But even if the qualification of priests and orders as organs of the Church should be successfully contested, the conduct still remains attributable per Art. 5, 8 or 11, the legal details of which were discussed above.

Not only the Catholic Church, the congregation of the first transatlantic en-

---

1130 Plumelle-Uribe (2008), 97.

1131 Legal status of the Holy See, downloaded from http://en.wikipedia.org/wiki/Legal_status_of_the_Holy_See (accessed 28.6.2012).

1132 E-Mail by Prof. Ludger Müller (Director of the Institute for Church Law at the University of Vienna), 29.6.2012 (on file with author).

1133 Crawford (2002), 98.

1134 Society of Jesus, downloaded from http://en.wikipedia.org/wiki/Society_of_Jesus (accessed 28.6.2012).

slaver states Spain and Portugal, was heavily engaged in the crime, but also the Anglican Church as well as smaller denominations such as the Moravians. The Anglican's church's Society for the Propagation of the Gospel (SPG) owned plantations and held Africans enslaved throughout the Caribbean. It had its seal branded into the flesh of the enslaved. When slavery was abolished in the British dominions in 1834, the SPG received compensation for its loss in slaves by the British Crown, as did other criminal enslavers.

Additional to direct involvement in slavery, religious education – catholic and protestant – served the formatting of enslaved Black people and making them more submissive to their condition as slaves.[1135] Numerous churchmen, acting in that role, were involved in this endeavor without which transatlantic slavery arguably could not possibly have gone on for centuries and which was thus constitutive for the crime. Numerous individual acts of priests in transatlantic slavery may therefore also be attributed to the Holy See and the Catholic Church via Art. 16 (Aid or assistance in the commission of an internationally wrongful act).

3. CONTINUING VIOLATION OF INTERNATIONAL LAW AND COLONIAL FORCED LABOR ON THE AFRICAN CONTINENT

Pertaining to what has been sustained so far concerning the fundamental illegality of transatlantic slavery at its time, the legal responsibility of perpetrating states and their ensuing obligation to make reparations, a decision rendered in 1853 by a United States-Great Britain Mixed Commission is very interesting. It concerned the conduct of British authorities who had at several instances seized several American slave vessels and freed enslaved Africans belonging to American nationals after Britain had abolished its naval slave deportation business. These incidents had occurred at different dates, and the Commission set out to determine for the moment at which each incident had taken place if slavery had then been "contrary to the law of nations" or not. Though the commission considered that it had been lawful at the time of the earlier incidents, thus entailing British responsibility, the later ones occurred at a time when the "slave" "trade" had been "prohibited by all civilized nations" and as such did not engage Britain's responsibility for violating naval rights of another nation by seizing the slave ships.[1136] Yet, we have seen above that by the law of nations and constitutional national laws transatlantic slavery had really always been illegal. So in that regard, the commission's decision relied on a mistake in law for the periods for which it judged Britain responsible for an internationally wrongful act for seizing the slave

---

1135 Plumelle-Uribe (2008), 87.
1136 Crawford (2002), 131.

ships. Thus, *argumentum e contrario* and following the general logic of the decision, it is really the responsibility of enslaver states that is engaged for the whole period of transatlantic slavery, because it was at all times illegal.

Additionally, and that is highly significant too in the case of transatlantic slavery, "once responsibility has accrued as a result of an internationally wrongful act, it is not affected by the subsequent termination of the obligation, whether as a result of the termination of the treaty which has been breached or of a change of international law"[1137]. So even if European powers could have unilaterally changed the law of nations to legalize genocidal chattel slavery in the 17th century – which they could not –, such a change of law would not have extinguished the already existent reparation claim for the 200 years of illegal enslavement and genocide that antedated these colonial slavery laws.

Yet, and that is indeed crucial to acknowledge, in international law "the breach of an international obligation by an act of a State having a continuing character extends over the entire period during which the act continues and remains not in conformity with the international obligation"[1138]. Now, many Africans and descendants of those deported claim that the basis for their claim to reparation is not only slavery, but the violation of sovereignty of African states and society at large and the genocide that began with transatlantic enslavement, continued with colonialism and is still perpetuated in the form of neo-colonialism up to today. The wrongful acts constituting the basis of the Maafa, that is the violation of African sovereignty and genocide, are continuing and have been perpetuated over more 500 years. This centuries-long breach of law constitutes the grossest human rights violation ever and gives rise to the vastest claim for responsibility and reparation that has ever been brought forth. In view of this reality, urgent action to redress this situation which continues to cost millions of lives would have to be one of the very top priorities in international relations and bodies. Yet, since these are controlled by the defendant western and European states, no one can seriously expect that to happen. Therefore, what is essential is the dissemination of knowledge about the firm legal anchorage of the right to reparation in international law to build people's power.

To further illustrate the point that we are in fact dealing with a continuing violation of international law, let us consider that whether a wrongful act is considered completed or has a continuing character in international law depends both on the primary legal obligation that is breached and the circumstances of a given case. "For example, the American Court of Human Rights has interpreted forced

---

1137 Ibid., 133.
1138 Article 14, International Law Commission (2001). Draft Articles on Responsibility of States for Internationally Wrongful Acts, November 2001, Supplement No. 10 (A/56/10), chp.IV.E.1, downloaded from http://www.unhcr.org/refworld/docid/3ddb8f804.html (accessed June 23, 2012).

or involuntary disappearance as a continuing wrongful act, one which continues for as long as the person concerned is unaccounted for."[1139] Now, the descendants of deported Africans for the most part still live in abject or relative material poverty in the places to where their ancestors were deported, structurally confined in conditions that may seriously reduce their life expectancies. Africans on the continent suffer very similar structural consequences. Now generally speaking, even in the case of a completed act with effects extending in time, such consequences would be subject to reparation, since the prolongation of such effects is relevant, for example, in determining the forms and amounts of reparations.[1140] However, and this is most important, the notion of the continuing violation has been applied by the European Court of Human Rights to establish its temporal jurisdiction in a series of cases. The issue arose because the Court's jurisdiction, like that of many other international tribunals, is limited to events occurring after a respondent state became a party to the Convention or the relevant Protocol by which it was established. In *Papamichalopoulos and Others v. Greece*, a seizure of property had occurred eight years before Greece recognized the Court's competence. Yet, because the Court held that since the property had not been returned, it constituted a continuing breach of the right to peaceful enjoyment of property under Article 1 of Protocol 1 to the European Convention of Human Rights. The Court declared itself competent even though the Convention entered into force only after the initial act of expropriation. In *Loizidou v. Turkey*, the Court assessed that in accordance with international law and in view of the relevant Security Council resolutions, no legal effects could be attributed to the 1985 Turkish Constitution which had provided for acts of expropriation. Thus, since the property was still withheld from its rightful owners, although this was covered by internal Turkish law, the wrongful act continued and the jurisdiction of the Court was established. There are more such examples of international jurisprudence to that effect, such as *Lovelace v. Canada* .[1141] Thus, the conceptualization of the crime as the Maafa, that is 500 years of warfare and genocide experienced by African people under enslavement and colonialism and their continued impact on African people throughout the world, makes possible the direct application of the Articles on state Responsibility that we have dealt with in detail to assess European states' legal responsibility to make reparations.

And indeed, Article 15 defines a "breach consisting of a composite act" as a violation that "extends over the entire period starting with the first of the actions or omissions of the series and lasts for as long as these actions or omissions are repeated and remain not in conformity with the international obligation". Genocide, apartheid, crimes against humanity, and systematic acts of racial discrimination are usually considered prime examples of such composite act-breaches.

1139 Crawford (2002), 136.
1140 Ibid.
1141 All cited in: Crawford (2002), 137 et seq.

"Genocide is not committed until there has been an accumulation of acts of killing, causing harm, (...) committed with the relevant intent, so as to satisfy the definition in article II. Once that threshold is crossed, the time of commission extends over the whole period during which any of the acts was committed (...). While composite acts are made up of a series of actions or omissions defined in aggregate as wrongful, this does not exclude the possibility that every single act in the series could be wrongful in accordance with another obligation. For example the wrongful act of genocide is generally made up of a series of acts which are themselves internationally wrongful."[1142]

As demonstrated throughout this work, this is exactly what happened in transatlantic slavery, colonialism and is still carried on through an abundance of internationally wrongful acts against African people and states today. The section that follows now therefore exposes examples of such acts and discusses their legal implications for the global African reparations claim.

In that context, it is important to acknowledge that "concerning the *ratione temporis*, it is not obvious, even from a legal point of view, that an event can be defined purely as past, as belonging to a different era, if its effects still persist in the present. International legal standards appear to be evolving rapidly in this area."[1143] The structures illegally set up through transatlantic slavery are still operational on a global level today. African people are still dying because they are Africans around the globe. Such as Raymond Hérissé, a Haitian youth killed with 100 rounds of ammunition by 12 Miami police officers while sitting unarmed in his car in 2011. Police then tried to destroy videotaped evidence. The incident remained without consequences for the acting officers.[1144] Such as Troy Davis, who was executed in October 2011 by the state of Georgia although grave errors had occurred during his trial and massive doubts existed about his guilt. The same state pardoned a "white" man a few days later who had confessed to the murder he was convicted of. Such as all those who die in the wars in Africa that are a consequence of the destruction of African civilizations by slavery and colonialism and that are led for the continued plundering of African resources for European, American, and more recently Asian, demand.

When assessing European and African responsibility it is important to keep in mind that official colonialism in Africa was really grown on the structures of trans-

---

1142 Ibid., 141 et seq.
1143 Ulrich, George (2002). "The Moral Case for Reparations. Three Theses about Reparations for Past Wrongs", in: George Ulrich and Louise Krabbe Boserup (ed.): Human Rights in Development, Yearbook 2001: Reparations: Redressing Past Wrongs, The Hague: Kluwer Law International, 369-385, 373.
1144 Allard, Jean-Guy (2011). In Miami, 12 Officers Shoot Haitian over 100 Times: Where Is International Press? downloaded from http://axisoflogic.com/artman/publish/Article_63221.shtml (accessed 6.12.2011).

atlantic slavery and itself relied on a slavery mode of production on the African continent. Transatlantic slavery had become less profitable due to the advancement of industrialization which had been rendered possible essentially through the accumulation of capital generated by slavery and which by then promised to yield higher profits, and because of the unstoppable quest for freedom of deported and enslaved Africans which had driven up costs for slave produce. This second aspect had been brought to the awareness of enslavers most drastically with the Haitian revolution of 1789 to 1804. But at the same time, European demand for African commodities and raw resources necessary for industrialization grew. Now, social and economic structures on the continent had to an enormous extent been shattered and destroyed through the past centuries of transatlantic enslavement, with large parts of the population killed in slave raids, deported, or dead from famines resulting from that general situation of European imposed violence. The European demand for African raw products necessary for industrialization coupled with this lack of population led to the imposition of forced labor by European states on Africans on the continent and official colonialism.[1145]

It is important to note in a connective perspective that at the same time that official colonialism was imposed on Africa, many southern US states passed "black codes" for offenses such as "enticement" or "vagrancy" which were punishable with forced labour only when committed by Black people. Simultaneously laws limited former slaves' freedom to pursue free work. Such legislation was in place well into the 20th century and pressed Black people into a situation of dependence and of, structurally or direct, forced labor. "[A] system of peonage and sharecropping emerged that held many former slaves and their descendants in involuntary servitude until the civil rights era of the 1950s".[1146] Since this forced labour had no legitimate legal coverage and indeed grew on the ruins of transatlantic slavery which had clearly been illegal, it was illegal too.

Former enslaver nations also did not enforce their prohibition of the "slave" "trade" with much vigour. France continued to deport enslaved Africans under the etiquette of *t*even after the abolition of slavery, until 1870. "For the slavers who were not successful and were captured by the British cruisers, little was done in terms of enforcement. (...) Occasionally a slaver was unfortunate enough to be caught. But the injustice of such cases was palpable. One Spanish captain who was sent to the Phillipine (sic) Islands for ten years, in 1832 applied for pardon. The government referred the case to Lord Palmerstone, and on his acquiescence, he was released in 1834."[1147]

Although this book focuses on responsibility and reparations for transatlantic slavery because that was the foundational crime, it is both factually consistent

---

1145 Inikori (1992b), 53.
1146 Peabody/Grinberg (2007), 100.
1147 Bailey, Anne C. "African Voices of the Atlantic Slave Trade", Ian Randle Publishers, Kingston/ Miami 2007, 136.

and legally appropriate to conceive transatlantic slavery in the wider context of the overall-crime of the Maafa, constituting a continuing violation of international law. Assessing responsibility for conduct of European states in colonialism in the same line that was maintained here to assess responsibility for transatlantic slavery would totally go beyond the scope of this book and will have to be dealt with in a different work. Still, a few concrete examples of atrocities perpetrated with colonialism shall be evoked now.

The beginning of "official" colonialism with the partition of Africa, such as conceived at the Berlin Conference of 1885, resulted in an understanding between the signatory powers according to which each obtained from the others carte blanche, to convert treaty relationships of "protection" with African states into relationships of absorption and annexation. According to Article XXXIV of the Berlin Act, all that a European power had to do was to notify the other signatories. However, such a side agreement with third European parties, that is other European states, could really have no effect on the legal standing of the African state, for pacta tertiis nec nocent nec prosunt. Alexandrowicz rightly assessed that these carte blanche arrangements between European powers were illegal when they provided for a breach of treaty or of the sovereignty of African states.[1148] This legal background always needs to be co-reflected when assessing responsibility for numerous instances of conduct of European states during colonialism.

Unlike pre-Maafa African servile labor, the practice of forced labor that all European powers imposed in their African colonies after abolition of transatlantic slavery and the transition to official colonialism indeed fitted the definition of chattel slavery. Like transatlantic slavery, it was characterized by a complete disregard for the humanity and lives of Africans. Maybe the most famous example is the terror regime brought over Congo by the Belgian King Leopold. The rubber collection system in this colony alone annihilated 10 million Africans in twenty years. The hacking-off of hands of whole villages, including children, which had failed to deliver the requested amount of rubber was common.[1149] What happened there under the direction of one and with the official approval of numerous European states was genocide, considerate of the legal requirements for qualification as genocide discussed earlier in this book.

The entire population of Congo was forced to collect rubber in the most ferocious and bloody conditions. This system was kept up for as long as the Belgians judged its cost economically preferable to the use of any technical support for rubber collection, well into the 20th century. "For centuries the investment in

1148 Alexandrowicz, C.H. (1975). "The Role of Treaties in the European.Afrcian Confrontation in the Nineteenth Century", in: A.K. Mensah-Brown (ed.): African International Legal History, New York: UNITAR, 27-68, 59 et seq.
1149 Hochschild, Adam (1998). Les fantômes du roi Léopold, un holocauste oublié, Paris, Belfond, 332.

Africa was inferior than the cost of the maintenance of even the breath of the African worker. To put him to work, a whole arsenal of legal, administrative and police measures was employed. This went from forced labor, 'obligatory labor', capitation tax to monetarisation coupled with unequal exchange and structural adjustment." [1150] As in transatlantic slavery, Africans were treated as a group of labor chattel while intentionally attacking and destroying them as human groups – their cultures, societies and physical lives.

Other European countries were also instrumental in bringing about the genocide in Congo. Austria sent a high delegation, consisting among others of an army officer, a count and the acting finance minister of the Habsburg Empire, Leopold Freiherr v. Hofmann, to the *Conference Géographique Internationale* (1876) where the fate of Congo was sealed. It was also the Austrian Minister v. Hofmann who proposed King Leopold as president of the *Association Internationale pour l'Exploration et la Civilisation de l'Afrique Centrale* under which banner the genocide was realized. Another association whose aim was to lobby for the "humanitarian crusade" of Leopold was founded in Austria as well. Austria also contributed to the Congo genocide financially and sent experts to assist the Belgian King. In 1885, an Austrian was appointed adjutant of the Belgian governor of Congo.[1151] Therefore, the responsibility of my birth country Austria, which is not readily associated with slavery and colonialism in Africa yet as all western nations profits economically and systematically from that system of exploitation, can be legally established under Art. 16 of the Articles on state responsibility (Aid or assistance in the commission of an internationally wrongful act) for the genocide in Congo. Today, the genocidal war in Congo is still going, still fuelled by European interference. This war started with the illegal and massive slaving operations of arming and pitting one group of the population against others by the Portuguese in the early 16th century and described in more detail in chapters II and IV. It continued in official colonialism with what Belgians did with the assistance of other European states, costing the lives of more than 10 million Africans. And with this violent pattern firmly entrenched after 500 years, the war is still going on, only that today the profits Europeans are making from it do not stem from plantation enslavement or rubber, but from coltan and uranium. Actually, the war is most ferocious in North Kivu and the other regions where European enterprises are most involved in mining these materials.

Given the implication in the genocide of African people by other European states such as Austria that generally uphold an image of themselves as having had

---

1150 Ki-Zerbo, Joseph (1998). 'La route mentale de l'esclave: brèves réflexions à partir de la condition présente des peuples noirs', in: Doudou Diène (ed.): La chaine et le lien. Une vision de la traite negriere, Paris: UNESCO, 175-181, 177.
1151 Sauer, Walter (2002). 'Schwarz-Gelb in Afrika. Habsburgermonarchie und koloniale Frage', in: Walter Sauer (ed.): k.u.k. Kolonial. Habsburgermonarchie und europäische Herrschaft in Afrika, Wien, Böhlau, 17-78, 59 et seq.

nothing at all to do with the enslavement and colonization of African people, it is most significant that Bruxelles is today the capital of Europe, and that in this city the apologia of genocide against African people is omnipresent and striking. In Bruxelles, a subway line carries the name of Leopold II, monuments in his honor are present at virtually every corner, and just behind the European parliament is the big Leopold-Parc. I don't think that European deputies would accept to go chill out at a Hitler- or Stalin-Park, but when it comes to African people's lives, standards are apparently very different. And this is not just about old monuments that have not yet been removed, but a conscious policy maintained to this day. The Afrika-Museum, the world's biggest showcase of robbed Central African art and artefacts and for colonialism propaganda, has in 1997, for its 100-years anniversary, been bestowed with a new monument starring King Leopold II in the center, sided by three tribal Africans whose legs have been amputated from below the knees, for whatever reason.

What Belgium and Austria did in Congo, however, was not a bad exception. In the colonies occupied by other European nations after the Berlin Congress, forced labor was also the most common form of labor in public works, on plantations and in mines.[1152] In Equatorial Africa, the French drafted laborers to build the Congo-Ocean railway from the Atlantic coast to Brazzaville. Workers were paid a minimum, but conditions were extremely bad and a high degree of coercion was applied. One African died for every tie laid in the rail bed.[1153] Adam Hochschild, historian and author of the highly acclaimed book "King Leopold's Ghosts", stated that as horrible as the genocide in the Congo was, what other Europeans did elsewhere in Africa at the same time was no less murderous.[1154]

Yet here again we encounter the manipulation of semantics. The French enslaved people under the ironic label "villages de liberté", where life conditions were horrifying, and people had no right to leave even though they were starved and many actually died from hunger. Up to 50% of local population was packed into such villages throughout Afrique occidentale française until 1905. Forced labor was used for the construction of railways and roads, clearing of forests, and on plantations producing for export. Porting was another much sought-after service by colonial Europeans that they recruited by force. Porters were not nourished and had to march 80 to 100 km at a time. To escape recruitment as porter, populations took flight in all directions, but as in transatlantic slavery, flight was punished with whip lashes, prison, deportation and death. Women and children

---

1152 Lawson-Body, Georges Latevi Babatounde (2000). "Du statut social de la force de travail sur les plantations aux Amériques du XVIe au XIX siècle", in: Serge Chalons, Christian Jean Etienne, Suzy Landau and Andre Yebakima (ed.): De l'esclavage aux réparations, Paris: Editions Karthala, 79-92, 81.
1153 Fegley, Randall (2010). "Death's Waiting Room: Equatorial Guinea's Long History of Slavery", in: Stephanie Beswick and Jay Spaulding (ed.): African Systems of Slavery, Trenton/Asmara: Africa World Press, 135-159, 138 et seq.
1154 Hochschild (1998), 332.

were taken hostage and locked up in huts where they were not given food until the men came out to work, and often to be worked to death.[1155]

All public and major work projects in "French" West Africa were carried out by forced labor. In Senegal, for example, this system was maintained until the 1940s. People were overseen by local commandants, just as slave drivers in the Americas were also enslaved Africans. The French state had legally bound itself to provide labor for its rubber *concessionaires* in French Equatorial Africa and for settler-owned cotton plantations in Ivory Coast, and apparently felt an urge to stick to these terms of engagement by all means. Thus, in Gabon, Congo, and Oubangui-Chari (part of the Central African Republic) the population diminished by one third in the first phase of colonial domination. Suret-Canale puts population decline at 40% between 1908 and 1916, and again at 40% for 1916-1924.[1156] Maes-Diop estimates that the total of Africa lost one third of its people in the time from 1880 to 1930.[1157] After that time, the catastrophe was not over however, as life conditions and hygiene had been damaged structurally and the Maafa was continuing in another form.

Of course Africans had resisted these developments, but as in transatlantic enslavement, resistance was broken with brute and unrelenting force. In Angola, for example, agitation against forced labor led to immediate imprisonment by the Portuguese.[1158] When considering all this, it is most crucial to keep in mind at all times that the imposition of genocidal slave labor and life conditions as well as of official colonialism as such, was only possible because 400 years of massive violence, directed and controlled by European states in illegal transatlantic slavery, had preceded them and permanently crushed indigenous forms of government and social coherence.

As in transatlantic slavery, Europeans also legislated on those colonial crimes. *The Code de l'indigénat*, promulgated by France for its colonies in 1887 and in force until 1947, codified an inferior status of the indigenous populations. Similar laws and strategies were employed by the other European powers, under the concept of indirect rule. Many laws provided that indigenous authorities, religious courts and native police carry out the colonial policy of tax burden, forced labor and arbitrary exercise of power. They created specific penalties for local populations and sanctioned the seizure of their lands. "Any white was free to impose summary punishment for any of 34 vaguely described infractions, such as 'disrespect' of France, its symbols or functionaries. The punishments ranged from fines to imprisonment to immediate execution. Theoretically punishment orders had to be signed by the colonial governor, but even that was almost always done in the

---

1155 Diop-Maes (1996), 239.
1156 Ibid., 253.
1157 Ibid., 256.
1158 Duodo, Cameron (2012). "What Frantz Fanon meant to African liberation (2)", in: New African N°513, London: IC Publications, 62-66, 64.

aftermath. In one region of the Kongo, 1,500 infractions were punished in this manner alone in 1908-1909".[1159] As in transatlantic slavery, the conduct that was constitutive of and at the very basis of colonialism was illegal. "Workers were supposed to be provided with food if working more than 5 km away from home, but this was often ignored. In 1930, the Geneva Convention outlawed the *corvée*, but France substituted a work tax (*Prestation*) in the AOF decree of September 12, 1930, whereby able-bodied men were assessed a high monetary tax, which they could pay via forced labor."[1160]

So, to take up the example of Senegal, after 400 years of massive enslavement directed by Europeans and entailing the corruption and destruction of indigenous political, social and economic systems, the French imposed forced labor up to the 1940s and peanut monoculture, thus further destroying any remnants of the social and economic fabric that could have served as a base to truly progressive development. It is that situation of hopelessness and poverty cemented in these (neo-)colonial structures that makes so many young African people risk their lives while trying to reach Europe via the Mediterranean sea.

Throughout, all the evidence reviewed for the purpose of accomplishing this work – and that was a lot – points to the fact that all instances of institutions approximating chattel slavery detected today in African societies are found in regions that have been seriously affected by transatlantic enslavement and/or colonial "forced labor". Native sub-officials and some chiefs appointed by the colonists made use of forced labor, compulsory crops, and taxes in kind.

"As the enforcers of the Indigénat, they were also, in part, beneficiaries. Still, they themselves were quite firmly under French authority when the French chose to exercise it. It was only in 1924 that chiefs du canton were exempted from the Indigénat, and if they showed insubordination or disloyalty they could still [as all Africans] be imprisoned for up to ten years for 'Political offences' by French officials (...). Part of the court system that the Code established relied on the principle of chief creation who were to replace traditional leaders with Africans who would be dependent upon the French. Consequently customary courts often served simply to place more power in the hands of official chiefs. After centuries of attrition through transatlantic slavery, there was still resistance, albeit most often indirect. Whole villages fled during the road building push in the 1920s and 30s, and colonial officials gradually relaxed the use of forced labor. Up to 2,5 million Mossi people fled from Upper Volta to the Gold Coast and Nigeria to escape forced labor."[1161]

1159 Martin, Phyllis (1995). Leisure and Society in Colonial Brazzaville, Cambridge: Cambridge University Press, 83 et seq.
1160 Indigénat, downloaded from http://en.wikipedia.org/wiki/Indig%C3%A9nat (accessed 5.5.2009).
1161 Ibid.

The importance of exposing these ugly truths about colonialism and its continuity with transatlantic slavery becomes very obvious at occasions such as a lecture in Social Anthropology at the University of Vienna, where the lecturer made
the remark that "everything should not be painted in black and white", and that
colonialism would also have had its good sides, such as the construction of railways. Yet the railways Congo-Ocean and Thiès-Kayes, for example, are side-lined
by non-declared cemeteries. In order to get the men to do the murderous labor,
women and children were locked into death houses, called so because the in-
mates were not nourished.[1162] In 1921, the French directed the construction of the
502-km-long Brazzaville-Pointe Noire railway line. Governor Raphael Antonetto
gave order to recruit local men to replace others who were dying massively on
the construction sites. Since most Congolese in that region were either dead already or had taken flight, the authorities went to look elsewhere, in neighboring
Oubangui-Chari, Cameroun and Tchad. Antonetti said that "we must consent to
the sacrifice of six to eight thousand men or give up on the railway". Construction went on, and in 1927 17,000 deaths were accounted for, although 30 km still
remained to be built. Other estimates assess that this railroad cost 30,000 lives.[1163]

This genocidal colonial concentration complex on the African continent was
maintained until the 1950s, when African people's struggle put an end to this
stage of the Maafa. Yet, after formal independence, most, if not all, progressive African leaders were eliminated by former European enslaver and colonialist states,
that is, killed or ousted from power. In Togo, President Sylvanus Olympio was
assassinated on January 13, 1963, two days before a planned break-away of the
Togolese financial system from the French national bank would have been signed.
The clan of his murderer Eyadéma has been ruling ever since. On the death of
Gnassingbé Eyadéma in 2005, French President Chirac honored him as a "friend
to France and a personal friend"[1164].

In Cameroon, popular leaders such as Felix Moumié in 1960 were eliminated
before and after independence. Moumié was poisoned in Geneva by William Bech-
tel, a French agent of the French secret service SDECE (Service de documentation
éxterieure de contre-éspionnage). Anti-colonial activist and economist Osendé
Afana was murdered by the French colonial army in 1966 on the border to Congo.
Anticolonial revolutionaries Ouandié, Fotsing und Tabeau were publicly executed
with the assistance of the French colonial army in 1971. A little better known is
the fate of President Thomas Sankara in Burkina Faso, who was also eliminated
with the assistance of French agencies by the collaborator Blaise Compaoré, who
alleged that Sankara had jeopardized relations with former colonial power France.
During his presidency, Sankara had sold all state limousines, including the presi-

---

1162 Ki-Zerbo (1978), 433.
1163 Plumelle-Uribe (2001).
1164 Plumelle-Uribe (2008), 164 et seq.

dential car, and replaced them with Renault 5s. As President, he received the same salary he had before his ascension to that position. His politics actively promoted equal rights of men and women, and were determined in fighting polygamy and female genital mutilation. Sankara affirmed that "when an African buys a weapon it is to use it against another African", and therefore limited armament expenses. The so freed budget was channelled into healthcare, education and housing. These politics went against the interests of former colonizer France and the arms industry. World Bank, IMF and France revoked credits. Yet, even without access to credits, Burkina Faso managed to considerably ameliorate life conditions for the people, whereas at the same time in other African countries austerity and structural adjustment programs proscribed by the IMF and World Bank worsened living conditions for the poor. Consequently, Sankara had become a reference of successful anti-colonial politics throughout the continent and beyond.

Sankara had also proven himself non-corruptible. The combination of all these factors made him a threat to the neo-colonial status quo. He had to be eliminated, and the neo-colonial powers easily found a collaborator who would do the dirty work, such as practiced uncountable times since the beginning of transatlantic slavery. Blaise Compaoré, a long time "friend" of Sankara, loved luxury and did not accommodate too easily to Sankara's politics of transparency. The only material assets Sankara possessed at the time of this murder was a modest house for which he had not yet finished paying off the mortgage.[1165]

These are just some examples of progressive African leaders killed by or with the assistance of former colonial powers in the 20th century. The list is much longer. All of these incidents must be assessed in detail with regards to legal responsibility and reparations. In light of what has been said above for transatlantic slavery by means of the ILC Articles, the continuing responsibility of European perpetrator states is clearly established.

It shall also not go unmentioned in that context that experts of the French army participated in the instruction of Rwandese militia, training them how to kill the greatest possible number of persons in the shortest time possible. The implication of France in the shooting down of the plane of Rwandese President Juvenal Habyarimana which triggered genocide in that country, is currently under judicial investigation. [1166]

Historians and political scientists such as Eric Toussaint have retraced pertinently how western governments impoverished and ruined their former colonies. In the 1950s, the World Bank granted vast credits to European colonial states such as Belgium, France and Britain for projects aiming at exploiting and robbing the natural resources of their colonies more efficiently. This happened not only in Africa, but was also done to other former colonies on the other side of the

---

1165 Plumelle-Uribe (2008), 164 et seq.
1166 Ibid., 196.

transatlantic slavery system, such as ex-British Guyana. These credits served to provide the colonial powers with minerals, agricultural produce and combustibles and helped to reduce dollar penury of these nations. When the African countries acceded to formal independence, the World Bank decided that the credits contracted and paid out to the colonial powers would be shifted onto the new African states. African states thus found themselves with huge and indeed criminal debts. Their monetary resources which would have been needed so urgently to construct health centers, schools and a stable infrastructure thus went back to the former colonizers in form of debt payment. The complicity of many African rulers in this was paid by new credits granted by World Bank and IMF, of which these collaborators kept and still keep large parts for themselves while their peoples are struggling to survive.[1167] Now all of this is possible only because of the structures set in place during transatlantic slavery, yet this situation continues to increase poverty and illness and to reduce the life spans of millions of Africans globally.

Most of what has been mentioned in this section can be attributed to the acting states through Art. 4, or Art. 8, because European enslaver states undoubtedly directed and controlled these settings and because the conduct in question was illegal and genocidal. What has been stated concerning transatlantic slavery in that regard, is analogously valid here.

Given this continuing genocidal situation, it is important to point out that the reparation claim for transatlantic slavery and the Maafa is not about attributing guilt to the descendants of European enslavers, but about responsibility. And if European descendants of enslavers are not guilty of the crimes of their ancestors, they are responsible for continuing to maintain and profit from a system that continues to take the lives of African people and for the foundation of which their states are also legally responsible. Examples of the practical consequences up to today of the crime of transatlantic slavery and of the continuing violation of law through colonialism and neo-colonialism for the descendants of the historical victims, who at the same time are victims of the continuing violation themselves, shall be discussed in the next chapter.

Some negationists argue that innocent beneficiaries of unjust acts have no obligation to make reparations. It is not really necessary to dwell on this point because there are really no "innocent beneficiaries" here since westerners today are collectively responsible for the perpetuation of this genocidal and illegal system. It is this system that makes it possible for them to savor cheap chocolate produced in slavery conditions, often involving child slavery, built on the structures of illegal transatlantic slavery in Africa. Fair trade chocolate is only slightly more costly, but most westerners are not even ready to make any concessions in such small matters and to change their consumption to fair trade. And for this they are

---

1167 Toussaint, Eric (2008). Odieux Prêts de la Banque Mondiale à la métropole coloniale belge pour coloniser le Congo, downloaded from www.cadtm.org/spip.php?article2421 (accessed June 16, 2008).

responsible, even if they are not criminally liable for the crimes of their ancestors.

V. Maafa Today - Legacy of Transatlantic Slavery, Continuing Genocide and the Urgency of Reparation

Having established that transatlantic slavery was genocide and a crime against humanity perpetrated over four centuries, some of the structures of oppression that were set in place through it and have in the following been characteristic of the Maafa in its entirety will now be analysed within a legal perspective. In order to make it pertinently clear how necessary and indispensable reparation is, this chapter will address some aspects of the perduring legacy of transatlantic slavery and the damage still generated through the continuing crime of the Maafa.

The final report of the seminal UNESCO experts conference in 1978 made the following assessment of the situation, and also drew a parallel between the position of diaspora and continental Africans who were both subjected by European states in colonialism to the kind of genocidal "forced labor" described above:

"Little changed except appearances. The relations of the masters and the newly emancipated did not improve. The condition of the emancipated was often worse, financially, than before. Under cover of the new legality, all sorts of schemes were introduced to enable the masters to perpetuate their control of the labour force (the 'gourmettes' of Senegambia and the 'freedom villages' of West Africa are examples). The existence of a free labour market meant that the masters could avoid part of the costs they had previously borne in connection with their slaves. Slavery was an obsolete system, but in addition it was now a less economical proposition than wage-earning labour. Moreover, when the labour market was saturated, wages fell. (...) The experts were generally inclined to conclude that abolition brought no radical changes, but simply led to the transition from one state of production and exploitation to another."[1168]

1168 United Nations Educational, Scientific and Cultural Organization (ed.) (1978). Meeting of Experts on the African Slave-Trade, Final Report, Port-au-Prince, Haiti, 31 January-4 February 1978, downloaded from http://unesdoc.unesco.org/images/0003/000333/033360eb.pdf (accessed 21.6.2012).

1. ON THE AFRICAN CONTINENT

Indeed, "none of the experts present" at that UNESCO conference "disputed the idea that the slave-trade was responsible for the economic backwardness of Black Africa"[1169], and it is this economic backwardness maintained by European ex-enslavers that fills our supermarket shelves with cheap blood chocolate. Unfortunately due to the commonly propagated historical misinformation, many people think that Africa before the 15th century had been "underdeveloped" and "primitive", and that the current state of material poverty on the continent would be nothing but the logic and more or less natural consequence of poor organization which would be intrinsic to African societies. Even if not sustained explicitly, this perspective is enforced implicitly through the mass media and dominant discourses. Yet, when reflecting with common sense on this situation, there can only be two explanations for the persistent state of poverty and violence in African societies. Given the facts of this persistent record of poverty and catastrophe, either something has to indeed be essentially wrong with Africans, or the firmly entrenched misery is due to the persistent and well-documented interference and imposition of violence by Europeans over centuries. In the latter case, there can remain no serious doubt for the necessity of reparations. Anyone denying the legitimacy of reparations must thus logically adhere to the first explanation, intrinsic social incapacities of Africans, and should openly say so, so we can advance from there, knowing who is who. Given the uncontestable historical facts, opposing reparations really comes back to nothing else but the defense of the racist anti-African attitude implicit in the first explanation.

Some argue that the so-called three-field crop rotation system would have been invented and known in Europe exclusively. This agricultural system is generally considered by mainstream European historiography as the precondition for any kind of progressive social development worthy of that name. Yet what is omitted is that African societies, such as the Serer, had practiced crop rotation for a long time, even if not necessarily on three fields.[1170] Multi-disciplinary research by Diop-Maes, widow of the great Cheikh Anta Diop, revealed that the levels of development and life standards of Black African people before European and Arab attacks had been quite elevated. She analyzed texts by Arab and Sudanese authors containing testimonies about the details of the lives of the inhabitants and the economic life of Black Africa from the 8th to the 17th century, and then

---

1169 United Nations Educational, Scientific and Cultural Organization (ed.) (1978). Meeting of Experts on the African Slave-Trade, Final Report, Port-au-Prince, Haiti, 31 January-4 February 1978, downloaded from http://unesdoc.unesco.org/images/0003/000333/033360eb.pdf (accessed 21.6.2012);
1170 Imfeld, Al (2007). Decolonizing African Agricultural History, downloaded from http://www.alimfeld.ch/African_Agricultural_History/Aghist.pdf (accessed 7.11.2010), 80.

confronted these texts with accounts written by early European navigators and envoys from the 15th to the 17th century. The findings were streamlined with contemporary archaeological research expertise on as many regions of Africa as possible. Mathematical models were also incorporated to assess demographical history. Diop-Maes' research shows that Black Africa, at least up to the 16th century, was rather heavily populated (comparable to the population ratio of India at the same time). Agricultural production was abundant and varied. The majority of the population was well nourished, and both craft production and trading were highly developed and diversified. Maes-Diop, along with other experts, also found that the socio-political systems of most African societies were humanist and favoured the development of a relative social well-being that was unknown in Europe at the same time. [1171]

Now, everyone is aware that the situation on the African continent is quite different today from those rather prosperous times. The situation has indeed been catastrophic throughout the times of official colonialism and of decolonization. Yet, the "before-those-times" remains a mystery in mainstream history discourses, when the main cause of the miserable situation in many parts really was the violence and decomposition of indigenous African social and economic structures through the transatlantic slavery system that ravaged the continent for over 400 years. The external demand for labor compromised and stopped economic development in Africa. Transatlantic slavery instituted insecurity and inter-ethnic and social tension, while creating an anti-productive economic mentality. As retraced already, this engendered a massive worsening, in both qualitative and quantitative terms, of indigenous servitude and slavery.[1172]

As discussed above, early accounts by European enslavers do speak of the availability of a few African captive slaves for purchase, which indicates that "slavery" existed, in certain forms, in Africa at that time. This historic fact of early African "slavery" as a marginal institution conforming to the law of nations at that time, has been misused to create confusion and to put the main blame for transatlantic slavery on Africans while exculpating Europeans. However, the whole transatlantic system was set up, directed and controlled by European states. The British abolitionist William Wilberforce, who today is celebrated by official England, wrote in the late 18th century that incontestably religious and civil institutions in Africa were gradually perverted and fashioned according to the exigencies of transatlantic slavery. He specifically pointed out how the administration of justice was seriously corrupted, and how many offences, even the smallest, became punishable by enslavement.[1173]

1171 Plumelle-Uribe (2008), 20, see also 39 et seq.
1172 Diop-Maes (1996), 211.
1173 Wilberforce, William (1814/1815). Lettre à l'empereur Alexandre sur la traite des Noirs a la suite du non-respect des dispositions signees par les Europeens lord du Congres de Vienne.

Now, it is really a perversion, but tragically a very powerful one, that reparation negationists advance the argument that the increase of internal African slavery after the end of transatlantic slavery would disprove any relation between external demand and African enslavement. Acknowledged slavery scholar Klein also pointed out that centuries of slave raiding left Africa with social and economic structures adapted to enslavement. The demand for tropical products in European markets made the exploitation of slave labor within Africa increasingly remunerative at the onset of official colonialism. New and more efficient weapons made it easier for those with access to them, that is the African elite of former collaborators in transatlantic enslavement or generally those willing to collaborate in colonization, to impose their will on large populations.[1174] Patrick Manning, another renowned scholar on the subject, comes to a similar assessment:

"The new system – the Atlantic slave trade and modern African slavery – became quite different from early African slavery. In the early days, war captives and other dependants who fell under the control of African rulers did the bidding of their owners. (...) But the number of persons held in slavery in Africa was small, since no economic or social system had developed for exploiting them. (...) After two or three centuries of the Atlantic slave trade, conditions in Africa had changed immensely. The 5,000 slaves purchased by the Europeans each year in the 16th century had risen to nearly 100,000 per year at the end of the 18th century. By the end of the 19th century, perhaps five or six million persons were held in slavery on the African continent, many times more than could have been enslaved before the Atlantic slave trade began."[1175]

Transatlantic slavery had brought about the emergence of new powerful elites, as only those who worked with European enslavers could maintain their positions, or in some cases, even save their lives. Thus, in many instances categories of powerful merchants and political rulers became merged. Military might became privileged to the detriment of ancient power control mechanisms and customs. These constellations were forcefully maintained, formed reality over a period of over 400 years and were cemented into enduring structures that still hold hostage the present.[1176] The debts that are crippling African and Caribbean economies, maintaining them in economic slavery as often argued, and keeping them from rising were for the most part imposed by European colonizer states and later by dictators who had been helped to power by European states and the USA, thus the same states who are profiting from debt payment and who had also been behind transatlantic slavery. It was with transatlantic slavery that European states commenced their practice of deposing African sovereigns and helping despots

---

1174 Inikori (1982), 42 et seq.
1175 Manning, Patrick (1994). "The Impact of the Slave Trade on the Socities of West and Central Africa", in: Anthony Tibbles (ed.): Transatlantic Slavery. Against Human Dignity, London: Merrell Holberton Publishers, 97-104, 97 et seq.
1176 Diop-Maes (1996), 211.

to power who were instrumental for their own economic agendas. The Maafa is really the biggest organized crime ever.

Although the extensive literature on human rights in Africa contains diverse assessments concerning the concrete normative value of such rights in African societies, it also reflects an impressively consistent descriptive pattern of traditional African societies embodying values that are consistent with and supportive of human rights, while recognizing the effects of slavery and colonialism in the erosion of these values. Dustan Wai argued that

"authoritarianism in modern Africa is not at all in accord with the spirit and practice of traditional political systems, but that its practices are aberrations facilitated by colonial legacies and reinforced by the agonies of 'underdevelopment'. (...) Colonial rule destroyed traditional institutions and relationships that protected people and constrained power; imposed authoritarian governments and reduced the rights exercised by individuals, conditioning Africans to repressive ways; left behind disastrously ill-structured economies and societies riddled with ethnic, social, economic, and political divisions; and imposed political boundaries that were arbitrary and incompatible with traditional social structures."[1177]

This process, however, did not commence only with official colonialism, but centuries earlier with transatlantic slavery. Since that time European states, enslavers, colonialists and neo-colonialists have always employed manipulation and violence to assure that local governments functioned to their best interests. This was and is effectuated by dividing, arming and corrupting. [1178]

Research confirmed that transatlantic slavery had significant negative repercussions for formerly egalitarian structured societies such as the Felupe on the Upper Guinea Coast, who had initially actively fought transatlantic enslavement for some decades. After being drawn into the transatlantic system as enslavers due to the need to defend themselves and acquire arms, these societies became hierarchized as those individuals engaging most in the enslavement of others acquired most wealth. Corruption of judicial institutions towards enslavement became common to both hierarchical and decentralized societies.[1179] This process was to a large extent responsible for the vassalage and slavery to which African people were increasingly reduced on the African coast itself. The testimony of a chief of Port Loko confirmed that those captives whom the Europeans did not buy were always put to work on the coast, whereas such a system had not existed before.[1180]

On the Upper Guinea Coast, where slavery had not existed prior to the engage-

---

1177 Silk, James (1990). "Traditional Culture and the Prospect for Human Rights in Africa", in: Abdullahi An-Na'im and Francis M. Deng (ed.): Human Rights in Africa. Cross-Cultural Perspectives, Washington DC: The Brookings Institution, 290-328, 292 et seq.
1178 Ajavon (2005), 196.
1179 Hawthorne (2003a), 98 et seq.
1180 Rodney (1966), 434 et seq.

ment of Europeans, a large number of people had been reduced to servile status by the end of the 18th century, whether as agricultural laborers, temporary members of households or as permanent residents of *roundes*. Many of them showed aversion to their oppression by escaping whenever the opportunity presented itself. Similar developments took place in the rest of Africa. In the 20th century, when "the European powers involved in the area [namely Britain, France and Portugal] intervened to end slavery and serfdom in their respective colonies, they were simply undoing their own handiwork"[1181] since, as we have seen, European states had not only been responsible for the emergence and then expansion of chattel slavery conditions through enslavement for the transatlantic system but all European colonial powers had also directly subjected Africans to brutal forms of forced labor during official colonialism.

Also among other societies that had known no slavery previously, such as on the Sierra Leone coast, slavery could be also confirmed by the middle of the 17th century. In areas that previously had known some kind of "slavery" and servile labor, these institutions had significantly expanded and changed in character, such as in the Yoruba and Dahomey regions.[1182] In major parts of Africa irregularity, unpredictability, distrust, hostility and violence had become firmly entrenched because of transatlantic slavery and, since there was no reparation and healing, continue to have grave repercussions on inter-ethnic relations up to today.[1183] Everywhere, it created tensions and violent conflicts between neighboring peoples.

The expansion of slavery in Africa was later further directly stimulated by colonial military activities, as food supply was vital, but not readily available for the colonial forces. "By 1894 an important grain market had emerged in Bamako which alleviated the acute problems of supplying the army and its outlying posts. The demand for cereals stimulated Banamba plantations, which also continued to feed the desert-side [slave] trade."[1184] France, for example, cemented alliances with collaborators by distributing captives as slaves after military victories, thus creating more tribalistic antagonisms. The *villages de liberté* have already been mentioned, set up by the French, and which were really slave villages, and "their primary function was to supply labor. (...) They were often seen as the commandant's slaves and frequently fled to other locations".[1185]

Recent years have seen a raise in awareness about present-day child slavery on cacao plantations in countries such as the Ivory Coast where many children from Mali and Burkina Faso are forcibly transported to.[1186] Hamady Bocoum, then

---

1181 Ibid., 440.
1182 Lovejoy (2000), 120.
1183 Hawthorne (2003a), 109 et seq.
1184 Roberts/Klein (1980), 378.
1185 Ibid., 383.
1186 Mistrati, M./Romano, U.R. (2011). Elfenbeinküste: Bittere Schokolade, Weltjournal, ORF2, 9.2.2011.

director of cultural patrimony of Senegal, sustained in that context that the centuries of transatlantic enslavement engendered an economy of violence and of man-hunting as well as a reflex to excessive auto-protection, all of which had and still have repercussions on development and induced a traumatism on the continent that resurges today as child slavery and other evils. [1187] Thus, when former European enslaver states maintain that they would not make reparations, because "the historic slave trade was not a crime against humanity or contrary to international law at the time when the UK Government condoned it", that they "today cannot take responsibility for what happened over 150 years ago", and that they would be "currently working (...) to combat the diverse forms of contemporary slavery, such as forced or bonded labour[1188], we need to respond instantly that transatlantic slavery was illegal at its time, that we are dealing with a continuing violation of law for which European governments are still responsible, and that it is not possible to combat present-day forms of slavery without healing and repairing the foundational crime of transatlantic slavery. In that vein and in recognition of this basic truth, the UN Working Group on Contemporary Forms of Slavery also referred to the "need for (...) compensation for victims of the slave trade and other early forms of slavery.[1189]

Not only western coastal African societies were affected by this but the whole of Africa. Kalck showed that captives were taken from as far as Nubia and Tchad and brought to Congo or the Guinea Coast in the 16th and 17th centuries.[1190] European slave raids are recorded to have taken place in the 16th and 17th centuries around Cape Town and in what is today Namibia. Communities there were armed and pitted one against the other. Initially, the thereby enslaved Africans were used to build the colony. Then, from the 18th century on they were also deported into transatlantic slavery by the Dutch, French and Portuguese. Women and children were raped and prostituted. This is more or less well-known for the Herero in present-day Namibia, but was done to many other communities as well. Researchers have assessed that these developments, together with the expulsion of one community into the area of another to make place for the Boer's cattle raising, are the main reasons for present-day instabilities in Namibia and Botswana.[1191]

1187 B.World Connection (2010). Esclavage. Commémoration et réparations, downloaded from http://www.bworldconnection.tv/index.php/Emissions/B.World-Connection-Esclavage-Commemoration-et-reparations.html (accessed June 24, 2010).
1188 Letter of January 2, 2003 by Gavin Tech, Deputy British High Commissioner, to "the RastafarI Brethren of Jamaica", c/o Mr. Howard Hamilton, Public Defender, 78 Harbour Street, Kingston.
1189 COMMISSION ON HUMAN RIGHTS, Sub-Commission on Prevention of Discrimination and Protection of Minorities, Forty-fifth session (1993). Study concerning the right to restitution, compensation and rehabilitation for victims of gross violations of human rights and fundamental freedoms, Final report submitted by Mr. Theo van Boven, Special Rapporteur, E/CN.4/Sub.2/1993/8,2 July 1993, 12.
1190 Diop-Maes (1996), 227.
1191 Gewald, Jan-Bart (1995). "Untapped Sources. Slave Exports from Southern and Central Namibia

It was also in the time of transatlantic enslavement that many groups developed a heightened consciousness of differences with their neighbors and started to exalt their specificities while denigrating others with terms such as mortal enemies, gorillas, snakes or hyenas. By diabolising a neighbor, one could more easily pretend to have a right to enslave or kill him. [1192] Ethnicity in the form of tribalism was not a cultural characteristic of the pre-Maafa African past, but was a consciously crafted ideological construct that was introduced during transatlantic enslavement and the colonial era.[1193]

Transatlantic enslavement not only led to the permanent instalment of chattel slavery on the continent, but also to enormous physical destruction, displacement and extinction of African communities. In Yorubaland, whole villages and towns were burnt down, and as many people killed as those caught in 17th and 18th centuries slave raids. This violence and diminution of population impeded traditional economic and cultural activities. "As one travels around villages and towns in northern Yorubaland today, one finds relics of abandoned habitations, (...) and defensive works (...), massive walls (...) erected to ward off or minimize the risk of attacks, (...) rampart walls and ditches (...)."[1194]

UNESCO research has confirmed that many people in Africa saw their villages, granaries and fields burnt during the slave hunting centuries, and had to take to the forest to live on its fruits and game to survive. In certain regions, the people had to abandon large villages to regroup themselves in small settlements in the interior of the forest that were only accessible through hidden path ways that were also secured by various snares. Interrogated elders unanimously recollected the "period of permanent horse ride kidnapping" ("la période des chevauchées permanents") as the main reason for the stagnation, or even regression, of African agriculture. Oral tradition maintains that the persistence of terror and death could trap the living at any moment of the day and night. One could no longer plan for the future or on elaborate ambitious projects, knowing that an enemy could at any moment come, burn down everything and take one away. This permanent fear fragilised the spirit of the people in many communities and installed a hesitant mentality focused on living from one day to the next. Oral tradition recorded in that UNESCO project also refers to transatlantic slavery as explication for the abandonment and decline of certain crafts and ancient occupations. The interlocutors in this project related with clarity how their societies passed

---

up to ca. 1850", in: C. Hamilton (ed.): The Mfecane Aftermath, Johannesburg: Wits University Press, 419-435.

1192 Guèye (2001), 20 et seq.

1193 Reader, John (1998). Africa: A Biography of the Continent, London: Penguin Books, 610.

1194 Usman, Aribidesi (2010). "The Landscape and Society of Northern Yorubaland during the Era of the Atlantic Slave Trade", in: Akinwumi Ogundiran and Toyin Falola (ed.): Archaeology of Atlantic Africa and the African Diaspora, Bloomington/Indianapolis: Indiana University Press, 140-159, 150 et seq.

from decentralized political organization, where the sovereign was assimilated to a "totem" incarnating the spiritual unity of the people, to systems that can be termed autocratic where the caprices of kings became considered law. Faced with a permanent state of insecurity, many societies proceeded to reforms in order to concentrate all power in the hand of sovereigns, in order to enable swifter reaction to imminent situations of danger, to the detriment of traditional reasoning and checks and balances.[1195] The multiplication of wars and slave raiding also led to hunger as fields often had to be abandoned due to general insecurity, to a rise in epidemics, and to hygiene regression. We have seen so far that before transatlantic slavery the life standard of common African people had generally been superior to that of Europe, but this sustained assault on Africans reduced life expectancy in many parts of Africa and the African diaspora.

Given these facts and relating to the struggle for the global enforcement of human rights, it is important to comprehend that

"(c)olonialism has contributed to the poor record of human rights in Africa. Human rights were not part of the Western law brought to Africa. The colonial government in Africa was 'authoritarian to the core', and its legacies in the areas of civil, political, and personal security rights, and in the administration of judicial rights were clearly undemocratic. (...) Colonial courts were used to (...) impose servitude on the African peoples as part of the apparatus of control. (...) The colonial state in Africa also created other situations that now militate against the adequate observance of human rights, for example, a very high degree of social stratification and the (...) intensification of parochial, tribal identities"[1196].

If the international community were serious in its loudly proclaimed commitment to secure respect and enforcement of human rights today, it would be necessary "that conceptions of human rights (...) draw on local cultural and legal norms and institutions (...). This is by no means an easy task, as it will certainly be resisted by the guardians of the status quo in the name of 'protecting' traditional African culture and/or religion. It is therefore imperative that these claims be challenged and tested by African scholars and activists who enjoy internal legitimacy and credibility within their communities. (...) It is the colonial framework that underlies the weakness of conceptions and protection of rights in African societies, rather than the cultures of those societies as such."[1197] As Mutua rightly asserts, it is necessary to "refigure a rights regime that could achieve legitimacy in Africa, especially among the majority rural populace, and become the basis for

---

1195 Guèye, Mbaye (2001). "La tradition orale dans le domaine de la traite négrière", in: Djibril Tamsir Niane (ed.): Tradition orale et archives de la traite négrière, Paris: UNESCO, 14-22, 17 et seq.

1196 Minasse, Haile (1984). "Human Rights, Stability, and Development in Africa: Some Observations on Concept and Reality", in: Virginia Journal of International Law, Vol.24, 591-592.

1197 An-Na'im, Abdullahi A. (2002b). "Introduction", in: Abdullahi A. An-Na'im (ed.): Cultural Transformation and Human Rights in Africa, London: Zed Books, 1-11, 2 et seq.

social and political reconstruction."[1198] Such an endeavour would need to uncover and draw on legal and humanistic African traditions that were destroyed or submerged in the violent times of transatlantic slavery and is thus not separable from reparations but is rather part of a comprehensive reparation strategy.

2. IN THE DIASPORA

Reparation negationists often bring up the argument that slavery would have ended such a "long time ago", and that it could not be permissible to go back "indefinitely" with reparation claims. However, transatlantic slavery is not so far removed from us in time. Not only are the legacy and structures still in full effect, but the overall crime of the Maafa is still continuing. In the United States where slavery was officially outlawed in 1865, "it continued, de facto, until as recently as the 1950s. This reparation claim is thus more recent in its root cause that the Shoa. National archive records reveal that in the 1920s and 1930s, the NAACP still received letters from African-Americans claiming to still be on plantations and forced to work without pay. Several claims were investigated and were found to be legitimate."[1199] Slave shipping, though outlawed by European states a hundred years earlier, continued up to the 1910s. In 1954, the Justice Department prosecuted the Dial brothers in Sumpter County, Alabama, "because they held blacks in involuntary servitude"[1200].

In Southern US states, practices of peonage and share-cropping which continued well into the 20th century were direct outgrowths of slavery that continued a system of complete control by the dominant "white" group. Peonage was a complex system where a Black person could at any time be arrested for "vagrancy", and ordered to pay a fine that he or she could not afford which then led to incarceration. A plantation owner would pay the fine and then "hire" him or her until the "debt" was paid off. "The peon was forced to work, locked up at night and if he escaped, was chased by bloodhounds until he was recaptured."[1201] Today, "African-Americans are more likely to go to jail, to be there longer, and if their crime is eligible, to receive the death penalty. They lag behind whites according to every social yardstick: literacy, life expectancy, income and education. They are more likely to be murdered and less likely to have a father at home."[1202] This of course needs to be appreciated in the context that many enterprises, such as Microsoft, Boeing, Honeywell, IBM, Revlon, Dell, Pierre Cardin, Compaq, TWA, Dial, Vic-

---

1198 Mutua (2002), 69 et seq.
1199 Farmer-Paellmann v. FleetBoston, Aetna Inc., CSX, in: Raymond A. Winbush (ed.): Should America pay? Slavery and the raging debate on reparations, Amistad, New York, 348-360, 351.
1200 Ibid.
1201 Ibid.
1202 Ibid.

toria's Secret, Starbucks and Wal-Mart have their products manufactured for as little as 21 cents per hour in US prisons where African-Americans are over-represented. Black women are among the fastest growing groups being imprisoned in the US. Most of the Black women and men incarcerated are poor and taken for non-violent offenses, sometimes for life due to "three strikes" laws. Racism in sentencing has been well documented, such as evidenced by the disparate federal sentencing laws for possession of crack (5 grams = 5 years in prison), used predominately by Blacks, and of cocaine (500 grams = 5 years), consumed more by whites, although they are pharmaceutically the same.[1203] In the United States, children as young as 13 and 14 years old are taken to adult prisons, and 94% of the children tried and convicted have been African American.[1204]

The 13th Amendment to the US Constitution indeed reads that "neither slavery nor involuntary servitude, except as a punishment for crime whereof the party shall have been duly convicted, shall exist within the United States, or any place subject to their jurisdiction". Thus, it is appropriate to say that slavery for Black people still exists to some extent in the United States. Since, as stated by Zimring, a criminologist at the University of Berkeley, "punishment became a political decision"[1205], it is also possible to define many African-American prisoners as political prisoners.

Right after the abolition of slavery in the USA, Jim Crow laws were effective for about one hundred years, from 1877 to 1972, in many states. They constituted a "government-mandated program of racial hegemony of whites". US President Ulysses Grant wrote during that time that the true objectives of southern "whites", thus the people who made these laws, were "by force and terror [intended] to (...) deprive colored citizens of the right to (...) a free ballot; to suppress schools in which colored children were taught, and to reduce the colored people to a condition closely akin to that of slavery". [1206] This legal subsystem, a direct outgrowth of transatlantic slavery, ended only in 1972 with the passage of the Equal Employment Opportunity Act, prohibiting racial discrimination and segregation in state and local employment markets.

Many US states had also passed laws containing prohibition of free Black land ownership. Thus, most descendants of enslaved Africans were locked out of the most significant wealth-building opportunity of the 18th and 19th centuries that was the availability of cheap public lands for sale in the United States. "It was a historic opportunity cost. For example, a major source of revenue in Georgia was the sale of lands 'ceded' by Native Americans to the state. These lands were sold to white citizens in lotteries (free blacks were excluded). (...) Although slave taxes had contributed to the funding of the Louisiana Purchase, slaves had no opportu-

1203 Asante, M. K., Jr. (2008). It's bigger than hip hop, New York: St. Martin's Press, 67.
1204 Asante, M. K., Jr. (2008). It's bigger than hip hop, New York: St. Martin's Press, 140.
1205 Asante, M. K., Jr. (2008). It's bigger than hip hop, New York: St. Martin's Press, 144ff.
1206 Brooks (2004), 2.

nity to settle a homestead themselves." [1207]

Scholars have assessed that long after the abolition of slavery, capital development and accumulation opportunities for Black people were not substantially different from those of the enslaved during transatlantic slavery.[1208] Black people were excluded from a range of professions.[1209] An assessment of reparations must also take into consideration that Black people, in the United States, for example, were and still are paid lower salaries than "whites" for the same work. They are also faced with structural discrimination that excludes them from works that they are qualified to do, not to mention the works that they are excluded from because they are structurally discriminated against in education, again as a consequence of the legacy of slavery. [1210] In a 2010 study, researchers predicted that the gap between Black and "white" wealth will increase further in the next years and decades. Black youth have the highest jobless rate among all races and ethnicities in that country, and it is rising. Whereas in July 2010 the "white" youth unemployment rate was at 16.2 per cent, it was double for Black youth (33.4 per cent).[1211]

In Martinique and Guadeloupe, still occupied by France, the *Békés* (descendants of "white" enslavers) today still possess 80% of land and control the quasi-totality of the economy and 99% of major enterprises.[1212] The vast majority of soils in these two countries were permanently contaminated with the pesticide chlordecone in the 1990s by Békés with the active assistance of the French state. Chlordecone, prohibited in the USA since 1976, is highly toxic and leads to a range of cancers. The descendants of the enslavers still have excellent contacts in the Elysée, the presidential palace, and obtained a special authorization to continue using the cheap yet deadly pesticide until 1993 although its effects were already well known. Clandestinely, it was used until 2002 in some parts of the French-occupied Caribbean. French doctors who conducted studies on the high incidence of certain types of cancer and children born with deformities in these islands came to the conclusion that there is a clear connection with the contamination of the soil. Lawyer Harry Durimel who prepared lawsuits for reparations in that regard received death threats. In Guadeloupe, around 80,000 people live in heavily impacted areas, but many more are affected because chlordecone infiltrated the water system of the island and finds its way in agricultural food produce. A 2010

1207 Outterson (2003), 142 et seq.

1208 Brooks (2004), 31.

1209 Dodson, Howard (2000). "Le prix de l'esclavage? Le prix de la liberté?'', in: Serge Chalons, Christian Jean-Etienne, Suzy Landau and Andre Yebakima (ed.): De l'esclavage aux reparations, Paris: Editions Karthala, 173-179, 177 et seq.

1210 Ibid.

1211 Ramos-Chapman, Naima (2010). A Generation of Black Youth Is Losing Its Future in the Jobs Crisis, downloaded from http://colorlines.com/archives/2010/11/will_great_recession_widen_racial_wealth_gap.html (accessed 24.11.2010).

1212 Ajavon (2005), 236.

university study confirmed a direct link between chlordecone and the high prevalence of prostate cancer in that country. Now, after France finally passed a ban on the use of chlordecone in 1993, many chlordecone stocks disappeared mysteriously. Traces of it were later found in Africa and South America.[1213] This is another reminder of how the legacy of transatlantic slavery and the continuing crime of the Maafa concern Africans and Black people globally and need to be addressed in an approach integrating local and global perspectives because Black lives are still considered expandable by the power elites on a global level. This is what international "organized crime" really is, and in order to combat it we, the people, have to organize. In "French" Guiana, part of the country and its inhabitants, that is indigenous and African communities, are poisoned by chemicals brought into the environment through gold mining – an enterprise that yields high tax revenues for the French state. In Ivory Coast, it was discovered not too long ago that western countries dumped their toxic waste in the Ocean just off the coast, also leading to a higher incidence in illnesses such as cancer. The problem is indeed global, and affects the African world as a whole.

For both the continent and the diaspora, it is a myth that the proclamations of formal independence, or of integration into the colonial "mother country" such as with the French Caribbean and Guiana, would have given back to Africans their sovereignty which is legally due to them. As the first President of Ghana Kwame Nkrumah wrote, "neo-colonialism is the worst form of imperialism: for those who practise it, it means power without responsibility, and for those who suffer it, it means exploitation without redress"[1214].

This continuity of the crime against African people is exemplified particularly drastically by the fate of Haiti. Since the devastating earthquake in 2010 many images testifying to the situation of grave poverty in that country, which was the first and only nation whose enslaved African people liberated themselves, have passed the newspapers and TV screens. Yet the true cause of their misery is seldom illuminated.

After the successful liberation, Haiti asserted in Article 44 of its 1805 Independence constitution "that any black person or indigenous native who arrived on the shores of Haiti would be immediately declared free and a citizen of the republic"[1215]. Jean-Jacques Dessalines, Haiti's leader at the time, offered captains of slave ships $40 per head for their enslaved African victims if they diverted their ships to Haiti instead of delivering them to slave holders in the Caribbean and the United States. Many captains took advantage of this offer, thereby frustrating common

---

1213 TF1 (2010). Le chlordécone, le poison des Antilles, downloaded from http://www.dailymotion.com/video/xeu64n_tf1-le-chlordecone-le-poison-des-an_news (accessed 22.12.2010).
1214 Affiong/Klu (1993), 7.
1215 Ifa Kamau Cush (2010). A tale of two countries, in: New African no 499, October 2010, 26-27, 26 et seq

European enslaver interests even further.

Already in 1801 during the revolution, Napoleon Bonaparte had said in an order to his foreign minister that "[m]y decision to destroy the authority of Haiti is not so much based on considerations of commerce and money, as on the need to block forever the march of blacks in the world"[1216]. After the revolution, all European nations and the United States refused to recognize Haiti's independence, and France declared it an illegal pariah state. France was only able to extort the horrendously high amount of money mentioned in Chapter IV from Haiti because Europe stood together in this. The final extortion payment was made by Haiti as late as 1947. In total, the amount of the extortion was equivalent to approximately 70% of that country's foreign earnings throughout the 19th century and part of the 20th century. The present-day value of Haiti's extortionate payments to France amounts to $22 billion.[1217] These "reparations" that France illegally extracted from the Africans it had previously held in illegal slavery laid the foundation for Haiti's poverty today, and also for the high death toll that the earthquake took. At the time when the earthquake happened, I was in neighboring Jamaica to do research for the present work, and I remember well hearing experts on the radio and TV stating that the same earthquake in Jamaica would not have been as deadly because infrastructure is better in that country. Damage would have been grave still because, although somewhat more solid than in Haiti, infrastructure and many buildings are still built poorly because of the legacy of transatlantic slavery.

It is also important to ponder on the fact that the United States and France upheld friendly relations with brutal Haitian dictators such as François and Jean-Claude Duvalier, but forcibly kidnapped and exiled President Jean-Bertrand Aristide shortly after he began to make serious moves to get payback and reparations from France, and set up a lawyer team for that purpose.

The tragic irony is that the horrible consequences of the intentional destruction of Haiti by former enslaver state France and other western nations, such as the humanitarian catastrophe since the 2010 earthquake and the ensuing cholera outbreak, are interpreted by too many other diaspora Africans as Haiti being "cursed". I bear witness to this again right now, in the context of the hurricane that recently struck Haiti in late August 2012 and left us with pictures of massively flooded streets and heightened misery. Instantly, on the Internet and on the Jamaican radio station Irie FM, there were Jamaicans and people from the French occupied Caribbean suggesting that Haiti was cursed and bringing that contention in connection with Haitian voodoo practice. When I was staying in Jamaica two years earlier, only a few days after the earthquake that killed so many people in Haiti I was sad to hear the widow of the deceased leader of one of the main Rastafari houses uttered that Haiti was "cursed", because of widespread

---

1216 Ibid., 26.
1217 Ibid., 26 et seq.

voodoo practice, whereas "Jamaica bless". This mind-set is the result of systematic and centuries-long brainwashing with Euro-Christianity, and we need to confront this attitude wherever we detect it with historical facts. And the facts are that the current unending misery of Haiti, being struck with one blow after another, is the result of the politics of intentional destruction and sabotage of this great nation of self-liberated Africans. If the people of Haiti were not kept so restrained in poverty by former slaver nations, then they would not have to cut down all their trees to make charcoal to cook and would have better infrastructure, making it more bearable when the country is hit by earthquakes or hurricanes. Given the significance of Haiti as the bulwark of African liberation, it is crucial that we get the perspective on its history and current condition right. Throughout this book it is argued that despite the solid and waterproof foundation of the entitlement to reparations in international law, Europeans will never make reparations. African people will have to take reparations, legally due to them, and that is really what Haiti has been striving to do from a long time. And it has been made to pay a very high price for taking reparations and aiming to restore African sovereignty in that country. People need to fully realize the implications of this for the struggle of African redemption and liberation, and resist the euro-christian subtle propaganda that Haiti would be cursed for liberating itself from slavery by taking strength from African spirituality in the form of voodoo! That propaganda is embedded in a vicious scheme of draining and keeping Haiti down politically and economically, resulting in lack of infrastructure, and then making it look as if it was Haitian people's incompetence when natural disaster joins to make things absolutely unbearable. If indeed there were any religious or spiritual implication in the fact that Haiti is taking one blow after another from earthquake and hurricane, it is not that this country would be cursed because of voodoo but rather that the Universe is sending us reminders that we need to honor Haiti and stick with it in the defense of African liberation. After all, it is only by such unity that taking reparations can work out, and Haiti shows us tragically what happens when only one African country is *taking reparations* alone: it will be crushed by European powers. And people must also never forget that it was Dutty Boukman, an enslaved African who had come to Haiti from Jamaica, who was instrumental in igniting the revolution in Haiti through the powers of voodoo. The African revolution knows no borders and can accept no borders, just as the enslavement and destruction also knew no borders. And in this liberation quest, African people scattered around the globe have always inspired one another. Nowadays, we just need to look at how uncountable rappers from Brooklyn to Dakar to Dar-Es-Salaam are citing Marcus Garvey, Malcolm X, Steve Biko, Cheikh Anta Diop or the Black Panthers. And Steve Biko in turn had attested that Black American soul music, a "culture of defiance, self-assertion and group pride and solidarity", was part of a "modern black culture that is responsible for the restoration of our faith in ourselves"[1218].

Although the case of Haiti is extreme, it is important to see it in connection with the rest of the transatlantic system and not as an unsystematic exception. The punishment of the people of Haiti for liberating themselves at the hand of the ensemble of western European nations serves as a deterrent reminder to other Africans who would try to recover their liberty and sovereignty. In that context, it is important to consider the following paragraph of the Final Report of the 1978 UNESCO conference:

"Slave revolts undoubtedly played a part in accelerating abolition and in the development of a wage-earning structure. The Haitian Revolution spread terror in the slave-trading colonies and metropolitan countries and the slaves regarded it as symbolic. Subsequently, during the period between the abolition of the slave-trade and that of slavery itself, frequent revolts occurred in the English- and Spanish-speaking Caribbean (...)."[1219]

Indeed, the French decree that abolished slavery in 1848 provided "reparations" for slave holders in Guadeloupe, Martinique and Guiana. Another law of April 30, 1849 stipulated that former slave holders were to receive a total of 120 million francs. These "reparations" were in part paid by the formerly enslaved Africans who received no compensation and no land, and many had no choice but to continue working on the same plantations for their former enslavers.[1220] In fact, most 19th century abolition policies forced former slaves to compensate slave holders for loss of property.[1221] In the British colonies, not only were slavers compensated for their loss of slaves, but the gradualist "free womb" policy that held that children born after the passing of that law were "free", kept them under their holders' will until 18 or 21 years old. Many northern US states and South American countries compensated enslavers by requiring former slaves to work without wages for a number of years.[1222]

In view of all these injustices perpetrated systematically over centuries, Akbar identified several areas where the disastrous legacy of transatlantic slavery is still manifest. He was referring specifically to the African diaspora, yet most of the points he makes also apply to the African continent. They concern: work; leadership; personal inferiority; and community division. Regarding work, Akbar assessed that

"(t)he slave was forced to work under the threat of abuse, or even death, but the work was not for the purpose of providing for his life's needs. Instead, he worked

---

1218 Biko, Steve (1978). I write what I like, Johannesburg: Heinemann, 46.
1219 United Nations Educational, Scientific and Cultural Organization (ed.) (1978). Meeting of Experts on the African Slave-Trade, Final Report, Port-au-Prince, Haiti, 31 January-4 February 1978, downloaded from http://unesdoc.unesco.org/images/0003/000333/033360eb.pdf (accessed 21.6.2012).
1220 Castaldo (2006), 29 et seq.
1221 Peabody/Grinberg (2007), 27.
1222 Ibid.

to produce for the slave master. He would neither profit from his labour nor enjoy the benefits of labour. A good crop did not improve his life, or his community. Instead, it improved the life and community of the slave master. Frederick Douglass (1855, 1970) describes the slave's work accordingly: (...) *the human cattle are in motion, wielding their clumsy hoes; turned on by no hope of reward, no sense of gratitude, no love of children; nothing, save the dread and terror of the slave driver's lash. So goes one day, and so comes and goes another.* Work, in natural society, is looked upon with pride, both because it permits persons to express themselves and because it supplies their survival needs. (...) Work came to be despised as any punishment is despised. Work became hated as does any activity which causes suffering and brings no reward for the doer. (...) Work became equated with slavery. (...) Consequently, slaves equated work with enslavement and freedom with the avoidance of work. Work was identified as the activity of the underdog and was difficult to be viewed with pride. Work is something approached unwillingly and out of necessity."[1223]

Chattel slavery and the mechanisms thus described were instituted in Africa on a large scale by European states during colonialism, even if not officially termed "slavery".

Concerning the second problem, namely leadership, Akbar assessed that

"(p)robably one of the most destructive influences which has grown out of slavery is the disrespect of (...) leadership. The allegory is seen throughout nature that the most certain way to destroy life is to cut off the head. From the turkey to the cow to the human being, the most immediate way to bring death to a body is to remove its head. This is especially true as a social principle. One of the things that was systematically done during slavery was the elimination of control of any emerging 'head' of leader. Slave narratives and historical accounts are full of descriptions of atrocities brought against anyone who exemplified real leadership capability. The slave holders realized that their power and control over the slaves was dependent upon the absence of any indigenous leadership among the slaves. Any slave who began to emerge as a natural head, that is, one oriented toward survival of the whole body, was identified early and was either eliminated, isolated, killed, or ridiculed. In his or her place was put a leader who had been carefully picked, trained, and tested to stand only for the master's welfare."[1224]

This correct historical assessment also pertains to the qualification of the Maafa as genocide, because it shows that the conduct of European slavers was directed at destroying Africans as independent human groups. Numerous examples throughout this work have demonstrated that this pattern was kept up throughout transatlantic slavery, colonialism and, up to the present, neo-colonialism.

Also relevant with regard to the qualification as genocide is the third prob-

---

1223 Akbar, Na'im (1996). Breaking the Chains of Psychological Slavery, Tallahassee: Mind Productions & Associates, Inc., 4 et seq.
1224 Ibid., 9.

lem that Akbar identified as "personal inferiority", the outcome of a systematic process of creating a sense of inferiority that was necessary in order to maintain Africans as slaves. "This was done by humiliating and dehumanizing acts such as public beatings, parading them on slave blocks unclothed, and inspecting them as though they were cattle or horses."[1225] In this context it must also be noted that the image of Africa and Africans globally has been systematically, and oftentimes still is, painted as inferior in order to maintain the exploitative system of the Maafa upon which western economies still depend. On a global level, dark skin colour was made to be associated with slave status, as well as with other kinds of subhuman traits. "On the other hand, the slave master's pale skin became equated with supernatural human traits. In fact, God, all the Saints and the entire heavenly hosts became identified with the pale skin. The logical conclusion of the abused, oppressed slave was that the basis for his condition was his skin color, and the way out of his condition was to change that color."[1226] Thus, we find, for example, the highly toxic practice of chemical skin bleaching not only in the African diaspora, but also on the continent. I have witnessed this many times when I lived in Senegal and travelled in Ghana. In Jamaica, I had a few encounters with school girls and boys who came up to me saying, "I like your color". While accompanying the Jamaica Reparations Commission to its public sittings, several students explained that "the youths of today don't think of themselves as anything of worth" and that this feeling of worthlessness expresses itself in the practice of cancer-causing skin bleaching. They reasoned that, as one part of reparation, balanced education is needed, to embed a solid background of "where you are coming from (...) in the minds of the youths".[1227] Reparation for transatlantic slavery is thus indeed a global imperative. "White" people also need to be healed from their global and structural superiority complex acquired with transatlantic slavery and colonialism.

Finally, Akbar assessed that "one of the most serious disturbances of community advancement coming from the slavery experience is disunity or 'community division'. The age-old pattern of divide-and-conquer was utilized along with so many other tricks in order to destroy African-American community life. Wedges of division were thrown among the slaves in order to insure that the possibilities for united efforts would be nearly impossible. The slave makers were fully aware that a disunited community would be easy prey for the continued control by the master."[1228]

Psychologist Akbar sustained that "[t]he slavery that feeds on the mind, invading the soul of man, destroying his loyalties to himself and establishing allegiance

---

1225 Ibid., 14.
1226 Ibid., 23.
1227 Jamaica National Commission on Reparations, May Pen Court House Sitting, 20.1.2010.
1228 Akbar (1996), 16.

to forces which destroy him, is an even worse form of capture"[1229]. Willie Lynch, a Barbados slave owner, was invited to Virginia in 1712 to teach his "effective" method of slave control to plantation owners there. In this seminar, Lynch explained that

"I have outlined a number of differences among the slaves; and I take these differences and make them bigger. I use fear, distrust, and envy for control purposes. Take this simple little list of differences, and think about them. On the top of my list is age but it is only there because it starts with A. The second is color or shade. Then there is intelligence, size, sex, size of plantation, status of plantation, attitude of owners, whether slaves live in the valley, on a hill, east, west, north, south, have fine or coarse hair or are tall or short. Now that you have a list of differences, I shall give you an outline of action... you must pitch the old Black against the young Black... you must use the dark skin slaves against the light skin slaves and the light skin slaves against the dark skin slaves. You must also have your white servants and overseers distrust all Blacks. But it is necessary that your slaves trust and depend on us. They must love, respect and trust us only. Gentlemen, these kits are your keys to control. Use them. Have your wives and children use them. Never miss an opportunity. My plan is guaranteed, and the good thing is that if used intensely for one year, the slaves themselves will remain perpetually distrustful".[1230]

This method was also employed in Africa, as retraced on numerous pages of this work. The enslaved person, both in transatlantic and colonial slavery in Africa, had no rights. "The virtues of being able to protect, support and provide for one's offspring, which is the cornerstone of true fatherhood, were not considered the mark of a man on the plantation. In fact, the slave who sought to assert such rights for his offspring was likely to be branded as a trouble-maker and either punished or killed. After several generations of such unnatural treatment, the [men] adapted and began to resist the role of a true father."[1231]

3. PSYCHOLOGICAL CONSEQUENCES

Various scientific studies have shown that the genocidal slavery laws, the systematic denial of the humanity of the enslaved, cruel and constant punishments, the deprivation of all legal rights and other psychological measures of extreme coercion over centuries and multiple generations, aimed at enslaving not only the body but also the mind, have resulted in psychological damages. African people could be sold, mortgaged, hired out, maimed, killed or injured. On the continent too many were exposed to live in a constant climate of fear and violence. On the

---

1229 Crawford/Nobles/DeGruy Leary (2003), 256.
1230 Crawford/Nobles/DeGruy Leary (2003), 256 et seq.
1231 Akbar (1996), 20.

plantation colonies the owner, or in many cases any "white" person, could do to a Black person and his loved ones whatever he desired. Experts have stressed that chronic disease, especially hypertension, the incidence of which are highest among Black people in the Americas, are direct results of the trauma of the Middle Passage and the plantation slavery system.[1232] "Those who made it to the Americas faced long-term physical and mental problems."[1233]

Now it is generally acknowledged by psychologists that the most common trauma stems from a serious threat or harm to one's life or physical integrity or to that of one's family and loved ones; from the sudden destruction of one's home or community; or from seeing another person who has been, or is being, seriously injured or killed as a result of an accident or violence. Yet all of the mentioned situations were the common and perpetual experience of enslaved Africans and their descendants. It has thus been assessed that "violence and abuse in a less severe form continued after slavery officially ended with lynchings, beatings, threats to life and property. Other individuals and groups commonly acknowledged to suffer from thus-induced post-traumatic stress disorder (PTSD) include victims of rape, war veterans, Jewish Holocaust survivors and their children. Black people need to be given assistance in handling this serious condition as another form of reparations."[1234]

The maintenance of family bonds was mostly beyond the control of the enslaved, not only because spouses and children could be sold or killed at any time, but also because slave masters actively fostered disunity among their captives. "During slavery, the Black man was valued as a stud and a workhorse and the Black woman as a breeder capable of having many healthy children that the white slave master could sell or work to death to make money for himself. Masters in the system of transatlantic slavery forbade marriage, a sacred rite in almost all human cultures."[1235]

Many slave ships had large numbers of captured children among their human cargo. They were objected to the cruel and barbaric conditions of the Middle Passage, torn from their parents and families, all alone in hell. We cannot even imagine the trauma that this experience induced in children who survived the genocidal Middle Passage. Psychology confirms that the years of childhood are crucial in the shaping the future adult. The constant witnessing of death, dying, and violence without the palliative of traditional customs passed on by family and loved ones must have done immense damage to these youths. [1236] "What did the wilful killing of innocent men, women, and children do to the psyche of those left behind? For those who survived and made it to the Americas, must they not have

---

1232 Satchell, Vermont (2003). Reparation and Emancipation, Emancipation Lecture 2003, Kingston: unknown publisher, 11.
1233 Quirk (2009), 56.
1234 Crawford/Nobles/DeGruy Leary (2003), 267 et seq.
1235 Ibid., 266.
1236 Ibid.

brought with them the horror of seeing so much death?"[1237] Children who grow into adults and never get a chance to heal a massive hurt done to their psyche and spirit will pass it on and have serious difficulties building healthy communities.

In many parts of the Americas enslaved Africans came to constitute the vast majority of the population. In order for a minority to hold the majority in complete subjugation, it has to engage extreme coercion as well as psychological measures aimed at enslaving both the body and the mind. This was done with rigid slave laws, aiming at stripping the enslaved Africans of their humanity with the whip and stiff punishments. In the transatlantic system slaves were not treated as human beings and had no legal rights, but were defined as property, chattels or commodities. The consequences that continued exposure to such genocidal living conditions over generations and generations has for a people cannot be anything else but catastrophic.[1238]

To sum up, it has been clearly found by scholars of various disciplines that many health problems of African Americans and other diaspora Africans are deeply rooted in the history of slavery. This is not only true in the sense of structural psychological harm causing physical illness, but also in the sense that poor material living conditions are not only stemming from and rooted in transatlantic slavery and leading to physical sickness and death for descendants of the enslaved but also that they are the consequence of the continuing crime of the Maafa.[1239] That assessment is accurate for almost every region of the African world, as it was in its totality affected by the transatlantic slavery system which fathered the global capitalist system. The empoisoning of most of the soil in Martinique and Guadeloupe by the descendants of "white" slave masters, assisted in this by the French state, leading to a high rise of cancer, or the dumping of toxic waste on the Ivorian coast, are just two random examples.

Studies conducted in the USA of the 1990s revealed that infant mortality rates in Black communities were 2,5 times that of "white" communities, and that Black people live five to seven years less than "whites". The death rate for the age group 25-44 is 2,5 times that of "whites". One reason for this is that landfills and sites that emit toxic substances are often located near Black communities. Other studies have shown that chemicals that can potentially cause birth defects, neurological, renal, and liver impairment, cancer, and disorders of other bodily systems can be detected at such sites. Black people in the USA are known to have higher rates of certain cancers. Childhood cancers such as leukaemia and neurological malignancies have increased in recent years in Black communities.[1240] Asthma, lead poisoning, malnutrition, anaemia, ear infections are problems that touch dispro-

---

1237 Bailey (2007), 134 et seq.
1238 Satchell (2003), 11.
1239 Ibid., 270 et seq.
1240 Ibid.

portionately many Black children because their families are structurally obliged through racism induced poverty to live in substandard housing conditions. All such problems may lead to permanent impairments and futher falling back in the school systems and employment sector, thus further aggravating the vicious cycle of poverty.[1241] Analogies to such situations can be found throughout the African world, both on the continent and in the diaspora, and all of them have their roots in the structures set up through transatlantic slavery and still illegally maintained in the current phase of the Maafa.

4. GLOBAL APARTHEID

This situation has been qualified as global apartheid by researchers and scholars. Apartheid is defined as "a policy of enforced separation between races, but the term is also used to characterize any invidious structure and practice of racial inequality – intended or unintended"[1242]. Vast amounts of sources reviewed for this work definitely confirm that the global situation stemming from transatlantic slavery fulfils all these elements. Gernot Köhler[1243], a peace researcher, is right to state that the

"notion of apartheid is most apt for denoting the current world situation in which a minority race (of whites and honorary whites) dominates the majority of humanity, which is composed of a variety of 'peoples of color.' In its global, de facto form, apartheid is even more severe than its South African exemplar. The disparities in wealth, power, military control, health, and life expectancy that characterize the world system or global macro-society are extremely wide and growing. (...) [G]lobal apartheid with its built-in forms of structural violence is consistent with what sociologist Howard Winant (...) describes as the global racial entity we know as capitalism, whose genealogy implicates the compounding and interdependence of race and class. Winant reminds us that in virtually every corner of the earth, dark skin still correlates with inequality. Although race is clearly internationalized, Winant points out that 'we cannot assume an overarching uniformity. (...) Thus the global similarities, the increasing internationalization of race, can only be understood in terms of prevalent patterns, general tendencies;

1241 Asante, M. K., Jr. (2008). It's bigger than hip hop, New York: St. Martin's Press, 52.

1242 Winant, Howard (1994). Racial Formation and Hegemony: Global and Local Developments in Racial Conditions: Politics, Theory, Comparisons, Minneapolis: University of Minnesota Press, 123; cited in: Harrison, Faye V. (2008). Outsider Within. Reworking Anthropology in the Global Age, Urbana/Chicago: University of Illinois Press, 221.

1243 Gernot Köhler (1978). Global Apartheid. Working Paper No.7, World Order Models Project, New York: Institute for World Order; reprinted in. Haviland, William A./Gordon, Robert J. (2002). Talking About People: Readings in Comtemporary Cultural Anthropology, Mountain View: Mayfield, 262 et seq.

in no sense can such generalizations substitute for detailed analyses of local racial formations."[1244]

Haviland defined "global apartheid" as "internationalized White supremacy", and assessed that life in South Africa until 1994 and the situation in the world were and are strikingly similar at large.[1245] On a global level, apartheid is

"a de facto structure ... which combines socio-economic and racial antagonisms and in which (1) a minority of whites occupies the pole of affluence, while a majority composed of other races occupies the pole of poverty; (2) social integration of the two groups is made extremely difficult by barriers of complexion, economic position, political boundaries, and other factors; (3) economic development of the two groups is interdependent; and (4) the affluent white minority possesses a disproportionate share of the world society's political, economic, and military power." [1246]

Haviland stresses that the system of global apartheid reposes on structural violence, engendering "situations" such as world hunger and pollution, and traces the source of humanity's major contemporary problems back to enduring race-class inequalities and thus, in last consequence, to transatlantic slavery.

The International Convention on the Suppression and Punishment of the Crime of Apartheid declared apartheid a crime against humanity, and legal experts categorize apartheid either as genocide or crime against humanity which theoretically in law obliges all states to contribute to bring this unbearable situation to an end. Please consider in that context that then US President Richard Nixon once stated, "There are times when an abortion is necessary. I know that. When you have a black and a white. (...) Or a rape". Such utterances must not be lightly dismissed as only expressions of craziness or wickedness of a racist individual. It is the structures that bring forth such screwed thinking that must be pondered upon from a legal angle of reflection. The Nazi built both ideologically (aiming at the extinction of Jews, because they were perceived as a mix between white and Black, in order to prevent a "bastardizing" of the "white race") and "technologically" on the Eugenics movement in the United States, and many leaders of that US Eugenics movement were direct descendants of slave holder elite. Jewish people got and get reparations, but the reparations claim for African people, the oppression of whom lies at the base of the persecution of the Jews, still remains to be effectuated.

Until then, global "white" supremacism, the other side of global apartheid, continues to express itself in everyday aspects of life such as speech. Many things considered bad are termed "black", such as "black Friday", "black sheep", "black-

1244 Winant (1994), 221

1245 Haviland, William A (1990). Cultural Anthropology. Sixth Edition, Fort Worth: Holt, Rinehart and Winston.

1246 Harrison, Faye (2010a). "Anthropology as an Agent of Transformation: Introductory Comments and Queries", in: Faye Harrison (ed.): Decolonizing Anthropology. Moving Further toward an Anthropology for Liberation, Third Edition, Arlington: American Anthropological Association, 1-15, 3.

heart" or "Schwarzfahren" ("driving black"; an Austrian expression for taking public transport without paying the fare). Yet, "most white people fail to recognize, and indeed refuse to recognize when it is pointed out to them, how their very own and daily behaviours and language help to uphold the system of white supremacy".[1247] This sad diagnosis is unfortunately confirmed by my own experiences with family members and acquaintances. "White" people are conditioned to take their advantaged position in the world for granted as if it were some sort of natural order, and many will also vehemently deny that instances of racism today would have anything to do with slavery and its legacy. One time when returning to Austria from Jamaica and waiting at the passport control line at the airport in London, it was disturbing to observe that while we were all in the "European citizens" line, only Black people got pulled to the side and had their suitcases taken apart. The officers even made an old granny go through this. Yet when I told them about this, a relative of mine refused to see that this had anything to do with racism and the legacy of slavery. He belittled the incident as nothing at all. Yet, it is highly distressing to imagine being subjected to such discrimination on a permanent and daily basis. And of course, such "minor" incidences of expression of global apartheid have of course psychological, social, economic, and spiritual consequences since they occur structurally and on a permanent basis.[1248] This situation of global apartheid has also recently been recognized by the UN Working Group of Experts on People of African descent, which affirmed "structural discrimination" of African people on a global level, and issued recommendations to counter this state of affairs.[1249]

That the legacy of transatlantic slavery flows into the continuing and on-going crime of the Maafa, its present forms of (neo-) colonialism and global apartheid, may be one reason why even the recollection of transatlantic slavery is a sort of taboo in former enslaver nations. At the UNESCO conference in commemoration of the abolition of slavery by France held on May 10, 2011, also falling together with the 10-year anniversary of the French law recognizing transatlantic slavery as crime against humanity, Françoise Verges, president of the government-instigated *Comité pour la mémoire et l'histoire de l'esclavage*, stated that there were more than a dozen demonstrations taking place all over France, but that the media had conspired not to report about this "non-évènement". No large newspaper reported on it. At the same time, she sustained that there were still grave racial inequalities in areas such as land ownership or access to education, while French

---

1247 Secours, Molly (2003). "Riding the Reparations Bandwagon", in: Raymond A. Winbush (ed.): Should America pay? Slavery and the raging debate on reparations, New York: Amistad, 286-298, 297.
1248 Secours (2003), 288.
1249 Working Group of Experts on People of African Descent, IX Session, April 12-16, 2010, III. CONCLUSIONS AND RECOMMENDATIONS, downloaded from http://www2.ohchr.org/english/issues/racism/groups/african/docs/session9/Conclusions_RecommandationsIXSession.doc (accessed 3.11.2010).

prisons are filled with young people from the *Départments d'Outre-Mer* (DOMs), that is, the French occupied Caribbean, Guiana and Réunion.

During the debate ensuing at this UNESCO conference, a young man from *Brigade Anti-Négrophobie*, an association militating against anti-Black racism, stated that "on this day, by the silence of the media (...), France declared war on us, (...) with this masquerade of commemoration. (...) After today, I can no longer tell the youth to stay calm. (...) After the 2005 riots I saw Ariel Wizman on TV because France burned. I say that if we are not listened to when we try to dialogue and find a peaceful solution to the problem, it will be necessary that we reply to this declaration of invisible war".[1250] Earlier that same day, members of the association wearing black Tee-shirts imprinted with "Brigade Anti-Négrophobie", had been refused entrance to the official French commemoration ceremony where then-President Nicholas Sarkozy gave a speech that can arguably be considered malicious (and will be discussed in more detail in Chapter VI), although they all held invitations. They were forcefully removed from the *Jardin de Luxembourg* by security personnel. In transatlantic slavery times, the *Jardin de Luxembourg* was a ground where African captives were displayed and sold. Video footage showed that the first rows of this official event by which France honored its abolition of transatlantic slavery were seated exclusively with "white" people. The children's choir that sang at the event consisted of "white" children, who were all dressed in white. One day earlier, at the occasion of a commemoration march in Nantes, several members of the association had also been arrested. The daughter of Malcolm X, Malaak Shabaaz, who was present at the UNESCO conference, asked how it was possible for the French state to "acknowledge" the abolition of slavery, yet still arrest the descendants of those it had illegally enslaved once they have the audacity to commemorate as they see fit. She also assessed that France is not allowing "Afro-French" identity, and that "clearly something needs to be done in this country".

Two years later, in 2013, France had a new government and a "left" President, François Hollande, but nothing has changed in how that country deals with African people. Again, members of the Brigade Anti-Négrophobie followed the procedure and acquired invitations to the official event for the commemoration of the abolition of slavery, yet were again barred from entry because of their wearing shirts imprinted with "Brigade Anti-Négrophobie". This time, they were not only refused entrance and taken to the commissariat for a few hours, but they were brutalized, arrested, kept in police lock-up overnight and charged with "rebellion". When I called at the police station to ask about the reason of the arrests, I was passed from one officer to another six times, until the commander told me that he had no information at all to give to me. At the end of our short conversa-

---

1250 Unesco Conference, Paris, 10 May 2011.

tion, I asked whether France would proceed like this every year and arrest African people when they choose to commemorate as they see it fit, and got the response that "this is a question I cannot answer".

In the content of his speech, Hollande also remained in line with his right-wing predecessor Sarkozy, qualifying transatlantic slavery as "an outrage committed by France against France". Hollande lashed out against reparations claims, with which his country is currently confronted by several Black activist groups, stating that "reparation is impossible. What has been has been". Misusing a quotation by Aimé Césaire, "to pay a bill and then it would be finished (...). No, this will never be settled", he went on to state that "history does not efface itself. One does not erase it. It cannot be object of transactions in the sense of accountability that would in many points be impossible to establish. The only available option is that of memory, of vigilance, of transmission."[1251] Again, here we have another European head of state that denies the application of international law for transatlantic slavery and colonialism since international law holds that reparation must be comprehensive and include material, structural, historical, and other forms of reparation.

In El Ejido near Almeria, in France's neighboring country Spain, about 90,000 Africans work presently in slavery-like conditions to produce ever cheaper vegetables, including "organic", for the whole of Europe. "They have no papers, live in slum-huts made from construction waste, with no toilets. Dirty water is all they have access to to cook and drink. There is no medical care. Human rights organizations speak of 'modern slavery' (FIAN or German Watch); they earn 2,5 Euros per hour, working up to 16 hours with temperatures reaching up to 40°C. Their passports are confiscated by plantation owners, and their settlements are guarded. They have to start working at five in the morning until late into the night. Whoever flees and gets caught, gets a beating. In a rebellion in 2010, the police came in and 34 African workers were wounded."[1252] Even if not officially termed "slavery", this situation has factual resemblance to plantation chattel slavery as it was imposed on Africans in both the Americas and Africa by Europeans in the times of transatlantic slavery and colonialism. And the main reason of why so many young Africans risk their lives to come to Europe where they are then subjected to such conditions, is the abject material poverty in many African societies whose root cause in turn is, again, transatlantic slavery.

In 2011, a boat with 72 African passengers, including women and young chil-

---

1251 Speech of French President François Hollande at the Ceremony for the Commemoration of the Abolition of Slavery, Paris: Jardin de Luxembourg, 10.5.2013. ("(...) "C'est l'impossible réparation. Ce qui a été a été. 'Il y aurait une note à payer et ensuite ce serait fini. (...) Non, ce ne sera jamais réglé.' L'Histoire ne s'efface pas. On ne la gomme pas. Elle ne peut faire l'objet de transactions au terme d'une comptabilité qui serait en tous points impossible à établir. Le seul choix possible, c'est celui de la mémoire, et c'est la vigilance, et c'est la transmission.")
1252 Tanzer, Oliver (2011). Der Preis der Sklaverei, in: Die Furche Dossier (22.6.2011), 21.

dren trying to reach another country in that region, Italy, was left to drift in the Mediterranean for 16 days by European and Nato navy authorities who ignored their cries for help. All but 11 of those on board died from thirst and hunger. The migrants used the boat's satellite phone to contact the Italian coastguard, and soon a military helicopter tagged with the word "army" appeared in the sky above the boat. The pilots, who were wearing military uniforms, lowered bottles of water and packets of biscuits and gestured to passengers that they should hold their position until a rescue boat came. No such rescue ever came however. A few days later, the boat was carried near to a Nato aircraft carrier – "so close that it would have been impossible to be missed. According to survivors, two jets took off from the ship and flew low over the boat while the migrants stood on deck holding the two starving babies aloft"[1253]. Yet, the Africans were ignored and left to die. After the boat was washed ashore on a beach near the Libyan town of Zlitan, no country has yet admitted sending the helicopter that made contact with the migrants. The Nato aircraft carrier is likely to have been the French ship Charles de Gaulle, which was operating in the Mediterranean at that time, but France has denied so, claiming the carrier was not in the region then. After being shown news reports which indicated this was untrue, the government spokesperson declined to comment. Of the 11 Africans still alive on April 10 when the boat washed up on the Libyan beach, one died almost immediately upon reaching land, while another survivor died shortly afterwards.[1254]

This was no single tragedy however. According to a 2007 study by the German Institute for Human Rights, information bulletins about boats overloaded with Africans in acute distress transmitted via NAVTEX (Navigational Information over Telex) are systematically ignored by national and Nato maritime organs in the Mediterranean. For example, in 2007 a Maltan military aircraft sighted a boat visibly overloaded, carrying 53 persons and definitively in distress. The aircraft returned to its base. The boat was never seen again. In 2006, a boat with African migrants trying to reach the Canaries sank because it was pushed away by a boat of the Spanish sea guard. Other reports allege that 30 Africans were actually thrown into the sea by Greek coast guards in 2006. Some of them would have drowned while some could have rescued themselves to the Turkish coast.[1255] Considered together with the facts and analyses presented in the above chapter about the legally required elements of genocide, these examples abet the claim that the Maafa constitutes a continuing genocide against African people, since in instances such as these people are clearly targeted and killed because of their Africaness.

The list of structural atrocities against Black Africans could go on and on. Am-

---

1253 Shenker, Jack (2011). Nato units left 61 African migrants to die of hunger and thirst, The Guardian, May 8, 2011, downloaded from http://www.guardian.co.uk/world/2011/may/08/nato-ship-libyan-migrants (accessed 15.6.2011).
1254 Ibid.
1255 Weinzierl, Ruth/Lisson, Ursula (2007). Grenzschutz und Menschenrechte. Eine europarechtliche und seerechtliche Studie, Berlin: German Institute for Human Rights, 19 et seq.

nesty International recently released a report that assesses among other findings that Black Africans are victims of torture, displacement and murder by militia of the new regime in Libya. Yet there is no Nato sending bombs to protect civilian populations now. Apparently Black African lives are not considered to have the same value as others or even as the economic and political interests that the European countries and the US pursued when overthrowing Libya's Muammar Khaddafi in the first place.[1256]

At this point, I also want to recall some more personal observations from everyday situations that are expressions of global apartheid. On a flight from London to Jamaica, I was asked to give up my economy class seat in exchange for a place in the premium class cabin so that a married couple that insisted to be seated together could do so. Our flight was going to Jamaica, a country with a predominantly Black population, yet the composition of the upper class passengers was quite different from the economy class in terms of skin color. The seats of the bursting economy class of the Airbus were occupied by mostly Black and Brown Jamaicans, with a ratio of approximately one "white" person for every 40 people, whereas the passenger composition of the upper-deck premium class was strikingly lighter in skin colour. I counted only eight Black and Brown passengers during my various trips to the toilet. The majority of the 30 passengers in this class were very light skinned Jamaicans, often of seemingly Chinese or Lebanese-Jamaican ancestry, and Europeans. And honestly, I was really glad that they gave me this seat upgrade – not only because it enabled me to make these observations that I can now present in this research, but also because my legs had already started hurting after being cramped for only one hour into the tiny space that one has in the economy class. Yet, most Black Jamaican passengers, due to socio-historical circumstances rooted in transatlantic slavery, do not have opportunities to access premium services. This is not to say that the majority of "white" people has, but the fact remains that those who can are predominantly "white" or "light-skinned" in a world where global apartheid remains a reality.

While living in Jamaica for this research, I saw every day in the community where I stayed and also in other parts of the country how materially poor and needy the majority of the people are. I rented a one-room studio in an old apartment building in Port Antonio, up on a hill above the town. Behind the apartment complex leads a small dirt trail to self-built squatter houses made out of wood and cardboard where one of the complex's caretakers and his family also live. At one time it was raining more or less continuously for about two weeks, not quite uncommon for Port Antonio. After the worst part of the rain was over, I walked over to my neighbors to have a chat and also share the outcome of a cake recipe that

1256 Libya militias out of control: Amnesty, downloaded from http://www.brecorder.com/world/africa/45981-libya-militias-out-of-control-amnesty-.html (accessed 16.2.2012).

I had just developed. The trail was completely muddy, and it was a serious challenge to walk without slipping, yet the children have to make their way through every day to go to school, even during the heavy rains. And they need to arrive at school clean to get entrance. How they manage to do this remains a mystery to me. When I sat on their porch, I could smell how the place was soaked and had developed mildew. This is a serious health concern, as long-term exposure to mildew is very toxic. Yet these people have nowhere else to go and live, they barely make ends meet and get through. They are parked in this situation because of transatlantic slavery. Their fore parents were brutally kidnapped from Africa and illegally enslaved to Jamaica, where they were not allowed to build anything for themselves. Even after abolition and emancipation they were not given anything, no land, no assets, nothing, while all the wealth remained in the hands of a powerful few. They are in this place and in this condition basically because of transatlantic slavery. The European countries that profited so immensely from the sweat and blood of their ancestors and which continue to reap enormous profits from the economic dependency that is forced upon people like Jamaicans refuse to step up to their legal and moral obligation to give these people what is rightfully theirs. I remember another day when I was at my neighbors' house when they could not find a few cents to buy a half pound of flour to make dumplings for supper. Also, while looking out of the minibus windows on my trips to the capital Kingston, I could not help but see the striking legacy of slavery neither. Though there are a few solid and beautifully built houses everywhere, Jamaica is really a naturally beautiful ghetto full of shacks and shambles. Yet living costs are extremely high, something which I would never have expected. It seems evident that one day this whole setting will explode. During my research stay, I suffered poisoning from unripe ackee fruit which is potentially deadly. Ackee is the national fruit of Jamaica and basis of a national dish, yet when picked unripe and forced open, it is highly toxic. Usually I bought my ackees from vendors displaying the whole fruits, so buyers can see and be sure that they are actually pursuing ripe fruits that have opened up by themselves. But with time I had gotten less vigilant and sometimes purchased ackee in pre-prepared bags, containing only the flesh of the fruit. And apparently one time I purchased from somebody who was in dear need of a quick dollar and had forced open unripe fruits. Although this almost made me to transition permanently into a different dimension and though I acknowledge that there are simply greedy and vicious individuals everywhere, I also see that there are many hungry and desperate people in Jamaica who are struggling to survive and meet their most basic needs on a day-to-day basis. Somebody may indeed have found him or herself in a situation of acute despair, making him or her sell unripe ackee that almost killed me.

Indeed, in every country worldwide the regions with a high concentration of Black and Indigenous peoples are also the economically poorest regions, where illiteracy, unemployment and disease are most rampant. In some countries, life expectancies vary greatly for "non-whites" and "whites". In Colombia, 151 Black children out of 1,000 die before reaching their first birthday, whereas the national average is 39 babies. A 76% of the Afro-Columbian population live in absolute poverty, with a per capita income (PNB) of $500, whereas the national PNB lies at $2,100.[1257]

And yet, several Latin American countries still celebrate October 12 (known in other places as Columbus Day, what is already bad enough) as "Dia de la Raza" (Race Day), that is Day of the "white" race. The late President of Venezuela Hugo Chavez stopped that practice in his country in 2003 and renamed the day into "Day of the Memory of the Indigenous Resistance", because it was on that day in 1492 that both the biggest genocide of human history and the resistance against it began, as Chavez declared. In Bolivia, Evo Morales announced that he would also put an end to the "Day of the Race".

Not too long ago I saw a TV documentary about *quilimbola*-communities, communities of descendants of Maroons in Brazil, showing how their lives are constantly threatened by *faziendero* (large estate owners) who are mostly "white" descendants of slave owners. Brazil has a booming and expanding agro-industry and aims to become the world's largest agricultural producer in the next decade. Thus, land is big business, and the Maroon communities are often perceived as an obstacle. The documentary was filmed in the state of Maranhão, where several *quilimbola*-leaders have already been killed by militias, and about 50 more have been directly threatened. One "white" *faziendero*, Dr. Brito Ferreira Klinger, spoke quite openly when he erroneously thought that the camera had been turned off. He told the team, "Those pigs, I will never again let them in. Never again! There will be no blood bath, because I employ technics. I kill them, I set the whole territory under current. 220 Volt. Is this not how they did in the Jew camps?! The German knew how it is done. Give me electricity here, and the problem is solved."[1258] These are not just void words, as several *quilimbolas* were already killed. These people need to permanently, meaning 24/7, protect their lands, which are constitutionally granted to them, otherwise they will be taken over by *fazienderos* such as Klinger in the wink of an eye. Unfortunately, these communities are materially poor and have access only to weak weapons for self-defense. Although the documentary is very important and its makers undoubtedly had good intentions, I also found it significant that the film does not speak of the ancestors and founders of the *quilimbola*-communities as "Africans who liberated themselves" or such, but rather constantly of "their ancestors, the slaves" even though at the time they founded the *quilimbolas* they had no longer been slaves, but had recovered their freedom. This indicates once again how persistent and deeply embedded the

1257 Plumelle-Uribe (2008), 123.
1258 Laurent Garcia, Nicolas Ransom und Angela Aguiar (2011). Brasilien: Der Krieg ums Land, Arte Reportage, 29 Oct. 2011, 22min.

global psychological legacy of transatlantic slavery and the "white" supremacism complex are. And that it is so firmly entrenched is really no surprise after 500 years. In the US during slavery times, "white" men were required to serve in "pattie rollers" militias, patrolling with arms and preventing rebellions of enslaved Africans. They were instructed to viciously whip any African without a written pass. The militias were funded by tax money, and "white" men had to serve. It is only logic that this structured and impregnated mentalities.[1259]

In 2010, a Saudi prince was convicted in Britain for beating his Black servant to death at a luxury hotel in London. Only slightly prior to that incident, a Black man had been beaten to death in Riyadh by 10 members of the Saudi religious police, and no charges were brought against them. Abuse of Black people is common in Saudi Arabia. A journalist argued that the "killing of the black man by Saudi police was not an isolated incident. It reflects the policy of the Saudi monarchy, which bars black people from becoming judges and holding senior military posts. In addition, black women are not allowed to work as on-camera reporters for Saudi state television stations, a former reporter told me. 'We can only use your voice,' her manager told her".[1260]

While living in Paris, I have had several experiences that showed me how deeply embedded anti-Black racism still is, on the part of both European and Arab people. When a burglary happened in my building, both my European and Arab neighbors stressed explicitly several times that the suspected housebreaker was "Black". A few years ago when I was staying at a hotel in Paris a friend, African-Guianese, came to pick me up there, and his way was barred by the Arab keeper who told him "tu n'rentres pas ici" ("you don't enter here"). All of this shows the need for comprehensive reparations, that of tackling the legacy of the illegal enslavement of Africans by both Europeans and Arabs. According to a recent late-2011 study, racism is on the rise in many European nations, most notably in Norway, the UK, the Netherlands, Austria and Russia.[1261]

Because of this unbearable situation of global apartheid, the Working Group of Experts on People of African Descent, established by the Commission on Human Rights' resolution 2002/68 (April 25, 2002), came to the following *Conclusions and recommendations* in 2011, after almost ten years of research. Large parts of this document will be quoted because it shows that reparation for transatlantic slavery is not a claim by a few extremist militants, but that the need for repair of this global damage is recognized as very urgent by one more UN body. The Working

---

1259 Asante, M. K., Jr. (2008). It's bigger than hip hop, New York: St. Martin's Press, 155f.

1260 al-Ahmed, Ali (2010). Justice, even for princes, downloaded from http://www.guardian.co.uk/commentisfree/2010/oct/20/saudi-prince-murder-justice (accessed 17.3.2011).

1261 Briggs, Billy (2011). Racism on the rise in Europe, downloaded from http://www.aljazeera.com/indepth/opinion/2011/09/201192182426183450.html (accessed 29.10.2011).

Group declared to be

"conscious of the fact that structural discrimination against people of African descent has deep historic roots and manifests itself in a unique and multi-dimensional manner due to the double legacy of slavery and colonialism. (...) The Working Group emphasizes the profound and persistent nature of structural discrimination against people of African descent, including in countries where they represent the numerical majority. The consequences of structural discrimination against people of African descent, even if such discrimination appears to be unintentional, can be as pernicious as direct discrimination. (...) The Working Group notes that an holistic approach, encompassing education, healthcare, the administration of justice, employment and housing, is imperative to breaking the cycle of poverty, social, economic exclusion and marginalization in which the majority of people of African descent are trapped. The Working Group stresses that the Millennium Development Goals should be achieved for all sectors of society, including people of African descent."[1262]

What the Working Group is recommending here, in fact, is reparation; that is to repair to the extent possible this global and genocidal situation brought about by transatlantic slavery and the Maafa. The Working Group went on to state that it

"regrets that many people of African descent do not have access to quality healthcare as they are unable to afford health insurance due to the situation of poverty they endure. (...) The Working Group stresses the need to address the over-representation of people of African descent who are subject to the criminal justice system, including mental institutions and child welfare system, as well as double standards in sentencing. The Working Group notes the prevalence of structural discrimination, severely affecting persons of African descent, at all stages and levels of the administration of justice, including, inter alia, legislation, law enforcement, courts and tribunals. This has far-reaching consequences in terms of poverty, education, and employment and undermines the fundamental democratic principles of political participation."

In the *Recommendations* part, the "Working Group urges States and specialized agencies of the UN, as appropriate, to implement, as a priority, the provisions pertaining to people of African descent in the Durban Declaration and Programme of Action and the Outcome Document of the Durban Review Conference, as well as previous recommendations of the Working Group"[1263].

Now, the Durban documents explicitly recognize the relationship between transatlantic slavery and the current unequal condition of African people worldwide. Both the Declaration and Programme of Action adopted at the UN World

---

1262 Working Group of Experts on People of African Descent, IX Session, April 12-16, 2010, III. CONCLUSIONS AND RECOMMENDATIONS, downloaded from http://www2.ohchr.org/english/issues/racism/groups/african/docs/session9/Conclusions_RecommandationsIXSession.doc (accessed 3.11.2010).
1263 Ibid.

Conference Against Racism in Durban call for reparations. In these documents, the international community

"strongly reaffirm[ed] as a pressing requirement of justice that victims of human rights violations resulting from racism, racial discrimination, xenophobia and related intolerance, especially in the light of their vulnerable situation socially, culturally and economically, should be assured of having access to justice, including legal assistance where appropriate, and effective and appropriate protection and remedies, including the right to seek just and adequate reparation or satisfaction for any damage suffered as a result of such discrimination, as enshrined in numerous international and regional human rights instruments, in particular the Universal Declaration of Human Rights and the International Convention on the Elimination of All Forms of Racial Discrimination"[1264],

and urged:

"States to take all necessary measures to address, as a matter of urgency, the pressing requirement for justice for the victims of racism, racial discrimination, xenophobia and related intolerance and to ensure that victims have full access to information, support, effective protection and national, administrative and judicial remedies, including the right to seek just and adequate reparation or satisfaction for damage, as well as legal assistance, where required", and to "reinforce protection against racism, racial discrimination, xenophobia and related intolerance by ensuring that all persons have access to effective and adequate remedies and enjoy the right to seek from competent national tribunals and other national institutions just and adequate reparation and satisfaction for any damage as a result of such discrimination. It further underlines the importance of access to the law and to the courts for complainants of racism and racial discrimination and draws attention to the need for judicial and other remedies to be made widely known, easily accessible, expeditious and not unduly complicated", and to "adopt the necessary measures, as provided by national law, to ensure the right of victims to seek just and adequate reparation and satisfaction to redress acts of racism, racial discrimination, xenophobia and related intolerance, and to design effective measures to prevent the repetition of such acts"[1265].

In pursuit of this, the Working Group also highlighted its recommendation for the establishment of an observatory within the Office of the High Commissioner for Human Rights to review and report on progress in the implementation by member states and specialized agencies of the UN of the Durban Declaration and Programme of Action, as well as on recommendations by the Durban follow-up mechanisms pertaining to people of African descent. It called "on the United Nations to promote further discussion on the use of the term 'Afrophobia' in its

---

1264 Declaration World Conference Against Racism, Racial Discrimination, Xenophobia and Related Intolerance, UN Doc. A/ CONF.189/12 (2001), downloaded from http://www.un.org./WCAR/durban. pdf (accessed 25.3.2011).
1265 Ibid.

work in order to highlight the special and unique discrimination faced by people of African descent".[1266]

Dilip Lahiri, member of the UN Committee on the Elimination of Racial Discrimination, stressed in his presentation to the Working Group that there

"are approximately 150 million people of African descent in Latin America, representing about one-third of the total population. Most Afro-descendants live in rural areas. In a region characterized by great disparities between wealth and poverty, a disproportionate number of Afro-descendants suffer a lack of infrastructure and utilities, no health services, few schools, high unemployment and low income. Afro-descendants make up over 40 per cent of the poor in Latin America while being only a third of the population. In many countries, Afro-descendants are considered to be the 'poorest of the poor'. In Ecuador, for example, 81 per cent of Afro descendants live below the poverty line. (...) With the lack of economic resources and education, the pattern of poverty becomes inherited for Afro-descendent families, and generations are left with the inability to access any of the resources of empowerment, education and wealth. The lack of jobs that provide a living wage also causes more members of the family to be active in the job market. This affects children the most because many families make less than minimum wage; therefore, they are often responsible for contributing to the family income. Since these children have an inadequate education they have no other choice but to take on these low paying dangerous jobs. This not only hinders the children from growing up and being able to move out from poverty, but their lack of education also provides them with a higher rate of facing job discrimination(s) in the future. (...) Of equal concern is the content of the education programmes. One of the chief concerns is the lack of a proper education programme which includes African history. Many Afro descendants are isolated, impoverished, excluded by the rest of society and abandoned by their governments. The denigration of black people is long-standing and far-reaching. Education functions as a means of promoting European values and Eurocentric versions of history, in which people of African descent have contributed nothing to the world and in which Africans are seen as inferior to other races. There is a deliberate omission of the contribution of Africans to history of Latin America which is not to be found in any history books. Little wonder that there are low levels of esteem and confidence among Afro descendants, because they are bombarded with images of a poverty-stricken and destitute Africa, whilst simultaneously being denied the knowledge of their true history". [1267]

1266 Working Group of Experts on People of African Descent, IX Session, April 12-16, 2010, III. CONCLUSIONS AND RECOMMENDATIONS, downloaded from http://www2.ohchr.org/english/issues/racism/groups/african/docs/session9/Conclusions_RecommandationsIXSession.doc (accessed 3.11.2010).

1267 Structural Discrimination against people of African descent in respect of access to education, Presentation by invited panelist Dilip Lahiri, Member, CERD, IX session of the Working Group of Experts on People of African Descent Geneva 12 to 16 April 2010, downloaded from http://www.ohchr.

It is because of this reality which is global in its general structures with varying local concrete implementations and for which the situation on Latin America is just one example, that the claim for global African reparations has been increasingly recognized by UN bodies. In 2002, the Sub-Commission on the Promotion and Protection of Human Rights issued a resolution in which it drew "the attention of the international community to the cases of massive and flagrant violations of human rights which should be considered as crimes against humanity and which have, to date, benefited from impunity, in spite of the tragic suffering which slavery, colonialism and wars of conquest have inflicted on numerous peoples in the world", and "*[r]ecalling* its resolution 2001/1 of 6 August 2001" considered "that it is not possible to combat racism and racial discrimination, struggle against impunity or denounce the human rights violations which persist in the world without taking account of the deep wounds of the past"[1268]. The resolution, while taking reference to the framework of the World Conference against Racism, Racial Discrimination, Xenophobia and Related Intolerance, stated the necessity "that the international community should consider the causes and consequences of those ills which, historically, have been brought about largely by slavery, colonialism and wars of conquest", and recalled that "the historic responsibility of the relevant Powers towards the peoples whom they colonized or reduced to slavery should be the subject of solemn and formal recognition and reparation. (...) [T]his responsibility is all the more well-founded since the periods of slavery and colonialism have brought about a state of economic collapse in the countries concerned, serious consequences in the social fabric and other tragedies which continue even today to affect entire peoples throughout the world"[1269].

The resolution goes on to state that

"*Considering* that the solemn and formal recognition of this historic responsibility towards the peoples concerned should include a concrete and material aspect such as rehabilitation of the dignity of the peoples affected, active cooperation in development not limited to existing measures of development assistance, debt cancellation, implementation of the 'Tobin tax', technology transfers for the benefit of the peoples concerned and progressive restoration of cultural objects accompanied by means to ensure their effective protection, *considering* that it is essential that the implementation of reparation should effectively benefit peoples, notably their most disadvantaged groups, with special attention being paid to the realization of their economic, social and cultural rights, *convinced* that such recog-

---

org/Documents/Issues/Racism/WGEAPD/Session9/DilipLahiri.doc (accessed 14.12.2011).

1268 Recognition of responsibility and reparation for massive and flagrant violations of human rights which constitute crimes against humanity and which took place during the period of slavery, colonialism and wars of conquest, Sub-Commission on Human Rights resolution 2002/5, downloaded from
http://ap.ohchr.org/documents/E/SUBCOM/resolutions/E-CN_4-SUB_2-RES-2002-5.doc   (accessed 23.3.2011).

1269 Ibid.

nition and reparation will constitute the beginning of a process that will foster the institution of an indispensable dialogue between peoples whom history has put in conflict, for the achievement of a world of understanding, tolerance and peace."[1270]

Thus, we see once again an UN body recognizing the duty and necessity of reparation for transatlantic slavery and colonialism. The resolution then requests

"all the countries concerned to acknowledge their historical responsibility and the consequences which follow from it to take initiatives which would assist, notably through debate on the basis of accurate information, in the raising of public awareness of the disastrous consequences of periods of slavery, colonialism and wars of conquest and the necessity of just reparation". It also emphasized the "importance for school curricula, university training and research, as well as the media, to place adequate emphasis on the recognition of the flagrant and massive human rights violations which occurred during the period of slavery, colonialism and wars of conquest (...)"[1271].

It is also significant that the resolution stressed that "crimes against humanity and other flagrant and massive violations of human rights, to which statutes of limitation do not apply, should be prosecuted by the competent courts", and that it requested "the United Nations High Commissioner for Human Rights to initiate, in a concerted fashion, a process of reflection on appropriate procedures for guaranteeing the implementation of the present resolution, in particular with regard to acknowledgement and reparation" [1272]. I have contacted the UNCHR to find out whether any such steps have yet been taken by that agency, but never received a response.

On the other hand, not only the deprivation, exploitation and oppression of Africans persist as the legacy of transatlantic slavery and consequences of the continuing crime of the Maafa, but also the profits that European nations still make from them. Slavery and colonialism were not enough in and of itself to create the prosperous economies of capitalist Europe and the USA, as the present relative economic decline of Spain and Portugal, despite their substantial engagement in transatlantic slavery and gigantesque plunder of colonial riches, indicates. However, slavery was clearly a *conditio sine qua non*, without which the economic rise of Europe would have been possible to that extent. Yet still, the current economic crisis in Portugal may have more to do with transatlantic slavery than one might suspect at first sight. Brazil, the principal slave colony of the Portuguese, was too big to be kept under control permanently, such as the British and French could do with their Caribbean colonies after the end of transatlantic slavery and even after official colonialism. In fact, it was only very shortly after the abolition of slavery in 1888 that Brazil broke off from the Portuguese crown one year later, whereas the British and French Caribbean colonies remained under the direct economic

---

1270 Ibid.
1271 Ibid.
1272 Ibid.

and political control of these former enslaver nations for much longer and in some regards up to today. Independence movements were violently repressed, something which was not so easy in Brazil, a country that is not only huge but that also has a large population. So the fact that the Portuguese state found itself cut off from colonial produce and revenue from Brazil may well be one reason why today they are off so much worse than France, a country that is still taking much of its wealth today from robbing Africa and the maintenance of their Caribbean colonies. It may also be worth further investigation in that perspective that much of Portuguese transatlantic slavery had been handled by Jewish merchants who did not let their profits flow back into the Portuguese economy to the extent that French and British enslavers did to their nations. This problem calls for much further attention and research, but what we definitely see is that former and present colonial powers still have not only massive, but indeed vital interests, in their global African colonies. One prominent example of this is the coltan that we all need for our mobile phones and which fuels both the genocidal war in Congo and the profits of non-African telecom and arms firms.

As just mentioned, France has not yet loosened its grip on Guadeloupe, Martinique, Guiana and a few others since it still has huge economic interests there. It is because of these territories, covering eleven million km^2 of Exclusive Economic Zone, that France is the second maritime power in the world, only after the USA and equal with Russia. Of course this Zone is a huge source of revenue. New Caledonia is the world's third producer of nickel, and in Guiana studies are currently underway to assess the exploitation of nickel, and other minerals. Additionnally, the DOMs et TOMs (Départements d'outre- mer – Territoires d'outre-mer) are popular tourist destinations. The flux of these tourists creates a large market for French private and state air companies. Guiana is used by France, and other nations such as Russia that pay France, to lance satellites. Yet, the people of Guiana do not benefit from job creation as most personnel is brought in from France. What they reap is only high levels of environmental pollution. After the launch of a satellite, people are advised not to go swimming for a few days. Most, if not all, satellites contain nuclear components.

The economy of the French colonies is totally monopolized in the hands of a few Béké families, descendants of slave holders who up to this day uphold a white supremacist ideology of blood-"purity". They still gain a fortune through a system in which the descendants of the Africans that their ancestors held in illegal and genocidal slavery have to work for them on the plantations or elsewhere to pay them for the products they need to live and for which the Békés alone set the prices because they still monopolize the economy.

Yet, when descendants of illegally kidnapped and enslaved Africans set out to change something about this situation, they are immediately prosecuted. That happened recently to Elie Domota, leader of a syndicate in Guadeloupe. At the occasion of a general uprising in Guadeloupe, Martinique and Guiana in 2009,

Domota said that those employers who refuse to raise salaries had to "leave Gua-deloupe" and that he would "not let a gang of Békés re-establish slavery". Even though his proposal is very reasonable in view of the social and historical back-ground and all the facts that have been assessed in this work, it caused a general outcry and condemnation within the French political spectrum from right to left, and led to the judicial persecution of Domota for "provocation of racial hatred".[1273]

When I was in French-occupied Guiana, I felt uneasy being in a Black coun-try that is still directed and controlled officially by the "white" ex-enslavers. The continued occupation and control of France is indeed a blatant violation of the Declaration on the Granting of Independence to Colonial Countries and Peoples, adopted by the General Assembly as resolution 1514 (XV) on December 14, 1960, where it is affirmed that "the subjection of peoples to alien subjugation, domina-tion and exploitation constitutes a denial of fundamental human rights, is con-trary to the Charter of the United Nations and is an impediment to the promotion of world peace and co-operation". This Declaration furthermore makes it clear that "all peoples have the right to self-determination; by virtue of that right they freely determine their political status and freely pursue their economic, social and cultural development". But France has crushed the independence movement in Guiana, Guadeloupe and Martinique with state repression and violence in the past decades, especially in the 1970s and 1980s. The colonial partition of territories and imposition of borders in the Guiana region according to the dominions of the former enslaver states Britain, Netherlands and France as well as the current immigration regime imposed in French-occupied Guiana are an obstacle to the communal life of Maroon and indigenous peoples in the region whose territorial bases stretch over several such neo-colonial territorial entities. Thus, continued neo-colonial occupation of "French" Guiana by France constitutes a "disruption of the national unity and the territorial integrity of a country" and is as such "incom-patible with the purposes and principles of the Charter of the United Nations"[1274].

Another important point that is often brought up or implied by detractors in the reparations debate also relates to the continued violation of international law by France and other former enslaver states. It holds that some Asian countries that were also colonized still rose to their present prosperity, thereby implying that the catastrophic material situation in many parts of global Africa would be the sole fault of Africans. This argument has very obvious flaws. The followings quotes taken from a magazine illustrate this. "The Taiwan Miracle/Miracle of the Asian

---

1273 Poursuites pour provocation à la haine raciale : "une manoeuvre", downloaded from http://tempsreel.nouvelobs.com/speciales/social/guadeloupe_dom_la_crise/20090309.OBS7874/poursuites_pour_provocation_a_la_haine_raciale_une_man.html (accessed 10.03.2009).

1274 Declaration on the Granting of Independence to Colonial Countries and Peoples, General As-sembly resolution 1514 (XV) of December 14, 1960, downloaded from http://www2.ohchr.org/en-glish/law/independence.htm (accessed 16.8.2012).

Tigers (...) [is] quoted so often out of context to spite Africa (...). Ghana and South Korea, Nigeria and Malaysia (...) were on a par economically at independence and now look at the gap between them! (...) [There is a] subliminal insinuation that says there might be something wrong with the Africans which prevents them from developing." Yet the people who sustain this regularly omit what Malaysian Prime Minister Mahathir bin Mohamad explained in October 1999 at the Africa-Asia Business Forum in Kuala Lumpur, "(...) Taiwan had been in conflict with mainland China since 1949, and was still in conflict with China, when America and the private investors from developed countries went there to build industries that brought benefits to all. South Korea and North Korea had been at war; in fact South Korea was a broken country when the Americans arrived."[1275] And when Washington and its allies decided to occupy and reconstruct Japan after the World War, one of the first things was that they sent a whole delegation of economic experts and redistributed land to make it accessible to the largest number of people. By 1950, 89% of Japanese agricultural land was owner-operated. They proceeded similarly in Taiwan. When mainland China became communist in 1949, the USA and European states set out to halt the spread of communism in the region by making countries like Taiwan, Japan, South Korea and other East Asian Tigers paragons of economic prosperity. The USA pumped $1,48 billion of free money into Taiwan between 1951 and 1968. When in 1958 Ghanaian prime minister Kwame Nkrumah approached the same government for a loan of $70 million to embark on an industrialization policy to make it an economic tiger and a model for the whole of Africa and which would have immensely improved Ghana's productivity in one generation, he was turned down and advised by President Eisenhower personally to go see the American aluminium magnate Henry J. Kaiser. "Kaiser did help, but before the dam was completed, he was already planning (by February 1964) with the American and British governments to overthrow Nkrumah's government. The coup was two years in the works, and finally succeeded in February 1966". Even before that, Nkrumah had been obliged to turn to the World Bank which imposed so many conditionalities on Ghana that the original concept of an integrated industrial project was killed. The US government "would not give Ghana a loan of $70m in 1958 to build the Akosombo Dam, it gave Taiwan $81,6m that same year for free"[1276]. Thus, we see a superficial comparison between the Asian Tigers and Africa is not justified. Indeed, the explicit argumentation and implicit assumption propagated by mainstream media coverage on Africa focusing exclusively on disaster, poverty and hungry children, suggesting thereby that something would be intrinsically wrong with Africans because they are so "underdeveloped", while some Asian countries have made it, is deeply racist and stems from "white" supremacist structures set in place from the times of transat-

---

1275 Ankomah, Baffour (2010). All issues great and small, in: New African No.501, November 2010, London: IC Publications, 62-69.
1276 Ibid.

lantic slavery. The same is true for hegemonic comparisons between present-day Haiti and the Dominican Republic which are not only totally ahistorical but also impregnated with covert racism, blaming a supposed incompetence of Black people for running their country properly while their more light-skinned Dominican neighbors would know how to do things.

So instead of getting the loan, Nkrumah was overthrown with the active assistance, if not under the direct control of former colonial and enslaver powers. Most other African leaders did not even stay alive. Just as Europeans got rid of African royals and leaders who obstructed or were not participating in enslavement for the transatlantic system, they got rid of Lat Dior Diop or Samory Touré during official colonialism. Later, they eliminated those who fought and worked for real and not just formal independence such as Patrice Lumumba, Ruben Um Nyobe, Thomas Sankara or Amilcar Cabral.[1277] And the criminal pattern still goes on, as we have seen very recently in 2012 Ivory Coast. I am no supporter of Laurent Gbagbo, but neither of Allasane Ouattara who had then-French President Nicolas Sarkozy as groomsman at his wedding. It is a historic fact that Gbagbo aimed at putting an end to the colonial financial pacts that oblige Ivory Coast to park a large share of its national money reserves in the French national bank. It is another fact that most serious allegations of election fraud were reported to have taken place in the regions controlled by Ouattara, yet the "international" community refused to look into these allegations, while at the same time giving credit to allegations against Gbagbo without proof and examination. Therefore, the author of an article published in the *New African* magazine reminded readers that, "(...) Joseph Pierre Belloc wrote about a century ago 'whatever happens, we have the Maxim gun and they have not'. (...) France used this maxim gun again to help get a candidate into power who they think will look after their interests in that country and provide a precedent for other Francophone African countries who may want to opt out of the Colonial Pact and CFA Franc agreements that France imposed on its colonies at independence."[1278] It is indeed tragic that this intervention was backed by the UN, allowing France to once again stabilize neo-colonialism, not only because by such actions the UN lose even more of their credentials as a genuine peace keeping institution. It is also tragic because even with the "rigged" (how Gbagbo contends) 46% of the votes in the second round, he has a large following among the people. They will feel that a huge injustice was done, and that is a very dangerous situation in a country that was just coming out a few years ago of another civil war.[1279] These recent events in Ivory Coast events displayed once again that Africa can still be taken overnight by any former colonial enslaver nation that wants to do so for its own economic and strategic interests, and highlight the imperative of

1277 Popo (2010), 184 et seq.
1278 Ankomah, Baffour (2011). Who are the people of Libya? in: New African May 2011, Nr. 506, London: IC Publications, 8-9,9.
1279 Ibid.

building African defence industries. Europeans intervened militarily in the more distant past of transatlantic slavery, in the less distant past of colonialism and are still ready to do so in the present anytime that their interests are menaced. This long history of aggression has established clearly that nothing but real power and force will stop them from continuing on that criminal path of global destruction.

What seems also crucial to acknowledge and highlight at this point is that the reparations debate is intrinsically linked with the immigration debate in Europe. Africa is the cradle of civilization and, in regions that are not ravaged by wars and catastrophes induced by the Maafa, it is still one of the best places to live. Yet the structures of exploitation that were set in place from the time of transatlantic slavery make it hard to survive there for many people. Thus, for example, many Malian immigrants in Europe come from the Kayes region where massive gold exploitation is financed by several public European state banks and the World Bank. Yet, while they finance the infrastructure that is necessary to get hold of the precious mineral, they give no money for environmental protection against the pollution caused by the mining. Gold mining produces dust that is charged with mercury, arsenic, lead, cadmium and antimony. The population suffers from respiratory problems, water pollution, child death and stillbirths, and dies from non-diagnosed diseases, many of them induced through the cyanide that is used to treat the mineral. [1280] Now, Kayes was a region that was also heavily impacted by transatlantic enslavement and colonial forced labor. African and indigenous people on the other side of the Atlantic, in "French" Guiana, for example, are exposed to the same kind of dangers and attacks engendered by gold exploitation from which the colonial slave master France is still reaping revenue.

When uranium was discovered in Niger in the 1970s, President Hamani Diori wanted to index its price on oil, yet as soon as he proclaimed this plan he was ousted from power by the former sergeant in the French army, Seyni Kountche. Not surprisingly the price for uranium crumbled once Kountche was in power, and Cogema, then the main French society stopeing uranium, succeeded in making France the world's fourth biggest producer of uranium, even though they only possesses 4% of global resources, and the first producer of nuclear energy (80% of French energy is nuclear). EDF, the French state energy company, claims to provide the "cheapest energy of Europe". In the meantime Nigerians remain without electricity, but are exposed to radioactivity. In the region where the uranium is stoped, there is a high incidence of cardiovascular disease, allergies, ectopic pregnancies and malformations. [1281]Another example that rose to the attention of the world because of the execution of activist and writer Ken Saro-Wiwa, is the Ogoni oil in Nigeria and the violence that is connected with its exploitation by western

---

1280 Labarthe, Gilles/Verschave, Francois-Xavier (2007). L'or africain. Pillages, trafics & commerce international, Marseille: Agone.
1281 Plumelle-Uribe (2008), 172 et seq.

oil companies, resulting in war and death for African people there. In Congo, there is a direct link between the exploitation of coltan, the continuation of war and the extermination of people. This situation was brought before the UN Security Council. In 2000, a group of experts clearly established this link and advocated for an embargo of mining products coming from Congo before the Security Council. The experts were subsequently advised twice by the Security Council to review their findings, what they did, but still always came to the same conclusions. So the Security Council ignored the findings of the final report in 2002 in which the group also listed enterprises and individuals against which sanctions should be taken, and told the group of experts to present all incriminating documents to the enterprises so that they could defend themselves. [1282] This action, or rather non-action, of the Security Council thus only served to further encourage the enterprises to continue their doings and to intensify the war in Congo.

African people globally, like other human beings, have a right to lead their lives in dignity and to enjoy all human rights, including economic, social and cultural rights. However, these rights cannot be realized until the effects of slavery and colonialism – effects that continue to cause havoc in many parts of the African continent and diaspora – are adequately addressed.[1283] And adequately addressing them is synonymous with reparation. Reparation for this crime coincides with the respect of a series of acknowledged human rights. And demanding human rights must never be perceived as too radical.

Cognizant of the massive depopulation that was caused through transatlantic slavery and the fact that those deported constituted a vital part of the productive forces of the affected African communities, it is safe to say that if transatlantic slavery would never have occurred, African economic conditions would be on a significantly healthier level today.[1284] Not only were the most productive young men and women taken away from Africa, but with them also a lot of know-how.[1285] Transatlantic slavery caused an endemic under-development on the African continent through economic, social and cultural destructuration over several centuries. Flourishing civilizations were destroyed, historically grown systems of governance mowed down, millions and millions of citizens brutally murdered or deported. From all of this emerged a pattern of poverty and under-development that not only still affects practically every African on the continent, but is also actively maintained by the former European perpetrator states of transatlantic slavery.

1282 Ibid., 182 et seq.
1283 Thipanyane, Tseliso (2002). 'Current Claims, Regional Experiences, Pressing Problems: Identification of the Salient Issues and Pressing Problems in an African Post-colonial Perspective', in: George Ulrich and Louise Krabbe Boserup (ed.): Human Rights in Development, Yearbook 2001: Reparations: Redressing Past Wrongs, The Hague: Kluwer Law International, 33-57, 53.
1284 Ibid.
1285 Boschiero (2004), 205.

Likewise on the other side of the Atlantic, slavery left a heavy heritage of under-development to the descendants of the enslaved Africans.[1286] As Jamaican lawyer and former member of the British House of Lords, Anthony Gifford stated during a parliamentary debate, the "under-development and poverty which affect the majority of countries in Africa and in the Caribbean, as well as the ghetto conditions in which many black people live in the United States and elsewhere, are not, speaking in general terms, the result of laziness, incompetence or corruption of African people (...). They are in a very large measure the consequences, the legacy of one of the most massive and terrible criminal enterprises in recorded human history; that is the transatlantic slave trade and the institution of slavery"[1287].

The system of slavery gave rise to poverty, landless populations, under-development, the destruction of culture and language, identity loss, inculcation of inferiority among the African population and the indoctrination of "white" people with a racist mentality. Today all of this continues to affect the perspectives and life quality and expectation of Africans in the Caribbean, the United States, Canada, Europe, Africa, and globally.[1288] On the reverse, European states and the USA, and "white" people collectively, continue to profit from political and economic structures established through transatlantic slavery and violently maintained up to the present. Now, of course the subject-matter of general and overall profiteering by Europeans from the Maafa has to be approached truthfully; and truthfully also means differentiated. As we have seen throughout this work, there is no margin of doubt that European rulers and economic elites profited enormously from transatlantic slavery, as did Western European societies in general since, at least, the industrial revolution – made possible through the capital accumulated per the transatlantic genocide crime – and especially so in the past 50 years. This is in no contradiction with the fact that life remained hard for a very long time for the average European man, woman and child whose blood the European capitalists and colonialists were also sucking, until they were forced by the labour and socialist movements during the early and middle decades of the 20th century to give up a piece of their cake baked with the blood of Africans and of other brutally and illegally colonized peoples. My grandmother who labored for decades as a housemaid for rich people, getting up during the long and cold Austrian winters at 3 o'clock in the morning to wade for two hours through the snow to reach the bus to take her to her workplace, lost her first child to diphtheria. This sickness was caused by contaminated well water, the only water supply available to my grandmother, combined with unsanitary and cold housing conditions and malnutrition, all poverty related. So my father's brother died in her arms at the age of three, and

---

1286 Ibid., 259.
1287 Slavery: Legacy. The official record from Hansard of the debate initiated by Lord Gifford QC in the House of Lords of the British Parliament on the 14th March 1996 concerning the African reparations, downloaded from: http://www.arm.arc.co.uk/LordsHansard.html (accessed 25.7.2010).
1288 Gifford (2007).

my father, her only remaining child, also fell ill of diphtheria a few years later and only escaped death scarcely. How could I say that my grandmother would have benefitted in any way from the Maafa in the earlier decades of her life? I cannot. The European power elites that fundamentally built their positions and power on slavery and colonialism also sucked her blood. It was through hard work that she built all she ever possessed; and up to her last days this was very little. Yet I do acknowledge that in later decades of her life, due to the persistent and also violent, knocking on the door of the capitalists by the European labor movement, my grandmother came to see some modest material benefits that the western European system had by then been obliged to open up to all of its citizens, if it was to persist. And if it was only for the coffee she was by then able to drink every day, cultivated by African and South American workers exploited in the structures set in place with transatlantic slavery and maintained throughout the Maafa. I can detect no blame whatsoever to put on my European granny; yet I recognize that the greater the benefits we Europeans, and other structural profiteers, are taking and consuming from the genocidal Maafa system, the greater our individual guilt becomes, within the general global setting of European societies' responsibility and obligation to make reparations.

Inside the USA, even the ascendancy of the first Black President Barack Obama did not change the racist structures of society within a setting of the Maafa and global apartheid. Only one remainder of this was the Jena 6 incident, where the directing board of a high school did not punish the "white" perpetrators of blatant racist provocation and death-threats, but the Black students who stood up against it. The directing board judged it a bad "joke" and not a racist provocation that three slipknots were found hanging from a tree in the schoolyard that was commonly known as the "white tree" because Black students were not allowed to sit under it by the unwritten laws of the school. Yet one day some Black students refused to comply and sat under the tree, entailing confrontations between Black and "white" students. In what ensued the prosecutor told the Black students after they had organised a small demonstration under the said tree that he could be their best friend or their worst enemy and that he could destroy their lives with the stroke of a pen. This encouraged the racist white students who proceeded to call them "niggers" and so forth. It was at this point that fistfights started, in which none was seriously hurt, yet the police came to arrest six Black students and they were finally charged with attempted murder. One student was later condemned for assault and battery to prison by an all "white" jury, but freed in the revision. Yet he was granted no bail while awaiting his new trial even though he was only 16 years old. Reverend and Civil Rights activist Al Sharpton declared that the world should know that Jena was not a singular case but repeated throughout the country, that there had been hanging slipknots at Columbia University in New

York, in North Carolina, in California, and even at the 9/11 memorial site.[1289] In this context, I would like to mention an incident that occurred about two years after Jena in my birth country Austria, where Hitler was also born. A high school history teacher went on a field trip with a group of students to Mauthausen, the labor death camp that the Nazi maintained in Austria. Upon sighting the reminders of horror there, one of the shocked students exclaimed, "but what could these people have done that they were treated like this!" This was overheard by a supervisor of the site and it turned into a scandal. The teacher found himself held responsible for the "racist" behavior of the student in a country where apologia of the Shoa is a criminal offense. Yet, and not surprisingly so, the ascension to the head of the most powerful state of US-President Obama is inevitably brought up by reparation negationists. I remember well how after a presentation I had done, one man in the audience mockingly asked whether repatriation as one form of reparations would mean that Obama could go back to Kenya. Many people contend that if a Black man can make it to the position of President of the USA, then the legacy of slavery cannot be so disastrous after all and that we would no longer need reparations. In that regard it is important to point out that during transatlantic slavery and colonialism there have always been African individuals who fared well in those systems. That Obama as an individual made it so far is due to a variety of factors, among them surely his intelligence and determination, but that does not necessarily change anything about the structural damage that needs to be redressed through reparations. Obama's election changed nothing for the vast majority of African people globally, except for a mental uplift to some extent. The ghetto dwellers in Kingston, South Central L.A. or Zimbabwe still hustle to make a living from day to day. Black people still have the same one per cent of the US's wealth held in 1865.[1290] "Despite the Black faces that now seem to call the shots in the story, the conditions of the masses of Black people haven't changed", or as stated by Malcolm X, "you don't stick a knife in a man's back nine inches and then pull it out six inches and say you're making progress".[1291] Opera singer Leontyne Price has in this context spoken of "token blacks" ("because pointing at us token black eases the conscience of millions, and I think it is dreadfully wrong").[1292]

Some have sustained that it was indeed the growth of the global reparations movement over the past two decades, culminating in the WCAR in 2001 that is in fact partly responsible for the ascendancy of Obama to presidency. Just as the pressure of the enslaved and colonized had at one time reached a point where there was a real danger that the whole system of exploitation of Africa and her people would be overthrown, had made it imperative to abolish slavery and later official colonialism, it may now have been high time to give a superficial impres-

---

1289 Plumelle-Uribe (2008), 125 et seq.
1290 Ball, Jared (2011). I Mix What I Like! A mixtape manifesto, Oakland: AK Press, 21.
1291 Asante, M. K., Jr. (2008). It's bigger than hip hop, New York: St. Martin's Press, 238f
1292 Asante, M. K., Jr. (2008). It's bigger than hip hop, New York: St. Martin's Press, 240.

sion of equality to take the steam out of the well founded claims of the reparations movement so that the global system of exploitation of Africa can go on.

Indeed, the global African reparations movement has gained a lot of magnitude during these last decades and years, but it has really been here since the beginning of the crime, as will be retraced in the next chapter.

VI.   The Legal Doctrine of *Laches* and the Reparations Movement

Naturally, there were always African people who actively resisted and fought for reparations in one form or another throughout the centuries since the beginning of the Maafa. Even if the global African reparations movement has indeed gained significant amplitude, especially since 1993 when the First Pan-African Conference on Reparations was convened under the auspices of the OAU in Abuja[1293], the movement is much older and really goes back in an unbroken line to the first illegal enslavement and deportation of Africans. In the fore field of the Abuja conference the OAU installed a Group of Eminent Persons to appraise the issue of reparations in relation to the damage done to Africa and its Diaspora by enslavement, colonization, and neo-colonialism, as the "damage sustained by the African peoples is not a 'thing of the past' but is painfully manifest in the damaged lives of contemporary Africans from Harlem to Harare, in the damaged economies of the Black World from Guinea to Guyana, from Somalia to Surinam".[1294] That the movement has grown stronger and louder in the past decades can surely be attributed in part to new and more decentralized technologies of communication. Not only are books more readily available than ever, but hip-hop and reggae mixtapes and the internet make it easier to communicate and organize for Africans scattered around the globe through the to-be-repaired crime. Yet the reparation claim has always been here, long before the 20th century, and the contention by reparation negationists that the claim for reparations would come too late and be time-barred is without any empirical basis, as we shall see in this chapter.

In international law, the legal doctrine of *laches* holds that a legal right or claim will not be allowed if a long delay in asserting that right or claim would prejudice the adverse party as a sort of "legal ambush"[1295]. It is based on the maxim that eq-

---

1293 First Pan-African Conference on Reparations For African Enslavement, Colonisation And Neo-Colonisation, sponsored by The Organisation Of African Unity and its Reparations Commission April 27-29, 1993, Abuja/Nigeria.
1294 Declaration of the first Abuja Pan-African Conference on Reparations For African Enslavement, Colonisation And Neo-Colonisation, sponsored by The Organisation Of African Unity and its Reparations Commission April 27-29, 1993, Abuja/Nigeria.
1295 Laches, downloaded from http://dictionary.law.com/Default.aspx?selected=1097 (accessed

uity aids the vigilant and not those who slumber on their rights. It thus operates against whoever neglects to assert a claim when such neglect, considered in the passage of time, would harm the adverse party.[1296]

It is often contended that reparation claims for transatlantic slavery would come too late, and that they would be barred because of *laches*. But they really are not late, the claims have just always been ignored by European and US governments. And the legal doctrine of laches does not take effect when the reason for why a claim has not been taken up is not neglect but refusal of acknowledgement.

Since the Maafa, comprising transatlantic slavery, can be defined as a continuing crime according to Art. 14 of the ILC Articles, as shown above in Chapter IV, it would not even be necessary to elaborate in depth on the doctrine of *laches* with regard to assessing legal responsibility. *Laches* is only relevant for terminated violations, but is logically irrelevant when it comes to continuing violations. Still, it might be expedient to spend a little ink on this aspect since that will demonstrate even more clearly how well justified the reparation claim for transatlantic slavery is in international law. To substantiate this point, we will now retrace a short review of some examples of the historic reparation movement. It should also be remembered in that context that it was only in 1996 that Polish victims of the Nazi turned with an insistent appeal to German Chancellor Helmut Kohl and demanded reparations, which were granted.[1297]

1. BRIEF HISTORICAL SKETCH OF THE UNBROKEN STRUGGLE FOR REPARATION

In 1570, Gaspar Yanga, originally from Gabon, led a revolt in Mexico and established the *Cofre de Perote palenque* Maroon community. He and his comrades justified assaults on "white" persons and property as a means of compensation for what the enslavers had taken from them over the years.[1298] As such, these Africans *took* reparations which were legally due to them. In Cuba, Maroons travelled up to twenty and even fourty miles, over hills and through forests, to attack plantations to obtain goods. In Columbia, a group of Maroons set fire to the city of Santa Maria in the early 16th century.[1299] In Venezuela, Guillermo Rivas acquired a Zorro-like image with his Maroon group, dispensing their form of justice against

---

8.7.2010).

1296 Obadele, Imari Abubakari (1989). "Reparations Yes!" in: Chokwe Lumumba (ed.): Reparations Yes!, Baton Rouge: House of Songhay, 23-66, 32.

1297 Winkler, Hans (2002). Entschädigung für Sklaven-und Zwangsarbeit durch Österreich, Wien: Diplomatische Akademie Favourtite Papers, 3.

1298 Thompson (2006), 135.

1299 Ibid.

enslavers. They occupied haciendas and liberated the enslaved people.[1300] Guillermo Rivas and a number of other Maroon leaders also punished slaveholders for their treatment of their enslaved captives.[1301]

Some Maroon communities seem to have been fully dedicated to the destruction of "white" settlements, for example in Cuba and Mexico.[1302] It is important to see that this pressure the Maroons asserted on the slavery system was significant and contributed significantly to its downfall. Such attacks aiming to destroy "white" enslaver settlements were a measure focused on bringing to an end the illegal conduct of Europeans and repair the violation of law. "Slavery would have remained an important social system throughout the Americas. (...). The pressure created by (...) Maroons and other insurgents ensured that there could only be one ultimate solution: freedom for all enslaved persons."[1303]

While the Maroons fought a practical reparation struggle, others sought justice through the legal system. In 1783, an African woman named Belinda brought a petition against her former master Isaac Roxall to receive reparations before the Massachusetts legislature. She argued in the petition that her labor had enriched her enslaver and that she had a right to lay claim to his estate. This appeal for her and her daughter was successful, and she was granted 15,12 shillings per year from the wealth that had been accumulated by the Roxall family, owners of the Ten Hills Plantation, as compensation for her enslavement.[1304] However, it is important to acknowledge that this woman was one very rare example of enslaved Africans who due to fortunate circumstances and determination was able to even make it to a court. Except for another few individuals, most of the millions and millions of enslaved Africans were structurally and violently prevented from ascertaining their rights before judicial institutions. That they were prevented to do so by the colonial states and slave masters did not make their claim to freedom and reparation invalid. And it was clearly recognized by this and other courts and at the time of transatlantic slavery that their claim was valid.

Ottobah Cugoano wrote in 1787 that "I wish to go back as soon as I can hear any proper security and safe conveyance can be found; and I wait to hear how it fares with the Black People sent to Sierra Leone. (...) This would be doing great good to the Africans, and be a kind restitution for the great injuries that they have suffered."[1305] He continued by stating an obligation "to restore to their fellow-creatures the common rights of nature, of which especially the unfortunate Black People have been so unjustly deprived (...)"[1306]. Cugoano stressed in his argument for

---

1300 Ibid., 142.
1301 Ibid., 325.
1302 Ibid., 202.
1303 Ibid., 329.
1304 Winbush (2009), 23.
1305 Cugoano (1787), 7.
1306 Ibid., 9.

reparation that "the just law of God requires an equal retaliation and restoration for every injury that men may do to others, to shew the greatness of the crime; but the law of forbearance, righteousness and forgiveness, forbids the retaliation to be sought after, when it would be doing as great an injury to them, without any reparation or benefit to ourselves".[1307] For according to the law of God, "(...) if any manner of theft be found in a man's hand, the law requires a retaliation and restoration; that is, that he should restore double (...)". In a footnote, he also added that the law of reparation had a long and well-observed tradition in Africa.

After the first abolition of slavery in the French Caribbean in 1795, the people rebelled in 1797 because the problem of compensation of former slaves had not been solved. These insurrections were severely repressed by the French state.[1308]

When slavery had been abolished in the USA, some individual claims lodged by former slaves against their former masters were brought to court, as it resorts for example from a letter sent by one Jourdon Anderson to his former owner Colonel P.H. Anderson on August 7, 1865, claiming payment for 32 years of labor.[1309]

In Cuba, one Andrea Quesada in the early 20th century sued for reparations to compensate herself and other slaves for their labor prior to abolition in 1886.[1310] She asserted that she had been illegally held in bondage for a decade on the Santa Rosalia plantation by the heir of her former owner, Manuel Blanco, despite the willed intent of her prior owner, José Quesada, to free her. Upon her example, within a few months, 27 other men and women using the surname Quesada brought suit.[1311]

Five anonymous authors published *Jamaica's Jubilee; or What We Are and What We hope to Be* in 1888 where they claimed "the interest, sympathy, and protection of those who were instrumental in effecting the expatriation of our ancestors", thereby indicating that they expected some sort of reparations.[1312]

At the end of the 19th century, Callie House organized the National Ex-Slave Mutual Relief, Bounty and Pension Association. She was appointed its secretary in 1898 and eventually became the leader of the organization. She traveled through the southern United States to rally for the cause of reparations. By 1900, the nationwide membership for this organization militating for reparations was estimated to be around 300,000 people. Following the pattern maintained since the beginning of transatlantic slavery, the government attempted to stop her and other leaders of the Association. In 1916, just as they did with the great Black leader and organizer Marcus Mosiah Garvey, indictments were passed against leaders of the Association claiming that they had obtained money from ex-slaves

---

1307 Ibid., 52.
1308 Coco (2005), 92.
1309 Brooks (2004), 6.
1310 Peabody/Grinberg (2007), 27
1311 Ibid., 167 et seq.
1312 Cited in: Thomas, Deborah A. (2004). Modern Blackness. Nationalism, Globalization, and the Politics of Culture in Jamaica, Durham/London: Duke University Press, 35.

by fraudulent circulars proclaiming that pensions and reparations were forthcoming. Callie House was convicted and served one year in prison.

The entire philosophy of Marcus Garvey, focused on African redemption and "Africa for Africans", really adds up to achieving reparation for the damage brought about by the Maafa, albeit less by claiming reparations from the oppressor than by taking reparation. Garvey was the most unrelenting advocate of repatriation to Africa, one form of reparations by international law, through his United Negro Improvement Association.[1313] The UNIA's 1920 Declaration of Rights of the Negro Peoples of the World, penned by Garvey stated that, "We declare that Negroes, wheresoever they form a community among themselves, should be given the right to elect their own representatives to represent them in legislatures, courts of law, (...) We hereby demand that the governments of the world recognize our leader" and that Black people get "complete control of our social institutions". In pursuance of "the inherent right of the Negro to possess himself of Africa", Garvey's and Garveyites goal was to "build up Africa as a Negro Empire [for] every Black man, whether he was born in Africa or the western world", and thus the UNIA sought "immediate establishment of an African nation". Garvey's ultimate goal of African redemption is convergent with the re-establishement of African sovereignty which is in turn, as highlighted and argued throughout this work and elsewhere, the ultimate aim and task of reparation such as provided by international law. His United Negro Improvement Association had over 1,900 divisions in more than 40 countries and 6 million members by 1920. Of course he had to be shut down by the powers perpetrating the Maafa, as they had done with Callie House and countless others.

Still, Queen Mother Moore (1898-1997) continued to lobby persistently for reparations, and in 1957 and 1959 brought petitions before the UN asking for reparations and self-determination. Another champion for reparations in the 20th century was James Foreman.

Historian L. Bennett Jr. assessed that there was a mass demand for land by freemen after and during the Civil War, when Black people asked en masse for some sort of reparation to be able to make their living in freedom. W.E.B. DuBois also documented land rebellions fought by freemen in their struggle for land in the post-Civil war area. Alston assembled old news articles, letters and other documents from the late 1800s and early 1900s, showing that Black reparation organizations organized tens of thousands of *New Afrikans* behind the demand for reparations.[1314]

Too many people are not aware of this, but Martin Luther King Jr. also advo-

1313 Garvey, Marcus (ed. 2004). Selected Writings and Speeches of Marcus Garvey, Mineola: Dover Publications, 18ff.
1314 Lumumba, Chokwe (1989a). "Proposed Reparation Amendment", in: Chokwe Lumumba (ed.): Reparations Yes! Baton Rouge: House of Songhay, 13-20, 15.

cated reparations. In his historic "I Have a Dream" speech, he phrased the demand for justice in terms of reparations and sustained concerning the "guarantees of life, liberty, and the pursuit of happiness" that "instead of honoring this sacred obligation, America has given the Negro people a bad check; a check which has come back marked 'insufficient funds'. We refuse to believe that there are insufficient funds in the great vaults of opportunity in this nation. And so we've come to cash this check, a check that will give us upon demand the riches of freedom and the security of Justice". [1315] At another occasion Dr. King stated that "no amount of gold could provide an adequate compensation for the exploitation and humiliation of the Negro in America (...). Yet a price can be placed on unpaid wages" [1316] and suggested a "massive (...) settlement" payment to represent compensation for stolen labor.[1317]

By these few examples, we clearly see that this is not a claim being raised for the first time some 150 years after abolition, but one that goes back to the very beginning of the crime.[1318] The position shared by too many people today that formerly enslaved Africans did not want or expect reparations is not based on facts and is wrong. Governments only actively refused to comply.[1319]

Réunion, Martinique, Guadeloupe and Guiana became French departments only in 1946, one century after the abolition of slavery, during which they had remained official colonies and its people did not have democratic citizen rights.[1320] Even today these countries are not yet independent from their former enslaver nation. There was a solid movement for recognition and redress in Guadeloupe, Martinique and Guiana in the 1960s and 1970s, but it was destroyed and its claims ignored by the France state and French society.

In fact, any form of rebellion against enslavement and seeking restorative justice for wrongs done to the victims of transatlantic slavery can be regarded as a

1315 Ogletree, Charles J. Jr. (2003). Repairing the Past: New Efforts in the Reparations Debate in America, downloaded from http://www.law.harvard.edu/students/orgs/crcl/vol38_2/ogletree.pdf (accessed 4.6.2010), 5.

1316 King, Martin Luther Jr. (1964). Why We Can't Wait, New York: Signet Classics, 150f.; see also: Cook Anthony (2000). King and the Beloved Community: A Communitarian Defense of Black Reparations, in: George Washington Law Review 68, 959-1014.

1317 Wenger, Kaimipono David (2010). From Radical to Practical (and Back Again?): Reparations, Rhetoric, and Revolution, downloaded from http://works.bepress.com/kaimipono_wenger/1 (accessed 20.8.2012).

1318 Brooks, Roy L. (2007). "Redress for Slavery - The African-American Struggle", in: Max du Plessis and Stephen Peté (ed.): Repairing the Past? International Perspectives on Reparations for Gross Human Rights Abuses, Antwerpen/Oxford: Intersentia, 297-313, 301.

1319 Farmer-Paellmann, Deadria (2003). "Excerpt from Black Exodus: The Ex-Slave Pension Movement Reader", in: Raymond A. Winbush (ed.): Should America pay? Slavery and the raging debate on reparations, New York: Amistad, 22-31, 28.

1320 Taubira, Christiane (2006). "Introduction", in: André Castaldo (ed.): Codes Noirs de l'esclavage aux abolitions, Paris: Editions Dalloz, XXVIII.

quest for reparations. "[S]lave rebellions can be considered the earliest and most violent expression of reparations on the part of Africans because they sought to secure their denied freedom by any means necessary including retaliatory and defensive violence. (...) These Africans wanted to *repair the damage* done by their kidnapping from West Africa and the restrictions placed on them by laws that incrementally removed their rights (...). 250 documented slave rebellions took place *before* the Civil War, but historian John Hop Franklin estimates it was far more since rebellions were often unreported and caused economic and political embarrassment to slave owners and local governments."[1321]

Numerous proclamations by Africans (sometimes passed in connection with physical acts of resistance and taking reparations) throughout the continent and the diaspora express a claim for the restoration of the inalienable rights of enslaved Africans. This includes declarations of sovereignty by such leaders of the resistance against colonization on the continent and in the diaspora as Samori Touré, Moro Naba Wobogo, Nana Yaa Asantewa, Queen Amina, Queen Nzinga, Mbuya Nehanda, Me Katilili, Frederick Douglass, Antonio Macao, Marcus Garvey, W.E.B. DuBois, Frantz Fanon, Dedan Kimathi, Patrice Lumumba, Pierre Mulele, Josina Machel, Mma Ngoyi, Malcolm X, Martin Luther King, George Jackson or Huey P. Newton. It includes declarations by those leading rebellions against enslavement such as Toussaint L'Ouverture, Nanny, Cudjoe, Tacky, Sam Sharpe, Paul Bogle, Nat Turner, Harriet Tubman or Sojourner Truth. It includes the Declaration of the Rights of the Negro Peoples of the World, the resolutions of the Aborigines Rights Protection Society of the then Gold Coast, of the National Congress of British West Africa (NCBWA), of the Rassemblement Democratique Africain (RDA), of the South African Native National Congress (SANNC), of the UNIA, of the Pan-African Congresses, of the All-African People's Conferences or of the Organization of African Unity (OAU), the Abuja Declaration, the Durban Documents and others.[1322]

The repatriation or Back-to-Africa-movement mounting from the first African captives who disembarked from the African shore is of course also an essential part of the reparation struggle.[1323] "Resettlement was seen as a means of righting a wrong that had begun two centuries earlier. (...) [T]he return to Africa was understood to be a specific, narrowly tailored form of restitution for slavery."[1324] Formerly enslaved African Paul Cuffe viewed repatriation to Africa as a form of

---

1321 Winbush (2009), 18 et seq.

1322 Affiong/Klu (1993), 4.

1323 Brooks, Roy L. (2003). History of the Black Redress Movement, in: Guild Practioner, Vol. 60, Nr. 1, Los Angeles, 1-12.

1324 Johnson, Jr., Robert (1999). "Repatriation as Reparations for Slavery and Jim Crowism", in: Roy L. Brooks (ed.): When Sorry is Not Enough. The Controversy Over Apologies and Reparations for Human Injustice, New York: New York University Paperback, 428 et seq.

slave redress. He financed the return of 38 free Black people, including himself, to Africa in 1816. However, he stressed that the US government had the responsibility to repatriate both slaves and free Blacks to their homeland.[1325]

When Brazil became independent in 1822, a law was promulgated that provided for those identifying themselves as slave descendants to return to Africa. A large group of descendants of Angolas thus asked to return. They installed themselves in the Angolan province of Namibe.[1326]

The Rastafari movement in Jamaica and in the following elsewhere, has continuously claimed repatriation and linked it to reparations.[1327] Gong Leonard P. Howell, who stands at the beginning of the Rastafari movement in Jamaica in the early 20th century, and Alexander Bedward who was also important in its consolidation, both advocated repatriation to Africa and reparations from the British colonial state for slavery and colonialism. Both were locked up in mental institutions by the colonial perpetrator state. When the Rastafari movement started to take off in Jamaica, hundreds of brethren and sistren who espoused demands for repatriation and reparation were ruthlessly incarcerated, their dreadlocks shaved, they were medicated with powerful psychotropic drugs against their will, and many were also killed.[1328]

Letters written by Prince Emmanuel, leader of the Bobo Shanti Rastafari order (Ethiopia Africa Black International Congress), addressed to the British governors of Jamaica and dating back as far as 1948, also express the claim to repatriation to Ethiopia/Africa for all Africans desiring so.[1329]

In 1961 a Rastafari mission went to Ethiopia, Ghana, Nigeria, Liberia and Sierra Leone to assess possibilities for repatriation to these countries. Several brethren met UN officials in 1964, but the officials explained that the UN had no power to take up the case unless the Jamaican Government presented a case to the Organization.[1330] Yet up to now, no Jamaican administration has taken steps to bring the matter before the UN. In that context it needs to be mentioned that although the explicit mission of the Jamaica National Commission on Reparations, installed by the Jamaican government in 2009, was to promote the cause of reparations, then-Prime Minister Bruce Golding reportedly said at an IMF conference at a time when the commission that his own government had set up was still working, that he was against reparations. Apparently, claims to reparations and to aid money are mutually exclusive. The following quote should be appreciated in this context:

"Nine years of lobbying with the African Group bore fruit at the 1998 session

1325 Brooks (2004), 4f; Brooks (2007), 301.
1326 Kwenzi-Mikala (2003) 11.
1327 Reparation Is A Must, in: Jahug Vol.4, London: Congo Call Production (year unknown).
1328 Hickling (2009), 3.
1329 Presentation to Reparation Commission at Liberty Hall Thursday, October 15, 2009, Hon Empress Petrona Simpasa Voice of Woman E.A.B.I.C.W.F.L.L., downloaded from http://www.black-king.net/english/library/presentation%20to%20reparation%20commission.htm (accessed 5.11.2009).
1330 Repatration Is A Must, in: Jahug Vol.4, London: Congo Call Production (year unknown).16.

of the Commission on Human Rights (CHR). The African Group unanimously proposed a resolution calling for the Declaration of the Transatlantic Slave Trade and Slavery as a Crime Against Humanity. (...) Senegal was chairing the African Group when this resolution was proposed. In an ironic coincidence, President Bill Clinton was on his way to Senegal to present the African Growth and Opportunity Act. Rumors have been consistent that President Clinton actually called Senegal's President Diouf from Air Force One to tell him that it would not be in Senegal's best interest to continue to push this resolution. (...) The next day Senegal withdrew the resolution from consideration."[1331]

Unofficial reports also hold that, when at one point Jamaica was considering to bring forth a lawsuit for reparations, the UK government let the Jamaican authorities know very quickly that such behavior could easily lead to the loss of aid and other assets.

Indeed, as sustained in a Rastafari communication, "from the days of Prophet Marcus Garvey unto Hon. Leonard Howell the British governments had imprisoned I'n'I Leaders of VISION to try to kill every righteous Movement for African Liberation". Yet still, the Rastafari movement shall never ever give up the claim for African redemption that is the mystical and historical reason for its emergence and existence, indeed its heart piece, and African redemption reposes on reparation and repatriation. Recently, the Rastafari community has also petitioned the Bahamas government on matters pertaining to reparations and compensation for our community for the many horrific human right violations committed by agents of the Bahamas government against the community and other poor people contrary to human rights law.

In 2010, the Caribbean Rastafari Organisation (CRO) called upon member states of both the African Union (AU) and of the European Union (EU) to include Reparations for Chattel Slavery and the Trans-Atlantic Slave Trade within the framework of the Second Action Plan (2011-2013) to be adopted at the 3rd Africa EU Summit in Tripoli on 29 and 30 November of that same year. The CRO referred specifically to the inclusion of reparations in the United Nations Durban Plan of Action (POA, 2001), as Section IV (i) recommends "provision of effective remedies, recourse, redress, and other measures at the national, regional and international levels", and (ii) proposes "facilitation of the welcomed return and resettlement of the descendants of the enslaved Africans". The CRO also highlighted the necessity of a careful distinction that must be made between reparations and various aid packages conceded to "alleviate the persistent poverty created by the colonization of African peoples, forced removal from their homelands and enslavement in the plantations of the Americas. Matters of trade and mutual cooperation are a normal component of international negotiations which are quite separate from

---

1331 Wareham, Roger (2003). "The Popularization of the International Demand for Reparations", in: Raymond A. Winbush (ed.): Should America pay? Slavery and the raging debate on reparations, New York: Amistad, 226-236, 221.

compensation for the specific historical injustice that continues to dog the lives of Africans. The misery perpetuated in Haiti strongly suggests the need for such distinction."[1332] The brethren and sistren also once again repositioned the Rastafari claim of repatriation to receptive African countries as one form of reparations.

In late 2011, the CRO further submitted a document to the African Union in which it was clearly stated that "for Rastafari, Repatriation is synonymous with themes of Emancipation, African Liberation and Reparations". What the Rastafari movement aims at is "no(t) Migration, (but) Repatriation!"[1333]. It rightfully conceptualizes repatriation as their "right to go home with recompense and free transportation to take I and I home to Africa", and therefore speak of *Reparations for Repatriation*.[1334] Indeed, Rastafari know that reparation without repatriation is not possible, since the coming home of the stolen children of Africa is the "trumpet call for African Redemption".[1335]

In a recent appeal for reparations to the British government, Rastafarians stated once again that "for those whose choice is to return to where we were taken from, (...) a sound economic empowerment in our home land is what we expected from the descendants and benefactors of the slave monsters. Governments in the Caribbean, England and all previous colonies surely should be prepared, where necessary, to negotiate with various leaders of African States to remove the barriers brought about by colonizers. The sons and daughters should not be forced to seek permission, visas, etc. to return to a home they were so savagely forced from."[1336] The Rastafari movement really needs to be credited for the sound and unrelenting analysis that reparation is not possible without repatriation since Mama Africa needs her lost children to heal while at the same time repatriation is recognized as possible only if it is part of a larger comprehensive reparation strategy.

The First Pan-African Conference on Reparations convened by the OAU in 1993, as well as the 2001 World Conference Against Racism in Durban at which reparations were also the hot topic, have already been briefly mentioned.

Reparation activists from all corners also came together in an "All African" meeting in Vienna/Austria in May 2001, aiming at unifying the struggle of the late

---

1332 Statement of the Caribbean Rastafari Organisation, Repatriation and Reparations Lobby, November 15, 2010.

1333 Christian, Ijahnya (2011). Return of the 6th Region: RastafarI Settlement in the Motherland. Contributing to the African Renaissance, Rabat: Codesria, 13eme Assemblée générale, 3.

1334 Christian, Ijahnya (2011). Return of the 6th Region: RastafarI Settlement in the Motherland. Contributing to the African Renaissance, Rabat: Codesria, 13eme Assemblée générale, 4.

1335 Christian, Ijahnya (2011). Return of the 6th Region: RastafarI Settlement in the Motherland. Contributing to the African Renaissance, Rabat: Codesria, 13eme Assemblée générale, 14.

1336 Letter of January 15, 2003 by the All Mansion's Secretariat of the Ethiopian Peace Foundation, Jamaica Branch, International RastafarI Community, RastafarI Brethren of Jamaica to Her Royal Majesty Queen Elizabeth II, Buckingham Palace, Attention: Mrs. Kay Brock, Assistant Private Secretary, c/o Mr. Gavin Tech, Deputy British High Commissioner, Kingston.

1990s and solidifying strategies of focusing on three core themes: the Declaration of the Transatlantic Slave Trade and Slavery as a crime against humanity; Reparations for people on the African continent and in the diaspora; and The Economic Basis of Racism.[1337]

2. NO CASE OF *LACHES*, YET WHO COULD FILE THE CLAIM?

Apart from the fact that African people have always struggled for reparation and have historically also manifested their claim in legal terms, thus frustrating any application of the doctrine of laches in this case, we also know that we are dealing with a continuing crime up to the present since "when slavery was abolished (...), it was succeeded by colonialism. The exploitation of the colonies and the deported Africans who lived there continued, it was a transformation from one subjugation to another. Colonialism ended for most of us only 30 years."[1338] France never even formally emancipated its colonies, and neo-colonialism remains a global reality. "The period of colonialism which succeeded the period of slavery, continued the exploitation of Africa and the Caribbean in new ways. Further acts of brutality were committed, and the peoples of these regions, until recently, were denied the status of sovereignty and independence with which alone they could themselves demand the redress of the wrongs which were done."[1339] Since the crime of the Maafa, of which transatlantic slavery was only one phase, is still continuing, it is obsolete to even consider *laches* in this case.

The OAU Group of Eminent Persons stressed in that context that

"[w]e are not out to penalize the present generations who are descendants of slave-owners and slave-traders. What we put before the world is the fact that certain countries today and certain sections of the present generation are placed in a better position, economically, politically and socially, than the claimants, as a result of the unjust enrichment enjoyed by their ancestors at the expense of claimants. (...) It is most important for us to grasp the linkage [between slavery and colonialism]. The Atlantic slave trade used European capital to take African slaves to the New World. With abolition, European capital turned its attention to the exploitation of African labour, land and mineral resources in Africa itself. The Atlantic slave trade had identified slavery solely with the black person, perpetually in a degraded and dehumanized position. Colonialism in Africa was based on

---

1337 Winbush (2009), 48.

1338 Facts on reparations to Africa and Africans in the Diaspora. Prepared by The Group of Eminent Persons on Reparations (1993). Lagos: The Group; cited in: Reparation Is A Must, in: Jahug Vol.4, London: Congo Call Production, 20.

1339 Grillitsch, Johanna (2007). Gedenkjahr 2007. Der Reparationsdiskurs in England, in: Stichproben. Wiener Zeischrift für kritische Afrikastudien 13/2007, 7. Jahrgang, 137-161, 145 et seq.

the racial foundations laid by the slave trade. Because the world failed to recognize the inhuman slave trade as a crime against humanity, European powers went in to commit equally heinous crimes against Africans under colonialism. (...) Even after nominal independence had been granted, with African human and material resources already depleted by the slave trade and colonialism, the Western world continues to control African economies and to manipulate its governments for their own ends. They bear a lot of responsibility for the increasing degradation, collapse of States, hunger, disease and gloomy prospects. (...) The effects of the slave trade was not felt by the immediate victims only but by all black peoples. The impact on Africa in the loss of people, destruction of agriculture and trade, insecurity of life, social degradation, etc. was disastrous and no black people, even those who participated in the trade, could escape its destructive consequences. One of the effects of the Atlantic slave trade has been racial prejudice. (...) All Africans suffered from this, whether enslaved or not. This was the foundation of colonialism and neo-colonialism in Africa: Prejudice against black people spread almost everywhere in the world and we have to redress this problem. The cost of this world-wide prejudice against black peoples is incalculable. It is revealed in such incidents as the recent Los Angeles riots, and it is beginning to show itself in some parts of Germany, Britain and France. It is even said to exist in Mauritania and other parts of Africa; thus the psychological damage is one of the things we have to redress."[1340]

Chief Moshood Abiola, who was the Chairman of the Group of Eminent Persons of the OAU, announced that, acting on behalf of the Black people of the world, it should soon be expected that a demand be placed on the agenda of the United Nations, after having secured support by the OAU.[1341] Not long after, he was killed in circumstances that remain dubious up to today. He ran in the Nigerian presidential elections, and had announced that as president he would continue to push the reparations agenda on the international parquet. Voices have been raised that this is the real reason why he was eliminated.

In view of all these facts it is more than upsetting that then-French President Sarkozy said in his speech at the 2011 ceremony for the commemoration of the abolition of slavery that "the descendants of slaves never asked excuses. They asked and they still ask that their wounds are recognized. They have not asked reparation, they asked comprehension and respect of their singularity, of their murdered identity. They have not asked special rights (...)."[1342] Even if Sarkozy does not know that the 1797 rebellions in Martinique and Guadeloupe were really for reparations and were brutally suppressed by France, he must know that French

---

1340 Facts on reparations to Africa and Africans in the Diaspora (1993), 22.
1341 Ibid., 20.
1342 Speech of French President Sarkozy at the Ceremony for the Commemoration of the Abolition of Slavery, Paris: Jardin de Luxembourg, May 10, 2011.

tribunals are currently reviewing claims for reparations against the French state filed by the Mouvement International pour les Réparations (MIR) in Martinique. Sarkozy's country and the US also illegally kidnapped Haiti's President Bertrand Aristide when that man started to make serious moves for claiming reparations for the illegally extorted millions that France forced Haiti to pay after the revolution. Yet the then acting French President had the nerve to, in that same speech, pay "homage to Toussaint L'Ouverture and the people of Haiti" who "died for liberty". He omitted to mention that it was France that killed Toussaint when he aimed to restore Haitian African independence and sovereignty.[1343] What is most sad though, is that this speech did not create any debate, but was rather positively received, even by many diaspora Africans in France. The psychological and social conditioning that is responsible for this state of affairs is a huge road block to reparation and will be further discussed in upcoming chapters.

Sarkozy is not the first European politician trying to recycle Europe's historical denial of reparation claims into an argument against reparations. A few years back, for example, the Viscount of Falkland had sustained in the seminal debate on reparations in the House of Lords that in his "experience, the African people are immensely forgiving. They have forgiven the iniquities that they suffered in recent times. To encourage the kind of attitude of fervent desire for reparation here would go against the grain, certainly among Africans, because it is not in their nature"[1344].

As seen throughout this work and highlighted in the first part of this chapter, African individuals, communities and states have historically demanded reparations. The defense of *laches*, also contained in the ILC Articles, can therefore not be invoked by responsible respondent states. Art 45 deals with the loss of the right to invoke responsibility and holds that "the injured State is to be considered as having, by reason of its conduct, validly acquiesced in the lapse of the claim". Such conduct includes unreasonable delay, as the determining criterion for the lapse of the claim. However, mere lapse of time without a claim being resolved is not, as such, enough to amount to acquiescence, in particular where the injured party does everything it can reasonably do to maintain its claim. [1345] In *Certain Phosphate Lands in Nauru* the ICJ stated that "(...) international law does not lay down any specific time-limit in that regard. It is therefore for the Court to determine in the light of the circumstances of each case whether the passage of time renders an application inadmissible"[1346]. Once a claim has been notified to a respondent state,

---

1343 Ibid.
1344 Slavery: Legacy. The official record from Hansard of the debate initiated by Lord Gifford QC in the House of Lords of the British Parliament on the 14th March 1996 concerning the African reparations, downloaded from: http://www.arm.arc.co.uk/LordsHansard.html (accessed 25.7.2010).
1345 Crawford (2002), 267.
1346 Certain Phosphate Lands in Nauru (Nauru v. Australia), Preliminary Objections, ICJ Reports 1992, 240, para.13.

delay in its prosecution cannot usually be regarded as rendering it inadmissible. We have just seen that deported Africans and their descendants have, incessantly, claimed reparations in one form or another from the very beginnings of transatlantic slavery, but the claims were suppressed by European slavers and states. [1347]

So who could today, in consideration of the legal affirmation of responsibility and the ensuing right to reparation, bring forth this reparations claim? One critical point in that regard is that international law was traditionally occupied only with relations and claims between states and has few considerations and mechanisms for harm suffered by individuals at the hands of governments. As seen in previous parts of this work, historical African states were violated in their rights by the conduct of European enslaver states, but none of them are still in existence today, partly as a consequence of the crime. Furthermore, millions and millions of Africans were violated in their most basic rights through genocidal transatlantic slavery.

The Paris Reparations Agreement was an earmark in that regard since it included also war reparations for stateless and non-repatriable victims of Nazi action, and provided a special reparations pool by liquidating German assets and heirless assets of Nazi victims, transferring proceeds to an international organization tasked with the resettlement of Nazi victims. It was the first legal document to recognize an individual right to redress for state crimes in contemporary European international law.[1348] Legally, neither the state of Israel nor Jewish organizations were entitled to raise claims, since that state did not exist at the time of the events, and Jewish organizations were not bodies recognized under international law. The Paris Reparations Agreement treaty, however, transcended these restrictions.[1349]

In that regard, is also important to acknowledge that the "establishment of the State of Israel is based on biblical claims to that land as the homeland given by God to the Jewish people. It is a claim based on something that happened over two thousand years ago. (...) [T]he same western governments that claim slavery happened too long ago for compensation by people of African descent accept as legitimate the right of European Jews to claim land based on theological interpretations that happened even longer ago."[1350]

Yet, even the recent formulation of the law of state responsibility by the ILC conceptualizes the state as the sole subject of wrongs whose victims are its nationals.[1351] It has not been pertinently clarified in contemporary international law doctrine if such a thing as individual claims to state responsibility exists. That be-

---

1347 Crawford (2002), 268 et seq.
1348 Ludi, Regula (2007). "Historical Reflections on Holocaust Reparations", in: Max du Plessis and Stephen Peté (ed.): Repairing the Past? International Perspectives on Reparations for Gross Human Rights Abuses, Antwerpen/Oxford: Intersentia, 119-144, 125.
1349 Ibid., 128.
1350 Tutu (2003), XVIII.
1351 Falk (2006), 489.

ing so, African unity – culturally and politically on a states level – is fundamental to push the global African reparation claim forward and to get to a position from where it will not only be possible to claim but to take reparations. Now, such African unity will not be easy to achieve given the structural damage brought about by the crime, yet it is not only an imperative but it also is neither illusionary nor an impossibility. In fact, there is a documented tradition of assembling different populations in vast, stable and prosperous entities in Africa. African empires were often of a superficie comparable to that of the whole of Europe, such as Kemet, Kush, Axum, Wagadu, Mali, Kanem, Kongo, or Songhay.[1352] It is highly significant that toponymic and onomastic analyses show a great dispersion of many names of persons and places between the East and West of the continent. One may find the same or very similar names in Senegambia, Cameroun and Ethiopia.[1353] On the other hand, Europe, praising its unity so much these days, is the place where globally the majority of wars and the most murderous wars took place during the past 200 years. [1354] In fact, ethnicity in the sense of tribalism was not a cultural characteristic of the pre-Maafa African past, but was a consciously crafted ideological tradition that was introduced during transatlantic slavery and colonial times by Europeans.[1355]

The International Law Commission in a study defined serious breaches "on a widespread scale of an international obligation of essential importance for safeguarding the human being, such as those prohibiting slavery, genocide and apartheid" as "international crimes" [1356]. In addition, the Commission related the concept of "injured state" to all other states than the offending state if the internationally wrongful act constitutes an international crime. International customary and treaty law also provide that all states can take action against the offending state for *erga omnes* and *ius cogens* violations.[1357] Art. 48 of the ILC Articles holds that all states are entitled to invoke responsibility for breaches of obligations to the international community as a whole. Art. 53 of the Vienna Convention on the Law of Treaties concretizes that a "peremptory norm of general international law is a norm accepted and recognized by the international community of States

1352 Popo, Klah (2010). Histoire des ‚Traites Négrières'. Critique afrocentrée d'une négrophobie académique, Paris: Anibwe, 59f.
1353 Popo, Klah (2010). Histoire des ‚Traites Négrières'. Critique afrocentrée d'une négrophobie académique, Paris: Anibwe, 60.
1354 Soulier, Gérard (1994). L'Europe. Histoire, civilsation, institutions, Paris: Armand Colin.
1355 Reader, John (1998). Africa: A Biography of the Continent, London: Penguin Books, 610.
1356 Commission in Human Rights, Sub-Commission on Prevention of Discrimination and Protection of Minorities, Forty-fifth session (1993). Study concerning the right to restitution, compensation and rehabilitation for victims of gross violations of human rights and fundamental freedoms, Final report submitted by Mr. Theo van Boven, Special Rapporteur, E/CN.4/Sub.2/1993/8,2 July 1993, downloaded from http://www.unhchr.ch/Huridocda/Huridoca.nsf/0/e1b5e2c6a294f7bec1256a5b00361173? Open document (accessed 25.5.2010), 13.
1357 Ibid., 17 et seq.

as a whole as a norm from which no derogation is permitted and which can be modified only by a subsequent norm of general international law having the same character" [1358].

In *Barcelona Traction*, the ICJ concretized that in "view of the importance of the rights involved, all States can be held to have a legal interest in their protection; they are obligations *erga omnes*", and clarified that the outlawing of genocide and principles and rules concerning the basic rights of the human person, including protection from slavery and racial discrimination, were such obligations *erga omnes*.[1359] Thus, theoretically, any state could take up the case of responsibility for transatlantic slavery.

Now, Art. 40 of the ILC Articles, dealing with serious breaches of obligations arising under peremptory norms of general international law, states that a "breach of such an obligation is serious if it involves a gross or systematic failure by the responsible State to fulfil the obligation". Obligations covered by this Article prohibit conduct that threatens the survival of states, people and the most basic human values. There is widespread agreement that at the core of this norm are prohibitions against slavery and the slave trade, genocide, and racial discrimination and apartheid. [1360]

And Art. 41 holds that states "shall cooperate to bring to an end through lawful means any serious breach within the meaning of article 40" and that no "State shall recognize as lawful a situation created by a serious breach within the meaning of article 40, nor render aid or assistance in maintaining that situation." This obligation to cooperate applies to states whether or not they are individually affected by the serious breach. States are thus under obligation not to recognize as lawful situations created by serious breaches in the sense of Article 40, that is for example slavery, genocide and apartheid, and not to render aid or assistance in maintaining such unlawful situations. This does not only refer to the formal recognition of these situations, but also prohibits acts which would imply such recognition. The existence of such an obligation of non-recognition in response to serious breaches of obligations arising under peremptory norms also finds support in international practice and in decisions of the International Court of Justice.[1361] "In particular, all States in such cases have an obligation to cooperate to bring the breach to an end, not to recognize as lawful the situation created by the breach, and not to render aid or assistance to the responsible State in maintaining the situation so created (Art. 40, 41)".[1362] That a number of egregious breaches of fundamental obligations

---

1358 United Nations, Vienna Convention on the Law of Treaties, May 23, 1969, United Nations, Treaty Series, Vol. 1155, 331.
1359 Barcelona Traction, Light and Power Company, Limited, Second Phase (Belgium v. Spain), Judgement of February 5, 1970, ICJ reports 1970, 3.
1360 Crawford (2002), 245 et seq.
1361 Ibid., 250.
1362 Ibid., 192.

require a response such as non-recognition by all states is also reflected in general international law, and includes obligations against genocide, aggression, apartheid and forcible denial of self-determination, constituting wrongs which "shock the conscience of mankind".[1363]

Thus, all states not only could take up the reparations case, they are arguably in a legal obligation to bring the continuing crime of the Maafa to an end, and could see their responsibility engaged if they continue to recognize the continuing serious breaches of international law.

Furthermore, continental and diasporan African states are justified to take counter-measures according to Chapter II of the ILC Articles, not only against Britain, France and other former enslaver nations, but against all European (and other nations) who do not comply with their obligation to bring the continuing crime of the Maafa to an end. Because there is "no requirement that States taking countermeasures are limited to suspension of performance of the same or a closely related obligation" (Art. 49), such counter-measures could include the refusal to make debt payments.[1364] Such proceedings would appear even more appropriate given the facts that not only were industry groups throughout Europe co-dependant on one another and thus on the transatlantic slavery system and the profits it generated, but that even smaller European states such as Sweden and Denmark had colonies.[1365] Many European industries contributed to maintain and continue the system of illegal and genocidal inhumane slavery. "The shipping and railroad industry benefited and profited from the transportation of slaves. The railroad industry utilized slave labor in the construction of rail lines. These transportation industries were dependent upon the manufacturing and raw materials industry to utilize the slaves they shipped. The cotton, tobacco, rice and sugar industries thrived on profits generated from their use of slave labor, and relied upon financial and insurance industries to finance and insure the slaves that they utilized and owned. All industries: raw market, retail, financial, insurance, and transportation, benefited from the reduced costs of slave-produced goods."[1366]

Beyond all of this, it is important to highlight that the legitimacy and legal anchorage of the right to reparation for the massive crime of transatlantic slavery and the Maafa is grounded in fundamental principles of international law that have been recognized in an unbroken line since before the beginnings of the crime. The concrete modalities of how and by whom that basic claim could be lodged today are only details of much more recent international law developments and must as such in no way be considered a hindrance to making the established right prevail.

1363 Ibid., 38.
1364 Ibid., 283.
1365 Peabody, Sue & Grinberg, Keila (2007). Slavery, Freedom, and the Law in the Atlantic World. A Brief History with Documents, Boston/New York: Bedford, 20.
1366 Farmer-Paellmann v. Fleet Boston, Aetna Inc., CSX, in: Raymond A. Winbush (ed.), Should America pay? Slavery and the raging debate on reparations, Amistad, New York, 348-360,356.

If legally due reparations will not be awarded by institutions or mechanisms of international law, they will have to be taken by any means necessary in order to make right and international law prevail. All current perpetrators of the continuing crime of the Maafa, especially western heads of states and leading politicians of ex-enslaver nations that have never desisted from violating international law and human rights of Africans should also be reminded publicly and regularly that one day they may well find themselves on trial for genocide.

VII. Additional Aspects and Developments in Current International Law Strengthen the Legal Force of the Reparations Claim

Now that we have reached the point to see clearly that reparations are legally due, anchored in the fundamental illegality of transatlantic slavery at the time when it was perpetrated, it is also significant to see that additional developments in current international law would, even independently of that affirmative assessment, make a strong case for transatlantic slavery reparations. Some of these developments shall be discussed in this chapter. That we deal with them would not even be necessary, since it has already been elaborated pertinently that transatlantic slavery was illegal at the time of facts and since the problem of non-retroactivity is therefore no decisive aspect in the legal reparations debate and no hindrance to the claim. But since it does no harm to present these additional elements either, we shall take a brief look at them still since they only further highlight the legal appropriateness of the claim.

Generally speaking, scholars like Quéguiner and Villalpando have convincingly argued that when dealing with questions of responsibility and reparations for historic crimes not defined as illegal at their time, but which continue to generate negative consequences for the descendants of the direct victims, it must be legally admissible to subordinate the principle of non-retroactivity of legal norms to still engage the international responsibility of states in the name of the fundamental character currently attributed to certain legal concepts like human rights and the condemnation and repression of genocide.[1367] A similar perspective is expressed in a UN General Assembly resolution (60/147) of December 16, 2005, where it

---

1367 Quequiner, Jean-Francois/Villalpando, Santiago (2004). 'La réparation des crimes de l'histoire: état et perspectives du droit international public contemporain', in: Boisson de Chazournes, Laurence, Jean-François Quéguiner and Santiago Villalpando (ed.): Crimes de l'histoire et réparations: les réponses du droit et de la justice, Brussels: Editions Bruylant, 39-72, 59.

was emphasized that "where so provided for in an applicable treaty or contained in other international legal obligations, statutes of limitations shall not apply to gross violations of international human rights law and serious violations of international humanitarian law which constitute crimes under international law"[1368]. Rosa Amelia Plumelle-Uribe has argued from the text of this Resolution that "the descendants of the victims of the chilliest utilitarian genocide of modern times as well as the indigenous survivors and all the other victims of colonial barbarity are founded in law to demand from the former enslaver and, until recently, colonialist States reparation that is legally linked to crimes against humanity committed against them, the temporal non-limitation of which is recognized by international law"[1369]. Additional arguments such as the importance of the notions of *ius cogens* and *crime against humanity*; the enduring fatal consequences of the crime/continuation of the crime (Maafa) up to this day; and that several European states and the USA have in the last years issued declarations of "regret", would further advocate for an exception to non-retroactivity in this case – if there would be a legal need for such an exception to ground the reparations claim, which there is not because the claim is fundamentally anchored in the illegality of transatlantic slavery.

1. *IUS COGENS*

The prohibition of slavery is today considered part of *ius cogens*. *Ius cogens* is the category of international law consisting of a body of norms recognized as so fundamental to the existence of the international community that they cannot be derogated by states. The Vienna Convention on the Law of Treaties defines *ius cogens*, a "peremptory norm of general international law", as "a norm accepted and recognized by the international community of States as a whole as a norm from which no derogation is permitted and which can be modified only by a subsequent norm of general international law having the same character"[1370]. Such a norm of imperative character obliges the states even without their consent. *Ius cogens* and natural law are based on the same foundation in that they recognize the existence of a certain number of fundamental rules linked to the universal conscience and inherent to any international society worthy of this name. And as we have seen in Chapter II concerning the legal status of slavery, natural law was

---

1368 UN General Assembly Basic Principles and Guidelines on the Right Remedy and Reparation for Victims of Gross Violations of International Human Rights Law and Serious Violations of International Humanitarian Law, resolution adopted by the General Assembly, 16 December 2005, A/RES/60/147.

1369 Plumelle-Uribe (2004), 188 (t.b.a.).

1370 United Nations, Vienna Convention on the Law of Treaties, May 23, 1969, United Nations, Treaty Series, Vol. 1155, 331.

accepted as positive law in the era of transatlantic slavery in both European and African societies.

The imperative character of *ius cogens* originates in the protection of the superior interests of the international society common to all its members, and must therefore be excluded from individual disposal by the states. Thus it serves to prohibit "immoral" or "anti-social" behavior that would be destructive for the international community or its components.[1371] Now, it is acknowledged in international law doctrine that there always exists a "certain" public order, the precise content of which evolves with the level of organization of the society.[1372] It logically follows that this "certain" public international order also existed at the time of transatlantic slavery. Given this utilitarian character of *ius cogens*, it would be hard to think of anything more important for the superior interests of international society than the interdiction of mass murder and genocide. Thus, the Geneva Conventions of 1949 referred in their definition *of ius* cogens to the "laws of humanity and the dictates of the public conscience"[1373] and qualified slavery as "crime against humanity".[1374] The interdiction of genocide is naturally at the core of *ius cogens*, and it is therefore evident that, even if detrimental to the individual economic interests of the European enslaver states, they were bound to respect it and could not rightfully declare its violation as being legal. The consequences for violations of *ius cogens* are particularly severe, leading in any case to the nullity of a contrary legal act.[1375] Thus, the slave codices and other European legislation that aimed to legalize genocidal transatlantic slavery must be considered as having been legally void at any time. This is indeed also confirmed by the refusal of national Parliaments and courts to register these *Codes Noirs* and to administer transatlantic slavery, but rather confirmed the freedom of plaintive Africans.

It is true that a *ius cogens* norm has to be recognized as such by the international community at large, yet this brings us back to the reasoning about the international legal personality of African states and the illegality of genocidal slavery in both Africa and Europe discussed at length in Chapter II. From that assessment it can be concluded that the illegality of genocidal slavery was indeed acknowledged as a fundamental norm of natural law, recognized as such by that international community at large at that time.

Transatlantic slavery was officially recognized as crime against humanity in important legal sources such as the French law of May 21, 2001 or the Durban Declaration, adopted at the United Nations World Conference Against Racism.[1376] Apartheid and slavery are listed as crimes against humanity in the Rome statute

---

1371 Carreau (2007), 89.
1372 Ibid., 93.
1373 Ibid., 88.
1374 Ibid., 92.
1375 Ibid., 87.
1376 Boschiero (2004), 211 et seq.

of the International Criminal Court.

It has been demonstrated pertinently above that transatlantic slavery meets the definition of genocide, such as stipulated in the Convention on the Prevention and Punishment of the Crime of Genocide and accepted by international law doctrine and jurisprudence. We have also seen there that the concept of genocide and its legal suppression are rooted in both *ius cogens* and in the notion of crime against humanity or international crime, and had not been explicitly formulated before the time of the creation of the International Military Tribunal of Nuremberg in 1948. Yet, the Tribunal employed the concept of genocide in the conviction of bringing on point an interdiction that had already existed in international law. It is commonly agreed that the Charter of the Tribunal did not create new law, but really only declared and confirmed international law concepts that had found acceptance over the past centuries.[1377]

Significantly, the Convention against Genocide provides for an exemption to non-retroactivity in so far as it requires member states to pursue authors of genocide for acts realized before the entry-into-force of the Convention. The application of the Convention against Genocide is thus also stipulated for events that antedate it.[1378] In the *Application of the Convention on the Prevention and Punishment of the Crime of Genocide* case, the International Court of Justice validated such a retroactive application of the Convention when it states that "(...) the Court will confine itself to the observation that the Genocide Convention (...) does not contain any clause the object or effect of which is to limit in such manner the scope of its jurisdiction *ratione temporis* (...)"[1379]. The ILC specified in this context that the principle of inter-temporality or non-retroactivity does not apply to the Convention on Genocide, and that the obligation to persecute perpetrators is valid whatever the moment it was committed.[1380]

Although it is the states that are legally responsible for its observation, the Convention really deals with the persecution of individual perpetrators of genocide. This however, only strengthens the argument that non-retroactivity can also recede in the realm of state responsibility. Non-retroactivity in fact has its roots and is indispensable in criminal law, for it serves to protect the individual against arbitrary state power. Penal sanctions and legal consequences established in the

---

1377 Gifford, Anthony. The legal basis of the claim for Reparations, downloaded from http://www.arm.arc.co.uk/legalBasis.html (5.9.2010).

1378 Condorelli, Luigi (2004). ''Conclusions générales'', in: Boisson de Chazournes, Laurence, Jean-François Quéguiner and Santiago Villalpando (ed.): Crimes de l'histoire et réparations: les réponses du droit et de la justice, Brussels: Editions Bruylant, 291-306, 299.

1379 Application of the Convention on the Prevention and Punishment of the Crime of Genocide, Preliminary Objections, ICJ Reports 1996, 595, para. 26.

1380 Brown, Bertram (2004). ''Etat des lieux des droits de l'homme, du droit international humanitaire et du droit international pénal face aux requêtes en 'réparation' des crimes de l'histoire'', in: Boisson de Chazournes, Laurence, Jean-François Quéguiner and Santiago Villalpando (ed.): Crimes de l'histoire et réparations: les réponses du droit et de la justice, Brussels: Editions Bruylant, 73-84, 76.

aftermath of a fact would sabotage confidence in a legal order and would be destructive to liberty and freedom. "The principle of non-retroactivity surely possesses the quality of *jus cogens* in criminal matters"[1381], while it can be repealed for other domains, such as indicated explicitly in intruments of international law, as in Art. 28 of the Vienna Convention on the Law of Treaties. And it is very reasonable that in criminal law it must be indefeasible, leaving no room for exception.[1382] Years spent behind bars or lives wasted in executions cannot be brought back. Scholars have argued however, and rightfully so, that it is only in the realm of individual criminal responsibility that the non-retroactivity demands such strictness while it does not dispose of absolute character in other domains.[1383]

The words of Hans Kelsen, one of the most renowned law scholars and a staunch positivist, should be taken into consideration in that regard. He wrote that the "principle forbidding the enactment of norms with retroactive force as a rule of positive national law is not without many exceptions. Its basis is the moral idea that it is not just to make an individual responsible for an act if he, when performing the act, did not and could not know that his act constituted a wrong. If, however, the act was at the moment of its performance morally, although not legally wrong, a law attaching *ex post facto* a sanction to the act is retroactive only from a legal, not from a moral point of view. Such a law is not contrary to the idea which is at the basis of the principle in question. This is in particular true of an international treaty by which individuals are made responsible for having violated, in their capacity as organs of a State, international law. Morally they were responsible for the violation of international law at the moment when they performed the acts constituting a wrong not only from a moral but also from a legal point of view. The treaty only transforms their moral into a legal responsibility. The principle forbidding *ex post facto* laws is – in all reason – not applicable to such a treaty."[1384]

Thus, given the sense and rootedness of non-retroactivity in criminal law, and that even in that domain exceptions are admissible under certain circumstances, an exemption must also be admissible in the realm of state responsibility in cases of grave human rights violations and genocide, such as transatlantic slavery the legacy of which continues to produce fatal consequences. That is even more accurate since, even in criminal law, the principle became fundamental in Europe's justice systems only in the late 1800's.[1385]

1381 Condorelli (2004), 305.
1382 Ibid., 299.
1383 Ibid.
1384 Kelsen, Hans (1943). Collective and Individual Responsibility in International Law with Particular Regard to the Punsihement of War Criminals, in: California Law Review Nr. 31, 530-546, 544.
1385 Bassiouni (1992), 87.

2. ACTS OF RECOGNITION

In addition, several former European enslaver states have in one form or another expressed their "regrets" for transatlantic slavery in recent years. One example of this is the French law of May 21, 2001 in which France recognizes that "the transatlantic slave trade as well as the trade in the Indian ocean for one part, and slavery for another, perpetrated from the 15th century in the Americas and the Caribbean, in the Indian Ocean and in Europe against African, Amerindian, Malagasy and Indian populations, constitute a crime against humanity"[1386]. In the declaration adopted at the World Conference Against Racism, Racial Discrimination, Xenophobia and Related Intolerance held in Durban in 2001, participating states also acknowledged that "slavery and the slave trade, including the transatlantic slave trade, were appalling tragedies in the history of humanity not only because of their abhorrent barbarism but also in terms of their magnitude, organized nature and especially their negation of the essence of the victims, and further acknowledge that slavery and the slave trade are a crime against humanity and should always have been so, especially the transatlantic slave trade"[1387].

Even though such declarations remain silent on the question of responsibility and reparations, and although words are always chosen very carefully in order to prevent that any legal steps in such a direction could be based on them, such statements may be legally significant. Boschiero has argued that once perpetrator states affirm that transatlantic slavery constitutes a crime against humanity and that it "should always have been so", these affirmations imply a retro-active and voluntary recognition of their responsibility.[1388] Yet, nonetheless the problem remains that western states clearly intended to only "recognize" their responsibility on a moral level. Thus, the Durban Declaration and Program of Action are non-compulsory and highlight "the political obligation" of the states responsible for slavery to negotiate in good faith with the affected people to arrive at a just and legal solution to the question of reparations.[1389] At the Durban Conference, European states also sustained that the present poverty in Africa would be the consequence of several factors, among them colonization, but above all of political instability, wrong development policies and corruption.[1390] Yet, all of these three factors are really only consequences of colonization and the Maafa. In order to guarantee a restrictive interpretation of the Durban Declaration, Canada de-

---

1386 Law n° 2001-434 of May 21, 2001 (JORF/LD 08175), downloaded from www.adminet.com/jo/20010523/JUS9903435L.html (accessed 23.4.2009) (t.b.a.).

1387 Durban Declaration and Program of Action, downloaded from http://www.un-documents.net/durban-d.htm (accessed 4.5.2010).

1388 Boschiero (2004), 256.

1389 Ibid., 259.

1390 Garapon, Antoine (2008). Peut-on réparer l'"histoire? Colonisation, Esclavage, Shoah, Odile Jacob, Paris, 154.

manded to insert a caveat emphasising that a "crime against humanity cannot be persecuted if it was not qualified as such at the time when it was committed". [1391] European states did not present any "apologies" at all at the WCAR, but restricted themselves to admitting "faults".[1392]

However, in view of the exceptional gravity of the crime of transatlantic slavery and its persistent legacy, it cannot be that easy for perpetrator states to shake off legal responsibility by way of unilateral declarations. There is a significant difference between the existence of an illicit fact on one hand, and the responsibility and legal consequences that this fact may entail, on the other. Now, the legal scope and effect of recognition is limited to the stipulation of facts.[1393] The recognizing party does not have the power to determine unilaterally the legal consequences of the recognized facts. Would it therefore be possible to interpret such declarations in a way that could make them a basis for reparation claims? To answer this question, legal doctrine and practice need to be scrutinized.

Unilateral acts of a state are not subjected to any constraint of form.[1394] Recognition can even be given tacitly.[1395] The International Court of Justice pronounced in the *Nuclear Tests* case that "it is well recognized that declarations made by way of unilateral acts, concerning legal or factual situations, may have the effect of creating legal obligations"[1396]. Yet in the same ruling the Court also pronounced that a declaration has to express such an intention of submitting to an obligation. The interpretative search of intention in a declaration is the task of the judge who should seek inspiration from the context and circumstances of the public unilateral act.[1397]

The Permanent Court of International Justice had stated earlier that "in any case a neutrality order, issued by an individual State, could not prevail over the provisions of the Treaty of Peace"[1398]. Primacy was accorded to the peace treaty over a unilateral act. In the same vein, the already mentioned international legal instruments and principles against slavery and genocide, most of them *ius cogens*, must weigh heavy in the interpretation of any such unilateral act of recognition by a former enslaver state.

In the interpretation of unilateral acts international jurisprudence has often referred to certain elementary principles of humanity and justice. One famous

1391 Hazan, Pierre (2004). 'Durban : le repli victimaire', in: Boisson de Chazournes, Laurence, Jean-François Quéguiner and Santiago Villalpando (ed.): Crimes de l'histoire et réparations : les réponses du droit et de la justice, Brussels: Editions Bruylant, 277-290, 287.
1392 Ibid.
1393 Carreau (2007), 220.
1394 Hummer/Neuhold/Schreuer (1997), 100.
1395 Ibid.
1396 Nuclear Tests (New Zealand v. France), Judgement of December 20, 1974, ICJ Reports 1974, p. 457, 19.
1397 Carreau (2007), 224.
1398 The SS 'Wimbledon' (UK v. Germany), Judgement of August 17, 1923, PCIJ Series A, No.1, 29.

case is *Cayugas Indians* (1926) where the tribunal invoked "general and universally recognized principles of justice and fair dealing" and sustained that "the claim of the Canadian Cayugas (...) is founded in the elementary principle of justice that requires us to look at the substance and to not stick in the bark of the legal form"[1399]. In the *Corfu Channel* case, the International Court of Justice based its decision on "certain general and well recognized principles, namely: elementary considerations of humanity"[1400].

Denis Diderot had written in 1765 in his famous *Encyclopédie* that transatlantic slavery was against "natural laws and all laws of human nature"[1401]. He explicitly noted that in transatlantic slavery, Africans were not enslaved in conformity with the international legal modalities of war captivity, and that the criminal African princes who sold them had no right to do so, because they were not their property. For this assessment of the fundamental illegality of transatlantic slavery, Diderot also referred to the "laws of humanity and equity". And these same principles of humanity and equity are still cited today by courts in their decisions.

Thus, in the *North Sea Continental Shelf* cases, the ICJ invoked principles of fairness and justice, and specified that the application of a legal rule must be based on prescriptions of fairness.[1402] What the Court proclaimed in the *Continental Shelf* affair (Libya v. Tunisia) is most important in the context of reparations for-transatlantic slavery:

"The result of the application of equitable principles must be equitable. (...) It is (...) the result which is predominant; the principles are subordinate to the goal. The equitableness of a principle must be assessed in the light of its usefulness for the purpose of arriving at an equitable result. It is not every such principle which is in itself equitable; it may acquire this quality by reference to the equitableness of the solution. The principles to be indicated by the Court have to be selected according to their appropriateness for reaching an equitable result. From this consideration it follows that the term 'equitable principles' cannot be interpreted in the abstract; it refers back to the principles and rules which may be appropriate in order to achieve an equitable result. (...) Equity as a legal concept is a direct emanation of the idea of justice. The Court whose task is by definition to administer justice is bound to apply it. (...); the legal concept of equity is a general principle directly applicable as law. Moreover, when applying positive international law, a court may choose among several possible interpretations of the law the one which appears, in the light of the circumstances of the case, to be closest to the requirements of justice."[1403]

1399 Carreau (2007), 297; see also http://untreaty.un.org/cod/riaa/cases/vol_VI/173-190_Cayuga.pdf.
1400 Corfu Channel case (UK and Northern Ireland v. Albania), Judgement of April 4, 1949, ICJ Reports 1949, p. 4, 22.
1401 Diderot, Dénis/d'Alembert, Jean Lerond (1765). Encyclopédie ou Dictionnaire raisonné, Vol. 16, Paris: Briasson, 532 et seq.
1402 Carreau (2007), 298 et seq.
1403 Continental Shelf (Tunisia v. Libya), Judgement of February 24, 1982, ICJ Reports 1982, p. 18.

Following the logic of the reasoning of the Court, it would seem evident that, given the particular gravity and monstrosity of the crime of transatlantic slavery and its enduring legacy, a categorical denial of legal responsibility and reparations, crouching behind a formal argument of "legality" and non-retroactivity would stand in blatant contradiction to the "legal concept of equity", "directly applicable as law" that the Court "is bound to apply". This reasoning by the most important contemporary institution of international jurisprudence must be included in the evaluation of all legal arguments concerning transatlantic slavery reparations, and thus also in the interpretation of the unilateral acts of "recognition" and their legal consequences. In that respect, it should well be possible to derive some recognition of legal responsibility from these declarations of former enslaver states, providing an additional basis and fuel for the reparations claim.

3. EVEN AN EXCEPTION TO NON-RETROACTIVITY ADMISSIBLE IN THIS CASE

What has just been assessed also needs to be reflected within the context that norms prohibiting slavery today are of imperative character and their violation is unambiguously recognized as crime against humanity. We also know that the disastrous legacy of genocidal transatlantic slavery still weighs on the lives of millions and millions. Former enslaver states have recognized a certain degree of responsibility[1404]. Legal principles of justice, equity and humanity have repeatedly been relied upon as basis for decisions by the highest institutions of international jurisprudence. These arguments and the ratio of the principle of non-retroactivity clearly reveal that this principle does not stand in the way of transatlantic slavery reparations. This view is also supported by an international legal practice that arrived at just and innovative legal solutions, overcoming eventual flaws of the positive law, when faced with manifest and insupportable injustices. Ingenious solutions dealing with the same problem of inter-temporality were successfully found in a series of other cases. Yet the dominant opinion of reparation negationists holds that those examples would have no repercussion for transatlantic slavery reparations because there would be no conclusive system of precedents in international law. Although it is true that international law knows no system of precedents in a strict sense, the decisions of international jurisdictions still leave their print mark. After all, jurisprudence is listed as a subsidiary means for the determination of rules of law in the inventory of international legal sources, that is, Article 38 of the Statute of the International Court of Justice. So whenever there was and is the will to do so, satisfactory legal responses to serious injustices

---

1404 Boschiero (2004), 256.

were and can be found through adequate interpretation of international law.[1405]

After WWII, the gravity and specificity of the Nazi crimes rendered the application of the then accepted legal principles of international responsibility morally inadequate. These crimes raised specific legal problems, especially regarding persons of Jewish origin and German nationality. A great number of persecuted people had been German citizens at the time of the facts and could therefore not benefit from the protection of a victor state. The state of Israel, representing Jewish interests, did not yet exist at the time of the Shoa.[1406] However, once it was recognized that the standard principles of international responsibility were inadequate to deal with Nazi crimes, it was possible to surpass and adapt them so that justice could be done.

The judgements of the Nuremberg tribunal made it clear that the principle of non-retroactivity must not hinder the persecution of crimes that were "criminal according to the general principles of law recognized by the community of nations". [1407] More recently, the UN-Tribunals for ex-Yugoslavia and Rwanda continued to follow this path by convicting individuals of war crimes for acts committed in armed conflicts that had no international character and were therefore not wars in a strict legal sense. This approach has been criticized by certain jurists as departing from existing international law. Yet the Security Council and the Tribunals maintained that international law must adapt to contemporary requirements. All of this is further testimony to the fact that international law disposes of possibilities to provide a legal basis for state responsibility and reparations for transatlantic slavery.[1408] At the same time these examples also indicate the absolute necessity of volition on the part of the international community.

The final Report of the Special Reporter of the Commission of Human Rights of the United Nations, entitled "The right to restitution, compensation and rehabilitation for victims of grave violations of human rights and fundamental freedoms", states that "the application and interpretation of these principles and guidelines must be consistent with internationally recognized human rights law and be without any adverse distinction founded on grounds such as race, colour, gender, sexual orientation, age, language, religion, political or religious belief, national, ethnic or social origin, wealth, birth, family or other status, or disability "[1409]. This

---

1405 Boisson de Chazournes, Laurence/Heathcote, Sarah (2004). ''Mise en œuvre de la réparation des crimes de l'histoire: une possible (ré)conciliation des temps passés, présents et futurs ?'', in: Boisson de Chazournes, Laurence, Jean-François Quéguiner and Santiago Villalpando (ed.): Crimes de l'histoire et réparations: les réponses du droit et de la justice, Brussels: Editions Bruylant, 99-130, 130.
1406 Ibid., 108 et seq.
1407 Jos (2000), 141.
1408 Brown (2004), 78.
1409 The right to restitution, compensation and rehabilitation for victims of gross violations of human rights and fundamental freedoms,Final report of the Special Rapporteur, Mr. M. Cherif Bas-

approach was also embraced in the resolution adopted during the preparation of the Durban Conference by the Sub-Commission on the Promotion and Protection of Human Rights in which it was stipulated that states which reduced to slavery and colonized other people have a "historic responsibility", and that this responsibility "should be the subject of solemn and formal recognition and reparation"[1410]. Taking all these aspects and developments of international law and the ratio and conceptualization of non-retroactivity into consideration, we see that this principle is no obstacle for transatlantic slavery reparations at all.

In fact, the claim for transatlantic slavery reparations can be buttressed by so many tenets of international law and documents by International Organizations that we could fill another book with them. Nontheless, some of the more important ones should be briefly mentioned here. One is the UN Basic Principles and Guidelines on the Right to a Remedy and Reparation for Victims of Gross Violations of International Human Rights Law, where it reads that,

"there is an obligation on States to respect, ensure respect for, and enforce the norms of both international human rights law and humanitarian law. These norms are contained in customary international law, as well as in the treaties to which a particular State is a party. States are obliged to prevent violations; to investigate any violations which do occur and, where appropriate, take action against the violator (...); to provide victims with equal and effective access to justice; to provide appropriate remedies to victims; and to provide for or facilitate reparation to victims. (...) Where there has been a violation of internationally recognized rights, a State has responsibility to make just and adequate reparation to all persons within the offending State. Reparation should respond to the needs and wishes of the victims and be proportionate to the gravity of the violations and the resulting harm. It should include restitution, compensation, rehabilitation, satisfaction and guarantees of non-repetition. In addition to providing reparation to individuals, States should make adequate provision for collective reparations for groups of victims and special measures should be taken to afford opportunities for self-development and advancement to groups who, as a result of human rights violations, were denied such opportunities".[1411]

Again we see how very well founded in international law the claim for reparations is.

---

siouni, submitted in accordance with Commission resolution 1999/33, downloaded from http://www. unhchr.ch/Huridocda/Huridoca.nsf/0/42bd1bd544910ae3802568a20060e21f/$FILE/G0010236.doc (accessed 16.4.2011).

1410 Recognition of responsibility and reparation for massive and flagrant violations of human rights which constitute crimes against humanity and which took place during the period of slavery, of colonialism and wars of conquest, Sub-Commission on Human Rights resolution 2001/1 E/CN.4/ SUB.2/RES/2001/1, August 6, 2001, downloaded from http://www.unhchr.ch/Huridocda/Huridoca. nsf/(Symbol)/E.CN.4.SUB.2.RES.2001.1.En?Opendocument (accessed 28.3.2010).

1411 Peté/Du Plessis (2007), 13 et seq.

The International Convention on the Elimination of All Forms of Racial Discrimination prohibits both purposive and intentional discrimination. When discrimination happens, its Article 2 paragraph 2 stipulates that "States parties shall, when the circumstances so warrant, take, in the social, economic, cultural and other fields, special and concrete measures to ensure the adequate development and protection of certain racial groups or individuals belonging to them, for the purpose of guaranteeing them the full and equal enjoyment of human rights and fundamental freedoms"[1412]. Given the systematic nature of the violation of law that transatlantic slavery constituted and of the legacy it entails, the only way to fully realize this obligation is through comprehensive reparation. It is crucial to never forget that African people globally are not only descendants of those deported, enslaved, killed and violated in the foundational crime of transatlantic slavery who suffer from its legacy, but are also at the same time themselves victims of the continuing crime of the Maafa. According to the "Basic Principles and Guidelines on the Right to a Remedy and Reparation for Victims of Violations of International Human Rights and Humanitarian Law", a "person is 'a victim' where, as a result of acts or omissions that constitute a violation of international human rights or humanitarian law norms, that person, individually or collectively, suffered harm, including physical or mental injury, emotional suffering, economic loss, or impairment of that person's fundamental legal rights".[1413] We have seen that transatlantic slavery was at all times illegal and contrary to historical contemporary law systems that protected what is today conceptualized as "human rights", and that African people globally are still suffering harm from that crime, physically and mentally. The Basic Principles and Guidelines hold that victims must get (a) access to justice; (b) reparation for harm suffered; and (c) access the factual information concerning the violations. Furthermore they state that in "cases where the State or Government under whose authority the violation occurred is no longer in existence, the State or Government successor in title should provide reparation to the victims".[1414] Thus, even potential internal re-organization of European perpetrator states or state succession is not an obstacle to transatlantic slavery reparations.

In that regard also needs to be considered "the fact that the responsibility of the State continues has been used against African States in the payment of debts accumulated by previous and illegitimate regimes. The clearest and most recent example is that of South Africa, where the majority government is now paying the debts for loans taken by the apartheid regime. The nationalist government of South Africa used many of the loans it received to bolster its ability to oppress

---

1412 UN General Assembly, International Convention on the Elimination of All Forms of Racial Discrimination, December 21, 1965, United Nations, Treaty Series, vol. 660, 195.
1413 Basic Principles and Guidelines on the Right to a Remedy and Reparation for Victims of Violations of International Human Rights and Humanitarian Law, UN Commission on Human Rights, Fifty-sixth session, E/CN.4/2000/62, January 18, 2000, downloaded from http://www.unhchr.ch/Huridoc-da/Huridoca.nsf/0/42bd1bd544910ae3802568a20060e21f/$FILE/G0010236.doc (accessed 12.4.2010).
1414 Ibid.

black South Africans, yet today it is those who fought against apartheid who are called upon to repay those debts."[1415] Present-day African states are forced to take responsibility for debts that colonizer states accrued for their better exploitation although they had not even been existent then. There is therefore no intelligible reason why European colonizer and enslaver states should not take responsibility for their own acts, even if their internal organization should have changed, such as with France which is today constituted as the Fifth Republic and was a monarchy in slavery times.

4. UNJUST ENRICHMENT

Although the claim for reparations is basically grounded in the illegality of genocidal transatlantic slavery, it may also be possible to further anchor it in the cause of unjust enrichment. Generally speaking, compensation for unjust enrichment may be due for injurious consequences of conduct which is not necessarily prohibited by international law.[1416] The law of unjust enrichment is not expressly defined in international law, but it has its place in many national legal systems and as such can be said to constitute a general principle of international law.[1417] The late great Dudley Thompson, former foreign minister and ambassador of Jamaica, defined it as such that "in law if a party unlawfully enriches himself by wrongful acts against another, then the party so wronged is entitled to recompense. There have been some 15 cases in which the highest tribunals including the International Court at The Hague have awarded large sums as reparations based on this law."[1418] Sometimes, it may even be sufficient for a claim of unjust enrichment that the party bringing the suit has a better claim to the disputed benefit. Now, in the United States, for example, chattel slavery was maintained from 1619 to 1865, and was followed by another century of legislated racial discrimination. The legacy of transatlantic slavery and global apartheid are still in effect. "This overwhelming oppression of one group of humans by another allowed some to create wealth, while the oppressed group was first forbidden and then harshly constrained from accumulating any wealth. These uncontroverted facts meet the legal definition of unjust enrichment (...)."[1419] Descendants of former slave owners and indeed "white" people as such have, generally speaking, an enormous economic advantage over the majority of those who are descendants of enslaved Africans and

---

1415 Tutu, Nontombi (2003). 'Foreword', in: Raymond A. Winbush (ed.): Should America pay? Slavery and the raging debate on reparations, XV-XIX, XVIII.
1416 Crawford (2002), 76.
1417 Schreuer, Christoph (1974). Unjustified enrichment in international law, in: AJCL Vol. 22, 281–301.
1418 Robinson (2000), 221.
1419 Van Dyke (2003), 58 et seq.

continental Africans whose continent was systematically devasted over centuries, an advantage that can be linked directly to the wealth accumulated from the labor of the enslaved and to the oppression that continued thereafter.

Unjust enrichment was also a major legal cause in Jewish reparation claims after WWII.

"The claimants who signed the Agreement in September 1952 were the State of Israel, on behalf of the half million victims of the Nazis who had found refuge in its borders, and the Conference on Jewish Material Claims against Germany, on behalf of the victims of Nazi persecution who had immigrated to countries other than Israel and of the entire Jewish people entitled to global indemnification for property that had been left heirless. (...) Much of the impetus behind the Jewish demand for group compensation was the realization that, because so many of the Nazis' Jewish victims had perished, the new German State would reap the material benefits of Nazi crimes. Like abandoned Japanese property on the West Coast which escheated to the State and was auctioned off, heirless Jewish property in Germany provided yet another classic example of unjust enrichment."[1420]

The same, at a significantly greater level of unjust enrichment, is true for transatlantic slavery.

European states have continuously and criminally appropriated vast material wealth in the form of labor and resources as well as cultural artefacts from Africa and have unjustly enriched themselves from transatlantic slavery, colonialism and neo-colonialism, perpetuating poverty, disease and death of Africans globally. The cause of unjust enrichment therefore provides a further legal basis for transatlantic slavery reparations.

We have seen that the claim can be pertinently based on so many causes – illegality at the time of facts, recognition, principles of equity, and unjust enrichment. It is a very solid legal case, as solid as a legal claim can get. Yet since nothing in international relations, including international law, moves without force and power, it remains indispensable to build serious people's power around the knowledge about this legally sound claim. For as the great Marcus Mosiah Garvey was right to say, "if we must have justice, we must be strong; if we must be strong, we must come together; if we must come together, we can only do so through the system of organization .... Let us not waste time in breathless appeals to the strong while we are weak, but lend our time, energy and effort to the accumulation of strength among ourselves by which we will voluntarily attract the attention of others."[1421]

Therefore the next chapter will deal with aspects of popular consciousness about reparations since consciousness is at the base of any effective organization.

1420 Westley, Robert (2003). "Many Billions Gone: Is It Time to Reconsider the Case for Black Reparations", in: Raymond A. Winbush (ed.): Should America pay? Slavery and the raging debate on reparations, New York: Amistad, 109-134, 120 et seq.
1421 Marcus Garvey cited in: Tafari, Jabulani I. (1996). A Rastafari View of Marcus Mosiah Garvey, Florida: Greatcompany Inc., 40f.

VIII. Popular Legal Consciousness & Reparation

Thus, this following chapter is less focused on the strict legal appraisal of the reparations claim, but rather deals with aspects of popular legal consciousness regarding transatlantic slavery reparations. To combine the two approaches is useful because in international law, even more so than in the national legal field and in life in general, nothing moves by itself only because a claim is well substantiated. Power is always decisive to get things going. In the case of reparations for transatlantic slavery, there is currently no African, continental or diasporan, state or other entity that politically would be in the position to take up the case and to actually push it forward on a global level. In fact each and every single currently constituted state is set up by western imperial design or modelled after it. As such, they all seem a priori unfit to represent the legitimate African interests behind the reparations claim.[1422] Yet this situation of powerlessness on the international parquet is part of the damage brought about by transatlantic slavery that would itself need to be addressed through reparations. Given this vicious circle, the movement for reparation has to build on people's power. As UNESCO's Ali Moussa Iye sustained at a public round-table at which I was also participating, the problem of reparations is really not a legal problem, it is a political problem to which a political solution must be found. Though I do agree with that, I also think that the legal case for reparations can help birth the political solution, and may indeed be necessary to facilitate getting to such a political solution.

International law scholar Lassa Oppenheim observed that the balance of power is "an indispensable condition of the very existence of International Law"[1423]. Thus, as stressed by the African Reparations Movement (ARM-UK),
"Unless our struggle for Reparations leads to the Pan-Africanist revolutionary conscientization, organization, and mobilization of the broad masses of African people throughout the continent and the diaspora to achieve, first and foremost, their definitive emancipation from the impeding vestiges of colonialism and the still enslaving bonds of present-day neo-colonialism, to smash the yoke of White

---

1422 Ball (2011), 28.
1423 Oppenheim, Lassa (1912). International Law, Vol.1, London: Longmans, Green & Co., 193.

racist supremacy and utterly destroy the mental and physical stranglehold of Eurocentrism upon Africans at home and abroad (...), we shall have no power to back our claim for restitution and to give us the necessary force of coercion to make the perpetrators of the heinous crimes against us to honour the obligations of even the best fashioned letter (...) of International Law."[1424]

Since this assessment is all too true, it is high time to put in extra efforts to build people's power and knowledge for reparations. Some Shoa reparations claims were settled only very recently. One survivor of Auschwitz asked, "Why did it take the German nation 60 years to engage the morals of the most brutal form of death, death through work?"[1425]. Now, that reparation process had been primarily driven by moral and political pressures while law took on a facilitating role.[1426] The lesson for the global African reparation struggle is that people's and political pressure needs to be mounted at every level; politically, culturally and legally. And law, also in the sense of a legal awareness of the right to reparation, has its role to fulfil in this. Nothing moves without power. The accuracy of this assessment was again showcased at the occasion of the rendition of an Advisory Opinion by the ICJ of the Israeli Wall. "As the 2004 Advisory opinion on the legal statues of the Israeli security wall clearly reaffirmed, there does exist in international law a well-established entitlement for the victim of legal wrongs to appropriate reparations. But between the affirmation of the legal right/duty and its satisfaction there exists a huge contextual gap. In this instance, Israel, backed by the US government, immediately repudiated the World Court decision, and the prospects of compliance are nil. The international legal standard is authoritative and context-free, but its implementation is context-dependent."[1427] It is essential to build people's power, and to do so efficiently it is necessary to analyze the emergence and development of consciousness in that regard.

While doing archive and library research in Jamaica and "French" Guiana for this book, I had many everyday encounters with people while using public transport, waiting in cashier lines or simply walking the streets. It is these encounters that led me to a series of observations concerning the state of consciousness about the right to reparation among people in Jamaica and "French" Guiana, who are in both countries majorily descendants of Africans captured and deported during transatlantic slavery. In both countries, many people asked me what brought me to their respective country. Yet, when I responded that I was there to do legal research work for reparations, I got highly divergent reactions in both places, respectively. In Jamaica, it was mostly silence, maybe a "yeah" or "alright", while

---

1424 Affiong/Klu (1993), 3.
1425 Falk, Richard (2006). "Reparations, International Law, and Global Justice", in: Pablo de Greiff (ed.): The Handbook of Reparations, Oxford: Oxford University Press, 478-503,493.
1426 Ibid.
1427 Ibid., 491.

in "French" Guiana people at first showed more positive reactions and sometimes even thanked me. One minibus driver regularly had me as a passenger without accepting that I pay the fare because he appreciated that work so much.

Given the just described decisiveness of power in international law and the fact that I am convinced that reparations for transatlantic slavery are not only legally due, but also indispensable to bring back a much needed balance in international relations, indispensable for the continued existence of human life on this our planet, I acknowledged that it is necessary to embark on a legal anthropological research that aims to identify factors that make people in a certain community or area have or not have a consciousness of their right to reparation. After having stayed in Jamaica for almost four months and in "French" Guiana for one-and-a-half months for library and archive work and thereby making the just mentioned observations, I decided that it was necessary to go back again to both locations to find out more about the (legal) reparations consciousness of the people.

In that small research, I aimed to give special consideration to the dialectical relationship between the scholarly investigation and affirmation of a legal claim, and the emergence and development of legal consciousness. As already mentioned, the latter is indispensable for the realization of any legal steps. This assessment is of universal validity, yet carries special importance when dealing with reparation for transatlantic slavery, since the dominant legal and political opinion holds that there would be no right to reparation for this most massive crime against humanity. This hegemonic point of view has unfortunately deeply impacted thought and action of the descendants of the original victims and heirs to the legacy of the crime.

Before proceeding further, it seems expedient at this point to let the reader know that when I came to Jamaica and "French" Guiana I had already been researching the topic intensively for two years. By that time I had gotten a fair overview of the relevant legal and historical materials and knew definitely that transatlantic slavery had been illegal at the time when it was perpetrated, that legal responsibility could thus be established and that reparations are therefore legally due.

1. SOME BACKGROUND INFORMATION AND FACTS ABOUT JAMAICA AND "FRENCH" GUIANA

The island of Jamaica is located in the Caribbean Sea between Cuba and Haiti. "French" Guiana is situated on the northern Atlantic coast of South America, neighboring Brazil and Surinam. Both are countries with a population majority of descendants of Africans captured and deported within the transatlantic slavery system. In "French" Guiana there remains a minority population of indigenous inhabitants (5-10%), whereas they have been totally wiped out in Jamaica by the European aggression. "French" Guiana also features a small minority of South-east Asian immigrants who were transplanted there by the French following their wars in South-east Asia.[1428] It has a population of about 229,000 on 83,534 km2, while there are 2,847,232 people living in Jamaica whose much smaller territory accounts for 10,991 km2. Half of the population of "French" Guiana lives in the capital city Cayenne while Kingston, Jamaica's capital, accounts for about one-fourth of the population.

The people of Jamaica fought hard first for emancipation from slavery, then for independence from Britain, which they attained in 1962, though Jamaica still remains part of the Commonwealth with the British queen as head of state. There was also a growing independence movement in "French" Guiana, but it was crushed and some of its leaders killed or deported by France in the 1970s.[1429] We will come back to this below. The status of "French" Guiana was changed by France from a colony to a département in 1946, and the French Guianese became, at least on paper, French citizens. As such they have access to French social security and so on. However, the GPD per capita is only at about 14,204 €, thus the highest in South America, but only 47% of that of metropolitan France. Most things, from telecommunication to transport to food items, are significantly more expensive than in metropolitan France, partly because French enterprises or individuals have a quasi-monopoly on the import business, embedded in structures that are traceable back to transatlantic slavery and colonialism. High unemployment is another major problem, figuring at about 20% to 30%. The Jamaican GPD is significantly lower, slightly varying around $5,000, all while life is rather expensive there, even basic food stuffs, and this state of affairs can also be accounted to the legacy of transatlantic slavery and the perduring structural violence of the Maafa. Many people also work in precarious and self-employed situations, such as street vending and hustling.

Both Jamaica and "French" Guiana are infamous for their high levels of violence. Jamaica has one of the world's highest incidences of murder, some even say the highest in relative figures, with 1,428 people murdered in 2010.[1430] Though not reaching nearly that level of violence, "French" Guiana still has the highest murder rate of any French department (about 40 people for 100,000 killed in 2010). Although officially a part of France, I have seen ghetto slums there that look the same as those in Jamaica. Houses and dwellings are constructed from wasted

---

1428 Französisch-Guayana (Wikipedia), download from http://de.wikipedia.org/wiki/Franz%C3%B-6sisch-Guayana (accessed 13.10.2011).

1429 Interview Max (entrepreneur & activist, Saint-Laurent-du-Maroni/F.Guiana, 24.9.2011); Interview Laurent (police officer, Cayenne/F.Guiana, 18.9.2011).

1430 Wingall, Mark (2011). Why has Jamaica's crime rate fallen, downloaded from http://www.jamaicaobserver.com/columns/Why-has-Jamaica-s-crime-rate-fallen_8329778 (accessed 10.10.2011).

wood and cardboard, built very close to one another, with no canalization or run-ning water. I was told that most inhabitants of such settlements are Guyanese, Brazilian, Haitian or others, but there are also "French" Guianese citizens living in such dwellings.

Most streets in Cayenne have no pedestrian sidewalks and are narrowly con-structed. Where there remains a small weeds-strip beside the road, it is normally plastered with glass splinters. This situation seems rather dangerous for children on their way to school. I asked some people and children and they confirmed this; there are many accidents. If a child is hurt or even dies, there is not much talk about it. The public apparently has gotten too habituated to this situation. As for the glass, it could be said that it is the responsibility of the people not to throw away glass like that. However, public rubbish bins are non-existent in most parts and since France is still in charge of its department colony, it should not only provide broader roads and sidewalks, but also trash cans. Yet France makes 1 billion euros per year with the Kourou Space Center in Guiana from which many European states launch their telecommunication satellites, while telecommunica-tion remains incredibly expensive for the Guianese people, and local Internet and mobile phone connections of bad quality.[1431]

2. REPARATIONS GROUNDINGS WITH MY BROTHERS AND SISTERS

The reasonings with people on reparations consciousness were built on loosely structured interviews. "Can you please tell me a bit about what you think about reparations?" served as the standard opening question. It always brought to light interesting information, in one way or another. Even if people first did not know what I was talking about, or refused to talk about the subject which happened rarely, such behavior carried valuable information. As Wolcott stated: "Interview-ing is not all that difficult, but interviewing in which people tell you how they really think about things you are interested in learning, or how they think about the things that are important to them, is a delicate art. My working resolution to the dilemma of assessing what informants say is to recognize that they are always telling me *something*. My task is to figure out what that *something* might be."[1432] If people's responses showed that they were familiar with reparations, whether as an explicit concept or only from the content matter, I subsequently asked, "What do you think reparations could be?" Usually a general reasoning about their feel-

---

1431 Interview Stenli (entrepreneur, Cayenne/F. Guiana, 22.9.2011).
1432 Kidder, Robert L. (2002). "Exploring Legal Culture in Law-Avoidance Societies", in: June Starr and Mark Goodale (ed.): Practicing Ethnography in Law. New Dialogues, Enduring Methods, New York: Palgrave Macmillan, 87-107, 91.

ings and thoughts about reparations and how they link reparations to their lives, ensued. During the conversations, I also asked, "What would you say if you heard that reparations are legally due to you/Jamaica/global Africa? Would you support a movement that sincerely works for that?" I also took an effort to guide our talks in order to perceive whether people included continental Africa in their conceptualization of who should get reparations, and, in Jamaica if they made a connection between the catastrophic situations in neighboring Haiti that had just been shook by the devastating earthquake and the need for reparations.

Just a few months earlier, the Jamaican government had initiated the Jamaica National Commission on Reparations whose task it was to study the feasibility of reparations and assess attitudes among the population through the holding of public meetings across the country.[1433] I therefore also asked whether people had heard of this Commission, what opinion they had of it, and if they thought that such initiatives were fit to advance the cause of reparations. Subsequently, I inquired whether people thought that cultural movements such as reggae (which features the demand for reparation in many lyrics, mostly in the concrete modality of repatriation) contribute to sensibilize and advance the cause of reparations. To conclude, and in order to get a better appreciation of the information brought forth during the conversations, I asked people to tell me a bit about their lives in general and about what was important to them. Finally, after having conducted a few such reasonings, I began to ask whether people went to church. This last question came about through empirical observation, because I had come to remark during the first conversations that there was a negative correlation between church adherence and reparations consciousness.

I had first aspired to record the conversations, but soon again desisted from that idea because people either outright told me that they did not want their statements recorded or showed great reluctance to answer once I put my dictaphone before them. I found it most beneficial to engage in normal talk with my reasoning partners, taking a few notes during the conversation when necessary, and then after each interview immediately searched a quiet corner where I would write down all important information I had retained.

3. THEORETICAL BACKGROUND

Research into legal consciousness has a well-established tradition in socio-legal

---

1433 I could accompany the Commission to some of these public meetings on invitation of Anthony Gifford and the late Prof. Barry Chevannes. I also assisted the Commission with legal advice on the subject.

study.[1434] It started in the 1960s and 70s with the observation that persons of low status and income were treated unequally by judges and other actors in national legal systems. Scholars assessed among the main reasons for this that poor people did not perceive of themselves as fully-fledged rights-bearing citizens, and that there prevailed a lack of relevant legal knowledge and a general sense of "power-lessness" or resignation among them. [1435]

More recent analysis has shown that anthropological research about identi-ties can have concrete consequences on a legal situation and thus on the lives of people. One example of this is the research of Hoffmann French, who has worked in north-eastern Brazil with two neighboring and related communities that have come to define themselves as Indigenous and Black, respectively, over the years even though they all descend from the same African, Indigenous and European ancestors, and are not distinguishable by exterior features. Each community, first the Indigenous, then later the Black, was recognized by a different federal gov-ernmental agency. In the 1990s, the process of self-identification as Black and descendant of *quilombo*[1436] survivors was triggered by legal changes in the con-stitution that recognized such descendants of *quilombo* communities as definite owners of the land they were living on.[1437] Just as with the people who had be-come the Xoco, that is the Indigenous community, the residents of neighboring Mocambo, realized that the use of the new *quilombo* clause in the constitution, which brought with it the possibility of land ownership, also meant reconsider-ing racial self-identification. The ensuing transformation of self-identification of Mocambo's residents was fostered through a series of legal categories, which il-lustrated that identities may be revised as laws are invoked and rights are put into practice. [1438] The residents found that the struggle for land came to define itself by new categories that valorized being Black.[1439] Anthropologists were involved in these developments through the compilation of expertise about the identities of communities. Also participating were liberation theology priests who highlighted to the people that an identification with their Indigenous or African roots could have concrete legal and, in consequence also, materially positive consequences for them. It is important to note that the involved anthropologists sustained that racial categories are always social constructs, yet the courts recognized these opt-ed-for identities. The courts acknowledged that self-identification and a lifestyle

---

1434 McCann, Michael (2006). "On Legal Consciousness: A Challenging Analytical Tradition", in: Benjamin Fleury-Steiner and Laura Beth Nielsen (ed.): The new civil rights research: a constitutive approach, Aldershot: Ashgate Publishing, IX- XXiX, iX.
1435 Ibid., X et seq.
1436 Quilombo is the term for Maroon (Africans who liberated themselves from slavery by running away) settlements in Brazil.
1437 Hoffmann French, Jan (2009). Legalizing Identities. Becoming Black or Indian in Brazil's North-east, Richmond: University of North Carolina Press, XI.
1438 Ibid., 78 et seq.
1439 Ibid., 99 et seq.

that differs from the social norm are the decisive points.[1440] That people develop a consciousness of their rights is always based on a certain identity. How they conceive their identity may mobilize them to get legally active. Observation and interviews cannot be separated from their context, but influence this context and the subject of inquiry itself. As such, knowledge generation is always a political process, whether one likes it or not. [1441]

These developments in Brazil draw the lesson for the reparations struggle that Black people need to identify as African in order to be able to really rally powerfully behind the demand for global African reparation. It is essential to realize that the deported people were deliberately robbed of their African identity. This was done through a thorough and systematic denigration of everything African; through a net of laws and practices that forbade the use of African languages, spirituality and even music; and through the entire system of transatlantic slavery as such since it equalized African identity with a pretended natural inferiority and slave status. The extreme length of over five centuries of this massive crime that spanned large parts of the globe has resulted in a psychological and mental situation that constitutes an immense barrier for seeking justice and reparation. Thus, one very important task for legal anthropologists would be to assist in the consolidation of a new global African identity, also in a perspective of attaining reparation. Law was co-formative in the damage that needs to be repaired and healed, and was intrinsically linked with identity. Colonial slave laws codified the unimaginable atrocities; they denied the humanity of the victims because of their descent from Africa and defined them as movables. The people were de-Africanized, and lies about Africa were systematically disseminated. It is not surprising that this has repercussions on the legal consciousness regarding reparations today. The urgent need for African unity built around an African identity that still remains to be well anchored is also highlighted by facts such as that there existed an unwritten rule of fraternity between European slavers on the African coast. They would, regardless of their nationality and whether their national governments were at a given time engaged in wars or hostilities in Europe, come to one another's assistance in dealing with their slaves, particularly in moments of rebellion. Collectives regrouping slave-ship captains of varying European nationalities sometimes indeed acted as a sort of government on the coast of Africa. When an issue of concern to all slavers in a given area had to be addressed, someone called a council meeting to be attended by nearly all captains.[1442] Since the oppressors facilitated their crime through unity, Africans will need to practice unity to get to reparation.

1440 Ibid., VIV et seq.
1441 Starr/Goodale (2002a), 4 et seq.
1442 Rediker, Marcus (2008). The Slave Ship. A Human History, London: John Murray, 211.

Activist anthropologist approaches that deny the existence of "neutral" observers, but actively seek to create knowledge and to provide assistance for empowering the people anthropologists work with, have always been in minority positions, but nevertheless have a long tradition, especially in South America and the Caribbean.[1443] Legal anthropological expertise and publications have also been used and accepted by courts and government agencies as evidence, such as in the Xoco case in Brazil.[1444] It is important to acknowledge in this context that new categories of self-identification were not something that people opportunistically made up to have access to material gains, but rely on aspects that were always part of their identity which they had rejected because of structural judgements of society.

If such mobilization of identity was possible and beneficial for the Indigenous Rights Movement, it is not illusionary to think that similar actions could and should be made for the Global African Reparations Movement. Quite on the contrary, the example of the movement for social justice of Indigenous people in the Americas should be taken up to forward other social justice causes as well. Identity is a highly significant analytical and legal category, because claiming rights requires assuming an identity that fits with the claim in question.[1445] Individuals' consciousness of their right can mobilize them to take legal action, but to gain consciousness of their right, they must first gain consciousness of identity. In the case of transatlantic slavery which produced such huge damage on a global and structural level, it is therefore of utmost importance to encourage and promote a new global African identity that is necessary for adequately bringing forth reparation claims.

Without massive popular legal consciousness about the legitimacy of the reparations claim, nothing at all will be able to progress in that perspective. Yet, "legal consciousness is constituted in relation to the legal processes available to people, the ideas and practices of legal professionals and lay people, and also discourses circulating locally and internationally. (...) This global/local interaction is crucial to the development of legal consciousness among people at all levels of society. The challenge is to identify which local imperatives, structures, and processes, how these discourses meet in a given context and thereby how they influence consciousness. (...) Researchers should address conventional questions and through their research provide answers leading to social transformation. (...) Data should be gathered and shared in order to effect social change and political transformation, specifically to reduce poverty and oppression. (...) Consciousness comes

---

1443 Brysk, Alison (2000). From Tribal Village to Global Village: Indian Rights and International Relations in Latin America, Palo Alto: Stanford University Press, 18.

1444 Ibid., 54 et seq.

1445 Coutin, Susan Bibler (2002). "Reconceptualizing Research", in: June Starr and Mark Goodale (ed.): Practicing Ethnography in Law. New Dialogues, Enduring Methods, New York: Palgrave Macmillan, 108-127, 111 et seq.

through involvement in the exchange of information. (...) The production and reproduction of knowledge is central to consciousness and consciousness-raising (...). Studying deliberate attempts to alter legal consciousness, including those planned by the researcher, can illuminate the content of consciousness and the process of legal change. (...) Legal consciousness, in the sense of an individual's understandings of law (...), an interactive, participatory approach often stimulates changes in consciousness (...)."[1446]

The building of legal consciousness may of course not only be beneficial in view of prospective formal claims before international courts or agencies, but also as a brick in the larger mobilization strategy of the global African reparation movement. "A right is not merely a claim of ownership; it is a claim about justice, legitimacy, and power (or resistance to power). Rights (...) often are fundamental to strategies for social reform."[1447] When people think that they enjoy a right, they will seek to vindicate it and are less likely to put up with a situation that goes back to the violation of their right.

Scholars such as McCann examined how legal rights "raise expectations". They provide a legal language to claim harms, the knowledge of which is necessary to become legally active, and also serve to catalyze social movements. People may be motivated to take some action by the idea that they have a "right" to something, and thus "rights" have effects even when no legal action in the strict sense has occurred yet. They may have subtle, but cumulative, effects on people's consciousness and actions.[1448]

Thus, unity with a shared consciousness about the right to reparation, is indispensable to achieve reparation, and should not be debased by futile discussions about whether claiming reparations would be a waste of time. Though there are different frontlines and multiple roles to fulfil, this is one war. Ayi Kwei Armah, one of my very favorite writers, wrote to me in a private correspondence that he does not occupy himself with the question of reparations because to do so would be based on the foolish expectation that one day western governments would wake up, recognize their wrongs and want to make up, which, I agree, would be going totally against the logic of their historically documented rationale of acting. Yet when Armah argues that the "rediscovery, development, clarification and expression of ameliorative African values are requirements underlined by our revolutionaries as an indispensable part of the decolonization process", that's really reparation. "Culturally and intellectually, decolonization means the search

1446 Hirsch, Susan F. (2002). "Feminist Participatory Research on Legal Consciousness", in: June Starr and Mark Goodale (ed.): Practicing Ethnography in Law. New Dialogues, Enduring Methods, New York: Palgrave Macmillan, 13-33.
1447 Nielsen, Laura Beth (2004). "The Work of Rights and the Work Rights Do: A Critical Empirical Approach", in: Austin Sarat (ed.): The Blackwell Companion to Law and Society, Oxford: Blackwell Publishing, 63-79, 83.
1448 McCann, Michael (1994). Rights at Work: Pay Equity Reform and the Politics of Legal Mobilizations, Chicago: University of Chicago Press, 64.

or research for positive African ideas, perspectives, techniques and values."[1449] That's what reparation means too, and more. Claiming reparations is important not because it would one day make western nations wake up to the realization of the claim's fundamental and striking appropriateness, but simply because African people will get aware that they have a legally well-established right to reparations because they have been violated in their legal rights for more than 500 years. African people globally need to realize clearly that western perpetrator states have a legal obligation to them to provide massive and comprehensive reparations. This, I hope and think, can be an important catalyzer to take African liberation and reparation in own hands and to finally take reparations.

This constant is nothing new indeed in the international African reparations debate and has been advocated by reparations activists since a long time ago. For example, a book review by Derrick Bell of Boris Bittker's book *The Case for Black Reparations* suggested that "the white power structure would never support reparations because to do so would operate against its interests. The initiative must come from blacks, broadly, widely, implacably."[1450]

It is crystal clear that full reparation such as due by international law will never be made by European perpetrator states; to do so would be suicidal for the system that they have violently built and maintained by any means for centuries. But the legal reparation argument remains essential, just as it is essential to continue pushing individual and national legal reparations claims before tribunals. And even if such individual reparations quests are not apt to bring about the reparation that is legally and morally due, it is important to lead these battles, because they do make a difference for the lives of individual victims of the Maafa. At the same time it is important that the people who do not wish to give their energy to pursuing getting reparations from the oppressors, perceiving it a waste of time, continue their work of economic self-empowerment of African people globally. Power only respects power and the most persuasive power is material and economic, so finally the way to reparations and reparation will come through the establishment of Black enterprises and cooperations. Yet there are different roles on several battle lines to fulfil in this war, including the legal front. The validity and truth of such an integrated perspective was evident in the personalities of Malcolm X and Martin Luther King Jr. who superficially pursued different approaches but really worked for the same goal and were thus able to grow on one another.

All African liberation movements from the first Maroons and the brigades that were organized on the African coast to fight enslavement and deportation up to today were really movements for reparation. And in last consequence, it will also be in their tradition of *by any means necessary* that African people will have

---

1449 Ayi Kwei Armah (2010). Remembering the Dismembered Continent. Essays, Per Ankh, Popenguine Senegal, 118.
1450 Robinson, Randall (2000). The Debt. What America Owes to Blacks, New York, Penguin Group, 205.

to take reparations. There are European people who have their mind, heart and spirit in the right place in that regard. I have witnessed them again and again at different events and reunions for African liberation and reparation. But they are far too few and will always be too few to make their governments and societies change course in their dealings with African people and to make full reparation on a voluntary basis.

Most African people have the impression that reparations are an unrealistic dream with no substantial hope for realization, so it is indeed crucial to make the people know that they have a sound legal claim, and if they unite behind this claim and take justice, they can again rule the world, so that as Marcus Garvey said, Africa's "hands of influence throughout the world" may "teach (...) man the way of life and peace, the way of God".

In view of that necessity, it is important to remind ourselves that one of the operational modes of ideology, defined as a process of meaning making that serves power[1451], is legitimation. "Legal ideologies and corresponding legal consciousness are ways in which social organizations produce the means of authorizing, sustaining, and reproducing themselves." [1452] In this perspective, it is crucial to recognize that the dominant legal opinion concerning transatlantic slavery reparations, claiming that slavery would have been legal at that time and that, thus, there would be no right to reparations, is in essence nothing else than the ideological legitimization for upholding an international situation that was anchored through transatlantic slavery and continues to exploit, oppress and kill the descendants of the original victims.

Critical Race Theory emphasizes how law and race are mutually constitutive.[1453] This school of thought concentrates mostly on US developments, yet its endeavours to uncover "how law was a constitutive element of race itself: in other words, how law constructed race"[1454] is very apt for application on the system of transatlantic slavery in its globality. Critical Race Theorists look into how race as racial ideology has shaped legal doctrine. Just as some scrutinized the role of the ideology of "white" supremacy in shaping US Supreme Court doctrine on the Fourth Amendment[1455], it is also necessary to assess how this same ideology of "white" supremacy has shaped international law doctrine on the question of the legal status of transatlantic slavery and of reparations.

1451 Ewick, Patricia (2004). "Consciousness and Ideology", in: Austin Sarat (ed.): The Blackwell Companion to Law and Society, Oxford: Blackwell Publishing, 80-94, 85.
1452 Ibid., 86.
1453 Gómez, Laura E. (2004). "A Tale of Two Genres: On the Real and Ideal Links Between Law and Society and Critical Race Theory", in: Austin Sarat (ed.): The Blackwell Companion to Law and Society, Oxford: Blackwell Publishing, 453-470, 453.
1454 Crenshaw, K/Gotanda, N./Peller, G./Thomas, K (1995). Critical Race Theory: The Key Writings That Formed the Movement, New York: The New Press, XXV.
1455 Gómez (2004), 462 et seq.

Both Pierre Bourdieu[1456] and the school of thought called "law and society scholarship" have also pointed out the dialectic relation between law and society. Legal systems are not only disputed terrains where rights and obligations are negotiated, but identity as well. Thus, law has a transformative impact on culture and identity. Law is recognized as a cultural system, a way of "imagining the real". Laws foster new relations, meanings and self-understandings. Legal systems are seen as contested sites of meaning where not only rights and obligations, but where identities are also constantly under negotiation, always within the context of historical processes. "In the course of that negotiation, law exercises transformative effects on culture and identity." [1457] The study of the power of law is important to make and to change social relations. Connections between legal activism, international law, and social movements need to be scrutinized. [1458]

Identity is both "precursor as well as a consequence of rights", and rights are "a result as well as a cause of change".[1459] Thus, "(l)egal knowledge (...) can matter as both an end and means of action; law provides both normative principles and strategic resources for the conduct of social struggle (...). Legal rights can give rise to a rights consciousness so that individuals and groups may imagine and act on rights that have not been formally recognized or enforced by state officials."[1460] Rights discourses may lead people who ordinarily consider themselves helpless to come to think that they do have some capacity to alter their lot.[1461] Abel has shown in this regard how "speaking law to power" in South Africa provided a powerful orienting frame for mobilizing challenges to apartheid.[1462] Even in situations of oppression, law can thus be conceived not only as an institution to be resisted, but also as a discursive resource for resistance to bring about social change.[1463]

In that regard, I think that further research needs to be conducted to assess the implications between "kréyol" identity and legal reparations consciousness. Several people have indicated to me that defining oneself as kréyol hinders the identification with Africa. Yet, the identification with Africa is a necessary pre-condition for claiming global African reparation. Most people in the "French"

1456 Bourdieu, Pierre (1987). The Force of Law. Toward a Sociology of the Juridical Field, in: Hastings Law Journal 38 (July 1987), 805-853.
1457 Hajjar, Lisa (2004). "Human Rights", in: Austin Sarat (ed.): The Blackwell Companion to Law and Society, Oxford: Blackwell Publishing, 589-604, 590.
1458 Ibid., 590.
1459 Hoffmann French (2009), 10 et seq.
1460 McCann, Michael (2004). "Law and Social Movements", in: Austin Sarat (ed.): The Blackwell Companion to Law and Society, Oxford: Blackwell Publishing, 506-522, 507 et seq.
1461 Ibid., 512.
1462 Abel, Richard (1995). Politics by Other Means. Law in the Struggle Against Apartheid, 1980-1994, New York: Routledge.
1463 Fleury-Steiner, Benjamin/Nielsen, Laura Beth (2006a). "A Constitutive Perspective of Rights", in: Benjamin Fleury-Steiner and Laura Beth Nielsen (ed.): The new civil rights research: a constitutive approach, Aldershot: Ashgate Publishing, 1-13, 6.

Caribbean and Guiana consider themselves kréyol.

In order to apply the assessments of all these mentioned schools of thought in a practically beneficial manner, it is necessary to empirically and individually identify factors that are responsible for why or why not people identify problems in their lives as legal or not. The linkage of factors may be rather complex, such as in Jamaica or "French" Guiana where the majority of the people did not have any rights at all recognized over several centuries, and only have access to education on a very limited basis up to today. Additionally and generally speaking, even if people know that they have a right, a variety of reasons may cause that they will not even attempt to have it enforced. Some factors that people have mentioned or displayed in the course of my small research are fear of overall negative repercussions for them; a certain habituation effect; and the general legal cultures of the respective countries.

4. LEGAL REPARATIONS CONSCIOUSNESS IN JAMAICA AND "FRENCH" GUIANA

"Whether or not individuals identify problems as legal ones (or as breaches of their rights) is complex. (...) Individuals exist in socio-economic, race, and gender hierarchies that affect their ability and willingness to pursue legal claims. (...) Individuals often do not know what rights they enjoy and when they have been breached. (...) Even when individuals understand that they have a legal right that has been breached and they know who is responsible, they may not choose to pursue it for a variety of reasons. They may fear retaliation; they may have become accustomed, due to their social location, to being harmed without redress; or they may not believe that legal actors will believe their claims or be responsive to them."[1464]

Considerate of this multidimensional problematic and of the importance of reparations for transatlantic slavery, it really would be necessary to individually research for each country and region of the African diaspora and continent what its respective time-space-specific factors for the emergence of legal reparations consciousness are. This is what I aimed to do on a small scale in Jamaica and "French" Guiana. While working on that endeavour, I have experienced myself that interactive and participation-oriented research can trigger changes in the legal consciousness of the people. People who, because of the various factors addressed were initially sceptic or unaware of reparations, started to display an altered and more positive view about the topic in the course of our conversations.

1464 Nielsen (2004), 68 et seq.

As explained already above, the inspiration for this small empirical research about legal reparations consciousness came to me while I was in Jamaica and "French" Guiana to dig archives and encountered many people who asked me about the purpose of my stays and whose responses were divergent in a way quite contrary to what I would have expected. In Jamaica, home of a long tradition of militant and rebel music, the most common reaction was silence. In "French" Guiana, where many things are still directed from and towards France and which was never officially decolonized, the reactions were far more positive. I had encounters there such as one with a very old man in a supermarket cashier line who after hearing my response to his enquiry about my journey's purpose broke into a wide smile and told me, "*Féliciations! Merci, c'est important ... Merci et beaucoup de force pour vous!*" ("Congratulations! Thank you, this is important ... Thank you and much strength to you!"). I already mentioned the minibus driver who always let me ride in his vehicle without paying because he appreciated so much that I was working for reparation. I was not only deeply touched by these encounters, but also very surprised by these observations, and felt like something that definitely deserved more attention had reached me. Since I am deeply convinced that reparations for transatlantic slavery, legally due, are a necessary precondition for fair chances to a prosperous and healthy life for the many African people who have received and treated me with much love and care during my private and research travels in the diaspora and on the continent, I determined that I needed to start researching out factors that are responsible for the presence or absence of legal consciousness about transatlantic slavery reparations, seeking thereby to promote the cause of global African reparation.

The reasonings in Jamaica revealed that, generally speaking, an explicit conceptualization of "reparations" is not widely present in the awareness of the people there. When posing my opening question of, "Can you please tell me a little about what you think about reparations?" I very often encountered reactions such as "... repatriation ... repatrutation, ... ehm, could you repeat that for me, please?"[1465] When I repeated my question, people sometimes told me, "... can you tell me a bit what it [reparations] really means?" I answered that it basically means that European states and former slave holders who were responsible for and profited from transatlantic slavery, would have to take financial and other measures to repair the damage done, as far as possible. Most people then cut me short with statements such as, "Yeah, yeah, ah dat, we haffi get compensation, yes, ah true dat".[1466] When I then asked whether people had previously heard about reparations, I was often told that this was indeed the first time that many people heard the term

---

1465 Interview Gloria (market vendor, Port Antonio/Jamaica, 20.1.2011).
1466 Interview Joanna (market vendor, Port Antonio/Jamaica, 29.1.2011) ("yeah, yeah, that's it, we have to get compensation, yes, that's true).

"reparations". I learned from these experiences that even though most people do not have a concept in their minds that is explicitly labelled "reparations", one can see very easily when only reasoning a little bit further with them that the content and essence of this legal concept is well present with the people. In their vast majority the people think that reparations are due to them. They may not conceptualize this claim in the legal language of "reparations" because they are simply not exposed to the knowledge about such terms. This again is due to their socio-economic position which in turn is largely a consequence of the legacy of slavery, the crime for which reparations need to be made. A vicious circle. In order to have a chance to break it, factors which impact in one direction or the other on the legal reparations consciousness of a given part of African people need to be searched out. Some of such factors which I think to have identified will now be presented.

A. CHURCH DOCTRINE, DEMONIZATION OF AFRICA AND REPARATIONS CONSCIOUSNESS

The reasonings revealed a negative correlation between church adherence and reparations consciousness. People who regularly go to church generally showed more reluctance to speak out in favour of reparations. Please bear in mind that Jamaica is the country with the highest prevalence of churches, relative to population size.

One active Christian woman in Jamaica told me, "… you know if I was not a Christian, I would be very bitter, from what I learn and hear in school, how they did to us in slavery, but we haffi forgive and move on (…)."[1467] Concerning the myth of the curse of Ham and Canaan, she told me, "(…) I believe it, it is in the Bible, so I have to believe it. (…) It all goes back to sin."[1468] She was sincerely convinced that transatlantic slavery happened because of "inter-generational sin" that would have entailed this curse against the children of Africa (Ham). Furthermore she told me, "If I think about it, if the Europeans didn't come to take us to the West Indies, we would still be heathen. In Africa, they have all kind of witchcraft, obeah, ancestor worship. (…) I don't want to go there and live; go there and see yes, but I have to prepare, pray and fast to be ready, so I can teach them."[1469]

Another man who very regularly attends church, told me, "Yes, but still we really just have to cope with it and do with it, and let it be because otherwise it will be to dangerous."[1470] I asked him why it would be dangerous to expose the poisonous legacy of slavery and claim reparations. He responded that, "Well, it would be dangerous … retaliation. Retaliation you know. So it better fi just let it rest and go on." I persisted to ask: "But don't you think that with just letting it rest,

---

1467 Interview Gladys (high school teacher, Port Antonio/Jamaica, 15.1.2011).
1468 Ibid.
1469 Ibid.
1470 Interview Will (retired mechanician, Port Antonio/Jamaica, 20.1.2011).

you still continue to suffer from the consequences, no true?" He said: "Yes, ah true, sufferation still ah gwaan because of it" and admitted a need for reparations, yet insisted that it was a delicate matter.[1471]

A taxi driver once told me that he would not go to Fi Wi Sinting, a festival celebrating Jamaicans' African heritage, because he was a Christian. This logic seemed so strange to me that I asked a Jamaican friend of mine about it, and she said that many Jamaicans don't want to have anything to do with drums or Africa. Because my friend highlights her African ancestry, her own sister does not want her children to be alone with her.

Thus we see that the words of Malcolm X have lost nothing of their relevance: "They made us think that Africa was a land of jungles, a land of animals, a land of cannibals and savages. It was a hateful image (...). They were so successful in projecting this negative image of Africa (...) we looked upon Africa as a hateful place. Why? Because those who oppress us know you can't make a person hate the root without making them hate the tree. You can't hate your origin and not end up hating yourself. (...) You can't make us hate Africa without making us hate ourselves. And they did this very skilfully (...). We ended up with twenty-two million Black people here in America who hated everything about us that was African. We hated the African characteristics (...). We hated our hair. We hated (...) the shape of our nose, and the shape of our lips, the color of our skin. Our color became a chain, a psychological chain (...), because we were ashamed of it. We felt trapped because our skin was Black. We felt trapped because we had African blood in our veins. This is how you imprisoned us. Because we hated our African blood we felt inadequate, we felt inferior, we felt helpless."[1472]

I mention in another chapter that some European people sometimes make statements to the end that descendants of Africans deported in transatlantic slavery would be glad today that they are not in Africa. Such arguments really hurt since the current misery in Africa also goes back to transatlantic slavery and the continuing crime of the Maafa, even more so if they are metted out by African people.

"We look at Africa today, and see how bad it is. We see poverty over there, AIDS, they're killing each other. And so we are in 2002, and we black folks can look at Africa and say I'm glad they made me a slave and brought me over here and put me through three hundred years of abuse, so that today, I am not over there, poor, diseased, and at war. But we also have to remember that small, elite group of Europeans not only took people from Africa to control those natural re-sources – that same mind-set also went throughout the whole continent of Africa and colonized it and (...) they had a sort of slavery right there, throughout the con-tinent."[1473] In that regard, the biased reporting of mainstream media on Africa, fea-

1471 Ibid.
1472 Malcolm X, cited in: Crawford/Nobles/DeGruy Leary (2003), 264 et seq.
1473 Winbush, Raymond A (2003a). "Interview with Chester and Timothy Hurdle, Barbara Ratliff,

turing only famine and wars, is definitely contra-productive for the development of reparations consciousness and should indeed be identified as a weapon of mass destraction in that regard. The same goes for the ever-present aid-campaigns and advertisements. What is due is not aid but reparations, and constantly portraying an image of a destitute Africa does not help build the consciousness that is needed to push reparation but rather serves to debase it.

In a school project on the effects of slavery on Black people described in Ray Winbush's seminal book, several teachers in Brooklyn/NY distributed to students quotes such as: "I am an African", and: "If it were not for chattel slavery I would still be home in Africa". The quotes were mounted on red, black, and green (the colors of the African liberation flag) paper and put on walls outside the classroom. The teachers were ordered to take the quotes down and some were even fired. Another teacher was fired because she told her pupils that they were Africans and as such had to live up to a high standard. "The black students in both classrooms saw nothing unusual about Asian children born in America calling themselves Asians, but had a difficult time referring to themselves as Africans. Many students of African descent have a distorted view of Africa. They see Africa as barbaric and uncivilized."[1474] The fact that they crushed this progressive project only further highlights that *Education for Reparation* is indeed most important[1475], because like one woman at a sitting of the Jamaica Reparations Commission said, the children are the future and they have to get the right perspective on what is going on.

N'COBRA (National Coalition of Blacks For Reparations in America) rightly stresses that as long as Black people globally do not identify as Africans, they "have no human rights as a people, and are individual clones of our various oppressors, always at their mercy"[1476]. In that regard, it is important to also accelerate research into the historical unity of African people. Ayi Kwei Armah assessed that "in our historical behaviour, we the people of Africa have tended to regard the continent – all of it – as our home". It was the regimes imposed by Europe and Arab invaders who are at the root of tribalism in Africa.[1477] Malian anthropologist Youssouf Tata Cissé also documented the unifying ethos prevalent in ancient Mali.[1478] More research in that direction needs to be done and be streamlined with

---

and Ina Hurdle-McGee", in: Raymond A. Winbush (ed.): Should America pay? Slavery and the raging debate on reparations, New York: Amistad, 315-320, 318.

1474 Nzingha, Yaa Asantewaa (2003). "Reparations + Education = The Pass to Freedom", in: Raymond A. Winbush (ed.): Should America pay? Slavery and the raging debate on reparations, New York: Amistad, 299-314, 301 et seq.

1475 Ibid., 310.

1476 Afrik, Baba Hannibal/Elijah, Jill Soffiyah/Benton Lewis, Dorothy/Worril, Conrad W. (2003). "Current Legal Status of Reparations, Strategies of the National Black United Front, the Mississippi Model, What's Next in the Reparations Movement", in: Raymond A. Winbush (ed.): Should America pay? Slavery and the raging debate on reparations, New York: Amistad, 363-383, 380 et seq.

1477 Armah, Ayi Kwei (2010). Remembering the Dismembered Continent. Essays, Popenguine: Per Ankh, 304.

1478 Ibid., 303.

reparations research and activism.

B. HISTORY DISCOURSES, LEGAL IDEAS AND EDUCATION

The dominant history discourse(s) are, not surprisingly, highly significant for the state of reparations consciousness. Another myth that is still fully functional is that "slavery was always there, people always got enslaved"[1479], as I witnessed several people say in Jamaica. However, I have remarked that all people who first came up with this kind of statement or attitude were very interested and appreciative when I stated that not all of what is commonly denominated as "slavery" constitutes the same reality that their ancestors went through, and that transatlantic slavery was both qualitatively and quantitatively different from other servile conditions, even if they are all commonly labelled "slavery". All of the persons I reasoned with subsequently changed their conclusions regarding reparations, and told me that they had not considered this before, but that now that they reflect upon it, it makes sense that they must get reparations. One woman, for example, initially told me that "slavery was always there, people always got enslaved (...)"[1480]. Yet when I interjected that not all "slavery" was the same thing, she was very responsive. She asked me: "How they treated us, chain us in the ships and everything ... you think it was different?" In the ensuing conversation she continued to drop phrases such as "Africans enslaved their brothers and sisters", but remained responsive to the information I offered in return, like that many African collaborators may not have known what cruel destiny awaited the people they sold, because African "slavery" had been so different from transatlantic slavery, as proven by historical evidence. Confronted with information such as this, she became more and more appreciative of the idea of reparations. She asked me, "But do you think we will ever get money for it?", and told me that she feared that reparations would foster "blame and hatred today" while she was "all about forgiveness". I expressed my opinion that reparations were not exclusively about money but about structures, and that there is damage that needs to be repaired before forgiveness can take place. Africa was at least as wealthy as Europe before transatlantic slavery (she was very surprised to hear that), while today the continent and many Jamaicans and other people in the African diaspora are materially suffering.[1481] After digesting this information, she finished my sentence "it is not about blame and hatred, but about..." with "bringing into balance"[1482]. Reasonings such as this one confirm general assessments by scholars that ethnography, observation and interviews cannot be separated from their context, but influence

---

1479 Interview Gladys (high school teacher, Port Antonio/Jamaica, 15.1.2011).
1480 Ibid.
1481 Ibid.
1482 Ibid.

this context[1483], and how rights discourses may be an important step to social change. Legal consciousness always develops in relation to the legal ideas that are circulating. Such ideas can be brought to the table by legal practitioners and scholars, but also through local and international discourses. Legal claims elevate expectancies and are as such already important for social reform movements. Legal claims feed our imagination of what is possible and therefore have an important strategic function. In this respect, legal knowledge and consciousness is both an end and a means of action. This is also the case for rights, or the interpretation of a right, that has not yet been officially recognized. The sole conviction of having a right and the argumentation that backs it up can be a motivation to become active and militate for one's cause.[1484]

Education is decisive for legal reparations consciousness. Yet education here does not necessarily mean formal education, but also street education, such as through the Black Power or the Rastafari movement. One interlocutor who was familiar and in favour of reparations, told me that he "(...) got to know a lot of things from reasonings with Rasta elders, and from the way I was raised too, you know, my mother is Rasta ... but otherwise, cho!.. in school dem teach you about Christopher Columbus and how dem wicked men great, but nothing about Marcus Garvey."[1485] Concerning this factor, I have diagnosed a strong urban-rural-divide, with country people being much less exposed to general and specific discourses relating to history and reparations. Socio-economic factors once again play high in this. Some interlocutors have told me that many people in Jamaica are busy with managing to survive and cannot afford to occupy themselves with issues such as history or reparations. I was also told that history is taught in Jamaican schools only from high school, but that many people merely attend elementary school. This, again, has socio-economic roots in the legacy of transatlantic slavery, the crime that needs to be repaired. In a situation like this, it is crucial that people continue to pass on historical knowledge from one generation to the next. One young man, who was a stern supporter of reparations, told me that he had reasoned on topics such as slavery with his granny: "From what mi hear, nuttin no change from then. You can do nuttin here, they will always keep you down ... Now foreign people like US-American or else, they come in fi run the business and shops dem, and we outta business because dem have cheaper access."[1486]

Other factors that the statements of people in Jamaica have indicated as inhib-

---

1483 Starr, June/Goodale, Mark (2002a), 4 et seq.
1484 Nielsen (2004).
1485 Interview Omeri (unemployed youth, Kingston (Sandy Gully community)/Jamaica, 19.1.2011).
1486 Interview Kenneth (market hustler, Port Antonio/Jamaica, 18.1.2011) ("From what I hear, nothing has changed from then. You can do nothing here, they will always keep you down ... Now foreign people, like US-Americans or else, they come to run the businesses and shops, and we are out of business because they have cheaper access.").

itive for claiming their right to reparations concern the general political and legal culture in Jamaica which is intrinsically violent and in itself a direct product of the damage that needs to be repaired. I was told by one interlocutor that people fear to militate and march for reparations because "they may shoot them up"[1487]. When asked who "they" was, and of whom the people were afraid, he said "the system ... the bigger man dem. Nuff people are for reparations, but they 'fraid". Jamaica has a long history of political violence. Indeed, political violence has always been a decisive factor of Jamaican life from the day when Europeans first set foot there. In colonial and post-colonial times, protesters and participants of political rallies have repeatedly been shot and killed.

Concerning fear in another sense, one interlocutor in "French" Guiana brought up that people there were afraid to lose French social security rights.[1488] In this context, another man made a link between an old enslavers' precept of always assuring that slaves were nourished and clothed sufficiently to satisfy the basic needs of survival to avoid problems on the plantation, and the functioning of French social security system in "French" Guiana today.[1489]

C. FRUSTRATION FACTOR

The conversations in Jamaica have furthermore indicated that a certain frustration factor may have instilled itself in segments of the society. What is meant by this? Contrary to Jamaican country areas and poor inner-city communities that were never really touched by these discourses, reparations was a well discussed topic in the capital Kingston, and there again mostly in intellectual circles, in the late 1970s and 80s. However, as I was told by one interlocutor (who was of the opinion that the present situation was "slavery in a different way, the result is the same"), the fact that there was a lot of talk during quite some time but entailed no results, brought about frustration.[1490] "People feel like it will never come, just a lot of talk. Them get disillusioned."[1491]

If this is indeed so, this situation also needs to be seen as a product of the damage that needs to be repaired, as it is part of a larger international setting that still holds the formerly illegally enslaved and colonized nations in a position of relative powerlessness in the international arena. The experience of "only being able to talk" and not being able to effectuate any substantial changes has repercussions on the motivation of the people to get active for change, disclosing once again the vicious circle in which the damage of the crime demanding reparation is structured in such a way that it hinders the people from acquiring the

---

1487   Ibid.
1488   Interview Dada (unemployed, Cayenne/F.Guiana, 18.9.2011).
1489   Interview Max (entrepreneur & activist, Saint-Laurent-du-Maroni/F.Guiana, 24.9.2011).
1490   Interview Paulette (landlady, Kingston (Liguanea)/Jamaica, 15.2.2011).
1491   Ibid.

necessary (legal) consciousness for change. Another interlocutor told me in this context that she did not care too much about the subject of reparations because "yes, Jamaica has a right to this [reparations], yes we have a right to this. But mi no know if it will ever happen so mi just stay with what I know and work with that. Mi haffi be independent and work and take care of myself, nobody else going take care of mi."[1492] From these utterances, I draw the conclusion that it may be counter-productive for the rooting of legal consciousness if only knowledge and information about a right is communicated over an extended period without any practical progress following. One of the reasons why people in general seemed to be more aware about reparations in "French" Guiana could be that the reparations debate is much more recent there and has really entered the public discourse only about thirteen years ago when the Guianese deputy to the French parliament, Christiane Taubira, started to lobby for a law that recognizes transatlantic slavery as a crime against humanity and which was passed in 2001. Originally Taubira's draft had also included a paragraph calling for reparations, but when the law was finally adopted that part had been cut out. Yet the whole process surrounding the emergence of that law seems to have played a crucial role in mediatizing for the first time in "French" Guiana the question of reparations on a larger scale. Several interlocutors confirmed this to me. "Yes, it was mostly from the Taubira law on that the term started to enter the minds"[1493]. I reasoned with many young people (<30 y.o.) in "French" Guiana who were, more or less, aware of the claim for reparations, but sustained that this heightened familiarity of Guianese people with reparations had nothing to do with the Taubira law. Some told me that this consciousness has just always been with them, "passed down from the ancestors"[1494]. Although I do not wish to question the validity of these claims, I think that it is also a possibility that they were too young when this law was discussed in Guianese society and therefore cannot easily assess its real impact. This is a question that still deserves further investigation.

D. LEGAL DISCOURSES
AND CULTURAL MOVEMENTS

It really seems only logical that legal intercourse interacts with other institutionalized discourses about history, politics, work, and so on to shape people's legal consciousness, understood as both the awareness that people have about their legal position(s) and the dynamic process through which actors draw on le-

---

1492 Interview Misty (small farmer & market vendor, Port Antonio/Jamaica, 27.9.2011) ("yes, Jamaica has a right to this [reparations], yes we have a right to this. But I don't know if it will ever happen, so I just stay with what I know and work with that. I have to be independent and work and take care of myself, nobody else will take care of me.")
1493 Interview Henriette (student, Cayenne/F.Guiana, 14.9.2011) ("Oui, c'est surtout a partir de la loi Taubira que le terme a commencé à rentrer dans les esprits").
1494 Interview Marietta (waitress, Cayenne/F.Guiana, 10.9.2011).

gal discourse to construct their understanding of and relation to the social world. That process takes place within a social context already structured in part by law itself. It is thus important to acknowledge that the dominant legal opinion about global African reparations, upheld by European ex-enslaver states, defining transatlantic slavery as legal at its time and blaming Africans for selling their brothers and sisters, fulfils in itself an important function of continuously alienating the descendants of the original victims from their ancestral roots and blocks the way to healing. As such it is crucial to analyze the role of law as an institutionalized discourse that gives meaning to social life and reproduces social structure. Law legitimates the patterns and categories of social life so that they seem natural, normal, and inevitable. Law discourses may even be more dominant than others, particularly if they are part of historically entrenched and long-standing social institutions.[1495] This is definitely the case with transatlantic slavery. However, law is but one of many available schemas through which actors makes sense of the social world. Albeit that it is a rather important one, it is not completely determinative for people's actions. It is therefore important to detect and scrutinize alternative social and cultural discourses that may empower people and thus also have repercussions on legal consciousness. Austin Sarat, a pioneer in studies of legal consciousness, has shifted much of his research agenda to representations of law in popular culture and their implications for both public attitudes and the deeper formation of legal consciousness. He sustains that studies of individual consciousness and of mass legal culture can very productively enrich and inform one another, allowing deeper insights into the social context in which subjectivity and legality are produced. [1496]

Because of this realization and the prevalence and popularity of rebel music traditions like reggae and hip-hop in both Jamaica and French-occupied Guiana, I aimed to seek out by means of the maintained reasonings to what extent these cultural movements had an influence on people's consciousness about reparations. And, not really that surprisingly, several people told me that music, referring specifically to hip-hop and reggae, had played an important role in their own conscientization. Two persons also mentioned that "la weed"[1497], that is, marijuana, was one factor in their becoming more conscious of their socio-historical situation. Not only cultural movements but popular discourses in general make a difference. One person in Guiana said that he became conscientized as a youth because he lived next to a bar from where he heard certain discourses that he never was told about in school.[1498]

In total, five people in Jamaica and six in "French" Guiana explicitly stated that

---

1495 Albiston, Catherine R. (2006). "Legal Consciousness and Workplace Rights", in: Benjamin Fleury-Steiner and Laura Beth Nielsen (ed.): The new civil rights research: a constitutive approach, Aldershot: Ashgate Publishing, 55-75, 56 et seq.
1496 McCann (2006), XXVI.
1497 Interview Laristo (musician/mailman, Cayenne/F.Guiana, 18.9.2011).
1498 Interview Max (entrepreneur & activist, Saint-Laurent-du-Maroni/F.Guiana, 24.9.2011).

they thought that cultural movements such as hip-hop and reggae have an impact on the level of consciousness of the people and/or that they themselves had become more aware of certain things through listening to such music.

However, another important aspect with regard to reparations, legal consciousness and music that surfaced during the conversations, and which I had not thought of before, concerns the negative impact of an apparently prevailing confusion between "reparation" and "repatriation" in Jamaica. Many reggae artists promote repatriation to Africa in their music. Although repatriation is one form of reparation recognized by international law, it is important to conceptually distinguish the two and to make clear that repatriation is but one form of reparations. When approaching them to reason about reparations, the first thing several people told me instantly was that they don't want to go anywhere, they don't want to repatriate.[1499] I was confronted with statements such as "Mi nah go Africa! I am from here, I'm not from Africa!"[1500], or "No, mi ah tell you, mi love Jamaica, mi love here so much, mi don't want to go anywhere, not even travel. Mi don't go Africa"[1501] at several occasions when asking about reparations. It is due to this confusion that several people at first spoke out against reparations in general, when they really only did not want to repatriate to Africa but got the concepts mixed up. Of course this brings us back to the diabolization of everything African during 500 years being instrumental in the realization of the crime and the need for a new global African identity as a pre-condition to effectuate reparation, but even then not all descendants of deported Africans would want to go back to Africa. And although Africa needs her scattered children to heal and rebuild, it is only right if not all go back to the continent, if only because that would leave the Caribbean and other territories in the possession of the enslavers, since they have exterminated the indigenous population. So in that regard, it is crucial that the political activist reparations movement joins together even more with artists to be able to lead matters in the direction we need to go. We will get to this point again in the chapter on "Hip-Hop, Reggae & other cultural movements" at the end of the book.

1499 Interview Joanna (market vendor, Port Antonio/Jamaica, 29.1.2011).
1500 Interview Misty (small farmer & market vendor, Port Antonio/Jamaica, 27.9.2011).
1501 Ibid.

5. SUMMARY FINDINGS ON POPULAR REPARATIONS CONSCIOUSNESS

A. CONSCIOUSNESS OF WHAT IS RIGHT, BUT LITTLE AWARENESS OF THE LEGAL CONCEPTUALIZATION OF THE RIGHT

Maybe the most important finding both in Jamaica and "French" Guiana was that practically all people I talked with, even if they were not familiar with the explicit concept and term of "reparations", really held the opinion that reparations, in the sense of the substance of what that term designates, are due to them. Yet when one thinks about it, this is really less surprising than it may sound to some, since "justice is a timeless concept. It may be suppressed, it may be denied, and by means of clever legal doctrines it may be suppressed, it may be denied, and by means of clever legal doctrines it may be made to disappear from sight altogether. Its timelessness, however, is something that all men and women understand."[1502]

However, it does constitute a problem that many people do not conceptualize what is due to them as "reparations" because of non-exposure to the legal and social discourses that carry that term, since it is not possible to rally behind a cause when concerned people are kept away from its instrumental concepts. This inaccessibility of legal and political knowledge is due to the socio-economic structures rooted in transatlantic slavery and as such part of the damage that demands reparation. Yet that situation constitutes a serious barrier to getting the reparations process going. Committed activists, legal anthropologists and scholars are needed in the breaking of this vicious circle. I would even go as far as to say that, given its constitutive role in the colonial oppression of Black and Brown people, anthropology has a duty to make reparations as well, and assisting the global reparations movement by providing empirical data could be one way of doing that. Now of course, this could not in any way be handled by anthropologists for whom this would just be another professional interest in the construction of their careers, or who may even let themselves be instrumentalized by the forces whose very existence is threatened by the prospects of reparation. It can only be done by individuals and groups who recognize the appropriateness and necessity of global African reparation.

And the fact that the overwhelming majority of African people apparently acknowledge that, in essence and content, they have a right to reparations for transatlantic slavery, is indeed a further indication of the fundamental illegality of transatlantic slavery at the time it happened. The descendants of the original victims, who are even structurally denied access to the legal concepts that would em-

---

1502 Peté/Du Plessis (2007), 26 et seq.

power them to take legal actions against their oppressors, know that some form of redress is due to them because what happened was wrong. They know this while being kept away from exposure to the corresponding legal concepts and that is a strong indication of the essential illegality of genocidal slavery such as practiced in the transatlantic system. In Jamaica, fourteen out of fifteen persons spoke out in favour of reparations in substance, in "French" Guiana fifteen out of sixteen. But only six in Jamaica and nine in "French" Guiana had been familiar with the explicit term "reparations" prior to our conversations. Many of the people told me that I was the first person from whom they ever heard the term "reparations". Yet during our ensuing reasonings it became apparent that they knew exactly what reparations are all about. One man even concluded that "justice and universal law" would demand reparations for African people although he had not heard the term before. But apparently he had reflected on its content before.[1503] In fact most of the people who at first did not know what "reparations" really means, spoke out instantly "yes, we must be compensated, a true dat" [1504] once I explained the term.

In "French" Guiana, I was told that it was also a challenge for the dissemination of reparations discourses and awareness that in some regions many people do not speak much French, but rather Taki-Taki which is a Maroon language. This contributes to a situation where some people, including my interlocutor, had not heard anything at all about the above-mentioned Taubira law, which brought the reparations debate to a larger public in France and the countries occupied by France. [1505]

One woman in Jamaica who was first sceptical about reparations, partly because she associated it with "repatriation" and thought that reparation activists wanted her to go back to Africa, responded to the question of whether she thought that the British and other European nations who operated slavery should pay – and take measures to repair – for what they did to the ancestors and the profit they are still making from the structures set in place with slavery: "Yes, Jamaica has a right to this, yes we have a right to this (...)"[1506].

Several people displayed some kind of scepticism with regard to reparations, although in principle they were supportive of the notion. One young woman stated, "Yes, I am for it, but it's complicated, too much time has passed also. (...) It is good and we are owed this, but then again is it realisable ?... One has to keep the feet on earth still"[1507].

1503 Interview Kenny (sculptor, Saint-Laurent-du-Maroni/F.Guiana, 24.9.2011).
1504 Interview Gloria (market vendor, Port Antonio/Jamaica, 20.1.2011).
1505 Interview Fabience (plumber, Saint-Laurent-du-Maroni/F.Guiana, 23.9.2011).
1506 Interview Misty (small farmer & market vendor, Port Antonio/Jamaica, 27.9.2011).
1507 Interview Henriette (student, Cayenne/F.Guiana, 14.9.2011) ("Oui, je suis pour, mais c'est compliqué, ça fait trop longtemps aussi. (...) C'est bien et on nous le doit, mais après est-ce que c'est réalisable ? ...Il faut garder les pieds sur terre aussi").

Other interlocutors who knew the explicit concept of reparations made statements like, "Yeah, reparations … that is right … reparations. It a good thing you know, an important thing you know, for if you oppress and destroy people for so long, and exploit their labour, you haffi pay up and repair at one time"[1508]. Another young woman who was already initially familiar with "reparations", exclaimed, "That's good! (…) [But] I don't think that they will give them"[1509]. Another man sustained that "(…) other people, they get paid, the Jewish, the Japanese … all others get something, only the Blackman dem no want fi give wi nothing." [1510] Someone else simply stated that "every crime demands reparation"[1511].

The chief of Apatou, one of the remaining Maroon communities in "French" Guiana, responded to my question of what he thought about reparations, "Well, you know, they gave us 2 kgs of rice, 4 kgs plantains and 1 kg onions per person per week …. The enslaver women drowned our children when they felt disturbed by them … they burned us alive. (…) It was eradication by any means. (…) The enslaver women, they cut the bellies of slaves whom their husbands had made pregnant … These are things that happened that need to be told"[1512]. He then told me that if I wanted to reason more about reparations, I should come back with a good translator because this is an important topic and he speaks only a little French and otherwise Taki-Taki.

With some people, I could not assess definitively whether or not they were familiar with the term "reparations". For example, I asked one man if he knew about reparations, and he told me "*oui oui*"[1513]. I proceeded to ask what he thought about it, and he said "yes, that's a good thing". When I proceeded to ask whether he thought that European states owed reparations to his people, he just responded "yes yes… but I don't know too much about that". He then let me feel that he did not wish to engage in any further reasoning, but deferred me to his daughter for that purpose. This man and his wife, who are of Maroon ancestry, have no electricity or running water at their house, as his daughter told me.[1514] This is a big shame for France and evidence for the continuing crime that this state is re-

---

1508 Interview Omeri (unemployed youth, Kingston (Sandy Gully community)/Jamaica, 19.1.2011).
1509 Interview Marietta (waitress, Cayenne/F.Guiana, 10.9.2011) ("c'est bien! (…) [Mais] je n'pense pas qu'ils vont leur donner").
1510 Interview James (musician, Kingston (Sandy Gully)/Jamaica, 31.1.2011).
1511 Interview Laurent (policeman, Cayenne/F.Guiana, 18.9.2011) ("tout crime demande réparation").
1512 Interview Pierre Sida (traditional chief of Apatou, Apatou/F.Guiana, 25.9.2011) ("Bon, vous savez… on nous donnait 2 kgs de riz, 4 kgs de plantains et 1 kg d'oignons pour une semaine par personne… Les femmes coloniaux ont noyé nos enfants si elles se sentaient perturbées… on nous brulait vivants. (…) C'était l'éradication par tous les moyens. (…) Les femmes des coloniaux, elles coupaient le ventre des esclaves que leurs maris avaient mis enceintes… Ces sont choses qui se sont passées qu'on doit dire").
1513 Interview Mr. Boké (market vendor, Cayenne/F.Guiana, 10.9.2011).
1514 Interview Henriette (student, Cayenne/F.Guiana, 14.9.2011).

sponsible for. After illegally enslaving, deporting and murdering African people and viciously persecuting and fighting those who strived to liberate themselves and restore their sovereignty, France still upholds a system where descendants of these Maroons, who still work very hard as small farmers for their subsistence, have to live in such conditions in the 21st century.

All, and I really mean all, people expressed and supported the view that the present poverty in their countries has its roots "(...) from what happened with slavery"[1515]. This was expressed in statements such as "the suffering goes (...) back to slavery,"[1516] "yes, yes, it [poverty] goes back to that time"[1517]; "the consequences are here [1518]; or "(...) basically it is the white man who rules... (...) already with religion... one has to be catholic, there is nothing else, but these are not our origins. (...) for 400 years (...) we still work for them"[1519]. People agreed therefore that the states responsible for transatlantic slavery need to give global African reparations.

B. WHAT IS DUE EXPRESSED BY THE PEOPLE

To the question of what they understood by reparations and what forms reparations could take, people stated that "it all comes back to financial, whether it be school, education health-care funding. (...) The planters got money, so why shouldn't we."[1520]; "better ... it haffi better than money"[1521]; or "'well, already that there is recognition and also some kind of compensation. (...) to let us better know our identity... at the end of the day it has to be like for the others [who got reparations], financial recognition."[1522]. One person stated that reparations were not about money but about "letting us live like we choose ... and create a society that more just and solidary (...) a real education, an education of traditional knowledge, of tembee art which is a means of writing, an art of hairdressing to pass on messages. (...) Preserving the traditional knowledge, that is reparation."[1523]

1515 Interview Miss Rachel (market vendor (83 years old), Port Antonio/Jamaica, 29.1.2011).

1516 Interview Joanna (market vendor, Port Antonio/Jamaica, 29.1.2011).

1517 Ibid.

1518 Interview Laristo (musician/mailman, Cayenne/F.Guiana, 18.9.2011) ("les consequences sont là").

1519 Interview Dada (unemployed, Cayenne/F.Guiana, 18.9.2011) ("à la base, c'est le Blanc qui dirige... (...) déjà avec la religion...faut etre catholique, il n'y a pas d'autre chose, mais se ne sont nos origines. (...) Pendant 400 ans (...) on travaille toujours pour eux".

1520 Interview Paulette (landlady, Kingston (Liguanea)/Jamaica, 15.2.2011).

1521 Interview Kenneth (market hustler, Port Antonio/Jamaica, 18.1.2011).

1522 Interview Laristo (musician/mailman, Cayenne/F.Guiana, 18.9.2011) ("bon, déjà, qu'il y a une reconnaissance et aussi de dédommagement de quelque sorte.. (...) mieux nous laisser connaitre notre identité ... en fin du compte comme les autres, la reconnaissance à titre financier").

1523 Interview Max (entrepreneur & activist, Saint-Laurent-du-Maroni/F.Guiana, 24.9.2011) ("nous laisser vivre comme on nous l'entend ... et créer une société qui est plus juste et solidaire (...), une vrai éducation, une éducation du savoir traditionnel, de l'art tembee qui est un moyen d'écriture, un art de tressage des cheveux pour passer des messages. (...) Préserver le savoir traditionnel, c'est les

Young people also brought up the issue of identity and history discourses. They criticized that in the French school system they were taught that their ancestors were the Gauls and that the history of Africa was presented as if it had only began with slavery.[1524] They also demanded that, as part of reparations, kréyol language be used in schools. I was told that reparations meant to "give us a real possibility of emancipation, to decide our lives".

One person expressed the continuity between slavery and colonialism, or rather rightly defined transatlantic slavery as one phase of colonialism: "the real crime is colonialism"[1525], and stressed that colonialism was not yet over. He explained that at the end of slavery, the colonists were compensated, and the banks of Guyane, Martinique, Guadeloupe and Réunion were created with parts of this money while the former slaves received nothing at all until today. "Nothing has changed in Guiana, only that the word is no longer colonialism."[1526]

Yet although I am still of the opinion that in "French" Guiana more people have, at least a slight, familiarity with the explicit concept of "reparations", my second research stay led me to relativize this qualification to some extent, because I encountered several people there who, like in Jamaica, had not heard at all of that term before and/or did not wish to engage in any further reasoning about the topic.

Regarding the aspect of who should take up and present an international reparations claim, some Jamaican interlocutors expressed the view that it should be the government with the people being behind it[1527], while being aware that the present government is structured "in the same colonial ways" and "part of the same colonial set-up ... we still not free" or stating that "yeah we still under colonialism"[1528].

C. ANTHROPOLOGY OF / FOR REPARATIONS

This small empirical research into legal reparations consciousness was only a beginning. Some factors of why people have or do not have consciousness of their right to reparations have been illuminated. I was not able to reproduce and summarize all of the findings in this short chapter due to lack of space, but many more questions and aspects that would need to be researched have surfaced in the course of the research.

It would be a very important task for legal professionals and anthropologists

---

réparations".)
1524 Interview Kéké (mailman, Cayenne/F.Guiana, 21.9.2011) ("donner une réelle possibilité d'émancipation, de gérer nos lives").
1525 Interview Max (entrepreneur & activist, Saint-Laurent-du-Maroni/F.Guiana, 24.9.2011) ("le vrai crime est le colonialism").
1526 Ibid. ("Rien n'a changé en Guyane, sauf que le mot n'est plus colonialism.").
1527 Interview Will (retired mechanician, Port Antonio/Jamaica, 20.1.2011).
1528 Interview Gloria (market vendor, Port Antonio/Jamaica, 20.1.2011).

to work to generate legal and social knowledge that can then be of help for social justice movements. Social science and research have to aim at social change. Otherwise they have little justification for existence. In this view, an Anthropology of, or for, Reparations would be a useful endeavour to engage in for committed activist anthropologists. Factors for legal consciousness development for reparations need to be researched in all parts and regions of the African diaspora and continent. The global reparations movement needs this kind of information in order to adapt and optimize its activities according to the respective local realities on the ground. At the same time, endeavors of activist anthropologists to empirically research about the state of people's consciousness on their entitlement to reparations through global reasonings on the ground will also help to familiarize the people with the relevant technical terms for legal action and mobilization, such as "reparations".

Although anthropology has a history of producing knowledge to oppress, some anthropologists, many of them diaspora Africans such as Eleanor Leacock and Faye V. Harrison, have stressed the importance of the discipline's ability to produce knowledge aligned with the promotion of social justice and liberation.[1529] Leacock stressed "that given an able and conscientious researcher, advocacy leads to fuller and more accurate understanding than attempted neutrality. To attempt neutrality (...) means to align oneself, by default, with the institutional structures that discriminate against and exploit poor and non-white people. (...) One can ignore realities of power and skirt the touchy question of conflict, and thereby fail to deal with the total structure of relationships in which people are involved."[1530]

Anthropological inquiry must be geared toward social transformation and human liberation. It must produce knowledge that "can be useful and potentially liberating for the world's oppressed". "Knowledge, production and praxis are inseparable. The conceptual separation built into the received tradition has served to shroud the role Western research and scholarship have actually played in rationalizing and providing useful information or 'intelligence' for socio-political control (...)."[1531]

Harrison, and I can only subscribe to her words from my own research journeys in Jamaica and Guiana, wrote of her experiences in Jamaica that they generated in her

"The confirmed conviction that anthropologists committed to a new science of humankind and a new world order must form pacts with their oppressed 'brethren and sistren', and these pacts must take precedence over many conventional professional expectations and requirements, which, as presently constituted, serve, ultimately, to reproduce (neo) colonial domination. Anthropology as a form

---

1529 Harrison (2008), 8.
1530 Leacock, Eleanor (1987). "Theory and Ethics in Applied Urban Anthopology", in: Leith Mullings (ed.): Cities of the United States, New York: Columbia University Press, 317-36, 323.
1531 Harrison (2010a), 10.

of politics has historically contributed to imperialist domination. For the discipline to gain a radically different political identity and agenda, it must be thoroughly decolonized and democratized. Anthropologists with dual and multiple consciousness have a central part to play in constructing an authentic science of humankind based upon the premises of equality and justice. (...) While multiple consciousness can engender more perspective and socially responsible field research, ethnographic experience can, in turn, enhance consciousness and commitment, and consequently influence the direction of long-term political activism (...)."[1532]

On the other hand, as Gordon stressed, even if not intentionally, anthropology per force empowers western elites by contributing to their general knowledge pool. Knowledge production is never and can never be value free. Therefore, "to be an anthropology which no longer serves the interests of the oppressors, it must be one which actively serves those of the oppressed. We must make decolonized anthropology positively, the 'anthropology of liberation'."[1533] Ulin also pointed out that a "genuinely critical and radical anthropology must challenge exploitative and hegemonic social practices and social formations"[1534].

One job of academics should be to analyze modes of struggle available under historically specific conditions. So far such research has revealed that the path to empowerment and structural transformation is usually indirect and full of contradictions, ambiguities, and reversals.[1535] This is clearly the case in the struggle for reparations and concerning legal reparations consciousness.

Harrison stressed that there is "no need for comparative research on Caribbean issues that draw boundaries that include or exclude on the basis of shared language and common colonial master rather than on the basis of factors that may actually be more significant for understanding the workings of cultural, economic, and political development".[1536] This is crucial to take to heart with regard to reparations consciousness. In that context, anthropologists need to carve out commonalities and differences in the largest number of locations possible, such as I aimed to do in "French" Guiana and Jamaica, and to produce knowledge that can be of practical help to the global African reparation movement.

The usefulness of such a multi-site research approach has been highlighted by recent trends in anthropology. Harrison therefore rejects the false dichotomy

---

1532 Harrison, Faye V. (2010c). "Ethnography as Politics", in: Harrison Faye (ed.): Decolonizing Anthropology. Moving Further toward an Anthropology for Liberation, Third Edition, Arlington: American Anthropological Association, 88-110, 105.

1533 Gordon, Edward T. (2010). "Anthropology and Liberation", in: Harrison Faye (ed.): Decolonizing Anthropology. Moving Further toward an Anthropology for Liberation, Third Edition, Arlington: American Anthropological Association, 150-169, 153 et seq.

1534 Ulin, Robert (1991). Critical Anthropology Twenty Years Later: Modernism and Post-modernism in Anthropology, in: Critique of Anthropology Vol.11, Nr. 1, 63-89, 81.

1535 Harrison (2008), 158.

1536 Harrison (2008), 206.

between "First and Third Worlds". "We must recognize the commonalties in the welfare problems faced by women trying to feed their families and keep their children alive, whether they live in drug-war-devastated inner cities of industrialized [or deindustrialized] countries or in militarized countries where conflicts are exacerbated by U.S. arms shipments."[1537]

If one takes a comparative look at the situation of average people in the former English Caribbean (which, though part of the Commonwealth, are politically independent states), the French Caribbean colonies and Africa, several things can readily be observed. For one, political without economic independence is not sufficient to enable a society to progress materially. I do not want to cast doubt here that formal independence is a big achievement in itself. The Jamaican people, for example, fought hard for their independence and are rightfully proud of it, and I think that especially on a cultural level it enabled many positive steps. Yet there may also linger a danger of illusion when full independence is not yet realized, an illusion that makes it impossible to tackle some structural problems that are absolutely detrimental to further and material progress. On the other hand, as tragic as this may be, political dependence of and incorporation into the former enslaver state, such as with the French occupied Caribbean and Guiana, may de-facto provide better living conditions for descendants of deported and enslaved Africans on a material level. Taken together, these observations speak loud for the necessity of full reparation – a reparation package that encompasses material and financial reparations, but also satisfaction in the form of acknowledgment of the fundamental illegal and genocidal character of transatlantic slavery and of full independence and sovereignty. Independence must be formal, political and economic, and go hand in hand with other forms of reparations.

Such a comparative perspective also leaves only two options with regard to an explanation of the disadvantaged position of African people globally; either it goes back to transatlantic slavery and colonialism, or African people must indeed be inherently incompetent and unfit for progress. The second position is so blatantly racist that it would generally be considered unacceptable; above that it is also clearly belied by the historical facts of great historical achievements by African people and the historical evidence of European direction and control of transatlantic slavery and its consequences. Since we are thus only left with the first explanation, who could still seriously challenge the necessity of reparations?

Indeed, "many savage inequalities expressing themselves in unemployment, subsistence insecurity, homelessness, drug abuse and violence implicate processes at the global level. In order to advance, people suffering from this condition need to (...) share their respective experiences to gain a broader perspective."[1538] Anthropologists may have an important task in mobilizing potentially power-

---

1537 Ibid., 225 et seq.
1538 Harrison (2008), 233 et seq.

ful knowledge and sharing knowledge in global networks, and therefore need to overcome limitations of individual fixation on personal careers.[1539]

Not only anthropology has a certain obligation to contribute to the reparation process, because of its constitutive contribution to colonialism. The same goes for other disciplines such as psychiatry and psychology. Books such as *"The Sanctioning of the Destruction of Lives Unworthy to Be Lived"* (1920) by psychiatrist A. Hoche and jurist K. Binding or *"The Priciple of Human Hereditary and Racial Hygiene"* (1924) by F. Lenz, E. Bauer, and the works of Eugene Fischer not only set the tone for the Shoa, but also propagated hatred toward Black people. The first president of the American Psychological Association (APA), G. Stanley Hall, theorized that Africans, Indians, and Chinese were members of adolescent races and in a stage of incomplete growth. Hall's thinking influenced the development of professional psychology in America immensely. With this notion of "adolescent races" western psychology legitimized colonialism to "save" African and other people from the liabilities of freedom.

Dr. Eugen Fischer, Director of the Kaiser Wilhelm Institute of Anthropology, Human Heredity and Eugenics, used psychology to justify the annihilation of Black children. Fischer claimed that Africans were of no value and useless for any employment other than manual work and servitude. Many "white" American doctors and psychiatrists approved of Nazi Germany's sterilization laws, providing for the sterilization of Jews and Black German children. "In fact, from 1902 up until 1931 (two years before the enactment of Germany's sterilization program), over 15,000 sterilizations were performed in the United States. The director of the United States Birth Control League, Dr. Lorthrop Stoddard, applauded Germany's efforts at cleaning up its 'race problem' and noted that Germany's sterilization laws weeded out the worst strains (Jews and coloreds) in the German stock. Stoddard's thinking had influenced and most assuredly continues to influence the idea and practice of population control in America." [1540]

Margaret Sanger, the founder of Planned Parenthood, still a huge and powerful organization in the United States today, devised a plan around 1939 to exterminate the Black population by convincing Black preachers to support birth control. Up to the 1950s, Black prisoners in New Orleans were routinely used for psychological experiments that involved surgically implanting electrodes into their brains. In 2002, the Citizen's Commission on Human Rights published statements "made by the directors of these experiments, Dr. Robert Heath from Tulane University and Dr. Harry Bailey from Australia, who boasted twenty years after the experiments that they used black people because it was 'cheaper to use Niggers than cats, because they were everywhere and cheap experimental animals'." The same Dr. Heath also received funding by the CIA to carry out drug experiments

---

1539 Ibid., 234.
1540 Crawford/Nobles/DeGruy Leary (2003), 256 et seq.

on African American prisoners in Louisiana State Prison. Many more such experiments, funded by government money, are well documented.[1541]

Mental health is an essential aspect of the human wellness and health of people. The consequences of "white" supremacism and racism, with its requisite negation and nullification of everybody and everything African, have resulted in more everlasting damage than the physical chains of bondage. Anthropology, psychology and psychiatry were the disciplines deployed intensively to justify and perpetuate the dehumanization of African people. The struggle for reparation is also about putting an end to the hatred of everything African and Black that was systematically propagated throughout centuries by European societies in general and those scientific disciplines in particular, and that has been internalized to some extent by African people themselves.

I have no doubt that there exists a dialectical relation between the scientific legal exploration and assessment of the entitlement to reparations and the emergence and development of legal consciousness in the population, an indispensable precondition not only for any start-up of international legal mechanisms but also and most importantly to get the people on a path which will lead them to take reparations. An activist-scholarly approach must thus be employed by an army of activists and anthropologists to engage people throughout the African diaspora and continent, and also Europeans and other people, in reasonings about reparations for transatlantic slavery. As Robinson stated, "the making of a well-reasoned case for restitution will do wonders for the spirit of African Americans"[1542] and Africans globally, but to realize that potential the case has to be brought to the people and built with the people.

Anthropologists and other African researchers would need to work together with lawyers and law people in order to identify the aspects that need to be incorporated into the legal argument which in turn must be employed to build people's knowledge, consciousness and power. Care needs to be taken in this since reparations are a topic far too important to be misused for wishy-washy researches. Research needs to be carried out on the premise that its aim is to expose certain factors and bring forth practically usable knowledge, while what finally would need to be implemented as reparations has to be decided exclusively by African people. As African American anthropologist Eleanor Leacock assessed, "The more serious a person's commitment is to helping some group obtain the information or skills it needs to improve its situation, the greater the care and accuracy devoted to research and support service should be."[1543] Such research projects also

---

1541 Ibid.
1542 Robinson (2000), 232.
1543 Leacock, Eleanor (1987). Theory and Ethics in Applied Urban Anthopology, in: Leith Mullings ed: Cities of the United States, New York: Columbia University Press, 317-36.

promise to add clarity to the debate about what concrete forms reparations would need to come in.

IX. Reparations NOW!!!
Reparations HOW?

Given the enormity and complexity of the damage and the severe urgency of global African reparation for the restoration of balance and for the healing that are prerequisites for the very continuity of life on our planet, I want to briefly discuss at this point what forms of reparation may be desirable and useful, as well as due by international law.

At the above mentioned UNESCO Conference in Paris on May 10, 2011, philosopher and reparations activist Louis Sala-Molins reminded the audience that the proposal submitted by Guianese parliamentarian deputy Christiane Taubira for the French law recognizing transatlantic slavery as crime against humanity had initially also contained a paragraph advocating reparations, and that when the law was finally passed, this part had been taken out. The responsible minister had explained regarding that deletion that reparations would be "too complicated".[1544] Indeed there remains little doubt that transatlantic slavery and the Maafa pose the most complicated reparation claim that ever had to be tackled legally and otherwise, but that is just so precisely because the crime is so enormous and has been continuing over such a long period of time, causing structural damage globally that is indeed incalculable. Yet, that the crime is so tremendous must be no reason for not even starting to engage in a reparation process, quite on the contrary. If reparations were only feasible for "uncomplicated" cases, well then the whole concept could be spared, devoiding much of international law of sense and purpose.

When then-French president Jacques Chirac said in a speech in Brazzaville in 1996 that "today, the west needs, not to make reparations, because neither the blood not the spiritual rape have a price, but to construct new bases of collaboration and aid in which each can recognize and respect the identity of the other"[1545], he must have been confused about some of the most basic aspects of international

1544 Intervention of Louis Sala-Molins, UNESCO Paris, May 10, 2011.
1545 Discours de M. Jacques CHIRAC, Président de la République, devant les deux chambres réunies du Parlement Congolais, Brazzaville/Congo, July 18, 1996, downloaded from http://www.jacqueschirac-asso.fr/fr/wp-content/uploads/2010/04/CONGO-18-juiillet-1996.pdf (accessed 24.3.2010) (t.b.a.).

law because many violations of international law concern the shedding of blood and violent oppression and they never "have a price", yet they generally and quite logically are subject to responsibility and reparations. If not caused by confusion, such a statement could only have been made in bad faith in order to secure the maintenance of the status quo of the legacy of slavery and colonialism and of the continuation of the crime of the Maafa, from which Chirac's country still benefits enormously in economic and political terms.

Generally speaking and drawing from personal experiences while conducting the small empirical research just retraced above, the notion that reparations would be synonymous with and restricted to financial compensation adds much counter-productive confusion to the reparations debate, and therefore needs to be deconstructed. In that endeavour, it may indeed be beneficial to depart from the various accepted forms of reparation that international law provides. Such an investigation into the legal forms of reparation may also lead to a relativization of some utterances made by various other statesmen. Thus, when Bill Clinton said that "(...) rather than reparation, the nation needs to continue to work to erase the effects of past discrimination (...)"[1546], he too must have been confused about the meaning of reparation in international law, because following the basic Chorzow rule, erasing the effects of a violation (thus, in Clinton's words, to "erase the effects of past discrimination") is exactly what any kind of reparations are aiming at; nothing more, but also nothing less. Then-President Abdoulaye Wade of Senegal, objecting to reparations on the grounds that four centuries of slavery cannot be evaluated in terms of dollars and calling the whole idea of reparations "absurd and even insulting", also confused reparations with purely monetary compensation. Wade pointed out that everyone, including his own ancestors would have practised slavery.[1547] Thus, we see once again how very crucial the analysis of semantics and of the manipulation of terms are, as well as the acknowledgment and diffusion of the assessment that "slavery" does not always equal "slavery".

Now, acknowledged law scholared Reuter stressed that "responsibility is at the heart of international law"[1548], and that responsibility as the corollary of international law is the best proof of its existence and the most credible measure of its effectiveness. De Visscher also sustained that state responsibility is the "necessary corollary" of the equality of states.[1549] Former Rapporteur of the International Law Commission Robert Ago, too, stated that reparations are the necessary corollary of law itself, and that "if one attempts (...) to deny the idea of State responsibility because it allegedly conflicts with the idea of sovereignty, one is forced to deny

---

1546 Satchell (2003), 6.
1547 Ibid.
1548 Pellet (2010), 1.
1549 de Visscher, C. (1924). La responsabilité des Etats, Leiden: Bibliotheca Visseriana, 90.

the existence of an international legal order"[1550]. If there is no responsibility, there is no law. In that perspective, the just quoted statements of western heads of states seem to imply a denial of the relevance of international law in the domain of transatlantic slavery and the Maafa, an assumption that needs to be refuted with all vehemence.

As indicated throughout this work, it could be seen at numerous instances that there is no scientific consensus as to exact numbers of how many direct victims transatlantic slavery made (UNESCO colloquium: 210 million deported or dead because of transatlantic enslavement[1551]; Maes-Diop: 400 million[1552]; others researchers: 15 million who actually reached the Americas[1553];...). In any case, the numbers are enormous and the legacy is still devastating. As Asante put it, "Numbers are only important to ascertain just how deeply the Transatlantic Slave Trade affected the continental African economic, social, physical, and cultural character. However, for purposes of reparations the numbers are not necessary since there can be no adequate compensation for the enslavement and its consequences"[1554]. Compensation is a necessary part of reparations, but full reparation such as due by international law comprises much more than money, including the destruction of the structures of the current world order that are anchored in transatlantic slavery and still based entirely on exploitation, colonialism and violence.

Reparations are due for mass murder and genocide, including the destruction of family life, for the stolen labor, and for other facets of the crime. "The result of the European invasion of Africa and the Caucasian perpetration of the crimes of enslavement, colonization and neo-colonization against Africans is the overthrow of the sovereign power of African people in their own homeland and the violently bloody imposition upon them throughout the continent and the diaspora of an unjust global law and order of White racist supremacy."[1555]

Transatlantic enslavement of Africans undermined not only contemporary lifestyles and survival chances of its direct victims, but also destroyed potentialities for their posterity, both on the continent and in the diaspora.[1556] People could not progressively learn and build skills for their development. It is in this context that one woman at a sitting of the Jamaica Reparations Commission uttered that

---

1550 Ago, Robert (1971). Third Report on State Responsibility, ILC Yearbook 1971, Vol II (1), 199, downloaded   from   http://untreaty.un.org/ilc/documentation/english/a_cn4_246.pdf   (accessed 4.3.2010).
1551 United Nations Educational, Scientific and Cultural Organization (ed.) (1978). Meeting of Experts on the African Slave-Trade, Final Report, Port-au-Prince, Haiti, 31 January-4 February 1978, downloaded from http://unesdoc.unesco.org/images/0003/000333/033360eb.pdf (accessed 21.6.2012).
1552 Diop-Maes, Louise (1993). Evolution de la population de l'Afrique Noire du neolithique au milieu du 20eme siecle, in: Ankh, Nr. 2, April 1993.
1553 Diop-Maes (1996), 209 et seq.
1554 Asante (2003), 8 et seq.
1555 Affiong/Klu (1993), 4.
1556 Asante (2003), 10.

"we are still in slavery; since independence poverty is even worse, more murder, more this, more that" [1557], and insisted that reparations would have to come in many forms, not just money.

It is also important to acknowledge that European states and the USA can only – but that they are in a legal obligation to do – deliver reparation<u>s</u>. However, the ultimate goal must be reparatio<u>n</u>, and that at last is only attainable if Africans globally are re-taking their rightful place in the world and effectuate healing for Africa. Legally due reparations by former enslaver states, also in the form of de-sisting from violently perpetuating the structures of exploitation set up through transatlantic slavery are a vital part of this endeavour, but they may never come. So while keeping in mind that Africans have a right to reparations from European perpetrators, Africans must really focus on attaining reparation, by any means necessary.

In order to further appreciate and assess the legal appropriateness of repara-tions in this case, let us take a brief look at some examples of reparations that have historically been effectuated.

One of the earliest records of a legal reparations arrangement stems from 341 BCE, when Rome and the Samnites concluded a *foedus*. However, the Samnites seem to have consistently violated it by interfering in a conflict with Palaipolis. Rome consequently demanded restitution and wanted to submit the dispute to arbitration by a third party. When Samnites refused this, war broke out again, which the Samnites lost. They then offered to give up as *a deditio* the body of their dead leader, Brutulus Paius, "in full satisfaction of the broken foedus."[1558]

Early legal systems in general unified goals of redress, deterrence, and punish-ment. Although most did not distinguish between public and private law, they recognized reparations as a necessary aspect of law. Retaliation, as a form of nega-tive restitution by equivalence, was permitted by several ancient legal codes, such as the Code of Hammurabi and Mosaic and Roman law. Roman law also knew compensation. Islamic law relied on *diya* (monetary compensation) and *qisas* (re-taliation). The Chinese Tang Code (619-906) contained rules about compensation, as did African societies, many of which provided for compensation and repair of social harmony instead of retaliation.[1559]

In African legal traditions, equity has always been a fundamental principle. Reparation, reconciliation and education about social requirements were always at the heart of African legal systems. [1560] Often, a prescribed punishment would not be applied, but transformed into reparation.[1561] The aim of a judgement was

---

1557 Jamaica National Commission on Reparations, May Pen Court House Sitting, 20.1.2010.
1558 Bederman (2001), 223.
1559 Shelton, Dinah (2006). Remedies in International Human Rights Law, Oxford: Oxford Universi-ty Press, 58 et seq.
1560 Camara (2004), 22.
1561 Elias, T. O. (1961). La nature du droit coutumier africain, Paris: Présence africaine, 144.

to re-establish harmony and to repair, not to chastise.[1562] A judge's job was not to punish but to advise and educate through speech[1563] and to help establish the truth as a necessary precondition to the reconciliation of adversaries and the reparation of eventual social imbalances that a conflict revealed.[1564] As such, the establishment of truth about transatlantic slavery and global education about that truth is another necessary and due form of reparations.

In the millenia-old legal tradition, reparations are considered to be an integral part of justice and law.[1565] Though not distinguishing between individual and state responsibility, Grotius conceded that "there arises an Obligation by the Law of Nature to make Reparation for the Damage, if any be done" from an injury caused by a violation of law. Vattel formally assimilated responsibility (though he did not use that term) to the obligation to make reparation.[1566] As stated above, the equation and limitation of reparations with and to financial compensation contributes to a considerable amount of confusion within the international debate. Thus, some Black people will say that they are against reparations, because accepting a sum of money would be tantamount to selling-out the enslaved ancestors. In this regard, it is helpful to look at the very foundation of the present reparation regime in international law. The concrete assessment and investigation of what forms of reparations are needed, has to be thorough and must of course be left to descendants of the enslaved and African people. Only a few ideas and food for further thought can be recalled and provided here.

Before embarking on our review of different forms of reparations due, it is crucial to keep conscious that these reparations are due by law. African people need to know that they have a sound legal entitlement to these measures. But these are not the reparations that will actually happen in reality, because they partly depend on the cooperation of the perpetrator states. And it is not very likely that this cooperation will ever happen, as indicated strongly by the persistent rationale of action maintained by European societies and states in the Maafa for the past 500 years. It would indeed be foolish to think that they will ever make real reparations. The reparations that will happen are those that will be taken by African people. But on the way to get there, mass mobilization is necessary and this mobilization can, I hope, be fuelled if people know what it is that the perpetrators owe them by law.

1562 Camara (2004), 37.
1563 Ibid., 45.
1564 Ibid., 55 et seq.
1565 Lykes/Mersky (2006), 590.
1566 Pellet (2010), 3.

1. BASICS OF REPARATION IN CONTEMPORARY INTERNATIONAL LAW

So for what exactly does the entitlement to reparations such as due by international law provide? The general and foundational rule of the international legal reparations regime was laid out by the Permanent Court of International Justice when it proclaimed in the *Chorzow Factory* case that "reparation must, as far as possible, wipe out all the consequences of the illegal act and re-establish the situation which would, in all probability, have existed if that act had not been committed"[1567]. Building on this fundamental principle, contemporary international law knows restitution, compensation, rehabilitation, satisfaction and guarantees of non-repetition as forms of reparation, or reparations. An injured state is entitled to select between these available forms of reparation as long as they are apt to redress the damage. In cases where the primary victim is a non-state, any state party to the relevant collective obligation has the right to invoke responsibility by seeking cessation, assurances and guarantees of non-repetition and, where appropriate, compensation in the interests of the injured person or entity.[1568]

In Art. 31, the International Law Commission also restated this basic principle of international reparation law, declaring that the "responsible State is under an obligation to make full reparation for the injury caused by the internationally wrongful act". Injury "includes any damage, whether material or moral, caused by the internationally wrongful act of a State" [1569].

"Injury" is generally broadly understood in the context of state responsibility.[1570] Paragraph 2 demands a causal link between the internationally wrongful act and the injury. It is only injury caused by an internationally wrongful act of a state for which full reparation must be made.

"The allocation of injury or loss to a wrongful act is, in principle, a legal and not only a historical or causal process. Various terms are used to describe the link which must exist between the wrongful act and the injury in order for the obligation of reparation to arise. (...) Thus, causality in fact is a necessary but not a sufficient condition for reparation. There is a further element, associated with the exclusion of injury that is too 'remote' or 'consequential' to be the subject of reparation. In some cases, the criterion of 'directness' may be used, in others 'foreseeability' or 'proximity'."[1571]

In any case, given the evidence presented in the chapters about the legal status

---

1567 The Factory At Chorzów (Germany v. Poland), Judgement of September 13, 1928, PCIJ Ser. A., No. 17, 40.
1568 Crawford (2002), 45.
1569 The Factory At Chorzów (Germany v. Poland), Judgement of September 13, 1928, PCIJ Ser. A., No. 17, 47.
1570 Crawford (2002), 202.
1571 Ibid., 204 et seq.

and about responsibility, these criteria remain unproblematic in the context of transatlantic slavery. There is no question, but indeed documented evidence, that European slavers and states knew quite well what they were doing and what the consequences would be. And if a state caused the harm deliberately, the link is usually beyond question.

"The notion of a sufficient causal link which is not too remote is embodied in the general requirement in article 31 that the injury should be in consequence of the wrongful act, but without the addition of any particular qualifying phrase." [1572] Even when two separate factors combine to cause damage, international practice has usually affirmed causality and responsibility, such as in the *Diplomatic and Consular Staff case*. In the *Corfu Channel case*, the ICJ assessed that the damage to the British ships was caused both by the action of a third state in laying the mines and by the conduct of Albania in failing to warn of their presence. Nonetheless, Albania saw its legal responsibility engaged. Even though the injury in question was effectively caused by a combination of factors, only one of which is to be ascribed to the responsible state, international practice and tribunals did not generally support a reduction or attenuation of reparation for concurrent causes. Thus, the UK recovered the full amount of its claim against Albania based on the latter's wrongful failure to warn of the mines even though Albania had not itself laid the mines.[1573] So even if, motivated by greed and manipulation at the hands of European enslavers, African individuals and societies collaborated in the transatlantic enslavement of others, this does not attenuate the responsibility and the obligation of European states to make reparations.

On the following pages now therefore, different means of reparations provided by international law and relevant to the case of transatlantic slavery will be briefly presented.

2. CESSATION, ASSURANCES AND GUARANTEES OF NON-REPETITION

Art. 30 of the International Law Commission's Articles stipulates that "the State responsible for the internationally wrongful act is under an obligation: (a) to cease that act if it is continuing; (b) to offer appropriate assurances and guarantees of non-repetition, if circumstances so require". [1574] The tribunal in the *Rainbow Warrior* arbitration case assessed "two essential conditions intimately linked" for the requirement of cessation of wrongful conduct to arise, "namely that the wrongful act has a continuing character and that the violated rule is still in force

---

1572 Ibid.
1573 Ibid.
1574 Crawford (2002), 194.

at the time in which the order is issued"[1575]. Both conditions are fulfilled in the case of transatlantic slavery. Since transatlantic slavery was only one phase of the continuing crime of the Maafa, encompassing transatlantic slavery, colonialism, neo-colonialism and global apartheid and characterized in its entirety by genocide and the violation of sovereignty of African states and of Africans, this Article proscribes that European states and the USA have to cease from their illegal conduct towards Africans and offer guarantees of non-repetition. The obligation to respect African sovereignty[1576] is still in force, and the violation of African sovereignty, perduring now for 500 years, has to stop.

The mechanisms employed to get transatlantic slavery started and running are the same that still continue to be used today in the ever-continuing exploitation of global Africa. Just like Europeans armed corruptible African individuals and interest groups and got rid of rulers and leaders who defended their people to the detriment of European economic interests, they also made sure to kill (or have killed by an African collaborator) many African leaders who worked for the upliftment of African people, thereby posing a serious threat to the structures that were set in place with transatlantic slavery. This is what happened to Patrice Lumumba in Congo, Thomas Sankara in Burkina Faso, Eduardo Mondlane in Mozambique, Barthelemy Boganda in the Central African Republic, Ruben Um Nyobe in Cameroun, Sylvanus Olympio in Togo or Amilcar Cabral in Guinea-Bissau. I do not wish to compare Laurent Gbagbo of Ivory Coast to these great leaders, but it seems very much as if he was violently removed because his politics did not suit French interests, confirming the same old pattern. Cessation of that line of internationally wrongful conduct is legally due and indeed one huge and essential component of reparation.

In fact, cessation is the first requirement in eliminating the consequences of an internationally wrongful act, thus of reparation. "The question of cessation often arises in close connection with that of reparation, and particularly restitution. The result of cessation may be indistinguishable from restitution, for example in cases involving the freeing of hostages or the return of objects or premises seized. Unlike restitution, cessation is not subject to limitations relating to proportionality."[1577] That means that even though the cessation of the violation of African sovereignty would seriously affect all European and US economies because cheap access to the resources and crude materials that are essential to western industry and lifestyle would no longer be secured, the obligation to cease from wrongful

---

1575 Rainbow Warrior (New Zealand v France), Decision of April 30, 1990, Arbitration Tribunal (1990) 82, ILR 499.

1576 Throughout this work, reference is repeatedly made to violations of "African sovereignty". Only States are considered "sovereign" in international law. Therefore, wherever allusion is made to "African sovereignty", this should be understood as referring to the sovereignty of African States and entities in general.

1577 Crawford (2002), 196 et seq.

conduct – and thus to do just that – remains.

Once the illegal conduct ceases, assurances or guarantees of non-repetition may be sought by way of satisfaction. Whereas assurances are normally given verbally, guarantees of non-repetition involve something more, such as preventive measures taken by the responsible state designed to avoid repetition of the breach.[1578]

In 23., the UN Basic Principles and Guidelines on the Right to a Remedy and Reparation for Victims of Gross Violations of International Human Rights Law and Serious Violations of International Humanitarian Law stipulate that *"Guarantees of non-repetition* should include, where applicable, any or all of the following measures, which will also contribute to prevention: (a) Ensuring effective civilian control of military and security forces; (...) (e) Providing, on a priority and continued basis, human rights and international humanitarian law education to all sectors of society and training for law enforcement officials as well as military and security forces".[1579] In the context of transatlantic slavery and the Maafa, this is a call for a balanced representation of Africa in the Security Council and other international bodies as well as for global education on the truth about transatlantic slavery. The First Pan-African Conference on Reparations hosted by the OAU in 1993 called in that respect "upon the countries largely characterised as profiteers from the slave trade to support proper and reasonable representation of African peoples in the political and economic areas of the highest decision-making bodies" and requested "the OAU to intensify its efforts in restructuring the international system in pursuit of justice with special reference to a permanent African seat on the Security Council of the UN".[1580]

3. RESTITUTION AND REPATRIATION

Article 35 deals with restitution, which together with compensation is the most prominent form of reparation. "A State responsible for an internationally wrongful act is under an obligation to make restitution, that is, to re-establish the situation which existed before the wrongful act was committed, provided and to the extent that restitution: (a) is not materially impossible; (b) does not involve a bur-

---

1578 Ibid., 198 et seq.
1579 UN General Assembly, Basic Principles and Guidelines on the Right Remedy and Reparation for Victims of Gross Violations of International Human Rights Law and Serious Violations of International Humanitarian Law, resolution adopted by the General Assembly, December 16, 2005, A/RES/60/147.
1580 Declaration of the first Abuja Pan-African Conference on Reparations For African Enslavement, Colonisation and Neo-Colonisation, sponsored by The Organisation of African Unity and its Reparations Commission April 27-29, 1993, Abuja, Nigeria.

den out of all proportion to the benefit deriving from restitution instead of compensation."[1581] Restitution has to be made to the extent that any changes that have
occurred in a situation may be traced to the wrongful act and can be reversed.
Restitution is often completed by compensation to ensure full reparation.[1582]

The UN Basic Principles and Guidelines on the Right to a Remedy and Reparation for Victims of Gross Violations of International Human Rights Law and
Serious Violations of International Humanitarian Law state in 19. that *"Restitution* should, whenever possible, restore the victim to the original situation before
the gross violations of international human rights law or serious violations of
international humanitarian law occurred. Restitution includes, as appropriate:
restoration of liberty, enjoyment of human rights, identity, family life and citizen-
ship, return to one's place of residence, restoration of employment and return of
property.[1583]

As mentioned earlier, it was in the *Factory At Chorzów* case that the Permanent
Court of International Justice set out clearly what would subsequently come to be
considered the basic rule of international reparation law. It held that the "essential
principle contained in the actual notion of an illegal act – a principle which seems
to be established by international practice and in particular by the decisions of
arbitral tribunals, is that reparations must, so far as possible, wipe out all the
consequences of the illegal act and re-establish the situation which would, in all
probability, have existed if that act had not been committed."[1584] Now, one thing
that is sure is that if transatlantic slavery had not happened, the descendants of
the deported would be living on the African continent today. Therefore, one primary reparations obligation is that those willing to return to Africa must receive
the means to do so. Before transatlantic slavery, African societies in general were
affluent, and it resorts clearly from the historic evidence that the illegal transatlantic slavery system is at the root of their present state of material misery.

The primary reliance on restitution, whenever practicable, has been recently
reaffirmed by the International Court of Justice in its opinion on Israel's security
wall. Although expressed in an advisory opinion, this was an important restate-
ment of international law because it was endorsed by fourteen of fifteen judges
very clearly:

1581 International Law Commission (2001). Draft Articles on Responsibility of States for Internationally Wrongful Acts, November 2001, Supplement No. 10 (A/56/10), chp.IV.E.1, downloaded from
http://www.unhcr.org/refworld/docid/3ddb8f804.html (accessed June 23, 2012).
1582 Crawford (2002), 213.
1583 UN General Assembly, Basic Principles and Guidelines on the Right Remedy and Reparation
for Victims of Gross Violations of International Human Rights Law and Serious Violations of International Humanitarian Law, resolution adopted by the General Assembly, December 16, 2005, A/
RES/60/147.
1584 The Factory At Chorzów (Germany v. Poland), Judgement of September 13, 1928, PCIJ, Ser. A.,
No. 17, 47.

"Israel is accordingly under an obligation to return the land, orchards, olive groves and other immovable property seized from any natural or legal person for purposes of construction of the wall in the Occupied Palestinian Territory. In the event that such restitution should prove to be materially impossible, Israel has an obligation to compensate the persons in question for the damage suffered. The Court considers that Israel also has an obligation to compensate, in accordance with the applicable rules of international law, all natural or legal persons having suffered any form of material damage as a result of the wall's construction."[1585]

Thus, one of the priorities of a comprehensive reparations approach must clearly be that those descendants willing to repatriate to Africa receive the means do so. Some Rastafarians have stressed in that regard that repatriation is different from migration. "Repatriation is about the slave masters and their following generation, paying up the obligations which are owed to Mama Africa and her people everywhere."[1586] In its reparations demands to the Queen of England, the Rastafari movement sustained that, for "those whose choice is to return to where we were taken from, strongly demand a sound economical empowerment in our home land is what we expected from the descendants and benefactors of the slave monsters. Governments in the Caribbean, England and all previous colonies surely should be prepared, where necessary, to negotiate with various leaders of African states to remove the barriers brought about by colonizers. The sons and daughters should not be forced to seek permission, visas, etc. to return to a home they were so savagely forced from. What we demand [is] that the present day government and economic power give those of us who desire Repatriation and Reparation the opportunity to do so and receive in a realistic and economically safe way home to Ethiopia [Africa]."[1587]

Restitution also encompasses the return of treasures and works of art looted from the African continent during slavery and colonialism, many of which are found today in European museums such as the Benin Bronzes in the Museum of Mankind in London or in the Parisian Quai Branly, as a result of theft and robbery during slavery and colonialism.

1585 Legal Consequences of the Construction of a Wall in the Occupied Palestinian Territory, Advisory Opinion of July 9, 2004, ICJ Reports 2004, p. 136.

1586 Ras Marcus (2010). Responding to Roy Augier, downloaded from http://www.rastafarispeaks.com/cgi-bin/forum/config.pl?noframes;read=106752 (accessed 19.6.2010).

1587 Letter of January 15, 2003 by the All Mansion's Secretariat of the Ethiopian Peace Foundation, Jamaica Branch, International Rastafari Community, Rastafari Brethren of Jamaica, to Her Royal Majesty Queen Elizabeth II, Buckingham Palace, Attention: Mrs. Kay Brock, Assistant Private Secretary, c/o Mr. Gavin Tech, Deputy British High Commissioner, Kingston.

4. COMPENSATION

Compensation is dealt with in the next Article (36): "1. The State responsible for an internationally wrongful act is under an obligation to compensate for the damage caused thereby, insofar as such damage is not made good by restitution. 2. The compensation shall cover any financially assessable damage including loss of profits insofar as it is established."[1588]

Respective of this precept of international law, the African World Reparations and Repatriation Truth Commission meeting held in Accra, Ghana, in 1993, consisting of attorneys, economists, and social scientists, issued a declaration in which it was calculated that enslavement, colonization, appropriation of land, extraction of raw materials and minerals (for example diamonds, gold, oil, mahogany, cocoa, etc.) out of Africa by Europe and the United States in the continuing crime of the Maafa cost the African continent *$777 trillion*.[1589] That sum was then claimed as compensation.

Inikori elaborated clearly in a project facilitated by UNESCO and assigned to him that the response of African societies to the external pressure gave rise to socio-economic and political structures and institutions that were not conducive to long-term economic development and competitiveness in the international economy. Between 1450 and 1870 export demand for captives kept the total population of tropical Africa at a level that was far too low to stimulate the growth of internal trade, diversification of the economy, transformation of technology and the development of commodity production for export. The political and social upheavals that transatlantic slavery engendered had serious negative effects on economic activities and restricted the inter-regional flow of goods. To procure protection against the activities of slavers, security became a far more important determinant of the choice of settlement than economic considerations, thus restricting the opportunities and incentives for economic growth, development and agricultural technology in Africa. The processes through which captives were produced for export engendered socio-economic structures that reinforced the economic consequences mentioned earlier. In combination, these factors acted as a chain on tropical African societies and facilitated the imposition of European colonial domination which aggravated the problem structurally, technologically and mentally.[1590] The high fatalities of military operations, slave raiding and wars associated with transatlantic slavery not only had serious consequences for the demographic process. It is not only logical but also documented that the polit-

---

1588 International Law Commission (2001). Draft Articles on Responsibility of States for Internationally Wrongful Acts, November 2001, Supplement No. 10 (A/56/10), chp.IV.E.1, downloaded from http://www.unhcr.org/refworld/docid/3ddb8f804.html (accessed June 23, 2012).
1589 Winbush, Omari (2003), 151.
1590 Inikori (1982), 28.

ical and social upheavals engendered through these developments had serious and lasting negative effects on economic activities. Inter-regional flow of goods was severely restricted, as were opportunities and incentives for innovation in agricultural technology. There can be no serious doubt that this pattern seriously restricted the chances for economic growth and development in Africa.[1591] The people kidnapped and enslaved were in the prime of life and at their reproductive peak. Additionally the survival rate in Africa during the transatlantic slavery area was reduced by the adverse conditions created by the enslavement.[1592]

Evidence shows clearly that all major regions of the world experienced considerable long-term population expansion between 1650 and 1850, even so among the survivors of the indigenous people in the Americas. Yet during the same period, the population of Africa declined absolutely or remained stagnant.[1593] Estimates departing from the presumption of a very reduced enslavement, touching two persons of 1,000 per year, only one-third of those being women, would equal a stop in population growth and even to a decrease. When one combines the fatalities of the hunts, captivity and transport with the birth and mortality rates of African societies, one arrives at the conclusion that the global population in Africa had to decline. This thesis has received some scepticism by some researchers, yet it was never scientifically challenged and defeated. This simulation also backed by the fact that it is based on an optimistic evaluation of life expectancy and mortality rate and only considers a part of the factual mortality provoked by transatlantic enslavement inside Africa. [1594] Manning also showed that areas most heavily impacted by transatlantic enslavement spread the thus-induced violence into regions more in the interior. This led to the widespread existence of slavery in many parts of Africa by the 19th century, not only in areas that had become directly enmeshed in the transatlantic system.[1595] While of course there can be no price on the lives of people killed, it is possible to calculate some of the damage that was inflicted on Africa through the loss of so much of its productive population, and for which there must thus be compensation.

Compensation generally corresponds to any financially assessable damage suffered by the injured state or its nationals, whereas satisfaction is generally more concerned with non-material injury.[1596]

Yet, the UN Basic Principles and Guidelines on the Right to a Remedy and Reparation for Victims of Gross Violations of International Human Rights Law

---

1591 Inikori (1982), 28.
1592 Ibid., 32.
1593 Inikori (1992b), 3.
1594 Manning, Patrick (1998). La traite negriere et l'evolution demographique de l'Afrique, in: Doudou Diene (directeur de la publication): La chaine et le lien. Une vision de la traite negriere, UNESCO, Paris, 153-173, 161f.
1595 Lovejoy (2000), XXI.
1596 Crawford (2002), 219.

and Serious Violations of International Humanitarian Law stipulate in 20. that *"Compensation* should be provided for any economically assessable damage, as appropriate and proportional to the gravity of the violation and the circumstances of each case, resulting from gross violations of international human rights law and serious violations of international humanitarian law, such as: *(a)* Physical or mental harm; *(b)* Lost opportunities, including employment, education and social benefits; *(c)* Material damages and loss of earnings, including loss of earning potential; *(d)* Moral damage; *(e)* Costs required for legal or expert assistance, medicine and medical services, and psychological and social services."[1597] Thus, mental and moral damage caused by transatlantic slavery are by international law also subject to be economically compensated.

In the context of assessing Iraq's liability under international law "for any direct loss, damage, including environmental damage and the depletion of natural resources (...) as a result of its unlawful invasion and occupation of Kuwait", compensation claims for pollution costs have been accorded by the United Nations Compensation Commission.[1598] Massive environmental pollution, still causing the deaths of countless Africans in Guadeloupe, Martinque (massive and illegal pesticide contamination), Ghana (illegal dumping of toxic electronic waste from Europe), Ivory Coast or Somalia (illegal dumping of toxic European waste before their coasts), just to give a few examples, is also rooted in transatlantic slavery and the continuing Maafa.

Reparation in this case needs to include without any doubt massive financial compensation, but must not be restricted to it. The sustenance of an integrative approach, departing from a clarification of what reparation can be by international law and what is mandated by international law in that specific case, will help generate the necessary support for reparations. This became very clear to me during a research stay in Jamaica, where I had the possibility to reason with people in everyday encounters and accompany the Jamaica Reparations Commission to its public discussions. At one such occasion a young man stated that reparations would diminish Jamaica's independence. He said that Africans should "not beg them help us, like children who cannot care for themselves". To which the late Prof. Barry Chevannes, chairman of the Commission, replied that reparation is not about begging, but "about justice and correcting a wrong". Another youth expressed the similar doubt that "reparations will [not] solve anything" (because they would come too little and too late), but could easily be misused to manipulate the people into a "here is the money, now shut your mouth" policy.[1599] A teacher

---

1597 UN General Assembly, Basic Principles and Guidelines on the Right Remedy and Reparation for Victims of Gross Violations of International Human Rights Law and Serious Violations of International Humanitarian Law, resolution adopted by the General Assembly, December 16, 2005, A/RES/60/147.
1598 Crawford (2002), 223.
1599 Jamaica National Commission on Reparations, Glenmuir High School sitting, 27.11.2009.

present at that discussion stressed the importance of equity and fairness and the fight against corruption as reparations; "even if we get reparation payments, we still have the political system ... wasting resources, wasting money". She also stated that "not everyone in this room is having African blood ... who will decide who should benefit from reparations?" Those statements highlighted the importance of making it clear to the large public what reparations are really about; the repair of the horrendous legacy of slavery, as far as possible, and the ending of the Maafa by any appropriate means.

A random example illustrates very well how many single acts of reparation necessary to redress the damage as far as possible will inevitably come back to economic measures, even if not in the sense of financial compensation. Public transport in "French" Guiana is practically non-existent, since France provides very limited public transport services, yet bars the people from organising public transports with coasters or shared taxis for themselves, as done in Jamaica under a state-supervised licensing system. Many people, who are in "French" Guiana for the sole reason that their ancestors were illegally kidnapped and enslaved under the responsibility of France, have to walk in the hot sun over long distances. Instead of doing something positive for the people after the abolition of slavery, France "invited" Maroons to integrate into society and to give up the "illegally" appropriated land they were living on while the slave holders could keep their estates and were compensated for the loss of the slaves. [1600]

It remains important to point out in the reparations debate that former enslaver states are in a legal obligation to provide redress by various means. A big part of such redress will logically come back to economic measures, such as in this illustrating example, even if strictly speaking they are not compensation. In fact, there is no reparation without economic reparations, simple as that. There is economic misery, caused by the most massive crime ever and motivated by economic profits, so there has to be economic reparations. Economic reparations are not exclusively about money being paid, but also about destroying the economic structures that were set in place through transatlantic slavery.

Any approach that aims at restricting the claim to ethical, historical, or moral "reparation" is not about reparation, and is not covered by international law. It is important to clearly state this at every opportunity. Recently, I have taken part at a panel discussion where some participants spoke out against "economic reparations" while advocating "moral" or "historical" "reparations". It seems that the global reparations movement has been knocking on the door increasingly and so vehemently during the past years that the European power establishment is getting seriously worried and now tries to engross the movement and coat it with divisive confusion. Yet, they can call such superficial measures "reparations" or

1600 Ajavon (2005), 216.

whatever else they want, but that changes nothing to the fact that it would not be reparation and would not satisfy the requirements of international law. Perpetrator states, who will be trying to get out of their responsibility by selling educational campaigns or cosmetic repentance as reparation, remain still in a legal obligation to provide real and full reparations such as demanded by international law.

Yet, since such opponents of economic reparations are seldom able to give pertinent reasons for their stance, it is not hard to prepare oneself to counter such manipulative manoeuvres. We just need to confront anyone speaking out against economic reparations with unrelenting questions about the why of their position. And we need to continue to point out that since there is huge economic damage, reparation has to be economic too, if it is to be worthy of that name.

Indeed, debates about whether what is needed would be financial, ethical, historical, educational or intellectual reparations are rather frustrating. Reparation by international law is full reparation; and if it is not that, including compensation, it is not reparation such as due by law.

5. SATISFACTION

Satisfaction, a less prominent form of reparation, also has an important role in full reparation for transatlantic slavery, as it is an important means of reparation in particular for moral damage such as emotional injury, mental suffering, injury to reputation and similar damage.[1601]

One modality of satisfaction is apology. Apology in that sense refers to the true and honest "acknowledgement of the legitimacy of the violated rule, admission of fault and responsibility for its violation, and the expression of genuine regret and remorse for the harm done"[1602]. It is not "by offering a justification or excuse for the offending behaviour, but by acknowledging that one has no excuse or justification for it"[1603]. Yet, making justifications and excuses is exactly what is presently done by European states and the USA. All European ex-enslaver states are arguing that African "slavery" would have antedated transatlantic slavery, that "slavery" would have been "legal" and that therefore no responsibility could be conferred on them. To "harm someone and then to question his or her perception of it is a double jeopardy, tantamount to 'soul murder'"[1604], and constantly denying the crime brings new pain to the victims. This, however, is what European ex-enslaver states are systematically doing. Satisfaction in its most basic form would mean a

---

1601 Falk (2006), 482 et seq.
1602 Jenkins, Catherine (2007). "Taking Apology Seriously", in: Max du Plessis and Stephen Peté (ed.): Repairing the Past? International Perspectives on Reparations for Gross Human Rights Abuses, Antwerpen/Oxford: Intersentia, 53-81, 58.
1603 Ibid.
1604 Ibid.

global and unambiguous recognition and declaration of transatlantic slavery and the Maafa as genocide and the naming of the truly responsible who direct(ed) and control(ed) the crime.

A meaningful and legally acceptable apology also needs to promise that the harmful act will not happen again; "in international law terms, a guarantee of non-repetition".[1605] Normally, an apology also implies a willingness to do whatever is appropriate to repair the harm caused, including the provision of compensation and restitution. Thus, we see that the different forms of reparation in international law are really destined to be combined with one another, and most definitely need to be applied in that manner for the transatlantic slavery and Maafa reparations claim.

It is therefore important in that regard to popularize the definition of reparation put forward in 1993 in Abuja by Chinweizu.

"Reparation is not just about money; it is not even mostly about money; in fact, money is not even one per cent of what Reparation is about. Reparation is mostly about making repairs, self-made repairs, on ourselves: mental repairs, psychological repairs, cultural repairs, organisational repairs, social repairs, economic repairs, political repairs, educational repairs, repairs of every type that we need in order to recreate and sustain viable Black societies ... More important than any monies to be received, more fundamental than any lands to be recovered, is the opportunity the Reparations campaign offers us for the rehabilitation of Black people, by Black people, for Black people, opportunities for the rehabilitation of our minds, our material condition, our collective reputation, our cultures, our memories, our self-respect, our religions, our political traditions and our family institutions; but, first and foremost, for the rehabilitation of our minds (...)".[1606]

Considering the damage brought about by the century-long demonization of anything African by the enslavers, still expressing itself today in a self-hatred of anything African by too many Black people in the diaspora and also on the continent, the UN Working Group of Experts on African people underlined the importance of states to encourage self-identification by people of African descent as a necessary precondition to adequately addressing discrimination against them in all areas and "underlined the importance of States facilitating self-recognition of people in the process of collecting disaggregated data". The Working Group called on states "to engage in comprehensive curricula reform to ensure that educational programs foster a positive self-image and pride among people of African descent and recognize the African and African descendants' contribution to world development, history and culture".[1607]

1605 Ibid., 59.
1606 Pan-Afrikan-Reparations-Coalition-In-Europe, downloaded from http://www.docstoc.com/ docs/17799955/PAN-AFRIKAN-REPARATIONS-COALITION-IN-EUROPE (accessed 7.6.2010).
1607 Working Group of Experts on People of African Descent, IX Session, April 12-16, 2010, III.

Earlier in 1978, the UNESCO experts meeting had recommended in that regard that, "African States should be asked to include the teaching of Caribbean cultures in their educational syllabuses at all levels and the Caribbean States should do the same with African cultures".[1608] Since responsible perpetrator states are in a legal obligation to provide the financial means –compensation – to realize this as part of reparation, this again exemplifies the intrinsic interlocking of the different modalities of reparation.

This approach is also covered by Art. 37 of the International Law Commission's Articles which holds that the "State responsible for an internationally wrongful act is under an obligation to give satisfaction for the injury caused by the act insofar as it cannot be made good by restitution or compensation. (...) Satisfaction may consist in an acknowledgement of the breach, an expression of regret, a formal apology or another appropriate modality".[1609] In the context of transatlantic slavery, this would also necessitate a clear assessment of responsibility and a rehabilitation of pre-Maafa and later African history, aimed at helping to heal the massive psychological damage discussed in Chapters II, III, V and VIII. "The appropriate form of satisfaction will depend on the circumstances and cannot be prescribed in advance. Many possibilities exist, including due inquiry into the causes of an accident resulting in harm and injury (...). One of the most common modalities of satisfaction provided in the case of moral or non-material injury to the State is a declaration of the wrongfulness of the act by a competent court or tribunal [such as in the] Corfu Channel Case."[1610]

The UN Basic Principles and Guidelines on the Right to a Remedy and Reparation for Victims of Gross Violations of International Human Rights Law and Serious Violations of International Humanitarian Law also stipulate *"Satisfaction"* in 22., and state that it "should include, where applicable, any or all of the following: *(a)* Effective measures aimed at the cessation of continuing violations; *(b)* Verification of the facts and full and public disclosure of the truth to the extent that such disclosure does not cause further harm or threaten the safety and interests of the victim, the victim's relatives, witnesses, or persons who have intervened to assist the victim or prevent the occurrence of further violations; *(c)* The search for the whereabouts of the disappeared, for the identities of the children abducted, and for the bodies of those killed, and assistance in the recovery, identification and reburial of the bodies in accordance with the expressed or presumed wish of the victims, or the cultural practices of the families and communities; *(d)*

CONCLUSIONS AND RECOMMENDATIONS, downloaded from http://www2.ohchr.org/english/issues/racism/groups/african/docs/session9/Conclusions_RecommandationsIXSession.doc (accessed 3.11.2010).
1608 United Nations Educational, Scientific and Cultural Organization (ed.) (1978). Meeting of Experts on the African Slave-Trade, Final Report, Port-au-Prince, Haiti, 31 January-4 February 1978, downloaded from http://unesdoc.unesco.org/images/0003/000333/033360eb.pdf (accessed 21.6.2012).
1609 Crawford (2002), 231.
1610 Ibid., 232 et seq.

An official declaration or a judicial decision restoring the dignity, the reputation and the rights of the victim and of persons closely connected with the victim; *(e)* Public apology, including acknowledgement of the facts and acceptance of responsibility; *(f)* Judicial and administrative sanctions against persons liable for the violations; *(g)* Commemorations and tributes to the victims; *(h)* Inclusion of an accurate account of the violations that occurred in international human rights law and international humanitarian law training and in educational material at all levels."[1611] Thus, we see that full and public disclosure on the truth about the responsibility for transatlantic slavery is due by international law, as are the financial means necessary to get there.

The comprehensive reparation approach that is commanded by international law also includes the obligation of former enslaver states to ensure an equitable presence of African/Black people at all levels within their organization; that they ensure full and effective access to the justice system for all individuals, including African/Black people and actively fight racist practices of the executive branches; and that they recognize ownership of ancestral lands inhabited for generations by descendants of enslaved Africans and assist them in the productive utilization of land and the comprehensive development of these communities, while respecting their culture and their specific forms of decision-making.[1612] This was endorsed by the UN's The Working Group of Experts on People of African Descent that highlighted the need to "combat discrimination against people of African descent in the administration of justice" by "appropriate training (...) for all those who are part of the justice system, including judges, prosecutors, law enforcement officers, and child welfare workers, to ensure they are sensitive to issues related to culture, diversity, racism and racial profiling".[1613] The Working Group also recommended "that States examine and revise laws and practices that have a disproportionate impact upon people of African descent in the criminal justice system and lead to their over-representation in prisons and other places of detention", and asked States to adopt measures facilitating "increased representation of people of African descent in the judiciary and in law enforcement".[1614]

States are also in a legal obligation to put a stop to the particular problems of

---

1611 Resolution adopted by the General Assembly [on the report of the Third Committee (A/60/509/Add.1)] 60/147. Basic Principles and Guidelines on the Right to a Remedy and Reparation for Victims of Gross Violations of International Human Rights Law and Serious Violations of International Humanitarian Law.

1612 Pan-Afrikan-Reparations-Coalition-In-Europe, downloaded from http://www.docstoc.com/docs/17799955/PAN-AFRIKAN-REPARATIONS-COALITION-IN-EUROPE (accessed 7.6.2010).

1613 Working Group of Experts on People of African Descent, IX Session, April 12-16, 2010, III. CONCLUSIONS AND RECOMMENDATIONS, downloaded from http://www2.ohchr.org/english/issues/racism/groups/african/docs/session9/Conclusions_RecommandationsIXSession.doc (accessed 3.11.2010).

1614 Ibid.

religious prejudice and intolerance that many descendants of enslaved Africans experience, such as brethren and sistren of the Rastafari movement which has also been one of the most prominent and consistent advocates for reparation and repatriation. Rastafarians are consistently persecuted and even killed because of their sacramental use of marijuana that they claim to have practiced from when they (their ancestors) still resided in the African motherland.

Satisfaction also incorporates the obligation of perpetrator states to change the names of streets and buildings that carry names of individuals who were instrumental in the realization of the genocide of transatlantic slavery and colonialism. Many countries and cities still have streets named after Christopher Columbus, as I have seen in "French" Guiana. Others are named after Leclerc, Napoleon's general responsible for reinstituting slavery. Philosopher Hegel was extremely racist, yet has numerous places and institutions throughout Europe named after him. Hegel sustained at a time when transatlantic slavery was in full effect that "the Negro exhibits the natural man in his completely wild and untamed state. We must lay aside all thought of reverence and morality – all that we call feeling – if we could rightly comprehend him: there is nothing harmonious with humanity to be found in his type of character ... [Africa] is no historical part of the world; it has no movement or development to show."[1615] Just as it is unacceptable by the standards of political correctness in western societies to praise Nazi scientists and personalities, never mind their eventual scientific contributions to their disciplines, such a degree of sensibilization must also be attained concerning personalities who helped or justified the African holocaust.

6. REHABILITATION

That last mentioned aspects bring us to the legal concept of rehabilitation which is generally associated with reparation for victims of human rights violations. Although the Articles by the International Law Commission do not mention rehabilitation as a specific form of reparation, as they relate in general to cases of international responsibility owed to other states, rehabilitation can be inferred from compensation and satisfaction.[1616] Since massive and systematic human rights violations were constitutive for the realization of transatlantic slavery, rehabilitation is one very important component of the needed reparation package.

1615 Robinson, Randall (2000). The Debt. What America Owes to Blacks, New York, Penguin Group, 27.
1616 Sandoval Villalba, Clara (2009). Rehabilitation as a Form of Reparation under International Law, London: Redress Trust, downloaded from http://www.redress.org/downloads/publications/The%20 right%20to%20rehabilitation.pdf (accessed 11.7.2012).

A. PSYCHOLOGICAL AND STRUCTURAL DAMAGE AND THE NECESSITY OF A MULTI-FACETED REPARATION STRATEGY

General reparations scholarship has highlighted that both the personal consequences of trauma and their socio-political context need to be addressed through reparations. Only dealing with the former, while leaving out the later can bring no progress for the victims on the long run. In societies rising out of political violence, reparations are recognized as a necessary part of the healing process, yet it is also widely recognized that it is extremely important to be prudent about the form in which reparations are made.[1617] "Wrong" reparations can have a counter-productive effect. It is essential that real recognition and condemnation of the crimes go hand in hand with compensation and with the establishment of structures that will ensure that such violations cannot occur in the future, while also taking care of individual needs of victims, in what concerns mental health and coping with trauma.

It is also generally recognized that it is essential that the process of reparation includes the naming of responsibility. This is crucial for healing because victims often partially internalize the blame if those really responsible are not exposed.

"At an individual level, financial reparations and other acts of reparations (e.g. building a monument) have the potential to play an important role in any process of healing, coping with bereavement, and addressing the impact of violence for victims. They can symbolically acknowledge and recognize the individual's suffering. Symbolic representations (e.g. a memorial) of what happened, particularly if relevant, can help concretize a traumatic event, aid an individual to come to terms with it, and help label responsibility. The final point is important because labelling responsibility can appropriately redirect blame toward those responsible and relieve guilt that survivors often feel."[1618]

Indeed, the entire context of how reparations come about and how society deals with the topic is essential. If not done comprehensively with the honest intention to repair, the objects of reparations may indeed further deepen wounds because they remind the victims that society is no safe place for them where their well-being is truly cared for. In the empirical research described in the above chapter I have related to this from comments of people who did not want to talk at all about anything that has to do with slavery or reparations, because they said that for them, this is like turning the knife once again in their wound.[1619] It is thus essential to acknowledge that true reparation and healing cannot come only or

---

1617 Hamber, Brandon (2006). "Narrowing the Micro and Macro: A Psychological Perspective on Reparations in Societies in Transition", in: Pablo de Greiff (ed.): The Handbook of Reparations, Oxford: Oxford University Press, 560-588, 574, 562.
1618 Ibid., 566.
1619 Interview Fabience (plumber, Saint-Laurent-du-Maroni/F.Guiana, 23.9.2011).

primarily through the furnishing of an object such as money or monuments, but also through the process of the delivery of such objects itself. What is really needed and due by law is full reparation, including material reparations accompanied by a process of true rehabilitation. In that context, it has been sustained that the "blemish of these inhumane conditions persists as a kind post-traumatic stress syndrome on the collective of Africans in America and though its original cause cannot be altered, the genesis can be understood. As is accepted in most insight approaches to mental healing (called psychotherapy), a confrontation with the original trauma and a restructuring of the mind's faulty adaptions to the assault" is warranted.[1620]

"The context in which reparations are granted needs to be one that demonstrates adequate levels of recognition, responsibility, social change and acknowledgement (...) within an environment where its meaning is felt to be genuine by those it directly affects. If not, the object itself can become (metaphorically speaking) the vehicle for re-evoking inner pain and suffering. (...) Reparations are a deep interpersonal and social barometer for victims. They tell the victim much about their place in society and signal whether there is social space for their grief, anger and feelings of injustice."[1621]

As Chinweizu stated, "the most important aspect of Reparations is not the money the campaign may or may not bring; the most important part of Reparations is our self-repair; the change it will bring about in our understanding of our history, of ourselves and of our destiny; the change it will bring about in our place in the World."[1622] Or as one woman at a sitting of the Jamaican Reparations Commission exclaimed, reparations and "self-reparation" must go hand in hand. [1623]

During the reasonings for the research and the sittings of the Jamaica Reparations Commission, some people responded to the effect that they were against reparations because "that would be like selling out once again the ancestors who were enslaved" and that it would be amoral to accept money as compensation for what happened. The general phenomenon of refusing reparations has been dealt with by scholars in the context of other human rights violations. Thus, the Madres de la Plaza de Mayo, the "mothers of the disappeared" group in Argentina, still refuse monetary compensation. In Brazil, some families of the murdered and disappeared during the dictatorship rejected attempts to compensate them "as the government's final attempt to buy their silence and close the book on the past without revealing the true facts of what happened."[1624] In all these instances, survivors or descendants perceive reparations as a form of "blood money", because they feel that reparations are being used to buy their silence in the absence

---

1620   Abkar, Na'im (1996). Breaking the Chains of Psychological Slavery, Mind Productions & Associates, Inc.: Tallahassee, i.
1621   Hamber (2006), 571.
1622   In: ARM-UK C, Affiong/ Klu, 4 (ohne genauere Angabe).
1623   Jamaica National Commission on Reparations, May Pen Sitting, 25.9.2009.
1624   Hamber (2006), 577 et seq.

of truth and justice. "Reparations, justice, and truth recovery need to be linked for reparation to be 'good enough' (...)."[1625] Considerate of this state of affairs, it is important to relativize expressions of rejection of reparations in the light of all the structural damage, and not to instrumentalize them as a waiver to reparations, such as attempted by western politicians. Many of the reasonings I engaged in in Jamaica revealed, unfortunately, that for many people "reparations" have come to equate monetary compensation exclusively, and that this is really the sole reason why some people are sceptical about "reparations" as such.

This detection points to another dilemma, mentioned above, that the people already need to have attained a certain level of legal consciousness in order to mobilize powerfully for the reparations process. Thus, a certain degree of "auto-repair" needs to have taken place, but in the case of transatlantic slavery the to-be-repaired structural damage is very much in the way of such auto-repair.

It is today recognized widely that trauma can perpetuate itself through generations, especially if it is the result of actions that erased fundamental moral boundaries in a society, yet were broadly permitted and often continue to be justified by the perpetrators and others. [1626] On both individual and social levels, "where gross human rights violations take place, predictability, trust, belonging, sense of self-agency and control – and hence meaning and meaning construction – are destroyed or severely affected."[1627] Traumatization is thought to be extreme if the causal actions took place over a long period and aimed at the destruction of the individual, his sense of belonging and his social activities. [1628] All of this was clearly the case in transatlantic slavery, over an extended period of almost 500 years.

Traditional psychological approaches assess that PTSD (Post-Traumatic Stress Disorder) represents a universal human phenomenon present in children and adults who have lived through war and organized violence, and that such persons need healing. More recent research has further confirmed that such traumas are chronic and intergenerational.[1629] While it is important to recognize that almost all African societies on the continent as well as in the diaspora, have lived through 500 years of war and organized violence, initiated with transatlantic slavery and not yet brought to an end, it is at the same time also crucial to stress that what are fundamentally political, economic, and psycho-social problems must not be pathologized or psychologized. These underlying structural attacks need to be identified and adequately addressed while at the same time helping people to individually cope with their individual damages suffered from these attacks.

"During war, communities are ruptured and relationships are stressed, some-

---

1625 Ibid., 577 et seq.
1626 Lykes/Mersky (2006), 592.
1627 Ibid.
1628 Ibid., 598.
1629 Ibid., 595.

times irrevocably fractured. Martín-Baró described the trauma of war as the concrete crystallization of dehumanizing social relations of exploitation and structural oppression. Friends and family members choose opposite sides of a conflict and many civilians are slaughtered in local attacks. Neighbours turn against each other, sometimes using the national/nation-wide political conflict to legitimize long-standing local conflicts. (...) It is not only the individual that is traumatized, but the social setting wherein social and cultural institutions are ruptured."[1630]

This turning of neighbors and neighboring people against one another under the mounting pressure of the transatlantic system is exactly what happened with transatlantic slavery, and is at the root of many psychological problems as well as much of contemporary warfare and violence in Africa and the diaspora.

Building on the general scientific model of PTSD, specialist medical scientists detected a disorder they baptized Post-Traumatic Slave Syndrome (PTSS) in communities of descendants of enslaved Africans. Long-term traumatic psychological and emotional injury is one direct result of slavery and continues to be perpetuated and reproduced by trauma caused by the national and global policies of inequality, racism, and oppression rooted in transatlantic enslavement. Although due to their resilience some Africans survived the immediate violence and disruption of family and home, many came out of this with serious injuries as a result of exceptionally harsh treatment at the hands of their captors, including severe psychological and emotional as well as physical damage. The recent unearthing of a slave cemetery in Washington DC is just one example testifying that enslaved Africans suffered physical injuries that have rarely been seen in recent history otherwise, and could only be the result of extreme exertion and physical deprivation.[1631] The trauma of this common and perpetual experience of Africans who could be killed and witness the killing of loved ones at any time, even after the ending of slavery and continuing to this day in some regions (for example in the form of the wars in the Congo and the gang wars in Jamaica) have to be dealt with through reparation.

After slavery had officially ended in the USA, violence and abuse continued in the form of "peonage, Black Codes, Convict Leasing, lynchings, beatings, threats to life and property, the rise of the Klan and other racist militant militias, segregation, racist killings through the police"[1632]. Individuals and groups generally acknowledged to suffer from a PTSD disorder include victims of rape, war veterans and Jewish Holocaust survivors and their children. Given the brutality and amplitude of transatlantic enslavement and the Maafa, Africans and their descendants globally are logically included in such an acknowledgement.[1633] The UN Basic Principles and Guidelines on the Right to a Remedy and Reparation

---

1630 Lykes/ Mersky (2006), 598.
1631 Crawford/Nobles/DeGruy Leary (2003), 267 et seq.
1632 Ibid., 267.
1633 Ibid.

for Victims of Gross Violations of International Human Rights Law and Serious Violations of International Humanitarian Law are also clear in that regard and provide that *"Rehabilitation* [as one form of reparations] should include medical and psychological care as well as legal and social services".[1634]

Such intergenerational trauma was researched mostly with Jewish Shoah survivors and their descendants.

"The need to historicize (...) responds to several challenges of working effectively with the psychosocial consequences of war, including trans-generational issues and what might be called social healing. A range of efforts in this respect suggests the importance for survivors and for their children and grandchildren of reconstructing identities, recognizing the agency of victims, survivors in historical, social and political processes, and providing some explanation for what happened to them. (...) Research with Holocaust survivors provides critical insight into how political trauma in the past experienced directly and indirectly several generations beyond the events. (...) This work confirms that 'breaking silence' has contributed importantly to individual and familial well-being as well as important historical protagonism in current political conflict involving this generation."[1635]

It is for these reasons that it has been acknowledged in legal scholarship on reparations that time limits for bringing forth reparation claims are highly problematic, because victims and descendants will often realize what really happened in its full scope and what rights they have only after a long time has passed.[1636] We have seen in the above chapter about the doctrine of *laches* that passage of time is no legal problem for the international transatlantic slavery reparations claim anyway because reparations have been claimed ever since the beginning of the overall crime of the Maafa, which is still continuing.

There exists an abundance of psychological and medical studies on trans-generational trauma in the African diaspora. Fred Hickling, professor at the University of the West Indies and leading Jamaican psychiatrist, for example, has assessed in a recently published study that 40% of Jamaicans suffer from personality disorders.

"In the Jamaican society, pervasive levels of stress and coping difficulties have led to the surfacing of a number of disordered personality traits. Jamaicans experi-

---

1634 UN General Assembly, Basic Principles and Guidelines on the Right Remedy and Reparation for Victims of Gross Violations of International Human Rights Law and Serious Violations of International Humanitarian Law, resolution adopted by the General Assembly, December 16, 2005, A/RES/60/147.
1635 Bar-On, Dan (1966). "Attempting to Overcome the Intergenerational Transmission of Trauma: Dialogue between Descendants of Victims and of Perpetrators", in: Roberta J. Apfel and Bennett Simon (ed.): Minefields in Their Hearts: The Mental Health of Children in War and Communal Violence, New Haven: Yale University Press, 165-188.
1636 Lykes/ Mersky (2006), 616.

ence racial, class, sexual, political and religious conflicts in their lives, which have originated from the historical experience of European imposed slavery. Slaves in Jamaica had no rights and, as such, any thoughts or concerns they had were often unheard. Jamaican slaves experienced dislocation from their African homeland, the horrors of the Trans-Atlantic middle-passage, and the genocidal enforcement of their labour on the British-owned plantations (...). They were forcibly separated from their families, their women raped and beaten by plantation owners and the men tortured and belittled by their masters. (...) Emotions had to be internalized for fear of punishment, thereby immortalizing these experiences and this way of life, which have become ingrained in the contemporary Jamaican psyche. Today, many members of Jamaican society have difficulty taking personal responsibility for their actions, preferring to put blame on something or someone else, or denying that they are even aware of what took place. Some Jamaicans turn a blind eye to illegal and immoral actions in order to avoid punishment, just as their ancestors were forced to do during slavery. (...) Most Jamaicans saw authority as social oppression, and colonization and the plantation system were the parents of the tarnished authority system. (...) No new authority systems had been established in independent Jamaica to replace colonialism."[1637]

Extreme levels of violence as a structural feature of Jamaican society have been passed on from one generation to the next for over 500 years and have their roots in the plantation society and ensuing colonialism that were based on violence against Africans as their very foundation. Enslaved persons had no rights and were permanently exposed to unimaginable levels of stress. Today, 60% of the 9-17-year-old Jamaican children declare to have a family member that was murdered. Some 17% of this age group do not think that they will get older than 25 years. [1638]

Extensive migration movements from the Caribbean to seek work, a better life, and escape unfavourable conditions are also a legacy of the structures of transatlantic slavery. Children left behind are often raised by relatives or neighbors. When this care-giving system breaks down, children may be left unprotected, unsupervised and vulnerable to harmful consequences such as physical, emotional and sexual abuse, child prostitution, and adolescent drug use.[1639] The involvement of young people in crime and violence in the Caribbean region is a serious problem, as is violence against children and also by children against other children. "In Jamaica, 25 per cent of those arrested for major crimes – including armed

---

1637 Hickling, Frederick W./Martin, Jaqueline/Harrisingh-Dewar, Allison (2008). "Redefining Personality Disorder in Jamaica", in: Frederick W. Hickling, Brigitte K. Matthies, Kai Morgan and Roger C. Gobson (ed.): Perspectives in Caribbean Psychology, Kingston: CARIMENSA, 263-288, 267 et seq.
1638 Matthies, Brigitte K./Meeks-Gardner, Julie/Daley, Avril/Crawford-Brown, Claudette (2008). "Issues of Violence in the Caribbean", in: Frederick W. Hickling, Brigitte K. Matthies, Kai Morgan and Roger C. Gobson (ed.): Perspectives in Caribbean Psychology, Kingston: CARIMENSA, 393-464, 398 et seq.
1639 Ibid., 400 et seq.

robbery, assault, rape and murder – were male youths aged 13-19 (...). Youths view violence as a useful tool for survival and social mobility, given their lack of faith in the efficacy of justice, law, and order."[1640]

A PAHO/WHO survey in nine CARICOM countries has shown that 16% of youths had been physically abused, mostly by an adult in their home. Some 10% reported sexual abuse.[1641] "The Caribbean communities of Barbados, Trinidad, Jamaica and the Leeward Islands have all been defined by sociologists as having fractured, unstable family lives and structures, resulting from slavery and the plantation system."[1642]

As long as the underlying structural problems are not addressed with its root cause – slavery – the various crime reduction initiatives can never bear fruit. As Hickling is right to highlight,

"the legacy of slavery and of the brutal plantation life is seen as a major contributor to the continued violence experienced in the Caribbean. Slavery was a form of domination in which the slave's body was not only property but turned into an object. Hickling (...) has written extensively about the historical origins of aggressive attitudes and behaviour among Caribbean people as being adaptive to the extermination of the indigenous peoples and to the brutal conditions of slavery and the post-emancipation period, and has suggested a historiographic psycho-analytical perspective on the development of violence in the region. (...) He concludes that the Jamaican people, who have survived in the New World with heightened attributes of adaptive aggression, have serious problems with authority, poor impulse control and difficulty handling power – all originating from the 500-year history of violence and migration born of European slavery and colonialism. (...) Caribbean countries have a history of armed conflict (e.g. Suriname, Grenada), riots (e.g. Jamaica), assassinations, military coups or insurrections (e.g. Guyana), and human rights crises (e.g. Haiti) in which there are reports of escalating violence, including government sponsored killing in poor neighbourhoods, arbitrary arrests, detention and shortages of food and medicine."[1643]

It resorts indeed from common sense that individuals with personality disorders are simply not able to make up an ordered and secure society. In a personal communication with Prof. Hickling, he stated that he very much acknowledges the necessity for reparations in this regard, necessary to be able to tackle these psychological problems in Jamaican society. "This mental health problem represents the psychological root of the conflicts that are endemic in this society. My work suggests that this is a condition that is passed down from generation to generation and had its roots in the authority conflicts and contradictions spawned in

---

1640 Ibid., 411.
1641 Ibid., 421.
1642 Morgan, Kai/O'Garo, Keisha-Gaye N. (2008). "Caribbean Identity Issues", in: Frederick W. Hickling, Brigitte K. Matthies, Kai Morgan and Roger C. Gobson (ed.): Perspectives in Caribbean Psychology, Kingston: CARIMENSA, 3-31, 5.
1643 Matthies/Meeks-Gardner/Daley/Crawford-Brown (2008), 394 et seq.

British plantation slavery, and midwifed in British colonialism in this country."[1644]
We thus see once again the need for an integrative approach such as already
outlined above. Hickling has written about his own psychological wound from
slavery: "One painful question reverberated in my mind as I explored the beauty
and vastness of the African motherland. Why did the Africans sell their brothers,
their sisters and us, their sons and their daughters? This was my wound of slavery,
of my history; an unspoken wound of all ex-slaves in the African Diaspora."[1645] The
structurally induced trauma cannot be healed without comprehensive reparation
and it has multiple dimensions, such as the painful question of why some African
ancestors sold one another; the experience of the genocidal Middle Passage and of
centuries-long denial of basic rights; economic marginalization; and the relationship to the international power structure that continues to propagate the myth of
non-responsibility of Europe and of Africans carelessly selling one another. While
researching for this work, I have had too many encounters with people, even
Rastafari and otherwise "conscious" people, who sustain that reparations would
be problematic since it would have been Africans who had sold their brothers and
sisters in the first place. It is therefore crucial to do away with this historic myth
that has been intentionally introduced by European slavers and maintained today
by reparation opponents, and disseminate wherever possible the real truth about
European direction and control and African collaboration with its legal technical
implications, such as pertinently elaborated in the previous part of this book, and
to thereby participate in the healing of the trauma.

In view of these assessments, it is also crucial to acknowledge that Jamaica is
an independent nation with its own research and university institutions that can
at least initiate such studies, as a first necessary step towards a solution of the detected problems, with professors such as Hickling highlighting the need for reparations in this context. "French" Guiana, on the other hand, is still occupied by the
former enslaver nation France, and I am not aware of any critical psycho-social
assessments of this sort there. This, again, shows that what is needed is an integrated and multi-faceted reparations approach, with specific implementations
according to specific local need on the ground. Jamaica has formal independence,
but no access to material assets of their ex-enslaver Britain, while the people of
"French" Guiana have not been restituted their formal sovereignty, yet have a
right to some material benefits that the French state provides for its citizens. Yet,
the entitlement to reparations such as legally due by international law provides
that all descendants of deported Africans have a right to all of this, both the respect of their sovereignty and to financial compensation.

Indeed in the formally independent Caribbean, political independence merely
represented a "redefinition of the legal status of [Caribbean] society, not bringing

---

1644 Hickling (2009), 35.
1645 Ibid., 37.

in its wake a profound social metamorphosis". [1646] The "paraphernalia of sovereignty" were transferred, but the societies remained shaped by (neo-) colonialism. The unfulfilled promises of decolonization have brought about deep rooted feelings marked by a profound sense of disappointment, alienation, frustration and anger. One way or another, such anger and frustration will find their outlets, as seen by the high levels of violence in the Caribbean. The "French" Caribbean, however, were never even officially decolonized. In both constellations, the *sufferers* and *likkle people* were never given a chance to recover their full freedom, sovereignty and material well-being. [1647]

One of the most devastating effects of transatlantic slavery was the damaging of the family. It has been assessed time and again that many of the present family problems suffered by Africans in the diaspora are rooted in slavery.

"During slavery, the Black man was valued as a stud and a workhorse. The Black woman's value to the slave master was as a breeder or sexual receptacle capable of having many healthy children. Healthy children that the white slave master could sell or work to death to make money for himself. The white man in the culture of slavery forbade marriage, a sacred rite in almost all human cultures. (...) Sale, inheritance of people, and the mobility of slave owners broke up many families. Traditional rites-of-passage ceremonies, an integral part of many African cultures, wherein the roles of the man and husband, woman and wife were explained to young people, were unknown to African descendants born into slavery. Despite the best efforts of the slave masters to destroy the Black family, poignant accounts remain of the extreme measures some African people took to maintain family ties. This included repeated trips by some brave Africans on the Underground Railroad (with its life-and-death risk) to liberate family members still held in bondage. The most well-known liberator of her people was Harriet Tubman, who returned to the South repeatedly to free her family members along with others."[1648]

In that regard, one teenager at a sitting of the Jamaica Reparations Commission in a high school suggested that reparations should help single-parent mothers to send their kids to school, since it is because of slavery that they are in the situation that they are in: poor and living in a society with structurally broken man-woman relationships.[1649]

In many regions of Africa, the shortage of men induced through the transatlantic system led to a modification of the division of labor between the sexes and to the assumption of some male tasks by the women. It also had great impact on matrimonial and family customs. Some researchers assessed that the women who

---

1646 Harrison (2008), 140.
1647 Ibid., 190.
1648 Crawford/Nobles/DeGruy Leary (2003), 266.Ibid.
1649 Jamaica National Commission on Reparations, Glenmuir High School sitting, 27.11.2009.

remained relatively numerous in Africa continued to have a usual number of children. Since more men than women (2:1) were deported, this suggests an increase in polygamous marriages and relations.[1650]
Reparation such as due by law in those regards would necessitate rehabilitation, thus a combination of compensation and satisfaction.

It has been shown throughout this work that transatlantic slavery inflicted serious devastations on the African continent. Reparations, sticking to the *Chorzow* rule, must not only deal with the legacy in the Americas, but also on the African continent and indeed globally, also in the form of rehabilitation. "Those who remained on the continent – that is, those who were not taken – were like war veterans in a war-torn land." [1651]
The general insecurity engendered by transatlantic slavery led to the erosion of customs and values, and undermined the traditional social structure. The ever-present acute or lingering violence destroyed the functioning of institutions. Political rivalries between different fractions inside societies disputing over power created a climate of perpetual civil war, such as in Senegambia or Nigeria.[1652] Warfare became the most lucrative industry and led to the development of military aristocracies throughout the continent.[1653] New power groups and short-time interests took overhand in the "national" interests of African communities, leading to a general climate that encouraged war with neighbors rather than peace. New states emerged whose very bases were the socio-political and economic structures of transatlantic enslavement, such as Ibadan. [1654] Inikori explained that the

"emphasis (...) is on the influence of the export slave trade on the character of the African states, particularly their militaristic character which gave the warrior class a great deal of influence in state matters. (...) It must be said too, that the export slave trade in many other ways created conditions for political warfare not specifically directed towards the acquisition of slaves for export. The kidnapping and sale for export of a few traders and other individuals from neighbouring territories, often led to complicated political problems ending up in some major wars. Good examples are the political complications which arose from the activities of the Ijebu slave traders in the western towns of the Ife kingdom, which eventually led to the Owu war in Yorubaland in the early 19th century. Similar political situations have been documented for Senegal and States in East Africa. Similarly,

1650 Manning (1998), 164 et seq.
1651 Bailey (2007), 151.
1652 Gueye, M'Baye (1995). "L'Afrique a la veille de la conquete", in: Elikia M'Bokolo (ed.): L'Afrique entre l'Europe et l'Amerique. Le rôle de l'Afrique dans la rencontre de deux mondes 1492-1992, Paris: UNESCO, 80-96, 94.
1653 Gueye, Adama (2003). "The impact of the slave trade on Cayor and Baol. Mutations in Habitat and Land Occupancy", in: Sylvaine A. Diouf (ed.): Fighting the Slave Trade. West African Strategies, Athens: Ohio University Press, 50-61, 52.
1654 Inikori (1992b), 33 et seq.

the proliferation of firearms in connection with the slave trade (...) contributed in some important ways to the incidence of warfare in sub-Saharan Africa during the slave trade era. Thus, it can be said that the export slave trade was a major cause of social conflict and warfare in pre-colonial Africa. This was so not because most of the wars of the period were specifically directed towards the acquisition of captives for export. Certainly some wars were so directed, and there were slave raids specifically to acquire captives for export. But the more important element is that the export slave trade helped to create values, political and social structures, economic interests, social tensions and inter-group or inter-territorial misunder-standings, all of which encouraged frequent warfare."[1655]

Transatlantic enslavement installed a permanent state of war, inter- and in-tra-community violence in the regions affected by it, that is the vast majority of the African continent. It also led to a deep corruption of indigenous African sys-tems of justice. For example, in the Gold Coast, adultery became punished with loss of freedom. Certain kings and rulers began to maintain a great number of "wives" who were employed to seduce every night young and inexperienced men who were subsequently charged with adultery, convicted and shipped.[1656]

It is very important to consider all of this when discussing solutions to the cur-rent problems of corruption and the rule of law in contemporary Africa. Pre-Maa-fa African systems of justice must be researched and rehabilitated as part of the reparation process. Yet, to draw the most benefit out of such an endeavour of researching pre-Maafa African structures and ways to do things and to organize society, it also has to be looked out for their smaller or bigger defaults which all known human societies possess to one extent or another. It seems evident that there must have been at least some seeds of disunity and other deficiencies present at the time of the arrival of the first European enslavers, because without them it would not have been so easy that Europeans impose illegal and genocidal transatlantic slavery. In any case, as evidenced by history in its chronological and relational order and clear documentation, despite such possible deficiencies, the ways of pre-Maafa societies were better in all respects of life standards and life expectancy for African people.

Throughout Africa, deep socio-political conflicts caused by the activities of Eu-ropean slavers and their African middlemen continued into the 19th century, and did not come to an end with the "abolition" of slavery, but were then utilized by France as an excuse to officially colonize Senegal.[1657] All of this needs to be addressed and the truth rehabilitated in reparations, combining measures of com-pensation and satisfaction.

Cognizant of that situation, UNESCO initiated the slave route oral tradition

---

1655 Inikori (1982), 50.
1656 Ki-Zerbo (1978), 220 et seq.
1657 Inikori (1992b), 34.

project to help to determine the present "conflict relations between ethnic groups and lineages, which, in these countries, are for certain the consequence of the slave trade and slavery".[1658] The editors of this compilation reported that the memory of the branding of slaves with hot iron for the transatlantic system still brought tears to the eyes of some of their interlocutors. They also stated that there remains a lot of bitterness and an "almost branded memory concerning certain groups within the societies for the part played by them in the Trans-Atlantic slave trade"[1659], and assessed that a lot of mending will be needed if such inter-community feelings are to be healed. Thus, Yoruba are still not happy to see Fon people, with repercussion on violence and elections in Nigeria today. We have heard and seen so much recently of the upsurge of violence in Nigeria, and given all the evidence reviewed in this work there remains little doubt that it is fundamental and urgent to finally begin with a thorough reparation process to prevent further escalation and deaths in Nigeria and elsewhere. Much more research is needed to assess the details of the damage, and that research of course necessitates financial provisions for its implementation (compensation), legally due from European perpetrator states in order to be able to bring forth truth (satisfaction) and to rehabilitate.

A colleague conducting historical research on different aspects of transatlantic slavery in Africa told me that she had been surprised to find that in the oral traditions of some peoples in Nigeria the "slave" "trade" features as an enriching activity that brought wealth. Research needs to be conducted to assess whether this is the case only for coastal former middlemen communities, but not for the interior victim communities, such as suggested by other authors.[1660]

In Ghana there are still conflicts between Ashanti and people from Southern Ghana from where many people were captured for the transatlantic system, such as from the Nzema people.[1661] Generally speaking, the UNESCO research project attested that transatlantic slavery remains a taboo subject in many parts of Africa that is not easily discussed.[1662]

Rehabilitation needs to bring to light memories of the ancient unifying ethos of Africa. As Ayi Kwei Armah reminds us, "African history antedates the Arab and European diaspora by millennia, so only part of the history of the concept of African unity involves the diaspora. You may want to argue that no thinkers conceived of the people's unity before the invaders came. In that case, you'd have to fight the documentary evidence, which we can look at, together."[1663]

1658 Simpson, Alaba (ed.) (2004). Oral tradition relating to slavery and slave trade in Nigeria, Ghana and Benin, Paris: Unesco, 5 et seq.
1659 Ibid, 5.
1660 Alagoa, E.J. (1992). Fon and Yoruba: the Niger Delta and the Cameroon, in: B.A. Ogot (ed.) General History of Africa V. Africa from the Sixteenth to the Eighteenth Century, Paris: UNESCO, 434-452, 451
1661 Simpson (2004), 41 et seq.
1662 Niane (2001), 11.
1663 Ayi Kwei Armah (2010). Remembering the Dismembered Continent. Essays, Per Ankh, Popen-

The establishment of the truth about pre-Maafa African past, transatlantic slavery and those powers responsible for it is an essential part of reparation. Given the evidence analyzed in this work and elsewhere, discourses like that of then French President Sarkozy, made in Dakar on July 26, 2007, must no longer be acceptable, just like it is totally unacceptable to blame any part of responsibility for the Shoah on Jews just because very few Jews were complaisant in the crime, or to say that Hitler also would have brought positive developments such as the construction of highways. Sarkozy in that speech said that "Africa has its part of responsibility in its own misery. It is Africans who sold other Africans to the slavers. And people killed one another at least as much in Africa as in Europe. (...) The coloniser took, but he also gave. He constructed bridges, highways, hospitals, and schools. He rendered the land fruitful; he gave his sweat, his work, his knowledge. Because not all colonisers were robbers, all colonisers were not exploiters". [1664] Possibly aware and alert that not only reparations for the past facets of the crime are at stake with the continuous acceleration of the reparations movement, but also present and future profits derived from the continuing oppression and exploitation of Africa, he continued: "Colonisation is not responsible for all present difficulties of Africa. It is not responsible for the bloody wars the Africans make between themselves. It is not responsible for the genocides. It is not responsible for the dictators. It is not responsible for corruption and prevarication. It is not responsible for the waste and pollution"[1665]. Nothing could be further from the truth, as testified by the abundant evidence presented throughout this work. Of course those who pull the triggers in the war in Congo and plant bombs in Nigeria are individually responsible for their actions, but European states remain nonetheless legally responsible for their illegal and centuries-long conduct that set the structures for such individual criminal acts and for still maintaining them. It is totally unimaginable that a German or Austrian head of state would come to Jerusalem to state that he had not come to speak of regrets and that no one could today ask young Germans or Austrians to atone for the crime of another generation.[1666] Such discourses are indicative of the determination of European ex-enslaver states to maintain the oppression and exploitation.

In that context and that of rehabilitation, it is also important to see in that "racism, as the practice of white supremacy, cannot be circumscribed by the petty injustices that individuals commit against individuals. Racism is a group practice. The theory of that practice is the viability of the race idea (...)"[1667]. The whole

---

guine Senegal, 304.
1664 Plumelle-Uribe (2008), 194 et seq.
1665 Ibid.
1666 Plumelle-Uribe, Rosa Amelia (2008). Traite des Blancs, Traite des Noirs. Aspects méconnus et conséquences actuelles, L'Harmattan, Paris, 196.
1667 Robinson (2000) Group, 17.

race idea itself is rooted in transatlantic slavery, thus contemporary problems due to "racism" cannot be solved unless reparations are made. Initiatives such as the French law punishing acts that make apology for racism are a good start, but without comprehensive reparations ensuing, will only remain superficial make-up, especially when the highest politicians of that state are at the same time holding speeches which are really nothing else than an apology of racism in its structural, genocidal and thus gravest form. Despite the awareness that the European perpetrator states will never make the reparations that they are legally obliged to make, we need to take up any possibility to remind them of this their responsibility and create public awareness. Since France has this law punishing acts that make apology of racism, people should really take them by the very heel of their own steps and bring in lawsuits in which it is elaborated that the refusal of reparations by France is really the greatest act of apologizing racism, even if it is only to create public awareness.

While doing research for this work, I came into contact with many people implicitly defending "white" supremacist positions, and that helped to sharpen my view for what arguments concerning the reparations debate are really crucial for the large public. These arguments regard questions of sovereignty of African states ("Is it really possible to say that the state criteria of territory was fulfilled for some nomads who lived in the jungle?"); the supposed "normality" of slavery ("'slavery' existed at all times, in many societies"); and the complicity of Africans in their enslavement. Too many "white" people who would consider themselves progressive refuse to engage in honest reasoning and exchange when confronted with historical facts in this context. Even in the face of (European) evidence testifying to the high development of some pre-Maafa African states and the largesse of some cities, one person persisted to refuse to acknowledge that these would have been in any way comparable to those of Europe at that time, and belittled them as having had "maybe some infrastructure" and "some chief" as king. Some Europeans told me that "people have always killed and oppressed one another", and that "the only reason why it was not the other way round – Africans enslaving Europeans – was that Africans are not be capable to do that". Now, that kind of "white" supremacists argument totally ignores such as European dominated mainstream history scholarship in general, historical research that has revealed not only that the Chinese had reached both the African and Pacific Mexican coasts before the Spanish and Portuguese without exterminating or enslaving the people there[1668], but also that Africans had voyaged to the American continent before the Europeans. The thesis of Van Sertima in that regard was credited as substantiated in a UNESCO publication. There are linguistic links between some

---

1668 M'Bokolo, Elikia (1995). La recnontre des deux mondes et ses repercussions: la part de l'Afrique (1492-1992), in: Elikia M'Bokolo (Directeur de la publication): L'Afrique entre l'Europe et l'Amerique. Le role de l'Afrique dans la rencontre de deux mondes 1492-1992, UNESCO, Paris, 13-30, 17.

pre-Columbian American and African languages, as well as architectural monu-ments in the Americas that indicate an early African presence. [1669] It was sustained in that UNESCO volume that research leaves no doubt today that interactions between the ancient Egyptians and the people of what would become the Amer-icas had taken place, such as evidenced by ancient heads sculptured from stone which display clearly African features and have been found in Veracruz, Mexico. Ancient Egyptian techniques of mummification, dating from a time when Kemet was still ruled by Africans, have also taken place at about the same time in Ol-meque culture and in Peru.[1670] There is in fact an abundance of pre-Columbian artefacts which clearly represent Africans and date back to the 13th and 14th centuries, such as the famous mixteque head displayed in the national museum of Mexico. Even Columbus had reported upon returning from one of his voyages in 1496 that the people of Hispaniola had told him that they had traded with Black people and in 1498 that the people on the coast south to Trinidad had offered him fabric such as he had also seen in Guinea. It is also documented that the emperor of Mali Aboubakri II had sent out a fleet on the Atlantic in 1310 or 1311, and that the great grandson of Sundiata, the founder of the Mali Empire, had participated in such an endeavour as well, although we have no information as to the outcome of these voyages.[1671]

Another "argument" that is often brought up is that "everyone just wants to get away from Africa, reparations don't interest anyone". It is true that many young Africans seek to leave their continent by any means, but that is due to the economic misery there which in turn goes back to the structures set up with transatlantic slavery and violently maintained ever since.

Now, evidence presented from several disciplines, such as psychiatry, psy-chology, sociology, economics, and anthropology, confirms that the ravages of transatlantic slavery have profoundly affected patterns of perception, thinking and behaviour of not only African people at home and abroad, but also of "white" people. Blacks and "whites" were both psychologically damaged. "While it in-stilled a false sense of superiority in 'Whites', transatlantic slavery discouraged independent judgement and self-reliance in Blacks."[1672]

This problem also concerns the fact that some prominent revisionist historians

---

1669 M'Bokolo, Elikia (1995). La recnontre des deux mondes et ses repercussions: la part de l'Afrique (1492-1992), in: Elikia M'Bokolo (Directeur de la publication): L'Afrique entre l'Europe et l'Amerique. Le role de l'Afrique dans la rencontre de deux mondes 1492-1992, UNESCO, Paris, 13-30, 19.

1670 Bondzie, Nana-Kow (1995). La ''decouverte'': un point de vue africain, in: Elikia M'Bokolo (Directeur de la publication): L'Afrique entre l'Europe et l'Amerique. Le role de l'Afrique dans la rencontre de deux mondes 1492-1992, UNESCO, Paris, 41-52, 44.

1671 Anselin, Alain (1995). L'Amerique et l'Afrique sans Christophe Colomb, in: Elikia M'Bokolo (Directeur de la publication): L'Afrique entre l'Europe et l'Amerique. Le role de l'Afrique dans la rencontre de deux mondes 1492-1992, UNESCO, Paris, 53-67, 64ff.

1672 Hickling (2009), 13.

such as Flaig in Germany and Petré-Grenouilleau in France give no references for their fictitious claims, maintained throughout dozens of pages, that "the majority of captives in Black Africa were produced by local authorities. (...) Generally, these remained masters of the exchange game, throughout the duration of the slave trade. (...) Black Africa entered the slave trade concretely and voluntarily"[1673]. And yet they provide not one single concrete example of a pre-Islamic or pre-European African institution approximating chattel slavery to back their contentions. Reparations need to aim at bringing a consciousness to global society where such proposals will no longer be given prominence. It is really not my intention to give exposure to such outrageous and indeed malicious proposals and I have been pondering on whether it would not be better to just treat them with the consideration they merit, that is none, but since they are written by "professors" who are given some attention by mainstream media, they must be mentioned and rectified. Flaig, among many other inaccuracies, alleges that Europeans succeeded to abolish slavery in Africa, thanks to their political efforts of will.[1674] The centrality of language and the power of its definition show through clearly here, even more so when we know that European imposed forced labor on the African continent in colonialism that was nothing else than genocidal slavery.[1675] Regarding transatlantic slavery, Flaig writes that the colonial slavery laws would have substantially limited the powers of punishment of masters, and that the observance of these "protective laws" would have depended on the extent to which a "specific public" became aware of what slave masters did and whether they condoned or condemned it. This professor seems not to be able to grasp in the least the fact that the majority of the "public" was violently enslaved and that the only part of the "public" that had any say on these genocidal laws and their implementation were the European oppressors or enslavers.[1676] This author then proceeds to sustain that the "military superiority of the natives" would not have permitted Europeans to enslave directly.[1677] We have seen at numerous instances throughout this work that the historical sources clearly show that Europeans did enslave directly and most of all relied on a vicious system of directing and controlling by military intervention. Historians such as these reveal their ahistorical and limited angle of vision when citing a king by the name of Eyo Honesty as an example of the presence and might of a great African enslaver when this king really reigned at the end of the 18th century[1678], thus at a time when Europeans and their collaborators had already wrecked the continent for 400 years. It really hurts to read proposals that the "trade in which enslaver Africans sold their African victims to European

---

1673 Pétré-Grenouilleau (2004), 74 et seq, Flaig (2009).
1674 Flaig, Egon (2009). Weltgeschichte der Sklaverei, C.H. Beck, München, 11.
1675 Flaig, Egon (2009). Weltgeschichte der Sklaverei, C.H. Beck, München, Flaig, Egon (2009). Weltgeschichte der Sklaverei, C.H. Beck, München, 15.
1676 Flaig, Egon (2009). Weltgeschichte der Sklaverei, C.H. Beck, München, 23.
1677 Flaig, Egon (2009). Weltgeschichte der Sklaverei, C.H. Beck, München, 171.
1678 Flaig, Egon (2009). Weltgeschichte der Sklaverei, C.H. Beck, München, 172f.

captains was not at all an 'unequal exchange' and by no means 'exploitation'.[1679] (...) The death rate was – compared to other transports – not very high; in the 19th century it did not figure above that of transatlantic transports of troops or convicts[1680]. (...) The material condition – food, clothing, shelter – of American slaves was better than that of European workers." [1681] Most of these proposals remain without any indication of sources. And as if that would not suffice, Flaig then goes on to call Toussaint L'Ouverture a "warlord" [1682] and to compare the situation in which Toussaint found himself obliged to institute forced labor in Haiti caused by acute food shortage in a country taken by revolution with the situation of the "colonial liberators" who would have chosen to intervene in Africa in the name of a "universal humanistic principle", that of the abolition of slavery. [1683] Flaig goes as far in his apology of genocide as to state that, "European colonialism suppressed the violent processes of enslavement, repressed the warlords and stabilized life conditions; after 1,000 years of bloodiest violence and genocides it opened the way to new possibilities. Certainly under colonial supervision. But the investions and expenses were higher than the profit drawn from the colonies."[1684] The list of such mindless statements without any anchorage in historical facts could go on and on, but here is not the place to duplicate large parts of Flaig's book. I just want to point out here still that at the end of his book Flaig explicitly refers to reparations claims and states that these would be fabricated by "African intellectuals".

Please don't be made insecure by such proposals. These historians cite no historical sources; and if they do, they cite mostly one another. We have assessed a great deal of solid sources to anchor the claims that transatlantic slavery was illegal, a genocide, that European states were legally responsible for it and that reparations are therefore due. And if not necessary for a special reason, also please don't go to buy their books and let them have your money. I have only given them some exposure here to rectify a wrong and to highlight the need not to trust blindly just because someone is made "professor" or is invited on TV. Always check their sources. And if you really feel like you have to see more of the lies that such authors propagate, check out their books in the library, but don't make them gain a dollar with maliciousness.

Yet, it remains tragic that proposals of "professors" who maintain this kind of malicious propaganda are given so much positive reception in mainstream media although it is perceivable even on a superficial basis that they do not work accurately since they trap themselves in obvious contradictions. Flaig, for example, writes that the average profits drawn from plantation economy would not have been high but would have stagnated around 10 per cent, whereas only a few pag-

1679 Flaig, Egon (2009). Weltgeschichte der Sklaverei, C.H. Beck, München, 176.
1680 Flaig, Egon (2009). Weltgeschichte der Sklaverei, C.H. Beck, München, 177.
1681 Flaig, Egon (2009). Weltgeschichte der Sklaverei, C.H. Beck, München, 187.
1682 Flaig, Egon (2009). Weltgeschichte der Sklaverei, C.H. Beck, München, 205.
1683 Flaig, Egon (2009). Weltgeschichte der Sklaverei, C.H. Beck, München, 213.
1684 Flaig, Egon (2009). Weltgeschichte der Sklaverei, C.H. Beck, München, 214.

es later he sustains that "against all expectations the slavery systems (...) did not break down, because they were economically highly profitable".[1685] It is important that reparations, in the form of rehabilitation of historical truth, be effectuated to reach a stage where the people will clearly know that such proposals have no scientific validity and that their real reason of existence is to weaken Africans and the reparations movement.

To counter this intellectual attack and as Kake diagnosed in his contribution to a UNESCO publication, the truth about transatlantic slavery must be taught in every school.[1686] Afrocentric schools, free of charge and open to all, that help reconcile Black children with their African heritage also need to be part of the comprehensive reparation package. This too would demand compensation as providing the financial means necessary for the implementation as well as satisfaction through re-establishment and access to truth.

In that regard, the then Mayor of May Pen/Jamaica, Milton Brown, also expressed "hope that reparations will end up with a people educated about its history", and mentioned that illiteracy is a big problem for the promotion of the cause of reparation. At the same time, slavery is at the root of mal-education and illiteracy, a truly vicious circle. He sustained that if people "got to really understand their history that would be the greatest benefit of reparations".[1687]

In order to fully comprehend transatlantic slavery, much research into original documents still remains to be done. And the time for this is running up, because many such thousand documents, dating back to before the 15th century and scattered in the ancient city of Timbuktu, are under acute threat. Up to 2009, they were kept in private collections due to lack of resources and constantly reduced by termites, rain and mice. The documents cover topics from medicine, history, theology, grammar and geography, and bear evidence to the remarkable intellectual history and the much overlooked pre-colonial heritage of Africa. "This is the proof," said Mr Boularaf, the curator of a new centre where these documents are preserved and studied, "Africa was not wild before the white man came. In fact, if you will excuse the expression, it was the colonising that was wild."[1688] After a visit of former President Thabo Mbeki in 2001, the South African government decided to help conserve these "most important cultural treasures". Today, they are again in acute danger given the current situation of Islamist militias occupying Timbuktu and destroying so much cultural heritage. Some manuscripts are

---

1685 Flaig, Egon (2009). Weltgeschichte der Sklaverei, C.H. Beck, München, 208.
1686 Kake, I. B. (1979). "The slave trade and the population drain from Black África to North África and the Middle East", in: The slave trade from the fifteenth to the nineteenth century, Paris: UNESCO, 164-174.
1687 Jamaica National Commission on Reparations, May Pen Sitting, 25.9.2009.
1688 Harding, Andrew (2009). Saving Africa's precious written heritage, downloaded from http://news.bbc.co.uk/2/hi/africa/8386866.stm (accessed 3.2.2010).

written in Arabic script, others in local African languages. They refute the notion that Black Africa produced only oral histories, with little or no written records. The director of that institute stressed that "there's a lot to be uncovered here. It's time we started re-looking at the history we were taught in school about Africa."[1689] Many other documents containing specific information about transatlantic slavery were taken away by European colonialists at independence.[1690] These need to be made accessible to Africans as part of the reparation process and that is what is also mandated by international law. The UN Basic Principles and Guidelines on the Right to a Remedy and Reparation for Victims of Gross Violations of International Human Rights Law and Serious Violations of International Humanitarian Law state in 24. that "victims and their representatives should be entitled to seek and obtain information on the causes leading to their victimization and on the causes and conditions pertaining to the gross violations of international human rights law and serious violations of international humanitarian law and to learn the truth in regard to these violations".[1691] Such rehabilitation of truth not only has to take place in what concerns transatlantic slavery, but also pre-Maafa African past, including that of ancient Kemet. As Ayi Kwei Armah sustains, written records of African history going back five thousand years are available in Arabic, the language of another invader, as well as in Sudani, Malian and other African languages. Children have to be taught in these languages to be able to appropriate themselves this past.[1692]

7. TRANSATLANTIC SLAVERY REPARATIONS BY AFRICAN STATES?

It seems to me that an, even superficial, examination of the various forms of reparation recognized by international law will also help to shed some light on some fundamental aspects of the debate about African collaboration in transatlantic slavery and about potential African responsibility with regard to reparations. This question is often overamplified by reparation negationists, and was expressed by Henry Louis Gates Jr. in his much discussed article for the New York Times. Gates argued that "the larger question just might be from whom they [reparations] would be extracted"[1693] and that any shared African and European

---

1689 Ibid.

1690 Niane (2001).

1691 UN General Assembly, Basic Principles and Guidelines on the Right Remedy and Reparation for Victims of Gross Violations of International Human Rights Law and Serious Violations of International Humanitarian Law, resolution adopted by the General Assembly, December 16, 2005, A/RES/60/147.

1692 Ayi Kwei Armah (2010). Remembering the Dismembered Continent. Essays, Per Ankh, Popenguine Senegal, 33.

1693 Gates, Henry Louis Jr. (2010). Ending the Slavery Blame-Game, in: New York Times, April 23,

responsibility would make reparations unfeasible in general. However, reparation in its legal conception generally aims at erasing the effects of a wrongful act, as far as possible. Now, as seen throughout previous chapters, Africa, in her entirety, has been devastated by wrongful transatlantic slavery. Relating to the question "from whom reparations would be extracted", a pertinent approach reflecting on the various forms of reparation provided by law and their fields of application leads to the conclusion that the only reparations that African societies and states can make, and may indeed be in a legal obligation to make, are satisfaction and rehabilitation. It is important to insist that this would not be a cheap or superficial way to absolution for African communities who were involved in enslaving. What it would need to be is a thorough and deep assessment of the past. Such an assessment is crucial since, as we have seen, the past of one group enslaving its neighbours, albeit under the systemic pressure of the European-induced transatlantic system and the gun-slave cycle, is at the root of many contemporary forms of warfare and violence in Africa today. This situation needs reparation and healing which will not come easy, but are nonetheless absolutely necessary. Furthermore the coming together of diaspora and continental Africans is a crucial precondition for the full recovery of African sovereignty, the focal point of any comprehensive reparation endeavour.

It is an undisputable fact that huge economic profits were extracted out of Africa to Europe and the USA through transatlantic slavery. That various individual African rulers, royal families or enslavers have also generated some short-term profits for themselves does not change this. Their profits were minimal compared to those channelled to Europe and most of them probably have since long evaporated in the general destructuration of African societies enacted by transatlantic slavery and the continuing Maafa. Thus, a comprehensive reparation endeavour that honours the legal sense and concept of the term needs to approach reparations as restitution (including the abandonment of the global economic and political structures set in place through transatlantic slavery; repatriation for Diaspora Africans willing to resettle in Africa; and much more), compensation, and satisfaction/rehabilitation (of African history, including the international declaration that pre-Maafa African servile labor did not, by any definition, equal transatlantic chattel slavery) at the hands of the responsible European entities. At the hands of any African state whose responsibility could be established, reparation in the form of satisfaction and rehabilitation – truth-finding of what African communities did to each other in order to make reconciliation with one another and with the descendants of the deported possible – is needed and is also well founded in international law. Beyond the anchorage of such an approach in international law, there also is factually no other way of reparation that contemporary African societies could make that would contribute positively to repair the damage inflicted

---

2010, A27.

by transatlantic slavery.

It may be indeed be recommendable for Africa and African states to start to take action in that regard. If African communities start to make reparation in such a manner, it will be much harder for former European enslaver states to argue that reparations could not be demanded from them because of any minor African co-responsibilities. And this has actually already begun. Ghana in 2000 provided in a law for the indefinite stay of Africans from the diaspora; under Section 17(1) (b) of the Immigration Law, Act 573, the authorities may grant the right to abode to a person of African descent in the diaspora with the approval of the President.[1694]

In that context, I want to stress once again that it seems highly important to de-emotionalize the reparations debate, to the extent possible given the monstrosity of the crime and the huge wounds caused by it, by sticking to what international law provides. Just recently, I was in a car with a Jamaican friend living in London and another friend from continental Africa, both of whom are active in the reparations movement, driving through Paris. They just got to know each other, but not even five minutes into driving they were shouting at each other over the question of whether "Africa must pay reparations too", as the Jamaican sustained. The matter was soon settled amicably, but only by arguing that all whose legal responsibility can be established, including African collaborator elites whose power and wealth today can be retraced to the crimes of their forefathers, must make reparations, but those who will have to pay reparations are the western states that directed, controlled and massively profited from the crime.

8. FULL REPARATION

Integrative of all these different modalities of reparation, international law postulates the requirement that "full reparation for the injury caused by the internationally wrongful act shall take the form of restitution, compensation and satisfaction, either singly or in combination, in accordance with the provisions of this Chapter" (Article 34 of the ILC Articles). That article makes it clear that full reparation may only be achieved in particular cases by a combination of different forms of reparation. For example, re-establishment of the situation which existed before the breach may not be sufficient for full reparation because, such as with transatlantic slavery, the wrongful act has caused additional material damage. "Wiping out all the consequences of the wrongful act may thus require some or all forms of reparation to be provided, depending on the type and extent of the injury that has been caused."[1695]

1694 Christian, Ijahnya (2011). Return of the 6th Region: Rastafari Settlement in the Motherland. Contributing to the African Renaissance, Rabat: Codesria, 13eme Assemblée générale, 26.
1695 Crawford (2002), 211.

This leads again, among others, to the direct correlation between the impact of transatlantic slavery and "ethnic" conflict in Africa today, as confirmed in recent studies. The largest numbers of slaves were taken from those areas of Africa that were most underdeveloped at the end of the 19th century and that today are the most "ethnically" fragmented.[1696]

Most people ignore that before the arrival of the Germans in Rwanda at the end of the 19th century, Hutus and Tutsis had lived together in relative prosperity in a kingdom that had been unified since the 15th century. But the German and later Belgian and French colonisers introduced racial criteria to create racial entities out of social categories. Thus, the Hutu and Tutsi races were created for the needs of the colonial domination that relies so often on the divide-and-rule stratagem.[1697]

Even though some of their descendants managed to survive in the Americas, there are groups which no longer exist in Africa due to the intense and multiple dislocations and violence that the continent and its people have experienced as a consequence of transatlantic slavery and colonialism. It has been clearly established that transatlantic slavery heavily impacted on many aspects of African societies and institutions, as well as on ideas of liberty, freedom and resistance on both sides of the Atlantic.[1698] The immediate effects of the transatlantic slavery system on the continent made warfare, displacement, and famine such a regular feature of life in some regions, such as in Senegambia, that people had to become so mobile, always ready to move in order to escape enslavers, that they were unable to carry on the exercise and development of acquired material culture and creativity as their ancestors had done. Many regions experienced poverty, technological decline, and minimalism in ceramic decorations in consequence.[1699] Redressing this damage will necessitate restitution in the form of repatriation, compensation and satisfaction.

African oral history still recalls and provides us with an idea of the impact that transatlantic enslavement had on the daily lives of African people on the continent. Bailey recounts the testimony of one Mama Dzagba of the Ewe community, recalling that "one man alone was not allowed to go single"[1700]. Chaos and fear installed themselves as permanent features of life. People were advised to travel in groups to prevent getting stolen or kidnapped. Lucy Geraldo, an over ninety-year-old woman, related that "when there is a commotion and you go there, you would never return. The Europeans would take you away. My mother said that

---

1696 Nunn, N. (2007). Historical legacies: A model linking Africa's past to its current underdevelopment, in: Journal of Development Economics Vol. 83, Nr. 1, 157-175.
1697 Plumelle-Uribe (2008), 186; see also Braeckman, Colette (1994). Rwanda. Histoire d'un genocide, Paris: Fayard.
1698 Ogundiran/Falola (2010b), 8.
1699 Ibid., 14.
1700 Bailey (2007), 35.

her grandma Agoshi was eating at home and went outside to see the commotion and she never returned". [1701]

A striking example of the prevalence that security concerns gained over other aspects such as productivity and agriculture is Ganvié, a lacustrine village in Benin. It is sometimes called the "Venice of Africa" and a tourist attraction, yet its people and other lacustrine villages were not attracted to settle there by the beauty of the landscape. Ganvié means "safe at last" and was founded during the period of transatlantic slavery when violence and fear created forced fleeing populations to seek a decent life in an environment that was then and still largely remains unattractive. Ganvié is probably the most well-known, but not the only one of such lacustrine villages that came into being as a consequence of transatlantic enslavement, though most of them no longer exist today. Its inhabitants suffer from ecological degradation, isolation, a drastic drop of fishermen's catch, lack of schools and health infrastructures and the highest rate of infant mortality (16,6%) in Benin, and, in many respects, can still be regarded as refugees. [1702] Other communities saw themselves obliged to take refuge in caves or in stilt houses, like on Lake Nyasa. This applies, among others, to communities of the Kabre, Dogon, Coniagui and Bassari. [1703] The people living in such conditions due to the illegal violence of transatlantic slavery need assistance in bettering their living chances. In legal reparation terms, this means a combination of cessation, satisfaction, restitution and compensation.

"Even years after transatlantic enslavement had ended, it is said that the sense of insecurity and fear associated with the preceding era was still there. On the other side of the Atlantic that fear was also all too real in the Diaspora communities, being exposed to lynching, segregation laws, abject poverty and pertinent discrimination. It cannot seriously be doubted that this centuries-long condition affected the psyches and minds of Africans on the continent and in the Diaspora in one way or another." [1704]

The multiplication of wars and slave raiding led to hunger (as fields often had to be abandoned due to the general insecurity), an elevation of epidemics, and hygiene regression. Doudou Diène, then division director at UNESCO, rightfully asserted that the persistence and amplitude of contemporary human rights violations in Africa are undoubtedly connected with the silence about these aspects of transatlantic slavery. [1705]

1701 Ibid.
1702 Soumonni, Elisée (2003). "Lacustrine Villages as Refugees", in: Sylvaine A. Diouf (ed.), Fighting the Slave Trade. West African Strategies, Athens: Ohio University Press, 3-14, 4.
1703 Ki-Zerbo (1978), 220.
1704 Bailey (2007), 143 et seq.
1705 Diène, Doudou (1998a). "De la traite négrière au défi du développement: réflexions sur les conditions de la paix mondiale", in: Doudou Diène (ed.): La chaîne et le lien. Une vision de la traite négrière, Paris: UNESCO, 21-23, 21 et seq.

Many regions became, even if not yet officially, colonies of the various European powers devoted entirely to the provision of captives for transatlantic enslavement. That was the case with the Portuguese colony of Angola in Central Africa from Cameroun to the Cape of Good Hope, which was structured in accordance with the requirements of large-scale production of captives. The Portuguese set in place a military regime, led by governor-traders, and had them raid neighboring kingdoms for captives and actively incited internal conflicts.[1706]

As recalled several times already, transatlantic slavery caused a dramatic increase in the use of domestic slaves on the continent. Oral history accounts and other sources give a multi-faceted picture of this domestic slavery. Slaves were used for many purposes and in many different ways. Their position depended on different parameters such as the family to whom they had been sold and the circumstances of their sale. In any case, and despite the aggravation that this situation represented compared to the pre-Maafa African types of servile labor, this slavery contrasted greatly with the transatlantic system of chattel slavery. African slavery remained at once a matter of business and family relationships, whereas transatlantic enslavement was a genocidal system that revolved ruthlessly around profits by any means and disdain for African life. [1707]

Many authors have highlighted that there is a clear relationship between the massive enslavement for the transatlantic system and the augmentation and worsening of servile labour and slavery in Africa in the course of that period and during colonialism. [1708] "There was a massive withdrawal of labour and skills from the peaceful production and distribution of commodities to the military production and distribution of slaves, as the slave trade was seen to be more profitable. As Hopkins observes, 'even when palm produce prices were at their highest in the middle of the nineteenth century, it still did not pay producers to turn from exporting slaves to shipping palm oil'."[1709]

Historical research established that the "evidence clearly refutes the contention that the transatlantic slave trade sprang from previously accumulated slaves in Africa. There was no process in place that regularly generated people for sale in the coastal societies of Western Africa before the coming of the Europeans. On the contrary, it was the power of European demand for captives to be exported as slaves that provoked large-scale gathering of captives for sale, which ultimately established a permanent process with supporting socio-economic and political structures. One part of the socio-economic structure was a large servile population, including slaves and serfs."[1710]

1706   Inikori (1992b), 36.
1707   Bailey (2007), 146 et seq.
1708   Manning (1998), 171.
1709   Inikori, Joseph E. (1982), 50.
1710   Inikori, Joseph (1996). "Slavery in Africa and the Transatlantic Slave Trade", in: Alusine Jalloh and Stephen E. Maizlish (ed.): The African Diaspora, College Station: Texas A&M University Press, 61-64, 62.

Diverse scholars such as Rodney, Lovejoy and Manning have demonstrated that transatlantic slavery radically transformed not only the character of servitude but also the societies on the continent themselves. This concerned the perversions of institutions and local beliefs, the lack of security, the proliferation of wars, and a general climate of distrust with an increase of accusations of witchcraft, adultery and other similar crimes.[1711] Since relatively young people at the peak of their productive capacity were exported, technological skills were lost to many African societies. Those who practiced them were simply not there any longer to develop and pass them on.

To sum up, transatlantic enslavement led to a massive expansion of slavery in Africa, and slave societies are generally not innovative since people with no perspective of freedom have little incentive to develop their efficiency. This situation in turn facilitated the imposition of European colonial domination which aggravated the problem structurally, technologically and mentally, thus hardening the chain imposed by transatlantic slavery, and not broken until today.[1712] Only a comprehensive reparation strategy, involving different forms of reparation such as restitution (repatriation), compensation (financial reparation for the genocide and stolen labor), satisfaction (assessment of what really happened and diffusion of that knowledge; as well as the naming of responsibility) and cessation (abandonment of genocidal structures of exploitation) can "repair" this global situation.

Many African elite and ruler groups emerged and firmly established themselves only through their collaboration with European slavers and through the use of firearms provided by these, for example on the Gold Coast in the 17th and 18th centuries. It was in these circumstances that the powerful Asante state developed. The dominant interest groups in all states who became or remained powerful during the long centuries of transatlantic enslavement were strongly linked to the export markets for captives in their respective regions.[1713] Conforming to the general line of reasoning of this work and the legal conclusions presented, it also needs to be assessed in the reparation process if and to what extent these dominant interest groups still constitute a political and economic elite in Africa today. If such continuities are detected, they must be brought to an end (cessation, satisfaction, restitution). Such a removal from power of those elites who are there because of their complicity in the Maafa is a requirement of any reparations approach since "our very spirits and souls need healing; for until this is done, reparations will be of no benefit to us, even when it is recovered. A people with a messed up mentality, which has been the trauma caused to us over the centuries of our enslavement, will not be able to handle reparations. Our leaders would simply cause any reparations to go right back into the hands of the west and the

---

1711 Rashid (2003), 135.
1712 Inikori (1992b), 1 et seq.
1713 Inikori (1992b), 34.

Arabs and Asians who have already benefited richly from the Maafa."[1714]

All forms of illegal enslavement of Africans, at the instigation of European or Arab states or rulers, need to be legally assessed and brought to reparation. As long as this is not done, the criminal and indeed still murderous legacy of slavery and enslavement will continue. In Mauritania, Black African children still disappear while out on an errand or on their way to school, to never be seen again. These children are brought to guarded camps in the interior of the country. When Mauretania deported thousands upon thousands of Black Mauritanians to Senegal and Mali during the Mauritanian-Senegalese border war of 1989, many children were left behind in the chaos and panic, and they were then picked up by these enslavers. Black Africans continue to be forced to work for Moorish masters without any pay. They are often beaten and tortured and only get to eat if there are leftovers. Many of them are not in possession of any kind of identity papers. Every possession that such a person might hold is considered to belong to the masters who often come to claim this "right" when an enslaved person dies.[1715]

Whatever the details of reparation will finally be, if we stick to the requirements of international law – that is to redress the damage as far as possible – and of African and European legal traditions, we will get where we need to get. Any reparations that do not respect these legal requirements and aim to restrict themselves to the sole payment of a certain amount of money could never be adequate to settle this claim.

The validity of this assessment has been affirmed in general in the relevant legal literature. "One of the main sources of dissatisfaction with most reparations awards is the fact that beneficiaries frequently consider them insufficient compensation. In this, they are usually correct, independently of the magnitude of the award, for reasons that have to do with the difficulty – and ultimately, the impossibility – of quantifying great harm. (...) There should not be anything in a reparations program that invites either the designers or their beneficiaries to interpret them as an effort to put a price on the life of victims or on the experiences of horror. Rather, they should be interpreted as making a contribution to the quality of life of survivors."[1716] A full package, involving all different forms of reparation, will need to be implemented.

Such an integrative approach to reparation, encompassing all of the mentioned measures and more, was also called for by the First Pan-African Conference on Reparations, hosted by the OAU in Abuja in 1994. The Conference stated that

---

1714 The Free Your Mind Movement (2007). The Abolition of Mental Slavery Act 2007, Pamphlet, 15.
1715 Cissokho, Aldiouma (2000). "Formes contemporaines de l'esclavage et necessité de réparation", in: Serge Chalons, Christian Jean-Etienne, Suzy Landau and Andre Yebakima (ed.): De l'esclavage aux reparations, Paris: Editions Karthala, 223-226, 223 et seq.
1716 De Greiff, Pablo (2006a). "Justice and Reparations", in: Pablo de Greiff (ed.): The Handbook of Reparations, Oxford: Oxford University Press, 451-477, 465 et seq.

"compensation for injustice need not necessarily be paid only in capital transfer but could include service to the victims or other forms of restitution and readjustment of the relationship agreeable to both parties".[1717] Participants also highlighted their conviction "that what matters is not the guilt but the responsibility of those states and nations whose economic evolution once depended on slave labour and colonialism, and whose forebears participated either in selling and buying Africans, or in owning them, or in colonising them", and that "the pursuit of reparations by the African peoples in the continent and in the Diaspora will itself be a learning experience in self-discovery and in uniting experience politically and psychologically". They demanded restitution for the "numerous looting, theft and larceny have been committed on the African People" and called upon "those in possession of their stolen goods, artefacts and other traditional treasuries to restore them to their rightful owners the African People". The Abuja declaration also exhorted "all African states to grant entrance as of right to all persons of African descent and right to obtain residence in those African states, if there is no disqualifying element on the African claiming the right to return to his ancestral home, Africa".[1718]

Yet it is regularly sustained, such as officially by the UK government on several occasions[1719], that, instead of making reparations, the way forward would be to sponsor aid programs for Africa and the Caribbean. This is totally unacceptable and could never bring about true healing and reparation. A lesson can be drawn from South Africa where while "(...) social upliftment [and development programs] implicitly recognized that communities suffered under apartheid, the direct links to who was responsible for this are seldom made publicly. (...) The current refusal (...) in South Africa to label some of the development work they are funding as being about 'community reparations' undermines the reparative social and psychological value of such actions."[1720] Accomplished reparation scholars such as de Greiff, Segovia and Hamber recognized in that regard that "based on (...) psychological analysis (...), development programs (...) are not really programs of reparations."[1721]

To sum up and considering the specific damage that has been done to Africa and African people globally through transatlantic slavery and the Maafa, reparations need to aim at "achieving nothing less than the total emancipation of all

---

1717 Declaration of the first Abuja Pan-African Conference on Reparations For African Enslavement, Colonisation And Neo-Colonisation, sponsored by The Organisation of African Unity and its Reparations Commission April 27-29, 1993, Abuja/Nigeria.
1718 Ibid.
1719 E.g. in the letters by the British High Commission in Kingston responding to reparation claims of the Rastafari Community of Jamaica in 2003; see also the position of European States at the WCAR in 2001.
1720 Hamber, Brandon (2006). "Narrowing the Micro and Macro: A Psychological Perspective on Reparations in Societies in Transition", in: Pablo de Greiff (ed.): The Handbook of Reparations, Oxford: Oxford University Press, 560-588, 574.
1721 Ibid., 575.

African people at home and abroad, (...) the uncompromising assertion of our full African sovereignty, particularly of our inalienable right to absolute self-determination (...)"[1722]. Since, according to the rule expressed in *Chorzow*, restitution has primacy over all other forms of reparation, this demand of restitution of African sovereignty[1723] is perfectly in accordance with international law. Huge sums of monetary compensation will surely need to be an integral part of reparation (also taking account of the fact that, after slavery ended, Black people in the west have been paid lower salaries than "whites" for the same work and were excluded from a range of working fields[1724], and that generally huge potentialities for Africans in the diaspora and on the continent were destroyed). But money can by no means be its only component. A comprehensive reparation approach is needed, in conformity with international law. The ultimate aim of reparations must be the destruction of the structures of exploitation that persist since transatlantic slavery.

True reparation has to be approached on an international and global level. European enslavers not only enslaved Africans from all over the continent and scattered them around their colonies, but they also worked together in this criminal conduct to varying degrees at various times. Ali Moussa Iye, director of the History and Memory for Dialogue Section at UNESCO, stressed that what was essential in transatlantic slavery was not so much the destination of the captives or the nationality of the enslavers, but the bestial and barbarous treatment Africans were subjected to.[1725] This is also why the UN Working Group of Experts on People of African descent called "for a UN interagency global study to collect data on people of African descent in their respective areas of work and to develop concrete recommendations that address the structural racism against people of African descent".[1726]

Yet, when it comes to concrete modalities of reparation, in the sense of repairing the damage to the extent possible, they will have to be country specific, both on the claimant and defendant side. Though the Portuguese royal house could, for example, well be obliged to give up all its assets in reparations, the country as such, due to its own present bad economic situation, may not be able to make any large compensation payments. However, the truth about transatlantic slavery and those responsible for it, that is historical rehabilitation, would still have to be taught in public education there. Portuguese firms in Africa may also have to contribute their part. Portuguese descent facienderos in Brazil would need to par-

---

1722 Affiong/Klu (1993), 5 et seq.

1723 In international law terms: "sovereignty of African States globally".

1724 Dodson (2000), 177 et seq.

1725 Châtel, Bénédicte (2011). Déconstruire le racism, Interview with Ali Moussa Iye, in: New African/Le Magazine de l'Afrique, Nr. 23, Nov-Dec 2011, 68-71, 68.

1726 Working Group of Experts on People of African Descent, IX Session, April 12-16, 2010, III. CONCLUSIONS AND RECOMMENDATIONS, downloaded from http://www2.ohchr.org/english/issues/racism/groups/african/docs/session9/Conclusions_RecommandationsIXSession.doc (accessed 3.11.2010).

take in reparations as well, the urgency of which is indicated by their continued crimes against Maroon descendants described above. Present-day African states, to which legal responsibility for their collaboration in transatlantic enslavement could eventually be attributed, might have to actively contribute to reparation mainly by satisfaction/rehabilitation of the truth and the acceptance of African descendants from the diaspora wishing to return to the continent.

The general goal of reparation, such as defined by law and justice, must be to "as far as possible, wipe out all the consequences of the illegal act and re-establish the situation which would, in all probability, have existed if that act had not been committed", that is the re-establishment of African sovereignty and the end of the genocide against African people and of global apartheid. Considerate of this it is evident that reparation for this crime, though demanded by law, would in last consequence result in a fundamental change of the global system and the end of capitalism such as we know it. Transatlantic slavery stood at the root of the capitalist system and was essential for its emergence and rise, as elaborated by historian and former Prime Minister of Trinidad and Tobago Eric Williams in his accomplished work *Capitalism and Slavery*[1727]. That would also mean, for example, the end of large agro-industrial firms like Monsanto and Ventria, who could no longer destroy natural food crops by forcing genetically engineered Frankenstein-products, such as a tomatoes containing fish genes (which revealed as carcinogenic in testing), on African farmers and make their very livelihood dependent on these firms.[1728] Ventria Bioscience currently assesses options to grow rice fused with human genes, to "help malnourished children" in Africa and other "Third world countries". Since developments such as these pose potentially irreversible danger to African people and others once the natural food crops will be permanently replaced and destroyed by the frankenstein-ones, the time to press for global African reparation is really now and must no longer be postponed.

Yet given the factual global power constellations and the fact that nothing moves by itself in general life and in international law without real power to back even the most well founded claim, it is African people globally who will have to start to *take* reparations, for example by organising campaigns not to pay taxes until France pays back the illegally extorted money to Haiti. The thus saved money could be transferred to an international fund at the disposal of the Haitian people. Such tax-refusal campaigns should be well grounded in a legal reparations argument, such as the one presented in this work.

1727   Williams, Eric (1944). Capitalism and Slavery, Richmond: University of North Carolina Press.
1728   Supreme Understanding/C'bs Alife Allah (2010). The Hood Health Handbook. Volume One, Altanta: Supreme Design Publishing, 106.

X. No Full Reparation Without Unity, No Unity Without Reparation. Random Reports

Of course such start-up campaigns of taking reparations will necessitate some degree of unity. And unity, indispensable to the achievement of full reparation, should not be hampered by overamplifying debates about whether claiming reparations would be a waste of time, time which should rather be spent in building the global African nation. Both approaches, the one of reminding African people and perpetrators of the legally long overdue reparations and of the legally due cessation of the Maafa, and the other one of building African political and economic power and self-reliance, have their importance in the same war which is fought on different frontlines and in which different roles have to be fulfilled to win. Ayi Kwei Armah wrote to me in a communication that he

"understand(s) the claim for reparations to be based on the assumption that some day Europeans and Americans will wake up and recognize that they did wrong when they came to Africa to set up a slaving enterprise, followed by a resource-pillaging economy that has gone under various names: empire, colonialism, apartheid, independence, structural adjustment, globalization, what have you. And that having woken up to their criminal liability, they will want to make amends. I see no basis in historical fact for either assumption. I see Europeans and Americans continuing steadfastly to maintain their crippling hold on us and our land, while their educational systems, churches and NGOs provide intellectual means for keeping us locked up in ignorance. Under these conditions, I'm for focusing our energies on our own awakening, not on anything we can expect from those who have worked so hard to destroy us. We've made things easy for them by remaining blind to our own potential (...)."[1729]

I totally agree with one of my very favourite writers that the expectation would be foolish that one day western governments would wake up, recognize their wrongs and want to make up. That would indeed be standing completely against Europeans' historically proven consistent rationale of acting, and it would indeed be a grave error to base the reparations struggle on any such expectations. As

---

1729 Private correspondence with Ayi Kwei Armah (on file with author).

Armah is right to state, "I'm interested in Africans developing ourselves and our land and our resources in such a serious way that Europeans will no longer dominate and exploit us, because we'll be too intelligent, and too strong, for anyone to destroy us. I'm satisfied to focus on that goal. So Europe and America exist for me only as negative vortices. I do not want to focus any of my productive attention on them." But as I understand it, what he is describing here is really nothing else than taking reparations. I have elaborated at various instances throughout this book that the main interest in the legal assessment of the anchorage of the entitlement to reparations in international law is that it may be helpful to get the people to the point where they will be ready to take reparation if Europe and America continued to refuse to give what is legally due. So, when Armah argues that the "rediscovery, development, clarification and expression of ameliorative African values are requirements underlined by our revolutionaries as an indispensable part of the decolonization process", that's really reparation. "Culturally and intellectually, decolonization means the search or research for positive African ideas, perspectives, techniques and values."[1730] That's what reparation is, too. Claiming reparations is so important not because one day western nations will wake up, but simply because African people globally need to know without any marge of doubt whatsoever which they have a legally substantiated right to reparations from western perpetrator states that have violated their legal rights for more than 500 years, and this can be an important catalyzer to take African liberation and reparation in their own hands. That is my hope.

While putting the last finishing touches to this book, Jamaica was celebrating its 50 years of independence on August 1, 2012. I have followed celebrations on the Internet, mostly via Irie FM, the world famous main radio station of the island. And indeed, the joy and pride with which Jamaicans celebrated their formal independence filled me with joy too. Now while witnessing the celebrations via the ether, I was physically in Paris, France. France never let its former plantation colonies accede to formal independence. In 1946, they were integrated into France as overseas departments, thereby doing away with the denomination as colonies and according limited material benefits such as French social security to the descendants of illegally enslaved Africans. But despite the change of terms, this constellation really still is colonialism. The descendants of the illegally enslaved and deported Africans still cannot dispose of their own destiny, have not been reconstituted in their sovereignty – which is legally due as part of reparation, and are still exploited by France.

So, on the contrasting background of Jamaica's independence joy, I also felt a certain unease at the same time about the acceptance, promotion and indeed celebration of "971", "972", and "973" – the colonial codes that France gave to its

---

1730 Ayi Kwei Armah (2010). Remembering the Dismembered Continent. Essays, Per Ankh, Popenguine Senegal, 118.

overseas departments Guadeloupe, Martinique and Guiana – by African Caribbean people hailing from there. Although it is true that "971", "972", and "973" are,
unfortunately, reality today and people may feel a need to represent this oppressive reality, it still seems somewhat disturbing that this representation is so rampant in general, but even more so in the domain of Rastafari and reggae culture. A
considerable part of reggae musicians, also claiming Rastafari, in France promote
these codes lyrically and visually in many ways. Now, though such displays and
assertions may also spring from a desire to reflect the social reality of still being
maintained in a colonized state, or to position oneself in contrast to metropolitan
France, albeit in an ambiguous manner, such representations fail to detect that
they are in fact also promoting the current colonial state that is still holding back
true progress from these countries and, most importantly, constitutes a serious
obstacle to global African unity. And for the repair of the damage caused over the
centuries of transatlantic slavery and for continued human existence on earth,
African unity and healing is vital. The psychological scopes that delimitate our
mental landscapes do limitate our possibilities. If African Caribbean people have
"971", "972", "973" or "974" as their reference point for identity, seeds of emancipation get buried.

On Facebook, I followed a few discussions ignited on the occasion of Jamaica's independence celebrations and the Olympic Games over the question of independence for the "French" Caribbean colonies. While most people expressing
themselves seemed to have no aversion to independence or autonomy as such,
quite a few stated their worries that without the subsidies and social security
from France, life standards in their countries of Guadeloupe, Martinique or Guiana would decline significantly. Some pointed to the high incidence of violence in
Jamaica and its corrupted political system with gang-related community warfare,
and suggested that the French occupied islands would fare a similar fate if independent. While some advocates of independence in these Internet discussions
pointed to other today independent former British plantation colonies that fare
better than Jamaica in these respects, I found it startling that none spoke up to
say that it really shouldn't even be a question of either independence – knotted to
material deprivation and poverty related violence – or the receipt of limited material profits from ex-slaver states – bound to the acceptance of continuing occupation and exploitation and the abandoning of any aspirations to recover African
sovereignty. All Africans, Jamaican, Guadeloupan, Martinican, Guianese, Haitian,
continental, or other have a right to reparation, and reparation by international
law and by the common-sense meaning of the term means sovereignty, independence, truth and material reparations. Only one such form of reparations without
the other is doomed to fail in every case, as seen on the examples of Jamaica
and Haiti on the one hand and Guadeloupe, Martinique and Guiana on the other.
Theoretically and in general, this is supported by reparation scholars who sustain
that reparation has to be multifaceted and adequate to every single case. "Wrong"

or insufficient reparation leads to the perpetuation of damage. The argument of better material living conditions in a continued setting of French colonial control seems even more disturbing in view of the debate that is going on simultaneously at this time about the derogation that the French government recently accorded to the "white" banana planters of Guadeloupe and Martinique, allowing them to continue spraying pesticides from air planes. This highly toxic practice has been banned by the European Union since 2009. Martinique is the country with the highest incidences of cancer worldwide, as high as in Tchernobyl. So even if Guadeloupans and Martinicans would lose some material guarantees through only formal independence without full reparation, they could at least decide to some extent what is done to them. But as artist Rara Difé Fonpanié adequately framed the problem, "It is rare that a revolution is made by a people with a full belly. The territories in the Caribbean occupied by France are held captive. Our prison is fear, our jailer the ghost of poverty, our revolution reflecting itself in the mirror of live conditions of the Haitian people and of the independent countries in the Caribbean."[1731]

Yet some participants in these Internet reasonings accused the advocates of independence of hypocrisy because they would continue to take subsidies from the French state. As if that would delegitimize their claim to independence! To state it again loud and clearly, both are due, sovereignty and money. To all Africans! One person even compared the acceptance of French social benefits while advocating independence with a child moving out but still coming back home all the time to eat, drink, watch TV, without ever giving anything in return! When I read things like this, I cry for the ancestors who had their lives taken so that France could build its empire on their blood.

And it is the direct descendants of enslavers, such as Groupe Bernard Hayot, and the French state who continue to massively profit from their de-facto colonies and are also responsible for the illegal and massive contamination with pesticides. This is indeed a very illustrious example of the continuation of genocide that started with transatlantic slavery. Apparently coco charbon has some abilities to remove pesticides and other chemicals from water, so France is actually in a legal obligation to provide the financial means to effectuate such a clean-up with coco, available abundantly in Guadeloupe and Martinique. It would indeed be interesting to have a group of African people from these islands sue the French state for this, basing their claim on the legal argumentation for reparations, eventually citing this book as evidence. I really don't see how a court could refuse the righteousness and accurateness of France's obligation to clean-up without providing

---

1731 "Il est rare qu'une révolution soit mener part un peuple qui à l'estomac plein. Les territoires occupées par la France dans la caraïbe sont maintenus captifs. Notre prison c'est la peur, notre geôlier c'est le spectre de la pauvreté, notre révolution se reflète dans le miroir des conditions de vie du peuple haïtien et des pays indépendant de la caraïbe ..."

space for large-scale exposure of the fundamental wrongness of European states' position in the reparations debate and thus for the promotion of the reparations movement. And such legal proceedings should be initiated urgently since people are dying from pesticide contamination right now!

Some Internet debaters argued that independence would not be necessary because they would be able to defend themselves against racism with diplomacy, and times would have changed since Malcolm X. This is a dangerous line of argument that blinds itself to the systematic nature of the Maafa that operates through methodical genocide, and not mainly through more or less spontaneous individual racist acts.

As brought up above, one gigantic problem with the continued colonial status and the identification of considerable parts of the people there with the colonial codes 971, 972, 973 is that this may be an obstacle to African unity. One can only be in solidarity with one nation, especially if they are at war with one another. And France and other former slaver nations have proven time and again their persistence to continue the Maafa, the genocidal war that they have been maintaining against Africans and groups of Africans since 500 years, as retraced throughout this book. "White" French people are still considering these territories as their colonies, such as put into evidence by an engaged journalist in the TV documentary "La Guadeloupe, une colonie francaise?" ("Guadeloupe, a french colony?").

Yet there were struggles for independence in these French colonies, throughout the 1940s, when they were formally elevated to the status of departments, and 1950s. This movement and its repression by France became more virulent in the 1960s, 70s and 80s, when more than a hundred people were killed by French security forces, and numerous leaders in Guadeloupe, Martinique and Guiana imprisoned and deported. Bomb attacks were directed against colonial administrations, such as police headquarters, yachts of French business men, hotels, and so on. One bomb was detected at the airport just before the arrival of President Francois d'Estaing in Guadeloupe, another one before take-off on an Air France Boeing 727. So, people wanted to be free and struggled hard for this, but the repression of the former slave master was even harder. Severe punishment was meted out for anyone giving support in any form to the *Groupe de Liberation Armée*. Yet the palace of justice in Martinque was burned down in 1981, and bombs also exploded in Paris, such as at the headquarters of Chanel next to the Ministry of Justice. In 1983, *the Alliance révolutionnaire caraibe pour les Antilles et la Guyane* staged bomb attacks in Guadeloupe, Martinique and Guiana in a coordinated effort. These attacks were directed against police cars, regional councils, court buildings as well as against the rocket base in Kourou, from which France launches in satellites, and against border control posts in Guiana, thus exclusively against agencies of the oppressive colonial state. More bombs went off in the following years, such as the one that destroyed the radio station of the French state agency promoting "white" French emigration to the colonies. In 1985, people convened the Conference of the last French colonies (Konferans a dènyè koloni fwansé) in Guadeloupe. July of that year also saw days of barricades and street fighting between the people in support of independence militants and the colonial state. France fired from a helicopter into the ghetto. In the following years and throughout the first half of the 1990s bombs continued to go off in Martinique and Guadeloupe and youths were killed by the French police. So it definitely is not as if the people of these countries have never claimed their independence, but this virulent history is rarely transmitted and silenced today. And this silencing of the memory of the ancestors and freedom fighters is abetted by the promotion of colonial codes by youth today who are not even fully aware that they may be contributing to promoting colonialism.

Given the sacrifices and fervour by the Rastafari movement to attain African redemption, I find it especially problematic that these colonial codes are also propagated in the Rasta colours of red, gold and green. The Rastafari international community, spearheaded by brethren and sistren in Jamaica, may have to acknowledge this misconception that is detrimental to what the ancients have fought and let their lives for, and make an effort to reason with and conscientize African Caribbean youth in France in this regard. The different Rasta mansions, the Nyahbinghi council and all Rastafari individuals with links to internationally loved artists such as Sizzla Kalonji should approach these artists on the importance of reasoning about this problem with artists and youths in France, Martinique, Guadeloupe and Guiana, whenever they go there for concerts and festivals. It is popular culture that is able to capture the minds of our youth these days, so all progressive movements aiming at African liberation must investigate ways to connect with cultural entertainers, also in what concerns the promotion of conscientization about the legal entitlement to reparations and related subjects.

One of the obstacles to African unity and reparation is also that the time-space specific modalities of oppression vary with respect to the respective former enslaver and coloniser and that has a hugely divisive effect in a situation where the underlying and fundamental mechanisms of oppression are really one and would therefore have to be combated as one. We have just heard about the situation in the French colonies and Jamaica. Now, in the USA for example, the situation is different again to the extent that the "white" settlers there arrived at the same time as the enslaved Africans whose descendants therefore perceive themselves more as a foundational part of that nation. That is what the Republic of New Afrika was about, claiming a part of the territory of the United States. A progressive African anthropology of/for reparations should research for all concerned regions their specifities with regard to what reparations would have to be to live up to the meaning of that term. By comparison of local experiences such an approach could also serve to tailor a global reparation strategy that could actually lead to full global African reparation.

For example, if one takes a comparative look at the situation of average people in the former English Caribbean (though part of the Commonwealth politically independent states), the French Caribbean colonies and Africa, several things can readily be observed. First, that political without economic independence is not sufficient to enable a society to materially progress. I do not want to doubt here that formal political independence is a big achievement in itself. The Jamaican people for example fought for their independence, are rightfully proud of it, and I think that especially on a cultural level it enabled many positive steps. Yet there is also a danger of illusion of full independence attached to it, an illusion that makes it impossible to tackle some structural problems that are absolutely detrimental to further substantial progress. Second, on the other hand, as tragic as this may be, continued political dependence, such as in the "French" Caribbean, may indeed guarantee better living conditions for descendants of deported and enslaved Africans on a material level. Taken together, these two observations speak loud for the necessity of full reparation – a reparation package that will encompass material and financial reparations, but also satisfaction in the form of acknowledgment of the fundamental illegal and genocidal character of transatlantic slavery resulting in the final independence of the French occupied Caribbean all while maintaining financial claims and "benefits".

In all constellations, whether it be formal but not full independence such as in Jamaica, continued formal colonialism such as for the "French" occupied territories and propagated unconsciously by colonized youth through their celebration of the colonial codes "971", "972", "973" and "974", the following words of Akbar should be pondered upon. "After 1865, we had the illusion of freedom, which made the disenfranchisement even more cruel than to the slave who was clearly defined as 'without rights'. (...) It is important to keep in mind that the image of God, which a people or a person possesses will determine the potential limits of their minds. If people have a narrow image of God, then their minds are narrow. If people believe that the biggest reality is a tree, then that is the extent to which their minds can aspire. If one believes that God can be only as large as a river or a lake, then that is as large as that mind will be able to reach. Such an image prohibits you from conceiving of the clouds which feed the ocean, your potential for understanding 'Truth' and the competence which comes from Truth is unlimited. People with a limited or narrow concept of God, then, have an automatically limited and narrowed psychology."[1732] In the same way, people who are constantly told that their reference point of identification is "971" will not reach Africa. And if they think that independence is not more than formal, people will attain neither full independence nor Africa.

[1732] Abkar, Na'im (1996). Breaking the Chains of Psychological Slavery, Mind Productions & Associates, Inc.: Tallahassee, 52

Another substantial problem that African people in other parts of the diaspora should also know about is that French society employs a subtle mechanism to uproot any emancipatory Black movement from its very springs. That mechanism is the ever-ready accusation of "communitarism" and its bedevilment. "Communitarism" is a word that creates fear in the French, and any campaign that is labelled as communitarist has already lost all chances of ever gaining broad acceptance. Anyone taking any steps at uniting people based on origin, religion, "race" or whatsoever, finds him or herself instantly accused of "communitarism" and as such already delegitimized. Now of course, this is only valid for colonized populations while the "white" French majority's communitarism continues to express itself through genocide, such as when the "white" enslaver-descendant planters link up with "white" French ministers to perpetuate exploitation and sufferation in the colonies. One day I found myself involved in a minor reasoning in an African bookstore in Paris on that question, and the shop keeper as well as another customer explained to me that this "communitarism" cudgel was employed only when Africans or Arabs were concerned, but not when Indian or Pakistani people were organizing and regrouping based on their origin. They explained this with the fact that Indians and Pakistanis were not colonized by France and thus need to be kept in check less. It is only Black and Arab youth who are harassed constantly by police identity controls, although many are French citizens. Yet when people want to mount campaigns to address this, they are taxed with the communitarism accusation.

XI. Strategies of Confusion to Weaken the Reparations Movement

Yet in spite of such manoeuvres to keep the people down, the reparations movement has gained much force in the past decades and the capitalist system, going back to and reposing in its very foundation on transatlantic slavery, is experiencing a serious crisis in these last years. It therefore is only logical that the perpetrators and profiteers of this system get increasingly worried and devise strategies to counter these developments. Thus, we need to be more than vigilant and not take all that appears progressive at first sight as also really being so in substance. For example, in May 2012, I attended a conference about reparations in a Paris bookshop and cultural center. One of the participants of the round table, an African Africanist of some local prominence, self-proclaimed reparations agitator and alleged former agent of Muammar Khaddafi, maintained with vehemence that two components would have to be kept strictly separated with regard to reparations. He explained that it would be the "civil track" on which reparations for forced labor should legally be pursued, whereas the "penal track" would have nothing to do with the reparations claim, since there could be no reparations for the murdered ancestors. I intervened to insist that the two tracks can in fact not be separated, because the very reason of why the imposition forced labor in this case was illegal is that it was extracted through illegal violence and genocide. Forced labor as such does not suffice to sustain a "civil" reparations claim, since forms of forced labor were always legal under certain conditions, such as punishment, war captivity or inheritance of servile status. Under certain conditions it is also still legal today, such as in prisons. The legal foundation for the entitlement to reparations, even from a "civil" lawsuits perspective, lays in the fact that transatlantic slavery was illegal because its genocidal ferocity was not normal and was explicitly prohibited by the laws of that time. Not even to mention again the fact that reparation is not only about money, though economic reparations are an essential part of it. So to argue that reparations are to be claimed only for the stolen labour as such, while refusing to engage the foundational aspect of transatlantic slavery as genocide, plays in the hands of reparation opponents who sustain that "slavery" would have been legal at that time.

Another highly problematic point that this professor insisted on was that he and his organization wants to see reparation claims restricted against private companies. He repeatedly said to "not attack France", because "I too am French". He spoke endlessly about how everything had been registered, what enslaved African had worked for how long for which estate and company, and that every descendant of deported Africans could file a claim against such private entities for the stolen labor on that basis. A man from Guadeloupe interjected that what interests him is not money, what interests him is that, if he is in Guadeloupe today and not in Africa, it is because France brought him (his ancestors) there. Therefore, what he wants is land to be independent. To which the "professor" responded that if he wants land, he would have to follow the same procedure the professor had just outlined concerning money claims against individual enslavers. He effectively told the man to go with his documents about his individual enslaved ancestors to the Békés, the "white" descendants of slavers in Guadeloupe and Martinique who still hold 90% of the land, and see with them who has the better claim to the land! In any case, "don't attack France!". Well, even if I had not heard rather compromising things about this professor before, these statements would have made me realize that bigger interests are most probably behind his proposals.

It is indeed most imperative that reparation claims are addressed first and foremost against the European states that instigated, controlled and directed the genocide of transatlantic slavery. It was they that gave out licences, chartered shipping companies, determined genocidal policy on the plantation colonies and pocketed huge revenues in taxes. It was France who gave the land to the Békés and still lets them have it while murdering the African population with pesticides. This event strongly indicated to me that France, as other former enslaver states, is well aware of the mounting pressure for reparations and that its fire may soon burn Europe. So they are now trying to engross the reparations debate and infuse confusion by trapping people into equating the quest for reparations with individual money claims against companies. And since they aim at ensuring to limit claims to forced labor as such as the sole legal basis while excluding the genocide component, these claims are already determined to fail before any court. Courts will contend that slavery and forced labor were legal at that time. The outcome of this will be a programmed frustration of some people who bought into it and got nothing, engendering a negative perspective on slavery reparations as such.

To take the cake entirely, the representant of this "reparations initiative" told the public that all Black individuals would have a valid legal claim for reparations against companies which are proven to have enslaved their individual ancestors, "no matter if your mother has already been reimbursed, you have nothing to do with that, you can demand restitution again for yourself". With promises like that, they are really taking the people for fools. Even Jews whose parent generation already received reparations for the Shoah cannot come and claim to be paid again. Even without any legal education, it is not hard to see that this is total non-sense, and that the only objective of such discourses can be to trap the people and lead them into pre-programmed frustration about reparations as such. Such divide-to-rule strategies need to be unmasked and rejected vehemently. These manoeuvres aimed at infiltrating and bringing confusion to the African liberation and reparation movement highlight once and again the importance of promoting a holistic and all-comprising reparations approach. Yes, companies and private entities need to be held responsible too, but that does not absolve the states of their – bigger and primordial – responsibility to repair for this state-organized crime that is still continuing – by the states as well as by private entities. Yes, huge sums of money are due, but so are land, satisfaction, cessation of the crime, and so on. One sister at the event said, "The money of the oppressor, I don't want it". Thus, the reparations movement also needs to succeed at making it clear to the people that the money that reparations are also about is not the money of the oppressor, but the wealth of African people that was illegally taken away from them through the greatest organized crime ever. Why would you want to let those who committed the worst atrocities imaginable, on a systematic scale and over centuries, keep the fortunes they have made from it? No, by all legal and moral standards, this wealth is due to those who created it, left their lives for it and their descendants. Reparations are not about charity, are not about buying peace or absolution without delivering justice. They are about justice, about repairing what can be repaired today for the descendants of the original victims, without taking away anything of the guilt of those who perpetrated the crime.

Another such desperate campaign aimed at taking some steam from the reparations movement is the Lifeline expedition, registered in Britain, in which "white" people march in chains through Jamaica and other countries making "apology" for transatlantic slavery. Fortunately there are brethren and sistren present who step up to tell these people that they don't want their apology, and that what is due is reparations.

Considerate of all of what I have reflected in this book so far, I really don't see any other way for humanity than that Africa heals herself and in the following, the rest of the world. Besides my love and need for justice, this conviction is one of the driving engines that made me do legal research work for reparations. A work that is also for my still unborn children; for the little Jamaican boy who begged in front of Sovereign Mall in Kingston and was so sweet and kind to me every time; for the little girls who sell water bags on the highway in Dalifort, a ghetto before Dakar, Senegal; it is for the children in Fukushima and all others whom we have to save from the destruction of our planet and to whom we owe a viable future through global African reparation and healing. The crime of transatlantic slavery and the Maafa is so foundational to the current destructive system of capitalism that there is no alternative to global African reparation. Africa, mother of all humanity, has to heal and retake her positive role in global relations. For this, unity and economic self-empowerment of African people globally are essential, and the way to get there has to be bolstered by the consciousness of the people that they have a legal entitlement to African redemption.

This is also what the Rastaman and Rastawoman have been highlighting from a long time in slightly altered terms. "Repatriation [and reparations] itself has been defined as sustainable development. I an'I who really want Repatriation learn to love Mother Earth Nature, while Western society depreciate her with un-necessary mass production, motivated by greedy men of destruction. When Earth react, her sons and daughters suffer ... drought, famine, earthquake, volcano eruption (brimstone), fire, hurricane, long winter, heatwave, pestilence ... Repatriation is also a return to the way of life that is friendly towards the Earth".[1733]

In the west, and in all nations "successfully" emulating the western model of mass production and consumption by any means, such as China, people in general will have to consume less and differently to save Mother Earth. That's a fact. The hegemonic western model that most states seek to emulate as "politically correct" with its holy grail of perpetual economic growth at any costs, is killing us and our earth. It just doesn't work out, neither with "alternative" energy sources such as bio fuel, which are currently investigated with the aim to allow us to continue and even further expand our mass consumption. Just at this very moment, prices for basic agricultural foodstuffs are going up crazy and will probably trigger famines in Africa and other parts in a few months, also because so much farming land is now used to grow crops for bio fuel.

Now, when I say people in the west and many other places need to consume less or differently, don't get scared. It wouldn't mean that you would have to walk around barefoot, or that you won't be able to pop that DVD into your player to-night. But just think how fifteen or twenty years back, electronic devices and machines could actually last for twenty years, whereas they are almost guaranteed to break down as garbage two or three years into purchasing today. Now, that's supposed to be industrial progress!? Something is clearly fishy here. Capitalist corporations are purposefully building their products in such a deficient way that you will have to pay them soon again to get new ones. So when we are talking about the need to consume less and differently, that is where we start. I know that there are European people, and increasingly more in these times of capitalist crisis, who are indeed poor and struggling hard to make basic ends meet. It is not they who will have to make great concessions for African reparations. Consumption will need to become more egalitarian, meaning that those global elites who proportionally are wasting away huge resources will indeed consume much less once global African reparations are implemented.

1733 Ras Iah C cited in: Christian, Ijahnya (2011). Return of the 6th Region: RastafarI Settlement in the Motherland. Contributing to the African Renaissance, Rabat: Codesria, 13eme Assemblée générale.

If not and if we keep our greedy consumption pattern up, not even to talk of expanding it, one way or another we in the west will always need to outsource the misery caused by its real costs to more or less geographically distant "others". But one day, that is sure, it will turn back on us, and that fire will not be nice. We in western industrialized societies need to consume less and differently if we want to survive, and other countries need to stop emulating the western model of economic growth by any means. That less is consumed in the west will also be a logical and inevitable consequence of global African reparation. It is therefore important that the global reparations movement acknowledges and promotes these interdependencies to link up with global environmental and social justice movements to brace one another in this struggle for the survival of humanity.

XII. Global African Reparation, a Must for Global Survival in Times of Nuclear Holocaust Menace and Deadly Pollution

It is not only essential that reparations are made, it is indeed crucial that they be made now. Any more delay will not make the legal entitlement disappear but only render its resolution much more complicated and conflictual. Even persons only randomly interested in Africa may have acknowledged recent developments of increasing Chinese involvement and investment on the continent over the past years. Chinese are not only buying up large portions of agricultural land, leaving the Africans who used to live there land-, shelter-, and food-less, and mines, but the African Union has even allowed them to construct their new headquarters in Addis Ababa. It is important to comprehend that with this move African statesmen and women have indeed consented to taking what should be their most important deliberations inside a Trojan horse, as, given the economic and geopolitical interest stakes in the continent, it can be presumed that China made sure to use its best technologies to wiretap the entire building. All important deliberations inside the AU building are in all probability followed by Chinese policy makers. Some observers greet the growing involvement of China as an opportunity for continental African countries to detangle themselves from the grips of their respective European ex-colonizers and the West as such, and welcome the Chinese as promising partners for business to curb African economies on a basis of more equal exchange.

But this will not happen and it is crucial to acknowledge that China is another major player in the world capitalist system that the west was able to force upon the world only as a consequence of transatlantic slavery and through the maintenance the Maafa.

Now, since sticking to international law and the obligation it holds to re-establish the situation which would, in all probability, have existed if the violation had not taken place, the entitlement to reparations for this crime encompasses the abandonment of capitalism. China may call itself communist and maintain a fair degree of internal oppression justified in the name of that ideology, yet its functioning and its global economics are highly integrated into the system and ideology of capitalism; that is, making profits by any means and no matter the human and environmental costs.

So taking away land from Africans to give it to China and further debasing continental sovereignty by housing the AU in Chinese property holds no perspective for progress whatsoever. What is needed and is due by law is reparation, including a global restructuring of the economy, which once accomplished will leave neither "need" nor space for European, US or Chinese neo-colonial policies.

Prominent author and former World Bank consultant Dambisa Moyo predicts that the west would lose its economic and political predominance in the coming decades to countries such as China, India and Brazil. She basically argues that this would be because the west would have maintained "bad" economic policies over the past 50 years and has cultivated a culture of debt while neglecting worth-generating productive work. Though there may be some truth to this point, the analysis is short-sighted in that it fails to detect that this is no new trend but that indeed the west has always relied on the productive work of others whom it enslaved and colonized, albeit to different degrees and in various implementations, in the past 500 years to build and maintain its economic strength. In the times from the industrial revolution up to the 1960s, "real" productive work inside the countries of Europe and the United States was more rampant than today, but the economic base for even this industrialization was at all times the wealth extracted from Africa and other colonized regions in the form of labor and raw materials. So what we are seeing today, the recession of "real" work in western countries, is really not that new.

So Moyo's question of who – the west, China, India or Brazil – will resort as the winner in the race over the position of the greatest global exploiter, may have some relevance in a short and mid-term perspective, but in the long run global African reparation is a must. If we continue within the logic of a capitalist world – profits by any means and real costs – let there be no doubt, none of us or them, Europe, the US, China, India or Russia will be able to maintain a top-of-the-world-position, because the planet will be gone. Blown up in a nuclear holocaust, made uninhabitable and toxic from major pollutions due to chemical agriculture and petro-industry, swallowed up by Frankenstein plants and creatures produced by the capitalist logic of short-time profits by any means and doomed to get out of control.

Even the figures that Moyo gives in her argument help to sustain this analysis and the fact that it's all about the control of resources, and African resources in particular. Farmland makes up only seven per cent of China's territory. So, in a situation of globally diminishing food security, the Chinese are massively buying up agricultural land in Africa – the continent holds one-third of the world's unspoilt farming land. The engagements between Russian Gazprom and Khaddafi's

Libya concluded in the years up to 2011 were arguably part of a Russian strategy to get control over Europe's energy supply.[1734] Now we all know how Khaddafi and Libya have fared since. So we see, it all comes back to control over natural resources and labor in ex-colonized countries, most importantly African. That also means that Africa has the key to lock off this tide of global policy that will bring massive destruction to all. And since China, Russia and others are already seriously competing against the west as main global exploiter and economic dominator, the west may indeed have a vital interest to bring the African reparations issue to justice as soon as possible. Because if Moyo's short-time prognosis becomes reality, and in a short perspective that may be well possible, the west and its people, once cut off from their ex-colonies' resources and wealth by China and others, will for sure suffer greatly.

The west has already instigated two world wars in the past century, both for reasons of control over colonies. As we see, the race for control over these dominions, which is decisive for the maintenance of political power in any given western "democratic" state of a certain size and population, is still not settled. Stakes could not be higher in this race of competing capitalist economies. Do we really want to wait for the next world war to happen over this question? I think that there is very little doubt that we must not let things take that course at all. We must rather push on global African reparation by any means, because that is the only way, going back to the source, for the world to get back some vital balance. If we want to keep planet earth habitable, then we need to come to reparation for this most massive crime and catastrophe ever.

I am convinced that comprehensive and full reparation is necessary if this planet and human life is to continue as we know it. I don't see another way than the healing of Africa, the mother of all humanity, and her retaking her positive power in global relations. As was sustained in a UNESCO publication, the rehabilitation of this chapter of human history which concerns all continents and people, will be the federating element for a universal conscience, without which we will undoubtedly continue to destroy our planet. As suggested in that book, UNESCO must therefore put together and sponsor an international team of researchers – led and directed by African – that will take up this most important task.[1735]

The whole debt crisis that is currently holding western public's attention in a stranglehold retains some fundamental mysteries. Europeans and US-Americans, generally speaking, have the materially highest life standards globally, so we need to ask to whom they are indebted. Apparently to China, but also among

---

1734 Moyo, Dambisa (2012). Der Untergang des Westens. Haben wir eine Chance in der neuen Wirtschaftsordnung? Berlin: Piper, 204.
1735 Deveau, Jean-Michel (1998). Pour une pedagogie de l'histoire de la traite negriere, in: Doudou Diene (directeur de la publication): La chaine et le lien. Une vision de la traite negriere, UNESCO, Paris, 507-526, 525.

one another. Some have suggested that this "crisis" has been staged to prepare in advance for transatlantic slavery reparations claims that have gained so much amplitude lately and promise to push forward even more fervently in the coming decades. European states and the US may prepare to say for when the moment comes, "Sorry, we have no money, we can give in reparations".

But even if that would really be the case, it would be no hindrance to reparations. Quite on the contrary, reparations would indeed solve the current economic crisis because in last consequence, if sticking to international law requirements, they would be accompanied by the abolition of the capitalist world system. Therefore, the global African reparations movement must seek to popularize this information and share it with anti-capitalist and environmental activists all over the globe. These activists and movements, even if not a priori interested in African reparations, should know that there is in fact an international law entitlement to the end of capitalism. Another world is not only possible, another world is also legally due. The current world system has been built on organized crime on a massive scale for over 500 years.

Indeed, global African reparation also holds the key to resolve the mounting threat by Islamists that so many in the west fear. The full reparation package, as due by international law, will also take account of the millennia-long illegal enslavement of Africans by Arabs and Muslims. Rehabilitation as serious and pertinent appraisal of that past would entail and allow to objectively criticize some features of systematic historical Muslim practice that relied to a considerable extent on oppression and intolerance of others. Please take note that I stress "practice", not Islam as such, about which I don't know enough to pass any judgement.

Such a historical rehabilitation endeavor as part of the reparations process might also diminish some of the attraction that radical Islamism reportedly currently has on young people of some African regions and which has led some commentators to express worries that Africa might become a new base for radical Islamism, and one that might be very difficult to control. At the same time, full reparation by Arab countries would also have to include a financial component. Since trans-saharan enslavement went on for more than a millennium, it can already be estimated that the amount due is not small neither. Arab countries, such as Saudi Arabia, would thus have to loosen up large sums of money and transfer them to Africa, thereby diminishing their possibilities of funding Islamic terror networks.

Comprehensive African reparation promises furthermore to take steam out of the Middle Eastern conflict since it will incriminate parts of both Jewish and Arab Muslim society as collaborators in the enslavement of Africans and oblige them to make amends, thus reducing their power to war among themselves. The three major world religions Judaism, Christianity and Islam have all been involved in the historic and systematic oppression, enslavement and exploitation of Africa and African people. We have seen above that at the beginning of transatlantic slavery the Portuguese linked up with light-skinned Moors in Mauretania who had already illegally enslaved Black Africans for several centuries and continue to do so up to today.[1736] Jewish individuals had often handled the process of enslavement and castration of Africans for these Arabs. After the fall of Grenada in 1492, and the expulsion of Muslims from Iberia, the Spanish crown also put Jews before the choice to either christianize or to leave. Many, such as Christopher Columbus, took off. When he arrived in the Americas, this was to set off the biggest genocide ever, exterminating many Indigenous peoples and killing hundreds of millions of Africans over the centuries. Many Jewish were among the first slavers and colonizers who came to Jamaica, for example, in the early 16th century. That is also the reason why the Caribbean islands have some of the oldest Jewish cemeteries in the western hemisphere. So to some extent it is arguable and also documentable that these three major religions which are currently threatening to throw the world into another major war, battled among themselves for pre-dominion in the exploitation of Africa. Arabs, Jews and Christians were all behind African enslavement and the Maafa. Comprehensive African reparations would re-assess and rehabilitate this past and detangle it, while also requiring the delivery of massive financial reparations by entities domiciled in all these three religions, leaving them with other concerns than fighting one another and keeping the world in a permanent and ever-present threat of nuclear holocaust.

Finally, for true healing, Africans would also need to re-evaluate their allegation and relationship to not only Christianity, but also Islam since, in their presently dominant forms, both religions came to the continent predominantly with enslaver invaders and continue to trigger violence in too many countries.

That leads to another important point. Global African reparation, as due by international law, also has to include massive disarmament, especially the nuclear powers. According to the basic relevant rule in international law, "reparation must, as far as possible, wipe out all the consequences of the illegal act and re-establish the situation which would, in all probability, have existed if that act had not been committed". Now, it is a fact beyond reach of doubt that western countries that hold nuclear weapons today would not have been in the position to develop them without their massive violation of international law that was transatlantic slavery and is the Maafa. Not only did the industrial revolution as such get going only on the basis of the primitive accumulation of wealth generated through illegal transatlantic slavery, but the uranium for the bombs was extracted illegally from Africa, such as from Congo. Now, of course it is not only the United States, France or Britain that have nuclear bombs, but also Russia, China and

---

1736 Wolf, Kenneth Baxter (1994). "The 'Moors' of West Africa and the Beginnings of the Portuguese Slave Trade, in: Journal of Medieval & Renaissance Studies 24, Nr. 3, 449-469.

Israel. Yet fact remains that Africans, as all other human beings on the planet, live under the constant threat of nuclear extinction, and this situation would not exist if the crime of transatlantic slavery and the Maafa would not have happened. Thus, international law gives Africans a right to a world free from nuclear danger. Of course it is the people who will have to get the major player countries in today's international relations to agree to an acceptable resolution, and this will not be an easy task, but it has to be done if we want to stay on this planet and it is also due by law.

Russia and China are currently both massively mining uranium in Africa.[1737] That African uranium is used mostly not for bombs, but for energy generation. Nuclear energy also poses a constant and most eminent threat to life on this planet, maybe even more than nuclear weapons, and part of the entitlement of African reparations is that Africans are freed of this danger, since that situation would not exist had transatlantic slavery not happened.

Global Africa has the power; if united, it holds the key to global survival. And this is not only about the prevention of nuclear extinction, there is so much more to this. Just look at the aluminium industry. Aluminium is used for so many products constitutive of the western lifestyle, yet making us and the planet sick and really killing us. In its exploitable form, it is mostly found in red earth; and red earth is common in Africa, South America and the Caribbean where multinationals are mining bauxite for aluminium extraction at knock-down prices, leaving the local populations deprived and polluted. Aluminium is a common ingredient in industrial deodorants. Its connection to breast cancer has been established medically. It is not accidental that most cases of breast cancer develop in the areas bordering the armpits. Aluminium is used in cosmetics, linked to allergies and auto-immune illnesses. It is an intrinsic component of vaccines. Right now the WHO is conducting vaccination campaigns world-wide and especially in Africa and other exploited regions of the globe. They put aluminium in our water. Sickness is indeed an industry, or at the very least necessary to keep many branches of industry, such as the pharma-industry, going. Yet, the aluminium that the powers-that-be use to maintain their industrial power complex and build weapons and indeed a very substantial part of what they need to keep African and other people down, comes from African lands on the continent and in the diaspora, and they use it to pollute the earth and to make people worldwide suffer and die from fabricated sicknesses.

By these few examples we see how crucial to world politics global African reparations really are. Not only for world politics, but indeed for world survival. All of our major problems that acutely threaten peace and the prospects of a viable future on this planet, can be traced in their roots to transatlantic slavery, and in their germs further back to Arab enslavement of Africans. This is true in what

---

1737 http://www.wise-uranium.org/upafr.html

concerns industrial pollution since the capitalist logic that reposes on economic growth by any means is rooted in transatlantic slavery. It is true in what concerns the devaluation of women and the violences committed against them since many such abuses are also engrained in the systematic devaluation of human life of the capitalist logic which is today emulated globally. It is true in what concerns famines around the world since they all are connected to situations of colonial exploitation. And the colonial exploitation of other parts of the world such as in Asia by European countries only became possible on the basis of the capital accumulation previously generated through transatlantic slavery. The world is one and all is connected. We are all connected to one another, and we are all connected to the past and to the future, together.

It is crucial that activists currently involved in the Occupy movement, in the environmental movement, in the peace movement, in the World Social Forum and all other progressive movements globally acknowledge that their claims are connected and legally substantiated in the entitlement to global African reparation. International law covers the African reparation claim, and this claim includes the freedom from life-threatening pollution and from biological, chemical, nuclear and indeed industrial[1738] warfare. It includes the cessation of the exploitation and theft of raw material in Africa, without which global industrial production in general will have to develop ways of production that depend less on resource spoliation. This will automatically lead to a drastic decrease in global pollution. Global African reparation will halt the deforestation of the Amazonian forests, the principal lungs of our planet, under the pressure of capitalist economic interests. Global African reparations will seriously and pertinently engage the world in a serious examination of racism. This must then be taken up to deal with ethnic conflicts all over the world, and also lead to a mitigation of the conflict in the Middle East.

Fundamental to all of this though, is that we must bid bye-bye to the hegemonic ideal of economic growth. The concept of economic growth has been fed to all of us in western societies and by now many other parts of the world as sacrosanct. "Economic growth" has become a mantra that is sung to us on a daily basis to the point that we accept it unquestioningly almost as if it was a natural requirement for life itself. Now, it is clear that when there is population growth, the economy has to grow simultaneously. If not, the portion of wealth available for everyone will get lesser and smaller, leading to conflict and violence. But if all of those "more" people also continue to participate in the productive process, logically and naturally there will also be economic growth. So far so good. Problems come in when economic growth as such is made a sacred cow, even more so in economies with declining populations, such as in western Europe where total population fig-

---

1738 Ayi Kwei Armah (2010). Remembering the Dismembered Continent. Essays, Per Ankh, Popenguine Senegal, 9ff.

ures would have been falling, if it was not for immigration. At the current phase of our capitalist lifestyle which devours and wastes massive resources, economic growth can only be perpetuated at the price of crude oppression and exploitation of "other-fied" people and of the earth. One does not have to be an economist to grasp this. It is simply logic. Truth is that, globally speaking, what we really need is not economic growth, but really economic recession because we are simply producing and consuming too much blood, sweat and tears for our planet to take it any longer. But no politician of the established western democracy model is going to tell us this, since the only possible consequence of this truth would be to produce and consume less. Much less for the "rich", but some less still for almost all in western economies, except the real poor. No five pairs of shoes a year, no new play station every year, no new mobile phone every half year, no new wardrobe with every fashion season. But we'll all be equipped with those basics still, and look and feel good. Better even, because healthier and less stressed.

Now to get there, the western democratic model is a serious obstacle because it comes with its inherently built-in principle that the politician who is the best short-time liar and charmer will get the most votes. Plenty of people will vote for the guy who promises "more economic growth, more money, less taxes" for the next coming years, but who will vote for the one who comes to tell the plain truth that if we all want to stay here at all, we will have to cut down and change some major ways of how we are used to do things? You got me ....

Yet, we have already reviewed the reasons why African reparations, although so well founded in international law, will never be given by any perpetrator state or an international institution, such as a court, because they are running international relations today as a consequence of the crime. African people globally will have to take reparations. The same goes here. At one point, and we have reached that point now if we want to save our planet, we will have to find a better solution to replace the system of professional liars that have come to be called politicians in the western system and indeed in all democracies world-wide that have taken up the western model. The western model may in theory be a pragmatic way of transmitting the generalized will of citizens to policy makers, but because of the intrinsic problem just outlined, it is programmed to lead to the destruction of the planet, since it always favors the one who promises the people most material benefits in a short time frame at no matter what real costs. That cannot be remedied by reforms such as more direct citizen participation. What is needed is that political leaders retain some kind of accountability for their policies even when they are no longer in office, so they will take better heed to how they are preserving or spoiling our children's resources. This of course is not compatible with the western conception of democracy. Again, comprehensive African reparations kick in and hold a perspective of resolution. As briefly mentioned above and exposed in detail in the works of other researchers, pre-Maafa African societies disposed of political systems that relied both on checks and balances and people's representation, and held leaders responsible for their actions. The details of such prospects to be recovered from ancient and traditional African politics will have to be assessed in another study, but what can and should already be retained is that such historical investigation is not only due as part of reparation for African societies as such, but also crucial in finding ways to lead us out of our present global and existence-threatening crisis.

It is indeed an essential and inbuilt feature of the western democratic model that the winner of periodically held elections will be who can best gloss up things and succeeds in promising and providing his constituency with material profits, by any means and with a very short-term cost calculation. After the next election, a politician or party might not be in power again, so why care who will then have to carry the long-term real costs. This system of democracy relies on the outsourcing of the exploitation that is necessary to provide western societies with cheap industrial products, constitutive of their current lifestyle, out of the field of vision and living environment of the voters. Western democracy has in the past fifty years only functioned because it has succeeded in outsourcing the most rampant, widespread and systematic human rights abuses, fundamentally undemocratic mechanisms, exploitation and oppression, which are in turn necessary to cover the costs for the smooth maintenance of power inside western societies. Thus, this model of democracy is not apt for export to the whole world; to do so would be factually impossible. Thus, African and other leaders must stop striving to get there and to have their policies measured and judged on that model. In order for the western democracy system to "function" in one place, that place has to outsource the crude exploitation and oppression that is necessary to produce the material wealth that its voters continuously demand more and more of. Supply failure would almost surely cost governments and politicians their jobs. We see, it really is no contradiction that western states buttress dictators in other parts of the globe. It is only when some of these dictators act totally out of the accepted way or when western governments feel like they have to state another example to periodically demonstrate their commitment to "democracy" worldwide, that a few dictators get put off from time to time. Now of course, if additionally a dictator also happens to have oil in his country, his stepping down will probably become due at one time or another. That's what happened with Saddam Hussein and Muammar Khaddafi lately; two birds killed with one stone, in each case.

In colonial Africa, specifically, "Western enterprise (...), as far as politics went, was a systematic apprenticeship in the establishment and reinforcement of dictatorship as a way of life", Ayi Kwei Armah reminds us. "Colonial institutions in Africa were inherently anti-democratic and dictatorial. From veto-wielding governments to legislatures selected by patronage, to bureaucracies accountable to no public constituency, all colonial social, political and administrative practices were determinedly hostile to democratic initiatives. Neo-colonial institutions and practices are continuing this tradition of hostility to democratic practice, but such is the strength of the Western power of self-deception that Western propaganda still" sustains "that colonialism was a preparatory process for democratic governance."[1739]

It is therefore vital to un-earth and re-assess pre-Maafa African political systems and ways of organizing society through pertinent research to add to what we already know from great ancestor researchers such as Cheick Anta Diop. In ancient Kemet, Ethiopia and Sudan, it was considered that if the king was not legitimate, the entire nature would be sterile, draught plague the lands, and epidemics destroy the people.[1740] The role of the pharaoh and other traditional Black rulers was that they were Guardians of the Temple, that is, of nature and cosmic order. Power was thus a heavy charge, and indeed not an obligation of means but of results. In such African system, elections were held among the assembly of sages to choose the one best suited for increasing the holistic well-being of the community.[1741]

Meanwhile, it is often sustained that the fact that capitalism is still around whereas communism has abdicated, would prove capitalism as better. I say that capitalism and communism, such as practised, were both rotten and evil. Moreover, that is simply no explanation. Just because one evil went down doesn't mean another is morally superior. The reason why capitalism is today the global system and communism has disappeared is not a question of moral superiority, but due to the simple fact that western capitalist countries could and can rely on their colonies and ex-colonies for massive resources, revenue and armament.

And this again, fundamentally concerns the question of human survival. As I have argued in an article published in the *New African* magazine, governments of western and eastern nations have, even in the eye of nuclear disaster that logically and only as a matter of time struck again at Fukushima in Japan, proven once again their determination to never cease by their own volition from using nuclear power.[1742] As with African reparations in general and as a part of these reparations, people, spearheaded by Africans who are legally covered by their entitlement to reparation, will have to take what is due.

While Japan was battling with the acute emergency situation, then-French President Sarkozy firmly declared that his country would never give up on nuclear

---

1739 Ayi Kwei Armah (2010). Remembering the Dismembered Continent. Essays, Per Ankh, Popenguine Senegal, 111.
1740 Camara, Fatou Kiné (2004). Pouvoir et Justice dans la Tradition des Peuples Noires. Philosophie et Pratique, Paris: L'Harmattan, 133.
1741 Camara, Fatou Kiné (2004). Pouvoir et Justice dans la Tradition des Peuples Noires. Philosophie et Pratique, Paris: L'Harmattan, 134f.
1742 Wittmann, Nora (2011). The scramble for Africa's nuclear resources, in: New African, June 2011, Nr. 507 (IC Publications: London), 72-74.

energy. That would be totally out of question since more than 80% of France's energy comes from nuclear plants. EDF, the state-dominated French main electricity supplier, prouds itself with providing the cheapest energy in Europe to households. They are able to live up to this because they are stealing uranium from, for example, Congo, a country that has systematically and illegally been subjected to genocidal enslavement and colonial exploitation costing many millions of lives and that has systematically been undermined in its sovereignty. Congo's leaders aiming to end the centuries-long exploitation got ruthlessly killed over centuries. Then-French President Sarkozy himself, as well as ministerial deputies on a continuous basis, made the journey to Kinshasa to secure a deal with Joseph Kabila to the effect that Areva, the state-owned nuclear energy giant of France, can exclusively exploit Congolese nuclear materials. Now, the bloody and genocidal war that is going on in Congo today is mainly centred on the exploitation of minerals such as coltan, a necessity for all our mobile phones, and uranium. Access to money and wealth in this country that has been continuously ravaged over centuries comes only through these crude materials. Nord-Kivu and Katanga are the provinces where the war ravages most ferociously, the provinces where Areva is mining most intensively and not incidentally also where the Portuguese imposed transatlantic slavery most ferociously and massively.

The French have also constructed the only nuclear plant on the continent in South Africa. Koeberg nuclear plant has brought with it a share of incidents with workers, acknowledged to be, contaminated. Right now the South African government is fostering plans with the French to expand nuclear power plants over the country. This was again confirmed recently by Deputy President Kgalema Motlanthe. These plans are madness. Even if Europe, Russia, China, the US and whoever would really need nuclear energy (which they do not, because nuclear energy is simply deadly in last consequence, in any way), Africa would not need it because Africa has the sun. Now, have we heard anything yet of this thing called solar energy? Not to mention electricity generation by means of the ancient Kemetic ankh, such as described in *The ANKH: The Afrikan Origins of Electromagnitism*[1743], a subject upon which historic research should also be facilitated as part of reparations.

Unfortunately, Algeria too, another country on the African continent under the tutelage of France for a long time, has pledged to immerge into nuclear energy production. Several African countries including Egypt, Nigeria, Algeria, Morocco, Tunisia, Ghana and Kenya are at different stages of nuclear development. More than twenty African countries have taken the political decision to go nuclear. It is argued by the lobbyists of the nuclear industry in Africa that "no country worldwide has ever industrialized on wind, solar and other renewable forms of

---

1743 Nur Ankh Amen (2001). The ANKH: The Afrikan Origins of Electromagnitism Hunlock Creek: EWorld Inc.

energy"[1744], and that African ambitious industrialization and development goals and programs would necessitate the building of nuclear reactors on the continent. But this argument seems to forget that all countries that laid the foundation to modern industrialization and remain its leaders, are in cold regions with no sun, and that they exploited human beings and materials stolen from Africa for their industrilization! So that argument holds no reason at all why Africa cannot industrialize with solar energy.

Right now, just surfing around the net a bit to update my knowledge on current happenings concerning nuclear energy in Africa and being hit by these devastating news that twenty countries would have made the decision to go nuclear, has me going mad. The time for global African reparations is now; it is not in two weeks or even tomorrow, it is now. One of the main reasons why they love nuclear energy so much and are totally unready to ever give it up, is that it is intrinsically centralized; its functioning depends on the control by the state and the corporate nuclear elite, even when it is no longer operational and no longer produces energy. Once the reactors are there, this control remains a necessity virtually eternally. Whereas solar energy is essentially decentralized; everyone who has a panel and access to sunlight is the boss. So we must not, by any means, allow them to plant their monster reactors on the continent – all constructed, maintained and to be maintained for a long, long future – by European ex-enslaver and colonizer state operated companies.

Almost every African country is at the moment also being mined or examined for prospective exploitation, often resulting in the eviction of the indigenous people living in the areas. Yet, by this, we also recognize easily that Africa is indeed in a powerful position. A united Africa, that is. Because if Africa is not giving out its nuclear resources, then the nuclear madness that ultimately will lead to global nuclear catastrophe, will be seriously downshifted, in the least. But the fact that the continuing crime still assures that any progressive Africans leader, such as Lumumba in Congo, are erased, makes it evident that although the nursing of progressive forces in Congo and other conflict areas on the continent are essential, a huge effort must come from Africans in the diaspora as well as from honestly solidary people from other backgrounds to make their states desist from wreaking havoc in African countries and violating the sovereignty of African states and people. It is one war, but there are many frontlines to consider simultaneously.

Not only in Congo but also in Niger, for example, another country that is massively mined for uranium by France, China, India and Korea, France has intervened violently and illegally in the same structural pattern put in place in transatlantic slavery and maintained ever since when it ousted Hamani Dior from power in 1974. Dior had wanted to index the price for uranium.

1744 Buyuka, Basset (2012). Kenya: Nuclear Energy Can Speed Up Vision 2030, in The Star: Nairobi, downloaded from http://allafrica.com/stories/201203060041.html (accessed 30.7.2012).

We need to fully acknowledge, and that also needs to be taken up and diffused by the anti-nuclear energy movement, that the contention that nuclear energy would be "cheap", which is the main argument of politicians and nuclear industry to have western populations accept it, is a blatant lie. A lie that reposes on the violent shifting of the real costs to Africa – through robbery and in the forms of war, poverty and death.

We must not in any case let them continue to go on with their criminal and genocidal system that will soon cost many more lives, even inside Europe and the United States. The European Union's ban on traditional lighting bulbs and their forced substitution with energy-saving lamps which contain mercury and have already ruined the lives of quite a few families is criminal and they are only in the position to push that on us because of the power they hold going back to transatlantic slavery.

And as this state of affairs and those developments clearly ring emergency, there is no more time to lose at all. Thus, we must ponder the words of Ayi Kwei Armah who stated,

"Now we're ready to do our work. If there is something left in the universe that will not obey their furious will, it's not because they overlooked some detail of control. It's just that fraud and violence, however powerfully organized against the balance of the universe, have their limits. Those limits were reached long ago. At the end of the time of violence comes a time of beginnings. Time for us to do our work."[1745]

To do this work, we have to build power and movement by any and various means. We have to build it through individual lawsuits for reparations[1746]; we have to build it through more empirical activist research; we have to build it through the publication of books; we have to build it through the arts, not just musically, but also visually and through fashion. After all, not everyone has the right access to books, and to what music one listens one chooses at least to a certain extent. But with visual arts and fashion, occupying the public space while advocating for reparations, people are confronted with our message, whether they choose to or not. And to do this work, and as Marcus Garvey highlighted, not only by speech but by his practice, we have to organize. And to organize in these days of planned confusion, people first have to unite around ideas again. In this regard, it is crucial to penetrate other means of communication than books, such as fashion activism. Pieces of fashion or accessories that are appealing to the eye and carry a revolutionary message can serve to bring reasonings to a larger number of people than

---

1745 Kwei Armah, Ayi (2002). KMT: In the House of Life, Africa (Senegal): Per Ankh, 134ff.
1746 Such as the lawsuit that Deadria Farmer-Paellman filed in a US federal court in 2002 against a variety of corporate defendants, or the lawsuit that reparation activists have filed against France in Martinque and which is currently under consideration.

they would normally reach through more conventional means of dissemination. In that perspective, cultural movements such as hip hop and reggae also hold essential potentials for reasoning and organizing.

Contemporary global threats to life stemming from spatial arms race to nuclear fallout to the danger of another world war can only be pertinently averted by global African reparation. To get there, we need to look into the past to build that future of global African redemption which is the only way to save our planet for us humans. In particular, we need to study the UNIA, the one organization through which Marcus Garvey united four million members, until they locked him up. We need to acknowledge that he succeeded in doing so in a time when telecommunication technology was in its very beginnings. How far could we go today if we made proper use of the technologies we have now – and of the cultural movements that already unite African and other youths around the globe?

In the powerful and significant coming together of Bob Marley and Mumia Abu-Jamal for an interview in 1979, Marley highlighted the quintessential necessity of reparation when he said:

"The problem is, our people must be united. And then all problem solve, and then every problem solve. 'Cause if the Black man check it him have the knowledge, wisdom and understanding enuff to do it. (...) Black man get the rootical gift, him maintain the God business, dat purpose why earth was created. I and I have to maintain dat.(...) And God say dem fe unite! Because when you unite, that is the power of God, you know. God love Love, which is unity. So when you unite, you get the whole power of God. That's what him want. (...) If Black people don't unite, the world, no one, no one can live good. (...) Cause the white man not living good, you know. The China man nah live good, either. Why? Because the Blackman is not united. Because the Blackman, him are the cornerstone pon earth! When time him shaky, the whole earth shaky. You see? When him solid, everything solid. And it a long while since we have been solid. You know. It's been a long long time. So you find out how much war, fight and dem tings go on."[1747]

So in that interview, Bob Marley really phrased the necessity of global African reparation for global survival. And, significantly, one year later this global African superstar was dead, and Mumia Abu-Jamal locked away on death row. That Mumia was framed by police is common knowledge, and there are indications that Bob Marley may indeed have been poisoned by intelligence agents, leading to his fatal cancer condition.[1748]

1747 http://ilhowibowo.blogspot.fr/2010/06/bob-marley-interview-with-mumia-abu.html; Bob Marley Interview with Mumia Abu-Jamal, Philadelphia, USA 1979.
1748 Potash (2007), 185f.

XIII. Hip-hop, Reggae and Cultural Movements

Indeed, it is crucial that cultural workers, like musicians such as Bob Marley have a huge task in the global African reparation struggle, and that they join forces with researchers, other activists, and the political reparations movement, such as with journalists like Mumia Abu-Jamal.

As writer Ayi Kwei Armah highlighted, "If we are to wake from [Europe's] spell and remake our society and our continent, Africans will have to retrieve our suppressed ability to conceive of our wholeness in both spatial and temporal terms; that we can begin doing this by re-articulating our dismembered society and remembering our suppressed history, philosophy, culture, science and arts; that for this awakening, all necessary intellectual information exits here and now, though in scattered form; that it requires the work of groups of determined researchers to bring it together, to process it, and to make it widely *available in forms accessible to all*. These being the requisite preparations for Africa's intellectual awakening. Any such awakening, it should be needless to point out, will ultimately take political and social forms. However, our recent history reminds us that no matter how huge the energy that goes into it, any attempted political awakening will be abortive unless it is preceded by a *preparatory process of cultural rebirth*, the kind of renewed self-awareness that enables a people long and relentlessly misrepresented – as essentially childish, stupid, incapable of management, averse to challenging intellectual undertakings, with an aptitude only for the easier occupations of rhythmic work, music and dance, seeing life only and eternal entertainment – to re-evaluate and re-imagine itself as fully human, fully intelligent, and therefore capable of facing and solving the problems now blocking our paths to a future of our own".[1749]

Music is one of the most important mediums of communication in global Africa. But as Armah is right to criticize, it has been stripped of its progressive quality of disseminating knowledge, education and reasoning. To a large extent, today it really is "only and eternal entertainment"[1750]. Yet, fact remains that hip hop and

---

1749 Armah Ayi Kwei (2010). Remembering the Dismembered Continent. Essays, Per Ankh: Popenguine Senegal, 9ff.
1750 Ibid.

reggae are *the* means of communication that connect African youths from Dakar to Paris and New York to Guiana or Jamaica like nothing else. It is not books, since in these times many are not exposed to books due to lack of time, money and education in this struggle for survival. Therefore we need to rely on these cultural movements and link them with the political movement for reparation and justice. As Armah further contends rightfully, "for any society to reach such a level of cultural awareness, it needs to nourish itself from the work (...) committed to the search for real, accurate data, however long suppressed or deeply buried, and willing to devote time and intelligence to the slow, steady research needed to unearth the buried data for presentation to an awakening universe. It is work that can only be done by committed intellectuals finding each other."[1751] We need to make the millions and millions of youths involved in the hip-hop and reggae movement realize that "no movement is about beats and rhymes. Beats and rhymes are tools"[1752], and expose them to the work of researchers and activists through music, other forms of cultural "edutainment" and indeed by all means necessary and available.

Now, of course, what is crucial is who owns, who runs and who controls content and exposure. Hip hop was born out of rebellion, as an outcome and tool of rebellion, created by the same force that created Malcolm X, as Asante writes, "A visceral energy aimed at transforming (or at least voicing) the conditions of oppressed people"[1753]. Yet in the past decades it has been lulled into a non-uplifting conservative instrument that promotes little challenge to the global structures of oppression. Thus, as Asante puts it, it is also crucial to acknowledge the "dangers and limitations of being collectively identified by a genre of music that we don't even own"[1754], whereby one major part of the problem is stemming from the distribution mechanisms for hip hop which is, together with reggae, the cultural expression of African youth globally. But it is not Black people who control how this cultural expression is disseminated. That is decided by multi-national corporations such as Viacom, Clear Channel, and Vivendi, the media corporations that own most major TV and radio channels such as MTV. Thus, they control how people perceive hip hop, and the mainstream picture of hip hop that they fabricate suggests a model of success that relies on promoting a self-destructive, capitalist lifestyle for young Black people, "while the positive ones, reflecting and talking about real issues in a progressive and positive way are termed 'alternative', as such already equalized with limited economic success prospects".[1755]

Throughout the Maafa, during and after transatlantic slavery, the "white" corporate and political structure recognized that this control over the Black and Af-

---

1751 Ibid.
1752 Asante, M. K., Jr. (2008). It's bigger than hip hop, New York: St. Martin's Press, 71.
1753 Ibid., 10.
1754 Ibid., 5.
1755 Asante, M. K., Jr. (2008). It's bigger than hip hop, New York: St. Martin's Press, 5.

rican image is not simply important to enslavement and oppression but indeed central. The images so produced by "whites" of Black people as lazy, amoral, not stable, only fit for menial work, sport and music, not only served and serve to justify the oppression of Africans but also to debase Africans in their confidence in and love of self.[1756]

As Assata Shakur was right to state, "Hip hop can be a very powerful weapon to help expand young people's political and social consciousness. But just as with any weapon, if you don't know how to use it, if you don't know where to point it, or what you're using it for, you can end up shooting yourself in the foot or killing your sisters or brothers. The government recognized immediately that rap music has enormous revolutionary potential." And they knew that they had to control this movement if they wanted to maintain their system of exploitation and oppression.

Thus, in this most important quest to raise the awareness of the youth for African reparations for global survival, it is crucial that the reparations movement takes up every occasion and opportunity to highlight that some of the most important hip-hop artists ever were backing the claim for reparations, such as the great Tupac Shakur. As pointed out in chapter VIII.4.d, popular discourses do have an impact on people's legal consciousness of their rights. In "White Man'z World", Tupac rapped, "In time I learned a few lessons, never fall for riches, apologize to my true sisters, far from bitches ... Help me raise my black nation, reparations are due, it's true... (...) We are under attack, I never meant to cause drama ... to my sister and mama, will we make it to better times, in this white man's world ... This is dedicated to my (...) teachers: Mutulu Shakur, Geronimo Pratt, Mumia Abu-Jamal, Sekou Odinga."[1757] The song and album were released eight weeks after Tupac's assassination, and at the time he had written it, all four of the mentioned Black Panther leaders, thus African people who had actively started taking reparations by any means necessary, were serving long-term prison sentences for exactly this activism. One of them, Mumia Abu-Jamal, was on death row. In fact, the *don killuminati* album in general represented a return of Tupac to more explicit and militant progressive Black lyrical activism, such as know from his very first album. And it is for this reason that the powers-that-be would not let him continue on this path of illuminating the Black and African youth world-wide, especially since he had by then risen to the most prolific and loved of all rap superstars. *All Eyez On Me*, released in January 1996, had been the second highest first-sales ever, only topped by the Beatles' *Anthology*. Not only the lyrical promotion of truth worried the establishment, but also the fact that Tupac had in interviews announced a return to more direct activism, such as finishing a movie script about his mother Afeni Shakur's journey with the Panthers, becoming involved around indepen-

---

1756 Asante, M. K., Jr. (2008). It's bigger than hip hop, New York: St. Martin's Press, 21.
1757 Tupac Shakur (1996). White Man'z World, in: Makavelli: Don Killuminati, The 7 Day Theory.

dent electoral politics, and opening community centers. Contrary to what the media have pushed so long and so hard that most people take it for reality today, Tupac was highly engaged in unifying East and West Coast rappers, in a situation of "war" that had purposefully been instigated by US intelligence and police to keep the hundred-thousand-strong armed Black gangs from coming together against their common enemy. For details on how and why Tupac was assassinated by US intelligence, apparently with the help of Tupac's last label, Death Row, I recommend to read the excellently researched book: "The FBI War on Tupac Shakur and Black Leaders"[1758] by John Potash. Potash retraces that police covered up the circumstances of the shooting over months, refused to hear eye-witnesses, and that the whole scenario of the shooting indicated the involvement of Suge Knight's Death Row, Tupac's label for about a year before his death and which he was about to leave. Police officers worked for Death Row and some of them had family – and other ties to officers and intelligence agents who had apparently played key roles in special units such as the Compton gang unit, which had been instrumental in pitting young Black people in poor neighborhoods against one another in bloody violence. Reportedly, and going totally to the contrary of what was the general standard within the company, Death Row management ordered Tupac's bodyguards not to carry guns to the boxing event in the aftermath of which Tupac was killed. According to officer Russell Poole, who later quit the police force due to his frustration that the evidence he had investigated on the implication of police officers in the murder of Biggie Smalls was ignored by police superiors, LA police investigators even went as far as stating that "they had loads of evidence in Tupac's murder and that they didn't plan to follow up on any of it. The Vegas detectives told Poole that police superiors said they were not supposed to actually investigate Tupac's murder."[1759]

No doubt, Tupac was getting really dangerous for the demonic system that has fed on Black and poor people for centuries. While he was alive, each of his solo albums sold more than double of the previous one. Since he was about to leave Death Row and had already laid the foundations for his own record label, managed by another former Panther friend of his family Yaazmyn Shakur, he would prospectively have made even more money that he already announced he would put into uplifting projects. In one of his last interviews, he had in fact said that he was about to "mix the street life with respected, known, and proven military philosophy"[1760]. At the time of his murder, he was also engaged to Kidada Jones, daughter of *Vibe* magazine owner Quincy Jones, and thus gaining access to a mainstream hip-hop publication as another platform to spread truth. It is evident

---

1758 Potash, John (2007). The FBI War on Tupac Shakur and Black Leaders. US Intelligence's Murderous Targeting of Tupac, MLK, Malcolm, Panthers, Hendrix, Marley, Rappers & Linked Ethnic Leftists, Baltimore: Progressive Left Press.
1759 Potash (2007), 118f.
1760 Ibid.

that all of this made him a major danger for the powers-that-be, so it really would be no surprise that they felt they had to eliminate him physically. But why are we, we who claim to advocate reparations and healing of Africa and African people as a pre-condition for global survival, and we who claim to love Tupac, letting the knowledge that the most revered MC of all times, loved and indeed idolized by Black and "white" youth alike, was advocating reparations slip into oblivion? He was doing so not only in his lyrics, but in fact by the very way he was raised and lived. Tupac was also national chairman of the New African Panther Party, which was and is calling for reparations, and this involvement in the leadership of the New African Panthers and the New Afrikan People's Organization was not an exceptional or minor episode in his life, but was grounded in its essence. Tupac, son of New York 21 Panther Afeni Shakur, who at age 23 was instrumental in getting herself and most of the other Panthers incarcerated for several years on a police and CIA frame-up acquitted, was raised and socialized as a revolutionary and actively continued to pursue on this path throughout his lifetime. Tupac was in contact with top foundational Panther Huey P. Newton in the year leading up to the assassination of Newton by US Intelligence services.[1761] The Black Panthers have always advocated reparations; in fact they did not only advocate reparations but they started to take reparations. Throughout the early 1990s, Tupac hired former Black Panther lawyer Chokwe Lumumba to represent him in his legal battles with the police. In 1993, Lumumba got him cleared of all charges of shooting two police officers in Oakland. It is no incident but in line with Tupac's politics that Chokwe Lumumba was at a given time a very important figure in the legal struggle for reparations and wrote and published: "Reparations Yes!: The Legal and Political Reasons why New Afrikans, Black People in the United States, Should be Paid Now for the Enslavement of Our Ancestors and for War Against Us After Slavery", a foundational literary document in the global African reparations struggle.

In the early 1990s, Tupac and Mutulu Shakur, the father who raised him and also a Black Panther, devised the Thug Life plan, and started, successfully, to politicize gangs throughout the US. Armed Black and Brown gangs with memberships going into the hundred thousands were becoming revolutionized and shifting their focus from killing each other to attacking the "white" capitalist power structure that was their real enemy. These activities coupled with his global stardom and influence made Tupac a major danger, and after a few unsuccessful murder attempts by US Intelligence, he was executed. Mutulu Shakur still remains imprisoned on a police frame-up today. Just days after Tupac's assassination, after several years of truce, the ghetto war between Bloods and Crips flared up again, and considering convincing evidence, Suge Knight of Death Row as a henchman of US Intelligence may have been instrumental in this as well.[1762] Is it not a huge betrayal by us, Tupac fans around the world, that we let this essential mission

---

1761 Ibid., 48ff.
1762 Potash (2007), 120f.

of his, the one that cost him his life, slip away and don't continue on the way he showed us? In my opinion, the global reparations movement needs to visually, vocally and musically incorporate Tupac in its activities in order to pass on this most important and urgent part of the message that he was actively militating for in his lifetime, and to attract more young people, Black and "white" and whatever hue, into the boat in this survival fight.

In the same perspective, it is also crucial to make young people aware that the Hip-Hop Summit Action Network founded and headed by hip-hop mogul Russell Simmons is advocating reparations. Point 9. of its "What We Want" program reads: "We want reparations to help repair the lingering vestiges; damages and suffering of African Americans as a result of the brutal enslavement of generations of Africans in America".[1763] Top mainstream rapper Sean 'Diddy' Combs is part of the board, and even though representatives of Warner Music and Virgin Music Group, arguably representing the interest of the establishment in formatting the minds of the people into sheeps and (self-) destructive behaviors through the mass media, are also sitting on the board, the reparations movement should seek to highlight that hip-hop and mainstream top artists are heading organizations calling for reparations. And even if it is only to direct the attention of a few more youth to the concept of reparations. At the same time we activists and strategic thinkers must also not neglect to reach out to hip-hop and other popular artists and encourage them on the path of conscientization and their role in spreading the message, just as the Black Panthers, directly and indirectly, did with Tupac since his very first days of his lifetime.

Yet, even the continuous attacks on revolutionary hip-hop artists such as Tupac and the implicit threat they represent to other artists have not succeeded in entirely silencing the progressive moments in hip-hop. Stic.man and M-1 who together form the group Dead Prez were co-instrumental in that my own life journey led me to effectuate this research work for reparations. They have been dealing with reparations explicitly in their music at several instances. In an interview, M-1 stated that "the question of reparations does not boil down to the money. It boils down to self-determination (...). The implication of this parasitic system is the question at hand. Reparations are only useful in a movement that understands the larger questions of power and is willing to assert that it will mean a better future for our people."[1764]

The global African reparation movement and its legal minds must continue to and even put heightened efforts into reaching out to hip-hop and reggae artists, directly and via organizations such as the National Hip-Hop Action Network and community organizations. Hip-hop and reggae need to provide the soundtrack for

---

1763 http://www.hsan.org/content/main.aspx?pageid=27
1764 Lulaine Compere M1's Thoughts to Professor Gates' New York Times Editorial
http://www.thesource.com/articles/49548

any successful reparation movement. There is no way around this since it is these musical cultures that shape the consciousness of global African youth. In many local African liberation struggles, be it in Haiti, in the US Civil Rights Movement or in the Mau Mau struggle, fire songs and drums invigorated and called people to action. Music is important to "prepare people for struggle, to elevate their consciousness."[1765] It is essential that we come to fully grasp again what KRS-1 so rightfully reminded us, that "hip and hop is more than music. Hip is the knowledge, hop is the movement. Hip and hop is the intelligent movement."[1766]

The reparations movement must not only reach out to hip-hop artists, but also to artists and people involved in reggae and Rastafari. Despite its militant origins centred around and aiming at African redemption, too many people identifying with Rasta today are following a misplaced conception of "One love" and don't even know what one is talking about when speaking of reparations. On the other hand, there is much mistrust at a practical level. A few years back I went to the Ethiopian World Federation office in Brixton/London to see if they had any materials relevant for this present research, and the bredren opening the door asked me if I deal with reparations or repatriation. When I said foremost reparations, but also repatriation as a form of reparations, he just stated, "Nah, we don't deal with that", and I was already out again. It is crucial that the Rastafari movement strengthens its roots that have always been in African resistance and liberation movements on both sides of the Atlantic such as the Mau Mau, the Nyahbinghi or the UNIA. In that regard it is also most important to highlight time and again that reparation is not only about money, but comprises many aspects, including repatriation. It is crucial to disseminate this knowledge, given the influence of the Rastafari movement on young people worldwide and their need for guidance. We really should aim at reaching at a stage where, when Jamaican reggae artists – having a following of millions worldwide – come to play a concert, be it in Paris, Trinidad, Guyana, Dakar, or even Austria, there is a stall present at the venue where people can familiarize themselves with the concept of reparations. Artists should also mention it on stage. In that regard, the Nyahbinghi council in Jamaica and other Rastafari houses, collectives and individuals may have to approach artists to see how this process can best be implemented. And the moment seems to be ripe just now. International reggae star Sizzla Kalonji has recently taken up the subject of reparations and repatriation in a speech in which he also said that the Rastafari movement would "put in place a legal constitutional representation of the Indigenous People and culture of Jamaica, to address the relevant Government who are able to assist us as a Government. We are now putting in place ourselves as the true Indigenous Government of Ras Tafari with a President Elect for the black people in the Diaspora" and made reference to the "Sovereign rights to gov-

---

1765 Asante, M. K., Jr. (2008). It's bigger than hip hop, New York: St. Martin's Press, 254f.
1766 Asante, M. K., Jr. (2008). It's bigger than hip hop, New York: St. Martin's Press, 256.

ern themselves"[1767] that have been denied for too long and are still due legally to African people globally. When popular artists like Sizzla are starting to talk international law, and recognizing and promoting that Rastafari, as the righteous government of Black people, will seek reparations on a government-to-government basis, the political reparations movement must surely not let this moment pass, but all sides and angles have to come together to inform and re-inforce one another.

Hip hop, reggae or other cultural movements by themselves will of course not bring us where we need to reach, but they participate in that journey, as other strands of work such as exemplary lawsuits; lobbying and mobilising by the political reparations movement; or fashion activism. All of these fields of work need to join together. Substantial change will have to be effectuated by political, economic and most of all practical action, but in order for the people to get to that stage they have to be prepared through culture. Bob Marley has been chanting "Africa Unite!" for a long time now, and we are still far from the African unity that is needed to bring about true reparation and world healing. But let there also be no doubt that these chants do have a most important effect. They uplifted the spirits of Zimbabwean freedom fighters and contributed to conscientization and movement that culminated in a situation where today it could no longer be delayed that a Black man take the office of President of the United States – and if it was only so that the powers-that-be are able to carry on their camouflaged system of global apartheid based on systematic and structural oppression of the majority of African people worldwide. What is important is that people had through persistent resistance and struggle set the stage to where this taking-off of steam had become necessary for the system. That already constitutes progress, and no doubt musicians played a huge facilitating role in that process. So what we need to do now is not get discouraged, acknowledge the progress that has been made because of the determination of the people and take it off from where Bob Marley left us physically, and that is reparations. Check again the passage from the interview with Mumia Abu-Jamal a few pages above. What Bob Marley left us with is the message that when "Blackman solid, everything solid" and that African people have to retake the "God business" to re-balance the earth, which is nothing else but reparation. We need to take this mission that Bob Marley left us to effectuate to the millions and millions of youth who glory in his music.

Another illustrious example of the importance of cultural popular movements for the building of consciousness for reparation comes through the, by now split, iconic French hip hop group *La Brigade*. Not only that this group, which consisted of up to fourteen members, established itself as one of the most successful French hip hop groups, all while maintaining consistently militant and political contents

---

1767 Collins, Miguel Orlando (Sizzla). Nyahbinghi Council Presidential Speech of October 21, 2012.

and dropping some of the best albums that this part of the globe has seen to this day. They also managed to do all of this without a manager. Today, Franco, one of the former rappers of *La Brigade*, is the extremely eloquent and analytically on-point spokesperson of *Brigade Anti-Négrophobie*, the association that has been mentioned above in context of the shameful official celebration of the abolition of slavery in that country in 2011 and which is one of the associations most active for reparation among young people in France. The music of *La Brigade* was, along with hip-hop from the US, such as dead prez, and reggae, most important for my own conscientization concerning global apartheid and the necessity of global African reparation. Without this musical education, I would most likely not have done the work that is now in your hands in the form of this book. Hip hop and popular cultural movements are not enough but they remain essential for our struggle.

The fact that different approaches of promoting and working for reparations, be it lawsuits, research, marching and rallying, people's tribunals, fashion activism and music, all have their roles to play in this struggle and are all necessary to get where we need to get, is brought on point by M-1 of Dead Prez in the context of a lawsuit that this group was maintaining against the NYPD after being harassed. M-1 declared that "our campaign cannot simply be legal, there also needs to be people campaigns that put the pressure on Doomberg or Bloomberg [then mayor of NY] to make decisions he wouldn't normally have to make. We have to use the legal aspect to provide an out for any community pressure that he might face and he may get a rock thrown at him in a press conference (...). Knowing your rights is almost like turning your lights on with the roaches because they scatter and with the lights on there is your protection. (...) Knowing your rights is one of the chief ways that you can defend yourself. But the struggle continues, the resistance is hot. (...) We know that our first job is to be soldiers and be defenders of our right so we began organizing ourselves."[1768] The relevance of a sound legal case, such as presented in this book, is to lay a foundation on which to make people realize that a fundamental change in the global order is legally due to them, and hip hop, reggae and other forms of cultural activism such as visual arts and fashion need to be used to get this knowledge across to as many people as possible. Finally, it will be the people who have to put the pressure on the policy-makers and authors behind the continuing crime of the Maafa "to make decisions they would normally not have to make", to paraphrase M-1, and to, last but not least, take reparations.

1768 Asante, M. K., Jr. (2008). It's bigger than hip hop, New York: St. Martin's Press, 165f. 153f.

XIV. Closing Remarks

According to the relevant laws – African, European, international – of that time, transatlantic slavery was most definitely illegal. Considerate of the central tenet of non-retroactivity not only in present-day international law, but also in African laws at that time, the question of the legal status, at the very basis of the reparation debate, must be assessed by those contemporary historical laws. Such an assessment constitutes the heart-piece of the first part of this book and it clearly confirmed the illegality of transatlantic slavery. Responsibility of European perpetrator states and the obligation to make reparations are thus established. Furthermore, the fact that we are dealing with a continuing violation of law, transatlantic slavery being only one stage of the Maafa, makes it possible to directly apply present-day international law and the International Law Commission's Articles on state responsibility as well as historic law. It also makes it possible to apply today's law provisions concerning genocide.

All of this notwithstanding, it is highly unlikely that any court or any other international institution will accord these legally due reparations. The current international power constellation, including its legal component, is to a big extent a consequence of and rooted in this crime. Therefore, people's power has to be created by all means, and especially through the raising of consciousness about the right to reparations and the global practical implication that true reparation would entail.

Given this factual power constellation in the world and the fact that nothing moves by itself in life in general as in international law without power to back even the most well founded claim, I suggest that African people globally start to take reparations, for example by organising campaigns not to pay taxes until France pays back the illegally extorted money to Haiti. The thus saved money could be transferred to an international fund at the disposal of the Haitian people. Such tax-refusal campaigns should be well grounded in a legal reparations argument.

Yet it seems clear that no court or tribunal or any other institution set up by Europeans and Euro-Americans will ever give the reparations that are necessary and legally due, even if confronted with the most solid and waterproof legal case. It is very important that organizations such as *Mouvement Internationale pour les Réparations* (MIR) in France and in its colonies continue to take legal actions in the courts against France and other enslaver states, because single victories may both bring reparations and legally due benefits to a number of individuals and groups of people. Taking such concrete legal action is also important to raise awareness, push the topic into the public arena and to make the people know that they have a legal right to reparations for the most massive crime ever that was perpetrated against their ancestors and is still perpetrated against them. But ultimately, it will have to be the people who will have to *take* reparations and make European states, societies and individuals give what they have been in legal obligation to give for the past 500 years.

As already mentioned above, while working on this research, I wanted to get to know the perspective of one of my favorite writers, Ayi Kwei Armah, on the subject. So I contacted him, and he let me have his opinion which is not very supportive of the struggle for reparations, since he "understand(s) the claim for reparations to be based on the assumption that some day Europeans and Americans will wake up and recognize that they did wrong when they came to Africa to set up a slaving enterprise, followed by a resource-pillaging economy that has gone under various names: empire, colonialism, apartheid, independence, structural adjustment, globalization, what have you. And that having woken up to their criminal liability, they will want to make amends. I see no basis in historical fact for either assumption. (...) Europe and America exist for me only as negative vortices. I do not want to focus any of my productive attention on them." I agree with Armah, whose books have made my heart beat like no other and opened mental channels for me, that Europeans will never ever give reparations voluntarily. They have known that what they did was wrong and illegal from when they first started the crime. They did, however, do the best to make everyone, including Africans, believe that the crime was "normal" and "legal". The most important thing about the global struggle for reparations is to make African people realize that they have a legal right to reparation, and to continue pushing until the people will be ready to take it. The struggle for reparations is fundamentally about "our own awakening, not on anything we can expect from those who have worked so hard to destroy us". The information that constitutes the basis of this international legal reparations claim is also the same information that "will end our blindness and prepare us to repair the damage of centuries of deliberate abuse, our selves"[1769].

It is crucial to see that lobbying and people power can move things in this matter. Thus in 1994, after the 1993 United Nations World Conference on Human Rights in held Vienna, Austria, the December 12th Movement and its International Secretariat lobbied successfully for the appointment of a Special Rapporteur on Contemporary Forms of Racism, Racial Discrimination, Xenophobia and Related Intolerance.[1770] Departing from that, further lobbying has brought about the

---

1769 Private correspondence with Ayi Kwei Armah (on file with author).
1770 Wareham, Roger (2003). The Popularization of the International Demand for Reparations, in: Raymond A. Winbush (ed.), Should America pay? Slavery and the raging debate on reparations,

World Conference Against Racism in Durban in 2001, and 2013-2023 will be a UN Decade for People of African Descent.

Due to the enormity of the crime of transatlantic slavery and consequently of the reparation claim, it was not possible to fully address in this study all technical details that might seem relevant, such as the question of what international court or institution could in theory handle this international claim, and what legal entities could figure as plaintiffs and defendants. State succession is also a legal issue in that regard that will have to be scrutinized in more detail in a further research. That these detail aspects were put back for now does not, however, diminish the validity and utility of the general argument elaborated here, since the clarification of the basic questions of the true legal status of transatlantic slavery at its time and of legal responsibility, is the pre-condition of the assessment of those other aspects. Furthermore it is not to be expected that this reparation claim will be settled in a legal procedure in which the perpetrator states cooperate.

Yet as demonstrated throughout this work, the claim for reparation rests on a sound legal basis and does not depend on the goodwill of the former enslavers.[1771] The question of reparation has to be appreciated on an *ex iure* basis and not *ex gratia* approach. The victims of this massive crime need to see their *rights* recognized and to acknowledge that these rights do not depend on their former enslavers' good will. That acknowledgement by the people will in itself be a small step of reparation.

As closing remarks, I would like to recall some personal experiences which, among many others, brought me to realize the urgent necessity of reparations and healing for transatlantic slavery and the Maafa. Though such remarks illustrating the underlying motivations are commonly placed at the beginning of a work, it would not have been appropriate to do so in this case, since they incorporate many references to concepts that were only, and could only be, explained in later parts of the work. Presenting them in the introduction may have caused confusion and incomprehension.

Such motivations were mostly small everyday encounters, such as walking from Parade to Eaststreet in downtown Kingston, a part of the city bordering the ghettos and feared for gang and police violence, and coming by a group of about five or six 15-to-16-year-old youths, leaning on a car. When I passed them, one of them stepped up to me and said that his friend liked me but he was too shy to tell me. I told the youth-man that I really appreciated that but that they were all way

---

Amistad, New York, 226-236, 229f.
1771 Gareau, Jean-Francois (2004). "Insoutenable imprescriptibilité à la lettre: Note sur l'interaction du temps, du droit et du symbole dans la problématique de la réparation des crimes de l'histoire", in: Boisson de Chazournes, Laurence, Jean-François Quéguiner and Santiago Villalpando (ed.): Crimes de l'histoire et réparations: les réponses du droit et de la justice, Brussels: Editions Bruylant, 25-38, 33.

too young for me. The youth just said, "Oh, ok, well miss have a very nice day". I had already anticipated some little botheration from them when approaching from the way they were looking at me a little provocatively, but finally they were just little youths stuck in the ghetto because of slavery, without much perspective. It made me sad when I walked away to think that these lively, positive and kind youths could well be the next victims of police murder or politically motivated gang violence – all a legacy of slavery with its unbroken neo-colonial world system structure. These things happen regularly in the place where they were born and live. Not far from where I met them, police had not long before killed the son of dancehall artist Spragga Benz who was about the same age while he was riding his bike. It breaks my heart to know what could happen to any of them at any time – basically because their fore-parents were kidnapped and taken to this land as slaves for the profit of European enslavers. Generally, I met so many people in Jamaica who showed me much love, although they are poor because they are Black in a situation of global apartheid, and I am European.

Millicent, a market vendor in the town I stayed in for the second part of the research, befriended me and often brought me wild green leaf vegetables as a gift, although I seldom bought from her because she only had a very limited range of produce. She never accepted money from me for this, and when I insisted on paying for the vegetables, she insisted more, telling me, "No man, it just grow free". I had had somewhat similar experiences on the African continent when I was living in Senegal a few years back.

When I walked home from town in Port Antonio, I crossed through settlements that are best described as ghetto dwellings made from cardboard and rotting aluminium sheets. Yet people were so respectful and nice to me, greeted me with "hi", "how are you, miss?", "good evening" and so on without ever harassing me. People gave me plants and flowers as presents when I passed. At the same time, the people in neighbouring Haiti suffered a massive cholera outbreak, due to their material poverty rooted in transatlantic slavery turned into absolute catastrophe by the 2010 earthquake. It is only by pure chance that my friends and neighbors live in Jamaica and not in Haiti that their ancestors were deported to Jamaica and not to a few kilometres further east to Haiti. People are poor and suffer from high levels of violence in Jamaica, but in Haiti people died *en masse* because of the to-be-repaired damage of transatlantic slavery and the continuing Maafa. It was such little interpersonal experiences that made me know that I had to contribute what I can to help realize justice for the people.

At Papine market in Kingston, another poorer neighborhood of that city with elevated levels of violence, I once asked a market lady who sold bagged spices if she had salt too. She didn't have it, but asked the seller next to her to pour some salt in a small bag for me. Another man standing nearby started to cuss about this, saying, "When we thirsty them neva give wi no drink and now yuh ah give them salt, cho !" ("when we are thirsty, they never give us water to drink and now you give them salt, cho !"). The market woman responded, "The woman just want some salt, give her some salt ...", and insisted on accepting no money from me in return.

In "French" Guiana, all, and I mean really all, grocery stores are operated by Chinese people. Once I was waiting in a cashier line of a grocer when the very old African man before me, who had just complained to me that the Chinese store owner was taking all his small money, turned again and asked me the reason of my visit to his country. When I told him that I was there for legal works for reparations, his face brightened in a wide smile, he took my hand and said, "Merci, merci! C'est important ... félicitations et merci!". These experiences were priceless, moved me very much and encouraged me not to give up on this work even when it kept me in some financial hardships and consumed most of my time for almost four years. I love Africa and African people so much and have been extended so much love and warmth, and that just made me know from my very inner being that if I could contribute something beneficial with this research work, it would well be worth the effort trying to contribute a little so that my African brothers and sisters globally will finally get what is rightfully theirs and can live in peace.

Given the extreme violence and genocidal racial oppression that was instituted by Europeans in the transatlantic system, I find it remarkable that so many Africans continue to live up to a faith in the principal and fundamental unity of mankind. Historically, the Brazilian Palmares communities, for example, also accustomed runaway "whites". Especially "white" women found refuge from oppressive and murderous European colonial society and a new home with them. In Haiti, people proclaimed after their accomplished revolution that all "whites" who declared themselves in solidarity with the aims of the new Republic could stay and were from then on also considered as "Black".

It is also important not to omit that there were at all times European people who actively stood up against slavery, such as a group of Quakers who drafted an anti-slavery resolution in 1688 in Germantown, Pennsylvania.[1772]

Numerous scholars and experts have stressed what common sense already tells us; that western demands for human rights enforcement in poorer countries will not be effective if European countries and the US themselves are not willing to acknowledge the injustice that they have perpetrated in the past and accept responsibility for those massive human rights violations. As Freeman puts it, the "denial of the case for reparations can therefore poison the present, and thus undermine

---

1772 Harper's Magazine (2003). "Does America Owe a Debt to the Descendants of Its Slaves?" in: Raymond A. Winbush (ed.): Should America pay? Slavery and the raging debate on reparations, New York: Amistad, 79-108, 104.

prospects for justice in the future."[1773] Throughout this work we have come upon quite a few utterances by western statesmen, such as Bill Clinton when he was US President, the British High Commissioner in Jamaica, or the British Communities Minister Andrew Stunell who dismissed reparations by claiming that "we don't believe that reparation is a way of tackling the issue of slave trade. Championing the cause against slavery is the main issue high on our agenda. Britain has been working closely with other nations and institutions along this line. (...) I want to say that the (...) government is highly committed against slavery, focusing on the international issues such as modern-day slavery and the sex trade"[1774]. Yet, it really remains impossible to effectively combat both racism and modern day slavery if reparation for transatlantic slavery and the Maafa is not made. Most, if not all, forms of modern slavery in some way go back to structures set in place through transatlantic slavery. Without willingness to address this issue, western endeavors in that regard unmask themselves as rather hypocritical in their commitment to tackle present-day exploitation and human rights abuses, when millions still suffer and die because Europeans and the USA are still profiting from the legacy of transatlantic slavery while continuing to perpetrate the Maafa. That was also recognized, in general terms, by Resolution 2001/1 of the Sub-Commission on Human Rights, unanimously adopted on August 6, 2001, where it is sustained "that it is not possible to combat racism and racial discrimination, struggle against impunity or denounce the human rights violations which persist in the world without taking account of the deep of the past", whereas "the historic responsibility of the relevant powers towards the peoples who they colonize or reduce to slavery should be the subject of solemn and formal recognition and reparation"[1775].

Considering the war in Congo, for example, and its direct link to genocidal slavery and colonialism in the region, the denial of reparation and the continuing interference of former enslaver and colonial European states in that conflict factually translate into a denial of the right to life of African Congolese people. Doudou Diène, former Director of the Division of Inter-cultural Projects at UNESCO, confirmed that the persistence and amplitude of present human rights violations in Africa have without a doubt a link with the silence and forgetfulness about transatlantic slavery. Because the defence of human rights is also a struggle for memory, occulted, unexplained and un-assumed tragedies come back to life.

1773 Freeman, Michael (2007). "Back to the Future: the Historical Dimension of Liberal Justice", in: Max du Plessis and Stephen Peté (ed.): Repairing the Past? International Perspectives on Reparations for Gross Human Rights Abuses, Antwerpen/Oxford: Intersentia, 29-51, 42.
1774 Cited in: Eze, Mercy (2010). Slavery Remembrance Day observed, in: New African, Nr. 499, October 2010, London, IC Publications, 28-29, 28.
1775 Recognition of responsibility and reparation for massive and flagrant violations of human rights which constitute crimes against humanity and which took place during the period of slavery, colonialism and wars of conquest, Sub-Commission on Human Rights resolution 2002/5, downloaded from
http://ap.ohchr.org/documents/E/SUBCOM/resolutions/E-CN_4-SUB_2-RES-2002-5.doc   (accessed 23.3.2011).

The construction of the ideology of race inequality, foundation of racism, is directly linked to transatlantic slavery, because the consciences of the times had to be calmed and the justification of the transformation of human beings into commodities justified.[1776]

As discussed above, some sustain that the Presidency of Barack Obama would have made the idea of reparations oblivious. Yet, for the vast majority of Black people globally and also in the USA things have not improved in practice, except maybe for an important uplift of their spirits. Some will say that the election of Obama was a next step in the right direction and that time will heal all wounds. Given the deep structures and high interests at stake, I do not think however that "time" will be enough. In any case, we cannot afford to wait for time to fix it, because each day that passes means not only death, suffering, and discrimination of African people, but also the continuation of a global system rooted in transatlantic slavery and its disregard for life that puts human existence as such at peril because its very foundation is the pursuit of profits by any means, resulting in industrial and nuclear pollution and blood spills at an extent that our planet can simply no longer take it.

I don't really want to enter here into the debate as to whether or not the election of a Black President in the United States was an event of fundamental change, or if Barack Obama is a necessity for this stage of neo-colonialism, such as argued for example by the Uhuru Movement. I think it is probably both; the struggles of African people globally did advance and achieve important things and without these struggles a Black President would not have become possible. Because of these historical struggles and especially the growing reparations movement, it was time to take some steam out in order to keep the machine of global African exploitation running and to give a superficial impression of equality. Yet, the fact itself that a Black man became president is important for the psyche of African people worldwide, and that positive effect cannot be taken away even if the election of the person Obama as such would indeed have been part of a neo-colonial scheme. But the fact remains also that socially, economically and politically, this election changed nothing for the vast majority of African people globally. All remains to be repaired. The ghetto dwellers in Kingston and Zimbabwe still hustle to make a living from day to day. [1777] And time is running out since everywhere from Brazil, to the Caribbean area, to the United States, to the African continent elderly witnesses able to provide both information on the enslavement and transatlantic slavery are disappearing. In Africa, a systematic mapping should be urgently undertaken of destroyed or deserted villages wherever they can validly

---

1776 Diène (1998a), 21 et seq.
1777 United Nations Educational, Scientific and Cultural Organization (ed.) (1978). Meeting of Experts on the African Slave-Trade, Final Report, Port-au-Prince, Haiti, 31 January-4 February 1978, downloaded fromhttp://unesdoc.unesco.org/images/0003/000333/033360eb.pdf (accessed 21.6.2012).

be linked to the slave trade.

The current regime of international law is depicted as promoting stability, justice and peace in the world. However, if the contention that this regime of international law would not offer any legal remedies for the massive crime and catastrophe of transatlantic slavery is maintained, it will be exposed as rather barbaric and not enlightened at all. International law, as it is today, must then be considered as a legal system in the sense of a system of legal rules and regulations, but certainly not in the sense of a legal system whose *raison d'être* is to promote justice.

It is crucial to highlight at every occasion that reparation for transatlantic slavery is not about making the current generations of descendants of slave owners and enslaver nations guilty for actions of their ancestors, but about the historical legal responsibility of their states and societies, about their own continued responsibility for perpetuating and profiting from the structures that were set in place through this genocide, and about global survival.[1778]

I hope that this work can make a small contribution in showing for good that transatlantic slavery and the Maafa have always been criminal and illegal, and that Africans globally have a right to reparation. So far, the ideas presented here have been well received by a number of international lawyers. The claim for reparation is just. Africans have known and ascertained this since the time of the first deportations. It is also well grounded in international law and legally due. Yet, to paraphrase Malcolm X, nobody will give you sovereignty. Nobody will give you equality or justice or true reparation or anything. If you're a man or a woman, you take it. *Ubi ius, ibi remedium...* by any means necessary.

1778 Thompson, Dudley J. (2000). "Réparations", in: Serge Chalons, Christian Jean-Etienne, Suzy Landau and Andre Yebakima (ed.): De l'esclavage aux reparations, Paris: Editions Karthala, 167-172, 169.

XV. List of Abbreviations

ARM-UK	African Reparations Movement-United Kingdom
BCE	Before Common Era
CARICOM	Caribbean Community
CE	Common Era
ICJ	International Court of Justice
ICTR	International Criminal Tribunal for Rwanda
ILC	International Law Commission
IMT	International Military Tribunal
N'COBRA	National Coalition of Black for Reparations in America
PAHO	Pan American Health Organization
PCIJ	Permanent Court of International Justice
R.I.A.A.	Reports of International Arbitral Awards
t.b.a.	translated by author
UNIA	United Negro Improvement Association
VCLT	Vienna Convention in the Law of Treaties
WCAR	World Conference Against Racism
WHO	World Health Organization

XIV. Bibliography

Abel, Richard (1995). Politics by Other Means. Law in the Struggle Against Apartheid, 1980-1994, New York: Routledge.

Adu-Boahen, Albert (ed.) (1985). General History of Africa, Vol. VII, Africa Under Colonial Domination 1880-1935, California: Heinemann & UNESCO.

Affiong Southey, Julie/Klu, Kofi Mawuli (1993). Charting an African Self-Determined Path of Legal Struggle for Reparations, Birmingham: African Reparations Movement- United Kingdom Committee.

Afrik, Baba Hannibal/Elijah, Jill Soffiyah/Benton Lewis, Dorothy/Worril, Conrad W. (2003). "Current Legal Status of Reparations, Strategies of the National Black United Front, the Mississippi Model, What's Next in the Reparations Movement", in: Raymond A. Winbush (ed.): Should America pay? Slavery and the raging debate on reparations, New York: Amistad, 363-383.

Ago, Robert (1983). The First International Communities in the Mediterranean World, British Year Book of International Law, Oxford: Clarendon Press.

Ajavon, Lawoetey-Pierre (2005). Traite et Esclavage des Noirs. Quelle responsabilité Africaine Paris: Editions MENAIBUC.

Akbar, Na'im (1996). Breaking the Chains of Psychological Slavery, Tallahassee: Mind Productions & Associates, Inc..

Albiston, Catherine R. (2006). "Legal Consciousness and Workplace Rights", in: Benjamin Fleury-Steiner and Laura Beth Nielsen (ed.): The new civil rights research:a constitutive approach, Aldershot: Ashgate Publishing, 55-75.

Alexandrowicz, Charles H. (1975). The Role of Treaties in the European-African Confrontation in the Nineteenth Century, in: A.K. Mensah-Brown (ed.): African International Legal History, New York: UNITAR, 27-68.

Alexandrowicz, Charles (ed.) (1968). Studies in the history of the laws of nations, The Hague: Grotian Press Society.

Allott, Antony (1975). Boundaries in Africa: A Legal and Historical Survey, in: A.K. Mensah-Brown (ed.): African International Legal History, New York: UNITAR, 69-86.

Ani, Marimba (1988). Let The Circle Be Unbroken: The Implications of African Spirituality in the Diaspora. New York: Nkonimfo Publications.

Ankomah, Baffour (2010). All issues great and small, in: New African Nr. 501, November 2010, London: IC Publications, 62-69.

Ankomah, Baffour (2011). Who are the people of Libya? in: New African Nr. 506, May 2011, London: IC Publications, 8-9.

Andrade, Elisa Silva (1995). "Le Cap-Vert dans l'expansion européenne", in: Elikia M'Bokolo (ed.): L'Afrique entre l'Europe et l'Amerique. Le rôle de l'Afrique dans la rencontre de deux mondes 1492-1992, Paris: UNESCO, 69-79.

An-Na'im, Abdullahi A. (ed.) (2002a). Cultural Transformation and Human Rights in Africa, London: Zed Books.

An-Na'im, Abdullahi A. (2002b). "Introduction", in: Abdullahi A. An-Na'im (ed.): Cultural Transformation and Human Rights in Africa, London: Zed Books, 1-11.

An-Na'im, Abdullahi/Deng, Francis M. (ed.) (1990a). Human Rights in Africa. Cross-Cultural Perspectives, Washington DC: The Brookings Institution.

An-Na'im, Abdullahi/Deng, Francis M. (1990b). "Introduction", in: Abdullahi An-Na'im and Francis M. Deng (ed.): Human Rights in Africa. Cross-Cultural Perspectives, Washington DC: The Brookings Institution, 1-14.

Apfel, Roberta J./Bennett, Simon (ed.) (1966). Minefields in Their Hearts: The Mental Health of Children in War and Communal Violence, New Haven: Yale University Press.

Armah, Ayi Kwei (2010). Remembering the Dismembered Continent. Essays, Popenguine: Per Ankh.

Asante, Molefi Kete (2003). "The African American Warrant for Reparations", in: Ray Winbush (ed.): Should America pay? Slavery and the raging debate on reparations, New York: Amistad, 3-13.

Asante, M. K., Jr. (2008). It's bigger than hip hop, New York: St. Martin's Press.

Asare, William Kweku (2002). Slavery reparations in perspective, Victoria: Trafford Publishing.

Baba Kaké, Ibrahima (1998). "La vulgarisation de l'histoire de la traite negrière", in: Doudou Diene (ed.): La chaîne et le lien. Une vision de la traite négrière, Paris: UNESCO, 25-29.

Bailey, Anne C. (2007). African Voices of the Atlantic Slave Trade, Kingston/Miami: Ian Randle Publishers.

Ball, Jared (2011). I Mix What I Like! A mix tape manifesto, Oakland: AK Press.

Ballong-Wen-Mewuda, Joseph B. (2002). "L'esclavage et la traite négrière dans la correspondance de Nzinga Mbemba (dom Afonso I), roi du Congo (1506-1543): la vision idéologique de l'autre", in: Isabel Castro Henriques and Louis Sala-Molins (ed.): Déraison, esclavage et droit. Les fondements idéologiques et juridiques de la traite négrière et de l'esclavage, Paris: EDITIONS Unesco, 301-314.

Bar-On, Dan (1966). "Attempting to Overcome the Intergenerational Transmission of Trauma: Dialogue between Descendants of Victims and of Perpetrators", in: Roberta J. Apfel and Bennett Simon (ed.): Minefields in Their Hearts: The Mental Health of Children in War and Communal Violence, New Haven: Yale University Press, 165-188.

Barry, Boubacar (1998). Senegambia and the Atlantic Slave Trade, Cambridge: Cambridge University Press.

Barry, Boubacar (1992). "Senegambia from the sixteenth to the eighteenth century: Evolution of the Wolof, Sereer and 'Tukuloor'", in: B.A. Ogot (ed.): General History of Africa V. Africa from the Sixteenth to the Eighteenth Century, Paris: UNESCO, 262-299.

Bassiouni, M. Cherif (1992). Crimes Against Humanity in International Criminal Law, Dordrecht/Boston/London: Martinus Nijhoff Publishers.

Batsikama ba Mampuya ma Ndawla, Raphaël (1999). L'Ancien royaume du Congo et les baKongo, Paris: L'Harmattan.

Baum, Robert (2010). "Slaves without Rulers: Domestic Slavery among the Diola of Senegambia", in: Stephanie Beswick and Jay Spaulding (ed.): African Systems of Slavery, Trenton: Africa World Press, 45-66.

Bederman, David L. (2001). International Law in Antiquity, Cambridge: Cambridge University Press.

Benezet, Anthony (1767). Some Historical Account of Guinea, Cirencester: The Echo Library (ed. 2005).

Benoit, Norbert (2002). "L'esclavage dans le Code jaune ou code Delaleu", in: Isabel Castro Henriques and Louis Sala-Molins (ed.): Déraison, esclavage et droit. Les fondements idéologiques et juridiques de la traite négrière et de l'esclavage, Paris: EDITIONS Unesco, 95-104.

Benoiton, Laurent (2010). "Le droit de l'esclave d'ester en justice contre son maître. Réflexions sur une disposition du Code noir protectrice de l'esclave", in: Tanguy Le Marc'hadour and Manuel Carius (ed.): Esclavage et Droit. Du Code noir à nos jours, Arras: Artois Presses Université, 15-41.

Beswick, Stephanie/Spaulding, Jay (ed.) (2010). African Systems of Slavery, Trenton: Africa World Press.

Biko, Steve (1978). I write what I like, Johannesburg: Heinemann.

Blackburn, Robin (1996). "Slave exploitation and the elementary structures of enslavement", in Bush, M.L. (ed.): Serfdom and slavery: studies in legal bondage, New York: Longman, 158-180.

Blackburn, Robin (1998). The Making of New World Slavery. From the Baroque to the Modern 1492-1800, London/New York: Verso.

Black's Law Dictionary (1979). 5th edition, St. Paul: West Publishing.

Blom, Philipp/Kos, Wolfgang (ed.) (2011). Angelo Soliman. Ein Afrikaner in Wien, Wien: Wien Museum/Christian Brandstätter Verlag.

Boisson de Chazournes, Laurence/Heathcote, Sarah (2004). "Mise en œuvre de la réparation des crimes de l'histoire: une possible (ré)conciliation des temps passés, présents et futurs ?", in: Laurence Boisson de Chazournes, Jean-François Quéguiner and Santiago Villalpando (ed.): Crimes de l'histoire et réparations: les réponses du droit et de la justice, Brussels: Editions Bruylant, 99-130.

Boisson de Chazournes, Laurence/Quéguiner, Jean-François/Villalpando, Santiago (ed.) (2004). Crimes de l'histoire et réparations: les réponses du droit et de la justice, Brussels: Editions Bruylant.

Boschiero, Nerina (2004). "La traite transatlantique et la responsabilité internationale des Etats", in: Laurence Boisson de Chazournes, Jean-François Quéguiner and Santiago Villalpando (ed.): Crimes de l'histoire et réparations: les réponses du droit et de la justice, Brussels: Editions Bruylant, 203-262.

Bourdieu, Pierre (1987). The Force of Law. Toward a Sociology of the Juridical Field, in: Hastings Law Journal Nr. 38, July 1987, 805-853.

Braeckman, Colette (1994). Rwanda. Histoire d'un génocide, Paris: Fayard.

Brevié, J.C. (1904). Rapport sur l'esclavage, Bamako: ASAOF.

Brooks, Roy L. (2004). Atonement and Forgiveness. A New Model for Black Reparations, Berkeley: University of California Press.

Brooks, Roy L. (2003). History of the Black Redress Movement, in: Guild Practitioner Vol. 60, Nr. 1, Los Angeles, 1-12.

Brooks, Roy L. (2007). "Redress for Slavery – The African-American Struggle", in: Max du Plessis and Stephen Peté (ed.): Repairing the Past? International Perspectives on Reparations for Gross Human Rights Abuses, Antwerpen/Oxford: Intersentia, 297-313.

Roy L. Brooks (ed.) (1999). When Sorry is Not Enough. The Controversy Over Apologies and Reparations for Human Injustice, New York: New York University Paperback.

Brown, Bertram (2004). "Etat des lieux des droits de l'homme, du droit international humanitaire et du droit international pénal face aux requêtes en, réparation' des crimes de l'histoire", in: Boisson de Chazournes, Laurence, Jean-François Quéguiner and Santiago Villalpando (ed.): Crimes de l'histoire et réparations: les réponses du droit et de la justice, Brussels: Editions Bruylant, 73-84.

Browner Stahl, Ann (2010). "Entangled Lives: The Archaeology of Daily Life in the Gold Coast Hinterlands, AD 1400-1900", in: Akinwumi Ogundiran and Toyin Falola (ed.): Archaeology of Atlantic Africa and the African Diaspora, Bloomington/Indianapolis: Indiana University Press, 49- 76.

Brysk, Alison (2000). From Tribal Village to Global Village: Indian Rights and International Relations in Latin America, Palo Alto: Stanford University Press.

Bush, Michael L. (ed.) (1996). Serfdom and Slavery: Studies in Legal Bondage, New York: Longman.

Camara, Fatou Kiné (2004). Pouvoir et Justice dans la Tradition des Peuples Noires. Philosophie et Pratique, Paris: L'Harmattan.

Capdevila, Nestor (2002). "Las Casas et les Noirs: quels problèmes ?" in: Isabel Castro Henriques and Louis Sala-Molins (ed.): Déraison, esclavage et droit. Les fondements idéologiques et juridiques de la traite négrière et de l'esclavage, Paris: EDITIONS Unesco, 41-58.

Capela, José (2002). "Ethique et représentation de l'esclavage colonial au Mozambique", in: Isabel Castro Henriques and Louis Sala-Molins (ed.): Déraison, esclavage et droit. Les fondements ideologiques et juridiques de la traite negriere et de l'esclavage, Paris: EDITIONS Unesco, 329-348.

Carreau, Dominique (2007). Droit international, Paris: Editions Pedone.

Castaldo, André (2006). Codes Noirs de l'esclavage aux abolitions, Paris: Editions Dalloz.

Chalons, Serge/Jean-Etienne, Christian/Landau, Suzy/Yebakima, Andre (ed.) (2000). De l'esclavage aux reparations, Paris: Editions Karthala.

Châtel, Bénédicte (2011). Déconstruire le racism, Interview with Ali Moussa Iye, in: New African/Le Magazine de l'Afrique Nr. 23, Nov-Dec 2011, 68-71.

Chinweizu (1987). The West and the Rest of Us, Lagos: Pero Press.

Christian, Ijahnya (2011). Return of the 6th Region: RastafarI Settlement in the Motherland. Contributing to the African Renaissance, Rabat: Codesria, 13eme Assemblée générale.

Cissé, Youssouf Tata (1991). Soundjata, la Gloire du Mali, Paris: Karthala-Arsan.

Cissokho, Aldiouma (2000). "Formes contemporaines de l'esclavage et necessité de réparation", in: Serge Chalons, Christian Jean-Etienne, Suzy Landau and Andre Yebakima (ed.): De l'esclavage aux reparations, Paris: Editions Karthala, 223-226.

Clarke, John Henrik (1998). Christopher Columbus and the Afrikan Holocaust. Slavery and the Rise of European Capitalism, New York: A&B Publisher Group.

Cleaver, Kathleen Neal (1995). The Antidemocratic Power of Whiteness, in: Kent Law Review Nr. 70, Chicago, 1375-1387.

Cleeve, George Van (2006). Somerset's Case Revisited: Somerset's Case and Its Antecedents in Imperial Perspective, in: Law and History Review Vol.24, Nr. 3, 601-645.

Coco, Lémy Lémane (2005). Regards sur l'esclavage dans les colonies françaises, Paris: Menaibuc.

Cohen, Ronald (1993). "Endless Teardrops: Prolegomena to the Study of Human Rights in Africa", in: Ronald Cohen and Goran Hyden (ed.): Human Rights and Governance in Africa, Gainesville: University of Florida Press, 3-38.

Cohen, Ronald/Hyden, Goran (ed.) (1993). Human Rights and Governance in Africa, Gainesville: University of Florida Press.

Condorelli, Luigi (2004). "Conclusions générales", in: Boisson de Chazournes, Laurence, Jean-François Quéguiner and Santiago Villalpando (ed.): Crimes de l'histoire et réparations: les réponses du droit et de la justice, Brussels: Editions Bruylant, 291-306.

Cook Anthony (2000). King and the Beloved Community: A Communitarian Defense of Black Reparations, in: George Washington Law Review 68, 959-1014.

Coutin, Susan Bibler (2002). "Reconceptualizing Research", in: June Starr and Mark Goodale (ed.): Practicing Ethnography in Law. New Dialogues, Enduring Methods, New York: Palgrave Macmillan, 108-127.

Crawford, James (2002). The International Law Commission's Articles on State

Responsibility. Introduction, Text and Commentaries, Cambridge: Cambridge University Press.

Crawford, James/Pellet, Alain/Olleson, Simon (ed.) (2010). The Law of International Responsibility, Oxford: Oxford University Press.

Crawford, Jewel/Nobles, Wade W./DeGruy Leary, Joy (2003). "Reparations and Health Care for African Americans", in: Raymond A. Winbush (ed.): Should America pay? Slavery and the raging debate on reparations, New York: Amistad, 251-281.

Crenshaw, K/Gotanda, N./Peller, G./Thomas, K (1995). Critical Race Theory: The Key Writings That Formed the Movement, New York: The New Press.

Cugoano, Quobna Ottobah (1787). Thoughts and Sentiments on the Evil of Slavery, London: Penguin Classics (ed. 1999).

Curto, José C. (2002). "Un butin illégitime: razzias d'esclaves et relations luso-africaines dans la région des fleuves Kwanza et Kwango en 1805", in: Isabel Castro Henriques and Louis Sala-Molins (ed.): Déraison, esclavage et droit. Les fondements ideologiques et juridiques de la traite negriere et de l'esclavage, Paris: EDITIONS Unesco, 314- 327.

Daes, Erica-Irene (2009). The Contribution of the Working Group on Indigenous Populations to the Genesis and Evolution of the UN Declaration on the Rights of Indigenous Peoples, in: Rodolfo Stavenhagen & Claire Charters (ed.): Making the Declaration Work. The United Nations Declaration on the Rights of Indigenous Peoples, Copenhagen: IWGIA, 48- 78.

Dass, Sujan (ed.) (2010). Black Rebellion. Eyewitness Accounts of Major Slave Revolts, Atlanta: Supreme Design.

Davidson, Nicol (1975). "Preface", in: A.K. Mensah-Brown (ed.): African International Legal History, New York: UNITAR, i-ii, i.

Davidson, Basil (1969). The African Genius. An Introduction to African Cultural and Social History, Atlantic Monthly Press Book, Boston/Toronto.

Davidson, Basil (1961). The African Slave Trade, Boston/New York: Back Bay Books.

De Frouville, Olivier (2004). L'intangibilité des droits de l'homme en droit international. Régime conventionnel des droits de l'homme et droit des traités, Paris: Editions Pédone.

De Greiff, Pablo (2006a). "Justice and Reparations", in: Pablo de Greiff (ed.): The Handbook of Reparations, Oxford: Oxford University Press, 451-477.

De Greiff, Pablo (ed.) (2006b). The Handbook of Reparations, Oxford: Oxford University Press.

De las Casas, Bartolomé (ed. 1989). Historia de las Indias, III, Editions des Obras completas, Madrid: Alianza Editorial.

De Moirans, Epifanio (1682). A Just Defense of the Natural Freedom of Slaves. All Slaves Should be Free, Lewiston: Edwin Mellen Press (ed. 2006 by Edward Sunshine).

Deng, Francis M. (1990). "A Cultural Approach to Human Rights Among the Dinka", in: Abdullahi An-Na'im and Francis M. Deng. (ed.): Human Rights in Africa. Cross-Cultural Perspectives, Washington DC: The Brookings Institution. 261- 289.

De Pommegorge, Pruneau (1789). Description de la Nigritie, Amsterdam/Paris: Maradan.

Derman, William (1973). Serfs, Peasants, and Socialists: A Former Serf Village in the Republic of Guinea, Berkeley: University of California Press.

De Visscher, C. (1924). La responsabilité des Etats, Leiden: Bibliotheca Visseriana.

Diagne, Pathé (1992). "African political, economic and social structures during this period", in: B.A. Ogot (ed.): General History of Africa V. Africa from the Sixteenth to the Eighteenth Century, Paris: UNESCO, 23-45.

Diderot, Dénis/d'Alembert, Jean Lerond (1765). Encyclopédie ou Dictionnaire raisonné, Vol. 16, Paris: Briasson.

Diène, Doudou (1998a). "De la traite négrière au défi du développement: réflexions sur les conditions de la paix mondiale", in: Doudou Diène (ed.): La chaîne et le lien. Une vision de la traite négrière, Paris: UNESCO, 21-23.

Diène, Doudou (ed.) (1998b). La chaîne et le lien. Une vision de la traite négrière, Paris: UNESCO.

Diop, Cheikh A. (1987) . L'Afrique noire précoloniale, Paris: Présence Africaine.

Diop-Maes, Louise Marie (1996). Afrique Noire. Démographie, Sol et Histoire, Paris: Présence Africaine/Khepera.

Diop-Maes, Louise (1993). Evolution de la population de l'Afrique Noire du neolithique au milieu du 20eme siecle, in: Ankh April 1993, Nr. 2.

Diouf, Sylvaine A. (ed.) (2003a). Fighting the Slave Trade. West African Strategies, Athens: Ohio University Press.

Diouf, Sylvaine A. (2003b). "Introduction", in: Sylvaine A. Diouf (ed.): Fighting the Slave Trade. West African Strategies, Athens: Ohio University Press, IX-XXVII.

Diouf, Sylvaine A. (2003c). "The Last Resort. Redeeming Family and Friends", in: Sylvaine A. Diouf (ed.): Fighting the Slave Trade. West African Strategies, Athens: Ohio University Press, 81-100.

Dodson, Howard (2000). "Le prix de l'esclavage? Le prix de la liberté?", in: Serge Chalons, Christian Jean-Etienne, Suzy Landau and Andre Yebakima (ed.): De l'esclavage aux réparations, Paris: Editions Karthala, 173-179.

Dumett, Raymond E. (2010). "The Work of Slaves in the Akan and Adangme Regions of Ghana in the Nineteenth Century", in: Stephanie Beswick and Jay Spaulding (ed.): African Systems of Slavery, Trenton/Asmara: Africa World Press, 67- 104.

Duodo, Cameron (2012). What Frantz Fanon meant to African liberation (2), in: New African Nr. 513, London: IC Publications, 62-66.

Du Plessis, Max/Peté, Stephen (ed.) (2007). Repairing the Past? International Perspectives on Reparations for Gross Human Rights Abuses, Antwerpen/Oxford:

Intersentia.

Durand, Jean-Baptiste (1807). Voyage au u Sénégal fait dans les années 1785 et 1786, Paris: Dentu.

Egharevba, Jakob U. (1968). A Short History of Benin, Ibadan: Ibadan University Press.

Elias, T. O. (1972). Africa and the Development of International Law, Leiden: A.W. Sijthoff.

Elias, T.O. (1975). "International Relations in Africa: A Historical Survey", in: A.K. Mensah-Brown (ed.): African International Legal History, New York: UNITAR, 87-106.

Elias, T. O. (1961). La nature du droit coutumier africain, Paris: Présence africaine.

Ewick, Patricia (2004). "Consciousness and Ideology", in: Austin Sarat (ed.): The Blackwell Companion to Law and Society, Oxford: Blackwell Publishing, 80-94.

Eze, Mercy (2010). Slavery Remembrance Day observed, in: New African Nr. 499, October 2010, London: IC Publications, 28-29.

eZurara, Gomes Eanes (1453). Chronique de Guinée, Paris: Editions Chandeigne (ed. 1994).

Fage, J.D. (1980). Slaves and Society in Western Africa, c. 1445-c. 1770, in: The Journal of African History 1980, Nr. 21, 289-310.

Falk, Richard (2006). "Reparations, International Law, and Global Justice", in: Pablo de Greiff (ed.): The Handbook of Reparations, Oxford: Oxford University Press, 478-503.

Farmer-Paellmann, Deadria (2003). "Excerpt from Black Exodus: The Ex-Slave Pension Movement Reader", in: Raymond A. Winbush (ed.): Should America pay? Slavery and the raging debate on reparations, New York: Amistad, 22-31.

Fegley, Randall (2010). "Death's Waiting Room: Equatorial Guinea's Long History of Slavery", in: Stephanie Beswick and Jay Spaulding (ed.): African Systems of Slavery, Trenton/Asmara: Africa World Press, 135- 159..

Fernyhough, Timothy (1993). "Human Rights and Precolonial Africa", in: Ronald Cohen and Goran Hyden (ed.): Human Rights and Governance in Africa, Gainesville: University of Florida Press, 39-73.

Fischer, Peter/Köck, Franz Heribert (2004). Völkerrecht. Das Recht der universellen Staatengemeinschaft, 6. Auflage, Wien: Linde Verlag.

Flaig, Egon (2009). Weltgeschichte der Sklaverei, München: C.H. Beck.

Fleury-Steiner, Benjamin/Nielsen, Laura Beth (2006a). "A Constitutive Perspective of Rights'', in: Benjamin Fleury-Steiner and Laura Beth Nielsen (ed.): The new civil rights research: a constitutive approach, Aldershot: Ashgate Publishing, 1-13.

Fleury-Steiner, Benjamin/Nielsen, Laura Beth (ed.) (2006b). The new civil rights research:a constitutive approach, Aldershot: Ashgate Publishing.

Florentino, Manolo/de Goes, Jose Roberto (2002). ''L'enfance asservie: les esclaves du Brésil aux XVIIIe et XIXe siècles'', in: Isabel Castro Henriques and Louis

Sala-Molins (ed.): Déraison, esclavage et droit. Les fondements idéologiques et juridiques de la traite négrière et de l'esclavage, Paris: EDITIONS Unesco, 349-363.

Fouchard, Jean (1972). Les marrons de la liberté, Paris: Editions de l'Ecole.

Freeman, Michael (2007). "Back to the Future: the Historical Dimension of Liberal Justice", in: Max du Plessis and Stephen Peté (ed.): Repairing the Past? International Perspectives on Reparations for Gross Human Rights Abuses, Antwerpen/Oxford: Intersentia, 29-51.

Gates, Henry Louis Jr. (2010). Ending the Slavery Blame-Game, in: New York Times, April 23, 2010, A27.

Gareau, Jean-Francois (2004). "Insoutenable imprescriptibilité à la lettre: Note sur l'interaction du temps, du droit et du symbole dans la problématique de la réparation des crimes de l'histoire", in: Boisson de Chazournes, Laurence, Jean-François Quéguiner and Santiago Villalpando (ed.): Crimes de l'histoire et réparations: les réponses du droit et de la justice, Brussels: Editions Bruylant, 25-38.

Garvey, Marcus (ed. 2004). Selected Writings and Speeches of Marcus Garvey, Mineola: Dover Publications.

Gayibor, N.L. (1990). Le Genyi, un royaume oublié de la coté de Guinée au temps de la traite de Noirs, Lomé: Editions Haho.

Gewald, Jan-Bart (1995). "Untapped Sources. Slave Exports from Southern and Central Namibia up to ca. 1850", in: C. Hamilton (ed.): The Mfecane Aftermath, Johannesburg: Wits University Press, 419-435.

Gifford, Anthony (2007). The Passionate Advocate, Kingston: Arawak Publications.

Giradin, Jean-Claude (2002). ''De la liberté politique des Noirs: Sonthonax et Toussaint Louverture'', in: Isabel Castro Henriques and Louis Sala-Molins (ed.) : Déraison, esclavage et droit. Les fondements idéologiques et juridiques de la traite négrière et de l'esclavage, Paris, EDITIONS Unesco, 213-237.

Gisler, Antoine (1981). L'esclavage aux Antilles francaises (XVIIe-XIXe siècle), Paris : Karthala.

Gómez, Laura E. (2004). "A Tale of Two Genres: On the Real and Ideal Links Between Law and Society and Critical Race Theory", in: Austin Sarat (ed.): The Blackwell Companion to Law and Society, Oxford: Blackwell Publishing, 453-470.

Goodell, Rev. William (1852). Slavery and Anti-Slavery: A History of the Great Struggle In Both Hemispheres; With A View of The Slavery Question In The United States, New York: William Harned Pub.

Gordon, Edward T. (2010). "Anthropology and Liberation", in: Harrison Faye (ed.): Decolonizing Anthropology. Moving Further toward an Anthropology for Liberation, Third Edition, Arlington: American Anthropological Association, 150-169.

Green, L.C./Dickason, Olive P. (1989). The Law of Nations and the New World,

Edmonton: The University of Alberta Press.

Greenawalt, Alexander K.A. (1999). Rethinking Genocidal Intent: The Case for a Knowledge-Based Interpretation, in: Columbia Law Review, Vol. 99, 2258-2294, 2266.

Grewe, Wilhelm G. (1984). Epochen der Völkerrechtsgeschichte, Baden-Baden: Nomos Verlagsgesellschaft.

Grillitsch, Johanna (2007). Gedenkjahr 2007. Der Reparationsdiskurs in England, in: Stichproben. Wiener Zeischrift für kritische Afrikastudien 13/2007, 7. Jahrgang, 137-161.

Grotius, Hugo (1609). The Freedom of the Sea, Ontario, Batoche Books (ed. 2000).

Grotius, Hugo (1625). The Rights of War and Peace, Indianapolis: Liberty Fund (ed. 2005).

Gueye, Adama (2003). "The impact of the slave trade on Cayor and Baol. Mutations in Habitat and Land Occupancy", in: Sylvaine A. Diouf (ed.): Fighting the Slave Trade. West African Strategies, Athens: Ohio University Press, 50-61.

Gueye, M'Baye (1995). "L'Afrique a la veille de la conquete", in: Elikia M'Bokolo (ed.): L'Afrique entre l'Europe et l'Amerique. Le rôle de l'Afrique dans la rencontre de deux mondes 1492-1992, Paris: UNESCO, 80-96.

Guèye, Mbaye (2001). "La tradition orale dans le domaine de la traite négrière", in: Djibril Tamsir Niane (ed.): Tradition orale et archives de la traite négrière, Paris: UNESCO, 14-22.

Hajjar, Lisa (2004). "Human Rights", in: Austin Sarat (ed.): The Blackwell Companion to Law and Society, Oxford: Blackwell Publishing, 589-604.

Hamber, Brandon (2006). "Narrowing the Micro and Macro: A Psychological Perspective on Reparations in Societies in Transition", in: Pablo de Greiff (ed.): The Handbook of Reparations, Oxford: Oxford University Press, 560-588.

Hamilton, C. (ed.) (1995). The Mfecane Aftermath, Johannesburg: Wits University Press.

Harms, Robert (2010). "Slavery in the Politically Decentralized Societies of Equatorial Africa", in: Stephanie Beswick and Jay Spaulding (ed.): African Systems of Slavery, Trenton/Asmara: Africa World Press, 161-172.

Harper's Magazine (2003). "Does America Owe a Debt to the Descendants of Its Slaves?", in: Raymond A. Winbush (ed.): Should America pay? Slavery and the raging debate on reparations, New York: Amistad, 79-108.

Harris, J.E. (1992). "The African diaspora in the Old and the New Worlds", in: B.A. Ogot (ed.): General History of Africa V. Africa from the Sixteenth to the Eighteenth Century, Paris: UNESCO, 113-136.

Harrison, Faye V. (2010a). "Anthropology as an Agent of Transformation: Introductory Comments and Queries", in: Faye V. Harrison (ed.): Decolonizing Anthropology. Moving Further toward an Anthropology for Liberation, Third Edition, Arlington: American Anthropological Association, 1-15.

Harrison, Faye V. (ed.) (2010b). Decolonizing Anthropology. Moving Further toward an Anthropology for Liberation, Third Edition, Arlington: American Anthropological Association.

Harrison, Faye V. (2010c). "Ethnography as Politics", in: Faye V. Harrison (ed.): Decolonizing Anthropology. Moving Further toward an Anthropology for Liberation, Third Edition, Arlington: American Anthropological Association, 88-110.

Harrison, Faye V. (2008). Outsider Within. Reworking Anthropology in the Global Age, Urbana/Chicago: University of Illinois Press.

Haviland, William A (1990). Cultural Anthropology. Sixth Edition, Fort Worth: Holt, Rinehart and Winston.

Hawthorne, Walter (2003a). Planting Rice and Harvesting Slaves. Transformations along the Guinea-Bissau Coast, 1400-1900, Portsmouth: Heinemann.

Hawthorne, Walter (2003b). "Strategies of the Decentralized. Defending Communities from Slave Raiders in Coastal Guinea-Bissau, 1450-1815", in: Sylvaine A. Diouf (ed.): Fighting the Slave Trade. West African Strategies, Athens: Ohio University Press, 152-169.

Hazan, Pierre (2004). "Durban: le repli victimaire", in: Boisson de Chazournes, Laurence, Jean-François Quéguiner and Santiago Villalpando (ed.): Crimes de l'histoire et réparations: les réponses du droit et de la justice, Brussels: Editions Bruylant, 277-290.

Heers, Jacques (2008). Les négriers en terres d'islam, Paris: Librairie Académique Perrin.

Henriques, Isabel Castro/Sala-Molins, Louis (ed.) (2002). Déraison, esclavage et droit. Les fondements idéologiques et juridiques de la traite négrière et de l'esclavage, Paris: EDITIONS Unesco.

Hernaes, Per (2001). "Les forts danois de la Côte de l'Or et leurs habitants à l'époque de la traite des esclaves", in: Djibril Tamsir Niane (ed.): Tradition orale et archives de la traite négrière, Paris: UNESCO, 112-119.

Hess, Penny (2000). Overturning the Culture of Violence, St. Petersburg: Burning Spear Uhuru Publications.

Hickling, Frederick W./Martin, Jaqueline/Harrisingh-Dewar, Allison (2008). "Redefining Personality Disorder in Jamaica", in: Frederick W. Hickling, Brigitte K. Matthies, Kai Morgan and Roger C. Gobson (ed.): Perspectives in Caribbean Psychology, Kingston: CARIMENSA, 263-288.

Hickling, Frederick W./Matthies, Brigitte K./Morgan, Kai/Gobson, Roger C. (ed.) (2008). Perspectives in Caribbean Psychology, Kingston: CARIMENSA.

Hickling, Frederick W. (2009). The Cycles of Elmina: Healing Our Memories, Overcoming the Wounds of Our History, Kingston: CARIMENSA.

Hill, Polly (1976). From Slavery to Freedom: The Case of Farm-Slavery in Nigerian Hausaland, in: Comparative Studies in Society and History Vol. 18, Nr.3.

Hilton, R.H. (1969). The Decline of Serfdom in Medieval England, London: Macmillan.

Hirsch, Susan F. (2002). "Feminist Participatory Research on Legal Consciousness", in: June Starr and Mark Goodale (ed.): Practicing Ethnography in Law.
New Dialogues, Enduring Methods, New York: Palgrave Macmillan, 13-33.

Hoffmann French, Jan (2009). Legalizing Identities. Becoming Black or Indian in
Brazil's Northeast, Richmond: University of North Carolina Press.

Huber, Ulrich (ed. 1722). Eumonia Romana on D.1.5.5.1, Amsterdam: ?.

Hugh, Thomas (1999). The Slave Trade. The Story of the Atlantic Slave Trade:
1440-1870, New York: Simon & Schuster.

Hummer, Waldemar/Neuhold, Hanspeter/Schreuer, Christoph (1997). Österreichisches Handbuch des Völkerrechts, Vol.1, Wien: Manz.

Ifa, Kamau Cush (2010). A tale of two countries, in: New African Nr. 499, London:
IC Publications, 26-27.

Imani, Pablo M. (2007). Afrikan Yoga. A Practical Guide to Wellbeing Through
Smai Posture, Breath and Meditation, London: TamaRe House, 20.

Inikori, J.E. (1992a). "Africa in world history: the export slave trade from Africa
and the emergence of the Atlantic economic order", in: B.A. Ogot (ed.): General
History of Africa V. Africa from the Sixteenth to the Eighteenth Century, Paris:
UNESCO, 74-112.

Inikori, Joseph E. (1982). Forced Migration. The impact of the export slave trade on
African societies, New York: Africana Publishing Company.

Inikori, Joseph (1996). "Slavery in Africa and the Transatlantic Slave Trade", in:
Alusine Jalloh and Stephen E. Maizlish (ed.): The African Diaspora, College
Station: Texas A&M University Press, 61-64.

Inikori, Joseph E. (1999). "Slaves or Serfs? A Comparative Study of Slavery and
Serfdom in Europe and in Africa", in: Isidore Okpewho, Carole Boyce Davies
and Ali A. Mazrui (ed.): The African diaspora: African origins and New World
Identities, Bloomington: Indiana University Press, 49-75.

Inikori, Joseph E. (1992b). The Chaining of a Continent. Export Demand for Captives and the History of Africa South of the Sahara, 1450-1870, Kingston: Institute of Social and Economic Research, UWI.

Isaac, Ephraim (1985). "Genesis, Judaism, and the 'Sons of Ham'", in: John Ralph
Willis (ed.): Slaves and Slavery in Muslim Africa, Volume I. Islam and the Ideology of Enslavement, London: Frank Cass and Company, 75-91.

James, C.L.R. (1938). The Black Jacobins, London: Penguin Books (ed. 2001).

James, George (1993). Stolen legacy, New York: Africa World Press.

Jenkins, Catherine (2007). "Taking Apology Seriously", in: Max du Plessis and Stephen Peté (ed.): Repairing the Past? International Perspectives on Reparations
for Gross Human Rights Abuses, Antwerpen/Oxford: Intersentia, 53-81.

Johnson, Marion (1976). The Economic foundation of an Islamic Theocracy- the
Case of Masina, in: Journal of African History, XVII, 4, 488-489.

Johnson, Jr., Robert (1999). "Repatriation as Reparations for Slavery and Jim
Crowism", in: Roy L. Brooks (ed.): When Sorry is Not Enough. The Controversy

Over Apologies and Reparations for Human Injustice, New York: New York University Paperback.

Jos, Emmanuel (2000). "Esclavages et crime contre l'humanité", in: Serge Chalons, Christian Jean-Etienne, Suzy Landau and Andre Yebakima (ed.): De l'esclavage aux reparations, Paris: Editions Karthala, 135-148.

Kake, I. B. (1979). "The slave trade and the population drain from Black África to North África and the Middle East", in: The slave trade from the fifteenth to the nineteenth century, Paris: UNESCO, 164-174.

Kelsen, Hans (1943). Collective and Individual Responsibility in International Law with Particular Regard to the Punsihement of War Criminals, in: California Law Review Nr. 31, 530-546.

Kidder, Robert L. (2002). "Exploring Legal Culture in Law-Avoidance Societies", in: June Starr and Mark Goodale (ed.): Practicing Ethnography in Law. New Dialogues, Enduring Methods, New York: Palgrave Macmillan, 87-107.

King, Martin Luther Jr. (1964). Why We Can't Wait, New York: Signet Classics.

Ki-Zerbo, Joseph (1978). Histoire de l'Afrique Noire, Paris: Hatier.

Ki-Zerbo, Joseph (1998). "La route mentale de l'esclave: brèves réflexions à partir de la condition présente des peuples noirs", in: Doudou Diène (ed.): La chaine et le lien. Une vision de la traite negriere, Paris: UNESCO, 175-181.

Klein, Martin A. (2003). "Defensive Strategies – Wasulu, Masina, and the Slave Trade", in: Sylvaine A. Diouf (ed.): Fighting the Slave Trade. West African Strategies, Athens: Ohio University Press, 62-78.

Klein, Martin A. (1988). "Slave Resistance and Slave Emancipation in Coastal Guinea", in: Suzanne Miers and Richard Roberts (ed.): The End of Slavery in Africa, Madison: University of Wisconsin Press, 203-219.

Klein, Martin A. (2010). "Slavery in the Western Sudan", in: Stephanie Beswick and Jay Spaulding (ed.): African Systems of Slavery, Trenton/Asmara: Africa World Press, 11- 43.

Köhler, Gernot (1978). "Global Apartheid". Working Paper No.7, World Order Models Project, New York: Institute for World Order; reprinted in: Haviland, William A./Gordon, Robert J. (2002). Talking About People: Readings in Comtemporary Cultural Anthropology, Mountain View: Mayfield.

Kolawole, Mary E. (1994). "An African View of Transatlantic Slavery and the Role of Oral Testimony in Creating a New Legacy", in: Anthony Tibbles (ed.): Transatlantic Slavery. Against Human Dignity, London: HMSO, 105-110.

Kopytoff, Igor/Miers, Suzanne (1977a). "African 'Slavery' as an Institution of Marginality", in: Suzanne Miers and Igor Kopytoff (ed.): Slavery in Africa: Historical and Anthropological Perspectives, Madison: University of Wisconsin Press, 3-81.

Kordes, Hagen (1998). "De la traite négrière au 'tri' des immigrants", in: Doudou Diène (ed.): La chaine et le lien. Une vision de la traite négrière, Paris: UNESCO, 313-325.

Kusimba, Chapurukha M. (2010). "The Collapse of Coastal City-States of East Africa", in: Akinwumi Ogundiran and Toyin Falola (ed.): Archaeology of Atlantic Africa and the African Diaspora, Bloomington/Indianapolis: Indiana University Press,160- 184.

Kwenzi-Mikala, Jérome T. (ed.) (2003). Tradition orale liée à la traite négriere et à l'esclavage en Afrique centrale, Paris: Unesco.

Labarthe, Gilles/Verschave, Francois-Xavier (2007). L'or africain. Pillages, trafics & commerce international, Marseille: Agone.

Lara, Oruno D. (1997). Résistances et luttes, in: Diogène, Nr. 179, 169-170.

Law, Robin (2004). Ouidah. The Social History of a West African Slaving 'Port' 1727-1892, Oxford: James Currey.

Law, Robin (2008). The Impact of the Atlantic Slave Trade upon Africa, Wien: Lit Verlag.

Lawson-Body, Georges Latevi Babatounde (2000). ''Du statut social de la force de travail sur les plantations aux Amériques du XVIe au XIX siècle'', in: Serge Chalons, Christian Jean Etienne, Suzy Landau and Andre Yebakima (ed.): De l'esclavage aux réparations, Paris: Editions Karthala, 79-92.

Leacock, Eleanor (1987). "Theory and Ethics in Applied Urban Anthopology", in: Leith Mullings (ed.): Cities of the United States, New York: Columbia University Press, 317-36.

Le Marc'hadour, Tanguy/Carius, Manuel (ed.) (2010). Esclavage et Droit. Du Code noir à nos jours, Arras: Artois Presses Université.

Lemkin, Raphael (1944). Axis Rule in Occupied Europe. Laws Of Occupation, Analysis Of Government, Proposals For Redress, Washington: Carnegie Endowment for International Peace, Division of International Law.

Levtzion, Nehemia (1985). "Slavery and Islamization in Africa: A Comparative Study", in: John Ralph Willis (ed.): Slaves and Slavery in Muslim Africa, Volume I. Islam and the Ideology of Enslavement, London: Frank Cass and Company, 182-198.

Levtzion, Nehemia/Hopkins, J.F.P. (ed.) (1999). Corpus of Early Arabic Source for West African History, Cambridge: Cambridge University Press.

Lohlker, Rüdiger (2006). Islamisches Völkerrecht. Studien am Beispiel Granada, Bremen: Kleio Humanities.

Lovejoy, Paul (2000). Transformations in Slavery. A History of Slavery in Africa, Second Edition, Cambridge: Cambridge University Press.

Ludi, Regula (2007). "Historical Reflections on Holocaust Reparations", in: Max du Plessis and Stephen Peté (ed.): Repairing the Past? International Perspectives on Reparations for Gross Human Rights Abuses, Antwerpen/Oxford: Intersentia, 119-144.

Lumb, D. (1968). "Legality and Legitimacy: The Limits of the Duty of Obedience to the State", in: Charles Alexandrowicz (ed.): Studies in the history of the laws of nations, The Hague: Grotian Press Society, 52-82.

Lumumba, Chokwe (1989a). "Proposed Reparation Amendment", in: Chokwe Lumumba (ed.): Reparations Yes!, Baton Rouge: House of Songhay, 13-20.

Lumumba, Chokwe (ed.) (1989b). Reparations Yes!, Baton Rouge: House of Songhay.

Lykes, M. Brinton/Mersky, Marcie (2006). "Reparations and Mental Health: Psychosocial Interventions Towards Healing, Human Agency, and Rethreading Social Realities", in: Pablo de Greiff (ed.): The Handbook of Reparations, Oxford: Oxford University Press, 589-622.

MacGaffey, Wyatt (2010). "Indigneous Slavery and the Atlantic Trade: Kongo Texts", in: Stephanie Beswick and Jay Spaulding (ed.): African Systems of Slavery, Trenton/Asmara: Africa World Press, 173- 201.

Malowist, M. (1992). "The Struggle for International Trade and its Implications for Africa", in: B.A. Ogot (ed.): General History of Africa V. Africa from the Sixteenth to the Eighteenth Century, Paris: UNESCO, 1-22.

Manning, Patrick (1990). Slavery and African Life: occidental, oriental and African slave trades, Melksham: Redwood Press.

Manning, Patrick (1982). Slavery, colonialism and economic growth in Dahomey, 1640-1960, New York: University of Cambridge Press.

Manning, Patrick (1998). "La traite négrière et l'évolution démographique de l'Afrique", in: Doudou Diène (ed.): La chaine et le lien. Une vision de la traite négrière, Paris: UNESCO, 153-173.

Manning, Patrick (1994). "The Impact of the Slave Trade on the Societies of West and Central Africa", in: Anthony Tibbles (ed.): Transatlantic Slavery. Against Human Dignity, London: Merrell Holberton Publishers, 97-104.

Martin, Phyllis (1995). Leisure and Society in Colonial Brazzaville, Cambridge: Cambridge University Press.

Matthies, Brigitte K./Meeks-Gardner, Julie/Daley, Avril/Crawford-Brown, Claudette (2008). "Issues of Violence in the Caribbean", in: Frederick W. Hickling, Brigitte K. Matthies, Kai Morgan and Roger C. Gobson (ed.): Perspectives in Caribbean Psychology, Kingston: CARIMENSA, 393-464.

Mazrui, Behnaz A./Montana, Ismael Musah/Lovejoy, Paul E. (ed.) (2009). Slavery, Islam and Diaspora, Trenton: Africa World Press.

M'Bokolo, Elikia (ed.) (1995a). L'Afrique entre l'Europe et l'Amerique. Le rôle de l'Afrique dans la rencontre de deux mondes 1492-1992, Paris: UNESCO.

M'Bokolo, Elikia (1995b). "La rencontre des deux mondes et ses repercussions: la part de l'Afrique (1492-1992)", in: Elikia M'Bokolo (ed.): L'Afrique entre l'Europe et l'Amerique. Le role de l'Afrique dans la rencontre de deux mondes 1492-1992, Paris : UNESCO, 13-30.

M'Bow, Mahtar Amadou (2002). "Les théories esclavagistes à travers la presentation du cahier des doléances de Saint-Louis du Senegal aux Etats bénéraux de 1789", in: Isabel Castro Henriques and Louis Sala-Molins (ed.): Déraison, esclavage et droit. Les fondements idéologiques et juridiques de la traite négrière et de l'esclavage, Paris: EDITIONS Unesco, 284- 300.

McCann, Michael (2004). "Law and Social Movements", in: Austin Sarat (ed.): The Blackwell Companion to Law and Society, Oxford: Blackwell Publishing, 506-522.

McCann, Michael (2006). "On Legal Consciousness: A Challenging Analytical Tradition", in: Benjamin Fleury-Steiner and Laura Beth Nielsen (ed.): The new civil rights research: a constitutive approach, Aldershot: Ashgate Publishing, IX- XXiX.

McCann, Michael (1994). Rights at Work: Pay Equity Reform and the Politics of Legal Mobilizations, Chicago: University of Chicago Press.

Meillassoux, Claude (1986). Anthropologie de l'esclavage, Paris: Quadrige Presse Universitaire de France.

Mensah-Brown, A.K. (1975b). "Notes on International Law and Pre-Colonial Legal History of Modern Ghana", in: A.K. Mensah-Brown (ed.): African International Legal History, New York: UNITAR, 107-124.

Mensah-Brown, A.K. (ed.) (1975a). African International Legal History, New York: UNITAR.

Menu, Bernadette (2006). Egypte pharaonique. Nouvelles recherches sur l'histoire juridique, économique et sociale de l'ancienne Egypte, Paris: L'Harmattan.

Miers, Suzanne/Kopytoff, Igor (ed.) (1977). Slavery in Africa: Historical and Anthropological Perspectives, Madison: University of Wisconsin Press.

Miers, Suzanne/Roberts, Richard (ed.) (1989). The End of Slavery in Africa, Madison: University of Wisconsin Press.

Miéville, China (2006). Between Equal Rights. A Marxist Theory of International Law, Brill: Leiden.

Miller, Joseph C. (2002). "Stratégies de marginalité. Une approche historique de l'utilisation des êtres humains et des idéologies de l'esclavage: progéniture, piété, protection personelle et prestige – produit et profits des propriétaires", in: Isabel Castro Henriques and Louis Sala-Molins (ed.): Déraison, esclavage et droit. Les fondements idéologiques et juridiques de la traite négrière et de l'esclavage, Paris: EDITIONS Unesco, 105-161.

Minasse, Haile (1984). Human Rights, Stability, and Development in Africa: Some Observations on Concept and Reality, in: Virginia Journal of International Law Vol. 24, 591-592.

Morgan, Kai/O'Garo, Keisha-Gaye N. (2008). "Caribbean Identity Issues", in: Frederick W. Hickling, Brigitte K. Matthies, Kai Morgan and Roger C. Gobson (ed.): Perspectives in Caribbean Psychology, Kingston: CARIMENSA, 3-31.

Moyo, Dambisa (2012). Der Untergang des Westens. Haben wir eine Chance in der neuen Wirtschaftsordnung? Berlin: Piper.

Mtubani, C. D. Victor (1983). African Slaves and English Law, in: PULA Botswana Journal of African Studies Vol. 3, Nr. 2, 71-75.

Muhammad, Akbar (1985). "The Image of Africans in Arabic Literature: Some Unpublished Manuscipts", in: John Ralph Willis (ed.): Slaves and Slavery in Muslim Africa, Volume I. Islam and the Ideology of Enslavement, London: Frank Cass and Company, 47- 74.

Mullings, Leith (ed.) (1987). Cities of the United States, New York: Columbia University Press.

Mutua, Makau (2002). "The Banjul Charter: The Case for an African Cultural Fingerprint", in: Abdullahi A. An-Na'im (ed.): Cultural Transformation and Human Rights in Africa, London: Zed Books, 68- 107.

Nawaz, M.K. (ed.) (1976). Essays on International Law. In Honour of Krishne Rao, Leiden: Sijthoff Publishing.

Niane, Djibril Tamsir (ed.) (2001). Tradition orale et archives de la traite négrière, Paris: UNESCO.

Nielsen, Laura Beth (2004). "The Work of Rights and the Work Rights Do: A Critical Empirical Approach", in: Austin Sarat (ed.): The Blackwell Companion to Law and Society, Oxford: Blackwell Publishing, 63-79.

Niort, Jean-Francois (2010). ''Homo Servilis. Un être humain sans personnalité juridique: Réflexions sur le statut de l'esclave dans le Code Noir'', in: Tanguy Le Marc'hadour and Manuel Carius (ed.): Eslavage et Droit. Du Code noir à nos jours, Arras: Artois Presses Université, 15-41.

Nmehielle, Vincent O. (2001). The African Human Rights System. Its Laws, Practice, and Institutions, The Hague/NY: Martinus Nijhoff Publishers.

Nunn, N. (2007). Historical legacies: A model linking Africa's past to its current underdevelopment, in: Journal of Development Economics Vol. 83, Nr. 1, 157-175.

Nur Ankh Amen (2001). The ANKH:The Afrikan Origins of Electromagnitism Hunlock Creek: EWorld Inc.

Nussbaum, Arthur (1954). A Concise History of the Law of Nations, New York: Macmillan Co.

Nzingha, Yaa Asantewaa (2003). "Reparations + Education = The Pass to Freedom", in: Raymond A. Winbush (ed.): Should America pay? Slavery and the raging debate on reparations, New York: Amistad, 299-314.

Obadele, Imari Abubakari (1989). "Reparations Yes!", in: Chokwe Lumumba (ed.): Reparations Yes!, Baton Rouge: House of Songhay, 23-66.

Ogot, B.A. (ed.) (1992). General History of Africa V. Africa from the Sixteenth to the Eighteenth Century, Paris: UNESCO, 262-299.

Ogundiran, Akinwumi/Falola, Toyin (ed.) (2010a). Archaeology of Atlantic Africa and the African Diaspora, Bloomington/Indianapolis: Indiana University Press.

Ogundiran, Akinwumi/Falola, Toyin (2010b). "Pathways in the Archaeology of Transatlantic Africa", in: Akinwumi Ogundiran/Toyin Falola (ed.) Archaeology of Atlantic Africa and the African Diaspora, Bloomington/Indianapolis: Indiana University Press, 3-45.

Okpewho, Isidore/Davies, Carole Boyce/Mazrui, Ali A. (ed.) (1999). The African diaspora: African origins and New World Identities, Bloomington: Indiana University Press.

Ollesson, Simon (2007). The Impact of the ILC's Articles on Responsibility of States for Internationlly Wrongful Acts, London: British Institute of International and Comparative Law.

Omotunde, Jean-Philippe (2004). La traite négrière européenne: vérité et mensonge, Paris: Editions Menaibuc.

Oppenheim, Lassa (1912). International Law, Vol.1, London: Longmans, Green & Co.

Oriji, John N. (2003). "Igboland, Slavery, and the Drums of War and Heroism", in: Sylvaine Diouf (ed.): Fighting the Slave Trade. West African Strategies, Athens: Ohio University Press, 121-13.

O'Shea, Andreas (2007). "Reparations Under International Criminal Law", in: Max du Plessis and Stephen Peté (ed.): Repairing the Past? International Perspectives on Reparations for Gross Human Rights Abuses, Antwerpen/Oxford: Intersentia, 179-196.

Outterson, Kevin (2003). "Slave Taxes", in: Ray Winbush (ed.): Should America pay? Slavery and the raging debate on reparations, New York: Amistad, 135-149.

Palmer, Colin A. (1998a). "Introduction", in: Colin Palmer (ed.): The Worlds of Unfree Labour: From Indentured Servitude to Slavery, New York: Ashgate, 1-11.

Palmer, Colin (ed.) (1998b). The Worlds of Unfree Labour: From Indentured Servitude to Slavery, New York: Ashgate.

Paradisi, Bruno (1951). L'amitié internationale: les phases critiques de son ancienne histoire, in: Recueil des cours, Académie de Droit International de La Haye Vol. 78, 325-378.

Parkinson, F. (1975). "Pre-Colonial International Law", in: A.K. Mensah-Brown (ed.): African International Legal History, New York: UNITAR, 11-26.

Patric, Adibe/Boateng, Osei (2000). Portugal, the mother of all slavers, in: New African Nr. 385, London: IC Publications.

Peabody, Sue (1996). "There Are No Slaves in France". The Political Culture of Race and Slavery in the Ancien Régime, New York/Oxford: Oxford University Press.

Peabody, Sue/Grinberg, Keila (2007). Slavery, Freedom, and the Law in the Atlantic World. A Brief History with Documents, Boston/New York: Bedford.

Pellet, Allan (2010). "The Definition of Responsibility in International Law", in: James Crawford/Alain Pellet/ Simon Olleson (ed.): The Law of International Responsibility, Oxford: Oxford University Press, 4-15.

Perbi, Akosua (2004). A History of Indigenous Slavery in Ghana: From the 15th to the 19th century, Accra: Ghana: Sub Saharan Publishers.

Peret, Benjamin (1999). La Commune des Palmares, Paris: Editions Syllepse.

Péroz, Etienne (1889). Au Soudan Francais: Souvenirs de Guerre et de Mission, Paris: ?; cited in: Roberts, Richard/Klein, Martin (1980). The Banamba Slave

Exodus of 1905, in: Journal of African History Vol. 21, Nr. 3, 375-394.

Peté, Stephen/ Du Plessis, Max (2007). "Reparations for Gross Violations of Human Rights in Context", in: Max du Plessis and Stephen Peté (ed.): Repairing the Past? International Perspectives on Reparations for Gross Human Rights Abuses, Antwerpen/Oxford: Intersentia, 3-28.

Pétré-Grenouilleau, Olivier (2004). Les traites négrières, essai d'histoire globale, Paris: Editions Gallimard.

Pétré-Grenouilleau, Olivier (1998). Nantes au temps de la traite des Noirs, Paris: Hachette Litératures.

Plumelle-Uribe, Rosa Amelia (2001). La férocité blanche. Des non-Blancs aux non-Aryens: génocides occultés de 1492 à nos jours, Paris: Editions Albin Michel.

Plumelle-Uribe, Rosa Amelia (2004). "Les crimes contre l'humanité et le devoir de réparation", in: Boisson de Chazournes, Laurence, Jean-François Quéguiner and Santiago Villalpando (ed.): Crimes de l'histoire et réparations: les réponses du droit et de la justice, Brussels: Editions Bruylant, 187-202.

Plumelle-Uribe, Rosa Amelia (2008). Traite des Blancs, Traite des Noirs. Aspects méconnus et conséquences actuelles, Paris: L'Harmattan.

Police, Gerard (2003). Quilombos dos Palmares. Lecture sur un marronnage bresilien, Guyane: Ibis Rouge Editions.

Popo, Klah (2010). Histoire des,Traites Négrières'. Critique afrocentrée d'une négrophobie académique, Paris: Anibwe.

Potash, John (2007). The FBI War on Tupac Shakur and Black Leaders. US Intelligence's Murderous Targeting of Tupac, MLK, Malcolm, Panthers, Hendrix, Marley, Rappers & Linked Ethnic Leftists, Baltimore: Progressive Left Press.

Purves, R. (1968). "Prolegomena to Utopian International Projects", in: Charles H. Alexandrowicz (ed.): Studies in the history of the laws of nations, The Hague: Grotian Press Society, 100-110.

Quenum, Alphonse (2002). "Regard chretien sur l'esclavage et la traite négrière: l'action des papes au XIX siècle", in: Isabel Castro Henriques and Louis Sala-Molins (ed.): Déraison, esclavage et droit. Les fondements idéologiques et juridiques de la traite négrière et de l'esclavage, Paris: EDITIONS Unesco, 203-211.

Quequiner, Jean-Francois/Villalpando, Santiago (2004). "La réparation des crimes de l'histoire: état et perspectives du droit international public contemporain", in: Laurence Boisson de Chazournes, Jean-François Quéguiner and Santiago Villalpando (ed.): Crimes de l'histoire et réparations : les réponses du droit et de la justice, Brussels: Editions Bruylant, 39-72.

Quirk, Joel (2009). Unfinished Business: A Comparative Survey of Historical and Contemporary Slavery, Paris: UNESCO.

Randles, W. G. L. (1969). De la traite à la colonisation: les Portugais en Angola, in: Annales Économies, Sociétés, Civilisations Vol. 24, Nr. 2, Paris, 289-304.

Rashid, Ismael (2003). "A Devotion to the Idea of Liberty at any Price. Rebellion and Anti-Slavery in the Upper Guinea Coast in the Eighteenth and Nineteenth Centuries", in: Sylvaine A. Diouf (ed.): Fighting the Slave Trade. West African Strategies, Athens: Ohio University Press, 132-151.

Reader, John (1998). Africa: A Biography of the Continent, London: Penguin Books.

Rediker, Marcus (2008). The Slave Ship. A Human History, London: John Murray.

Reynolds, Edward (1994). "Human Cargoes: Enslavement and the Middle Passage", in: Anthony Tibbles (ed.): Transatlantic Slavery. Against Human Dignity, London: Merrell Holberton Publishers, 29-34.

Richard, Jérémy (2010). "Du Code Noir de 1685 au projet de 1829: De la semi-réification à l'humanisation de l'esclave noir", in: Tanguy Le Marc'hadour and Manuel Carius (ed.): Eslavage et Droit. Du Code noir à nos jours, Arras: Artois Presses Université, 15-41.

Roberts, Richard/Klein, Martin (1980). The Banamba Slave Exodus of 1905, in: Journal of African History Vol. 21, Nr.3, 375-394.

Robinson, Randall (2000). The Debt. What America Owes to Blacks, New York: Penguin Group.

Rodney, Walter (1966). African Slavery and Other Forms of Social Oppression on the Upper Guinea Coast in the Context of the Atlantic Slave-Trade, in: The Journal of African History Vol. 7, Cambridge: Cambridge University Press, 431-443.

Rodney, Walter (1970). A History of the Upper Guina Coast 1545-1800, New York: Monthly Review Press.

Rouveroy van Niewaal, E./Zips, Werner (ed.) (1998). Sovereignty, Legitimacy and Power in West African Societies, Hamburg: Lit-Verlag.

Rubin, Alfred P. (1968). "The Use of Piracy in Malayan Waters", in: Charles H .Alexandrowicz (ed.): Studies in the history of the laws of nations, The Hague: Grotian Press Society, 111-135.

Ryder, Alan (1969). Benin and the Europeans 1485-1897, London: Longman.

Sala-Molins, Louis (1998). "L'esclavage en codes", in: Doudou Diène (ed.): La chaine et le lien. Une vision de la traite négrière, Paris: UNESCO, 288-293.

Sammons, Diane E. (2007). "Corporate Reparations for Descendants of Enslaved African-Americans", in: Max du Plessis and Stephen Peté (ed.): Repairing the Past? International Perspectives on Reparations for Gross Human Rights Abuses, Antwerpen/Oxford: Intersentia, 315-358.

Sarat, Austin (ed.) (2004). The Blackwell Companion to Law and Society, Oxford: Blackwell Publishing.

Satchell, Vermont (2003). Reparation and Emancipation, Emancipation Lecture 2003, Kingston : ?.

Sauer, Walter (ed.) (2002). k.u.k. Kolonial. Habsburgermonarchie und europäische Herrschaft in Afrika, Wien: Böhlau.

Sauer, Walter (ed.) (2007). Von Soliman zu Omofuma. Afrikanische Diaspora in

Österreich 17. bis 20. Jahrhundert, Innsbruck/Wien : Studienverlag.

Sauer, Walter/Wiesböck, Andrea (2007). "Sklaven, Freie, Fremde. Wiener 'Mohren' des 17. und 18. Jahrhunderts", in: Walter Sauer (ed.): Von Soliman zu Omofuma. Afrikanische Diaspora in Österreich 17. bis 20. Jahrhundert, Innsbruck/Wien: Studienverlag, 23-56.

Sauer, Walter (2002). "Schwarz-Gelb in Afrika. Habsburgermonarchie und koloniale Frage", in: Walter Sauer (ed.): k.u.k. Kolonial. Habsburgermonarchie und europäische Herrschaft in Afrika, Wien: Böhlau, 17- 78.

Scelle, Georges (1934a). Précis de Droit des Gens. Vol.1, Paris: Librairie du Recueil Sirey.

Scelle, Georges (1934b). Précis de Droit des Gens. Vol.2, Paris: Librairie du Recueil Sirey.

Schabas, William A. (2000). Genocide in International Law, Cambridge: Cambridge University Press.

Schabas, William A. (2008). Origins of the Genocide Convention: from Nuremberg to Paris, in: Case Western Reserve Journal of International Law Vol. 40, 35-55.

Schreuer, Christoph (1974). Unjustified enrichment in international law, in: AJCL Vol. 22, 281-301.

Schulte-Tenckhoff, Isabelle (1998). "The Function of Otherness in Treaty Making", in: E. van Rouveroy van Niewaal and Werner Zips (ed.): Sovereignty, Legitimacy and Power in West African Societies, Hamburg: Lit-Verlag, 9-21.

Schwarzenberger, Georg (1968). "Breisach Revisited. The Hagenbach Trial of 1474", in: Charles H. Alexandrowicz (ed.): Studies in the history of the law of nations, The Hague: Grotian Press Society, 46-51.

Schwarzenberger, Georg (1976). "Towards a Comparative History of International Law", in: M.K. Nawaz (ed.): Essays on International Law. In Honour of Krishne Rao, Leiden: Sijthoff Publishing, 92-106.

Secours, Molly (2003). "Riding the Reparations Bandwagon", in: Raymond A. Winbush (ed.): Should America pay? Slavery and the raging debate on reparations, New York: Amistad, 286-298.

Shelton, Dinah (2006). Remedies in International Human Rights Law, Oxford: Oxford University Press.

Silk, James (1990). "Traditional Culture and the Prospect for Human Rights in Africa", in: Abdullahi An-Na'im and Francis M. Deng (ed.): Human Rights in Africa. Cross-Cultural Perspectives, Washington DC: The Brookings Institution, 290-328.

Simpson, Alaba (ed.) (2004). Oral tradition relating to slavery and slave trade in Nigeria, Ghana and Benin, Paris: Unesco.

Smallwood, Stephanie E. (2007). Saltwater Slavery. A Middle Passage from Africa to American Diaspora, Cambridge: Harvard University Press.

Smith, Mary (1954). Baba of Karo: A Woman of the Muslim Hausa, London: Faber and Faber.

Somé, Roger (1998). "Esclavage, génocide ou holocauste ?", in: Doudou Diène (ed.): La chaine et le lien. Une vision de la traite négrière, Paris: UNESCO, 527-542.

Somé, Roger (2001). "Slavery, Genocide or Holocaust?" in: Doudou Diène (ed.): From Chains to Bonds. The Slave Trade Revisited, Paris: Unesco/Berghahn Books, 416-430.

Soumonni, Elisée (2003). "Lacustrine Villages as Refugees", in: Sylvaine A. Diouf (ed.): Fighting the Slave Trade. West African Strategies, Athens: Ohio University Press, 3-14.

Starr, June/Goodale, Mark (2002a). "Introduction. Legal Ethnography: New Dialogues, Enduring Methods", in: June Starr and Mark Goodale (ed.): Practicing Ethnography in Law. New Dialogues, Enduring Methods, New York: Palgrave Macmillan, 1-10.

Starr, June/Goodale, Mark (ed.) (2002b). Practicing Ethnography in Law. New Dialogues, Enduring Methods, New York: Palgrave Macmillan.

Strauss, Peter L. (ed.) (2002). The Fetha Negast. The Law of the Kings, Kingston: Miguel Lorne Publishers.

Supreme Understanding/C'bs Alife Allah (2010). The Hood Health Handbook. Volume One, Altanta: Supreme Design Publishing.

Tafari, Jabulani I. (1996). A Rastafari View of Marcus Mosiah Garvey, Florida: Greatcompany Inc.

Tanzer, Oliver (2011). Der Preis der Sklaverei, in: Die Furche Dossier (22.6.2011), 21.

Tardieu, Jean-Pierre (1984). Le destin des Noirs aux Indes de Castille XVIe-XVIIe siècles, Paris: L'Harmattan.

Testart, Alain (2001). L'esclave, la dette et le pouvoir, Paris: Errance.

Thiam, Iba D. (1995). "L'Afrique Noire a la veille de la découverte de l'Amerique", in: Elikia M'Bokolo (ed.): L'Afrique entre l'Europe et l'Amerique. Le role de l'Afrique dans la rencontre de deux mondes 1492-1992, Paris: UNESCO, 83-92.

Thipanyane, Tseliso (2002). "Current Claims, Regional Experiences, Pressing Problems: Identification of the Salient Issues and Pressing Problems in an African Post-colonial Perspective", in: George Ulrich and Louise Krabbe Boserup (ed.): Human Rights in Development, Yearbook 2001: Reparations: Redressing Past Wrongs, 33-57.

Thomas, Deborah A. (2004). Modern Blackness. Nationalism, Globalization, and the Politics of Culture in Jamaica, Durham/London: Duke University Press.

Thompson, Alvin O. (2006). Flight to Freedom. African Runaways and Maroon in the Americas, Kingston: University of the West Indies Press.

Thompson, Dudley Joseph (2000). "Réparations", in: Serge Chalons, Christian Jean-Etienne, Suzy Landau and Andre Yebakima (ed.): De l'esclavage aux reparations, Paris: Editions Karthala, 167-172.

Thornton, John (1992). Africa and Africans in the Making of the Atlantic World, 1400-1680. Cambridge: Cambridge University Press.

Thornton, John (1998). The African Experience of the '20.and Odd Negroes' Arriving in Virginia in 1619, in: William and Mary Quarterly, Third Series Vol. 55, Nr. 3, Williamsburg, 421-434.

Tibbles, Anthony (ed.) (1994). Transatlantic Slavery. Against Human Dignity, London: HMSO.

Tutu, Nontombi (2003). ''Foreword'', in: Raymond A. Winbush (ed.): Should America pay? Slavery and the raging debate on reparations, XV-XIX, XVIII.

Ulin, Robert (1991). Critical Anthropology Twenty Years Later: Modernism and Postmodernism in Anthropology, in: Critique of Anthropology Vol.11, Nr. 1, 63-89.

Ulrich, George (2002). "The Moral Case for Reparations. Three Theses about Reparations for Past Wrongs", in: George Ulrich and Louise Krabbe Boserup (ed.): Human Rights in Development, Yearbook 2001: Reparations: Redressing Past Wrongs, The Hague: Kluwer Law International, 369-385.

Ulrich, George/Krabbe Boserup, Louise (ed.) (2002): Human Rights in Development, Yearbook 2001: Reparations: Redressing Past Wrongs, The Hague: Kluwer Law International.

Usman, Aribidesi (2010). "The Landscape and Society of Northern Yorubaland during the Era of the Atlantic Slave Trade", in: Akinwumi Ogundiran and Toyin Falola (ed.): Archaeology of Atlantic Africa and the African Diaspora, Bloomington/Indianapolis: Indiana University Press, 140-159.

Van Dyke, Jon M. (2003). "Reparations for the Descendants of American Slaves Under International Law", in: Raymond A. Winbush (ed.): Should America pay? Slavery and the raging debate on reparations, New York: Amistad, 57-78.

Vasina, J. (1992). "The Kongo kingdom and its neighbours", in: B.A. Ogot (ed.): General History of Africa V. Africa from the Sixteenth to the Eighteenth Century, Paris: UNESCO, 546-587.

Vernet, Thomas (2009). "Slave Trade and Slavery on the Swahili Coast, 1500-1750", in: Behnaz A. Mazrui, Ismael Musah Montana and Paul E. Lovejoy (ed.): Slavery, Islam and Diaspora, Trenton: Africa World Press, 37-76.

Wareham, Roger (2003). "The Popularization of the International Demand for Reparations", in: Raymond A. Winbush (ed.): Should America pay? Slavery and the raging debate on reparations, New York: Amistad, 226-236.

Watson, Alan (1989). Slave Law in the Americas, Athens/London: The University of Georgia Press.

Weinzierl, Ruth/Lisson, Ursula (2007). Grenzschutz und Menschenrechte. Eine europarechtliche und seerechtliche Studie, Berlin: German Institute for Human Rights.

Westley, Robert (2003). "Many Billions Gone: Is It Time to Reconsider the Case for Black Reparations", in: Raymond A. Winbush (ed.): Should America pay?

Slavery and the raging debate on reparations, New York: Amistad, 109- 134.

Wiedemann, Thomas (ed.) (1981). Greek and Roman Slavery, London: Routledge.

Williams, Eric (1944). Capitalism and Slavery, Richmond: University of North Carolina Press.

Willis, John Ralph (1985a). "Introduction", in: John Ralph Willis (ed.): Slaves and Slavery in Muslim Africa, Volume I. Islam and the Ideology of Enslavement, London: Frank Cass and Company, 1-15.

Willis, John Ralph (ed.) (1985b). Slaves and Slavery in Muslim Africa, Volume I. Islam and the Ideology of Enslavement, London: Frank Cass and Company.

Winant, Howard (1994). Racial Formation and Hegemony: Global and Local Developments in Racial Conditions: Politics, Theory, Comparisons, Minneapolis: University of Minnesota Press.

Winbush, Omari I. (2003). "Reflections on Homer Plessy and Reparations", in: Raymond A. Winbush (ed.): Should America pay? Slavery and the raging debate on reparations, New York: Amistad, 150-162.

Winbush, Ray (2009). Belinda's Petition. A Concise History of Reparations for the Transatlantic Slave Trade, Bloomington: Xlibris.

Winbush, Raymond A. (2003a). "Interview with Chester and Timothy Hurdle, Barbara Ratliff, and Ina Hurdle-McGee", in: Raymond A. Winbush (ed.): Should America pay? Slavery and the raging debate on reparations, New York: Amistad, 315-320.

Winbush, Raymond A. (ed.) (2003b). Should America pay? Slavery and the raging debate on reparations, New York: Amistad.

Winkler, Hans (2002). Entschädigung für Sklaven - und Zwnagsarbeit durch Österreich, Wien: Diplomatische Akademie Favourite Papers.

Wiredu, Kwasi (1990). "An Akan Perspective on Human Rights", in: Abdullahi An-Na'im and Francis M. Deng (ed.): Human Rights in Africa. Cross-Cultural Perspectives, Washington DC: The Brookings Institution, 243-60.

Wittmann, Nora (2011). The scramble for Africa's nuclear resources, in: New African, June 2011, Nr. 507 (IC Publications: London), 72-74.

Wolf, Kenneth Baxter (1994). The "Moors" of West Africa and the Beginnings of the Portuguese Slave Trade, in: Journal of Medieval & Renaissance Studies 24, Nr. 3, 449-469.

ZeBelinga, Martial (1999). ''Productions, Impossibilités et renouvellements des asservissements du Noir'', in: Esclavages et servitudes d'hier et aujourd'hui, Actes du colloque de Strasbourg des 29 et 30 mai 1998, Strasbourg: Histoire et Anthropologie.

Decisions and Opinions:

Application of the Convention on the Prevention and Punishment of the Crime of Genocide, Preliminary Objections, ICJ Reports 1996, 595.

Application of the Convention on the Prevention and Punishment of the Crime of

Genocide (Bosnia and Herzegovina v. Serbia and Montenegro), Judgement of 26 February 2007, ICJ Reports 2007, 420.

Barcelona Traction, Light and Power Company, Limited, Second Phase (Belgium v. Spain), Judgement of 5 February 1970, ICJ reports 1970, 3.

Case concerning Right of Passage over Indian Territory (Merits), Judgment of 12 April 1960, ICJ Reports 1960, 6.

Case concerning the Northern Cameroons (Cameroon v. United Kingdom), Preliminary Objections, Judgement of 2 December 1963, ICJ Reports 1963, 15.

Certain Phosphate Lands in Nauru (Nauru v. Australia), Preliminary Objections, ICJ Reports 1992, 240.

CMS Gas Transmission Co. v. Argentina, Final Award of 12 May 2005, ICSID Case No.ARB/01/8.

Continental Shelf (Tunisia v. Libya), Judgement of 24 February 1982, ICJ Reports 1982, 18.

Corfu Channel case (UK and Northern Ireland v. Albania), Judgement of 4 April 1949, ICJ Reports 1949, 4.

Difference Relating to Immunity from Legal Process of a Special Rapporteur of the Commission on Human Rights, Advisory Opinion of 29 April 1999, ICJ Reports 1999, 62.

Duchy of Sealand, Judgement of 3 May 1978, Administrative Court of Cologne, ILR 1989.

EnCana Corp. v. Ecuador, Award of 3 February 2006, London Court of International Arbitration, 45 ILM 655 (2006).

Eureko B.V. v. Republic of Poland, Arbitral Award of 19 August 2005, Ad hoc Arbitration, Brussels.

Farmer-Paellmann v. FleetBoston, Aetna Inc., CSX, in: Raymond A. Winbush (ed.): Should America pay? Slavery and the raging debate on reparations, Amistad, New York, 348-360, 351.

Free Zones of Upper Savoy and the District of Gex (France v. Switzerland), Order of 6 August 1930, PCIJ, Series A, No.24, 12.

Gabĉikovo-Nagymaros Project (Hungary v. Slovakia), Judgement of 25 September 1997, ICJ Reports 1997, 7.

Greco-Bulgarian Communities (Bulgaria v. Greece), Advisory Opinion of 31 July 1930, PCIJ, Series B, No.17, 32.

Hasan Nuhanovic v. Netherlands, Appeal Judgement of 5 July 2011, Gerechtshof's Gravenhage (Court of Appeal), The Hague.

Interpretation of Peace Treaties (second phase), Advisory Opinion of 18 July 1950, ICJ Reports 1950, 221.

Island of Palmas (Netherlands v. USA), Award of 4 April 1928, R.I.A.A. (2), 829-871.

Legal Consequences of the Construction of a Wall in the Occupied Palestinian Territory, Advisory Opinion of 9 July 2004, ICJ Reports 2004.

Legality of the Threat or Use of Nuclear Weapons, Advisory Opinion of 8 July

1996, ICJ Reports 1996, 70.

Legal Status of Eastern Greenland (Denmark v. Norway), Judgment of 5 April 1933, PCIJ, Series A./B., No. 53.

Military and Paramilitary Activities in and against Nicaragua (Nicaragua v. United States of America), Judgement of 27 June 1986, ICJ reports 1986, 14.

Noble Ventures Inc. v. Romania, Award of 12 October 2005, ICSID Case No. ARB/01/11.

Nuclear Tests (New Zealand v. France), Judgement of 20 December 1974, ICJ Reports 1974, 457.

Peace Conference on the former Yugoslavia, opinion n°1 of 29 November 1991, Arbitration Commission, cited in: Pellet, Allain (1992). The Opinions of the Badinter Arbitration Committee: A Second Breath for the Self-Determination of Peoples, European Journal of International Law Vol. 3, Nr. 1, 178–185.

Phosphates in Morocco (Italy v. Fr.), Judgement of 14 June 1938, PCIJ, Series A/B, No. 74.

Prosecutor v. Dusko Tadic, ICTY, Appeals Chamber, Decision on the Defence Motion for Interlocutory Appeal on Jurisdiction of 2 October 1995, Case No. IT-94-1, 656-57.

Rainbow Warrior (New Zealand v France), Decision of 30 April 1990, Arbitration Tribunal (1990) 82, ILR 499.

Reparation for injuries suffered in the service of the United Nations, Advisory Opinion of 11 April 1949, ICJ Reports 1949, 174.

Reservations to the Convention on Genocide, Advisory Opinion of 28 May 1951, ICJ Reports 1951, 12.

The Factory At Chorzów (Germany v. Poland), Judgement of 13 September 1928, PCIJ, Series A., No. 17, 40.

The Prosecutor v. Jean-Paul Akayesu, Judgement of 2 September 1998, International Criminal Tribunal for Rwanda, Case No. ICTR-96-4-T.

The SS 'Wimbledon' (UK v. Germany), Judgement of 17 August 1923, PCIJ, Series A, No.1, 4.

Treatment of Polish Nationals (Poland v. Danzig), Advisory Opinion of 4 February 1932, PCIJ, Series A/B, No.44, 4.

United States Diplomatic and Consular Staff in Tehran (USA v. Iran), Judgement of 24 May 1980, ICJ Reports 1980, 29.

Western Sahara, Advisory Opinion, ICJ Reports 1975, 80.

Resolutions, Declarations, etc.:

Charter of the International Military Tribunal, downloaded from http://avalon.law.yale.edu/imt/imtconst.asp (accessed 29.6.2012).

Commission in Human Rights, Sub-Commission on Prevention of Discrimination and Protection of Minorities, Forty-fifth session (1993). Study concerning the right to restitution, compensation and rehabilitation for victims of gross violations of human rights and fundamental freedoms, Final report submitted by Mr. Theo van Boven, Special Rapporteur, E/CN.4/Sub.2/1993/8, 2 July 1993, downloaded from http://www.unhchr.ch/Huridocda/Huridoca.nsf/0/e1b5e2c6a294f-7bec1256a5b00361173?Opendocument (accessed 25.5.2010), 13.

Declaration of the first Abuja Pan-African Conference on Reparations For African Enslavement, Colonisation And Neo-Colonisation, sponsored by The Organisation of African Unity and its Reparations Commission April 27-29, 1993, Abuja/Nigeria.

Declaration on the Granting of Independence to Colonial Countries and Peoples, General Assembly downloaded from resolution 1514 (XV) of 14 December 1960, http://www2.ohchr.org/english/law/independence.htm (accessed 16.8.2012).

Declaration: World Conference Against Racism, Racial Discrimination, Xenophobia and Related Intolerance, UN Doc. A/CONF.189/12 (2001), downloaded from http://www.un.org./WCAR/durban.pdf (accessed 25.3..2011).

Durban Declaration and Program of Action, downloaded from http://www.un-documents.net/durban-d.htm (accessed 4.5.2010).

International Convention on the Suppression and Punishment of the Crime of Apartheid, downloaded from http://www.hrea.org/index.php?base_id=104&language_id=1&erc_doc_id=930&category_id=35&category_type=3&group= (accessed 16.11.2009).

International Law Commission (2001). Draft Articles on Responsibility of States for Internationally Wrongful Acts, November 2001, Supplement No. 10 (A/56/10), chp.IV.E.1, downloaded from http://www.unhcr.org/refworld/docid/3ddb8f804.html (accessed 23 June 2012).

International Law Commission (1996). Report of the International Law Commission on the Works of Its Forty-Eighth Session, UN GAOR, 51st Sess., Supplement No. 10 (A/51/10).

Recognition of responsibility and reparation for massive and flagrant violations of human rights which constitute crimes against humanity and which took place during the period of slavery, colonialism and wars of conquest, Sub-Commission on Human Rights resolution 2002/5, downloaded from http://ap.ohchr.org/documents/E/SUBCOM/resolutions/E-CN_4-SUB_2-RES-2002-5.doc (accessed 23.3.2011).

Recognition of responsibility and reparation for massive and flagrant violations of human rights which constitute crimes against humanity and which took place during the period of slavery, of colonialism and wars of conquest, Sub-Commission on Human Rights resolution 2001/1 E/CN.4/SUB.2/RES/2001/1, 6 August 2001, downloaded from http://www.unhchr.ch/Huridocda/Huridoca.nsf/(Symbol)/E.CN.4.SUB.2.RES.2001.1.En?Opendocument (accessed 28.3.2010).

Report of the International Law Commission on the work of its forty-eighth session, 6 May-26 July 1996, Official Records of the General Assembly, Fifty-first session, Supplement No.10, UN.Doc. A/51/10.

The right to restitution, compensation and rehabilitation for victims of gross violations of human rights and fundamental freedoms, Final report of the Special Rapporteur, Mr. M. Cherif Bassiouni, submitted in accordance with Commission resolution 1999/33, downloaded from http://www.unhchr.ch/Huridocda/Huridoca.nsf/0/42bd1bd544910ae3802568a20060e21f/$FILE/G0010236.doc (accessed 16.4.2011).

UN Commission on Human Rights, Basic Principles and Guidelines on the Right to a Remedy and Reparation for Victims of Violations of International Human Rights and Humanitarian Law, UN Commission on Human Rights, Fifty-sixth session,E/CN.4.2000/62, 18 January 2000, downloaded from http://www.unhchr.ch/Huridocda/Huridoca.nsf/0/42bd1bd544910ae3802568a20060e21f/$FILE/G0010236.doc (accessed 12.4.2010).

UN ESCOR (1947). Draft Convention on the Crime of Genocide, UN ESCOR, 5th Session, UN Doc E/447.

UN General Assembly, Convention on the Prevention and Punishment of the Crime of Genocide, resolution adopted by the General Assembly, 9 December 1948, 260 A (III).

UN General Assembly, Basic Principles and Guidelines on the Right Remedy and Reparation for Victims of Gross Violations of International Human Rights Law and Serious Violations of International Humanitarian Law, resolution adopted by the General Assembly, 16 December 2005, A/RES/60/147.

UN General Assembly, International Convention on the Elimination of All Forms of Racial Discrimination, 21 December 1965, United Nations, Treaty Series, Vol. 660, 195.

UN General Assembly (1946). Resolution 96 (I), U.N. Doc. A/63/Add.1.

UN General Assembly, Responsibility of States for internationally wrongful acts, resolution adopted by the General Assembly, 28 January 2002, A/RES/56/83, available at http://www.unhcr.org/refworld/docid/3da44ad10.html (accessed 2 April 2012).

United Nations Educational, Scientific and Cultural Organization (ed.) (1978). Meeting of Experts on the African Slave-Trade, Final Report, Port-au-Prince, Haiti, 31 January- 4 February 1978, downloaded fromhttp://unesdoc.unesco.org/images/0003/000333/033360eb.pdf (accessed 21.6.2012).

United Nations, Vienna Convention on the Law of Treaties, 23 May 1969, United Nations, Treaty Series, Vol. 1155, 331.

Working Group of Experts on People of African Descent, IX Session, 12 – 16 April 2010, III. CONCLUSIONS AND RECOMMENDATIONS, downloaded from http://www2.ohchr.org/english/issues/racism/groups/african/docs/session9/Conclusions_RecommandationsIXSession.doc (accessed 3.11.2010).

Internet sources:

Adibe, Patrick/Boateng, Osei (2000). Portugal, the mother of all slavers: Part 1, in:

New African, March 2000, downloaded from http://findarticles.com/p/articles/mi_qa5391/is_200003/ai_n21452668/ (accessed 18.7.2011).

African slave trade, downloaded from http://en.wikipedia.org/wiki/African_slave_trade#cite_note-Ethiopian_Slave_Systems-7 (accessed 28.3.2011).

al-Ahmed, Ali (2010). Justice, even for princes, downloaded from http://www.guardian.co.uk/commentisfree/2010/oct/20/saudi-prince-murder-justice   (accessed 17.3.2011).

Ago, Robert (1971). Third Report on State Responsibility, ILC Yearbook 1971, Vol II (1), 199, downloaded from http://untreaty.un.org/ilc/documentation/english/a_cn4_246.pdf (accessed 4.3.2010).

Allard, Jean-Guy (2011). In Miami, 12 Officers Shoot Haitian over 100 Times: Where Is International Press? downloaded from http://axisoflogic.com/artman/publish/Article_63221.shtml (accessed 6.12.2011).

Beckles, Sir Hilary (2010). Haiti destroyed by design, downloaded from http://rastareason.wordpress.com/tag/sir-hilary-beckles (accessed 3.2.2010).

Briggs, Billy (2011). Racism on the rise in Europe, downloaded from http://www.aljazeera.com/indepth/opinion/2011/09/201192182426183450.html   (accessed 29.10.2011).

Buyuka, Basset (2012). Kenya: Nuclear Energy Can Speed Up Vision 2030, in The Star: Nairobi, downloaded from http://allafrica.com/stories/201203060041.html (accessed 30.7.2012).

Crimes Against Humanity and War Crimes Bill 2000, downloaded from http://www.parliament.the-stationery-office.co.uk/pa/cm199900/cmbills/166/00166--a.htm#10 (accessed 15.11.2010).

Discours de M. Jacques CHIRAC, Président de la République, devant les deux chambres réunies du Parlement congolais, Brazzaville/ Congo, 18 July 1996, downloaded from http://www.jacqueschirac-asso.fr/fr/wp-content/uploads/2010/04/CONGO-18-juiillet-1996.pdf (accessed 24.3.2010).

Französisch-Guayana (Wikipedia), download from http://de.wikipedia.org/wiki/Franz%C3%B6sisch-Guayana (accessed 13.10.2011).

French Slavery, downloaded from http://etymonline.com/columns/frenchslavery.htm (accessed 29.5.2010).

Haïti, les récentes Opération "Bonaparte", Opération "Rochambeau". Ou quand la France insiste pour se venger, downloaded from http://www.bworldconnection.tv/index.php/Articles/Caraibe/Haiumlti-les-reacutecentes-Opeacuteration-quotBonapartequot-Opeacuteration-quotRochambeau-quot.-Ou-quand-la-France-insiste-pour-se-venger.html (accessed 24.5.2012).

Harding, Andrew (2009). Saving Africa's precious written heritage, downloaded from http://news.bbc.co.uk/2/hi/africa/8386866.stm (accessed 3.2.2010).

House of Lords Debate on Slavery Reparations, 14 March 1996, downloaded from http://www.publications.parliament.uk/pa/ld199596/ldhansrd/vo960314/text/60314-26.htm (accessed 5.4.2012).

Imfeld, Al (2007). Decolonizing African Agricultural History, downloaded from http://www.alimfeld.ch/African_Agricultural_History/Aghist.pdf   (accessed 7.11.2010).

Indigénat, downloaded from http://en.wikipedia.org/wiki/Indig%C3%A9nat (accessed 5.5.2009).

Jamaika (Wikipedia), download from http://de.wikipedia.org/wiki/Jamaika (accessed 13.10.2011).

Kim, Young Yoon (2009). Slavery in Imperial China, Korean Minjok Leadership Academy, downloaded from http://www.zum.de/whkmla/sp/0910/hersheys/hersheys5.html#ii (accessed 2.3.2011).

Laches, downloaded from http://dictionary.law.com/Default.aspx?selected=1097 (accessed 8.7.2010).

Law n° 2001-434 of 21 may 2001 (JORF/LD 08175), downloaded from www.adminet.com/jo/20010523/JUS9903435L.html (accessed 23.4.2009).

Legal status of the Holy See, downloaded from http://en.wikipedia.org/wiki/Legal_status_of_the_Holy_See (accessed 28.6.2012).

Libya militias out of control: Amnesty, downloaded from http://www.brecorder.com/world/africa/45981-libya-militias-out-of-control-amnesty-.html (accessed 16.2.2012).

Morell, Virginia (2001). The Pyramid Builders, downloaded from http://ngm.nationalgeographic.com/ngm/data/2001/11/01/html/ft_20011101.5.fulltext.html (accessed 11.3.2012).

Ogletree, Charles J. Jr. (2003). Repairing the Past: New Efforts in the Reparations Debate in America, downloaded from http://www.law.harvard.edu/students/orgs/crcl/vol38_2/ogletree.pdf (accessed 4.6.2010).

Pan-Afrikan-Reparations-Coalition-In-Europe,   downloaded   from   http://www.docstoc.com/docs/17799955/PAN-AFRIKAN-REPARATIONS-COALITION-IN-EUROPE (accessed 7.6.2010).

Poursuites pour provocation à la haine raciale: "une manoeuvre", downloaded from   http://tempsreel.nouvelobs.com/speciales/social/guadeloupe_dom_la_crise/20090309.OBS7874/poursuites_pour_provocation_a_la_haine_raciale_une_man.html (accessed 10.03.2009).

Presentation to Reparation Commission at Liberty Hall Thursday 15th October 2009, Hon Empress Petrona Simpasa Voice of Woman E.A.B.I.C.W.F.L.L., downloaded from http://www.black-king.net/english/library/presentation%20to%20reparation%20commission.htm (accessed 5.11.2009).

Ramos-Chapman, Naima (2010). A Generation of Black Youth Is Losing Its Future in the Jobs Crisis, downloaded from http://colorlines.com/archives/2010/11/will_great_recession_widen_racial_wealth_gap.html (accessed 24.11.2010).

Ras Marcus (2010). Responding to Roy Augier, downloaded from http://www.rastafarispeaks.com/cgi-bin/forum/config.pl?noframes;read=106752 (accessed 19.6.2010).

Return of the Charles-Town Maroons 1st November 1831 CO 140/121, downloaded from http://jamaicanfamilysearch.com/Members/M/MaroonsCharles (accessed 19.2.2011).

Sandoval Villalba, Clara (2009). Rehabilitation as a Form of Reparation under International Law, London: Redress Trust, downloaded from http://www.redress.org/downloads/publications/The%20right%20to%20rehabilitation.pdf (accessed 11.7.2012).

Shenker, Jack (2011). Nato units left 61 African migrants to die of hunger and thirst, The Guardian, 8 May 2011, downloaded from http://www.guardian.co.uk/world/2011/may/08/nato-ship-libyan-migrants (accessed 15.6.2011).

Slavery and the Law in Virginia; downloaded from http://www.history.org/history/teaching/slavelaw.cfm (accessed 20.3.2011).

Slavery: Legacy. The official record from Hansard of the debate initiated by Lord Gifford QC in the House of Lords of the British Parliament on the 14th March 1996 concerning the African reparations, downloaded from: http://www.arm.arc.co.uk/LordsHansard.html (accessed 25.7.2010).

Society of Jesus, downloaded from http://en.wikipedia.org/wiki/Society_of_Jesus (accessed 28.6.2012).

Structural Discrimination against people of African descent in respect of access to education, Presentation by invited panelist Dilip Lahiri, Member, CERD, IX session of the Working Group of Experts on People of African Descent Geneva 12 to 16 April 2010, downloaded from http://www.ohchr.org/Documents/Issues/Racism/WGEAPD/Session9/DilipLahiri.doc (accessed 14.12.2011).

THE SLAVE TRADE ARCHIVES PROJECT, Restricted Final Report 516INT5061, Paris February 2005, downloaded from http://portal.unesco.org/ci/en/files/18318/11159056237Slave_trade_archives_Final_Report.doc/Slave%2B-trade%2Barchives%2B-%2BFinal%2BReport.doc (accessed 14.3.2010).

Toussaint, Eric (2008). Odieux Prêts de la Banque Mondiale à la métropole coloniale belge pour coloniser le Congo, downloaded from www.cadtm.org/spip.php?article2421 (accessed 16 June 2008).

Visit to the Netherlands - Speech by M. Dominique de Villepin to the International Law Academy, The Hague 11.03.2004, downloaded from http://www.ambafrance-uk.org/Visit-to-the-Netherlands-Speech-by.html (accessed 7.3.2010).

Wenger, Kaimipono David (2010). From Radical to Practical (and Back Again?): Reparations, Rhetoric, and Revolution, downloaded from http://works.bepress.com/kaimipono_wenger/1 (accessed 20.8.2012).

What Lincoln and Other Yankees Knew: The evidence that pre-civil war U.S. slavery was illegal, downloaded from http://medicolegal.tripod.com/slaveryillegal.htm#2 (accessed 14.10.2010).

Wingall, Mark (2011). Why has Jamaica's crime rate fallen, downloaded from http://www.jamaicaobserver.com/columns/Why-has-Jamaica-s-crime-rate-fallen_8329778 (accessed 10.10.2011).

Wink, Marcus (2003). The World's Oldest Trade: Dutch Slavery and Slave Trade in the Indian Ocean in the Seventeenth Century, downloaded from http://www.historycooperative.org/cgi-bin/justtop.cgi?act=justtop&url=http://www.historycooperative.org/journals/jwh/14.2/vink.html (accessed 28.4.2011).

Yorke–Talbot slavery opinion, downloaded from http://en.wikipedia.org/wiki/Yorke%E2%80%93Talbot_slavery_opinion (accessed 19.10.2010).

Films and Wordsounds:

B.World Connection (2010). Esclavage. Commémoration et réparations, downloaded from http://www.bworldconnection.tv/index.php/Emissions/B.World-Connection-Esclavage-Commemoration-et-reparations.html (accessed 24.6.2010).

Laurent Garcia, Nicolas Ransom und Angela Aguiar (2011). Brasilien: Der Krieg ums Land, Arte Reportage, 29.10.2011, 22min.

Mistrati, M./Romano, U.R. (2011). Elfenbeinküste: Bittere Schokolade, Weltjournal, ORF2, 9.2.2011.

TF1 (2010). Le chlordécone, le poison des Antilles, downloaded from http://www.dailymotion.com/video/xeu64n_tf1-le-chlordecone-le-poison-des-an_news (accessed 22.12.2010).

Tupac Shakur (1996). White Man'z World, in: Makavelli: Don Killuminati, The 7 Day Theory.

Interviews:

Interview Dada (unemployed, Cayenne/F.Guiana, 18.9.2011).

Interview Fabience (plumber, Saint-Laurent-du-Maroni/F.Guiana, 23.9.2011).

Interview Gladys (high school teacher, Port Antonio/Jamaica, 15.1.2011).

Interview Gloria (market vendor, Port Antonio/Jamaica, 20.1.2011).

Interview Henriette (student, Cayenne/F.Guiana, 14.9.2011).

Interview James (musician, Kingston (Sandy Gully)/Jamaica, 31.1.2011).

Interview Joanna (market vendor, Port Antonio/Jamaica, 29.1.2011).

Interview Kéké (mail man, Cayenne/F.Guiana, 21.9.2011).

Interview Kenneth (market hustler, Port Antonio/Jamaica, 18.1.2011).

Interview Kenny (sculptor, Saint-Laurent-du-Maroni/F.Guiana, 24.9.2011).

Interview Laristo (musician/mail man, Cayenne/F.Guiana, 18.9.2011).

Interview Laurent (police officer, Cayenne/F.Guiana, 18.9.2011).

Interview Marietta (waitress, Cayenne/F.Guiana, 10.9.2011).

Interview Max (entrepreneur & activist, Saint-Laurent-du-Maroni/F.Guiana, 24.9.2011).

Interview Miss Rachel (market vendor (83 y.o.), Port Antonio/Jamaica, 29.1.2011).

Interview Misty (small farmer & market vendor, Port Antonio/Jamaica, 27.9.2011).

Interview Mr. Boké (market vendor, Cayenne/F.Guiana, 10.9.2011).

Interview Omeri (unemployed youth, Kingston (Sandy Gully community)/Jamaica, 19.1.2011).

Interview Paulette (landlady, Kingston (Liguanea)/Jamaica, 15.2.2011).
Interview Pierre Sida (traditional chief of Apatou, Apatou/F.Guiana, 25.9.2011).
Interview Stenli (entrepreneur, Cayenne/F. Guiana, 22.9.2011).
Interview Will (retired mechanician, Port Antonio/Jamaica, 20.1.2011).

Other:
Collins, Miguel Orlando (Sizzla). Nyahbinghi Council Presidential Speech of Oc-
    tober 21,2012.
Conversation with Colonel Frank Lumsden, Somerset Falls, Jamaica, 20.2.2011.
E-Mail by Prof. Ludger Müller (Director of the Institute for Church Law at the
    University of Vienna), 29.6.2012 (on file with author).
Facts on reparations to Africa and Africans in the Diaspora. Prepared by The
    Group of Eminent Persons on Reparations (1993). Lagos: The Group; cited in:
    Reparation Is A Must, in: Jahug Vol.4, London: Congo Call Production, 20.
Fragments of the ship's book of the Sao Miguel trading to Benin in the year 1522
    (A.T.T. Corpo Cronológico II, maço 149, no.29)
Intervention by L. Sala-Molins, UNESCO Conference/Commemoration of the Ab-
    olition of Slavery, Paris, 10.5.2011.
Jamaica National Commission on Reparations, Glenmuir High School sitting,
    27.11.2009.
Jamaica National Commission on Reparations, May Pen Court House Sitting,
    20.1.2010.
Jamaica National Commission on Reparations, May Pen Sitting, 25.9.2009.
Letter of 2 January 2003 by Gavin Tech, Deputy British High Commissioner, to
    "the RastafarI Brethren of Jamaica", c/o Mr. Howard Hamilton, Public Defender,
    78 Harbour Street, Kingston.
Letter of 15 January 2003 by the All Mansion's Secretariat of the Ethiopian Peace
    Foundation, Jamaica Branch, International RastafarI Community, RastafarI
    Brethren of Jamaica to Her Royal Majesty Queen Elizabeth II, Buckingham
    Palace, Attention: Mrs. Kay Brock, Assistant Private Secretary, c/o Mr. Gavin
    Tech, Deputy British High Commissioner, Kingston.
National Commission on Reparations. Commentary by Lord Anthony Gifford QC
    on Judge Robinson's Paper, 29th December 2009.
Private correspondence with Ayi Kwei Armah (on file with author).
Repatriation Is A Must, in: Jahug Vol.4, London: Congo Call Production (year
    unknown).
Speech of French President Sarkozy at the Ceremony for the Commemoration of
    the Abolition of Slavery, Paris: Jardin de Luxembourg, 10.5.2011.
Statement of the Caribbean Rastafari Organisation, Repatriation and Reparations
    Lobby, 15.11.2010.
Telephone conversation with Colonel Frank Lumsden, 18.2.2011.
Tour and Reasoning with Ms. Marcia (aka Kim) Douglas; Custodian of the Maroon

Museum in Charles Town, Portland, Jamaica, 17.2.2011.

UNESCO Conference/Commemoration of the Abolition of Slavery, Paris, 10 May 2011.

Wilberforce, William (1814/1815). Lettre à l'empereur Alexandre sur la traite des Noirs à la suite du non-respect des dispositions signées par les Européens lord du Congrès de Vienne.

INDEX

28800661R00308

Printed in Great Britain
by Amazon